PHOEBE APPERSON HEARST

A Life of Power and Politics

Alexandra M. Nickliss

University of Nebraska Press | Lincoln & London

Frontispiece: Phoebe Apperson Hearst wearing fur
coat with high collar. UARCPIC 13:3461.Courtesy of the
Bancroft Library, University of California, Berkeley.

Library of Congress Cataloging-in-Publication Data
Names: Nickliss, Alexandra M., author.
Title: Phoebe Apperson Hearst:
a life of power and politics / Alexandra M.
Nickliss.
Description: Lincoln, NE: University of Nebraska Press,
[2017] | Includes bibliographical references and index.
Identifiers: LCCN 2017026677
ISBN 9781496202277 (cloth: alk. paper)
ISBN 9781496205322 (epub)
ISBN 9781496205339 (mobi)
ISBN 9781496205346 (pdf)
Subjects: LCSH: Hearst, Phoebe Apperson,
1842–1919. | Upper class
women—United States—Biography. |
Philanthropists—California—Biography. |
Women philanthropists—California—Biography. |
University of California
(System). Regents—Biography. | Women civic
leaders—United States—Biography. |
Hearst, George, 1820–1891—Family. | Hearst family.
| California—Politics and government—1850–1950. |
San Francisco (Calif.)—Biography.
Classification: LCC CT275.H4865 N53 2017 |
DDC 305.48/21092 [B]—dc23 LC record available at
https://lccn.loc.gov/2017026677

Set in FournierMT Pro by Mikala R Kolander.
Designed by L. Auten.

In loving memory of my dearest mother, Mary Nickliss,
and father, George Eli Nickliss

Contents

Illustrations

Acknowledgments

This book was a labor of love. I started research on Phoebe Apperson Hearst before biographies became fashionable again. Little did I know that the book would be completed while the genre of biography rose in popularity, and that it would take over a quarter of a century to finish. There is much to think about and make sense of while researching and writing about someone whose life interacts so powerfully with a particular historical period. There are thrills to be gained in unraveling the mysteries of a subject's life across time. The discovery of even the smallest detail, along with random elements that form broader patterns, makes working on a book exciting and leads to new ideas and interpretations. (For more on the rise of biographies, see Jo Burr Margadant's *The New Biography* and the American Historical Review's roundtable on historians and biography in the June 2009 issue).

Researching and publishing a biography present a myriad of challenges. Overcoming them is made easier because turning a dissertation into a manuscript worthy of publication is a collaborative effort. Billie Jean Jensen taught me the craft of history many years ago and inspired me to study the history of women in the United States and to enter a doctoral program. Lack of finances and other life circumstances presented obstacles to getting the graduate degree and, ultimately, forced me to leave the program. I returned to the University of California at Davis to complete the dissertation after working for a few years at City College of San Francisco. I finished my dissertation while working full-time, teaching five classes a semester, sometimes six. Thanks to Ruth Rosen for reading my dissertation and raising questions. Roland Marchand, a wonderful scholar and teacher, now deceased, gave me invaluable intellectual and practical advice. Thanks also to Michael L. Smith for his comments and criticisms.

I owe a special debt of gratitude to Eileen Boris who generously provided essential information and support that helped guide me through the labyrinth of steps to get this book published. Many thanks to Estelle B. Freedman, Charles Grench, Karen Halttunnen, Al Hurtado, Karen Lystra, Peggy Pascoe, now-deceased Sandra Schackel, Nancy J. Taniguichi, and Virginia Scharff for offering advice and counsel about the academy and to Mary P. Ryan and Kathryn Sklar for teaching me valuable lessons about protecting my work and how to navigate entrance into, and advancement through, the academy.

Colleagues, friends, and the *Pacific Historical Review* and University of Nebraska Press reviewers helped improve the manuscript in many ways. I am deeply indebted to Anne M. Boylan for her assistance and support. She took time out of her busy schedule to review my manuscript and gave valuable expertise, insights, comments, and criticisms that clarified the manuscript and helped this historian avoid serious errors. My manuscript benefitted immeasurably from the feedback and suggestions of Blanche Wiesen Cook, Sarah Deutsch, Anne Hyde, Mary Beth Norton, and Jennifer Scanlon. Grey Osterud, Linda Shopes, and Karen Brown gave me expert editorial comments, suggestions, and assistance that taught me how to get the book manuscript ready for publication. Mary Adams, Jane Bernard-Powers, Sue Bowie, Geraldine Jonçich Clifford, Cita Cook, Ruth Crocker, Allen F. Davis, Rochelle Gatlin, Gayle Gullett, Nancy Hewitt, Timothy Killikelley, Gloria Ricci Lothrop, Valerie Mathes, Laurie Wu McClain and Charles McClain, Richard Orsi, Glenda Riley, Lois Scharf, Sandra Schlesinger, Jan Shipps, Deanne Spears, Carol Srole, Joan Wilson, Shirley Yee, and members of the Stanford Biographer's Seminar provided valuable suggestions and critiques on drafts of the dissertation and book manuscript. Jacqueline Braitman's comments improved a draft of a published journal article.

Thanks to Peter de Groot for assistance in editing letters that opened doors to gain access to research materials, to Jill Love and Larry Salazar for their translation from French to English of Henri Émile Bénard's letters to Phoebe Apperson Hearst, and to Bob Proctor for directing me to the Thomas Barry diary at the Bancroft Library at the University of California. I am grateful to Matthew Bokovoy, Senior Acquisitions Editor at the University of Nebraska Press, and the press reviewers, for providing valuable comments, critiques, and advice. Thank you also to Heather Stauffer at the University of Nebraska Press for assistance in dealing with the formatting and specifications for images included in the book and to Ann Baker for assistance with the publication process.

The Bancroft Library staff of the University of California at Berkeley made research a joy. Susan Snyder's unstinting assistance saved me time and effort. Work on this project also was made easier with the help of Bancroft librarians Tony Bliss, Terry Boom, Walter Brem, Rebecca Darby, A. Iris Donovan, Jason Eason, Franz Enciso, David Farrell, Peter Hanff, Bonnie Hardwick, Jim Kantor, David Kessler, Lorna Kirwan, Michael Lange, Irene Moran, Kathryn Neal, William Roberts, Theresa Salazar, Baiba Strads, Jack Von Euw, and many others. The staff at the Library of Congress, the University of California, Harvard University, San Francisco State University, the California Historical Society, University of Arizona Special Collections, the Huntington Library, University of Missouri, University of Maryland, Columbia University, Smith College, Stanford University, the Saint Louis Public Library, and San Francisco Public Library gave valuable assistance. More help came from the archivists at the Phoebe Apperson Hearst Anthropology Museum at the University of California and the University of Pennsylvania Museum, the San Francisco State University and City College of San Francisco Interlibrary Loan Services, and City College librarians, Rita Jones, former Dean of the CCSF Library, Carol Olivier, and Christopher Kox.

The Hearst Foundation, through the City College of San Francisco, generously supported this project with no strings attached. My appreciation goes to Brian Kenny of the Hearst Corporation in San Francisco who graciously arranged to provide me access to materials on Phoebe Apperson Hearst never seen by researchers. Several sabbatical leaves granted by the City College of San Francisco allowed time to work on the book. Helen Ely, Ralph Gregory, Mabel Reed, and Ken Middleton of the Phoebe Apperson Hearst Historical Society, the employees at Maramec National Park, the Wortham Foundation, Natalie Sliepcevich of the Hearst Free Library (Anaconda, Montana), Eleanor A. Kubeck, editor of the National Cathedral School's magazine, and Scott Butterwork, of the National Cathedral School, were all unfailingly helpful. Mareshi Gail of the San Francisco Bahá'í Faith, Dorothy Wick of the Young Women's Christian Associations, the staffs of the San Francisco Young Women's Christian Association, the General Federation of Women's Clubs, the Mount Vernon Ladies' Association of the Union, and the National Parent and Teacher Association all helped me with resource materials. Thanks to Sally Watkinson, a former student, and Lawrence Neuber, someone with a passion to learn about Phoebe Apperson Hearst, for their brief stint as research assistants.

Many thanks to Milanna and Hank Meyer, Sue and Bob Bowie, Steve and Jo Moorhouse, Mary Adams, Peter de Groot, Laurie Wu McClain, Charles McClain, Richard Oxsen, Marsha Oxsen, Danice Fagin, Paul Fagin, Betsy Uprichard, Barbara Tatum, Roxie Kellum, Leslie Brandt, Russell Piti, David Cash, Carol Peltz, Jim Blattner, Tom Callahan, and Bill Goodwin for keeping me sane while I taught many classes, graded papers, and worked on this book. I offer gratitude and thanks to anyone who gave me assistance but whose name has slipped from my memory during the many years it took to complete this project.

My parents, George Eli Nickliss and Mary Nickliss, both deceased, gave me love and support to spur me on when it felt as though there were too many obstacles to surmount. They have my undying love, respect, and gratitude. It would have been impossible to get this book published without the assistance and support of family, friends, and members of the academy. I am deeply grateful to all of them.

Introduction

Elite philanthropist Phoebe Apperson Hearst hosted an elaborate luncheon meeting for 350 women in September of 1916 at the St. Francis Hotel in a room draped with colonial tapestries. This was no society lunch, but rather a political event in San Francisco, convened to form a California branch of the National Woman's Party (NWP). How did the seventy-three-year-old Hearst come to chair and host such an event? This is the story of her unlikely evolution from an ordinary girl in rural Missouri to a powerful woman in local, state, and national voluntary associations and California academic politics. Hearst's parents had instilled in her ambition and an evangelical sense of duty and hard work that pushed her to become powerful and famous. Her upbringing laid the groundwork for her to become the first vice chair of the Campaign Committee and vice chair of the NWP of California. The NWP meeting of September 1916 addressed issues of personal interest to Hearst—women, power, and American politics. The gathering was held for multiple purposes: to establish a California branch of the NWP to work for a national suffrage amendment; to adopt a constitution; to consolidate the NWP's growing presence in the city; to appoint officers and members of a governing "central committee"; and to raise campaign funds to defeat President Woodrow Wilson in his November reelection bid.[1]

Hearst and the attendees advanced suffragist Alice Paul's argument that the women's right to vote in national elections could determine the outcome of the 1916 presidential election. "The talk was of political expediency" of "the fundamental idea of the hour—the use of power," of "fighting [against] those who have fought us," and of "votes for all the women of the country on the plain basis of justice," according to the *San Francisco Examiner*. Suffragist Ida Finney Mackrille stressed "wielding the power we possess." She advocated Alice Paul's position that the political party in power in Washington DC must be removed because of its opposition to a constitutional suffrage amendment. As Mackrille said, "The women voters in the States where women vote have in their power the distribution of ninety-one electoral votes, enough to decide the coming presidential elections." She emphasized that the Democratic Party refused to give "women the vote." So suffragists "must fight them, and give some other party the power to give it." Sara Bard Field, suffragist and poet, reminded the audience that President Wilson was "personally and directly responsible for the failure of the Susan B. Anthony amendment to be passed." She added, "And we must fight him and his party, for both are opposed to us." Hearst's public modesty and lack of an advanced education prevented her from making a speech. Although she was reticent to employ her own powers of persuasion in public, as other suffrage supporters did, she enjoyed wielding her economic might in the NWP. Her political contribution of one thousand dollars, "announced amidst a tumult of applause," spurred the fund-raising drive led by Doris Stevens, NWP's California branch organizer. Hearst's financial gift encouraged NWP donors and attendees to believe they could raise the money necessary to defeat Wilson. The total raised reached a little more than two thousand dollars "in less than twenty minutes."[2] Hearst's political event at the elegant St. Francis Hotel was typical of the way she exerted power and authority within the constraints of sex and class in American politics during the tumultuous and turbulent times produced by industrialism, immigration, and urbanism.

Most Americans know the Hearst name. And some are familiar with the name Phoebe Apperson Hearst. Many people, though, are unfamiliar with her accomplishments. Readers are probably most familiar with her son,

William Randolph Hearst, the newspaper mogul, and his father, George Hearst, the mining tycoon and United States senator, both very rich men. So they probably associate the Hearst name with George and William's extravagant wealth. Not many know that Phoebe Hearst controlled the entire family estate from the time she was forty-eight years old until she died at the age of seventy-six. Even fewer know how this ordinary young girl from rural Missouri, who knew virtually nothing about her husband's large estate when he passed away, grew to be a powerful, wealthy woman in her own right, known nationally and internationally.

At the heart of my understanding of Phoebe Apperson Hearst is the concept of power—its possession and exercise—elements that are difficult to separate. This book is about Hearst, gender, and how she leveraged her fortune, intelligence, and other resources, to accrue power as she navigated local, national, and international arenas of power and politics. It examines the opportunities and challenges she faced as she grew into a powerful woman in a world in which power was considered male and defined by men. But Hearst often directed her power toward a different set of goals than most men: women, children, education, and social reform. Hearst's success in acquiring and exercising power brought her authority, prominence, and status in local, state, and national organizations and academic institutions of higher education as well as worldwide recognition.[3]

Hearst's upbringing and access to resources defined her as a wealthy woman in the top tier of society with the ability to wield power. To address class fully as a "central concern outside of women's labor history," as well as the psychological basis for power, would be beyond the scope of this book.[4] This biography, nonetheless, attempts to provide a better understanding of the relationship between femininity, masculinity, religion, power, class, and diverse racial and ethnic groups in American politics as we explore the life of Phoebe Hearst.

This investigation aims to open up new avenues of inquiry and thinking into women and power. While previous studies have argued that women possessed power, they neglected to examine explicitly how women accrued power in a male world to realize their vision for society.[5] My goal is to explore Hearst's power, along with the personal interests that shaped and drove her politics, by studying how Hearst acquired and exerted private and public, informal and formal, control over money and resources.

This book is also a call to move beyond the hermeneutics of the last twenty-five years or so in women's and gender history and feminism in the United States. The first hermeneutic step was the argument made years ago by women anthropologists when they started to analyze the relation of women to power through the lens of culture. Their argument stressed that women were not taken seriously or were seen as legitimate because the path they used to control money and resources was shaped and limited by their association with domesticity.[6]

The second hermeneutic step was the argument for female power. I argue that before the passage of state suffrage and the Nineteenth Amendment, Hearst leveraged her intelligence and resources to accrue power as she moved into and through the male world. Hearst's life shows that power is not gendered. Like male philanthropists who controlled fortunes, Hearst used her power to advance issues of mutual interest to women and men, such as children and their education and social reform, including suffrage. Before the Nineteenth Amendment expanded voting rights, Hearst held and exercised power in political arenas such as nonpartisan voluntary associations and academic institutions of higher education.[7]

"Money is power" is a familiar cliché. But money alone is not power. Nor is it feminine or masculine. It is one resource among many that bring people power. Men possessed and controlled money. Women possessed and controlled money. True, men and women usually acquired money differently. Andrew Carnegie, for example, earned wealth through industry and business, while women like Hearst were married to husbands who gifted wealth to their female spouses, or they acquired it through inheritance. Hearst's skills allowed her to acquire, control, and use money, along with a range of resources, and this brought her power. Ultimately, Hearst used many of the same intellectual and diplomatic skills and talents wielded by men to accomplish the goals that made her a woman of authority in the larger society.[8]

Hearst knew it was hard to achieve what she did. As she once wrote to her husband, George, "You are greatly mistaken if you think it is easy to accomplish all I do." Even though she possessed and managed considerable wealth, it was a great challenge for any nineteenth- and early twentieth-century woman, within the constraints of sex and class, to control money and leverage her fortune and resources effectively in American politics. Men placed innumerable barriers in the way of women who wanted to exert power on equal terms with men. Men, moreover, rarely acknowledged openly, especially in public, that women held power. They usually referred to them as possessing "influence" and "authority," especially before women won both the state and broader constitutional right to vote. Hearst loved to exert power and be active in American politics. Her affection for nonpartisan American politics bordered on an addiction, according to one of her friends, even though the stumbling blocks placed in her way sometimes seemed insurmountable.[9] But Hearst refused to let these barriers defeat her.

I examine Hearst's life thematically and chronologically in this book to make sense of and highlight the significance of her experiences in getting and exercising power. Understanding Hearst's life of power and politics is a challenge because she left behind very little of her inner thoughts, feelings, and perspectives. Because so few materials exist to illuminate her private life, I will use as many of her own words as possible to help readers comprehend Hearst's decisions and actions. Studying Hearst's experiences is useful for gaining insight into how women acquired and exerted real power in many, but not all, of its forms—ideological, rhetorical, social, cultural, economic, political, legal, and symbolic—in the context of forces operating in the mid-to-late nineteenth century and the Progressive Era. There is much to study and contemplate regarding Hearst's life and the complicated relationship between herself and other women and men, and about power in culture, civil society, and the state.

Hearst's story tells us about her temperament, contradictory personality, and abilities. We learn about her dignified upbringing and her love of travel in her youth to educate herself and better her life. We examine how she used travel to escape from the taxing parts of her day-to-day experiences. We see how she struggled to maintain and restore her health and energy. We also gain knowledge and insight into the ways she adjusted to life. We study how she made deft use of the rhetoric of self-sacrifice and martyrdom, as well as social entertainments and high-society affairs, as tools to build the careers, reputation, and status of her husband and herself. We see the sophisticated ways she handled these tools as she grew older to form her political agenda at a time when numerous factors made it difficult for women to become potent forces in American society and politics. We gain understanding into her strategic involvement and exercise of power in nonpartisan, voluntary, woman-only and mixed-sex associations as well as in academic politics and traditional, partisan electoral politics. We learn what factors, especially those associated with her individuality, sex, class, and race, influenced her decisions and actions, including those related to the suffrage movement. As well, Hearst's story draws our attention to her interest in children. We also accompany her on her adventures in health and medical reform in the 1880s. We study how she perpetuated the myth that women need to be protected by men at the same time that she challenged the myth of male protection. Once she held official positions of power and authority, however, she shaped and altered institutional policies to help women, and some men, advance themselves. And finally, Hearst's successes in amassing power, in a male world, show how in fact she used many of the same forms of power that men used as she struggled with both the obstacles and limits of power.

Hearst, over the arc of her life, controlled and used her money and other resources, individually and collectively, in "creative" ways. Americans often expected wealthy women to spend money frivolously on high-society affairs, fashion, or other personal pleasures. Hearst met those expectations in order to gain acceptance into elite circles of the wealthy. But she also was different from most rich women. She utilized her money and array of resources on issues of interest to herself, as well as those she shared with other women and men, to take command over people and organizations. Her ideas and talents brought her fame, and her initiatives in gift giving served her well. Her knack for focusing her attention on specific issues of interest to herself and of widespread concern to the general public helped make her popular.

Hearst decided, for instance, to pursue her love of children and her intense interest in education. To this end, she established, in the early 1880s, free public kindergartens for the Golden Gate Kindergarten Association (GGKA). She participated in the advancement of women in education in the arenas of health and medical reform—a concern to herself and many Americans, especially women, who possessed little or no knowledge about their bodies and medicine. Her money ideas and skills made her a GGKA director and president of the Pacific Homeopathic Dispensary, a San Francisco hospital. Her work and activities in these groups were critical in promoting her name and building a good reputation in the city. Her intelligence, decisions, and skills helped her win election as the first president of the Century Club of San Francisco, as the first treasurer of the General Federation of Women's Clubs, as the president of the Columbian Kindergarten Association, and as the first female regent of the University of California. Her sophisticated ability to use power made her a cofounder and first vice president of the National Congress of Mothers and a vice regent from California of the Mount Vernon Ladies' Association of Virginia.[10]

Hearst's participation in the Panama-Pacific International Exposition (PPIE) and Young Women's Christian Association (YWCA) also show how she controlled and used her money and an array of resources in "creative" ways. Her innovative ideas transformed her into a candidate for elective national office and a representative of the YWCA. Her YWCA election victories provided an opportunity that led to her election as the ceremonial head of the PPIE Woman's Board that she transformed into a position with meaning and purpose. These triumphs made her an advocate for the YWCA's moderate yet progressive reform politics. She was instrumental in building the Asilomar compound on the Pacific Coast, the YWCA's first permanent conference and training center. Asilomar provided opportunities for women to learn about power and how to prepare themselves to carry out the YWCA's brand of politics at the PPIE and beyond.[11]

Hearst used her power in "coercive" ways as well. While Hearst often shared power with women and men in nonpartisan voluntary association and academic politics, there were times when she forced others to realize her ideas and plans and carry out her orders. She refused to share power with anyone when it came to the vast estate she controlled after her husband died in early 1891. She directed and supervised the Hearst estate overall, including her female and male employees, and the business operations. She made it obligatory for male physicians to support her positions and policies while she served as first president of the Board of the Pacific Homeopathic Dispensary. As a University of California regent, she was able to persuade the male regents to do what she wanted. She lobbied PPIE men to support her positions when she was head of the Woman's Board. Nonetheless, Hearst expressed elitist, condescending attitudes toward those she deemed inferior—typical views in her day for members of her class—not hesitating to use coercion to carry out her original ideas and plans to advance herself by advancing others, mostly women. Significantly, she worked to reduce the tension and conflict she helped create, as a wealthy woman with considerable clout, by helping others better their lives. As we will see, the ways Hearst used power were complicated and cannot be explained entirely by social-control theory.[12]

Hearst's life and complex political experiences were shaped by the American West where her individuality took root. The West was a place free of long-established tradition, making it easier for people to create "new landscapes, new property systems, new social relationships, and new political institutions," as one historian observed. Born in rural Missouri, Hearst was brought up to do what was expected of most white women—especially those in the eastern part of the country—to be pure, pious, submissive, and domestic, particularly to get married and have children. But she also was raised to be a true woman of the American West—to be a worker and "civilizer." Hearst's ancestors, parental lessons, and western experiences laid the foundation for her to become an independent woman. Life in the West gave her room to grow and provided opportunities to make a good name and reputation for herself while, at the same time, helping to shape regional identities in the West and distinguish America from other nations.[13]

Hearst was eager at a young age to leave her birthplace in rural Missouri and go to California to live out her dreams. Practically speaking, the only way she could get there was to marry a man who would take her there. So she needed to make a good choice of a future husband if she was to make her dreams come true. She did. She chose George Hearst. George gave Phoebe access to and control over his fortune early in their marriage. He trusted her ability to make the right decisions in giving away his money "for charitable and philanthropic purposes" at the same time that she spent money on fancy high-society affairs and personal luxuries to advance George's career and help them both to gain acceptance into elite circles. By the early 1880s, she was making monetary gifts and giving advice and guidance as she wished to family members and friends, mostly women, to help them achieve individual goals and realize their dreams.[14] One of her top political priorities became promoting the economic independence of young women, and her home in California became the base from which she dispensed her philanthropy to individuals and associations across California and in other parts of the nation and abroad.

Among the first to experience "the power of money . . . from dear Mrs. Hearst" was Mattie Wynn, a Southerner and one of Hearst's female friends, as well as Mattie's daughter, Emily Wynn.[15] Hearst believed it was a woman's duty to perform her domestic role. But it was her experience with economic uncertainty, when her husband lost his financial bearings during the mining boom that then went bust in the mid-1860s, which forged her beliefs about parental responsibilities, especially preparing children for self-support. Hearst urged parents to train "young people in the directive of their tastes and worthy predilections" and direct them "into channels of useful, productive occupation."[16] Emily Wynn's predilection was to become an artist. Her mother lacked the means to help her daughter get the proper training abroad, so Hearst provided the money for Emily's education to become a painter. She also contributed financially to Emily's wedding. Emily married Alfred Elias, an artist known especially for oil and pastel paintings of natural scenery and scenes or events from everyday life. Emily Wynn Elias herself became a successful painter of portraits, genre scenes, landscapes, and still lifes, exhibiting "in Paris in 1882, 1889 and 1890, and at the Royal Academy in London in 1884." Hearst encouraged Emily to marry but also to sell her paintings abroad, whether she married Alfred or not. From Hearst's perspective, her money was well spent in helping young women establish their own identities and gain a means of economic support, whether within or outside of marriage.[17]

Hearst's story demonstrates the real and intricate interrelationship between power and politics in the lives of both women and men. Hearst spent a good portion of her adult life actively involved in what men called "philanthropy," or "service," or in a few cases, "disorderly conduct," but which was really "politics"; and the worlds of voluntary associations and academia became important political arenas for her.[18] Her life encourages us to think more about a complex and nuanced understanding of many, but not all, forms of power—ideological, rhetorical, social, cultural, economic, political, legal, and symbolic—that Hearst and others exercised in American politics broadly conceived.

Recent scholarly and popular interest in wealthy Americans controlling and spending money and resources on political causes of personal and shared interest with other women and men can be traced back to wealthy women like Phoebe Apperson Hearst. Industrial tycoons captured the attention of nineteenth- and early twentieth-century Americans. Andrew Carnegie, John D. Rockefeller, Commodore Cornelius Vanderbilt, and his son, William K. Vanderbilt, and John Hopkins, among others, built reputations as well-known philanthropists. Rich women like Hearst, who married into wealth or inherited fortunes, also fascinated Americans. These rich women built distinguished reputations as well-known philanthropists. But few Americans, especially men, acknowledged and recognized their power.[19]

Hearst entered American politics while the field of philanthropy was going through a transition between 1873 and 1893. Pauperism emerged as a great problem during the depression following the Panic of 1873. Dedicated reformers charged that many of the gifts to the needy were "wasted on imposters"—people undeserving of the money. On the other hand, reformers argued that the money received by the deserving poor "tended to degrade rather than to elevate them." Alarmed by the increased amounts of money and taxation being collected "for public relief," they castigated private as well as public charity relief workers and groups of both sexes for wasting money on the undeserving poor. To address the problem, devoted reformers interested in efficient and effective giving argued for rigorous professional standards and scientific principles "to make philanthropy a science."[20] The influential forces of industrialism, immigration, and urbanism shaped Hearst's philanthropic decisions during the formative years of developing her abilities to donate and skillfully use her money and resources. Hearst's choices about how to spend her money and resources provided opportunities for her and other women and men to reshape American society and the nation-state.

Hearst's life of power and politics was shaped in part by her parents' belief in white superiority. While Randolph and Drusilla Whitmire Apperson instilled in her the acceptance of a life constrained by sex and class, they inculcated in their first child ambition and the drive to challenge traditional beliefs and constraints as well. This varied array of traits, beliefs, and principles inherited from her parents set the stage for Hearst to grow into a mature, though complicated woman of great importance. As well, the Appersons steeped their eldest child in the values and ideals of Cumberland Presbyterianism. The Cumberlands were an evangelical, radical reform wing of the Presbyterian Church. Randolph and Drusilla Apperson taught their daughter the power of moral authority and to do her religious "duty in all things," as Hearst explained when she was in her early twenties. She knew she was to marry and have children. But the Appersons also impressed upon her the importance of making something of herself. She learned from her parents that women's work was valuable and as important as men's. By the time she was a young woman, her parents' lessons pushed her to fulfill a need to find a useful role in life with meaning and purpose beyond the traditional domestic role.[21] To this end, she sought to advance herself by also helping those she considered less fortunate—including white, black, poor, and immigrant women and men—to advance themselves.

Phoebe Apperson Hearst showed signs, early in life, of her ability to make strategic decisions to satisfy her ambition and fulfill her ardent desire to rise in the world at the same time that she met American expectations about white womanhood. One of the first signs of her ambition emerged when she accepted George Hearst's marriage proposal, though Phoebe became disillusioned with her marriage not long after she wed George. Unhappy in her twenties, she thought having children would reduce her disenchantment. Her religious values, meantime, kept her from spending most of her husband's money frivolously, especially on fancy parties and fashions, like many women married to rich men. While a young woman, she refused to set out to amass power with her husband's money to satisfy herself, even though she was ambitious. Instead, she did her duty. She bore a child, behaved within the bounds of propriety, and remained dignified. But she was fortunate enough to be married to a rich man who gave her the opportunity to seek, through travel, a separate, independent identity from him with meaning and purpose. She discovered, moving from place to place in Europe, that she could use George Hearst's money in useful ways to help her find a place in the world by improving the lives of others, especially the poor.[22]

As I have argued, Hearst's choices and methods of achieving her goals were shaped in part by her Cumberland Presbyterian upbringing. They helped define her and her reputation. But they also helped her form and express her political agenda. She took a decidedly different path from other women married to rich men, such as Caroline (William) Schermerhorn Astor. Hearst fit Astor's notion of a wealthy woman, but only to a point. As Astor succinctly put it, in speaking of high-society women in general, "Each woman is for herself and trying to outdo the others in lavish display and mad extravagance, with little thought of any ultimate good or any ideal." While Hearst vied successfully with other wealthy women in spending money to hold ostentatious high-society affairs, her upbringing taught her that she would have to do more, especially to be successful in the nation's capital. To gain acceptance in the elite social and political circles of Washington, a wealthy woman needed to make careful, skillful choices about how to deploy that wealth. She needed to show refinement and talent in choosing guests and music. A demonstration of originality and artistic flare was required in putting on social entertainments. But Hearst's drive and personal interests told her she also needed to follow general evangelical principles at the same time, to lend meaning and purpose to her life by doing something more than simply entertaining guests at her fancy parties in San Francisco or Washington DC.[23] What Hearst did accomplish, both socially and by helping the less fortunate to better their lives, enhanced her power and fame.

Hearst went beyond what Americans expected from the elite among wealthy women in high society in Washington DC. She was "not alone a society woman—she is a great deal more. She is a level-headed business woman, thoroughly understanding all the ins and outs of her large mining and other interests," observed writer Juliette Babbitt in 1895. Hearst, moreover, believed "in fitting people to take care of themselves, and for many years has devoted a certain goodly sum to the education of young men and women in those branches of art best calculated to fit them for the battle of life," Babbitt declared.[24]

Hearst developed a businesslike approach to transforming herself into a powerful woman involved in progressive reform issues of shared interest to women and men within the largely male world of American politics. Some of her sumptuous social events not only entertained but advanced reform positions similar to those of Jane Addams. Hearst, beyond gifting money, promoted free, public coeducational kindergartens and pioneered ideas—especially through design and architecture at the University of California—to push forward her career and advance women in health and medical educational reform. Among other causes, she promoted a minimum wage and the ballot for women.

Hearst was a contradictory, imperious, and charming woman who was raised to be a dutiful, faithful, evangelical wife and parent. Yet she was not a devout evangelical. Nor, unlike Addams, was she a deep thinker or involved in traditional partisan politics. Hearst did become quite skilled at making connections, building networks, and trust. She excelled at working with people who could help her get what she wanted inside and outside of political arenas. Holding successful high-society affairs that were really political events, coupled with her involvement in nonpartisan voluntary-association politics, made her "one of the most popular women in Washington," observed writer Juliette Babbitt.[25]

Hearst was unwilling to wield power primarily for the sake of self-aggrandizement, thinking that it was more important to use her abilities and to spend her money and resources on individuals and organizations that addressed political issues that she and others, including men, cared about. The legally incorporated groups to which she belonged succeeded in giving their members formal public power and authority and the capacity to sustain political activities and agendas. Hearst's success in elevating her power and authority over others, individually and collectively, while she helped improve lives, thus brought her greater visibility and made her a national figure in American politics, one with an international reputation as well. The story of Phoebe Apperson Hearst's life of power and politics begins in the West in the early 1840s.

Author's Note

A few words about the correspondence and papers of Phoebe Apperson Hearst are in order. There are many unanswered questions about Hearst's personal thoughts and life because we have so few sources and little evidence to work from. Hearst was reserved and reticent to divulge what went on her in her private life, particularly after the 1880s, when she entered the national elite circle of the wealthy. She wrote few letters after the mid-1890s that are presently open and available to scholars and researchers, although she left bits and pieces of her thoughts and responses in notes on the pages of some of her correspondence. Her desire to remain closemouthed and secretive fuels the mystery that surrounds what power is and how she acquired and exerted it, making it a real challenge to depict her as a flesh-and-blood person of power and consequence.

Only a small number of letters written by Hearst are included in the George and Phoebe Apperson Hearst Papers at the Bancroft Library at the University of California, Berkeley. Most of the letters written by Hearst in this collection date from the 1860s through the 1880s. The rest of her papers in the Bancroft collection consist of correspondence written to and received by her. There are also boxes of unorganized letters written to her in the Family Archives of the Hearst Corporation in San Francisco. Some additional Hearst letters are scattered throughout library collections in the United States; for example, in the Peck Collection at the Huntington Library in San Marino, California, and the California Historical Society in San Francisco. The major source used for this biography was the George and Phoebe Apperson Hearst Papers at the Bancroft Library. Other sources used at the Bancroft were the William Randolph Hearst Papers; manuscript collections of University of California academics, administrators, and friends; the papers of women's organizations in which Hearst was involved; and contemporary newspaper accounts, articles, and government publications. Hearst's papers and correspondence generally contain a wealth of material on privileged, elite, and prosperous middle-class white women and men with whom she worked and was politically active. There is a dearth of material that explicitly expresses her thoughts about the working class and racial and ethnic groups. There is virtually no material on the views that diverse people, including her employees, possessed about Hearst or about their reactions to her and the power she exerted to control and change their lives. This lack of material leaves us with unanswered questions about many of Hearst's attitudes and actions and how she interacted with and exercised power over others, especially black, Chinese, Native American, working-class, poor, and immigrant women.

Scholars and authors have paid much more attention to Hearst's son, William Randolph Hearst. Will's letters in archival and manuscript collections are far greater in number. Phoebe Apperson Hearst's son will appear in the story when his relationship with his mother helps us gain insight into her personality and persona and how she mastered her life of power and politics.

The Phoebe Apperson Hearst Correspondence and Papers were rearranged and recatalogued under the title "George and Phoebe Apperson Hearst Papers" after the research was completed for this book. I have traced sources within the new arrangement where possible. Any questions concerning the material in the George and Phoebe Apperson Hearst Papers can be directed to the Bancroft Library at the University of California.

Finally, Randolph and Drusilla Whitmire Apperson spelled the first name of their newborn daughter "Phebe." Phoebe Apperson Hearst, as she approached her sixtieth birthday, took the advice of a male friend (Joshua Stallard) to change the spelling of her first name to Phoebe. The latter is the spelling I have used throughout.

PHOEBE APPERSON HEARST

I

Ability

Phoebe Elizabeth Apperson Hearst possessed "beauty, grace and charm." Those characteristics "left stamped upon my mind a picture of perfect womanhood," declared her friend and contemporary Elizabeth W. Allston Pringle, a South Carolina rice planter and plantation manager. Hearst and Pringle had served together on the Mount Vernon Ladies' Association (MVLA) Council. The MVLA was an organization devoted to the restoration of George Washington's Mount Vernon home in Virginia. As Pringle elaborated, Hearst "rarely spoke in Council, but listened most attentively to all that was said," adding, "[Phoebe] . . . devoted her powers of mind and heart as well as her material wealth to the good of this Association."[1] How did Hearst, an ordinary girl from a rough environment in rural Missouri, establish the foundation necessary to give her the ability to transform herself into such a refined, flawless, powerful representative of womanhood? What was the origin, or root, of her power?

Phoebe's life began when she took her first breath on December 3, 1842, in the Cumberland Presbyterian settlement of Franklin County, Missouri, about forty miles southwest of St. Louis. It was named the Whitmire Campground because so many settlers had the last name of Whitmire. Phoebe experienced the misfortune of coming into the world at a time when Americans possessed a deeply held belief in the attributes of "true womanhood"—purity, piousness, submissiveness, and genteel domesticity. True womanhood was a trope based on "Victorian prescriptive literature" that dogged white women from birth. It demanded that females be modest, moral guardians who married and generally held their tongues in public. Without these "cardinal virtues," "no matter whether there was fame, achievement or wealth, all was ashes." With them, women were "promised happiness and power."[2] Phoebe's parents, as soon as their firstborn child opened her eyes, began to shape the life of their eldest child by passing on the lessons they had learned while growing up in the South and the prevalent, popular ideas that permeated society and the nation.

Phoebe's grandparents, John and Alcey Favor Apperson and Henry and Ruth Hill Whitmire, came of age in Virginia and South Carolina, respectively, during the Revolutionary War era. Her Southern parents, Randolph Walker and Drusilla Whitmire Apperson, grew up in the early nineteenth century, steeped in reverence for religion and the virtue, charm, modesty, self-control, and submissive nature expected of a Southern lady. Republican ideology and principles of the time linked home and the state. They centered on a patriotic political role for females that stressed the duty of women to educate sons to be virtuous citizens and "demanded a well-educated citizenry" as a means to civilize society. The Appersons took these beliefs to heart and instilled them in Phoebe from birth. But they also reshaped them to fit women's experiences in what was considered a less sophisticated and cultivated region—the American West. Randolph and Drusilla, as they raised their daughter, struggled to impose order on and interact with the western rural environment in which they were living, and they relied on this regional understanding of women as "civilizers" and workers to shape Phoebe's distinctive character and abilities. Phoebe's individual qualities were thus laced with traits and values from the South along with notions of true womanhood and republican ideology that contributed to the development of a western regional identity.[3]

Phoebe's parents and ancestors contributed the natural aptitude and education she needed to achieve the goals, financial and otherwise, set by her family.[4] Her kind and enterprising father, Randolph, was born in Abingdon, Virginia, on April 10, 1809. He came of age in an era that emphasized a character ideal that encouraged men to set and achieve personal goals. Randolph had little schooling, but he grew up to be an ambitious, industrious, self-educated, and enterprising individual. He had an eye for design and was "public-spirited." He was, moreover, a Jacksonian Democrat with both conservative and liberal views by the time he grew into a young man. Phoebe's paternal grandparent, John Apperson, was a physician and farmer and served in the American Revolutionary War. John's wife, Alcey Favor Apperson, took care of the home and eleven children. Both John and Alcey were from Culpeper, Virginia. Phoebe's maternal grandparents, Henry and Ruth Hill Whitmire, joined almost one million Virginians going to the Deep South and West in 1819, several years after the Panic of 1817, to seek greater opportunities. This emigration emptied the state of human and economic resources during a national boom. The Appersons and Whitmires were drawn to Missouri by the extensive publicity that beckoned settlers to take advantage of opportunities in the West. They carried with them to Missouri their Southern sensibilities, a belief in male reliance on developing "inner resources," and a way of life based on hierarchy. At the time, Franklin County, Missouri, was a wide open, remote area that lacked established institutions of white civilization, providing the Randolph family with an opportunity to undermine a clearly delineated pecking order and room to move up the social and economic ladders.[5]

In 1830, when he was twenty-one years old, Randolph left the Methodist Episcopal Church, at the end of a democratizing era in American Christianity, and became a devotee of the Cumberland Presbyterians in rural Missouri. The Cumberland Presbyterians were a radical reform wing of the church that grew out of the Kentucky revivals in the early nineteenth century. They expressed and emphasized salvation by faith and tended "to depart from the Westminster standards"—church documents that represented the doctrinal standards of Presbyterian denominations. They promoted religious reform by rebelling against inflexible Calvinistic rituals and symbolism. They also gave up on traditional high standards of academic education for their ministers in order to make it easier to meet the need for licensed clergy in the South and West. These religious reformers held evangelistic camp meetings to practice and promote the faith.[6] Randolph came of age in an antebellum generation in which middle-class families valued respectability, material success, and "identification with a progressive model of human endeavor," so Randolph was raised an evangelical with more progressive views than most conservative Southerners.[7] Randolph grew to manhood in an environment that encouraged self-sufficiency and that was free, to a large extent but not entirely, of deep-rooted, long-held traditions and the ways of life in the East, setting the stage for him to pass on his individual traits, beliefs, and evangelical values to his daughter.

Phoebe's mother, Drusilla Whitmire (Apperson), passed on to Phoebe the personal qualities, convictions, and evangelical principles that helped her daughter develop the ability to understand herself primarily as a "lady," rather than a pioneer woman, growing up in the American West. Drusilla came of age in the same generation in the South as had Randolph Apperson. She was born on September 24, 1816, in Newberry District, South Carolina. She took her first steps in a big, elegant white house on the edge of a town named after her family, Whitmire. Her Cumberland Presbyterian parents, Henry and Ruth Hill Whitmire, steeped Drusilla in the world of commerce and trade, the church's religious principles, and Southern genteel domesticity. Drusilla's enterprising parents never owned a plantation or slaves, unlike many of their neighbors. Instead, the Whitmires were landowners and ran a tavern, or public house, that Drusilla visited. Economic realities meant the Whitmire family "could not afford the luxury of" placing women on pedestals, despite their adherence to the ideal of Southern ladies—an apparent contradiction.

To survive, Drusilla's family sold food, drink, and goods in the tavern marketplace, a center of economic self-sufficiency and financial power.[8] From an early age, then, South Carolinian evangelical, rural, and commercial values and forces comingled in Drusilla's daily experiences. The lessons in Southern sensibilities and Cumberland Presbyterian values and exposure to the tavern business on rural land her father owned shaped her outlook on life and contributed to the rise of the Whitmire family standing in their community.

The intelligence and efforts of the Whitmire family were good enough to make their business successful in a rough, rapidly changing, and unpredictable commercial economy that differed markedly from the world of slaveholders but embraced the hierarchical and patriarchal structure and way of life in the South. The Whitmires' accomplishments made them a part of the slow-rising *middling sorts*—a category based on family status at birth, level of education, manners, and property owned. A rebellious lot, the middling sorts set their sights on owning enough land to enjoy an economically self-sufficient and stable family life and decent physical and mental health, especially in their older years. The Whitmires rose to a higher class standing as the term *middle classes* replaced *middling sorts* between 1800 and 1850. The Whitmire family's crowning achievement: they were "for many generations the largest landowners in the [upper] section" of South Carolina. Drusilla's family joined other enterprising families in seeking new opportunities and adventures, particularly in the West, to maintain a prosperous class standing and to rise in status.

The Whitmires were aspiring parents like the Appersons. They traveled from South Carolina to the West during the period when the Panic of 1817 dealt a severe blow to their home state and signs of slow-growing inequality began to appear in the South more than in the North. They traveled to Missouri on an emigration train of ox carts with the Hearst and Clark families, among others. They established the Whitmire Campground in a territory seeking admission to the Union as a slave state, which was granted in 1821. Drusilla met her future husband, Randolph

Apperson, seven years her senior, in the campground, and they married in late January of 1841, some twenty years after Missouri entered the Union as a state and accepted the highly delineated order of the Southern way of life based on slavery.[9] So Randolph married up. He wed a woman who came from a higher family and community standing. Many other pioneer women in Missouri were not as fortunate as Drusilla to come from such a well-heeled, dignified family with manners and property. The Whitmire family work in the commercial world took precedence in their lives but not to the exclusion of their religious beliefs and concerns and Southern ways.

Coming into the marriage, Randolph Apperson held no property and was from a family with a lower social and economic position than Drusilla Whitmire's. He compensated by becoming a Cumberland Presbyterian elder and Sunday school teacher. Elected church elders were required to possess the qualities and abilities needed to take care of religious, business, and civil affairs. The teaching of Christian principles was a top priority, but they also handled church business and the concerns of ordinary citizens. Furthermore, they executed church laws and guarded "against the effects of power," as one minister noted. They also advocated equality and spread the principles of democracy at the same time that evangelicals supported slavery—an obvious contradiction. The Appersons possessed a Southern family heritage and came from slave states as well, but no evidence exists to prove conclusively whether they sympathized with or supported slavery. So it may have been Randolph's Cumberland Presbyterian occupation, rather than slavery, landownership, or commercial endeavors, which brought him power, authority, and respect. His job defined his family's community standing in the Whitmire settlement as the popularity of religious revivalism grew and talk of democracy came from the mouths of Protestant ministers.[10] Leadership in the religious world took precedence over commercial pursuits for Randolph and brought him and his family standing in the settlement.

The birth of the Appersons' first child—Phoebe Elizabeth Apperson—occurred about two years after Randolph and Drusilla married. There are only a few sources available to tell us about Phoebe's early life. One is an unpublished hagiographic biography written by Adele S. Brooks, Phoebe's friend and a contemporary. It provides some information useful to understanding Phoebe's childhood and teen years, particularly descriptions of the kind of attributes Phoebe possessed as a young person by the early 1860s. But Brooks's work must be used with caution. Phoebe experienced, Brooks wrote, "a lonely childhood" because relatives, friends, and neighbors were not nearby. But although it was not uncommon for women to experience loneliness on the frontier, the Appersons came to Missouri with a large number of homogenous people with a sense of community to establish a settlement in the "wilderness" with "Indians . . . around in every direction" and "some Spaniards but mostly French," according to George Hearst, a neighbor who lived close to the Appersons. Women in the West wrote and talked about feeling isolated. But "women's isolation was perceived more than real," according to one scholar. The Apperson family lived and socialized together with people in the Cumberland Presbyterian campground and with new settlers who were mostly like them. About a year after Phoebe's birth, Randolph and Drusilla had another daughter, Sarah Agnes, but she died in infancy. Phoebe's brother, Elbert (Eppy), came along in 1851.[11] Phoebe's experiences growing up with Southern parents in the middle class in a sparsely settled, but not entirely isolated, area in rural Missouri certainly differed from those of young daughters and sons in affluent, urban families, especially those on the East Coast and with Northern sensibilities. These children, unlike Phoebe, enjoyed the pleasures of wealth and participated in a cultivated, refined way of life in more densely populated areas.[12]

Phoebe's enterprising parents gave their firstborn child an ordinary upbringing for a girl with her ancestry, religion, and class in rural Missouri. They believed, like many Americans, that for women to be successful they had to possess "good sense or good luck" in selecting a man of means, "sharing his identity," and rising "with him." Randolph and Drusilla relied on parental control and home lessons to teach Phoebe the traits of, and respect for, true womanhood and republican ideology in the American West. They taught these attributes and values so she could attract a worthy suitor, marry and have children, and develop her ability to secure a bright future.[13]

To increase their daughter's chances of making something of herself by finding the right suitor, the Appersons drilled into Phoebe a sense of religious duty and the power of moral superiority influenced by their Cumberland Presbyterian beliefs and their Southern heritage. These were special characteristics Americans assumed white women possessed and could put to good use to "civilize" the West. Drusilla Apperson was "a woman of uncommon vigor of mind and body." She presumably held the primary responsibility for raising the Appersons' children. She was, more than likely, the disciplinarian and stabilizing force in the family. Randolph probably supported the lessons Drusilla taught their daughter— Cumberland Presbyterian and republican principles, including literacy, gentility, and domestic skills.

Having been raised by parents who owned a tavern, Phoebe's mother was familiar with the business world. She took business lessons to heart and became a capable household manager. She ran a well-ordered home and ruled with "unflagging diligence" and "efficiency," a hallmark value of rising industrialism. Drusilla also took a strict religious and cultural approach to training her first child in "impeccable conduct, the dignified grace, and the welcoming cordiality southerners . . . considered important in the schooling of an elite daughter." A "reserved and dignified" perfectionist, Drusilla educated her eldest child to have a noble, stately demeanor while she grew up in a world filled with pioneer women with less sophistication and polish. She drummed into Phoebe's head the "traditions of high character, sound principles, industrious living, religions thinking and gentle breeding; and in all . . . [the] ways of worthiness and grace" often taught to Southern ladies and which some Southerners thought "important in the schooling of an elite daughter." Drusilla raised Phoebe, in other words, to believe it was her sacred duty to God to be modest and conduct herself in a morally superior manner that matched people's expectations of what it meant to be a "lady" and "civilizer" in rural Missouri. So this girl with a customary upbringing was steeped in the beliefs and ways her parents thought would be useful for their eldest child in finding a worthy suitor, someone with the potential to help her rise into the elite class so she could avoid misery, misfortune, and public criticism.[14]

But the Appersons had more in mind than simply marital goals for their daughter. Randolph and Drusilla taught Phoebe the value and dignity of labor to help her realize her ambitions and rise in the world. The Appersons believed in capitalism and held a high regard for industry. But the lessons that centered on making money contradicted some of the religious principles of Cumberland Presbyterians, such as their concern about the corrosive and corrupt influence of wealth. Americans saw wealth as an avenue to comfort, power, and esteem in an era of growing industrialism, particularly in regions of the West. Cumberland Presbyterians, though, warned that riches produced temptations and led to idleness and damnation, threatening the social order. It was especially challenging for hardworking women in the home to obtain wealth. They went unpaid for their labor and thus failed to contribute "directly to the family income." There was little danger these women would face the temptations of wealth since they possessed virtually no riches of their own if married. These same women were "incorrectly labeled 'leisured' and endowed with other traits of the upper-class, ornamental, ideal lady." A Cumberland Presbyterian woman, married to a wealthy man still needed to avoid the destructive and sinful effects of riches.

But the Appersons distrusted the label "leisured." So what if Phoebe married someone with a fortune? Although Phoebe's parents did not want their daughter involved in any conduct that smacked of the appearance of leisure or self-indulgence, they still wanted their daughter to marry well. They schooled Phoebe in the appropriate ways of thinking, manners, disposition, and conduct to be a dignified and reserved evangelical woman and to believe in Cumberland Presbyterian evangelical and reform principles so she could achieve a respected position and reputation in her community. The Appersons gave Phoebe "that finest gift of God—an indomitable purpose *to do*." They raised Phoebe to value productive work for some meaningful purpose. As Phoebe explained years later, Drusilla taught her skills to perform useful work, such as "to sew, wash, iron, mend, and churn." Drusilla's "prime command" to Phoebe was to do her work well. Her parents' lessons were comingled in Phoebe's mind at an early age. She was raised to possess a strong respect for evangelical principles and the importance of habitual and useful work that could bring her life meaning, make her money, and contribute significantly to civil society.[15] Drusilla, after all, was raised a Cumberland Presbyterian and a capitalist. Phoebe, then, grew up believing it was her religious duty to do work that was as valuable and important as men's. The lessons Phoebe absorbed about the importance of being a "lady," doing meaningful work, and the significance of religious duty were at the heart of her ability to make something of herself and rise in the American West.

Phoebe's mother was a harsh taskmaster. She demanded that her daughter rip out unaligned "stitches in a long 'felled' seam" and sew them again if her work fell short of meeting her mother's exacting standards. Phoebe refused to take kindly to all of her mother's commands and relentlessly strict approach. Although a display of emotions was a hallmark of evangelicals at church gatherings, Drusilla admonished Phoebe to exercise "firm self-control" and not allow tears or any "other emotional lapses and demonstrations," no matter how frustrated she became—a sure sign she was a "lady." Phoebe rebelled, but to no avail. She bowed, eventually, to her mother's severe demands and conformed to Drusilla's mostly conventional beliefs. The pain Phoebe endured because of her mother's strict teachings alienated her emotionally. It created discord between the two. But her mother's tough lessons set the stage for Phoebe, later in life, to identify with and accept the need for improvements in workers' lives, especially economic self-support for women.

While it took Phoebe a long time to appreciate Drusilla's instructions because of the severe discipline she suffered at the hands of her mother, Phoebe cleverly exploited these lessons, eventually, to justify standing on her own two feet. As she commented years later, "Girls should be taught to do all kinds of useful work. I did not find her [Drusilla's] discipline altogether agreeable at the time, but I have learned to thank her since her teaching has made me independent." Instilled in Phoebe's core being at a young age was a belief that women's domestic work was to be taken seriously and on equal terms with that of men. These principles created internal tensions and conflicts between Phoebe and her mother. Women and Americans in society, in general, grappled with similar issues.[16] Phoebe struggled to learn lessons from her mother, but she accepted the fact that, as time passed, they were designed for her benefit and to improve her skills incrementally.

Phoebe possessed a deep love and respect for her father while she learned her mother's lessons. The Appersons' eldest child identified more closely with her father, in some ways, than with her mother, and so she was more receptive to the new lessons she learned from him. Randolph raised Phoebe like a firstborn ambitious son. He agreed with Drusilla that his daughter should be trained to believe that women's work was to be taken seriously and on equal terms with men's. But he instilled in her, as well, a deep sense of that legitimate authority often demonstrated by an eldest male child. Phoebe's "education in those early years was that of a boy," according to Pringle. Randolph gave his daughter the kind of religious education usually reserved for aspiring young boys, like those he ministered to in Sunday school, particularly of the lower class. Sunday school teachers gave orders. They commanded and enforced obedience. They controlled pupils in the classroom. Most of these teachers taught students to master specific tasks and build a moral, ordered life based on the basic tenets of the Bible. But they also educated girls and boys to be social, sensible, and logical human beings with the power of reason. Teachers instructed students in the ability to rationally justify their own actions and to be accountable to God for what they did. It is difficult to imagine Randolph deviating significantly from these lessons. Randolph's instructions to his firstborn, moreover, went beyond the doors of his home and classroom. He introduced her to a life outside the confines of domesticity and broadened her horizons. He took his eldest child wherever he went and taught her the joys of riding a pony bareback through the woods and fields.

Health reformers, meanwhile, especially "irregular" doctors, "Thompsonians, homeopaths, hydropathists, and electromagnetists, among others," started to tout cleanliness, outdoor exercise, and eating vegetables to restore health and prevent disease. Randolph showed Phoebe, at an early age, the importance of being healthy and physically fit and educated her about men's entitlement, or right, to travel about freely and exercise personal independence. Randolph's eldest child "spoke with delight of her early companionship with him [her father]," Pringle explained later.[17] Little surprise, then, that Phoebe grew up with her father's kind, ambitious temperament and his mixed conservative and liberal outlook. Phoebe also inherited from her father the decision-making and business abilities that she put to good use later in life. Randolph, like Drusilla, instilled in Phoebe the Cumberland Presbyterian's passion "for a broader education" and preference for reform.[18] Early in life, then, Phoebe's character was molded by Randolph, as well as by Drusilla, into one of a dignified, ambitious lady taught to believe that women's meaningful, useful work was the equal of men's.

When Phoebe was with her father, she subsumed her religious and academic education to the pleasure of her father's company. She grew close to him emotionally and relished the lessons he taught her about travel as an enticement to being her own active person. Randolph inculcated in his daughter traits of independence and business ability, associated later with western manhood and being an "industrial mining entrepreneur—the bonanza king who became a more enduring and creative force in the West." Phoebe later "attributed much of her executive and business ability to this early association with her father," according to Pringle.[19] Phoebe held a core set of attributes, beliefs, and values derived from her father and mother, by the end of the 1840s, that set the stage for her to become an able, mature, complicated, contradictory, and multifaceted person with the abilities to make something of herself as a wife, mother, and reform-oriented person within or outside the home.[20]

The Appersons became convinced by reformers that Phoebe needed education beyond home lessons to be able to meet her religious duties, republican obligations, and to rise in the world. But providing their daughter with an advanced education, especially more sophisticated skills and knowledge, would be difficult. Many Americans wondered: why spend time, energy, and money educating a girl, or young woman like Phoebe, if her destiny was to marry and have children? By the late 1840s, though, prospects started to improve for females to get an education. Andrew Jackson, in the late 1820s and early 1830s, had strongly defended systems in society that gave white men power and equal rights, but not women. Yet during the age of Jacksonian democracy, the belief in equality intensified. Faith and confidence in equality led to a profound change in the relations between women and men that impacted Phoebe's life.

Acceptance of the intellectual equality of men and women helped to provide an opening for females increasingly to move into public life and take the first steps to create a women's rights movement, in the late 1840s, that included suffrage. By the time Phoebe approached the age when young girls married, evangelical Protestants and supporters of republican ideology joined forces to argue that "the new nation required a new kind of educated woman." These reformers viewed females as human beings entitled to "the same moral and social rights as men." Reformers promoted the notion that female children get the same education as boys in moral character, literacy, and numeracy, essential elements of education if Phoebe was to make something of herself.[21]

Reformers, at the same time, impressed upon Phoebe and other girls the importance of the traditional, unpaid domestic role, while some reformers, like Catharine Beecher, acknowledged that teaching was strongly associated with a "missionary ideology" and "could be accepted as a *chosen* alternative to marriage for a woman of the educated classes." To ease the anxieties of Americans frightened by the thought of young white women getting schooling, reformers at the time that the women's rights convention took place in Seneca Falls, New York, in 1848, informed parents that education would make it easier for females to stay in the woman's sphere.[22]

The Appersons found the reformers' argument persuasive. They sensed that the more education Phoebe received the better her chance to make a good marriage and be successful. So they paid twenty-five cents a week for their daughter to attend a local pioneer log-cabin common school, or the Salem School, across the Maramec River. Phoebe walked over rolling hills on school days, found a place to cross the river, approached the one-room schoolhouse, and stepped into the classroom. She probably sat with seven or eight other girls and boys on wooden benches positioned in rows on a dusty, hardwood floor. She wrote her lessons, most likely, on slate and recited her spelling words out loud. Because good teachers were hard to come by in rural Missouri, a low-skilled itinerant teacher, almost certainly a female, taught Phoebe basic lessons in reading, writing, arithmetic, moral character, and good citizenship. Girls usually spent more time in school than boys did because parents pulled boys out of the classroom to help them tend the fields. Virtually no evidence exists, interestingly, that tells us about the early life, or education, of Phoebe's brother, Eppy.[23] It appeared the Appersons privileged their daughter over their son. They responded to the reformers' line of reasoning by providing Phoebe with an education that helped build her knowledge and that strengthened her sense of self-confidence.

Phoebe's chances of finding a suitable mate looked dim in the 1850s, despite the fact that, unlike many young girls, she possessed a rudimentary education and basic skills. There were few potential suitors in Franklin

County worthy of her attention, even though there were more white men than white women living there. More men came to the urban areas in Missouri than to the much larger, sparsely settled country where Phoebe grew up. She lacked fond memories of growing up in such an unrefined, uncultivated, and dangerous place. The Appersons had been lured to the West by stories and the publicity about the opportunities there, but it was also a place "fraught with danger." Settlers heard stories about a western environment, or "wilderness," that "bred savagery in man and beast alike"—not the ideal place for a reserved, cultivated lady. Missouri women, like Drusilla and Phoebe, also contended with conflicts, before the Civil War, between whites and Native Americans. "Disputes concerning runaway slaves," and hostilities between "antislavery and proslavery factions," occupied their time as well. Worries about money also plagued women in Missouri, especially Phoebe's family. Her immediate kinfolk struggled to handle the forces of nature and the vagaries in the economy as most of the money made from capitalism went to the cities in Missouri. The growth of industrialism and immigration, meanwhile, increased people's awareness of the wretched conditions of poverty in urban areas. Rural areas struggled with poverty, too, as was evident in Phoebe's description of her birthplace years later: "The country is so poor & rough. The people in Missouri have to work so hard & many are so miserably poor, it makes me almost sick to see it." Even worse, she continued, "they think this is a good place to live."[24] For Phoebe, her birthplace offered few chances to find a worthy mate.

The Whitmire Campground was located in a desolate, violent, and primitive environment that made Phoebe's daily existence, and chances to make something of herself, a real challenge. True, her parents raised her to be an industrious, "ambitious girl," according to Hubert Howe Bancroft, who interviewed Phoebe later for a biography of George Hearst. And she was familiar with, and valued, hard work. But why stay in rural Missouri if she had to work hard and still end up terribly poor? Why remain in her birthplace if she believed her chances to make something of herself, and rise in the world, were slim to none? Even though tales and news abounded about Missouri as a state that presented good chances for advancement or progress, these accounts pertained mostly to white men.[25] While some of the stories offered hope that she might find a suitable husband so she could make a better life and increase her standing in the world, Franklin County simply lacked such opportunities for an ambitious and young, refined girl like Phoebe.

Phoebe became captivated with the tales of gold miners returning to rural Missouri. The miners' yarns of incredible wealth and adventure got her thinking in her early teens about going west. Phoebe did not fit the stereotype of a woman reluctant to go west. She dreamed about going to California—a state believed by many to be the land of opportunities. It was a place in the 1850s that showed "the beginnings of becoming the cutting edge of the American Dream." Phoebe imagined getting a broader education there. She thought about living in a gorgeous home. She pictured herself being active in the Golden State. Realizing her dreams in California, she hoped, would make it possible to lift herself out of her limited rural life in Missouri. Usually the "power to move independently, to go where one wants, and to feel secure in going" was the privilege of men.[26] While Phoebe accepted that her "destiny" was to marry and have children, she fantasized about marrying someone to take her to California where she would have the opportunity to be active like a boy. Traveling, moreover, would give her the chance to see the world as a means of self-education.

But how would she fulfill her dreams and aspirations if the right beau never came along? What if she failed to choose the right suitor or never married? What if she became a widow or pauper? Randolph and Drusilla knew what it was like to survive in a volatile economy. Unsure of what the future exactly held for their daughter, Randolph and Drusilla took precautions. The Appersons were influenced by Mary Wollstonecraft's argument that parents ought to prepare young daughters for self-support in case the need arises. So the Appersons made arrangements for their daughter to learn more sophisticated lessons about how to be a "lady"

and how to become a teacher when job opportunities in public education for women were on the rise. Teaching was an occupation shaped by
republican ideology that gave women a public, political role. Notions of
western womanhood also gave Phoebe the chance to challenge the idea
of separate female and male spheres. Learning to fend for herself would
open the door for her to gain a measure of financial independence, which
might protect her from economic vulnerability and destitution.

Most Americans, by the 1850s, considered teaching the most promising, genteel, and suitable professional employment for a young woman
who wanted to engage in useful public work. The possible exception was
becoming a writer. But being a writer was an occupation that required skills
beyond Phoebe's experience, education, and realm of passions and preferences. To get the proper training to be hired as a public school teacher,
Phoebe needed more than a rudimentary common-school education.
"'Female' seminaries" existed, "where 'lady-like' accomplishments were
stressed, but these were not close at hand, and colleges for women were few
and too distant to be thought of as possibilities in her case," according to
Brooks. The Steelville Academy, established by the Cumberland Presbyterian Church in St. Louis, was a possibility and closer than Brooks thought.[27]

The Appersons' decision to provide Phoebe with advanced skills and
knowledge was driven primarily by practical economic, rather than religious, considerations, so instead of enrolling Phoebe in the Steelville
Academy to learn from pious strangers, the Appersons made plans for
their eldest child to get a "finishing school" education and work as a
governess and tutor in the home of William and Lucy Ann Dun James.
The Jameses were a wealthy couple who lived about one hundred and
fifteen miles southwest of St. Louis. Phoebe's parents knew the Jameses
probably through their neighbor, George Hearst. To work and live with
the Jameses would give Phoebe the chance to escape the watchful eyes
of her mother and father and to avoid hard physical labor in the Whitmire Campground. The Jameses, in essence, would become Phoebe's
surrogate parents.

William James's father, Thomas, came from the "Athens of the West" in Chillicothe, Ohio, to Missouri in 1825 to establish the Maramec Iron Works. Thomas's "third" son, William, grew up to be a dapper dresser, "stood well over six feet tall, weighed more than two hundred pounds, had dark wavy hair, and gave the impression of a dapper young college boy." He was nineteen years old when he married "his home-town sweetheart, Lucy Ann Dun," in 1846. Dun was a Presbyterian from a famous Scottish upper-class family and sister of Robert Graham Dun. R. G. Dunn owned the R. G. Dun Company, which later became the Dun and Bradstreet Company. William and Lucy took over his father's Maramec Iron Works in 1847 and raised three children. William James was a "merchant-capitalist." He ran Maramec like the eighteenth-century "iron plantations" of Pennsylvania. Maramec was a precursor to the company town. The land and the buildings belonged to James, including the local seminary he constructed. William was conservative but "open-minded," like Randolph Apperson. He was willing to experiment. He was connected to prominent men. He "made friends with influential politicians." He also held a paternalistic view of the white and nonwhite workers who rented houses from him.[28] His belief in paternalism must have meshed with the Appersons' Southern upbringing. William wanted to maintain his father's economic standing and make enough money to provide Lucy Ann Dun James and their children with the lifestyle to which she was accustomed. The Appersons' plans for Phoebe to live with and work for William and Lucy Ann Dun James were twofold. Phoebe would learn from Lucy James, a Christian woman, how to attract a worthy suitor while she received training for appropriate, paid, and useful work with purpose and meaning to bring her higher standing in the world, especially economically.

The Jameses became Phoebe's role models. Phoebe relied mainly on Lucy Ann to feed her drive, develop her ability, and teach her lessons in refinement so that she might turn into a sophisticated "lady" and prepare for self-support if the need arose. Lucy was a dignified, Presbyterian woman, reserved and cultured, living in Maramec, an unsophisticated place.

She eased her discomfort in such a rough environment by creating the well-meaning and kindly social and cultural work she had grown up with in Ohio. She brought an air of social and cultural refinement and order to a rural place that foreign travelers found abounded with rudeness, helping to stabilize a fluid class system.[29] Lucy took primary responsibility for holding social events. These social occasions gave people opportunities to make connections, build networks, and develop power-working relationships. She and William made a habit of inviting folks to their home as the Maramec Iron Works grew. Guests felt welcome and valued. Prominent citizens, business and civic leaders, and politicians and spouses enjoyed evenings of merriment. They experienced lively conversation on issues of personal interest. They consumed sumptuous meals.

Lucy held popular Fourth of July festivities, in particular, to help build community among the Maramec workers. Mob violence between whites and blacks often took place in the antebellum North during Fourth of July events because blacks protested a holiday celebrating the birth of a nation that kept them in chains. Lucy's social affairs at times, and in some ways, mimicked aspects of the Southern way of life in the East. These social occasions promoted and expressed nationalistic spirit and pride. The children of whites and of slave parents of a similar age that William hired, according to custom, played with each other at these celebrations.

Sometimes tension and conflict erupted during other holiday events. There were times when employees protested William's policy of forbidding the sale of liquor at the Maramec store, fought, and got drunk. But Maramec holiday celebrations, dances, and fiddling contests often brought the various classes together as well, knitting together the larger community. The social entertainments provided opportunities for exercise and pleasure and reduced tensions. They also drew women into the "politics of celebration." The Jameses welcomed the establishment of the Methodist Episcopal and Baptist Churches at the same time that William and Lucy were handling the challenges of running a business. Together the Jameses built the Maramec Iron Works into "the first successful large-scale foundry west of the Mississippi River." Maramec became an important, sophisticated social, cultural, and industrial complex, and prosperous community. Maramec, by 1861, was on its way to becoming a cutting-edge boom town and a place where frontier society and industry were linked in the American West.[30] Phoebe had the good fortune to have parents who made the right decision at the right time to place her with people with similar ambitions and religious and cultural values.

Phoebe's opportunities to grow her abilities could have taken a turn for the worse at the Jameses because the Civil War disrupted the national and local Missouri economy. But the Maramec Iron Works "escaped serious damage." William used part of the accumulated wealth from his business to hire Phoebe E. Apperson as a governess to the Jameses' children and as a tutor to the kids of the iron workers. Leaving her family and life in provincial rural Missouri behind, she traveled at the age of nineteen to Maramec to be a teacher (most female teachers in rural common schools were sixteen through twenty-five years old). Seeing an iron mill was a new experience for Phoebe. She heard the jarring, harsh noise of the iron works' forges, blast furnaces, and the rush of water when she arrived. She was introduced, as she walked into Maramec, to the world of business and expanded her world of coeducation. Living and working there gave her the chance to broaden her horizons and life experiences. Nonetheless, she anticipated marriage as she settled into the Jameses' household to absorb valuable lessons and develop her skills.[31]

Phoebe, at Maramec, was exposed to the Jameses' mixture of northern, southern, and eastern cultural and benevolent sentiments and values in the American West. She saw how their marriage worked. She observed how they set themselves apart from the masses. She learned about how separating from the common people could produce tension as William and Lucy Ann became part of the wealthy business and social elite. The tension and strife Phoebe experienced with her mother were absent as her life evolved at Maramec. The new governess "got along famously" with Lucy James. Lucy provided Phoebe with a sense of connectedness, belonging, and security that gave her self-confidence. The bond, meanwhile, grew between them at the same time Phoebe felt constrained by the limits of womanhood. Phoebe, when she was off from work, played with her employers' children and studied French. Learning French was "considered an 'indispensable accomplishment in a well-educated Female'" in an era when literacy was on the rise.

Phoebe built on the lessons her parents taught her as she observed, and gleaned a lot from her experiences with, William and Lucy. Her knowledge deepened about how to behave and function properly in the more cultured and refined world of powerful higher-ups. She learned how those with money helped deserving relatives and friends of limited means, including herself. She also grew into a young woman who was a bundle of complicated contradictions that were closely interrelated. She was modest but ambitious, a young evangelical middle-class governess. She possessed only a rudimentary education at the same time she was engaged in getting broader knowledge and experience. She prepared herself for marriage to a man who could bring her into elite circles while she prepared herself for public work and self-support. Governess Apperson controlled, commanded, and enforced obedience from students. In doing so, she found out what it meant to experience a measure of independence and reap the economic benefits earned at the Maramec Iron Works in a community growing into a city in the West during the Civil War.[32]

Phoebe's abilities were tested at Maramec. The contradictory nature of her individual traits led to tensions that were quite evident at Maramec when she tried to get paid what she thought she deserved. Most rural female teachers were restricted by sex segregation and low wages. The average weekly wage in 1861 for female rural teachers was $4.05 and for male rural teachers $6.30. Determining Phoebe's weekly wages is difficult because her pay seemed to vary depending on the number of students she taught and the length of time she devoted to each one. Phoebe, at one point, got paid $4 for schooling two children for two months. She also received approximately $40 in November 1861 as well as March 1862. There were times, though, when her work went unpaid. That was an awkward dilemma for a young, dignified woman in her first job. What should she do? Should she know her place? Should she defy the prevailing conventional view of nineteenth-century white women as deferential, demure, and submissive, and ask for or demand her wages?

After some contemplation, Phoebe dug deep down, made a decision, and asserted herself. She expressed her disapproval. She wrote a note to Lucy James in a modest, polite tone in an effort to make the tension vanish between herself and an employer she liked. She requested payment for her work. Her approach paid off. She got her wages. Emboldened by her accomplishment, she followed the admonitions of at least one nineteenth-century Protestant clergyman who preached "saving . . . as the true way to improve one's station." Phoebe decided to deposit twenty dollars in the local bank in May 1862. She could buy, with wages left over, a pound of butter for a little over eight cents, a pair of shoes at the community store for $1.75 or $2, a yard of muslin for just over thirty-seven cents, or a barrel of flour for $5. Her earnings appear to have given her an economic standing greater than Maramec iron workers who received average wages of about ten dollars per month.[33] Phoebe became aware of and gained an appreciation for the relationship and interplay between religion, money, and class while she lived with the James family, developed skills to assert herself, and met the challenges of work at Maramec.

With the James family, Phoebe could see how wealthy, elite Protestants operated. She gained knowledge about what it meant to be a teacher who earned her own way. She developed an invaluable skill—the ability to take action to get what she thought was rightfully hers. These experiences, born of complex contradictions, made an indelible, lasting impression. What Phoebe accomplished at Maramec set her apart from most white women who lacked the opportunities to test and grow their abilities to get an advanced education and broader experiences beyond their immediate family and home environment.

Phoebe E. Apperson got a chance to test and expand on her newly acquired skills when she entered public life, in 1861, to work as an educator. Local officials, who probably knew of her work experience at the Jameses, asked her to fill a teaching post at the Reedville School, a district school. There were no prospects of marriage to a suitable beau in sight, so she accepted the job that separated her further from her parents. Teaching at the Reedville School gave her a chance to get more work experience and shape her own destiny. Teachers acted as parent surrogates and moral and political guides. They molded student character and intellect. Common-school teachers engaged in intellectual pursuits. They taught pupils "ranging in age from toddlers to two or three to young men and women of nineteen or twenty." Lessons focused on the maintenance of emotional restraint and deference. Yet students also were taught to be thinking and independently active people and citizens. But this was at a time when many Americans and the law considered women and blacks to be dependent children and inferiors without citizenship rights. Phoebe was a young woman raised to be attentive to Cumberland Presbyterian beliefs and principles. So she asked God to "help me to do my duty in all things," she explained a few years later.

It is hard to imagine that a young Phoebe, raised to believe in the moral superiority and authority of women, deviated much from what most teachers did in the classroom. And what they did in the classroom was to protect, "civilize," and train boys and girls to be virtuous citizens. Westerners accepted educating young boys and girls together. It is difficult to say, without evidence, whether the girls in Phoebe's Reedville School classroom got exactly the same education as boys. Girls must have been exposed, though, to some of the same lessons boys received. In any case, Phoebe's background and teaching experiences call into question the argument that all country teachers lacked training and "status sufficient to grant any kind of real power."[34] As her twentieth birthday approached, Phoebe was a dutiful, dignified, evangelical, and reform-minded public school teacher who possessed and exerted power and moral authority skillfully over her students in the classroom.

Phoebe had a chance to think about attracting the right suitor to satisfy her parents' expectations and her dream to go to California while she taught. She knew her path to higher social standing, accomplishment, and hopes for living an active life in the state on the edge of the Pacific Ocean depended on her ability to choose and marry a worthy man. Phoebe's choice of a prospective husband made clear her ambition. She could have chosen an ordinary man about her age. She could have selected someone with few prospects for a bright future or a local man with lesser status and wealth. She accepted, instead, a marriage proposal from the most promising, ambitious suitor to come along, George Hearst. Phoebe's future husband lived on a farm nearby and was twenty-two years older, "old enough to be her father."[35]

Despite his declaration that "no record" existed of his birth, George was born in Franklin County, Missouri, on September 3, 1820, according to his autobiography. His ancestors and parents, like the Appersons, came from the South. George's father, William G. Hearst, was of Scottish heritage from the Abbeville District of South Carolina. He was raised a Presbyterian. He, unlike Phoebe's ancestors, owned "three or four slaves," George recounted inaccurately. William G. Hearst actually owned "19 of the 41 slaves in the [Maramec] Township," according to one historian. William Hearst was a hard-working farmer. He had "a great interest in public affairs." But, as George noted, he was not "very religious" or "very strict." Elizabeth Collins, George's mother, possessed English and Irish heritage. She came from Georgia. Elizabeth's family settled in Bigelow, Missouri, in 1805. A dignified, reserved Methodist with broad views, she married William in 1817.

The Appersons had three children. So did the Hearsts: George; a younger "unmarried" sister, Martha, or "Patsey," who did not have a will when she died; and Jacob, a disabled, unmarried brother. Jacob died when George was nineteen years old. Martha passed away when he was thirty-four. George's father, by the time he passed away, headed the wealthiest family in the Maramec Township. He owned six hundred to eight hundred acres of land. He also served as a commissioner of school lands and as an overseer of the first road district.[36] Evidence is lacking to tell us about Hearst family politics and dynamics, especially about their attitudes, religious or otherwise, and interactions with slaves and immediate family members, some of whom were disabled and died young. Thus, we know very little about Hearst family relations in the early years of George's life. What little evidence we have is primarily from George Hearst himself.

George was a mama's boy. He tagged along with his father, as a young boy, to political meetings. But he was closer emotionally to his mother, Elizabeth, than to his father for several reasons. His father died when he was a boy. So in his early years, George was "embedded in a feminine world" like most boys. In his autobiography, he admitted, "I was my mother's boy." Most American boys were taught that the way to become true men was through attributes of self-assertion, aggression, and independence. These traits could also include expressions of tender emotions. Young boys usually learned these qualities without guidance from "caring adults" and "without any significant emotional support." George's assessment of his mother downplayed traditional manly attributes and expressed a sentimental view. Elizabeth gave him the care and support he needed. No surprise, then, that he displayed gentle and sympathetic feelings toward his mother. George revealed his emotions toward Elizabeth by helping her with "a very hard life," he wrote, especially with chores around the farm.

George took over management of the place when he was fifteen. He still felt sentimental about his mother and praised her profusely when he was sixty years old. "She was quite a good woman, and very conservative under all circumstances," he wrote, "always cool and always gave good advice." She never got mad. She also was "a woman of some education," he remarked, and had a high class standing too. Elizabeth, like Phoebe's mother, came from a "very good family," he explained. "She had things you would not see nowadays, such as cashmere shawls [introduced to Europe during the Napoleonic wars, they were too expensive for the middle classes], leghorn bonnets, and things above the common." Elizabeth was devoted to her family. She possessed a reputation, much like Drusilla Apperson, as a good household manager.

George displayed loyalty to his mother but had ambition like his father. As he explained, "I . . . was very ambitious to learn everything, and it would worry me terribly if I could not succeed." Growing into manhood, George received scant and irregular education. He attended grammar school "for three months at age eight, and for fifteen months beginning at age fifteen." He recounted that he "did not go to school more than two years all told, outside of the few months when I was a mere child; or say two and a half years was all the time I ever spent in a school house." He graduated from the Franklin County Mining School in 1838. He hoped for a brighter future, possibly in politics, after graduation. But looking back on his life years later, he believed any success he had he owed mostly to his mother rather than to his father.[37]

The West, for George Hearst, held great potential as a place where he could apply the abilities he inherited and the lessons he learned from his parents to become rich and famous. Growing up in rural Missouri, stories of the discovery of gold in California captivated George. Lured by the promise of riches and opportunities, he went west in search of fortune in 1850. This was the same year California joined the Union as a free state. He acknowledged in his autobiography that he survived the potential dangers on the journey that included "a touch of cholera" near Fort Kearney, Nebraska. Once he reached his destination, he became a placer and quartz miner. He vied for riches with Argonauts, participants in the 1848 gold rush, and many foreign miners. Hearst amassed capital by using new technology to dig glittering ore out of the ground. He struggled, working with the latest mining machinery, to handle the intense competition from white and foreign miners in the diggings whom he thought took money out of the country and made it difficult for him to prosper financially.

George and his financial associates established the Ophir Silver Mining Company in April 1860 with a capitalization of $5.04 million. His company was a prime example of the new corporate businesses in an emerging economy. It was the biggest corporation in the West and "part of a global industry." The fruits of George's abilities and hard work led to his ownership in the Ontario Mine in Utah, the Homestake in South Dakota, and the Anaconda in Montana. His mining accomplishments made George Hearst a bonanza king, a status based chiefly on his wealth and a position comparable to industrial tycoons in the East.[38]

Bonanza kings claimed to share common values, identity, lifestyle, and institutions with elite businessmen in the East. George Hearst possessed inherited wealth and proven leadership skills like eastern industrial tycoons. But he fell short in some areas when compared to his eastern counterparts. He never joined elite male groups for instance. "I never had anything to do with affiliation societies, such as Masons Odd Fellows," he wrote. His father, a modest man and a good judge of character, had owned a large amount of property. Wealthy ancestors, to match those of eastern business moguls, however, were not included in his family tree. The value of the large amount of property his father owned paled compared to the value of the assets of eastern industrial tycoons. George also lacked the polished and sophisticated social skills that men in the New York and Philadelphia wealthy class possessed to be accepted by high society or the social elite.[39] But what he lacked in social skills he made up for in his abilities to find shiny ore and dig it out of the ground. George was more comfortable in a man's world than in a woman's. He preferred the rough-and-tumble world of miners in the West to rubbing elbows with the rich elite at high-society affairs in the East or West.

George's mother fell ill with tuberculosis in Missouri in the midst of his struggles to gain investment capital for his mining business. She asked him to come home. So he dropped his business pursuits and traveled to his mother's side in 1860. He became concerned more "than anything else" for his mother while at home. But he also thought about getting married. He was way past the age, at forty years old, when most men were expected to get "hitched," settle down, and have children. He knew the "advantage," he said, "of having a woman our [sic] West." "Of course, if she was a good woman," he wrote, "it was a good thing to have her; but outside of that there is not much that she could do. The first five years in California a woman was a curiosity," he explained. George probably agreed with many Americans that the definition of a good woman meant being physically attractive and neat and tidy in appearance. A virtuous woman also met a husband's sexual demands and bore and took care of children. She maintained family respectability as well. George wanted to marry a good-looking, virtuous woman, like his mother, who represented power and morality. Yet he recognized the constraints of womanhood.

The additional challenges he faced, while he handled law suits against his mines, temporarily drew his mind away from thinking about finding a good woman. To complicate matters, he was a secessionist. That resulted in his being thrown in jail for using "alleged seditious language." But he refused to let his political and business difficulties and interests overshadow entirely his need to find a potential mate. He took a local young woman, Josephine Renfro, to the county fair while his mother was ill. He also reacquainted himself with his "former neighbor" and distant relative, Phoebe Elizabeth Apperson.[40] George was not looking for female companionship or romance. He was not looking for a high-society socialite from the East or someone who would act as a sounding board for his business interests. He wanted a down-to-earth, respectable, physically attractive, virtuous, hometown girl sensitive to his own ambitions, someone who possessed the ability to give him a son and heir and help him make his way in the world, particularly in the sophisticated social and cultural world that his mother's family and wealthy elite men inhabited.

Elizabeth Hearst passed away six months after George returned to Missouri from California. Protecting himself from the emotional pain he suffered from his mother's death, George quickly transferred his affection for his mother to Phoebe E. Apperson. He made a practical decision to court Phoebe. He believed that there was not "much chance of" a real aristocracy "being established" in America. And he held "no fear that there ever will be any class rule here." He was driven to be successful nevertheless. Selecting an appropriate, proper woman to marry was important to George. But his decision was not as important to Phoebe for obvious reasons, particularly economic. Having little zest for social climbing and social power, he needed a future wife with a more refined and cultured upbringing, like his mother's, if he was to be successful.[41] George's age pushed him to choose the right mate sooner rather than later after his mother's death.

George's future wife, like his mother, was raised a Protestant. She was a Cumberland Presbyterian and considered by some a belle of her time. She stood five feet, four inches and had a deceptively slight build. People perceived her as physically frail and weak because of her diminutive body. But at the core of her small physique existed a strong constitution. Phoebe had a "quantity of smooth dark hair" that fell around an oval face. This physical trait represented beauty and a morally virtuous character at the time. She had "remarkably fine and delicately tinted skin, a gentle expression and large solemn [gray-blue] eyes of power—clear, penetrating and responsive, a gleam of humor in their change ful [sic] expression," Brooks noted. A medium forehead and mouth, a straight "aristocratic" nose and rounded chin completed the idealized picture of a young woman. Phoebe possessed a shy demeanor, was inclined to show courtesy, and be pleasant too.[42] Phoebe was the virtuous woman who possessed the traits and abilities George needed to help him fit into the world of the powerful with high standing in their community.

George Hearst and Phoebe E. Apperson had a lot in common. Both possessed Protestant and Southern roots. Both believed in hard work and were practical. Both wanted to take advantage of opportunities. Both had aspirations for a better life and to rise in the world. Both had experienced the loss of a sibling. Phoebe seemed to be the future wife George wanted. And George seemed to the future husband Phoebe wanted. Phoebe E. Apperson became a means to George Hearst's ambitious ends. George became a means to Phoebe's ambitious ends. George's and Phoebe's union would be beneficial to both.

But Phoebe's and George's devotion to religion, physical description, and personal deportment were as different as night and day. George was close to being a nonbeliever, rough and uncouth. He claimed his father was raised a Presbyterian but not very religious. But he knew he had to have religion to be considered acceptable. "When I was young I had very strong religious views," he explained a bit disingenuously in his autobiography. Phoebe saw George differently. She assessed her future husband by the religious standards set by her parents. She found George wanting. She registered her utter dismay at his lack of religious devotion. As explained in her diary, a year after the Civil War ended, he "was not a member of any church and comes so near being an infidel, it makes me *shudder*." George's lack of devotion to religion bothered her. But he possessed Southern attributes that must have appealed. He had a "drawling but musical voice," according to the *New York Times*, "and the pronounced accent of a [white] Southerner of the slave days." He stood over six feet tall, with a rough face, deep-set blue eyes, and a bushy, long beard. Yet he was unsophisticated. Observers described him later as loud, crude, flamboyant, "an illiterate man, but not an ignorant one." He was a stubborn individualist and a lazy, informal dresser. He never wore a dress suit. A story frequently told, but unsubstantiated, described him as "an inveterate tobacco chewer," a reporter explained, "and when he becomes animated in congenial company scatters the extract of the weed somewhat promiscuously over his front shirt." The newsman "could *not* [emphasis added] vouch for . . . [the] accuracy" of this tale. He also came from the wealthiest family in the Maramec Township. The rumor was that George Hearst was a philanderer. His passion, though, was mining. He thought everything, including a marriage, took a second seat to digging shiny rocks out of the ground.[43] For Phoebe, the differences between herself and George would make it a challenge and a lot of hard work to "civilize" her future husband.

George Hearst was one of the most eligible bachelors in Franklin County. He asked Phoebe Apperson, one of the most beautiful, single women in the same county, to become his wife in 1862, as a "marrying craze" swept the nation. Phoebe bowed to tradition and convention in that year. She did what Drusilla Apperson, Lucy James, and most women did—she accepted an offer of marriage. Brooks explained, "According to local tradition she [Phoebe] had refused a dozen offers of marriage," before she accepted George's. No proof exists to corroborate the story. Phoebe must have known that accepting George's marriage offer would mean a ticket out of the Missouri frontier to California. Brooks claimed that Phoebe's parents objected to seeing their only daughter wooed by a man twenty-two years older who would take her further west to California. The state seemingly was a land of opportunity. But it also was a dangerous and unstable place. The claim that Phoebe's parents objected also is unsubstantiated. An 1855 Missouri law, at the time George proposed to Phoebe, stated that a young girl "over the age of eighteen years and under the age of twenty-one years, shall have full power to make any marriage contract concerning any real or personal property, or any other matter, with the consent of her father, if living." The revision of the 1855 Missouri marriage consent law occurred in 1866, four years after George and Phoebe wed.[44] Phoebe, at the very least, must have had the consent of her father, unless the law was ignored or George and Phoebe took the matter into their own hands.

Some might think Phoebe wanted to marry George for his money. That was one way for a young woman to make something of herself. But no evidence exists, currently available to scholars and researchers, to suggest that George ever thought his fiancée was a gold digger. Hearst family legend says that Phoebe knew George mined precious metals and that she was aware George possessed money, but perhaps not a fortune. As the story goes, Phoebe bought a piece of brown merino wool to have a dress made before heading to San Francisco. George first ordered his new bride a black lace-trimmed silk dress. He then bought numerous colorful silk dresses when the Hearsts arrived in California. Phoebe was appalled at George's extravagance. But a friend told Phoebe, "Don't worry, dear. Your husband is part owner in one of the richest mines of the West."[45] It is hard to image George proposing marriage, or going through a wedding ceremony, if he had believed Phoebe wanted "to tie the knot" because of his money. A gold digger hardly fit his definition of what it meant to be a good woman or wife.

Phoebe realized her ambition, at the age of nineteen, to marry a man who would take her to California as the Civil War raged. She and her fiancé rode over bumpy, rugged, dirt roads from Franklin County to Steelville, Missouri, in Crawford County, in the summer of 1862 to get married. Minister W. P. Renick of the Steelville Presbyterian Church conducted the wedding ceremony on June 15. The legal ritual probably took place in the home of A. J. Seay, a "bachelor friend" of George's, a young lawyer, and veteran of the Civil War. The newlyweds and kinfolk celebrated after with sumptuous food, more than likely, in the James family home.[46]

Phoebe's ability to select the right husband was another important step toward making something of herself. She took on her new husband's identity and social standing on the day she and George married. They signed a prenuptial contract the day before. Phoebe, as the use of "separate estates" grew significantly in the antebellum era, did what was expected when she and George agreed to marry by mutual consent. She was self-sacrificing and abandoned her teaching job. George in return legally gave his bride-to-be fifty shares of stock in his Gould and Curry Gold and Silver Mining Company of Virginia City, Nevada Territory. The par value of the company stock in 1863–64 was 4,800 shares at $500. Phoebe, like her father, came into the marriage without any property. But she owned and controlled the shares George gave her for her natural life. Under no circumstances was she to use them to pay off debt or other liabilities. Her stocks reverted to George if she died before her husband.[47] George and Phoebe's prenuptial agreement made her a stock owner with an estate separate and independent from her husband. The fact that she had her own estate set her apart from most married women. Her marriage to George, which brought her property ownership, immediately improved her legal and economic status.

Does the prenuptial agreement signify that George Hearst bought a wife? Some might think so. It was true that nineteenth-century American marriage laws gave husbands the right to buy wives like a piece of property. Some men, by custom, did treat wives as property to be bought and sold. But George valued Phoebe's beauty and cultured background. He also understood the limits of womanhood. He adhered, moreover, to an 1849 Missouri law that gave married women the right to possess, use, and distribute property. Phoebe held control of her own financial resources separately from George unless he altered the agreement or divorced her. But the property Phoebe owned was small when compared to her husband's. It would not be enough for her to survive on her own for very long. George could also take away, at a moment's notice, what he had given to Phoebe. Phoebe, even with the prenuptial contract, was economically dependent upon him and vulnerable. George got what he wanted. He married a good, beautiful, and more cultured person, at least in his eyes. The property he gave Phoebe could protect her, economically, from being entirely at the mercy and whim of her husband. The prenuptial contract also allowed Phoebe to contribute to family support. But she could not use the assets George gave her to pay impatient creditors in case her husband was in a difficult position financially and lacked the ability to provide for his family or to pay his debts.

So George's motivation for the prenuptial agreement is hard to pin down. As one scholar stated, "The *only* [emphasis added] incentive for a husband to agree to settle property on his wife was fear of financial ruin."[48] George would have indicated that Phoebe could use her assets to pay creditors, and would have given Phoebe a much larger part of his estate, if his only desire was to protect his family against creditors. But that was not the case. So the exact reasons for George giving Phoebe a separate estate when they married remain unclear. The property Phoebe owned gave her a practical advantage regardless of George's real reasons for creating a prenuptial contract. Possessing a separate estate encouraged Phoebe to act and think for herself as an independent person.[49] In other words, the legal agreement gave Phoebe the opportunity to make her dreams come true and enhance her ability to stand on her own two feet—hardly a sign that George treated Phoebe like a piece of property. George, by signing a prenuptial agreement, sent a message that he would give his wife latitude, and possibly freedom, denied other white, married women.

Phoebe and George Hearst left Franklin County, Missouri, for St. Louis on the first leg of their journey to California in October or November of 1862. From St. Louis they went to New York. From New York they took the safest and most expensive way to get to California. They sailed on a ship, the *Ocean Queen*, to the Chagres River on the Caribbean side of Panama, then crossed the Isthmus of Panama by rail and traveled up the coast of Mexico to San Francisco. It was a long, slow, and potentially dangerous trip for passengers prosperous enough to be able to afford passage. Passengers on overcrowded steamers were exposed often to attacks from Confederates, who were also on the lookout for boats carrying troops and gold bullion to help the Northern cause during the Civil War. Travelers frequently experienced Panama fever, heat, cholera, and seasickness. Phoebe's maiden voyage turned out to be "an ordeal," according to Brooks. Phoebe had grown up with "a remarkably sound and resilient constitution" at a time when people, including her family, thought "that good health was within the reach of each and every citizen."[50] Maintaining the best of health on the trip to California was a challenge.

As well, Phoebe was pregnant on the voyage. As the steamer swayed back and forth, she became "seriously and alarmingly ill." It is unclear whether her pregnancy or the sea voyage, or both, made her sick. Unless people had known she was pregnant, her illness would have fed the contradictory mythical image of the "Victorian ideal of the perfect lady." The ideal was a lady who was "the symbol of conspicuous leisure and the agent of conspicuous consumption." It evolved into a symbol of a conspicuous consumptive or an invalid—a useless, frail, delicate, unhealthy, and disabled female. Phoebe struggled with her illness. George's voice about this trip, though, is virtually nonexistent. Women and men who were ill, nevertheless, were perceived differently. Viewing a Victorian woman as a conspicuous consumptive served as a justification in the minds of many Americans to deny women, like Phoebe, legal and political rights, even though some held property rights. On board, Phoebe met Margaret Hughes Peck, wife of David M. Peck who was part owner in a wholesale grocery called Wellman, Peck and Company. Traveling with them were the Peck's three children, Helen, Orrin, and Janet. George took a special liking to Orrin. And following the common practice of many nineteenth-century women who developed emotional ties to one another, Phoebe and Margaret developed a "mutual attraction" that brought Phoebe comfort.[51] The young, new bride came to understand, during the voyage to California, the importance of female friendships to help get her through physically and emotionally hard times and survive harm or injury so she could arrive unscathed in San Francisco to live out her dream.

Although Phoebe possessed the endurance and stamina to survive the unpleasant, dangerous trip, the port of San Francisco was a welcome sight. The *Sonora* fired her gun to signal the ship that brought the Hearsts to San Francisco. A colorful crowd of folks stood on the dock as the steamer approached the wharf. Cheerfully dressed women, Native Americans with blankets, Spaniards with large hats, and Chinese with queues and mandarin coats gazed upon the approaching steamers. Prostitutes, rich men wearing silk hats, hoodlums from the tar flats, gamblers, and throngs of people eagerly awaited "the newspapers and intelligence" the ship carried.[52] But the welcome greeting only lasted a short time. The Hearsts disembarked and walked into the "topsy-turvy" city of San Francisco after the steamer docked.

Most people, like George Hearst, came to San Francisco to get rich quick. George was probably not a new visitor to the city. Having been familiar with life in the mining West, he more than likely knew what to expect. Phoebe, though, was unprepared for what she found. It was a place associated with a rapidly changing urban environment triggered by the accelerated growth of industrialism, immigration, and urbanization. San Francisco was built "almost overnight." Life there had its "ups and downs." Everyday hazards and ordeals were common. Phoebe probably saw very quickly that San Francisco was no fairyland. She likely possessed, like other newcomers, a sense of bewilderment as she realized she was one of less than approximately 30 percent of women living among a "sea" of men who refused, especially in San Francisco, to abide by Victorian standards of decorum and respectability.[53] Was the trip to this unfamiliar place worth it?

San Francisco was a place "born cosmopolitan," meaning a place that consisted "of elements gathered from all or various parts of the world." Hotels, restaurants, and amusements welcomed customers from Asia, Latin America, Europe, and North America, and a handful of African Americans. Phoebe tried to get comfortable with her new surroundings. She strolled by commercial establishments in the city that served as centers of popular and consumer cultures and economic power. These places helped order and tame a disorderly and unstable society. She saw the people and places that introduced conflicts between capital and labor and created turmoil. She observed firsthand the inequality that plagued society. To complicate matters, the Committee of Vigilance of 1856 and its successor, the People's Reform Party, dominated the town. Political mismanagement and corruption prevailed. The foreign-born, meanwhile, came to the San Francisco of the 1860s in a flood. San Francisco teemed with foreigners by the time Phoebe was a permanent resident. More foreigners existed in San Francisco than in any other large American city in the 1870s, 1880s, and

1890s. Yet it was a place where a majority of residents were native-born.[54] The life Phoebe knew while growing up in rural Missouri, and working for William and Lucy Ann Dun James, faded away and then vanished for the most part when she entered San Francisco.

Phoebe began to show her ability to express herself and meet American, and George's, expectations during her early years in San Francisco. Most white, pioneer women wanted an ideal home with a stable family life. Phoebe was of a similar mind, even though her upbringing had shaped her into a refined and cultured woman who also wanted more from life than that. An ideal home became a symbol of the desire of pioneer women to bring "civilization" to the West. Phoebe got her wish to live in a gorgeous place. But any dream she held of getting a beautiful, ideal home, and a stable family life, was shattered quickly when George Hearst told her they would live in the dazzling Lick House Hotel on Montgomery Street between Post and Sutter. The Lick was San Francisco's first and finest luxury hotel. Walking through the lobby, people saw the "flagged marble" floor. Mirrors, plush velvet, and brass galore adorned the inside. The hotel had a dining room made of oak, walnut, ebony, mahogany, and lime wood imported from South America and the Orient. The arched roof, ground-glass skylights, and three crystal chandeliers that cost a thousand dollars each, enhanced the appearance. The Lick was the "most favored by the fortunate." It was the center of the city's fashionable, business, and community life until William Chapman Ralston, a banker known for his lavish lifestyle, opened the block-long Palace Hotel in October 1875. The Palace was proof of the city's financial good health.

But the hustle and bustle in the Lick from the comings and goings of middle-class and elite men and women proved too much for Phoebe and the lifestyle and trappings of the rich and prosperous made her uncomfortable. An unpretentious young woman, she expressed her desire to live in a homier, quieter place conducive to building a stable family life. Practical considerations seem to have trumped romantic ones when George proposed to Phoebe and she had decided to accept. But they loved each other in their own ways. Each wanted to please the other. George pleased Phoebe. They moved to the Stevenson Hotel near Market Street, several months later. Phoebe pleased George. She performed her wifely, Christian duty and George performed his husbandly duty once the Hearsts settled in. She and George showed their ability to have a child—a precious natural resource expected of a newly married couple. But Phoebe was the one who demonstrated her physical capacity to carry the child to term. She bore, on April 29, 1863, a healthy son and heir, William Randolph Hearst. The birth gave Phoebe "supreme joy" and a "deep sense of the responsibility of each generation for the welfare of the next," according to Brooks.[55] Phoebe had dutifully accomplished the godly aspirations she was taught to believe in. She did what the Cumberland Presbyterians and society expected of a refined, white woman. She had a child, became a parent, along with George, and accepted the responsibility to raise a son. Phoebe hoped bearing a child would help create a stable Hearst family unit as well as life in a disorderly, chaotic city.

But Phoebe's dream of a stable family unit never materialized because George Hearst left his wife and infant son, shortly after Willie's birth, to take care of his mining interests. His prolonged absences satisfied George but made life miserable for Phoebe and undermined her confidence in her skill to get what she wanted. George and Phoebe essentially began to lead separate lives. The separations were so trying that Phoebe wrote to her husband that she felt like "a fool for loving" him. George responded cleverly but a bit defensively: "I am sorry you think so. I do not know. I do not think I have done anything so unworthy of your love, I know I would be sorry to have done anything. . . . I am not sorry I have you and hope I never will be. . . . But I have the blue[s] and feel very bad." George, struggling to deal with his business ventures, felt homesick and "like giving up every thing [sic]," he wrote. But he added a telling note: "miss you for my self [sic]." He wanted to satisfy himself but at the same time avoid doing anything wrong in the eyes of his wife. Rumor had it, though, that he was pursuing another woman.[56] George's protracted absences and the rumors added stress and strain to Phoebe's marriage.

Phoebe's confidence in George was shaken. For all her upbringing, training at the James household, and experience teaching, Phoebe struggled, because of George's prolonged absences, to build a strong, reliable family unit. She felt pain and suffering in her marriage when George was gone. She was very low. She explained to Willie's Irish Catholic governess and wet nurse, Eliza Pike, in an innocent tone of voice, that she was "*terribly* lonely." Wet-nursing was a way that domestic employees such as Pike could earn "a living by selling what they produced." Eighteenth-century Americans relied on wet nurses to take care of babies experiencing difficulty eating. But new nineteenth-century views claimed that wet nurses threatened the family pecking order because of their control over infants. This situation often triggered class tension and conflict. Hearst hired Pike as nurture replaced fear as a central guiding principle of middle-class child rearing. Pike became Hearst's employee during a shift away from the authority of fathers to an emphasis on domestic affection. Pike became a replacement for Phoebe's domestic affection while she wet-nursed Willie. A further complication was that Eliza took Willie with her on trips and away from home. Phoebe, in the meantime, gave Pike instructions on how to handle Willie while they were gone. She expressed hope that Pike would wean him soon.

But Phoebe felt she held little control over her life or that of her child while Eliza and Willie traveled, even though she and Pike communicated with one another through letters. Phoebe also struggled with the example George set for their son regarding religious matters. Her husband was not a member of any church and was almost an infidel. "It is hard for me to contend against" George's lack of religious "influence on my boy," she wrote. Worse yet, she missed her "Baby every minute." To comfort herself, Phoebe wrote to Eliza as though she were a friend, hardly an acceptable arrangement for a woman married to a wealthy man. Meanwhile, Phoebe's

1. Phoebe Apperson Hearst and her baby, William Randolph Hearst, 1863. 1991.064-Ax, box 1:03. Courtesy of the Bancroft Library, University of California, Berkeley.

letters to her husband had little to no impact on getting George to return home sooner than he planned. He kept telling her he needed to do the work he loved. And he reminded her he would be away for long periods. There were times when he did tell his wife he expected to be home soon. But he refused to say what he meant by soon—a day, week, a month, or more?[57] Upset and desperate, Phoebe lamented, "I am so lonely I don't

2. A young George Hearst. BANCPIC 1991.064–AX, box 1:01. Courtesy of the Bancroft Library, University of California, Berkeley.

know how to live."[58] She was in an unfamiliar place far from George and her parents. She possessed few, if any, true friends. While she struggled to take care of her first child, she felt so forlorn and helpless. Marriage and raising a child were not what she had anticipated.

Phoebe must have wondered if she had made the wrong choice. Her marriage became strained to the breaking point when George's interest in California politics kept him away even more. George served in the California legislature at a time when mining and agricultural interests and leaders operated in an era of exploitation. Legislators believed that mining and farming would bring quick wealth to California and, by implication, to the federal government and the rest of the nation. So the state's nascent political ruling elite decided wealthy men like Hearst must be given top priority in formulating policies. That is, Hearst's economic power needed to be turned into political power. In 1865 Democrats nominated him to the California Assembly. Following the assembly swearing-in ceremony on December 6, legislative leaders assigned Hearst to the Committee of Mines and Mining Interests. George, a supporter of Thomas Jefferson, was a conservative Democrat. He was gone from his family much of the time during his 1865–66 term, because he was "constant in his attendance at the session(s), returning from Sacramento only for Saturday night(s) and Sunday at home," according to Brooks.[59]

Phoebe pined for her husband while he was away. She wanted him to come home and stay there for a long while. Unwittingly, she made her feeling of loneliness worse by keeping "strict account . . . of all his absence," she wrote in early 1866. Only when he was at "home" for an entire "winter" did she "begin to feel more like married people than before," she explained.[60] The unified and stable family life she wanted was not at hand because she had married an absentee husband and father. Getting George to stay at home for extended periods was out of the question. She agonized over her marriage and experienced little satisfaction from it. But she relied on her ability to make practical decisions to survive and endure.

Phoebe decided to make herself feel better by turning her personal sorrow into action. She intended to be "very busy," as she put it. She kept her body and mind active doing household chores like putting up fruit. She dreamed about becoming "a thorough French scholar," she remarked. Travel became another way to keep herself busy and engaged and to take her mind off of her unhappiness. Since George decided he could not come to her, she decided to go to him. Phoebe packed her "portly trunks," as it became increasingly acceptable for women to travel. George "was so glad to see me," Phoebe noted. She attended rounds of dances, luncheons, dinners, and legislative and "private masked ball[s]" once she arrived in Sacramento. Balls in the state capital served as expressions of civic culture, a tool of propaganda, and a way to arouse people to political action. But Phoebe found it difficult to leave George when the time came. "You know how foolish I am about leaving Mr. Hearst," she confided to Eliza Pike.[61]

Phoebe, after she returned, struck out more and more on her own. She traveled as much as she could. She visited friends by stagecoach. She went "to Yosemite falls but that is a very rough trip," she mentioned. She stayed with a friend, Camilla Price, for several weeks. She satisfied her passion for a broader education by seeing the exhibition of a local teacher, a Miss Patton, which stimulated her mind and gave her a chance to gather knowledge. It "was quite a success," she declared. She called on a local judge. She busied herself by pursuing her interest in design and architecture. She developed plans to make the Hearst "house made much larger." A young mother, she also engaged in the unexpected. She left Willie at home, in April 1866, possibly with his governess or her parents, and sailed, with her brother, Elbert, to the Sandwich, or Hawaiian, Islands. "The voyage proved an excellent tonic," according to Brooks. She enjoyed "moonlight parties with horseback quadrilles" and social entertainments. Traveling expanded her horizons and developed her abilities to handle life experiences outside the home. Being active and going from place to place helped her to rebuild her confidence and make herself happier. But her marital problems remained.[62]

George, meanwhile, was "homesick" and aware of Phoebe's problems, especially her loneliness. Concerned about his wife's situation, he came up with a solution that he must have thought showed his love for his wife. He paid for Phoebe's parents to move from Missouri to the Santa Clara Valley near Lawrence where "old friends and neighbors from Missouri" were located. Visits to her parents, from time to time, helped assuage her loneliness. But she wanted a permanent solution to make her happy in her marriage—for George to stay put and spend much more time at home. Driven and self-absorbed, George paid little attention to his wife or his son except for writing an occasional letter. Nor did he respond to Phoebe's request that he stay home longer. He needed to attend the sessions of the California legislature, and his mines in places far away beckoned because he needed to handle contests with competitors and extensive litigation battles that cost him dearly and threatened his success as a bonanza king.[63] Trips to see her parents and others were few and far between—hardly a lasting solution to her troubles. George's solution to Phoebe's problem was only a temporary fix.

A financial crisis that hit the Hearst family in mid-1866 made Phoebe's intractable problems even more complicated. George's modern corporate enterprises and industries experienced hard economic times because of the mining industry's "difficult transition into maturity" in a developing region, the West. George lacked investors to provide the needed capital to increase production. One reason was that the output of California gold mines declined precipitously. Miners lost their jobs. Most of George's fortune vanished. The adverse effects of the rapid economic decline that adversely impacted George's mining business, nonetheless, affected Phoebe, even though she was a property owner. She grew anxious and frightened. She possessed virtually no understanding of her husband's finances or knew how to protect herself and weather the economic storm. As the value of her husband's land and mining production plunged, she wrote, "Times are hard. my husband has lost a *great* amount of money lately. he is feeling low spirited." She feared George's mining companies would go under. "Mines that we have don't pay. all is a drawback, I don't see a bright futur [*sic*]," she wrote. She felt helpless and began to realize how economically vulnerable and financially dependent she was on George. Her husband's financial problems scared and distressed her.[64] George's financial crisis undermined her confidence and tested her abilities.

Phoebe decided to do what Americans expected of a genteel, white, married woman. She accepted the limits of womanhood circumscribed by men. She supported George as the mining crisis grew worse and his fortune dwindled. She concluded that a good way to help George was to concentrate on matters that she could control—the household finances and her domestic employees. She felt "quite discouraged" over money matters, especially since George's financial crisis had altered the class status of the Hearst family. She decided to follow the example set by her mother and mother-in-law. She made efforts to help stabilize the situation while she lived in San Francisco—a notoriously unstable place. She displayed financial savvy and autonomy in her home. She ran her household like a business with a degree of competence. Sensitive to "a great many [business] failures here," she explained, she economized on goods and the services of domestics who "were status symbols for" families. As she put it, "I feel that we must live more quietly & be economical."

She sold the carriage, horses, and harness. "I have sent the horses to Pas. Poor ney. I shall miss him. we have sold the Rockaway for two hundred dollars." "I don't like to see them on the streets," she wrote. It was painful for her to see others control goods that had helped set the Hearsts apart from the lower classes. She also let her domestic employees go to save money. But she needed to rationalize what she did to herself. "So many servants are only a nuisance," she explained, because it was hard work to train them.[65] She weathered the vagaries of the economy by mounting a reasonable moral and practical response to save her husband from what she thought might be economic failure and ruin.

But Phoebe saw a silver lining during the hard economic times, too. She was free from her husband's day-to-day control over her life because he was gone so much. That meant she possessed the time and opportunities to make decisions independent of George. The free time allowed her to grow into her own person, within expected constraints of sex and class, and acquire greater sophistication in her abilities and experiences— opportunities that were unavailable to most married women, including white women. But with the comfort she experienced despite misfortune, there were challenges.

Phoebe struggled with her ability to handle family finances appropriately during the period of crisis. She set aside lessons learned about the wealthy elite. She resisted the growing appetite for spending money on splendid fashion, high-society affairs, and excessive travel in order to survive. Making money and dressing to the hilt had become conventional marks of high class standing and respect in the 1860s. Phoebe grew reluctant, in the words of Thorstein Veblen, "to conform more nearly to the requirements of the instructed taste of the time." She shunned fancy clothing to appear beautiful to men or to express the wealth, power, and esteem "long associated with the upper strata of society." Phoebe resisted, moreover, being consumed with "genteel self-fashioning and the careful cultivation of appearances" as economic disaster enveloped the Hearst family. She believed that spending money frivolously, or engaging in conspicuous consumption, as Veblen later called it, was sinful. To properly display her evangelicalism required that she reject "showy clothes and everyday luxuries." When an invitation "to the finest party ever given in Cal . . . at the Lick House" arrived, she expected George would not go because he rarely if ever attended high-society events. But he "want[ed] to go to *this* party at the Lick—for a wonder," she wrote. She never revealed why George wanted to attend and thought seriously about whether to go herself. But the pain and suffering she was enduring during George's financial crisis placed things in proper perspective.

To appear at this party "she would have to get a handsome dress. It would be both troublesome and expensive and after all would not pay. I don't care about all the furbelows & vanity," she remarked. She understood that New York high-society women set the standard in fashion for the rich. She knew, moreover, that she fell considerably short of the standard. Her dresses were "very small potatoes," she wrote later, when compared to the magnificent clothes worn by wealthy New Yorkers. Phoebe believed that clothing need not be expensive to prove one worthy, admirable, and respectable. There was more to a person's character than fine clothing and attendance at lavish social entertainments, she thought. As Phoebe—or

Puss, as her family affectionately called her—noted, "dress does not *make* the person." Buying costly goods also gave the wrong impression at a time when the Hearsts struggled financially.

Convinced that individual traits took precedence over a personal image and persona, Phoebe turned down the party invitation and tightened her economic belt. She knew that "a great many are going to the World's fair. I wish I could go, but I can't and it does no good to think about it," she wrote. To further underscore their financial straits, she told Eliza that a friend "had no assistance from Geo for a long time because he *could* not give any more."[66] Phoebe's top priority and challenge was to use her abilities to help her husband and family survive hard economic times. She wanted to help George keep his mining business from going under. But the economic trade winds that coalesced around the Hearsts created status anxiety and difficulties for Phoebe.

Phoebe tried other ways to make herself feel better as business and money problems lingered like a dark cloud over the Hearst family. She kept herself busy. To comfort herself, she wrote in her diary, which allowed her to express herself in private while helping her to shape views that might one day become part of public opinion as she ventured out into the world. She turned to religion and was industrious, as well. "There is always plenty of work to be done," she wrote. She displayed her passion for learning, too. She attended public lectures that stimulated her intellectually. Not a regular churchgoer nor fervently religious, she believed nonetheless in following general evangelical principles. She enjoyed Dr. Wadsworth's "very fine" lectures on the Young Men's Christian Association, a nondenominational, nonpartisan, Protestant voluntary association. Wadsworth's lectures got her thinking, for one so young, about such weighty issues as secularism, life, and death. "Oh that we were so *worldly* life is so short we should be prepared to die at anytime," she wrote. She also "heard a *very* good sermon from Reverend O. P. Fitzgerald" and thought it had value. "I feel it did me good," she explained.[67] But she still needed to grapple with the realities and pressures of married life after her good feelings dissipated quickly.

Phoebe's abilities to handle the Hearst family crisis suffered a setback when the accumulated stress and strain of her marriage and financial problems took a heavy physical toll on her. She came down with "bilious fever, then inflammation between the Stomach & Bowels" in the fall of 1867. She was so ill that when she "was dressed thick & had on a shawl" she "only weighted 89 lbs (eighty nine lbs)," she explained. "I have not been so sick since my marriage." The "severe sickness has changed me terribly," she added. She felt the need to battle her illness to bolster her physical power and avoid strengthening people's perception of women as inferior, even though she was quite discouraged about her health. She thought it would help if she experienced a change of scenery to, among other things, "escape from the anxieties . . . of everyday life." A visit to a doting father in Santa Clara Valley, California, would provide comfort and support to help her get better. Free to make decisions centered on herself and her son, while her husband was gone, she rented out the Hearst's home for half a year and took a break from raising Willie and the burdens associated with the never-ending flow of guests. She would be "really glad to rest from having company & visitors," she noted. She was not physically debilitated enough from her illness to prevent traveling.

So she left Willie at home and followed a pattern established in America by the 1850s. Phoebe traveled for physical as well as mental and spiritual renewal. She would make her "home at Pa's for the summer," she explained, to recuperate and recover. Before she came back to San Francisco, she ate "enough to scarcely sustain life" and "came very near taking a long journey across the dark river from when no traveler returns," she wrote in a dramatic tone. Waxing philosophical about life and death, she counseled Pike: "It is a great burden but life has so many cares we must only try to be patient & do all the good we can. the end is not very far distant." Mentally and emotionally shaken by her illness, she thought about the paradox of prosperity—the paradox between wealth and morality: "We ought to think more of these things & less of the world with its gaudy trappings and emptiness," she wrote.

From the beginning of her ordeal, though, Phoebe felt gratitude. The Hearsts had enough money to live comfortably, and "that is much to be thankful for," she observed.[68] Experiencing difficulties in her marriage and George's financial crisis made a long-lasting, indelible impression. She would never forget the fear and anxiety she suffered. Time spent in independent rational thought, though, helped her get through her economic and physical ordeal and develop her skills and talents, as well as finding other ways to handle personal crises.

Faced with such intractable problems, Phoebe relied on a practical approach, with personal appeal, to cope. She experienced "a great increase in power and autonomy *within* her family," not "over sex and reproduction within marriage" but over raising and controlling her child. She took full advantage, unlike most evangelicals, of a shift in middle-class attitudes from male dominance and the importance of religion to the central role of the female parent for affection and protection of a child's education, survival, and welfare. This new attitude moved away from the reliance on Divine Providence to raise children. It implied that human beings possessed the ability to "shape and control the natural order." Phoebe and women of her generation followed the advice contained in the new model of nineteenth-century expert advice on raising children: be a good parent by watching over and building passionate relationships with sons and daughters.

Phoebe experienced a close emotional attachment to her doting father. So it seemed the right and natural thing to do to lavish attention and affection on her son, Willie. She also believed it her duty to meet George Hearst's and society's expectations to be a faithful, dutiful wife and a good parent. For her this meant she had to provide Willie with "a fine education, if nothing more," she wrote, so he would have an easier time of it than his father.[69] George's prolonged absences gave Phoebe the chance to develop herself and her abilities, become resilient, and build her physical strength. But taking concrete action to meet her husband's and society's expectations also undermined her individual growth. Phoebe felt frightened and helpless while she raised her son without George close by to guide and support her. Doting on her son helped her feel better. But this did little to relieve her anxieties while she pursued other practical solutions to help her cope.

To complicate matters, Phoebe's fear grew because she lacked knowledge about the human body and medicine. This restricted her ability to handle her, and her son's, health problems. "I am constantly afraid [Willie] will get sick," she wrote Eliza Pike. She was at a loss to know why anyone, including Willie and herself, became ill. Her fears about her son were particularly acute while "the plague or pestilence," which "is really awful," she noted, spread, and smallpox raged through San Francisco. As she explained, "I have not felt afraid for myself but for Willie. His system is now in such a weak state he would be more susceptible to any disease, I have been vaccinated 13 times in my life. it never took." But the lack of medical records makes it difficult to substantiate her claim. Her ignorance made it hard for her to take care of Willie. So she took precautions and was very careful. She became so scared that Willie "would not live" that she remarked three times in one letter about "how careful" she had to be. She made every effort to observe her son closely and do the best she could to protect him from colds, typhoid, the plague, and small pox. Small pox was "malignant & fatal in most cases," she wrote. She watched him "every minute" so no danger would threaten him.

When Willie "had a fever & a very severe cough," Phoebe stuck close to her son and nursed him back to health. She understood the inherent problems in such an approach, however. When Willie was with her "so constantly," she wrote, he would become "very babyish." So she was careful not to watch him too closely. She knew smothering him with constant attention would not prevent him from getting sick, either. Instinctively she wanted to strike a balance between doing what was expected of a good parent and turning conventional wisdom—good parents watch over their children—to her advantage. Willie "is a splendid big boy & so much comfort. I don't know how I could do without him," she explained. Phoebe's devoted son returned the compliment. He told Phoebe how much he loved her.[70] Phoebe's anxieties about disease and health helped her build a close emotional bond with Willie similar to the one she experienced with her father and that George Hearst had experienced with his mother. Willie provided Phoebe with the emotional closeness she craved but could not get from George. Developing a loving connection with her son helped fill the void created by the prolonged absences of her husband. But it also reinforced the limits placed on her by her domestic role. Her close relationship with her son, moreover, was not enough to rid Phoebe completely of her fears, especially about her body and disease, and the agony and dissatisfaction she experienced in her marriage.

Phoebe, then, relied heavily on her domestic abilities and role to solve her difficulties. Most women hoped to bear children after marriage. She thought having more children would be the solution to her problems, so she wistfully longed for a daughter. She exclaimed as early as September 1866, "I do wish he [Willie] had a little sister, but no signs yet!" Ten months later, she thought again about getting pregnant. Because George was gone a lot, she possessed little control over marital fertility. She knew having more children would be by chance. There were times when she thought she was pregnant. But she had incorrectly assessed her situation. The pressures of life, meanwhile, took a physical toll. She experienced fainting spells and suffered from dysentery. She was bored, too. "Times are very dull here," she lamented. Phoebe seemed to accept reality that summer: "There seems to be no hope of a little sister," she wrote.

Her ardent desire to have more children kept haunting her. A year later she wrote George that it had been almost a year since she had seen him. She could not figure out why she was unable to have another child. Phoebe agonized for yet another year. She hoped "for *something* but no change yet," she wrote Pike. "I am *always* sorry we have not six children, but cannot remedy the matter," she remarked to George several years later. She wanted "a little girl of my own," she lamented. Eventually, she assessed her regret against reality. As she explained to George, "I know you like boys best, but I am not likely to be soon blessed with either [a boy or a girl]." In an effort to put the problem to rest, she sternly informed her husband, "I will say no more on the subject."[71] She questioned her ability to have children and remained unsatisfied. If she and George produced no more children, would her marriage become one of convenience?

Phoebe and George's paths rarely crossed by this point. Phoebe, moreover, knew George would not console her about her love of children and her strong longing to have more. She and her husband, nevertheless, loved each other as best they could. They had an emotional bond, even though Phoebe had to remind herself of George's love for her. "I *must* comfort myself with the remembrance that you love me," she remarked, "even if you *never* say you miss me, we cannot all be demonstrative." Her marriage was far from ideal. So she sought solace from Eliza Pike. Pike provided her with the emotional intimacy and support she needed and could not get from her husband. She felt comfortable revealing her fears to Eliza. But Phoebe refused to accept completely the reality that she was unable to become pregnant again, even though she told George she intended to be silent on the subject. She solemnly confided to Eliza several years later: "There seems to be no hope for any more babies in this family. The other day a friend remarked that it was better to have one splendid boy than several ordinary ones. though that does not reconcile me."

Phoebe continued to keep herself busy, in the early to mid-1870s, so she could keep her mind off of getting pregnant and prevent boredom. She met her husband's and society's expectations and raised Willie and entertained company at expensive social affairs. "Our market bills were enormous," she recalled. She fell back on the lessons in self-sufficiency she learned from her mother to rectify the situation. She felt "obliged to do some sewing & mending—for it took all my money to buy something to eat" for her guests. She spent the rest of her time on housecleaning and putting up fruit and sweet pickles, an unpleasant task she was "not sorry to lose" to an employee. She built a stable to keep cows, chickens, and a pony. She also took short trips.[72] She led a separate life, for the most part, from George.

Even so, she felt something was missing. Unable to understand why she could not have another baby or control her fertility, she reasoned it was futile to keep thinking and dreaming about it. She possessed the intelligence to conclude there must be more to life. Ironically, George's decision to give Phoebe access to thousands of dollars of his fortune opened the door for her to search for meaning and purpose beyond her traditional domestic world.[73]

2

Money

At this new turning point in her life, disappointed that she and George had been unable to conceive more children, Phoebe Hearst relied on her husband's fortune to find a new identity and role for herself. She began in earnest to search for a way to live on equal terms with her husband beyond those duties required of a genteel woman married to a bonanza king. Traveling became one path that opened the door for Phoebe to further education and self-improvement. Her life experiences in Europe would give her the opportunity to find something more important to do besides being a dutiful wife, parent, and social hostess. Hearst would then became involved in both women-only and mixed-sex nonpartisan voluntary association politics, in which women sometimes had power over men. Her accomplishments brought her a good reputation, social and cultural capital, and status.[1]

While she sought a new identity and role, Phoebe became engaged in a delicate and challenging balancing act to find a life with meaning and purpose, moving back and forth between satisfying men, particularly her husband, and herself. The discoveries she made about herself and what she learned as she traveled throughout Europe, coupled with her passion for an education, led her to involve herself in the American kindergarten reform movement. There she spent her husband's fortune wisely and well. Her ideas and adroit handling of his money brought her recognition and status in the nonpartisan political world of voluntary associations. These accomplishments, in turn, moved her into the arena of health reform where she deftly acquired and used power successfully to advance herself by forcing male physicians to do what she wanted—advance women in medicine—as she continued to hold high-society affairs and in general do what was expected of women married to wealthy men.

Having plenty of money did not automatically create an idyllic life for Phoebe. Money got in the way, for example, of her expectation to celebrate the holidays with her husband and eight-year-old son as Christmas of 1871 approached. George's mines had been "looking fine" and were on the way to "making plenty of money again," Phoebe noted. Her husband, meanwhile, wanted to make sure his mining business was profitable over an extended period. So he wrote to his twenty-nine-year-old wife, "I will not be home at Christmas." In anticipation that his announcement would fall short of meeting Phoebe's desire for him to spend Christmas with his family, George tried to soothe her feelings when he delivered the bad news. "I never was so anxious to see you in all my life. I am homesick," he wrote. Driven to be successful, he exploited the idea of manhood for his own benefit to explain why he would not be home. "And sometimes I think I will start and go at once but that would not be manly," he wrote. The manly thing to do was to take care of his mining company and make more capital: "As long as I pretend to do anything to make money I must attend to business before my own happiness or wants," he explained a bit disingenuously. A loyal wife, Phoebe had begun to adjust to George's prolonged absences earlier, about eight years into their marriage, resolving to understand George and accept his ways. He was just not the kind of man who could "stay at home long," she explained to Eliza Pike.

She determined not to feel hurt this time. Nor did she express her displeasure when her husband was away. "I have made up my mind to not fret about it. I cannot help feeling lonely, but may as well take things quietly," she remarked. She decided, instead, to make light of her situation. She joked to Pike, "You know how fond he is of rocks." Phoebe's level of maturity must have pleased George. But humor alone probably was not enough to erase her disappointment that her husband would not be spending Christmas with his family. Phoebe resumed her regular schedule of activities to keep her mind off her disappointment while she waited for George to return. Possessing access to George's fortune, she increasingly spent her husband's money on holding elegant lunch parties and dinners, doing what Americans thought a woman married to a man interested in making a lot of money should do. She attended the opera, theater, concerts, and lectures in style to broaden her education.[2] She adjusted, by Christmas of 1871, to George's need to make money and the fact that she would celebrate the holiday without him. But at least she derived some satisfaction from spending George's money on social and cultural experiences that increased her knowledge and broadened her experiences.

Phoebe was dependent on George's money for her survival. He had control over his entire fortune, with the exception of what he had legally transferred to Phoebe in the Hearsts' prenuptial agreement. Fortunately for Phoebe and Willie, George survived the mining crisis in the 1860s. The mining bust ended. His business recovered, which increased his fortune by the early 1870s. His success likely emboldened him to think about setting his sights on the Hearsts rising into the elite. His and Phoebe's decisions show they sensed what they needed to do to get there. George took steps to provide his family with the luxurious lifestyle Americans expected of the rich and famous. To develop that lifestyle entailed social climbing. But he displayed little interest in being a social climber. He relied, instead, on Phoebe to become a successful socialite. To be a success meant the Hearsts needed a proper house in which to entertain. To obtain the appropriate house required that he spend money, of course, so he bought a "big, roomy house on Rincon Hill," "at Chestnut Street near Hyde," as San Francisco grew into the economic power and financial center of the West.[3] George's willingness to spend money on a large home for entertainment convinced Phoebe of his commitment to move the Hearst family into elite circles.

But the purchase of a large house alone was insufficient for the Hearsts to gain acceptance among the elites. Neither was it enough for the Hearsts to establish strong roots in the top tier of society. George realized it would take Phoebe looking and playing the part of a high-society woman married to a wealthy mining tycoon. Knowing he was not coming home for the holiday, he satisfied himself and tried to placate his wife at the same time. He gave Phoebe Christmas gifts in 1871 of an "elegant black silk dress & one thousand dollars in gold."[4] Phoebe sensed the need to act the part her husband wanted her to play. But would she accept George's gift, knowing her evangelical beliefs warned of the sins and evils of wealth? Would taking George's gifts help her develop the ability to make San Franciscans sit up and take notice of the Hearsts? High-society women were expected to demonstrate informal social power, or control, over the casual use of resources in their homes. But to rise in class, a woman also needed to get involved with charitable and nonpartisan voluntary associations outside the home where females could lord power over guests and members.[5] Phoebe, though, was not yet involved in such organizations, so accepting George's gifts became a first step toward getting members in the top tier of society to welcome the Hearsts into the elite.

Willing to dress and act the part of a woman of means, Phoebe made a practical decision for the sake of her husband and family. She set aside her religious concerns about the temptations of wealth and accepted George's gifts of a black dress and money. Such an elegant gown made possible the shaping of her public persona—a fictional presentation of herself to public guests within her home that they carried with them back to the outside world. She knew how to present herself properly to guests in the social and political elite within and outside her home. She ambitiously and ably spent George's money on high-society affairs in ways that garnered the approval of the elites during the era of the western bonanza kings when the impact of industrialism had created gaps in wealth between the rich and poor.

As 1872 approached, Phoebe began to enter the San Francisco social scene at a time when the view that socialites ought to equal or surpass "the English in their manners and appearance" fell "like a cloud upon the social world of San Francisco," a high-society reporter noted. Would-be San Francisco socialites like Phoebe felt pressured to follow the British high-society model. Phoebe accepted the burden of physical and mental distress associated with social climbing. And she knew the power of politeness and the value of making friends and good connections from the time she had spent with William and Lucy Ann Dun James. She began her rise by replacing her middle-class acquaintances with those in the upper tier of society. The middle class at the time had amassed control over visiting rituals. Phoebe, by the standards of the era, had been middle class when she married George. Joining members of the middle class, she filled up at least one entire day a week making rounds of public and political calls on "social equals," defined by class. She tolerated visits from a bevy of "flounced and crinolined ladies with snugly belted waists and modestly secluded feet," wrote Brooks, her biographer, friend, and contemporary. Female visitors "set out at half past ten in the morning on an all-day 'round of visits'" wearing clothes that suggested idleness because they constrained movement at the same time that women engaged in life's activities. Ceremonial rituals to say a quick hello usually lasted about fifteen minutes. Others took up to two hours. In one morning alone, Phoebe "counted 48 calls" to the Hearst home from bothersome company and "so many hangers on," she wrote. The visiting rituals, over which she possessed some but not entire control, were so vexing that she "had fainting spells." She was "completely exhausted," she explained.[6] In Phoebe's mind, nevertheless, spending time and energy on social calls from an array of guests, especially the wives of prominent men, was the proper self-sacrificing act for a woman married to a wealthy, powerful man.

3. Phoebe Apperson Hearst with shawl and black background, September 20, 1872. BANCPIC 1972.015 pic 1:1. Courtesy of the Bancroft Library, University of California, Berkeley.

Phoebe also changed her relationship to people and the social order between friendly visitors by spending money on affairs that mimicked those in the top tier of society, further separating and isolating the Hearsts from the middle and working classes. She orchestrated large, lavish, and impressive high-society lunch parties and elegant dinners. One of her first crowning social achievements was the celebration of their tenth wedding anniversary in August 1872. It was "a very handsome affair," she wrote. She sent out 125 invitations, because that was all her home could "comfortably accommodate," she explained. She scrupulously planned her guest lists and events. She used silver and a "new set of China and glass ware, with a very large, beautiful centerpiece of rare flowers." She "had excellent music." "Everything but the ice was made in the house," she proudly declared. Holding such events reflected the pride Phoebe held in the making and using of local products for her social entertainments and in providing jobs for residents close by. A society reporter understood and sounded a conservative note about the importance of Phoebe's consumerism. Entertaining by the rich benefited the poor, according to the reporter. As this writer noted, "I know the good it does, how many poor people are benefited by the lavish expenditures of the rich. I know that it encourages horticulture; I know that it keeps looms weaving, girls sewing, painters painting, printers printing, coach men in fares, and tailors in work, and the postman and messenger boys ringing the bell and making the servant-girls run up and down stairs." But what were the workers' views of all this? The reporter does not say.

The anniversary celebration appeared to fulfill all of Phoebe's expectations. "The supper was an entire success," she exclaimed proudly. Over time, though, Phoebe grew bored and impatient with holding high-society affairs, hobnobbing with elites dressed in the height of fashion, and discussing news and gossip with an endless stream of guests—writers, painters, businessmen, politicians and their wives. The social rituals, the constant flood of visitors, and attending a whirlwind of balls, hotel dances, luncheons, and dinners were tedious and physically draining. She "was so worn out" that she grew "very tiresome [*sic*]" of her "work," she remarked.[7] But she kept holding the parties because she believed it was her duty. Doing so would help George realize his class and political ambitions. Phoebe also was proud of the skills, talent, and good judgment she used to select the goods and services for her events, especially her anniversary party. Putting on successful high-society "shows" built the Hearsts' reputation for respectability. It boosted their status. It set them apart socially, economically, and politically from the lower and middle classes.

But there were times when Phoebe got fed up and reached a breaking point holding these many entertainments. She expressed her displeasure with having to do so much for people as early as the fall of 1867: "I will not wear myself out for people as I have done," she explained. Although Phoebe thought it was her duty to hold society affairs for the sake of her husband and family, when she had fallen seriously ill during George's financial crisis, she sensed she was destined to do more with her life. As she put it, "I have something of more importance to live for."[8] She had not been raised a "leisured" woman in the traditional sense of the word. She was raised a worker and "civilizer." She needed to nourish the core of her being by crafting an identity and role for herself, beyond that of a western wife, parent, and society hostess.[9]

In 1872 George opened the door for Phoebe to search for a life of consequence that would allow her to make something of herself. He suggested that she and Willie "go next April [1873] to Europe & attend the *world's* fair at Vienna" and "then go to Paris if we are blessed with good health," she wrote Eliza Pike.[10] He told Phoebe that he would meet them in New York to sail abroad, leading his wife to think that the entire family would travel around Europe together. But he reneged on his promise. Phoebe tried as best she could to get him to change his mind, but George was intransigent. She lacked the rhetorical power to convince her husband. It was "very difficult," she remarked, "to persuade him to go anywhere for pleasure" because of his work.[11] George's business and political interests took precedence over his wife and child. But his money increased the likelihood that the Hearsts would move into the elite and, at the same time, gave Phoebe the chance to satisfy herself.

Phoebe could have rejected her husband's proposal to go abroad. But faced with the choice of staying in her protected refuge, her home, or going without her husband, she accepted George's offer to cross the Atlantic. She reasoned it was the best thing to do for George as well as herself. "I really feel sad to break up my nice home," she lamented, "but now is such a good time to travel and I had best take advantage of it." Travel would give her a chance to alter and transcend the boundaries, established by men, which had constrained her. It was an offer she believed she needed to take. Would George ever again make another suggestion like this? Who knew? So she jumped at the chance to broaden her horizons. She was disappointed that George would not travel with her and Willie. But "we expect to have a splendid time," she wrote.[12] Her decision pleased George and herself.

The prospect of going to Europe to see the Vienna International Exhibition and stay in Paris would be a transforming experience of culture and refinement for Phoebe and her son. Her "first trip to Europe" was "so long and eagerly anticipated," according to Brooks. She prepared thoroughly for an active, public life abroad by intensely studying French and German. Such a long journey to places so far away would be a challenge for a woman with a young child. But Phoebe thought Willie was old enough to appreciate and benefit from the sightseeing. One of George's acquaintances, Peter Toft, an artist in Europe, thought Phoebe could handle the challenge. She was "genteel and quiet, but with all firm in her resolutions, and remarkable free of all kinds of nonsense. I think she can take good care of herself," Peter wrote George. "Americans found part of their national identity in the role they played as tourists in Europe," one scholar observed.[13] Phoebe and Willie might find part of their individual and national identities abroad, too. She was forced by societal convention to rely on her husband to provide the money for her adventure; yet having control of George's money, and spending it wisely, was no guarantee the trip would produce the results Phoebe desired.

In fact, Phoebe faced quite a challenge gaining control over the money George had promised for the trip. She knew how to manage household finances. She possessed property and gold. She also occasionally discussed George's business dealings with him. But she was not an owner of a company in partnership with George. She lacked an understanding of just how much money her husband controlled as well. George, furthermore, refused to teach her about the intricacies of his financial affairs and business dealings. Household employees, as late as 1890, did the everyday shopping for wealthy San Francisco women. Phoebe did get some experience managing finances beyond her household when she traveled on short trips to see George, relatives, friends, and local exhibitions. She could have learned more lessons about money as a member of charitable, benevolent, and female nonpartisan, voluntary associations in the 1870s. But she was not yet a participant in such groups by the middle of the decade. She was busy, instead, learning how to live without George. She spent much of her time and energy raising, protecting, and caring for their son. She also honed her skills as a high-society hostess. But few opportunities existed for her to manage finances outside her home or for her to learn about the inner workings and details of her husband's business affairs.

The limitations placed on women that prevented Phoebe from being adequately schooled in finances were so severe that success manuals "excluded women" and "associated failure," economic and otherwise, with her sex. The handful of women fortunate enough to learn how to handle money, or be successful businesswomen, were taught by their husbands.[14] George, though, was not interested in taking Phoebe into his confidence on money matters and his business affairs. Nor did he want to teach her how to handle finances in general or instruct her in the complexities of his mining companies. So Phoebe depended on George to take care of the management of family finances and business affairs outside the home. That meant Phoebe relied on George to make the financial arrangements for her 1873 trip.

Relying on George to take care of money matters for her trip produced painful lessons for Phoebe. Her husband promised she would have the money for her adventure. "As to the money you will need in or on your trip dont [sic] give your self any trouble about it. I will see that you have it at any cost," George wrote. George wrote a letter of credit to Lloyd Tevis, a capitalist and attorney, to provide her with ten thousand dollars. Phoebe, while she packed her bags and trunks, battled with her husband's business associates, Lloyd Tevis and James Ben Ali Haggin, a San Francisco lawyer and rancher in partnership with Tevis, over how much money George intended to give her. Phoebe expected the amount George promised. She thought it was her right to get it. Tevis and Haggin had other ideas. They refused to comply with George's promise. Phoebe felt comfortable revealing her true feelings to her husband in private. Angry over the prejudicial treatment Tevis showed her, she took action to get what she wanted. She expressed her displeasure adamantly to George: "I did not feel at all satisfied in regard to my letter of credit, for you *positively* told me the amount would be ten thousand dollars and assured me it would be right & Tevis would attend to it." Upset with what she saw as Tevis's disrespect, Phoebe wrote sarcastically, "I would just as soon have taken an ice bath at once. Haggin was polite & agreeable enough, but gave me the amount *he* thought necessary." She trusted George would provide her "with all *needed* funds but what wounded me," she remarked, "was to be set aside in that way, as though it was of no consequence."[15] It was obvious that money had become Tevis's tool to express a devalued and prejudicial view toward Phoebe.

Deeply hurt, Phoebe intensely resented how Tevis treated her. She wrote to George, "I dont [sic] mean to have you think that I feel myself of importance." She added, "I think at first Mr. Tevis was very indifferent & thought I did not amount to much." But her acute sensitivity to being devalued as a woman existed beneath her modest demeanor. The money George promised represented her husband's appreciation and respect. So she felt she was entitled to it. "I do feel that I have a right to respect *even* from [the] Tevises," she explained, assuming Tevis and his wife held the same views. She judged correctly that she needed to prove to Tevis she merited his esteem. Phoebe knew women were supposed to submit themselves to men. She understood she needed to seek Tevis's approval. Yet she possessed the good fortune to have married a wealthy man who gave her control over thousands of dollars of his money and allowed her to strike out on her own. Knowing George trusted her with his money, she went directly to her sympathetic, rich husband. She explained the situation and demanded that George take action. As she wrote George, "I was at first very angry, & would not trust myself to write to you fearing that I might say something to regret & you would feel annoyed." But she decided, instead, to set aside her fear. She asserted herself to express her views and feelings to her husband. Her anger born of pain was a sure sign she wanted to develop a mind of her own and control her own life.[16]

Phoebe knew it was acceptable to state her feelings honestly and directly to her husband in private. But she recognized it would be socially unacceptable for her to communicate her anger to Tevis in public. So she expressed herself positively and forcefully, acting decisively rather than engaging in an emotional, public outburst. She reined in her feelings as her mother had taught her. Then she used an approach similar to the one she used with Lucy James years ago. She made a polite but firm demand to Tevis to gain his respect. Once she "made it a point to show him in a very quiet way I had a head of my own, he finally became quite agreeable," she wrote George. Even so, the experience produced deep pain that stayed with her. Phoebe bristled later when she thought about how George's business partners controlled the money he intended for her to have. She lashed out. She told George she felt "as though Mr. Haggin knows every cent I spend & mentally comments on it." She added, "Sometimes the thought oppresses me like a heavy burden."

After she proved herself to Tevis, she and the Tevises discussed business (from time to time Phoebe discussed business affairs with George, but not in any depth) and what it was like for her to go it alone abroad. Tevis and his wife came to see that she possessed a mind of her own and the ability to take charge of her own life. Phoebe could take care of herself. Her traditional, dignified approach, laced with intellectual self-reliance, determination, and perseverance, brought a small personal victory. She got respect from Tevis. George, meanwhile, kept his promise about the money. He expected his business associates to do what he ordered. As he wrote in his autobiography: "I always had to have it my own way or not at all, and this has been my disposition all through life."[17] Phoebe's experience had moved her to invoke her rhetorical powers successfully this time. She spoke her mind to George and took steps to get what she thought was rightfully hers—the money her husband promised her for her trip.

Signs emerged of Phoebe's increasing self-confidence and desire to fashion herself into a more independent woman, once she controlled George's money. She rented out the Hearst house for a year. She then started to sign most of her letters to her husband and friends "P. E." Hearst rather than using Phoebe E. Hearst or her girlhood nickname, "Puss."[18] Her new signature, with abbreviated initials, gave her name an air of importance. It also made it difficult to determine the sex of the correspondent. Only people who knew her, or received letters from her with her full name printed on it, could tell she was a woman. If the male recipients of her correspondence thought she was a man, they might see the writer as an independent thinker and take the contents more seriously.

P. E. Hearst used George's money to turn herself into a serious, thoughtful, and adventuresome traveler. She left San Francisco with Willie, now her ten-year-old son, one glorious spring day in March 1873. This was the first of what would be many odysseys to Europe. She and Willie boarded the railroad train to travel across the country to St. Louis, Missouri, to visit relatives and friends. Climbing the steps of the railroad car, they joined the rapidly increasing American middle class who could afford the time and money to go on vacations and tour the United States. The growth of railroads made travel "quicker, easier, more comfortable, and cheaper." Railroad travel, in other words, democratized vacations.

Phoebe, like other tourists going from west to east, probably anticipated seeing enchanting places and beautiful landscapes—features that made the United States different from Europe. She knew Europe was, she wrote, "certainly superior in many respects" to a young American nation deficient in historical roots and tradition. Phoebe looked forward to learning more about America as well as to experience new people, places, and cultures abroad. She looked out the window of the railroad car and enjoyed the scenery and sights. Railroad travel would put her on the path to becoming a "purveyor . . . of modern values," like a social scientist. She was a "modern tourist . . . with a curiosity about" all kinds of people, poor, rich, "ethnic and other minorities."

Having a large amount of money created difficulties, however. She felt burdened by the duties and obligations Americans expected her to perform because she was a woman married to a wealthy man who gave her control of thousands of dollars. As she explained to George, "I mean to try & have a good rest. . . . I cannot help it & am responsible but somehow this way of shouldering others burdens will cling to me." She also hoped the trip would shed light on how she could meet American societal expectations and yet fulfill herself at the same time. The journey, she thought, would help her clarify what she should do with her life. There was "no reason why American women cannot come abroad & return clear headed," she noted.[19]

But the money Phoebe Hearst spent on the trip did little to protect her against the risks associated with travel. Traveling across the country was serious and dangerous business for Phoebe, as "vacationing . . . came into vogue in the West." The trip tested her physical stamina and courage. She learned what it was like to be unprotected from the physical hazards of railroad travel, horrible weather, and the spread of disease as the train moved closer to Missouri. Her experience challenged the myth of male protection. She secured comfortable accommodations "in the sleeping car." But dangers abounded. "The track was under water for a distance of about three miles. the water entirely covered the car wheels in many places. there were floating blocks of ice which by rapidly drifting against

& under our train threatened to throw us from the track." "[F]inally the train could proceed no farther," she recounted. In addition, having virtually no understanding of the human body, viruses, bugs, or medicine made the journey more of a challenge for Phoebe. The epidemics of spinal meningitis and smallpox sweeping the nation frightened her. She feared her young son might come down with a dreadful disease and die.

Additional difficulties traveling from Utica to Albany, New York, prevented her and Willie from catching the train to Boston. In Boston, though, her experience improved. Phoebe was reminded of the comfort and value she derived from female friends when she met Clara Anthony at the station. She enjoyed her visit with Clara and her husband. "Mr. & Mrs. Anthony have entertained me very handsomely," she wrote George. She attended "elegant" luncheons, "fine concerts," and visited "interesting places." She liked Boston and rubbing elbows with culturally refined people. "I should like to stay here about three months," she remarked.[20] Phoebe reaped the rewards of having the physical staying power and mental and moral strength to travel across the country to visit friends, even while money fell short of shielding her from the difficulties of travel or putting her at ease within herself. In fact, possessing the ability to spend such a large amount of money produced inner conflict.

On the next leg of her trip, Phoebe confronted an internal paradox between morality and wealth that "many Americans cared deeply about," as one historian noted. How she negotiated this contradiction provide clues as to how she came to understand herself. Phoebe and Willie Hearst, accompanied by Lloyd Tevis and his wife, boarded the elegant, opulent steamer *Adriatic* of the White Star Line for Europe on April 19, 1873, about three years after the "White Star liner *Oceanic* . . . marked the beginning of a new epoch in transatlantic passenger travel."[21] She carried on board with her the paradox between Christian principles and materialism. As she put it before she sailed to Europe, "We might want too much of this world's good[s] & forget our father who cares for us all." She was a Christian evangelical woman, generally speaking. She approached religion with appropriate respect. She was raised in an era that stressed parental duties and responsibilities to educate children for moral purposes, including work and citizenship. Little surprise, then, that Phoebe wanted God's help to do her duty in all things. She figured it was her Christian duty to work and "civilize" her son and to prepare him for citizenship. Yet she also possessed dignified detachment from evangelicalism. She was not deeply pious nor a regular churchgoer. So she raised Willie with "no church affiliations" nor was he ever "a member of any church," she wrote later. She came of age at a time, as well, when Sarah Josepha Hale's *Godey's Lady's Book* warned readers "about Americans who were guilty of copying aristocratic European manners and mores." Her faith in general evangelical principles made her fully aware of the temptation and corrosive influence of wealth. So her need to perform her Christian duties battled with her need to live the lifestyle that George and other Americans, though not Europeans, expected of a woman married to a wealthy man.[22]

No wonder she was conflicted about the enjoyment she received from spending George's money on travel. "There is a *pang* with the pleasure," she noted, referring to the twinge of guilt she felt because she could afford the luxury of travel when many Americans could not. "The stresses prosperity put on morality," as historians had noted, caught up with her. She missed George and felt "a little homesick," too. But these worries were exacerbated because she was "conscience stricken about having so much enjoyment & you at home worrying & working," she wrote her husband.[23] Thinking about the price of all sorts of things frequently curtailed her pleasure in spending. "Everything costs so much. I am sometimes discouraged and frightened," she wrote George. "I feel worried about spending so much."[24] Religious considerations filled her mind. But in fact she possessed virtually no understanding of the amount of money George had at his disposal.

Cost was on her mind shortly after Phoebe arrived at the St. James Hotel in London. The rooms she expected were not available. The staff gave her a room "that was desirable in every respect excepting the *price*," she remarked. She took it, but "with a determination to change as soon as I could do better," she wrote. She feared being seen as a self-indulgent woman spending a lot of money foolishly. She felt uncomfortable, moreover, spending George's fortune lavishly for pure enjoyment. So she looked for accommodations "in which I could feel settled & where I should not be at such enormous expense," she explained. But "every place seemed to be full. I tried less expensive hotels. they were full. . . . You would have been amused," she wrote George. The trip also severely strained her powers of endurance because the London season was in full swing. The celebrations planned for the visit of the Shah of Persia to Queen Victoria made finding accommodations even more difficult and physically draining. She discovered a pleasant, respectable place she "*thought* would suit" her and Willie after three days of searching. It was "better than in the hotel," more homelike and less expensive, but "far up town. the distances are something frightful. still I am learning how to manage," she wrote.[25] She wanted to make sure she was not spending dollars frivolously. Yet spending George's money abroad gave her the chance to deepen and broaden her ability to learn about how to handle finances beyond the confines of her home.

Along the way, Phoebe refused to admit to herself the class status she derived from being married to a wealthy bonanza king. She did "not assume to be superior to the rest," she wrote Pike. She stuck to her evangelical, middle-class ways and reined in her spending, even though she probably knew that lavish spending was necessary to be a successful social climber. She was "determined to not buy a single article for myself that I could do without. it only adds weight to the baggage & is more care."[26] She justified her decision by doing what Christian women were expected to do. She was self-sacrificing. But she satisfied her practical side, too. She persuaded herself that her self-imposed financial restriction helped her better handle the physical challenges and demands of travel. She kept expenses down in Vienna to about $8 a day ($163 in terms of 2015 purchasing power) while she visited the international exhibition. By the time she reached Munich, she knew she had to "attend to my *banking* & keeping accounts." She studied "all the new money and it changes in every country, keeping a person constantly calculating & watching to keep matters right," she wrote.[27] As her evangelical, middle-class convictions and morals continued to war with her status as a wealthy woman, Phoebe scrupulously watched her pennies, unlikely behavior for a wealthy elite woman learning to be comfortable in her own skin with spending large amounts of money.

Phoebe's ability to control George's wealth produced other problems as well. She struggled with being both dependent and independent. Societal expectations required her to appear dependent on men in public. Yet she wanted to grow into an independent woman. Just because she had money did not mean it was easy for Phoebe to be independent; she was, after all, traveling with her son. At first she wrote George, "Willie & I get along very well alone."[28] She possessed power as a parent to control her son and his life. But she felt frustrated. She realized the constraints placed upon her because she was responsible for raising a child. She loved her son dearly, but contending with him upset her from time to time. As she explained, "Willie interrupts me so constantly, I lose all my ideas," she wrote George. Trying to secure hotel accommodations in London with Willie in tow also proved challenging. Some places refused them because Willie had whooping cough. Taking care of an ill child restricted her public activities as well. "Willie cannot go to the Opera or Theatre for he would surely cough loudly just at the most unfortunate moment," she wrote George. She wanted to be independent, but she knew the limits of womanhood. As she explained, "I should be quite independent. he [Willie] could always accompany me, but as it is I am dependent upon others. have been with Dr. S & Mr. & Mrs. May."[29] Rather than travel on her own, then, Phoebe followed convention. She was a responsible parent who took care of her child. She behaved in company and in public as though she were dependent on men, even though privately she wanted to break free of these limits. No amount of money could make her absolutely independent unless she was willing to abandon her acceptance of the constraints of sex.

We have seen that Phoebe strongly believed that women's work was as valuable and as important as men's and thought of herself as "no idler," as she wrote George from abroad.[30] Several months into her European trip, she appeared to find the perfect rationale that could mesh her great wealth with her passion for education, allowing her to feel more comfortable about spending George's fortune—self-education. Americans of the Hearsts' generation were "more materialistic" than Europeans and maintained that "the possession of wealth was not only the way to creature comfort but to power and esteem." This was an age of increasing spending "to achieve 'self-realization or 'self-gratification.'" But some held that these beliefs "threatened to tear apart [American] society." Raised to shun looking and acting "leisured," Phoebe probably wanted to avoid the appearance of self-gratification: "I would rather spend the money to fill my mind with what will give me pleasure all my life, than to put it on my back," she wrote emphatically to Eliza Pike.

Phoebe had at last resolved in her own mind the internal contradiction between enjoyment of wealth and a life of purpose, and this justification freed her from guilt. Now if she desired, she could relax, enjoy herself, and take pleasure in using letters of introduction to get "invitations to luncheons, dinners, and teas" at the same time that she indulged herself in the freedom to travel and broaden her education. Her trip now became an American version of the British tradition of a Grand Tour of Europe, "undertaken . . . for education and pleasure." Taking the Grand Tour was a symbol of status. It gave Phoebe and other Americans an opportunity to discover "a sense of themselves as powerful and independent actors on a broad international stage." Her tour experience also gave her the chance to find and shape an American identity that included a new role for herself as separate and independent from her husband and from raising a child. By the time Hearst joined other American elites, who had enjoyed "touring and sightseeing for decades," she convinced herself that she held a duty and a right to spend George's money for activities Cumberland Presbyterians valued and enjoyed, particularly education.[31] Her reasoning satisfied her moral imperatives, and spending money on travel abroad for self-education was turned into a religious ritual.

On tour, Phoebe saw the sights she thought any proper Christian lady married to a wealthy and powerful mining tycoon ought to see, and she kept busy. "I have been as industrious as possible feeling it my duty to improve the time so kindly given to me," she wrote George.[32] She bought and read books, magazines, and newspapers like other ladies of her generation, reflecting her keen interest in human relations and contemporary issues. She stayed up late to read history books for the purpose of moral development, as she saw it. Her reading helped her understand the people and cultures of the countries she visited. Her eyes moved over, and interpreted, the words in Hawthorne's *Notes of Italy* and Shakespeare's *Two Gentlemen of Verona* and *Romeo and Juliet*. "I read every American paper or magazine we can find & try not to be in utter ignorance of what is going on over there," she explained. She delved into the meaning of articles in an English newspaper, wrote correspondence, and kept a journal to discover and create herself.[33] Her decisions about how she spent her money, time, and energy opened up new perspectives on herself and the world.

Phoebe's new understanding of herself justified her religious ritual of travel as hard work and made it more comfortable for her to spend a large amount of money. She sat for a portrait painting in Europe that cost three hundred dollars—a princely sum for most Americans. The more at ease she became about spending money, the more confident she became in educating herself about the luxurious lifestyle expected of a woman married to a wealthy man. It was almost as if she was preparing herself to become an accomplished high-society hostess and businesswoman. She studied guide books and immersed herself in learning about European life and culture, gaining knowledge as well about the cultural work that evangelicals valued and others expected cultured high-society women to perform. She made "a great effort to see all the most important sights," she wrote. She saw "interesting objects" including "the Piazza of San Marcos that is the center of amusement & business." She visited the Doge's palace in Italy. She gazed upon "large paintings" and the design and architecture of buildings. She visited the University of Sheffield, with a school of law and a distinguished school of medicine. She walked in and out of churches, palaces, galleries, museums, theaters, and public buildings. She listened to operas and concerts and much more. She educated herself about manufacturers. She grappled with exchange rates and attended to her finances. She was determined to "study all the new money and [how] it changes in every country, keeping a person constantly calculating & watching to keep matters right. Then I try always to see *everything* of special interest in each place," she explained. She was busy doing what she thought others expected her to see and do and coping with the challenges of travel; she had to "admit that sightseeing is *very* hard work." "I must work very hard to accomplish much. I have certainly not been idle for a minute & though I am frequently almost exhausted I feel repaid for it will all my life be a source of great pleasure to recall our [journeying]," she explained.

The way for Phoebe to avoid the destructive and immoral enticements of wealth and protect herself "from any negative association with leisure" was to convince herself that her pleasurable social and cultural travel activities were meaningful work. Most nineteenth-century Americans refused to call such activities "work," and thought that "work, not play, was the key to their success." Phoebe developed her own interpretation to justify what she was doing. She thought spending money to educate herself, and to build the cultural capital Americans expected of high-society women, was not only her duty but her obligation and responsibility as a woman married to a bonanza king. Her newly acquired self-confidence made her feel uneasy in the company of Yankee public schoolteachers, who represented America as they traveled through Europe, because Europeans laughed at them, considering Americans to be inferior in culture and history.[34] Phoebe's concept of travel for self-education and self-improvement was acceptable hard work for a woman married to a wealthy man.

Throughout her travels, Phoebe found herself taking on different functions that would do justice to the kind of western, evangelical lady her parents raised her to be—a woman created by God with natural or biological moral superiority. It was not enough, though, for her to feel entirely comfortable spending money. The new identity and role she sought needed to be suitable for a Christian woman married to a rich mining tycoon eager to gain acceptance into the top tier of American society.[35] She resolved this conflict by persuading herself, by the end of 1873, that it was acceptable to spend money for self-education.

She went to more operas, symphonies, and theaters in London, Antwerp, Dresden, and Munich where she rubbed elbows with wealthy aristocrats. She attended the International Exhibition in Vienna. She gleaned ideas from, and saw the arrangements and organization of, art objects and artifacts in exhibits she walked past in many galleries, museums, and libraries. Each depository was organized and designed to stir feelings of nationalistic pride and unity. She scrutinized furniture as she strolled past the displays. She went outside and took pleasure in seeing the old parliament building and the Queens' Court in Ireland—manifestations of the power of politicians and monarchies. She observed the "finely paved" streets, additional manufacturing buildings, palaces, and homes that were of interest in the daily lives of common people. The pleasure she took in travel kindled strong affection for her husband. She signed her letters "Your loving wife."[36] She loved her husband for providing her with the opportunity to absorb useful knowledge and information that would turn her into a suitable woman of culture and refinement while helping the Hearst family gain acceptance among wealthy elites.

Phoebe Hearst's ability to observe and learn about the relation of money to different socioeconomic classes was crucial in allowing her to figure out what she should do with her life. As she came face-to-face with the European aristocratic way of life and high culture, she took special note of the stark contrast between classes, especially how they spent money and lived. She began with what she called the "*very* rich people" that artists painted. They captivated her.[37] "The aristocratic families are very formal & there is no such thing as being able to form acquaintances with this class unless one brings letters of introduction from most reliable & cultivated people," she wrote George.[38] "The formality & distinctions of class seem a little strange to an American at first," she explained.

The ostentatious wealth of the European aristocracy truly astounded her. She was amazed by how the nobility handled their financial resources. "How they do spend money," she observed, "a dozen or more servants to each family, coachman, footmen, butlers, &c, horses, carriages, & every luxury." She was filled with wonder at the sight of aristocrats' "perfect palaces." She was forced to "admit, the English know how to live. they seem to get so much more for their money than we." She became aware of class differences by paying close attention to the design, architecture, and location of people with different amounts of money. She observed the distinctions between the "thousands of handsome & comfortable homes in the stylish & *elegant* parts" from "the old & poor parts" of cities."[39] But she felt most comfortable with "the well-to-do middle classes" who "are more approachable," she explained.[40] They were not so cold, formal, and proper. Phoebe had taken the view when she was younger that individual character was more important than the amount of money one spent on fashion. But her view was altered abroad. Money was central in understanding the character and class structure of Europeans. But she did not limit herself to finding out about the aristocracy and middle class and how they spent money.

Phoebe's interest in money spent and earned led her to develop sensitivity to the conditions of the poor while she traveled through Ireland. There she absorbed lessons about the working class during a period of intense cultural and political nationalism. Concern among the Irish was on the rise because of the erosion of their culture under the oppressive weight of British imperialism. The Irish called for home government (or home rule) after November 1873, which aroused the working class and poor to fight the tyranny of the English landlords. They wanted to create a separate, independent, democratic nation and government ruled by their own people. Phoebe learned about cultural events of interest to the working class and poor amidst the political turmoil. The inexpensive concerts and "out door amusements" for the masses in Germany surprised her. The low pay and poverty of the working classes grabbed her attention. As she put it, "The poor classes are *terribly* poor." She took particular note of German workers, in general, and female workers in particular. "Working classes recieve [*sic*] very small wages, an ordinary servant girl has only 4 Thalers," a German unit of money, "or at most 5 per month, a thaler is 75cts & they have few privileges," she wrote. "The finest cooks in families receive 15 thalers but a cook who can do just general housework has 10 per month." The meager wages and the impoverishment of the working class shocked her. Seeing people in poverty also made an impression on her son. "Willie wanted to give away all his money & clothes too, & really I felt the same way," Phoebe wrote a bit disingenuously.[41] Coming face-to-face with such poverty was a new experience that she would not forget easily.

Her experiences with money and socioeconomic class led Hearst to think of herself as different and separate from the "crowd of common people." With the weight of her duties, obligations, and responsibilities sitting squarely on her shoulders, she became "accustomed to bear much fatigue & to systematize & form plans, she wrote George.[42] And as Phoebe became increasingly able to think of herself as separate and independent from her husband, she came to some bold decisions. Why not use her husband's fortune for self-education, self-improvement, *and* to better the lives of people in the lower classes?

What Hearst learned in Europe, though, pushed and pulled her in opposite directions as she spent money on her quest to find a new identity and role. On the one hand, her wealth gave her the chance to fulfill her desire for independence. She became "quite independent and have been most of the time alone," she explained to Pike. She wanted to stay abroad for another year. On the other hand, she needed to do what was expected of a dutiful American wife. "But if Mr. Hearst cannot come over we will go home next June, for I do not think it right to be so long absent from husband & home," she remarked. She was frightened, though, about sailing home because of the loss of life in accidents at sea. But George told Phoebe to "spend whatever time is necessary for your pleasure & satisfaction." She had the money to stay abroad to please herself. So she did. But when he became lonely, George changed his mind. He had received no word from her in a month by the end of March 1874. Duty called when Phoebe found out her husband was sad from being alone. Regardless of the money she had, her acceptance of the constraints of marriage compelled her to return home. She took her time about getting back, though. She left Europe in October 1874 to cross the Atlantic. After "a very long and stormy voyage," she set foot "on my own native soil again," she noted.

George quashed Phoebe's independence immediately upon her return. He wanted her to come directly home from the East Coast without stopping to see anyone. George "does not want us even to go out of town again without him," she wrote after she came back to California. Phoebe's independent spirit, nonetheless, remained alive. She began to sign her letters P. A. Hearst (for Phoebe Apperson Hearst) rather than P. E. Hearst (for Phoebe Elizabeth Hearst). Was this a desire to place her birth family on par with her marital family or to show more determination to strike out on her own?[43] In any case, the financial means at her disposal abroad and safe return home gave her the self-confidence to stand increasingly on her own two feet while she met her husband's needs. Her trip gave her a solid foundation upon which to take action to move her closer to an equal power relationship in her marriage with George. The more travel for self-education and self-improvement she experienced, the more she could reduce being pushed and pulled in opposite directions and the closer she could get to creating a truly equal marriage-power relationship with George, a bonanza king and powerful California politician.

In 1876, the opportunity to attend the Philadelphia Centennial Exposition became another avenue for Phoebe to learn more and to deepen and broaden her experiences. George's financial position was not so adversely impacted by the Panic of 1873 as to prevent her from spending the money to visit the exposition. The exposition, organized by an elite group of prosperous citizens, diverted attention away from Washington DC's political corruption. It also got people to thinking about something more positive than the economic disaster and working-class unhappiness with industrialism. This national event "was a calculated response" to bolster faith in the power of American capitalism and democracy as well as culture and society. Some argued the centennial celebration depicted America as a "moral influence" and the exposition as "a moral compass." "If the exposition was a moral compass, present and future social, political, and economic choices could be judged as right or wrong, good or bad, by using the exposition as a fixed coordinate" to improve "America's material and moral standing in the eyes of the civilized world," one historian noted. People who passed through the front gates were reminded "of America's history, achievements, and progress" rather than the deleterious effects produced by industrial tycoons and venal national politicians, the economic crisis, or the growing Gilded Age class tension and conflict.[44] A visit to the exposition, paid for by George, would draw Phoebe's attention away from the ill effects of the Panic of 1873 and focus it on improving her marriage and exerting power to improve the lives of others.

The Philadelphia Centennial Exposition was of great value to Phoebe Hearst. The exposition introduced her to the reform issues of personal and shared interest to moral women and men. These issues played a central role at a national event that promoted and advanced "the ideas and values of the country's political, financial, corporate, and intellectual" establishment as well as the social and cultural elite. The elite presented their vision at the exposition "as the proper interpretation of" American culture, society, capitalism, and democracy. After paying the fifty-cent admission fee, Phoebe strolled around the grounds in sweltering heat, building her cultural capital as she went. She wrote George that "there were 257,000 people at the exhibition" on one day she attended. "What do you think of that; it was dreadful." It was far fewer people than the total of more than ten million who attended from opening day on May 10 to the day the exposition closed about two weeks into November. Hearst walked among a steady stream of "cosmopolitan" people from different countries, cultures, and classes.[45] But she refused to let the hot weather and the flood of humanity surrounding her prevent her from soaking up as much knowledge as she could.

Hearst saw "the exhibition thoroughly," she remarked. She acquainted herself with the male exhibition directors and with Elizabeth Duane Gillespie and the members of the Women's Centennial Executive Committee. Gillespie and her colleagues were wealthy elite women who contributed to American growth and prosperity. They oversaw women's achievements at the exposition. Gillespie was married to a wealthy man and was the daughter of William J. Duane, secretary of the treasury, and the great-granddaughter of Benjamin Franklin. Prominent in Philadelphia high society, Gillespie had accumulated powerful friends and developed important connections that helped her become the head of the Women's Centennial Executive Committee. She supervised women's national exposition work and activities that promoted products for mass consumption. The exhibits and commercial goods depicted the country's economic progress. The exposition, under Gillespie's leadership, also advanced the superiority and honor of white American "civilization."[46] What Hearst saw exposed her to women's contributions to "civilization."

It probably did Hearst's heart good, and gave her a sense of pride, to see the Woman's Pavilion. It was the first exposition building paid for, planned, and controlled by women. Women's work, achievements, and goals were on display. Hearst walked around exhibits inside that informed her about reform issues such as kindergartens and self-support for women. The exhibits reflected support for issues raised by the women's rights movement, although Gillespie and her colleagues refused to address women's rights issues in speeches, correspondence, and published accounts of their activities. Even so, the pavilion contained offices for the only published exposition newspaper, the *New Century for Women*. The newspaper addressed "the problems of the status of woman." Six hundred exhibits, a library, art gallery, and a "working kindergarten . . . in the Woman's Schoolhouse" dotted the exposition landscape as well. The "Centennial Kindergarten" was a big hit. "One of the most popular exhibits . . . was the separate Saint Louis kindergarten display managed by Susan Blow" that promoted the ideals of Friedrich Froebel. Froebel's ideals on education reform focused on cultivating children's good character, like strong will, and their innate spiritual, mental, and physical abilities. The popularity of the Centennial Kindergarten helped bring Froebel's ideals into vogue in the United States in the late 1870s. Hearst thought the entire exhibition to be "very fine . . . quite as fine as the Vienna Exhibition all except the picture gallery," she wrote. Impressed with what she saw, Phoebe noted, "There is enough to keep us hard at work for a long time."[47] The reform ideas and information in the exhibits spoke to Hearst about helping less-privileged women and children. Their appeal was irresistible to Phoebe—a woman with a personal interest in children and education. With her head crammed with knowledge and information, she returned to California.

Several years later, Hearst spent more of her husband's money on another important trip that helped transform her into something more than simply a knowledgeable wife, parent, and high-society woman who gave parties. She boarded the RMS *Russia* of the Cunard Line with William M. Lent—"an old San Francisco friend" and president of the Savage Mining Company—and his family to cross the Atlantic in September of 1878. Hearst hired Thomas Barry, a University of California graduate, to tutor Willie. Barry joined Hearst and her son months later to prepare Willie for admittance into a prestigious eastern school and, later, entrance into Harvard University.[48] Barry's assistance provided Phoebe the time to rest and devote herself to becoming a philanthropist—an identity and role that allowed her to find an answer to her internal struggle between materialism and moral principles.

Phoebe hoped to get some rest on her 1878 European excursion. But she could not shake her sense of obligation to help with the problems of others. She was exposed during this trip to the argument of "militant reformers" in America and Britain that the wealthy needed "to exercise greater care in the bestowal of charity" by making "philanthropy a science." They wanted to develop and use scientific methods to ascertain which poor were "truly deserving," or worthy, of material aid. Hearst enjoyed what she learned abroad. But there was also the sound of a martyr and disdain in her voice for those she was supposed to help as she gathered material on reform. "I wish I could forget all cares. I mean to try, & have a good rest. . . . I cannot help it & am not responsible. But somehow this way of shouldering others burdens will cling to me," she wrote George. She felt saddled with the burden of helping others improve their lives, actions Americans expected from a moral, ambitious, reform-oriented woman of Phoebe's social and economic standing. So she engaged in an active and full schedule to train for a new philanthropic role that met American expectations as she traveled through England, France, and Germany.[49] She was unable to rest for very long before she felt the need to work.

Phoebe set high standards of work for herself as she prepared to become a philanthropist, developing disciplined and efficient habits. She made definite plans for a daily routine and executed them. She ordered Thomas Barry to wake her son at six in the morning on a typical day. Barry tutored Willie usually until 10:30 a.m., sometimes until 12:30 p.m. Hearst wrote business letters for Barry to transcribe and send after her son finished his lessons. The rest of the day, rain or shine, she visited artists and picture dealers. She made and executed travel plans. She satisfied her interest in the arts and culture. She instilled in her son a love of these as well. She went to one palace and museum after another with Willie in tow. She learned about the Old Masters at L'École des Beaux-Arts. She reflected on, and talked to her son about, paintings by Giotto, Leonardo da Vinci, Rafael, Rubens, Van Dyke, Michelangelo, and Botticelli. She gazed at the Gobelin Tapestries. She walked around many museums—the Museum of Decorative Arts in the Pavilion de Flore in the Tuileries, the South Kensington and British Museums, the Rijks Museum, and others. She studied ceramics, Aubusson tapestry, glassware, lace, Egyptian and East Indian jewelry, and much more. She returned to her lodgings at sunset. She took dinner and sometimes a walk in the evenings. Hearst grew tired arranging her life while she performed her daily activities and work. She nonetheless cultivated the traits and habits of a professional to prepare herself for a new individual role as a reformer working to improve the lives of a "cosmopolitan" people. This new philanthropic role would be one that would help shape a regional identity blossoming in San Francisco and Northern California.[50]

The hard work of sightseeing and making plans to become a philanthropist exhausted Hearst and "undermine[d]" her "powers of endurance." She was in dire need of "a long rest and systematic medical and climatic treatment," Brooks explained. Phoebe decided it was the right time to take a break and visit a spa to take the "cure." She probably thought, like most of the French bourgeoisie, that spa medical treatments were good for her physical, mental, and moral well-being. So she visited Cauterets, a spa in the Pyrenees. In early August of 1879, she sent her mischievous, rebellious, sixteen year old son back to Paris to join Barry in making preparations for the trip home, despite the fact that she would miss "dear Will," as she did several years later on another trip. Phoebe then pampered herself and consciously adopted the best habits to keep her body, mind, and spirits in sound condition.

Cauterets was one of the health resorts that became a powerful place of rejuvenation, medical and otherwise, for ambitious social climbers and aspiring members of the economic and political elite in Europe. Others who took "pleasure in the acquisition and display of cultural capital" also enjoyed staying there. Her visit helped restore her energy and she became physically fit. Phoebe steeped herself in the trappings and lifestyle of the rich at the resort. She observed closely how sophisticated wealthy women behaved and acted. She learned about European social status, proper social circles, refined table manners, and elegant, stylish dress, all the while building more cultural capital, too. She enjoyed the architectural environment that honored the elite. Her visit formally conferred upon her the rights, prestige, status, and prominence accorded to ambitious members of the prosperous and wealthy classes. The place must have appealed to her because there she could reconcile and engage in work, rest, and pleasure. Having satisfied her love of travel and passion for education on this trip to Europe, she sailed back to New York and set foot on American shores in late November of 1879.[51] George's money continued to give her the opportunity to begin the work of turning herself into a wealthy elite woman and enjoy herself in other ways.

George and Phoebe moved into a larger home on Van Ness Avenue after she returned from abroad. This street was considered "the most fashionable" place for the wealthy to live in San Francisco. Women married to rich men, meanwhile, went downtown to spend their husband's money on clothing of the most current design. Some of these women, unlike Phoebe, "were powerless among the powerful without access to the incomes that they legally shared with their husbands."[52] Phoebe was different. She had access to her husband's fortune. Even so, it was a rare occasion when she enjoyed her husband's money for the sake of pleasure alone. She usually spent his fortune on activities that mixed pleasure with work. Her latest European trip had fit the bill. She had restored her mental and moral energy and physical constitution at the same time that she acquired the proper training to prepare herself to fit comfortably into elite San Francisco social, economic, and political circles. The fruits of her European trip were put to good use within and outside her new home as she settled into her new role as a philanthropist.

Once settled into their new house, Phoebe also began to think about spending George's fortune to provide Willie with a proper formal education. She wanted it to be easier for her son than it had been for his father to gain acceptance into elite circles.[53] With an eye on her son's future, she drew on the habits and skills she had acquired and cultivated abroad—a place steeped in history and tradition—to determine where Willie would go to school.

Money was probably no object in selecting a school for Willie. Phoebe decided to enroll him in an exclusive boarding school for the sons of the old and new wealth from "Boston and New York to Chicago and San Francisco"—St. Paul's School in Concord, New Hampshire. Americans, at the time, accepted "the growth in importance of the New England boarding school as an upper-class institution." These schools became crucial to "the creation of a national upper class." Willie attended classes with children of the Vanderbilts and Rockefellers, along with brokers, statesmen, and members of eastern patrician Episcopalian families. He made the "right" connections and networks with the sons of parents who had power, rank, and fame. But he paid a price. As he wrote his mother, "I feel very despondent & lonely all the time & wish for you to come awful bad. . . . It is all I can do to keep from crying sometimes when [I think] how much alone I am & how far away you are." While it may have been hard for Willie to adjust to being so far away from his mother and home, Phoebe was enjoying the fruits of her good judgment. She had selected and spent money on the right school. In the same year that Phoebe sent Willie to St. Paul's School, the Hearst name appeared in *The Elite Directory of San Francisco and Oakland* for 1879, the "first complete membership list" of the city's upper class—"2,341 men, women and children (1.2 percent of the city's total population)."[54] By the early 1880s, then, Phoebe had become a woman of means, with enough growing sophistication in cultural capital to take on the identity and role of a philanthropist. She had raised and educated Willie properly, establishing educational roots and connections for him three thousand miles away that would help the Hearst family continue to gain acceptance as official members of the San Francisco and East Coast elites.

Phoebe's accomplishments convinced George that his wife was indeed ready to take on the duties and obligations of a philanthropist. Ultimately, according to Brooks, he placed "the selection and management of their extensive mutual work for public charitable and philanthropic purposes" in his wife's hands, "to avoid duplication of effort."[55] While George did not appear to be involved to any significant degree in charitable and philanthropic endeavors himself, his decision unified Phoebe and her husband's philanthropic goals under her control. George trusted Phoebe to use his money wisely. His decision shifted the balance of economic power in their relationship in the early stage of their marriage, moving Phoebe even closer to the power and status her husband enjoyed. It heaped upon her shoulders the task of controlling and distributing the Hearst fortune for philanthropic purposes, providing her the means to define and determine the Hearsts' humanitarian interests and goals. Not long after she had the money in hand, Phoebe put it to good use to expand her travel experiences.

Phoebe loved travel. Travel was, as she wrote, "the most widening and deepening experience of my life. . . . I so love new scenes, new countries new people." So she left California again, in early January 1882, for constant traveling and socializing in Boston, Washington DC, and New York. On January 20 she sailed from American shores. But this time she went without her son, giving her the freedom to become a truly independent woman, although, as always, within the constraints of contemporary notions of sex and class.[56] She looked forward to her third trip to Europe in nine years and to visiting friends on the East Coast. She could gather more information on how to spend George's money on reform issues of personal interest, and she could continue to broaden her perspective on the world.

Hearst's judicious use of money during her travel adventures provided her with a deeper understanding of how Europeans, especially the aristocracy, developed interconnected relations to strengthen and broaden family contacts and power relationships. She took the lessons learned abroad and applied them to her son to help him increase his power and stature and make it easier for him to be accepted into the political elite. Phoebe paid for nineteen-year-old Will to attend Harvard University in the fall of 1882, deciding that Harvard was the place for her son to go to establish eastern roots. In attendance at this prestigious, private university he could build networks with the old money and blue bloods in New England and

Philadelphia and the new money in New York. Will explained later what he thought his mother's goal had been when she sent him there: "There is something which I know you always considered—the opportunity to make your offspring solid with a power in politics."[57] Phoebe's experiences at the Jameses and travels through Europe had taught her the importance of developing networks and meeting people who knew others with power, rank, and fame. Enrolling Will at Harvard was money spent wisely, she thought. Attending Harvard would help him meet the proper people to help turn him into a powerful elite politician.

Hearst now possessed the time and freedom, with Will at Harvard, to turn her money and resources toward helping other reform-minded women in arenas of politics and nonpartisan voluntary associations. Hearst had not been a member of any of these organizations in the 1860s and 1870s because she was so busy trying to adjust to her marriage, be a good parent, and become a social climber in San Francisco. But now that her son was at college, Hearst began, in the early 1880s, a lifelong involvement in political activities and in nonpartisan voluntary associations. Her participation in groups of women, and some with men, many of whom spent their entire lives as reformers, was of primary importance in giving her life meaning and purpose. She gave to the arts and music, although her commitment to nonpartisan voluntary associations, and the shared interests of female and male members in these groups, overshadowed her efforts in the worlds of art and music. Her work and activities in voluntary organizations helped to shape public opinion. When she did join these groups, she started to influence debate on political issues of personal interest to women and some men in the West—an environment that welcomed the formation of "new political institutions" like voluntary associations.[58]

Americans valued and expected wealthy, elite women in San Francisco to get involved in nonpartisan voluntary association politics, especially those that were aimed at a moral purpose and brought women moral authority.

For some this meant participating in women's clubs, settlement houses, and the suffrage movement. For Hearst it meant entering political arenas and organizational life through the American kindergarten reform movement inspired by Friedrich Froebel. The Woman's Christian Temperance Union (WCTU) enthusiastically promoted the American kindergarten reform movement, although Hearst never became a member of the WCTU or developed strong ties to the organization. In fact, she drank wine and enjoyed a glass of champagne for health purposes. What interested her more than temperance, later called Prohibition, was a movement that appealed to her passion for education and love of children. She took great interest in providing opportunities for women to protect themselves from economic hardship through self-support and in organizations that investigated political issues of interest to members.

Kindergarten education was a way to provide job opportunities for women to achieve economic independence and to educate girls and boys. Kindergarten supporters, like Hearst, also possessed keen interest in studying more about how to improve the lives of women and children. San Francisco, in the 1880s, was almost the only western American city that supported sex-segregated education in the schools. Female and male advocates of educating boys and girls separately argued for protecting "delicate and refined" girls from "ruffian boys." Yet there were parents and teachers who opposed sex-segregated education, including Hearst and the California superintendent of schools, John Swett.[59] Hearst had attended a log-cabin common school with boys in her youth. She had also taught in a coeducational district school for about a year. So it was little surprise that she advocated educating girls and boys together and participated in voluntary association politics centered on coeducation.[60]

White, wealthy, elite, and prosperous women had opened the first kindergartens in America before the Civil War to educate their children. Margarethe Schurz was the wife of Carl Schurz, a German immigrant and an effective political campaign orator for Abraham Lincoln in 1860. She established the first American kindergarten in 1855 in Watertown, Wisconsin, for children who spoke German. Elizabeth Peabody opened the first organized kindergarten in Boston for English-speaking children five years later. Bertha Semler, a student of Friedrich Froebel, came to California to establish a kindergarten while Hearst was on her 1873 European jaunt. The kindergarten closed one year later, probably because of lack of funds. Emma Marwedel was a German-born and Froebel-trained kindergarten advocate. She came from Washington DC to Los Angeles in the summer of 1876 where she started the California Model Kindergarten and Pacific Model Training School for Kindergarteners. Dr. Felix Adler then came from New York to San Francisco to give lectures on kindergartens. Adler and Marwedel later formed the San Francisco Public Kindergarten Society. The society raised enough interest and support to open Kate Douglas Wiggin's Silver Street Kindergarten, the only free kindergarten west of the Rocky Mountains to help those in need.[61]

Sarah Brown Ingersoll Cooper, inspired by a visit to the Silver Street Kindergarten, established the Jackson Street Kindergarten Association in San Francisco in 1883. It was "composed of ladies *and* [emphasis added] gentlemen belonging to the Bible Class of Mrs. Sarah B. Cooper, in Calvary Church." Cooper was a graduate of Emma Hart Willard's Troy Female Seminary; a governess for a prominent family in Augusta, Georgia; a kindergarten advocate; a suffragist; and the spouse of Halsey F. Cooper, an owner and editor of a prominent newspaper in Chattanooga, Tennessee. Cooper, in 1884, suggested that the Jackson Street Kindergarten Association be renamed the Golden Gate Kindergarten Association (GGKA) for purposes of incorporation. A vote was taken. The name change "was unanimously adopted," a GGKA report announced. The WCTU of San Francisco "established in connection with it [the GGKA] the first free kindergarten of the WCTU." The 1879 constitution and bylaws stated the object of the organization: "the establishment and maintenance of Free Kindergartens in San Francisco and environs; the sustaining of a Free Normal Training School for Kindergartners; and to further promote the work for needy, neglected children, as far as possible, in pursuance of the Articles of Incorporation of this Association." The GGKA opened up a new career for women as kindergarten teachers and, as Cooper said, helped "the needy and neglected little waifs of the by-ways and the high-ways" in the gloomy, decaying Barbary Coast and Tar Flat areas of San Francisco. One goal of the overall kindergarten movement was to train children for useful and good citizenship—"to rear virtuous, self-governing, law abiding citizens" by cultivating "honesty, industry and self-control" through education in the arts and trades.[62] The GGKA's reform business was kindergartens.

The GGKA, like other American kindergarten organizations, promoted the reform-minded ideas of Frederic Froebel, the father of the kindergarten reform movement and a supporter of the advancement of women in Germany. Froebel's movement gained momentum in late nineteenth-century Germany and the United States. The movement was strongly influenced by Christian values. Froebel's philosophy was a "systematic and practical" program "based on children's learning by doing." His thinking held out the promise that girls and boys could acquire the "practical power" to avoid crime and lift themselves out of poverty through education. He also promoted kindergarten teaching as an opportunity for women to achieve a sense of purpose, a measure of economic independence, and professional status. The power of teachers to train girls and boys to be politically independent, among "every power" at the GGKA, was "recognized and brought into activity," according to Cooper.[63] The GGKA with the support of the WCTU rallied Hearst and other women to acquire, build, and use resources to support the myriad of women's reform causes and claim an equal part in American politics to advance the position of women. The GGKA then got caught up in the reform aims of the women's movement, or what some later called "feminist goals."[64]

"Entirely without solicitation," according to a GGKA report, Hearst asked Sarah B. Cooper about kindergarten activities in which she was deeply interested. Cooper's response led Hearst to join other wealthy women, like Jane Lathrop Stanford, in addressing the needs of the working class, immigrants, and the poor. Hearst provided generous material gifts for teacher salaries. She also paid money to rent buildings in which classes were conducted. She hired a janitress. She provided for furniture, materials, and repairs for the GGKA. One of Hearst's donations established the GGKA Hearst Free Kindergarten, No. 1, at 512 Union Street in early October of 1883. By establishing a free public kindergarten, Hearst married and comingled her moral duty with her civic obligation, freely and individually chosen, that "authentically bound" her to the Constitution as a citizen. She, in effect, reshaped her duties as a wife and parent, understood as a "substitute for obligations to the state." Hearst exerted her economic, intellectual, and voting powers within the association to take control of urban space usually dominated by men. She then exerted power to fashion that space into a public arena to promote political issues that might help the downtrodden and less fortunate. Hearst's actions made her look "like a good angel" to the GGKA, Cooper wrote.[65]

But Hearst wanted to be more than a good angel and a money machine to the GGKA. She also was interested in GGKA operations and devoted herself to playing a meaningful and powerful role in GGKA politics. She kept track of her donations in writing. She gave specific instructions on how she wanted her money spent to buy clothing, shoes, and medicines for students. She also provided financial support for the operation of two additional free public kindergartens. In exchange, Cooper kept Hearst informed about the overall direction of her free kindergarten classes. Moreover, she accepted Hearst's control over her project. As Cooper explained to the GGKA patron regarding one project, "I will do nothing till I hear from you." Hearst by 1889 had funded 115 children in two free GGKA kindergartens. She established the "Hearst No. 3" kindergarten by spring of 1890 to provide women with more opportunities for self-support.[66]

Involvement in GGKA politics was a good fit for Hearst. She sympathized with the daughter of a woman friend and her "desire to study some art or profession." She revered, in addition, the notion of dignified, paid labor. As she explained to Hubert Howe Bancroft, a nineteenth-century historian, in an interview, "All persons should feel that labor is not only honorable, but that it is a necessary discipline and indispensable to the formation of sound character." Hearst was following the lead of the German Kindergarten Movement when she committed herself to the general principle "of the dignity of labor . . . as an essential element of citizenship." She and GGKA teachers promoted and advocated the professionalization of kindergarten teaching to increase women's status and provide them with a means to gain economic independence. They also focused on Froebel's ideas that students should be educated humanely and meet high academic standards.

Toward this end, Hearst's financial contributions to the GGKA gave her a voice in the association. She suggested rules for children and policies for teachers. She required students to prepare for class outside school. She set the time for teachers to start work. She established a rule that teachers needed to visit students' homes to enlist "the cooperation of the mothers." Her policies required staff to find out the reason for student absence after the first day of school missed. Perhaps because Hearst, as she had explained to Hubert Howe Bancroft in the same interview, "did not find her" mother's "discipline altogether agreeable," she rejected Froebel's policies on "corporal punishment, rote learning, and extended confinement." Hearst was adamant "that no corporal punishment or anything like shutting [a child] in a room that is *dark* is to be resorted to," she wrote.[67] During the many years of her participation in the GGKA, Hearst took a businesslike, professional approach to handling and keeping abreast of kindergarten reform issues and activities that appealed to her.

Hearst's ideas, decisions, major benefactions, and approach made her a director of the legally incorporated GGKA in 1884. Director Hearst exercised both legal and political power with Cooper over women and men in kindergartens—"the greatest moral renovator that San Francisco ever had," Cooper stated. Kindergarten teachers from the beginning saw themselves as professionals and part of the movement to advance women "moulding and training and shaping these little souls for usefulness," Cooper explained. To help make this happen, Cooper founded a GGKA teachers' training school in 1891. Meanwhile, cases against and for coeducation were argued across the nation. Hearst's active participation in the GGKA meant she was not only an advocate of the advancement of women but of educating girls and boys together and improving the lives of small children in poverty. Defenders of coeducation argued that men who controlled schools were biased. Coeducational schools would give boys and girls the chance to learn about each other and build respect, leading to "an equality of funding and instruction rarely available in [a] girls' school."[68]

Hearst, a believer in teaching "girls . . . to do all kinds of useful work," as she put it, wielded her power to convince Americans she represented "ideals" and possessed "special qualities" that were possibly "universally desired" and praised but that only members of the top tier of society possessed. At the same time, she strove to eradicate the very tensions and class divisions she was helping to create by endeavoring to ensure that no participant in the kindergarten movement felt isolated or unfairly treated and denied. Hearst's contributions to the GGKA turned the spotlight of the press on herself and the organization. In turn, that brought her and the GGKA praise and made her a well-known philanthropist in San Francisco nonpartisan voluntary association politics. Jane L. Stanford was impressed and commented on the reputation Hearst built. "Your name is a household word, for your sweet unostentatious charities have reached out far and wide."[69] For those who might be uncomfortable with women having and exercising power, Hearst's moral authority gave them comfort because it sanctioned the formal public power that she, and women like her, possessed and exerted in GGKA politics.

Hearst, Cooper, and the GGKA achieved success at a time when Americans handed over intellectual expertise to male academic professionals and teachers involved in the political world of education. G. Stanley Hall, one of the founders of American psychology, and John Dewey, a prominent philosopher and functional psychologist, both personified such male intellectual authority. Unfortunately for Hearst and the kindergarten movement, these academic professional men referred to kindergartens as "romantic" and "sentimental"—which were, of course, code words for "female," according to one historian.[70] Hearst ignored Hall's and Dewey's criticisms.

Hearst focused instead on building a good name and reputation in San Francisco by strategically and systematically donating her ideas and money to advance GGKA reform politics and the organization. She had by now exerted informal power, outside a legally incorporated body, in private and at home. But her ability to act and produce effects in the GGKA displayed her formal or "public" organizational power based on conventional politics. Traditional politics was a permanent guide for the exercise of control and authority for women and men within political arenas that included laws of incorporation. GGKA members exercised the vote granted them in the charters of incorporation. Americans usually accepted reform-minded women possessing and exercising control in nonpartisan voluntary organizations, like the GGKA. So Hearst felt comfortable with her involvement in the GGKA, an organization that served as Hearst's base of power to express and "act" on her "own interests." Her decisions as a GGKA director influenced and pressured partisan politicians into making changes kindergarten activists wanted in cities. Reform-minded women who helped establish kindergartens shaped "debates about neighborhood design and housing design." Some GGKA members probably joined California suffragists to lobby successfully for an 1874 California law that granted women the right to hold public office.[71] Her position as an official director of the GGKA was thus a political office invested and validated by the laws of California with formal public power to create social reform aimed at social justice, among other goals.

Hearst's work handling her varied affairs got the best of her, especially physically and medically, in the 1880s. She suffered from recurring and debilitating bouts of physical and mental exhaustion that resulted from the stresses and strains that built up at points of crisis. She fell seriously ill with muscular rheumatism. She feared the effects of disease, severe fatigue, and health complications. As she tried to avoid getting ill again, she was faced like many women with an unavoidable difficult and confusing problem: how could she stay healthy and physically fit to disprove a conventional "image of the woman as an invalid, as weak, delicate, and perpetually prone to illness" at the same time she educated and improved herself and helped others, mostly women? Could she mobilize her money and resources in the fight against illness and disease that prevented her and other women from fulfilling private duties and civic obligations? Would she be able to convince people to think of her as a reform-minded, wealthy woman citizen rather than a "conspicuous consumptive" or lady of leisure?[72]

Female and male medical experts assisted Hearst in answering this question. Hearst's successful kindergarten activities in the early 1880s helped build a name and reputation for herself that caught the attention of the emerging medical profession.[73] Most of the women admitted to medical schools before the 1880s lived in the Northeast. They were accepted into medical degree programs in "Washington DC, Maryland, and the Midwest and West" after the 1880s. Once they were admitted, they grappled with endless difficulties "from which their male colleagues were spared." "Women in any profession were having a hard time in those days," remembered Anne Fearn, "but women physicians seemed particularly obnoxious to the average man and woman of the eighties and nineties." The occupation of studying human illness was considered repugnant for a woman of a respected and superior social position. Women made some progress nevertheless. They increased the number of female physicians in the United States to approximately seven thousand in 1900. This number was much higher than in England, with 258, and in France, with 95. But American female physicians found that they needed to act like ladies to move forward in the emerging medical profession.[74]

Hearst began to throw her money and resources into homeopathy, a growing part of the American medical establishment. Homeopathy was a response to certain of the ineffective and dangerous treatments of mainstream doctors. Samuel Hahnemann, a German doctor, thinker, and founder of homeopathy, called these physicians "allopaths." Homeopathic practices existed "on the East Coast of the United States some 20 years before it arrived in California." Most were voluntary organizations kept open and in operation by gifts from wealthy women. The Board of Examiners of the California State Medical Society of Homeopathic Practitioners approved the practice of homeopathic physicians. A few San Francisco homeopaths met in Dr. J. A. Albertson's office in San Francisco in January 1881 to form "a homeopathic medical school" in California. The school ran into problems. It took until 1883 for homeopaths F. E. J. Canney, J. N. Eckel, C. B. Currier, and William Boericke to raise the money to establish the Homeopathic, or Hahnemann, Medical College of San Francisco. Boericke was from a prominent family in Philadelphia devoted to homeopathy. The new school created opportunities for students to get advanced medical and clinical training with homeopathic physicians at an affiliate—the Pacific Homeopathic Dispensary, or Hospital. The dispensary "offered the earliest hospital care by homeopathic physicians in San Francisco."[75] But homeopathy was threatened by late nineteenth-century opinions. Most mainstream orthodox physicians, or allopaths—the American Medical Association (AMA), as well as Andrew Carnegie and John D. Rockefeller—believed homeopathy was unconventional and opposed it. AMA members ridiculed homeopaths, charging that such practitioners were unorthodox and dogmatic. They also failed to meet AMA ethical standards. Some went so far as to call homeopathic physicians "quacks."[76] Hearst disagreed with the negative characterizations of homeopathy.

Sara A. D. McKee approached Phoebe Hearst in the fall of 1882 about the opening and development of the homeopathic hospital, which would be affiliated with the Hahnemann Medical College of San Francisco. McKee probably became aware of or met Hearst through her network of reform-minded women active in social welfare services in San Francisco. Dr. Laura Ballard, a homeopathic physician, was Hearst's private doctor in the early

1880s. During this period, Hearst became interested in homeopathy to develop a more harmonious, cooperative world and to integrate women into, and advance them in, medical education. State legislatures, meanwhile, passed laws that made it mandatory for female doctors to treat women patients in government institutions, hospitals, and asylums for the insane. Given to being rebellious from time to time, Hearst likely wanted to challenge the male bias that prevented her sex from getting advanced training as members of the emerging medical profession. One way to do that was to provide coeducational opportunities for women in the field of medicine, so she offered to "secure a suitable house and open the Hospital at once," providing the rent for the building "for the first year." Her offer led to an invitation from Ballard to become the president of the board of directors.

At the same time, the AMA was pushing ahead to take control of the licensing of physicians and turn male doctors into professionals. They wanted medical schools to adopt high academic standards and make crude medical methods passé. The professionalization of medicine and the transformation of hospitals from welfare into medical institutions was well underway when a growing chorus of reform-minded females criticized the lack of opportunities for women to study and practice medicine. Women comprised only 4.3 percent of the total number of physicians in the United States by 1890. Hearst sensed it was the right time to act on Ballard's invitation to become president of the Pacific Homeopathic Dispensary's board of directors. She accepted the invitation.[77] While president of the board, Hearst's decisions and actions provided women with the opportunity to become economically independent professionals in the male field of medicine and gain acceptance from and work with male physicians on equal terms. At a personal level, Hearst's involvement with the medical profession allowed her to learn more about the human body in ways that would help her maintain and sustain a strong physical constitution.

Being head of a hospital board was a new experience for Hearst, so she moved with caution and worked through a representative. Contributions of money alone was insufficient to accomplish her goals. Once again, Hearst displayed her knack for associating herself with people who were effective in advancing her personal and political interests. She chose to delegate authority to Sara A.D. McKee to act as her Pacific Homeopathic Dispensary representative in dealing with female hospital physicians and male physicians on the faculty at the Hahnemann Medical College. McKee helped Hearst cautiously and diplomatically navigate the intricacies of power relationships with physicians of both sexes at a time when professional medicine was in its infancy. Most American hospitals, moreover, served the poor. Homeopathic hospitals usually were run and staffed by women. That was the case initially at the Pacific Homeopathic Dispensary. Hearst engaged in a serious, private discussion with Dr. Ballard about the aims of the hospital during its early stage of development. Should the dispensary "be a Hospital for women and children alone, under women physicians—or a general Hospital" with male and female doctors on the staff?

Hearst decided, after discussion with Ballard, not to "confine her assistance to an Institution for women and children only." Both agreed: a hospital with female and male physicians to serve and treat all was "in the best interests of Homeopathy." It would advance the careers of both sexes in medicine. The founders of the new Hahnemann Medical College, meanwhile, agreed that "women should be admitted on an equal footing with men to all the privileges of the college." Hearst's cautious but dignified and professional approach as she worked through McKee and Dr. Ballard paid off. Her financial support and policies provided female graduates of the new medical college a way to get advanced medical and clinical training so they could serve the medical profession on equal terms with men. This egalitarian principle was promoted by advocates of women's advancement and other reform-minded males and females who demanded that both sexes have "equal access to scientific and sexual truths."[78] Hearst's network in the medical field continued to take shape as she carried out her duties and obligations as the head of the hospital board.

Hearst was neither militant nor strident in promoting the advancement of women in medicine. She became a major donor of the dispensary. She offered her home to advocates of homeopathy for meetings. Sensing it was the right time, she announced that "if desired she would be chairman of the meetings and open her house for them." It was in the self-interest of the hospital board to accept Hearst's offer if female and male physicians were to work together and Hahnemann Medical College graduates were to obtain advanced medical and clinical training at the dispensary or hospital. The staff knew that the hospital, McKee wrote, "had $1,065.65 and that it would have found it very difficult to succeed the first year without that money." They needed more financial support to keep the place open and running, so they enticed Hearst to provide financial support with an offer to chair the executive committee of the board of directors. She accepted. Several months before the executive committee convened, the stress and strain of dealing with her responsibilities took such a physical toll that Phoebe fainted. But she refused to let the pressure get the best of her. She recovered from "a fainting attack" and directed the meetings. She made friends with the participants and created a pleasant environment where better collegial relationships could be cultivated.[79]

Hearst needed most of her resources as she struggled to maneuver male physicians at the Hahnemann Medical College, located at 115 Haight Street, into working with female physicians from the Pacific Homeopathic Dispensary and accepting them as attending doctors. McKee's responsibility was to represent Hearst and persuade male physicians directly. As she explained, "Our founder—president—and largest single contributor [Hearst] might reasonably expect that her Physician, who holds an average standing among the profession in the city, might attend at the Hospital, as one, among the ten general physicians who have already given service there." The fact that Dr. Ballard might practice with male physicians on the hospital staff triggered a vehement reaction from the male faculty at the medical college in March 1883. The male physicians wanted control over the hospital and its staff. Dr. C. B. Currier, dean of the faculty and a professor of diseases of the throat and chest, "never lost the opportunity" to complain to McKee that "every man who had been in the Hospital during the attendance of a woman physician grumbled about it," according to McKee.[80]

Hearst boldly took issue with male physicians at the Hahnemann Medical College who criticized and opposed women physicians. She challenged their efforts to take control of her board of directors. She had every intention of placing members on the board whom she preferred. She responded skillfully, diplomatically, and directly to those who opposed her position. After she "consulted with a number of my associate directors," she explained to the Hahnemann Medical College physicians, "I am prepared . . . to outline the policy of the Board." Her board explained that they had "long realized the benefit of having the Hospital connected with the Hahnemann Medical College, and we look with favor on any satisfactory plan for their union, believing the interests of both college and Hospital will be subserved by the association of the two." But Hearst was opposed to the attempt by male physicians to place members they wanted on her board. She explained further that her board was not "prepared to accede to [board members backed by the college] for we are called upon to endorse in advance a Board whose names we do not know." She requested that the male physicians provide "a list of the names of the directors" they "propose, for we fear that in the preoccupation of your busy lives, you may not have been able to consult all the ladies." She made clear, then, her desire that the conflict be resolved. As she put it, "I am extremely anxious that a Board may be elected on Monday that will be acceptable to all & that every effort may be made to harmonize all discordant elements."[81] Hearst had little hesitation making decisions that reflected her policies and applying her power as head of the hospital board to formulate a board to her liking.

Hearst created a plan before the board election that used her money as leverage to gain support and acceptance for her policies, especially from the male physicians. She responded to Currier's criticisms and offered alternatives indirectly through McKee to resolve the problem. Hearst preferred harmony and order over confrontation and disorder. McKee served and represented Hearst. Hearst could avoid confrontation, distance herself from the male physicians, and lessen the likelihood she would alienate or offend anyone by going through McKee. In consultation with Hearst, McKee took a modest, tactful approach in getting the male doctors to accept and work with the female physicians on the hospital staff as well as accept members on the hospital board to Hearst's liking. "We did not seek a woman physician for a resident," McKee explained coyly, "but took the only available person we know of." McKee wrote Dr. Currier that "our Board has never deliberated over this matter of women physicians, as our constitution does not allude to it." She explained Hearst's position further: "I can speak for Mrs. Hearst, myself and some others when I repeat what we have often stated that while *we* manage the affairs of the Hospital . . . each Hom. Physician in whom we have confidence, and who is willing to work, shall have an equal chance to do so."

For those who might be offended by this policy and contemplated dropping out of the staff, McKee identified alternatives: "A few of the more public spirited physicians" could take control of the hospital; they could "form a new board of Directors who may manage things better"; they could attempt "disincorporation [*sic*]—and re-incorporation under such changed laws, and with such restrictions as shall be acceptable." McKee expressed Hearst's concerns. As she explained, "Some of the managers are in favor of disincorporation a measure that I hope will be used only as a last resort," she wrote Dr. J. N. Eckel. McKee went on: the last "and best remedy was "for . . . men and women to make a bold united front, and push this small beginning into a great work." If Currier rejected the best solution, the hospital would face, McKee added, "visibly shrinking pockets, month by month," a recognition that Hearst would withdraw her financial support and encourage other contributors to do the same. Hearst's policies prevailed. The new board consisted of members who supported her positions. "The proposed new Board must all become members of the Corporation," Hearst explained. Eight months later, graduates from the Hahnemann Medical College received training at the Pacific Homeopathic Dispensary that operated with both female and male physicians on the staff.[82]

Hearst's private life remained difficult while she enjoyed her accomplishments in advancing women's education and employment in medicine. In 1884, George bought the 670,000-acre Babícora Ranch in Chihuahua, Mexico. The land was located in Texas, "about 250 miles southwest of El Paso." John Gilbert Follansbee, Will's friend and Harvard classmate, wrote to Phoebe in early 1884 about the land-claim battles in Mexico near the Hacienda San José de Babícora Ranch. Responding to Follansbee's letters, Phoebe became secretive and protective of the Hearst family interests and business assets in Mexico. As Follansbee put it, "I did as you told me, and burnt up all the letters." Will traveled south of the border to help Phoebe protect the family assets by inspecting the Hearst Mexican property since George was gone dealing with his business operations. That left Phoebe alone again. She felt abandoned and hurt. Revealing her true nature in private to her son, she wrote to Will in April 1884: "May you have many happy years and never know what it is to be neglected by those you love. . . . I am suffering such great pain. I cannot write more." Phoebe expressed her pain in a dramatic tone of voice. For her, though, misery loved company. Rather than reduce the emotional drain on herself by reining in her feelings in private, she sensationalized emotions that drew attention to her suffering. The stress and strain from dealing every-day with visitors of "six to ten solicitous friends, enemies & beggars" added to her personal problems. As she struggled to stay healthy, she wrote to Will: "It does seem as if I had more than my share of aches and pains."[83] Phoebe took her son's actions personally rather than realizing that he had other responsibilities to take care of, particularly related to the Hearst estate.

Phoebe's personal problems grew more complicated because of George. His political career suffered a setback as Phoebe's name and reputation became well-known among educational and medical advocates and reformers interested in the advancement of women. George failed to get the

California Democratic Party's gubernatorial nomination in 1882. The party instead chose General George Stoneman, a Southern California wine grower, a member of the politically powerful railroad commission created in the 1879 California Constitution, and an anti-monopolist.[84] Having failed to secure the nomination, what political move would George make next?

Phoebe's relationship with Will grew tense while George thought about his next move to advance his political career. Phoebe, by this point, probably began to question whether the Hearst money she spent on Will's Harvard education was worth it. By 1885, she was desperate to get Will to buckle down and study and watch his pennies while he attended Harvard University. Will ignored his schoolwork in favor of partying and pulling pranks on friends and faculty. Phoebe begged him to "study & don't pay tutors to do the work that you should do yourself. Pay your board bills. Pay tutors & be reasonable. Don't run bills," she admonished her son. She even traveled to Boston to deal with the situation firsthand when her pleading from afar fell on deaf ears. But Will's problems continued. He did not meet the requirements for numerous courses and ended up on probation. Phoebe struggled to understand her son's lack of interest in carrying out her wishes. She was deeply grieved. She wrote to Will in a dramatic tone: "I cannot understand how it is possible for you to be so utterly indifferent to my wishes. I am mortified & grieved beyond your comprehension."[85]

Phoebe was "in such a state of anxiety & uncertainty." She was concerned about what would happen to the Hearsts' and her son's reputation, status, and future if he did not graduate from Harvard. As she explained to Will, "It would almost kill me if you should not go through college in a creditable manner." Will, though, thought it a dreadful idea that he had to attend another year of college, because he wanted to help his father with his business. Phoebe intervened. Will resented her intervention. Phoebe, meanwhile, felt frustrated and blamed George for undermining her attempts to get Will to study by giving their son money to do whatever he wanted. As she explained to George, "I will not be held responsible when you go on giving him the means to do just as he pleases. I cannot give you a full account of my conversation with Will upon" the subject of money. "It is very hard for me." Phoebe knew Will threw money away on dinners, parties, and drinking. She possessed faith in Will, but she wanted her son to redeem himself. For a while, she thought she was achieving some success. But her hopes and expectations went unfulfilled. Will left Harvard University without graduating.[86] Will for the most part ignored his mother's wishes when it came to studying because he knew he would get whatever money he needed from his father and, in time, from his mother. Phoebe's failure to exert control successfully over her son while he attended Harvard University was a great disappointment to her. From Phoebe's perspective, it appeared that the Hearst money had not been well spent on their son's education.

Phoebe's personal problems never seemed to end. She tried to handle more stress and pressure and got "*very* tired of always being ill," she admitted. Worse yet, she could not shirk her familial duties and social and political obligations. Her status anxiety grew. Her weak physical condition became so bad that it prevented her from being active. She must have wondered if Will's difficulties at Harvard could harm her reputation and rank. She tried to limit her fear and protect her family name and reputation by donating money to link the Hearst name for the first time to the University of California. The University of California was a state university and a public institution, led by elites, which developed American nationality and used power to "translate . . . national ideals into institutional and operational reality." She gave $3,500 to the university for a metallurgical laboratory in the Department of Mining in 1885.[87] Little did she realize at the time how prophetic her gift was as she increased her reliance on gift-giving to reduce her personal anxieties.

Phoebe grappled with her personal problems as George's economic and political fortunes improved. Her husband amassed more wealth and cultivated his political connections with Governor Stoneman between 1882 and 1886. Stoneman struck a deal with George Hearst to get reelected for a second term, and Hearst delivered the votes of the San Francisco delegation to Stoneman so he could extend his tenure as governor of California. Stoneman rewarded George Hearst for his support. He appointed the bonanza king, on March 23, 1886, to fill the U.S. Senate seat for California left vacant when Republican John F. Miller passed away in early March. The *Sacramento Bee* charged Hearst with buying control of the San Francisco delegation to secure the Senate appointment. The newspaper provided no evidence to support the charge. The California legislature voted to seat George Hearst as a U.S. senator in early 1887.[88]

Phoebe Hearst had displayed skill and good judgment in using the Hearst money by the time George took his seat as a United States senator. She held high-society affairs and advocated for and accomplished political goals, privately and through participation in nonpartisan voluntary associations. How she chose to use her money and resources brought her a good reputation and made her prominent in San Francisco, especially elite circles. Wesley Mitchell, husband of Lucy Sprague, the well-known educator, wrote years later about how most Americans were backward in the art of spending money, an art dominated by women, he claimed. Mitchell remarked in the *American Economic Review*, "To spend money is easy, to spend it well is hard." He chided women for lacking an efficient system for spending money like industrial tycoons used, "based upon accumulated empirical knowledge."[89] Hearst demonstrated throughout the 1880s that she had indeed learned to spend her money in an "enlightened manner"—on self-education, self-improvement, and kindergarten and medical reform issues. The orderly, deliberate, and adroit ways she used money and resources advanced her own interests and helped others, women mostly, do the same.[90] She proved Mitchell wrong.

Having achieved such success, Phoebe A. Hearst probably realized rather quickly, after moving to Washington DC, that if she and George were to be successful in the capital, she needed to direct her money and other resources in ways that expressed and advanced her own political interests and career while elevating the Hearst name and reputation as well. She had already demonstrated the sophisticated, diplomatic skills needed to handle money properly in accomplishing personal aims and helping organizations accomplish political goals before the Hearsts arrived in Washington DC. Her skill in handling her money and resources, along with her experiences in nonpartisan voluntary association politics, would open the door for her to see how she could shape her own political agenda while George served in the United States Senate.

3

Political Agenda

In 1885, just before the Hearsts moved to Washington DC, Phoebe bought letter paper with the monogram PAH printed on it—initials of her first, maiden, and married names joined together. Over time, she gradually signed her correspondence PAH rather than P. A. Hearst—an expression of a complex, more mature, self-confident, and self-governing woman.[1] Phoebe knew people expected her to appear submissive and respectable in public and to hide her longings to control her own life. Her decision to put pen to new personalized stationery was a delicate, acceptable way for her show her independence without offending the opposite sex or Victorian sensibilities.

Independence in the realm of American politics likewise required Phoebe to balance assertiveness with a respectable, public demeanor. Rather than express her politics directly and openly in public—because it was unacceptable for dignified and respectable wealthy women to do so—she relied on her money and resources to form and communicate a complicated political agenda. Her personality and skill in clarifying and acting on her political priorities, coupled with her organizational experience and refined techniques, widened her political network, increased her power, and led her into nonpartisan and partisan voluntary association politics at the local level. Her success and lessons learned in local politics contributed to her meteoric rise into national nonpartisan voluntary association politics where, on equal terms with men, she served as an official in one of the largest women's organizations in the late nineteenth and early twentieth centuries.[2]

During this period of the late 1880s and early '90s, Hearst's struggles with family crisis gave her a chance to gain insight into herself and her political values. Although she had the opportunity to increase her independence while George spent his time and energy devoted to national politics and service in the United States Senate, she found herself constrained by private relations, especially with immediate family members, which grew more difficult and complicated in 1886. Among her most pressing problems was her son. Will's trials and tribulations produced great stress for his mother. Will, as he grew into manhood, had become enchanted with Eleanor Calhoun, from Tulare County, California. He met Calhoun in New York during the 1881 Christmas holiday season. Calhoun was a reasonably successful, dramatic actress and protégée of George Hearst's business associates James Ben Ali Haggin and Lloyd Tevis. Phoebe grew concerned when she found out that her twenty-three-year-old son was smitten with Calhoun. Phoebe disapproved adamantly of the powerful attraction Will and Eleanor held for one another.

Annoyed with Will's goings-on with Calhoun, Phoebe treated her son as though he were a child rather than a full-grown man. She explained her feelings to Orrin Peck, the son of Margaret Peck, Phoebe's life-long friend whom she had met on the steamer coming to California in 1862: "I am so unhappy about my boy" because he "is *desperately* in love with Miss [Eleanor] Calhoun, the *actress*." Phoebe believed Eleanor wanted "to marry a man, who has money," namely Will. Calhoun was intelligent but unreliable, lazy, and a gold digger, according to Phoebe. "Calhoun is wonderfully bright and even brilliant but so erratic, visionary, indolent and utterly wanting in order & neatness with extravagant tastes and no appreciation of values. All she cares for is to spend money, enjoy luxury

& receive admiration," Phoebe wrote. She added, "I feel that it will ruin my boy's life to marry such a designing woman and he will have to be burdened with the whole family of *eight*." Phoebe had a very low opinion of Eleanor. She was, at one point, so upset with her son's involvement with Calhoun that she remarked to George, "How is it possible for him to devote his time & attention to a *prostitute* and utterly ignore his *mother*."

Phoebe was at her wit's end. "I don't know how I can *live* if he marries Eleanor Calhoun," she remarked. Status anxiety probably engulfed Phoebe while she thought about the distinct possibility of marriage between Will and Eleanor. Could a match between them undermine the Hearsts' efforts to gain approval from Washington DC elites or damage the family reputation and status? Not one to sit by idly and watch problems adversely affect her family, Phoebe took charge and intervened. She and George strongly opposed the marriage. It was Phoebe, though, who tried "to delay matters" with her husband's blessing. In time, Phoebe dealt successfully with her son's attraction to Calhoun. Will eventually broke off his relationship with Eleanor and the crisis disappeared. But Will's romantic dalliance with Eleanor drained Phoebe physically and emotionally.[3] From her perspective, the intervention had been well worth it because Will never married Eleanor. The difficulties with her son were resolved successfully, at least for the moment.

Mary W. Kincaid, meanwhile, understood Phoebe's mental and emotional state while she dealt with Will's problem. Hearst probably first met Kincaid in the early 1870s when she had sent Will to a pro-labor union school in San Francisco—the North Cosmopolitan Grammar School. "Foreign-born Democrats . . . lobbied" successfully to have German, French, and Spanish taught at the school. That was one way to Americanize the students from immigrant backgrounds. Kate Kennedy headed the North Cosmopolitan Grammar School from 1867 to 1887. She was an Irish educational reformer, an advocate for the advancement of and equal pay for women, a suffragist, and a member of the Knights of Labor. Kincaid was an honors graduate of Benicia Seminary. She became the vice principal and the loyal assistant of John Swett, the principal of Girls' High and Normal School in San Francisco. The school Swett supervised was established to maintain moral standards. Teachers educated students for marriage. It was separate from the Boys' High School where pupils were schooled to enter the University of California.

Swett, while he headed the Girls' High and Normal School, battled Christopher "Blind Boss" Buckley to get respect and tenure rights for teachers so they could keep their jobs "without fear of political reprisals." Buckley was an Irish saloon owner. He headed the San Francisco Democratic political machine. He had built an uneasy political alliance with George Hearst on antimonopoly issues. Buckley also used a smear campaign to force Swett to resign. When Kincaid took Swett's place as principal of the Girls' High School in 1889, "local politicians saw her as a Swett disciple, and therefore an enemy." Kincaid, like Phoebe, struggled with the challenges. But in Kincaid's case, dealing with partisan political officials while she did her job as principal of Girls' High School, helped her develop empathy toward Phoebe as her friend handled crises that involved Will and adjusting to George's political world as well.

Kincaid drew upon a "model of the social body" in sanitary science that had become became prevalent in the 1850s as she reached out to help Phoebe understand herself and her situation. The idea behind the model was for the "American people [including Phoebe] to have themselves explained to themselves." However, the paradigm became so tied together with conversations on biology that words to describe body parts turned into tropes that were believed to be "scientific truths." These figures of speech labeled various groups in society according to different parts of the body. They turned differences between individuals and groups in society into biological inequalities allegedly supported by "scientific facts." The heart represented emotions and women; the head, the intellect and male head of the household and society; and the hands, the workers.[4] Kincaid invoked these figures of speech as she warned her friend about the daunting personal and political challenges that lay ahead as the wife of a United

States senator: "I guarantee your hands and heart and brain will be full trying to keep him [George] satisfied." Phoebe knew her friend was right. George Hearst, considered to be among the wealthiest men in the Senate, was a handful. "I need not tell you," Phoebe wrote Orrin Peck, "how I have to manage Mr. Hearst and to keep him even near the right thing."[5] To understand herself and her situation, Phoebe turned the body metaphor to good use. She believed that "science," in the name of improving American society, justified her wifely duty to control and reform her husband. These beliefs helped move her closer in her mind to a balance in the power relationship between herself and George, a change in outlook that helped her feel better about her new life in the nation's capital.

But adapting to George's world of national partisan politics, during the Grover Cleveland presidency, seriously tested "Mrs. Senator Hearst" while she and George lived at 435 Massachusetts Avenue in Washington DC. Europeans used the term "Mrs. Senator" to mean a woman of substance, privilege, power, and distinction. Phoebe, as she took on the varied responsibilities of being Mrs. Senator Hearst, felt burdened by the steady stream of requests for aid as she struggled simultaneously with additional family crises. Democrats, meanwhile, blanketed the city, and the pace of high-society life picked up considerably.[6] The political and social demands alone for Phoebe were piled sky high. But she detested the arena of national politics, especially Democrat and Republican politicians. The partisan political realm consisted of personal affronts. Few standards of manners and decorum existed. Superficial social intercourse, moreover, was the general rule. Scandals, financial confusion, partisan squabbles, competitive elections were the norm. To top it all off, the "spoils system" plagued Washington DC residents. The spoils system often rewarded unqualified and incompetent party loyalists with public jobs.[7] Phoebe abhorred George's national partisan political world.

Even so, she liked living in Washington DC with George close by. But she knew she "could enjoy more there if not in [the world of male] political life," she remarked. As she explained to Orrin Peck, whom Phoebe considered a second son, "A Senator's wife has her trials I assure you, and I don't consider that there is much honor in politics." She went on, "I hate [Washington DC] politics so that it is difficult for me to mention the subject." She added, "I have *no* faith in politicians. One can never depend upon them." That was a telling statement, the roots of which she could trace to personal experience. Deeply distressed by her husband's involvement in what she considered the filthy cesspool of politics, she remarked to her son, "It troubles me very much for papa to be in politics." Phoebe became desperate for a solution to her problem. She turned to Will for help. She wanted her son to convince George to abandon his political career. "When you come home I hope you can induce him [George] to give it [politics] up," she wrote. Her request fell on deaf ears. She failed to get what she wanted from Will. Upset, she wrote Will, "I feel very unhappy about your utter indifference & extreme selfishness."[8] Phoebe tried to figure out a way to resolve her personal and family difficulties and get used to the fact that George refused to leave the world of political elites. George, meanwhile, continued to represent his constituents in the United States Senate and deal with his mining business.

Phoebe started to understand her political values more clearly when she acted as a family powerbroker during a longstanding crisis involving her alcoholic brother, Elbert Apperson (Eppy), while she lived in Washington. Phoebe knew she had "to be the anchor [in her family] for awhile longer" after close relatives contacted her for help. As she put it, "I am always obliged to carry all social responsibilities." Doing what was expected, especially regarding family issues, was a serious business to Phoebe. Her brother's loss of self-control, indolence, and persistent dependency were sins in her eyes. "He did nothing, would lie about in a stupor for days," she wrote. Eppy's disease distressed and depressed Phoebe and created emotional tensions and strains that afflicted Eppy's wife, Lizzie, and Eppy's "bright" young daughter, Annie. She believed, like pre–Civil War crusaders, that vices such as alcoholism, laziness, and poverty were sins and obstacles to redemption and worldly prosperity.[9]

Phoebe started to knit together her personal and political reform interests and values as she tried to understand Eppy's human frailty. She attributed her brother's condition at first to character defects. She did not have "much faith in [his individual] reform, but I do all I can to help," she remarked. Phoebe was doubtful that her brother would abandon his destructive ways. But she also was reluctant to reject conventional beliefs about womanhood by refusing to get involved. So how would she handle this family emergency? Understanding herself to be a strong woman and an instigator of reform-minded activities, her instincts took over. She decided to follow the model created by women in the arena of social science. She would exert the power and authority of a mother to protect, empower, and punish members of her family. Shifting American attitudes now advocating the belief that environmental factors, rather than individual character flaws, produced vices, such as poverty and alcoholism, influenced Phoebe's decision.[10]

Hearst thought that the best solution was to change Eppy's surroundings dramatically and provide for his family because she thought social and political conditions were responsible for his alcoholism. She became determined to do what she thought was best for Eppy. She "insisted upon radical measures" suggested by Lizzie, Eppy's wife, to split up the Apperson family. The plan was a form of punishment because it separated Eppy from his wife and daughter. But it also was practical. Lizzie came to San Francisco. Phoebe's brother went to his father's to "be taken care of." The strategy was intended to protect Lizzie and Annie from the adverse effects of Eppy's "personal failings." Eppy and Lizzie decided, with Phoebe's approval, "to let Annie stay with me for a year or more," Phoebe explained. Phoebe anticipated treating Annie like the daughter she never had. She planned to take Annie abroad as soon as possible "to make something of her," she remarked.

In effect, then, Phoebe was replacing her brother in caring for his family emotionally and financially. She provided mental and moral support and goods and services to Eppy, his wife, and child, which her brother could not provide while he battled the demon alcohol. Phoebe became

the head of the household and the family protector, provider, and pun-
isher. The radical plan to reform Eppy worked. He stopped drinking.
And his sister, as she managed the crisis, moved away from old views
about charity and embraced new ones centered on the importance of
environmental factors, rather than on individual character flaws and
human frailty, as the cause of vice.[11] Struggling with her brother's crisis,
she gained a new awareness about the central role of social and political
conditions in American society. These experiences helped her gain insight
into her relationship with her family, the rest of society, and the world.
She recognized that social and political forces were at the heart of her
understanding of Eppy's struggle with alcoholism.

The stresses and strains produced by family crises took their toll on
Phoebe. She became so upset, miserable, and ill she needed to abandon
her social and political activities. "I have suffered enough to kill most
women, and yet I am alive, though not *very active*," she wrote in the dramatic tone of a martyr. She lamented her situation and explained how her
health suffered. "My nerves were in such a state that neuralgia tortured
me and it became almost impossible for me to digest any food. Finally I
had rheumatic fever and during the last six weeks I have had three severe
operations performed," she added. Evidence is lacking, however, to corroborate that these harsh medical procedures actually took place. With so
many intractable problems, Phoebe feared getting "into a state of depression impossible to throw off." She cried out forlornly to Margaret Peck, "I
am so heartbroken I have no pleasure or pride in anything."[12] She wished
her health was better and admitted, as Margaret observed, "that she takes
the best of care of herself, and this she considers every woman's duty."

Over time, Phoebe's perspective had been shifting as older, fatalistic
views about "death and disease" were exchanged for the belief that it
was possible for every citizen to have "good health."[13] She relied on what
she knew of the body metaphor to understand herself and the causes of
her illness. She drew on that knowledge to assert mind over matter to
gain further insight into her situation as 1886 came to a close. "As I gain

strength, my courage increases and I have determined to keep my mind and heart in a better condition and rise above the trying influences that have so burdened me," she continued. It appeared that the hands that represented the workers, at the moment, were not a top priority for a wife of a U.S. senator. But her mind and heart were another matter. She wanted to alleviate the toll her brother's crisis had taken on her life. She anticipated the positive outcome: regain a measure of understanding of herself as a head of a household and increase her control over her life so she could resume her high-society affairs and reform-minded political activities.[14] To achieve the desired result, she needed to strengthen her bodily power—her emotional, intellectual, and physical condition and independent spirit.

Phoebe threw herself into her work as the wife of a U.S. senator as she got back on her feet physically and emotionally. With skill and sound judgment, she made strategic and systematic decisions to protect her husband and the Hearst name and family, in part by becoming "pretty close mouthed generally," according to Orrin Peck. She continued to hold high-society affairs that met the established social and political standards in the nation's capital. Phoebe knew very well that mere money and a desire to shine in high society were insufficient to the task. Higher-ups in Washington DC shunned the class who had "nothing but their money to recommend them." Displays of "vulgar ostentation" were frowned upon, and egotism was a "dreaded bane of society," a high-society writer noted. The use of terrible grammar, discussions in public about wealth, and unfashionable dress, needed to be avoided at all cost. Displaying proper etiquette (rules of correct, logical behavior and authority), and being refined, were crucial. In the meantime, neither Phoebe nor anyone else expected George to attend her social entertainments, since he was "not given to society."[15] Neither did she expect him to shorten or abandon his prolonged absences. George did not care about social climbing. He left that to his wife. But while the role of social hostess lacked meaning and purpose for "Mrs. Senator Hearst," she drew, nevertheless, on all the lessons of good breeding and the ways of worthiness and grace she had learned from her mother and Lucy Ann Dun James, to hold and orchestrate the social affairs she understood to be critical for her family's acceptance into the correct social and political circles. She paid particular attention to "official society's stern rules of precedence and [took] protocol very seriously," especially the power of politeness, to show that she and her family possessed what it took to fit into the proper elite groups at the national level.[16]

As a senator's wife, Phoebe would have to prove she controlled all the "gifts for entertaining" without exhibiting in public any signs of submitting to the stresses and strains produced by doing what was expected to establish the Hearsts in Washington DC. Newspaper articles and social visits from others exposed the Hearsts to Washington DC society. Reporters wrote about how the wives of national politicians spent an excessive amount of resources, especially money, time, and energy, on society teas, luncheons, evening receptions, and dinners. Phoebe probably knew she would need to compete with society women like Jane L. Stanford to impress. That meant spending money and resources on organizing and holding stunning dinner parties, balls, and receptions in the Hearsts' "adopted city," which the press incorrectly named "a city of leisure." Washington DC was hardly a city of leisure considering the extensive amount of time and exhausting activities required to hold successful high-society affairs.[17] Phoebe knew that how she handled these challenges would have an impact on her social standing and self-worth as well as the Hearst's family position among the Washington DC power elite.

High-society hostesses needed an appropriate home in which to do the requisite entertaining and perform the appropriate rules of etiquette and protocol. Phoebe diplomatically and cleverly prodded George into buying a Greek Revival—characterized as colonial at the time—three-story brick structure at 1400 New Hampshire Avenue, Northwest, in the "fashionable" and "beautiful" Dupont Circle neighborhood. Secretary of the Treasury Charles S. Fairchild owned the 1883 house designed by architect Robert I. Fleming. The design promoted the American principles of independence, freedom, and democracy that Phoebe favored. She refused to urge George to act against his "better judgment and" his "wishes," she explained, regarding the purchase, yet she understood, and wanted to satisfy, her husband's ambition as well as her own (it had even been reported that it was her drive, not her husband's, that was responsible for bringing the Hearsts to Washington). She developed a line of reasoning intended to appeal to her husband's business instincts. Relying on her rhetorical powers, sense of geographical location, and acumen in architectural design, Phoebe pointed out that the house was well located on a corner with a design that allowed air and light. She could make it pretty and attractive if George bought the house. He could then sell it and make money, she argued. She deferred to him to make the decision, a reasonable approach in George's eyes. But she also knew that George wanted to please her—he respected his wife and her aspirations to shine as Mrs. Senator Hearst. He understood that owning the property would benefit both of them. So he bought the place. It was said that the house "cost over $300,000."[18] Phoebe had taken a shrewd approach. George's purchase of a proper home for a senator and his wife was a way for the Hearsts to put down roots in Washington society.

Phoebe set about remodeling the new Hearst house into a home for entertaining. She must have sensed that official Washington society lacked sparkle—the place was in dire need of leadership and a good dose of cultural refinement and civic pride. In the new house, Phoebe showed herself to be a "remarkable example of the success of womanly pride and ambition sustained by indomitable will and perseverance," according to Dr. Silas Reed (a miner, practicing physician, and friend of George's from Missouri). Drawing on these strengths, Phoebe used complex, refined techniques and sophisticated skills to mount an ostentatious, but not vulgar, display of the Hearst wealth. She made herself happy at the same time by pursuing her interest in design and architecture—acceptable fields of activities for women. She supervised and completed her first architectural project. She likely recognized the intellectual and emotional connection between the home, domestic architecture, and cultural improvement. She saw a remodeled house, moreover, as a comfortable home. But she also experienced it as a place to make rational plans and a foundation from which to socially and culturally improve society and the national city.[19]

Washington architect Harvey L. Page, in 1889, was commissioned to enlarge and remodel the Fairchild house in the Henry Hobson Richardson Romanesque style Phoebe preferred. It was the first American architectural style that Europeans copied. Although this style was on its way to becoming passé at about the time Hearst began the remodeling, she probably liked the particular design because of the moral values and convictions it expressed that represented the standards she learned growing up. She most likely favored what others described as a design of "order and diversity, vigor and restraint, individuality and sensitive interpretation of precedent that provided a foundation for subsequent endeavors." The style linked the Victorian and academic worlds, an increasingly important association for Phoebe as she grew to become a mature, older woman.[20] This was the first time she was to use her personal interest in design and architecture as an expression of power and standing in society.

Phoebe persevered to complete the remodeling project. She was renovating the new house on New Hampshire Avenue as mansions became all the rage in San Francisco, Denver, New York City and northern Long Island, Philadelphia, and Rhode Island. The project also proved to be disruptive and a test of her abilities and endurance. Phoebe A. Hearst, the press noted, "has built the new house, turned it upside down, inside out, so to speak, and left little sign of the former structure except some of the bricks." The new house epitomized the transition she had made from San Francisco elite circles into the Washington DC elite circles that would alter her life. It was, for Phoebe, "very trying and tedious to live in this state [of renovation] when I was really quite ill and Mr. Hearst not very well," she explained to Sarah B. Cooper (her friend and colleague from the Golden Gate Kindergarten Association). Nevertheless, once the renovation project was finished, Phoebe lost no time in putting on high-society affairs, at great cost and generally without her husband's assistance or presence. Phoebe understood the importance of these extravagant dinners to her husband's political success. "The dinners given in" Washington DC hold "some object in view and, of course, that object is generally connected with politics," opined the *New York World*.[21]

Phoebe A. Hearst had now been transformed into Mrs. Senator Hearst, and George and Phoebe were well and truly members of the capital elite. At this point, the sheer sophistication, number, size (both small and large), and scope of Hearst's affairs overshadowed those she had held in San Francisco in the 1870s. She dazzled and impressed guests and society columnists. She crafted the invitation lists carefully. She hired musicians who performed unobtrusive background music, while discreet and competent staff waited upon her guests. She created a distinct style for each high-society dinner party. She used artistic hand-painted menus, some with gilt edges. She staged original floral decorations, personally arranging fresh-cut flowers. She selected and properly placed table ornaments of medium height in the best location so guests could see each other across the table. She mapped out the seating arrangements so that visitors with similar interests and views could enjoy interesting conversations with the people who sat next to them. General event preparation, serving food properly, and taking care of all the details took considerable thought, work, time, and financial resources. Jane Lathrop Stanford spent thousands on luncheons with twelve courses that "took two and a half hours to serve," one high-society observer noted. The largest high-society balls and receptions demanded even greater amounts of time and money, which only millionaires, or their spouses, possessed. And, of course, success demanded etiquette—displays of the proper courtesies and good breeding and proper dress acceptable to the national social and political elite.[22]

Phoebe put on a brave performance at her parties because she knew it was the right and proper thing to do. Egos were to be kept in check. Consideration of the needs of others was highly valued in Washington DC. In fact, Phoebe dressed "rather modestly for a woman of her wealth" at these affairs, one reporter noted. She behaved in a respectable and courteous manner. She focused on pleasing others. And although giving parties was a "terrible strain," she somehow managed to fool others into believing she took pleasure in being part of the world of the political elites: "During all this strain, I have smiled & entertained & been bored, when able to be out of bed. Good clothes, an artistic make up and a brave spirit, have deceived the world." But still she spared no expense on social entertainments that not only met but exceeded what people expected, and she bore her burdens quietly. Her high-society affairs sparkled and buzzed with excitement, and an array of guests from all over the country came to the Hearst mansion to mix and mingle and engage in sophisticated, absorbing conversation. She, too, after all, now had the opportunity to meet and converse with people with similar interests and contribute to shaping Washington DC into a truly representative city of the entire nation-state.[23]

It must have pleased Hearst that her cultural capital and high-society reputation began to skyrocket. People were impressed with her completed architectural project. They took note of her abilities as a "charming," "perfect" hostess who "dresses in exquisite taste," as one newspaper reported.[24] Frances Benjamin Johnston was an innovative, independent photographer, and an advocate for women's advancement. She made a living taking pictures of prominent social, professional, and political clients in Washington DC. Johnston hailed the Hearsts' remodeled mansion as "unquestionably the finest private residence lately erected in Washington, and stands [as] a veritable triumph of refinement of style in architecture and of decorative art, preaching a rousing sermon of good taste" in an age of extravagance.[25] Reporters, who described Hearst as a Democrat, assessed her abilities as a high-society hostess in "command of an income that many an English Duchess might envy." To give a thoroughly successful dinner in Washington "is the supreme social test," according to an 1889 article in the *New York World*.

Hearst met the test. Her dinners "are perfection, and remain green in one's memory for a long time," the newspaper noted. The *Illustrated Amer-*

ican proclaimed Hearst to be "a graceful and pleasing woman" who "has a low voice." When draped in an evening dress "with strings of diamonds around her beautiful neck," she was "handsome . . . [and] hospitable." The *Denver Union* called her the "most artistic entertainer at Washington."[26] Hearst's architectural project and parties were impressive, but it was the acclaim she received in the press that brought the Hearst family to the attention of the capital elite and made the Hearst name well-known across the nation.

The press attention, in turn, helped Phoebe A. Hearst's public persona and image garner authority and increase her status and prominence. Her clever and practical use of money and resources made her popular in elite social, cultural, intellectual, and political circles and brought her a reputation as a distinguished socialite and social leader, all of which assisted her husband and the advancement of his career. As Margaret Peck put it, "Your entertaining is such a help to Mr. Hearst."[27] Although Phoebe continued to struggle with the internal tensions and strain produced by her personal life and holding society affairs, through it all, she managed to turn her home into a center where various, but not all, forms of power—ideological, rhetorical, social, cultural, economic, political, and symbolic—coalesced and were on display for all to see. Newly positioned on the top rung of the ladder of the national elite as Mrs. Senator Hearst, she did credit to her husband's career, herself, and Washington DC.

Phoebe saw her participation in Washington DC social and political affairs as a self-sacrifice expected of the spouse of a rich, powerful U.S. senator, entitling her to public praise but also providing justification for personal, private rewards.[28] Exhausted from her activities, Hearst decided she needed a break. She wrote to Sarah Cooper, "I really am not equal to the care of opening a house there [in San Francisco] this year." Having accomplished so much as a high-society hostess in Washington, she decided not to return to the West Coast. Instead, she thought it best to go to Europe.[29] Phoebe, over the years, traveled abroad for a variety of reasons: for self-education, self-improvement, and to rest and escape unpleasant tasks and conflicts. This time she needed to relax and get away from the urban conflict and political corruption in San Francisco, and the "filthy cesspool" of partisan politics in Washington DC. Dealing with the burden to help and please others, along with tolerating the filth of national politics, was difficult enough. But she "was so hurt and astonished at" the class warfare, anti-Chinese and anti-labor riots, and the political mismanagement and corruption in San Francisco at a time when "machine-style party organization controlled access to city government," "she would have been glad to go away entirely & never return," one biographer noted.[30] Harmony and order were supposed to be the "friends" of a traditional self-sacrificing woman, like Hearst, rather than the conflict and stress that came from adjusting to national political life in Washington.

Hearst's involvement in nonpartisan voluntary association politics became one way for her to work through the stress and strains produced by family crises and to bring her life meaning and purpose, even though her organizational work and activities brought additional pressures. Phoebe wanted to make a contribution to the creation of a harmonious and orderly society, and to prove she deserved the title "Mrs. Senator Hearst." Her participation in reform causes might at the same time draw people's attention away from "charges" against George that he "had bribed his way to office." Since she possessed only a rudimentary education, she hired an assistant, Mary W. Kincaid—who became principal, after John Swett, of the Girls' High School in San Francisco—to teach and travel with her on an active, working vacation.[31] She needed someone like Kincaid, with advanced schooling and broader experiences, to help her study and steep herself in reform ideas and knowledge about social and political conditions.

Kincaid declared her belief "in the womanly dignity that relies on character and culture alone," as Hearst's and other benevolent women's understanding of themselves turned more and more political. Kincaid allied herself with Democratic Party leaders in the mid-to-late 1880s. Democratic

Party officials established the Committee of One Hundred to take the reins of power in San Francisco out of the hands of Christopher "Blind Boss" Buckley, which would help Swett's fight for teachers. Kincaid became, she explained at the time, "discouraged about matters" and struggled to "know the ways of politicians." Hearst, meanwhile, made Kincaid feel important by presenting an offer to her she would find difficult to refuse. Hearst showered Kincaid with gifts and money to lure her away from her position as principal. Kincaid's "whole life," she wrote to Hearst, "[is] made sweeter by the ideal world I am able to transport myself into when I people it with you and your surroundings amongst the beautiful things that your hand has put into my home." Caught up in San Francisco school and partisan politics, Kincaid felt "powerless at present to change much in the school," she wrote, in a city ruled by "Blind Boss" Buckley. The stress of duties that were so overly arduous made Kincaid's job as principal a disagreeable "task," Margaret Peck wrote Hearst. Kincaid's occupation became so distasteful, she first took a leave of absence and then formally resigned from Girls' High and Normal School, or what she called "this prison," on New Year's Day in 1892 to become Hearst's devoted full-time employee, teacher, and guide.[32] The decision to hire Kincaid showed Hearst's developing knack for choosing the right people to work with to advance herself and her husband. But it also displayed Hearst's determination to learn how to gather information to help clarify and formulate her top political reform priorities.

The power-working relationship Hearst and Kincaid formed was friendly, affectionate, and political. Mary referred to Phoebe as her "darling sister" as early as 1886. She also displayed personal concern for Phoebe's well-being. She warned Phoebe shortly after she arrived in Washington DC: "An amazing lot of parasites will attach themselves to your greenness, and *you* will be dried up." Phoebe, in return, considered Mary "such a loyal and loving friend." But Hearst held the upper hand. She was developing into a powerful, domineering woman with a sense of social responsibility and class and racial superiority. Hearst had taken on crass and arrogant attitudes about money and class as she became used to the pleasures that wealth and prominence brought as Mrs. Senator Hearst. Her views became evident in her disparaging comments about the lower classes and her blunt disdain for the rabble. As she put it later, "I'm not a bit proud but I do love the prestige that *filthy* lucre gives one and another thing, I do hate to come in contact with common people."[33]

Kincaid served Hearst's needs. She acted as a liaison between Hearst and the recipients of her largesse. Working through Kincaid, Hearst could distance herself from those in the lower classes without offending either her employee or the beneficiaries of Hearst's gifts. Kincaid was deferential to her employer and willing to do her bidding and carry out her agenda. She explained to Hearst: "I accept *any* office or appointment under the sun that you think best and will work my very best to perform the duties." Kincaid knew she worked for a privileged white woman with a rudimentary education in an America in which a growing number of female and male reformers were seriously troubled by the enormous gaps that existed between the wealthy and the poor and in which class demarcations were increasingly rigid.[34] There was no doubt in Kincaid's mind, in other words, that Hearst was the boss.

Hearst unapologetically ordered Kincaid to develop a systematic plan for the trip abroad that would help her pinpoint her top concerns and values and translate these priorities into a political agenda. Phoebe wanted to rest, relax, and enjoy herself. But she also wanted to absorb detailed knowledge and have broader and deeper experiences that would assist her in becoming a competent reformer in nonpartisan voluntary association politics. Hearst, moreover, possessed an ardent desire to provide an opportunity for her niece, Annie Apperson, her surrogate daughter, to make something of herself abroad. Phoebe knew what it was like to struggle with the vagaries of the national economy. Getting through George's financial crisis in the mid-1860s had been a painful experience that stayed with her and influenced her thinking and decisions. People needed to be prepared for weathering such economic crises by studying an occupation. As Phoebe explained to a female friend, "The training and influence coming from well-directed effort to learn a business are calculated to strengthen the character, ennoble the life, [and] benefit society as well as the individual." Parents were obligated to prepare youngsters for economic independence, according to Hearst. She thought "it a duty for parents to fit their children for self-support, even if the need never comes." Women who followed her advice would achieve "a finer womanhood, full of purpose and refined energy," Hearst wrote. Toward this end, Hearst planned to take her niece to Europe to educate and prepare her to stand on her own feet.

With the commanding presence of a general, in 1889 Hearst instructed Kincaid to plan for an active working vacation for herself and her niece. Kincaid drew up detailed plans for the trip. She asked Hearst "whether it [seemed] best to follow" them. Hearst studied and approved the plan. She then gave Kincaid a good deal of money to go abroad, live comfortably, and make preparations for her and Annie's arrival in Paris several months later.[35] Hearst and her niece left San Francisco and journeyed across America during a time when travel for small groups of women of a similar age was becoming common. They sailed on the ss *City of New York*, with Andrew Carnegie on board that summer, although they never met.[36] Hearst, nevertheless, looked forward to actively carrying out Kincaid's methodical plan created for her time in Europe, and that would help her form and establish her political agenda and philanthropic goals.

Hearst and Kincaid traveled to England after meeting in Paris, with Kincaid pursuing her investigations on Hearst's behalf in London, France, and Germany. Kincaid's work helped Hearst develop and expand the power of her networks across the Atlantic. Like Hearst, Mary was very intelligent. She also knew the "right" people and, according to Orrin Peck, "how to appease the begging public." Most likely it was Kincaid who put Hearst in touch with people who provided her with letters of introduction to Europeans interested in education and reform. On this trip, Hearst took note of "social and political conditions." She was, moreover, excited by the kindergarten movement and the "universal interest it so richly merits. It is as you say the great work of the age & God is moving human hearts to recognize it," she explained to Sarah Cooper. Hearst was interested in being introduced to social science reformers critical of the political economy. She wanted to meet and talk with people who supported and explained Froebel's ideas and were "the very soul of the [kindergarten] movement," she recounted. The letters that presented her to kindergarten reformers encouraged Hearst to strive intellectually, ethically, and morally to learn about and accomplish greater kindergarten reform. The more she learned about political issues of personal concern, ones that were also shared by men, like kindergartens, the more she gained insight into women's relationship to power and national reform politics in America and abroad.[37]

The letters of introduction Hearst carried with her to Europe opened the door to private discussions with some of the most prominent activists and writers in the German kindergarten reform movement. Meanwhile, back across the Atlantic, more upper- and middle-class women were getting involved in nonpartisan, voluntary association politics in America.[38] Hearst met "many charming people to whom I have letters of introduction & who are deeply interested in educational matters," she explained. She held productive conversations with Professor Wilhelm Preger, author of *The Soul of the Child*, and Baroness Berthe von Marenholtz-Bulow, Friedrich Froebel's outstanding student who adapted his work to urban and industrial settings. She met with Henrietta Shrader-Breymann, Froebel's niece and former student, who defined the traits assigned to teachers that "anticipated the role devised by Jane Addams in the 1880s for the settlement house worker," and which centered on teachers helping to solve urban problems and close the gap between rich and poor. Other meetings took place with Froebel's widow; with Miss Manning, a kindergarten reformer just returned from Bombay, India; and Miss Sheriff and sister Lady Gray, educational writers.[39] Hearst also took the opportunity to learn about "the development of scientific truths that would transform education" and help her "participate in the educational reform that would transform society."

Looking forward and to the past, Phoebe wrote to George that she has "gained information & seen much that will remain with me as long as I retain my faculties." She "most carefully" studied "the care & training of little children among the poor classes," she explained, to prepare herself for reform politics back home. She added, "There is much that can aid us in America for the experience here is surely worth something to us and there is a work to be done among our cosmopolitan population." She visited schools to train domestic help, wives, and parents. She saw "manual labor schools." She had "a long talk . . . with a very intelligent and agreeable woman who is doing admirable work . . . among the poor." She studied Froebel's kindergarten and "Sloyd" system for manual labor just as his ideas were gaining in popularity in America and elsewhere. She learned from her assistant but also enjoyed watching Kincaid teach Annie. "Kincaid's instruction is given in such an interesting and thorough manner that it will be a great advantage to Annie. The child has also a great benefit in seeing so much which she could never obtain from books," Hearst wrote. Both Phoebe and Annie enjoyed the experience of travel and learning how to make something of themselves. For Annie that meant being schooled in the European people, culture, and ways of life. For Hearst that meant paying more attention to social and political factors, as well as gaining more sophisticated cultural and political knowledge that would help her to make competent decisions about acting on her reform interests.[40]

Hearst clarified her political values and agenda while traveling abroad. She collected practical ideas and information she thought wealthy women interested in reform should know but which the masses often were denied. She learned about universities, libraries, the Hermitage Museum in St. Petersburg, Russia (which was closed to the public but open to Hearst), ethnographic and anthropological museums, galleries, palaces, monuments, zoological gardens, and Berlin—a center of commerce and trade. She continued to focus her attention on social and political conditions. Hearst and Annie relied on Kincaid's accurate and broad knowledge and skills as they toured the sites. Kincaid "explained all that we did not fully understand," Phoebe wrote George. "Her knowledge is so varied and exact and she has the most delightful way of imparting it," Hearst noted.[41] Sarah Cooper had introduced Hearst to the basic tools of social science while Hearst was a director of the Golden Gate Kindergarten Association. Kincaid helped Hearst take the next step: to familiarize herself with the fundamental skills of a social scientist—observation, investigation, facts, and analysis. Hearst, while Kincaid guided her, began to turn herself into an amateur social scientist as social workers in the United States and Great Britain were involved in a long, contested political battle over the transfer of power from evangelical women to trained professional social scientists and social workers.[42]

Hearst enjoyed building her knowledge and cultural capital with her dear friend Kincaid as the "professor." "What an education travel is! . . . . One learns more in such a trip as this than he could possibly do in a four years' college course," Kincaid remarked.[43] Hearst scrutinized in Vienna, Austria, "the school gardens, the cooking schools & the training schools where girls are taught to be good servants, and also for the preperation [sic] of good wives & mothers," she commented. Hearst "had not seen the exhibition in Paris." But she was so enthralled with her travels and the lessons learned that she wanted to visit Brussels to see "the model schools," she wrote. Unfortunately, she did not have enough time to fully develop her agenda because George wanted her to come home. She knew her husband would not come abroad. She was "entirely 'broke up,' as they say, by your telegram," that demanded she return to America, Kincaid explained to George, adding, "for she can not imagine what is the matter as long as you say you are well." George was worried about his wife "being worn out." But Phoebe felt "surprise and disappointment" when she heard of her husband's demand to interrupt her work.[44] The delicate balance she was trying to maintain seemed to George to be tipped too much in his wife's favor.

A young Hearst had submitted more readily to her husband's demands to keep the subtle balance on an even keel. But she refused this time. The older Phoebe Hearst had gained a refined knack for choosing sophisticated, skilled people, in this case Kincaid, to work with who could help her achieve her goals. Hearst presented Kincaid with a challenge. She called on Kincaid to intervene and haggle with George over when she should return home. Kincaid acted as an intermediary between Phoebe and George. She could explain to George what Phoebe was often reluctant or unwilling to say, and she was sensitive to Phoebe's need to avoid appearing frivolous. She understood her boss's work ethic and her need to learn more about educational reform. Showing she accorded the same value and respect to Phoebe's interests and activities as she did to George's, Kincaid argued that George should allow Phoebe to stay abroad longer because she "has worked every day the whole day at looking into the history and development of the people in this northern world." Kincaid explained further: "Not a single hour has" Phoebe "given to social life or show"—a distortion of reality to impress George. Phoebe was different, Kincaid argued to George, from another wealthy woman, Katherine Duer Mackay, a "queen of society" in New York and the spouse of the owner of the International Telephone and Telegraph Company. Mackay "came here in as much grand state as a queen, spent her time in foolish ostentation in dancing around the Court here and displaying her rare clothes and jewels, traveling about in private car, and all such unreality as a superficial woman would delight in," Kincaid remarked. Kincaid explained to Phoebe that she told George "how you had worked at study of everything in the north, what a benefit to his household and what prestige among the legations your intelligent observation gives you, what lovely invitations to visit fine people at their country homes, but if you had to sail Oct. 16th, you could not accept these invitations."

Phoebe, in other words, could deepen her knowledge and understanding and make important connections if she remained abroad. Those actions would help her prepare a political reform agenda to act on back home that would shield the Hearsts from attacks by moral critics and enhance the family prestige. It was up to Phoebe to protect herself and her son since George was an absentee husband and father. All George needed to do to reap the benefits was to approve of his wife staying abroad longer, according to Kincaid. She informed Phoebe that she and George "talked about your being worn out, and the change in you, and your grieved heart at not getting a word from Will." Kincaid knew Phoebe would feel it her duty to return to America if her husband was ill or unhappy, so she wrote her employer and friend that she "would telegraph" her "if Mr. Hearst did not seem well and happy."[45] Over time, Hearst would slowly submit to her husband's demand. But with Kincaid's help, she could satisfy herself and meet her husband's needs at the same time—always a tricky balancing act.

Kincaid provided Phoebe with an argument to justify learning what she needed to build a politically active career separate and independent from her husband at the same time that she made him happy. Kincaid tried to convince George that his wife was different indeed from wealthy women of leisure, like Mackay and Caroline Schermerhorn Astor. Mackay and Astor, Kincaid thought, engaged in conspicuous consumption the likes of which Thorstein Veblen disapproved. Phoebe, according to Kincaid, refused to spend money frivolously. Kincaid's assistance was essential if Hearst was to develop her political agenda and "train" herself adequately, furthermore, to be a competent philanthropist on par with other wealthy female philanthropists active in advancing American political reform causes within a competitive business and political world where men raced against each other for money, possessions, and power.[46]

Kincaid arrived at a solution. George needed to go "west on railroad matters on Senate Committee, he would take about two weeks on that, then go to California and *probably to Mexico*," Kincaid explained. So why shouldn't he allow Phoebe to remain abroad to engage in meaningful activities that she enjoyed while he was elsewhere doing what made him happy? George was impressed with Phoebe's devotion to preparing herself for advancement as well as with Kincaid's argument. He wanted, moreover, to make his wife happy. So he asked Kincaid to tell Phoebe she "had better stay as long as" she "thought best."[47] George's decision to give his approval for Phoebe to extend her visit abroad was a turning point in Phoebe's life. The more time she focused on fulfilling her own needs and ambitions, the less she thought about her desire to have more children. She also missed her husband and son less the more she felt fulfilled. George understood, fortunately for Phoebe, his wife's need to be active and experience an independent and separate life with meaning and purpose. He wanted to give his wife more time and freedom to do what she liked since he spent so much of his own time away doing what he liked. His decision pleased both Hearsts. Phoebe must have experienced a sense of relief and freedom after George granted her wish for an extended stay abroad.

Upon arriving home from her European tour, Hearst was ready to put her newly clarified ideas about educational reform into action, but this was not without a degree of personal conflict over her feelings about people in the lower socioeconomic classes. Hearst knew it was unacceptable for her to reveal publicly her disdain for the "rabble" because it would taint her public image and reputation, so she masked her condescension in public. Still, she went on to use her resources, especially her economic power, strategically and systematically, in concert with kindergarten reform organizations, to help her constituents, San Francisco women, in particular, achieve self-support and move up the social, cultural, economic, and political ladders.[48]

Emma Jacobina Christiana Marwedel, a disciple of Froebel and a member of the board of directors of San Francisco's Silver Street Kindergarten, noted the increase in Hearst's level of kindergarten expertise when Hearst returned home from Europe. Marwedel praised Hearst's ability to learn about kindergarten matters and flattered her by telling her she was "very anxious to know" what impact the knowledge and study abroad had had on Hearst's "ideas and noble mind." Hearst's decisions informed Marwedel's curiosity. Hearst was a strong believer in parents preparing girls and boys to protect themselves from economic vulnerability. So she decided to direct her expertise against funding an unsatisfactory, unspecified project. She put her money, instead, toward the establishment of a third Hearst Free Golden Gate Kindergarten Association class. She also thought about establishing a fourth to provide individual opportunities for educating children and for young girls and women to get training for jobs at the same time that she enhanced the collective power of the GGKA.

Hearst then hired Marwedel in 1890 to train San Francisco kindergarten teachers. This was at a time when women reformers had moved away from "moral suasion" and become increasingly involved in American women's nonpartisan voluntary association politics. Hearst's decision, however, concerned Sarah Cooper, according to Kincaid, because Marwedel had been "such a care and worry to her for seven years, and was so inharmonious and visionary that she feels that the sweet harmony now existing in the work in this city will be gone if Miss Marwedel comes actively into the field."[49] Somewhat ironically, the decisions Hearst made during this time, along with the ill-advised hiring of Marwedel, contributed to reinforcing the very anxieties and tensions that roiled the competitive world of kindergarten reform as she took her first step toward realizing the top priorities on her political agenda.

The *Daily Evening Post*, however, considered GGKA reform kindergartens to be "a noble charity," without reporting on any of the internal politics in the competitive world of kindergarten reform. In contrast, others saw the kindergarten reform movement through a more critical lens. John Dewey, the American philosopher, psychologist, and educational reformer, encouraged kindergarten advocates to turn their backs on the "abstract and outmoded" ideas of Froebel. Dewey and G. Stanley Hall, a founder of American psychology and a faculty member at Clark University, devalued the kindergarten because it was a female endeavor. Hall depicted females involved with kindergartens as prim, prudish women who never married. Hearst ignored these criticisms and characterizations. She continued her GGKA efforts as she split her time between living in Washington DC and

San Francisco. Her ideas and gifts made a public splash and helped turn the GGKA into a successful organization that by 1890 supervised 1,500 enrolled students as well as trained kindergarten teachers. Susan Blow, a prominent Froebel supporter and teacher instrumental in opening the first public school kindergarten in September 1873 in one section of her birthplace, St. Louis, Missouri, offered more acclaim. Because of the participation of wealthy women like Hearst, the Golden Gate Kindergarten Association of San Francisco was the best funded and organized in the kindergarten movement, according to Blow.[50]

Hearst's and Cooper's GGKA political successes attracted press attention and made both famous. Reporters praised their achievements. Flattery and acclaim for Hearst's philanthropic gifts, which had surpassed eighty thousand dollars by 1906, as well as her activities in the kindergarten movement, came from, among others, Jane Lathrop Stanford, honorary president of the GGKA in 1889. The kindergarten movement made Hearst so famous that Frances Folsom Cleveland, wife of President Grover Cleveland and a fellow Democrat, became a staunch advocate for the cause. The first lady asked Hearst for advice on kindergartens. After receiving Hearst's recommendations, she set up a tiny class in the White House for the Cleveland children, run by the mother of the first lady's niece, Mary Willard. Cooper's career also soared. She became the first president of the International Kindergarten Union in 1892. Hearst's GGKA activities linked her religious, domestic, and organizational roles. It brought her acceptance and prominence among the wealthy national elite and aroused interest among reporters. Rather than forcing her will directly on others in GGKA nonpartisan politics, her deft handling of ideas and money had enhanced her respect and good name and reputation.[51] Hearst's sophisticated, diplomatic approach and methods were proving successful in promoting herself and her political agenda to advance women. In turn, her systematic decisions and actions increased the GGKA's organizational power and placed her and the GGKA on the cusp of a national kindergarten reform movement.

While her reputation and prominence soared, Hearst took another step to promote and advance a top priority on her political agenda—economic independence laced with moral protection politics advocated by the Women's Educational and Industrial Union (WEIU). Hearst lived at a time, at the end of the nineteenth century, when virtually no protective labor legislation or minimum wage laws existed for women, and perilous working conditions, long hours, low pay, and exploitation, particularly economic and sexual, were too often the norm. Failure to protect women from danger to their health or economic and moral well-being grew during this period, a morally reprehensible situation. Wealth and income inequality increased, meanwhile, because of the growth in industrialism and capitalism and the failure of the patriarchy to function properly on behalf of both women and men. Knowing what it was like to feel economically vulnerable, Hearst chose to gift money and support to the nonpartisan San Francisco WEIU. The organization came as close as an organization could come to representing all the principles of women's advancement.[52]

The WEIU was a women's club established in 1888 and patterned after the first WEIU formed in Boston in 1877—an organization that stood "among women, a power for women; a shield against injustice, as well as a means of advancement," the Boston WEIU declared in 1879. The Boston WEIU established a parlor for women and rooms for them in which to have lunch and read. The organization provided classes to help females succeed in business and lectures on questions and topics of interest to women such as literature, religion, health, the trades, and political and legal rights. It also came up with the idea of municipal housekeeping—the notion that women possessed and must use their "special moral qualities" outside the home to achieve moral improvement or reform in society, especially in cities. The WEIU, like the GGKA, used resources to help "worthy" female wage earners and unemployed women avoid oppression and gain economic independence through unpretentious efforts and activities. Abby Morton Diaz, an American blue blood, was a WEIU founder and president from 1881 to 1892. She argued that "once women rid themselves of time-consuming and fruitless domestic labors, they must seize economic independence." The way for the WEIU to achieve moral improvement was to protect working-class and poor women by providing vocational training and helping them get jobs so they could stand on their own two feet economically and prevent men from making unethical use of women for their own advantage or profit.[53] The WEIU's moral protection politics that Hearst advocated rested on and was intertwined with the principle of helping women acquire the power to be economically self-supporting and independent.

The WEIU's moral protection politics challenged the myth of men protecting women from danger, especially economically, and opposed men who believed the work of women was degrading. This WEIU position appealed to Hearst because she saw herself as a worker, "civilizer," and protector of women, especially those in the working class. Hearst strongly believed in the dignity and value of women's and men's work. She wanted to impress upon girls "who *desire to* [emphasis added] or are forced to earn their own living the necessity of doing their work well—of preparing themselves to render excellent service, no matter where they are employed," she was quoted as saying in the *New York Herald*.

WEIU members were in the "grasp" of "the Mighty Power" of Christianity, according to Mary Grafton Campbell, WEIU president in 1888—the year the San Francisco branch was established. The power of Christianity interested Hearst. She thought evangelical women should do the right thing and fulfill their religious duties—marry and have children. She knew, though, like white women's rights advocates, that the protections men offered to women with middle-class backgrounds like herself—such as "financial support, supervision, polite courtesies, and general solicitousness" that were seen as "privilege"—could be taken away if she and other females deviated significantly from the behavior men expected. George, after all, could make a decision at any time to deny her access to his fortune. Yet the WEIU also "recognized mutual dependence and mutual support." The legally incorporated organization brought together proud, independent female workers, citizens, and prosperous and wealthy women who believed they "ought to help those who *do* need." WEIU members experienced an unequal power and class relationship to be sure. But education and training to do useful work well to achieve economic independence were crucial to Hearst. The skills, knowledge, and experiences women learned helped members develop an autonomous identity that made them and the WEIU powerful.[54] Hearst and the WEIU took issue with members of the opposite sex who argued that women needed men to protect them from other, unethical men who used women for their own benefit. What the WEIU did with the power of Christianity to benefit middle- and working-class women, economically or otherwise, interested Hearst.

Ironically, Hearst's support for the WEIU also reinforced the myth that women, particularly the working class and poor, needed the protection of wealthy or prosperous female patrons. WEIU members made it their mission to assist "all women," not only middle- and working-class women but also poor women who lacked resources. And because Phoebe was convinced that environmental factors were the cause of poverty, she thought the poor needed help and deserved protection from women of various classes in the WEIU and men who possessed resources. At the same time, she also assumed her superior class and race meant she was entitled to her views and actions being accepted by WEIU members and others, especially the poor. As she said to Hubert Howe Bancroft, in a condescending, superior tone common in her day and often used by privileged whites, she did "not think that people should be educated above their station in life." She added, "I have not the slightest idea that the advantages of education should be kept from the poorer classes; on the contrary I think they should be educated in a way that would enable them to make the most of their present position and cultivate them to fill any higher station to which they may be elevated."[55] So although Hearst challenged the falsehood that men shielded women from danger, especially economically, she also believed that many women, especially the poor and disadvantaged, needed the protection of more affluent women—a contradictory and elitist view to be sure.

Hearst was in fact sincere in her desire to assist middle-class, working-class, immigrant, and poor women, and some men, even though she saw it as a burden. Phoebe could remember what it was like to experience the uncertainties and insecurities produced by hard economic times. Being wealthy, she saw women in the lower classes, particularly wage earners and the downtrodden, as her nonpartisan constituents—those in need of help that she had a duty and obligation to serve and represent politically—even though Kincaid exclaimed, "What vultures they are!"[56] Kincaid's claim was a contradiction that was not particularly bothersome to Hearst and reformers like her. Giving women, particularly the poor, opportunities to secure various forms of power, especially economic and political, to move up the ladder in society, while shielding them from injury, pain, harm, or loss that resulted from the actions of immoral men, constituted moral protection politics for Hearst and the WEIU. In essence, Hearst's and the WEIU's position on moral politics replaced the dominant power of men as protectors of females with that of wealthy and affluent women.

Hearst and Louise Sorbier, a reformer, served and represented the same nonpartisan constituents on issues of self-support, laced with moral protection politics, and women's rights. Sorbier led the San Francisco WEIU during the 1890s and into the early twentieth century. President Sorbier declared that the WEIU, with its elitist characteristics, benefitted females of all classes, creeds, and nationalities. It also "promote[d] . . . by practical methods the educational, industrial, and social advancement of women." Sorbier and WEIU officials taught voting members how to acquire and control resources to advance themselves as well as obtain political and legal rights. Some have claimed the WEIU was "little more than an employment bureau for domestics." Members were trained "in Dress-making, Millinery, Stenography, Type-writing, Reading, Penmanship . . . [and] Arithmetic," and to be "Governesses, Teachers of all kinds . . . Seamstresses," and "Nurses." They received training as well "in French, German, Choral Singing . . . and Hair-dressing." But they also drew "intellectual power" from informal gatherings and learned about binding wage contracts. They received training on how to conduct legal battles against an employer who cheated them out of wages. They listened intently to lessons about how to find employment and investigate working conditions. They were schooled in how to become "free, independent, self-supporting women" in the world of business. The organization, moreover, lobbied "to compel the enforcement" of unenforced laws to benefit "the health or the financial or moral well-being of women," the *First Annual Report* proclaimed. The union at this point chose not to endorse the ballot for women publicly. Despite this position, some WEIU leaders supported suffrage. Others refused.[57]

Hearst's contributions to the WEIU made known her tolerant attitudes as well. Hearst's financial support had placed her at the top of the San Francisco WEIU's "Donations in Kind" list in the first year of the organization's existence. She was on the list of moderate donors in the second year and at the top of the list of "Cash Donations" in the seventh year. Donating to the WEIU had made evident Hearst's ladylike and businesslike approach to providing her female constituents with opportunities to achieve economic and political power. Meanwhile, in the middle of the second year of the WEIU, just over half of the leaders resigned because of a major internal political battle. Hannah Marks Solomons, a Jewish immigrant, had become president in 1890. Solomons struggled with antisemitism while she led the organization. One Catholic member complained that almost all of "its original founders" had left the group and that Jewish members predominated. Sorbier, a Catholic, led the charge against Solomons. She claimed that when Solomons headed the Domestic Training Committee in 1889–90 she engaged in wasteful and thoughtless handling of WEIU funds because she paid "the same bills twice." Two investigations cleared Solomons. But Sorbier became president in 1891.[58]

Hearst took a balanced political position. She only gave a modest amount to the organization during the controversy. Despite her decision to reduce her contributions, she showed respect and tolerance for the rights of Jews amid the political controversy and conflict. She refused to criticize Solomons. Nor did she disassociate her name with or withdraw her financial support from the WEIU. Hearst's support for Solomons and the WEIU showed that she was capable of advancing her political interests without rendering powerless men and women she did not consider to be of her own class status, religion, or cultural outlook, including Jews.[59]

Hearst became the WEIU's "greatest benefactor" and a life and advisory board member as the mid-1890s approached. Her good friend, Mary W. Kincaid, held elected positions as the corresponding secretary and as an associate director in 1893 and 1894.[60] Hearst possessed the opportunity, while Kincaid was a WEIU official, to keep informed about what was going on in the organization while she kept her distance from her middle- and working-class and poor constituents. Adeptly, Hearst could express her political position while she yet set herself apart from those she served by helping to fund the WEIU without becoming active in, or an elected official of, the organization.

Hearst now began to complicate and broaden her political agenda by acting on other priorities. She became politically active in the Century Club of San Francisco, a literary, educational club, composed of white and mostly middle-class women, devoted to improving "the condition of womankind." The Century Club threw itself into partisan electoral politics in San Francisco in the mid-to-late 1880s. Julia Ward Howe's visit to San Francisco in 1888 encouraged women who took "initial steps towards forming a club" to take additional steps. Sarah Dix Hamlin, the original organizer of the Pacific Association of Collegiate Alumnae, and other women, met in the home of Mrs. B. F. Norris to establish the Century Club on September 22, 1888. They wanted to establish a club to provide women with a place to freely exchange thoughts and views and develop "co-operation among women." They elected Phoebe A. Hearst club president and Hamlin a director at the September meeting. The first official meetings were held in Hearst's home at 1105 Taylor Street in San Francisco, beginning in December 1888. The Century Club was "one of the first large woman's clubs organized in California," according to Brooks. The club reached its limit of two hundred members the next year. It was necessary for a member to propose, two members to endorse, and the board of directors to elect women seeking admittance. "Intelligence, culture, and ability to advance the interests of the Century Club" also determined membership. Anyone who disturbed "the harmony of the Club" or damaged "its good name or prosperity," could "be reprimanded, suspended or expelled."[61]

Hearst was invited to become the first president about a year before the formal opening of the Century Club.[62] The club historian recounted that Hearst, demure as ever, had been "reluctant to accept the presidency because of her impending departure for Washington DC." Unwilling to wait until she returned from the nation's capital to take a vote to elect Hearst president, members forced a vote by acclamation before Hearst went back East, placing pressure on her to accept a two-year term as president before she left. The club possessed no record to explain why Hearst acceded to the presidency. But the group lacked funds. The voting members "assumed that the tenuous organization needed every possible advantage; and that Mrs. Hearst's prominence and her own worthy reputation as a force in the community, filled the requirements perfectly."[63] The club relied on her abilities to control resources, especially her ideas, connections, and political experience, to get the club up and running and make it successful.

Voting members believed Hearst to be the club's "good angel" with the ability and assets to make the organization into "an undoubted power." She paid the $125 per month rent for a suitable meeting place at 1215 Sutter Street for one year and gave additional financial support years after her term ended. Fifty-four percent of the charter members were elite, prosperous, and powerful women listed in the city's *Elite Directory*. Hearst and Kincaid were charter club members. Other members included University of California graduates as well as women who were nationally prominent, like GGKA president Sarah Cooper, Dr. Charlotte Brown, founder of San Francisco Children's Hospital, and suffragist Ellen Sargent, wife of a U.S.

senator.[64] Hearst's participation in the Century Club gave her the chance to expand her power networks.

President Hearst challenged people to think of and accept the Century Club as a training ground for women to jump into partisan electoral politics. While Hearst led the club, the organization became deeply involved in the San Francisco partisan political game. Hearst's friend Mary McHenry Keith later descried city politics as a "filthy pool" while "Blind Boss" Buckley controlled the city. Keith was an alumna of San Francisco Girls' High and Normal School, first female graduate of Hastings Law School, a suffragist, Democrat, and wife of William Keith, a prominent California "nature school" painter and later a recipient of Hearst's largesse. Crowded and dilapidated school buildings caused problems during Buckley's reign. Revenue needed to be raised to repair the structures or build new ones. But Buckley supported low taxes—a political position that must have appealed to voters. The Buckley-backed board, meanwhile, increased the school district's debt, dismissed teachers, slashed salaries, and closed schools.[65] Women reformers blamed Buckley for the decaying public school system. To improve the world of education they would have to get involved in the "cesspool" of local politics even though California women lacked the right to vote.

During Hearst's presidency, no state passed woman suffrage in the two decades after the Wyoming and Utah Territories granted women the right to vote in 1869 and 1870, respectively. Advocates of suffrage claimed throughout the 1870s that women were citizens legally. Thus, females were entitled to the ballot. The courts denied the claim. The California legislature, meanwhile, passed a law in 1874 that granted women citizens over the age of twenty-one the right to "be eligible to all educational offices within the State, except those from which they are excluded by the Constitution." San Francisco women followed the path the National Woman Suffrage Association established in 1869. They pursued a broad range of reforms "in the interests of women" after the 1874 law passed. The American Woman Suffrage Association, established in the same year, chose a different path. They recruited male supporters of abolition and Republican leaders and focused on one issue—woman suffrage. Hearst and San Francisco women, including members of the Century Club, tested the legislature's 1874 law. They got involved in educational reform issues in the city's partisan electoral politics. They mobilized to participate in and reshape the powerful American political party system, as black women had in Illinois, by taking part in pressure-group politics. They lobbied men to represent them. They also demanded a strong government and the use of its power to provide social services, especially at the local level, like kindergartens, to help the less privileged and to protect the rights of all citizens.[66]

Hearst and San Francisco female reformers believed it was their moral and political duty and obligation to improve the schools. So they were eager to boot off Buckley's supporters on the San Francisco School Board. The Public School Reform Association (PSRA) in 1886, led by Milicent Shinn, a member of the Pacific Association of Collegiate Alumnae, was formed rapidly to support the election of reform candidates opposed to Buckley. The nonpartisan Citizens' Independent Convention and the partisan Labor Party put together a slate of six candidates for the 1886 citywide election. The PSRA asked other partisan political parties to support these candidates for the school board election—Sarah Dix Hamlin, May Treat, Mary Campbell, Cordelia Kirkland, Mrs. G. K. Phillips, and Miss K. A. F. Green. There were twelve elected members of the school board. Five of the first fifteen leaders in the WEIU were Century Club members and participated in the partisan election campaign. The female politicians received support from "various independent groups" and the Labor and Prohibition Parties. The female candidates the PSRA backed, though, lacked the endorsement of the Democratic and Republican parties. They lost. But they garnered more votes than other reformers who ran and proved their viability and competence as political campaigners and candidates.[67]

Century Club president Hearst chose to put her money and other resources to good use in the 1888 San Francisco School Board election. Her participation in this election displayed her support for an emerging progressive liberalism—the use of "state power to regulate the capitalist economy and to improve the living conditions and 'security' [of] the citizenry, without abolishing private property or revolutionizing liberal democratic political institutions," as one scholar described it.[68] Hearst became familiar with the San Francisco electoral process and candidates in the 1886 election campaign. She invested her resources to get six female reform candidates elected in a second citywide election in 1888 for school board. All six candidates were suffragists. Most taught school. Half were Century Club members who advocated women's advancement. The club member candidates were Sarah Dix Hamlin, a Latin and Greek scholar who ran in 1886; Amelia Truesdell, a public school teacher; and Nellie Weaver, a lecturer on education with a national reputation.[69] Hearst believed women elected to democratic political institutions could solve urban social ills and evils that men had been unable or unwilling to solve.

Hearst and Century Club members joined and comprised one-third of the Committee of One Hundred. The Committee of One Hundred was a women's group that expressed confidence in and support for female candidates and ran their campaign. Almost half of the Century Club's leaders got involved in the 1888 election at a time when women lacked the right to vote in California. Hannah Solomons, president of the WEIU of San Francisco, backed them. The day after the Committee of One Hundred established itself, Hearst became the largest contributor. She pledged to pay off any remaining debts after the election. Hearst and Century Club supporters battled, a reporter noted, "a great many, who do not care to sanction" women's "intimacy with professional politics" as well as the opposition of the *San Francisco Chronicle*. Supporters of the female candidates made a house-to-house canvass to replace school board members in Buckley's camp with honest, progressive female reformers.[70]

In other words, San Francisco women relied on male political methods to get their candidates elected.

Hearst experienced a difficult time leading the club during the partisan 1888 election campaign. It was one thing for her to have the experience of being a director in the nonpartisan Golden Gate Kindergarten Association, where she often followed the lead of Sarah Cooper. But it was quite another for her to be an elected president of an organization in the West that took part in the difficult business of partisan politics. The job was demanding and draining. Hearst explained to Ellen Davis Conway that "in the East, you have the enjoyment of advantages that are impossible in this new country, and we [in the West] have to struggle to create conditions that are assured with you." Conway was the spouse of Moncure Daniel Conway (1832–1907), a pastor of the First Unitarian Church in Washington DC and a magazine editor and newspaper correspondent. He credited Ellen with making many of his accomplishments possible.

President Hearst faced a difficult challenge as she strove to figure out how to make a new role for herself as a president of a club with few precedents to follow and virtually no one, outside of possibly Mary W. Kincaid, she could talk to about her struggles and challenges. It became "a great trial for me to preside with composure over one hundred and twenty clever women," she wrote Ellen Davis Conway. Leading the club tested Hearst's abilities, courage, and endurance. "I am harassed by a mass of petty cares. . . . My house is full of company, and life moves on with me about the same as when you were here—only with more anxiety," she confessed. Her health, self-confidence, and idealism waned under the pressure as she grappled with the stress and strain of leadership. Phoebe struggled to present herself as a confident, adept, and effective leader and role model while the campaign was in full swing. She reined in her emotions. She confided to Conway that the members "shall never know what is going on inside—perhaps I can make them believe I am most courageous and competent." President Hearst experienced "a special burden on women"—the tension between upholding a traditional role while rebelling against it.[71]

Unscrupulous women teachers made Hearst's experience as Century Club president complicated and challenging. They engaged in messy politics and sometimes resorted to the same unprincipled, partisan political methods as men. These teachers needed Buckley's political support to keep their jobs. So they promoted religious bigotry and rumors that pitted Protestants against Catholics and Catholics against Jews. Having to deal with political women who appeared to lack moral scruples created more burdens for Hearst as she led a group that lacked religious and racial diversity. She was so discouraged that she wrote Conway that she would probably resign the presidency shortly because "this position brings many responsibilities." Raised by her parents to be honest and scrupulous, Hearst found the demands of the position difficult to handle. She also concluded that the unethical methods used in American women's nonpartisan voluntary association *and* partisan electoral politics were distasteful. She possessed little tolerance for either sex using them. The female candidates lost the 1888 election, but they claimed "a moral victory" because they had been competitive.[72] Trying to cope with her fear and anxieties, Hearst must have wondered whether it was worth it to contribute her resources to the campaign given the challenges, the underhanded methods used, and the painful defeat of the female candidates. But Hearst was too ambitious to allow these difficulties to cut short her term as president of the Century Club.

Hearst decided that serving out her term as president, focusing on a moderate political approach, was the right thing to do. In 1889, Sarah M. Severance, state superintendent of franchise for the Women's Christian Temperance Union, introduced a school suffrage bill in the California legislature. It passed the senate but failed to get a two-thirds vote in the assembly.[73] At about the same time, Hearst and Century Club members soured on participating in the rough-and-tumble world of partisan electoral politics in which men held dominant power. So she took the Century Club in a different direction. Under Hearst's leadership, the Century Club shied away from partisan electoral politics. The club centered its work on nonpartisan voluntary association politics that focused on receptions, developing women's abilities, training members to get power through debates and educational programs, and proper money management while they recruited talented women with leadership potential. The club increased its membership, possessing a good selection of published material in the reading room and two thousand dollars in the club bank account.[74]

Hearst's power to move the Century Club along a dignified political path was reflected in the bylaws of 1893. Section 7 declared: "No demonstration on behalf of any political or religious object shall ever be made by this Club; and sectarian doctrines or political partisan preferences shall not be discussed by this Club at any regular or special meeting thereof." The Century Club avoided participation in municipal or state elections after Hearst's term expired as president. But club members did debate political issues of interest to members. They also voted to approve positions on such political questions as the construction of a "drainage system" for San Francisco. Hearst's presidency, nonetheless, demonstrated her tacit support for helping women learn about nonpartisan association politics, power, and leadership at club meetings that trained members, as Mary McHenry Keith explained later, for involvement in the suffrage cause in partisan politics, among other political issues.[75] The defeat of female candidates in the 1888 election had been a painful experience that led President Hearst and club members to withdraw from partisan electoral politics. Yet Hearst refused to quit, sensing bigger and better things ahead. Moving the club in a different direction strengthened Hearst's public reputation for acting appropriately as a woman married to a wealthy man in American politics.

Hearst's decisions and actions brought her to the national level in nonpartisan club movement politics. She traveled to New York at the request of the members in the spring of 1889 as a representative and delegate of the Century Club. There she met, on April 23, 1890, with active people associated with the Woman's Christian Temperance Union and about one hundred members of white women's clubs from nineteen states with pride in woman's politics and worth. Jane (Jennie) Cunningham Croly revived a slightly different version at this meeting of a plan she had created in 1869 to form a General Federation of Women's Clubs to unite literary clubs in a national organization. Women's clubs in attendance in New York took up Croly's plan. They formed what would become one of the largest, independent, and most important female nonpartisan voluntary organizations in America, the General Federation of Women's Clubs (GFWC).[76]

The GFWC, comprising both conservative and progressive members, became a national umbrella reform organization "of great benefit to women individually," the *Chicago Tribune* observed. It advocated for dignified, white women club members to exert power as reformers to effect change, especially to pressure legislators to improve society. It was a woman-only group. "Not a Man Was Present," according to the *Chicago Tribune*, at the GFWC constitution ratification meeting at the Scottish Rite Hall. The attendees looked "forward to the complete emancipation of American women." The GFWC constitution created officers with power and authority. It granted female members the right to vote and elect officers. It held the governing officials responsible for their decisions and actions. Charlotte Emerson Brown from New Jersey became the first GFWC president. The National Federation of Afro-American Women established in 1895 advocated that all women vote. But its conservative white counterpart, the GFWC, established a rigid color line. The organization dragged its feet on suffrage even though members discussed the issue at meetings. The GFWC excluded black organizations until 1902 and was unwilling, as a legally incorporated body, to support suffrage until 1914.[77] Hearst's involvement with the GFWC merged her political agenda with the politics of a moderate, national, nonpartisan voluntary reform association.

Hearst's determination, good judgment, refined techniques, and political experiences led her from being the president of the San Francisco Century Club to election as an officer in the national GFWC. She accepted the nomination and won a unanimous election as the first treasurer of the GFWC "over every protest," according to biographer Brooks. The protests emerged probably because she was rich or possibly because of animosity directed at her son, Will. Treasurer Hearst helped to build "a fashionable, societylike reputation" for the GFWC because she, and other officers, were prominent, wealthy women. Brown and GFWC board members were kindred spirits who inspired and energized each other. Hearst's election as first GFWC treasurer made her a member of a group of ambitious, middle-class, and wealthy reform-minded white women interested in high society and American politics. She and her colleagues used the myth of woman as guardian of the home to their advantage—to teach females a "gospel" that valued women getting and wielding intellectual, moral, social, and physical power. But the organization also emphasized a complementary relationship between women and men. They would rise and fall together in the eyes of GFWC officials. The GFWC, furthermore, promoted efficiency and order during tumultuous, disorderly times. Hearst and her GFWC colleagues believed it their moral duty and obligation to get involved in moderate reform politics of personal and shared interest with men. National GFWC officers represented and solved urban problems to improve the lives of female and male citizens—mostly whites—and build a harmonious, whole society.[78]

Hearst's involvement as treasurer in the GFWC expanded her political agenda further, making it more complex by including consideration of a wide range of reforms at all levels of government. It mixed together her support for economic independence and nonpartisan and partisan political power for women and the use of federal power to achieve reform, which was forged in the California women's movement, with the GFWC's goal of preserving what was best in society—such as women's special abilities, particularly as a parent—applying it all to progressive reform that eschewed radical politics and aims. The GFWC mobilized older and younger generations of white women and trained them to think independently. They learned how to debate and formulate policies. They were trained to reduce class conflict. President Charlotte Emerson Brown explained that one goal was to "break down walls of separation and prejudice"—words that rang hallow because the GFWC excluded black women. But the GFWC also engaged in the accepted practice of backing members for elections to positions of power on school boards.

The organization took political positions on issues of concern to women and men alike. They also possessed an interest in partisan political leaders and in securing legislation, even though the organization refused to endorse suffrage officially. Hearst and GFWC members received training in how to lobby male politicians to pass local, state, and national legislation on many issues: education (including the establishment of public libraries and supporting members running for school boards); health; child rearing and labor; poor working conditions, especially for females; alcohol abuse; prostitution; educational and employment opportunities for women and children; clean milk; recreation; sanitation and street lighting; conservation; and suffrage. Susan B. Anthony, Lucy Stone, and Julia Ward Howe recognized the GFWC by attending its events at the World's Columbian Exposition in Chicago in 1893.[79] The GFWC, though, refused to publicly endorse suffrage until twenty-one years later.

Hearst continued to take a skillful and powerful role in advancing a progressive reform agenda in nonpartisan and partisan politics across the country. She challenged the common belief, based on "scientific" theories of evolution, that women "lagged behind men, much as 'primitive people' lagged behind Europeans." She managed finances so well that after looking over the books and official papers Hearst sent, GFWC president Brown proclaimed that "The books & documents reached me safely & I found them all *beautiful*, accurate, and in perfect order." Hearst's service as treasurer fed her reputation as having a "masculine grasp of financial affairs," as one of Phoebe's female friends described her skill.[80] A shy, modest woman in public, Hearst was emboldened to think in private that she could handle GFWC money matters as well as any man. Her GFWC experiences encouraged her to think she was a competent national official. She demonstrated that she handled assets and liabilities and exerted power as capably as wealthy, elite men and male treasurers involved in any other nonpartisan voluntary associations controlled, funded, and run by men. She contributed, as did elite men, to the existence of civil society, or the state, by being "a representative to act for it."[81]

Hearst commanded her estate and a large fortune while she sat on the GFWC board. To carry out her duties and responsibilities successfully, given the array of activities in which she was involved, meant "continual work, work, work," as Florence Bayard Hilles wrote to her. That "seems to be your lot in life," Hilles commented. Work to Hearst meant the supervision of the vast Hearst estate as well as being very active in various arenas of politics, especially public, nonpartisan voluntary associations. Hilles was part of Hearst's network. They met for the first time at the GFWC convention in 1890. Both happened to be Democrats. Hilles was a suffragist and the daughter of Thomas Francis Bayard, an idealistic Democrat, lawyer, and United States senator from Delaware, 1869–85. Her father had been appointed secretary of state by President Grover Cleveland in 1885.[82]

Exerting her power to influence and pressure partisan politicians into supporting political causes that were important to her had now become the core of Hearst's existence. Promoting her political agenda and herself at the national level brought her great satisfaction and made her happy. But Phoebe's GFWC politics were cut short in early 1891 when her family problems surfaced once again. She received distressing news as her first year as GFWC treasurer came to a close. Her husband was seriously ill with stomach cancer or possibly colon cancer. She grew anxious about George's deteriorating health, so she set aside her own interests and pleasures. She resigned as GFWC treasurer and dropped her GFWC politics in Washington DC to take care of her husband. Hearst's ever-widening circle of women friends and connections could see how her husband's decline was affecting her. Ada Butterfield Jones, a young woman married to William Carey Jones, professor of jurisprudence at the University of

California and someone Phoebe had assisted, heard the news of George's illness. She had empathy for her friend. Butterfield Jones remarked how Phoebe's love for excitement and the hustle and bustle of being very active in politics must have made it difficult for her to stop what she was doing to tend to George's illness, even though Ada thought that it might be a good thing for her friend to slow down. "What a recluse you have been these past months—quiet and lack of excitement is sometimes good for people," Butterfield Jones assured her.

Coping with her husband's illness was a challenge. Ordinarily, Phoebe was an active, independent, and self-confident woman. She lost her sense of security about her own power, though, as George's health declined and she experienced the fragile nature of her self-confidence. As she lamented, "Everything is so uncertain and I do not know just what I can do." Not knowing what to do, Phoebe like other nineteenth-century women took comfort from women friends like Hilles to get her through difficult and uncertain times.[83]

Mary Kincaid understood Hearst's predicament. She could see the burdens Phoebe was enduring while taking care of George yet also continuing to perform her social and political duties and obligations. Mary stepped in to protect Phoebe when George became unable to fill that role. She was interested in helping and bolstering the strength and courage of her dear friend. She reassured Phoebe she possessed the "nervous energy to hold out until all is over, which, in God's ruling, cannot be far off. Then you will have to let us look out for you," Mary insisted, turning the tables on her friend by presenting herself as Phoebe's protector. Vowing to shield and keep Hearst safe, Kincaid wrote her friend, "I am the self-appointed dragon to keep off all vampires, leeches, mendicants, and sycophants."[84]

Phoebe, sustained by her women friends, watched her husband's slow, "steady and uninterrupted decline" that yielded hard nights and more comfortable days. Eventually, George Hearst's health took a turn for the worse, and he died peacefully on February 28, 1891, at 9:10 p.m. from,

4. Phoebe Apperson Hearst in a tent at Camp Sesame, Sonoma County, California. BANCPIC 1972.015–PIC box 1, folder 2. Courtesy of the Bancroft Library, University of California, Berkeley.

according to the *San Francisco Examiner*, "a complication of diseases, resulting primarily from a serious derangement of the bowels." Phoebe was by his side at the Hearsts' Washington DC mansion. Their son, William Randolph Hearst, was present as were Jack G. Follansbee, Dr. Charles Ward, the attending physician, and nurses. Several minutes after George's death, Senator Leland Stanford visited Phoebe to offer his condolences. That night, the United States Senate and United States House of Representatives passed resolutions of sorrow and regret. Congress "adjourned after midnight," Phoebe's biographer and contemporary noted, for one day to respect and honor George Hearst and provide time for national mourning.[85]

Kincaid fretted about her friend's emotional and mental health and physical stamina while Phoebe deeply mourned her husband's death.

"I am so worried about you all the time, for these weeks of anxiety and mental and physical fatigue must leave you nearly at the end of your bodily power," Kincaid wrote Hearst. Phoebe tried to adjust while following the female tradition of not being socially active for six months after "a period of 'deep mourning'" when a close family member passed away. She felt the need during this period to connect to her rural roots. So she left the problems of the city for nature. She pitched tents at Camp Sesame in the Valley of the Moon at the foothills in Sonoma County.[86] She found solace and comfort in agricultural surroundings away from the hustle, bustle, and tensions of American politics and urban life. Hearst, a forty-eight-year-old widow, returned to San Francisco six months later. A woman with a grown adult son but without a husband, she was no longer expected to do her daily wifely and parental tasks. She was a widow and really on her own now. But exactly what lay ahead? Would she have the confidence and drive to continue working on her political agenda in American politics? What plans would she make for the future?

4

Power by Design

Phoebe Apperson Hearst became a millionaire in her own right when George Hearst passed away. Hearst held legal right to half of his property if he died first and any income earned before and after marriage, according to California inheritance laws in place on the day George died. State reform statutes considered Phoebe to be single regarding "inheritances, gifts, and, later, wages." But other coverture laws applied. George, before his death, had possessed faith and trust in his wife's ability to manage his fortune. According to Adele Brooks, he went beyond the law in his will to make his wife "a gift of the other half [of his property] absolutely unfettered by any bond or by any obligation to account for her management or disposition of it to court, Judge or any other authority whatever." Estimates of Phoebe's inheritance in early February 1891 ranged between five and twenty million dollars. George refused to leave his son, William Randolph Hearst, one cent. He was, according to one historian, "a hopeless spendthrift." That left Phoebe as the primary beneficiary and provider for the Hearst family in George's will, but he had also set limits on Phoebe. "If she married again one-half of the estate," the *New York Times* reported, "should revert to her son."[1] Sensitive to the provisions of George's will and her own desires, Phoebe never remarried. Why get married again and lose her freedom and independence as a widow and half of the Hearst estate?

Hearst faced several tests immediately after George's death. She needed to familiarize herself as soon as possible with her deceased husband's complicated business arrangements to understand the estate she inherited. She had displayed interest in, and occasionally given advice to George on, his business affairs while he lived. She had offered George, from time to time, her assessment of the character of her husband's business associates. And she tried to teach herself as much as possible about the details and inner workings of her husband's business dealings the summer before his death. These lessons, nonetheless, fell short of providing her with enough knowledge and understanding to manage the entire Hearst estate on her own. What she learned, moreover, hardly qualified her as a business expert. "It is not easy to understand the intricacies of so large an estate" worth millions, Phoebe's friend, Florence Bayard Hilles, noted.[2] Would Phoebe be able to rise to the challenges she faced after George passed away?

One of the first trials Hearst confronted was to battle professional men to gain control over her life and what she believed was legally and rightfully hers—the vast Hearst estate. Dr. Charles Ward, George's attending physician, in particular, gave her trouble. Ward tried to take advantage of her by charging excessive medical fees. "Words fail me absolutely," Hilles wrote, at the mention of Dr. Ward's bill. "It is without exception the most preposterous thing ever heard of," she complained to Hearst. Hilles was delighted "in the thought that you question paying it," she wrote Phoebe. Hearst's independent nature emerged to deal with Dr. Ward's bill. But her move toward independence faded quickly. Her self-confidence was low. She explained to Sarah Cooper how disgruntled she had become over the situation. "I was compelled to hold myself in readiness to see my lawyer or my business manager at any time, either to sign papers or to consider some details in settling our varied and scattered interests."[3]

Hearst needed to regain her confidence in order to stand on her own two feet and control her future. But how would she do that? She began by consulting with the legal and business professionals, and other male employees, who had worked for George; she already knew and trusted them. As she remarked: "I am gradually learning the details as I think it best. I should have a personal knowledge of everything connected with it [the vast Hearst estate]." But she almost immediately ran into difficulties learning the intricacies of her estate and dealing with George's business managers. Irwin C. Stump, who worked in her San Francisco office, was one of the business managers she inherited from George. Phoebe discovered one day that Stump had sent Charles M. Dobson to England, where Dobson falsely represented Stump. He had used the Hearst name in England without authority when he announced unexpectedly the sale of a "Prize" mine. Phoebe was surprised and unsettled by the news of the sale.

Phoebe's own parents had been raised in the South, a place where names stood for family pride and honor and held moral worth. Convinced that the Hearst name counted for something, especially in the business world, Phoebe took offense at Dobson's misuse of it. Once she heard about Dobson's perfidy, she fearlessly and forcefully expressed her own mind in a private letter to Stump. "I did not believe that you would send a man in your own interests, and use my name in that manner. I am now convinced that you did, and I protest most emphatically," she wrote. "Unless my name is withdrawn from this" she warned, "I will cable friends in London to publicly disclaim my connection with the business."[4] Phoebe held no qualms about making decisions on her own and using leverage to control Stump's behavior so she could protect her assets and the Hearst family name and good standing.

Few Americans would have expected someone like Phoebe, finding herself newly widowed, to learn how to control her own life and affairs. She was a woman, after all. But Phoebe acted quickly to learn about her vast estate. Even so, once she assumed control of the overall management of her estate—which consisted of a wide variety of properties spread across many locales and "owned in partnership with others"—she still felt "harassed with anxieties and uncertainties, in fact, knowing absolutely nothing in regard to my own affairs," she explained, exaggerating for effect. Despite these feelings, she decided to defy popular expectation. She had admonished Stump over his handling of the Hearst mine and made her priorities clear. "My business is unquestionably more important to me and should be to you," she wrote Stump. "I wish to know details [about my affairs] even though I may not be expected to use my own judgment in deciding them," she explained in a commanding tone. She announced her strong desire to familiarize herself "with all business transacted in connection with her affairs, to have all important matters referred to her before consummation, and all deeds sent to her for signature," according to Brooks. Hearst's declaration meant she had joined a rather small group of women. Only a handful of wealthy females with control over a vast estate existed in America at the time. Supported by friends in Washington DC, Hearst's confidence grew in her ability to exert command over her employees. She reduced her reliance on Stump and relegated him to a less trusted and menial position. Gently and delicately, she eventually removed Stump from her employ, replacing him with a relative as 1895 approached.[5] Hearst did the unexpected by taking charge of her own future and her employees.

Hearst usually avoided hiring relatives. This time, though, she made an exception. She hired a man she felt she could trust, the younger Edward Hardy Clark, her cousin and the son of a father with the same name. The younger Clark impressed her. A member of the family and honest, he refused to ask for, nor expected, favors. She sought his legal advice and learned from him what she needed to know. Clark advised her about her legal rights to use, allocate, and bequeath money, as well as other issues. When Phoebe became worried about her legal claim to control her estate, Clark explained to her: "You have the right, absolutely to do as you wish in all things. That Mr. Hearst [Phoebe's son] hasn't the slightest legal claim in any way, but if you enter into a partnership of course you can use only the income from half and only dispose of that account by gift or will."

Obtaining legal authority over the vast Hearst estate proved to be a lengthy, complicated, and tricky probate exercise. But at the age of forty-nine, Hearst had become, at the end of this legal process, an independent businesswoman in her own right with command, circumscribed by the constraints of sex and class, over her own life and a vast family estate worth millions.[6] The transition to widowhood had challenged her, but Phoebe had made clear her intention to control her employees and make her own personal and business decisions. It appeared, in fact, that she enjoyed having power and exerting it over her vast resources, even though she experienced insecurities and had needed to learn how to handle the inevitably complicated business affairs that came with her newfound power and authority.

As Hearst learned to contribute to the financial management of her estate, to build confidence, and to reassert her independence after George's death, it was time to think of the future and her own path forward to a rich and fulfilling life. A middle-aged widow with a rudimentary education, she had long held an ardent desire for a higher education, if only she could overcome the obstacles women of her generation faced in gaining admittance into, and graduating from, institutions of advanced education. But because of the prevailing and prejudicial American attitudes toward women, she sensed such an enterprise was out of the question. So what decisions could she make to determine her future and satisfy her ambitions, considering her limited formal education?

Spurred on and supported by relatives and women friends, Hearst slowly took steps to devise a strategy to achieve power by design—that is, to systematically carry out increasingly sophisticated and strategic decisions and actions to achieve her goals. Over time, she conceived of innovative ways to pursue and interweave her passion for education with her newfound enthusiasm for design and architecture. As it happened, her experiences traveling through Europe, and her visit to the World's Columbian Exposition in Chicago, in 1893, would inspire her to imagine new projects, to make sophisticated and strategic decisions about implementing her goals, and to select the most beneficial people for moving her ideas forward and gaining approval of them in America. Eventually, her achievements would bring her greater stature and the right to vote on equal terms with the opposite sex in the world of nonpartisan academic politics in higher education in America. But how did this extraordinary confluence of her enthusiasm for education and design come together for her?

Hearst's passion for education was first shared with her parents, and her interest in space and design seems to have been inherited from her father. Both pursuits became essential in shaping her strategic and systematic plan to achieve power by design. Phoebe would, by 1891, recall trips abroad where she had tried "to see just as much as any two pr. of eyes can do & gain all the information possible." She made telling comments in her letters during her 1873 European journey about the design and architecture of city buildings. The structures, cities, and streets that interested her told her something about herself and her core concerns and values. She was drawn to objects and structures that spoke to the power possessed by monarchs. The riches of aristocrats caught her eye. The Shah at the State Opera in London was "a perfect blaze of diamonds & precious stones," she wrote. The elegant buildings constructed by "Kings & Queens" for public and private use fascinated her. She took pleasure in describing buildings in her letters to George in great detail, down to the length of Westminster Abby, which was over 500 feet.

Important and powerful countries and cities captivated her. "I am in love with Italy," she wrote. She found Venice "a most interesting old city, yet retaining many evidences of its former greatness & power." "The old Parliament building and 'Four courts'" in Scotland, and residences in London, England, enthralled her. She paid special attention to the houses of the well-to-do and commoners. She closely observed street design too. "There are thousands of handsome & comfortable homes in the stylish & *elegant* parts are thousands of magnificent residences. Hundreds are perfect palaces." "In the old & poor parts [of London], *many* streets are very narrow, gloomy & crowded in the better portions," she wrote. She expressed her concern for a lack of city planning and need for improving the urban environment in Antwerp, Belgium. "The streets are not laid out upon any plan, but have followed the natural caprices of a growing population. They wind & turn so that a stranger has no small difficulty in finding their way," she remarked. The shabby, dilapidated buildings, disorderly and overgrown cities, and depressingly dark streets displeased and unsettled her. Gazing upon orderly physical environments, like the formal gardens of the Royal Palace of Herrenhausen in Germany, probably put her more at ease. Phoebe clearly displayed in her letters an emerging interest in design and orderly town and city planning to create and generate civic pride and help build a municipality's reputation among interdependent urbanites.[7] She enjoyed learning about the concrete structures that were manifestations of the power of kings, queens, and partisan politicians as well as the dwellings of the masses.

Hearst's fascination with design and architecture grew deeper on additional trips, in the late 1880s and early 1890s, to Europe. She scrutinized buildings located in splendid historical settings that expressed aristocratic manifestations of wealth and status in imperial Britain, France, Italy, and Germany—nations vying with each other for economic, political, and military power. When she traveled through Germany, professional organizations of architects, engineers, and well-read and well-informed reformers pressured administrators to replace affluent citizens—connected to the city leader who controlled public environmental policymaking—with appointed paid officials to handle urban growth. In 1892 Hearst was moved and gratified by the responses from the Berlin Bürgermeister, the most powerful, paid official in Berlin, and other officials to urban environmental concerns. German officials responded to the 1874 and 1875 laws passed by the national government to address environmental issues by planning new street networks and "town-extension planning." The results pleased Hearst. "I find Berlin wonderfully changed and improved since Will and I were here in 1873," she explained. One public structure in Berlin especially stood out and delighted her—the building that held importance to people involved in political struggles to improve urban conditions. "The new town hall is very handsome," she wrote. Commoners also were not far from her mind. Houses continued to fascinate her. "I enjoyed the privilege of going over these old homes, and seeing much that was rare and beautiful," she wrote. The architecture of Berlin's public and private buildings that in her view represented the legitimate power and authority of citizens and were located in public "physical space in which people made history," in Europe as well as in America, appealed to her.[8] She was inspired by what she saw and learned.

Back in America, Hearst arrived at a new way to satisfy her ambition for recognition and success, while pursuing her interest in education, through the Columbia Kindergarten Association (CKA). She developed a plan to use her money and resources to involve herself, along with other women and some men, in the nonpartisan politics of the American kindergarten reform movement in the nation's capital.[9] Louisa Mann, wife of Benjamin Pickman Mann, had first introduced kindergartens in Washington DC, organizing the CKA in 1893. While Hearst could have joined a group of all-female kindergarten supporters, she chose to build on past strategies and follow her political instincts instead. She attended a meeting of women and men, on March 17, 1893, to establish the CKA to lobby the United States Congress to pass legislation to introduce kindergartens into public schools in the District of Columbia. Hearst possessed a reputation in "education and the public welfare" that knew "no local boundaries, no difference of race or social condition," according to CKA officials. So organizers asked her to "consent . . . to connect herself with the cause . . . as President of the Society." Hearst agreed. With her consent, her name was put forward for election as CKA president, the head of the administration that governed the CKA. This action followed a frequent pattern, established by nonpartisan voluntary associations, to elect elite women and men as officers. Her election victory moved her up the ladder in reform politics in a Southern city known by advocates of female advancement to be a special place of work for successful professional women. Emma Marwedel, for instance, had lived in the federal city before she came to California to open a kindergarten.

Below Hearst in the official CKA pecking order was Carroll D. Wright, the elected first vice president. Wright, a social economist and statistician had organized the United States Bureau of Labor, established at first under the Department of the Interior and becoming the Department of Labor in 1888. He also became the first commissioner of labor. Wright was the leading public official involved in discussions on the problems of workers. He advocated gathering and using data to improve wages, industrial conditions, education, literacy, and housing. Next in line in the elected hierarchy of the CKA was the secretary, Benjamin Pickman Mann, the son of the prominent lawyer, Massachusetts legislator, and educator Horace. The reelection of these 1893 CKA officers occurred in mid-March of 1894. Hearst later was nominated to the executive board. "This nomination was put to vote and confirmed," according to *The Kindergarten News*.[10] Hearst's association with kindergarten reform politics in the nation's capital would help ensure that her name and reputation received national exposure in the press.

Benefiting from her past experience with organizing the Golden Gate Kindergarten Association in San Francisco, Hearst's decision to use her money and resources to help create the CKA, coupled with her good name and reputation derived from her previous nonpartisan voluntary association politics, served her well. Hearst, while serving two successful terms as a CKA official, possessed and exerted formal and legal public power and authority over a mixed group of kindergarten reformers dedicated to an educational venture with popular appeal in the federal city.

Hearst's CKA presidential election victories coincided with a period in which Americans saw education to be "a form of politics." Many considered it to be an essential ingredient of democracy and the best avenue for reform in the post–Reconstruction Era. Washington DC residents showed interest in building cultural and civic pride through educational reform when Hearst lived in the segregated national capital, but they were also struggling to eradicate juvenile delinquency and reduce crime at a time when poverty and inequality were on the rise across the country in the wake of the Panic of 1893. Yet for all the interest shown in educational reform, difficulties existed in securing money for teachers' salaries, desperately needed and adequate space, and to create a stable public school system in a segregated city. Social welfare services, moreover, were lacking, so folks living in Washington turned to Hearst and other philanthropists, among others, to receive help.

A secular, humanitarian movement emphasizing community spirit that had reached the nation's capital toward the end of the 1870s raised expectations among DC residents that prominent people, especially women like Hearst, might be willing to devote their assets to one, or possibly more, philanthropic reform causes. Addressing political reform issues gave wealthy philanthropists an opportunity to deepen their "enlightened self-interest" and intensify their "sense of public duty" at minimal sacrifice to themselves. Hearst's election to CKA president moved her to contemplate carrying out her civic obligations and responsibilities. She assumed her official position at a time, in the 1890s, when interest in social Darwinism was gaining prominence and a growing chorus of critics discouraged random, haphazard giving. These critics advocated and promoted providing aid to "only the 'worthy poor.'" They encouraged Hearst, and other public-spirited rich women and men, to support "scientific philanthropy." CKA members wanted to professionalize monetary donation by turning it into a science and then using this approach to philanthropy as a political tool for reform.[11]

CKA president Hearst accepted and adopted the political methods promoted by advocates of scientific philanthropy. Under her leadership, the CKA awakened Americans to the need for providing a public school education, based on Frederic Froebel's principles, for "a class of children, ineligible now by age for admission." Her sense of evangelical duty, interest in children, and need to subtly challenge American expectations regarding femininity, pushed her to insist that a model free kindergarten be established worthy of validating republican ideals and scientific rationality. She offered, after her election, financial support to the CKA Executive Committee if they agreed to handle the day-to-day kindergarten management responsibilities. They accepted her offer. Hearst adopted a businesslike approach used routinely by conservative women and men. She relied on her money and resources to carry out what she thought were her political obligations and responsibilities. Her approach was one that reconciled professionalism and reform. Hearst was "a first-rate business woman," one man exclaimed. The *New York Herald* agreed: "As a businesswoman she [Hearst] is very methodical and painstaking." She kept meticulous records, issued receipts, and tracked money that went to kindergarten reform advocates. She also hired a staff that relied on objective social-science techniques to express and promote the priorities on her political agenda—educational reform and the professionalization of kindergarten teaching.[12]

To achieve Hearst's reform plans and political goals, at the third CKA meeting, members agreed to appoint a committee "to prepare and present to Congress a bill to facilitate the institution of public kindergartens, and to establish a model kindergarten." President Hearst created high standards for her model free kindergarten that centered on developing the individual whole child. She also contributed the main financial support to get the CKA up and running. She gifted $764.50 to rent a house for half a year, located at 2037 H Street NW, in which to hold kindergarten classes. She paid for a competent teaching staff that she helped hire—Harriet Niel, supervisor to director Miss. S. E. Lobb, and her assistant, Miss S. S. Rawlins, both from Philadelphia. She employed "only . . . well educated thoroughly trained, conscientious teachers who love the work and believe it is the best means for laying the foundation for future good and usefulness in the child," she wrote. She stressed that educators "must be made to realize that children trained in the kindergarten are better prepared to go on with school work; this they can only do by having children thus trained in their classes."

The rest of the money to cover expenditures for the first year of CKA operations came from others, including Kate Douglas Wiggin. Wiggin was an author and kindergarten educator from Philadelphia who in 1878 became head of the first free kindergarten in California—the Silver Street Kindergarten. Advocates and supporters of scientific philanthropy, meanwhile, increased social pressure on the rich to rely on scientific methods. Carroll Wright promoted scientific techniques. But Mary W. Kincaid, years earlier, had already introduced Hearst to basic elements of social-scientific procedures. Hearst supported Wright's approach. She encouraged her staff to rely on a scientific approach to identifying neighborhood children who would be deserving applicants for admittance.

The first CKA free kindergarten opened with ten students on December 19, 1893. Twenty-five children attended by January 1, 1894. The enrollment increased to thirty shortly after.[13] Hearst rented and leased single domestic structures for these classes, viewing this as a way to enter CKA politics and increase her power to promote and advance her reform agenda and reputation. She provided opportunities at the same time for the working class, immigrants, and the poor to improve their circumstances while she enhanced the CKA's organizational clout to lobby Congress effectively.

Hearst, as an officer of the CKA, in time became instrumental in helping to integrate kindergartens "into mainstream academic and governmental structures under male leadership."[14] But first, Hearst and the CKA understood that they would have to get involved in the "filthy pool" of American politics. Unfortunately, Hearst's earlier experiences with local and national politics, both in San Francisco and Washington, had left her with a strong, scornful attitude toward conventional partisan politics. The values that government men held near and dear were an anathema to her respectable feminine values of honesty, cooperation, harmony, and virtue.

Refusing to join direct CKA lobbying efforts she considered undignified and dishonorable, Hearst chose to appear deferential and rely instead on male kindergarten lobbyists to pressure Congress to achieve the CKA's goals. She chose to work through a man with a prominent last name in

American education—the husband of Louisa Mann, Benjamin Pickman Mann. By doing so, she participated in shifting the intellectual authority within the kindergarten movement away from women and toward male academic professionals. Mann became Hearst's and the CKA's voice in the halls of the U.S. Congress—a deliberative partisan legislative body that limited and superseded the control Hearst and her teaching staff possessed in and over the CKA and Mann. Hearst believed that her choice of Mann to represent the kindergarten movement would protect her from criticism that she was stepping outside the bounds of propriety because she was president of an organization that lobbied Congress. Hearst, an amateur social scientist, her staff, and other kindergarten advocates provided Mann with statistical and detailed survey information to support his efforts on behalf of their shared goal of making "kindergartens a part of the public school system" and raise the professional status of kindergarten teachers. It appears the lobbying paid off. Circumstantial evidence indicates that the CKA convinced Congress to appropriate $12,000 "for kindergarten instruction" in the District of Columbia in 1898. All major cities in America had kindergartens by 1914.[15] Hearst's decisions as CKA president showed how a dignified, genteel woman could keep her distance from the corrupt, vile world of partisan politics and still be effective politically.

Hearst understood that her goals could be achieved only by accepting the limits circumscribed by men in general, and Mann in particular, even though she was president of the CKA. But she refused to discuss publicly the restrictions or obstacles she experienced as CKA president, and she never explained privately or publicly why she held herself apart from lobbying the U.S. Congress. She declined to discuss the barriers established by men that limited her participation, even though there were instances in which she held power over men like Mann. Hearst's decision to remain reserved and silent, depending on men to advance CKA politics, made it more difficult for others, women mostly, to understand her success. How did she manage to acquire and wield power so effectively in achieving her goals while at the same time negotiating the constraints of sex and class?

In the autumn of 1893, as the CKA lobbying efforts were underway, Hearst attended the 1893 World's Columbian Exposition at Chicago. She probably visited the exposition because it appealed to her nineteenth-century sensibilities and values at the same time that it satisfied her thirst for new ideas and knowledge, especially about design and architecture and reform issues. This national exposition ran from May 1 to the end of October 1893, the identical period CKA kindergarten reform classes contributed to making life better for the downtrodden in Washington DC. The "great show," as one of Phoebe's friends and others called it, expressed Americans' growing fondness for consumption and production and asserted the nation's claim to be an independent world power poised for empire. Adults paid fifty cents and "children under six years of age" were "free" to enjoy a celebration of nationalism.

Hearst, after she paid the fee, joined a total of 27,529,400 adults and children who attended and strolled around the grounds. She observed the handiwork of Bertha Honoré Palmer from Kentucky, the head of the Lady Board of Managers and spouse of Potter Palmer, owner of the Marshall Field department stores and the Palmer House Hotel in Chicago. She stopped to see the exhibits and read the messages of exposition elites, reformers, and social scientists largely united by class and social views. These folks called on Hearst, teachers, and others to save neglected, poor, and uneducated children suffering from the deleterious effects of the Panic of 1893. It was also seen as one way to counter a growing number of women getting involved in the socialist movement. It is possible she attended a lecture by a businessman and founder of the Oriental Club in Philadelphia, Robert Stewart Culin. It is conceivable that she met Zelia Nuttall and Alice Fletcher, who talked to Culin at his presentation. It also is plausible that she ran into Sarah Yorke Stevenson, an Egyptologist from Philadelphia who "described the Ceremonial Rites of the dead." As she passed the exhibits, Hearst learned about the reform activities of public-spirited elite, middle-, and working-class women interested in design and architecture and a variety of political reform issues exhibited at the exposition like kindergartens, anthropology, and suffrage.[16]

Hearst traveled abroad again after she visited the World's Columbian Exposition, where she came up with yet another unique idea and strategic plan to provide kindergarten opportunities for whites and blacks. "Having developed some ideas of her own, and wishing to be quite free to carry them out in her own way," Hearst wrote from Paris in 1895 that she wanted to resign from the CKA presidency. Robert Turner, an African American born in Virginia in the mid-1850s and who some have called her devoted servant, traveled with her. Turner could read and write, yet needed to improve his spelling, as was evident in one of his letters to his employer signed "From Your True Servient." Hearst assigned Turner significant responsibility. He was of the highest status and best paid among Hearst's domestics. He experienced a standard of living similar to that of a middle-class professional. Hearst considered him "useful as well as ornamental"—an attitude remarkably similar to the most limited and conservative view of women as submissive and ornamental fixtures to be placed on pedestals. This view was held widely by early nineteenth-century, upper-middle-class and elite Southern men.

Hearst, while she traveled with Turner, cited several reasons for her CKA resignation. "Ill health and the increasing pressure of business has forced me to consider" the resignation from the CKA presidency "for several months," she wrote. She also wanted to resign to carry out her idea to establish "three independent kindergartens in different parts of Washington, two for whites and one for colored children." Turner possibly influenced Hearst's plan. She knew the value of remaining associated with the CKA. "I do not wish, in any sense, to sever my connection with the Association and hope to take a warm interest in its working in the future as I have done in the past," she explained. This seemed to be the time for her to use what one of her female friends, Clara Anthony Reed, called her "god-like power" to give white and black children kindergarten educational opportunities and to open a National Kindergarten Training School for white and black women. Her idea and plan became a part of the "transnational traffic in reform ideas, policies, and legislative devices," as one historian described it.[17] Ironically, it was in Europe, rather than in America, that she became more clear-headed about how to assist whites and blacks.

The District of Columbia had been experiencing a large migration of black Americans from the South by the time Hearst returned home and began to act on her plan. Blacks and whites faced some of the same problems as they tried to educate their children—meager assistance and inadequate space. Black teachers received salaries that were 10 percent lower than whites and experienced heavier teaching loads. A white high-school teacher made $750 a year; a black teacher got $74.54 less than the white teachers, which were mostly women, in the 1890s. Whites and blacks sometimes joined forces in their efforts to build a stable school system and change Washington DC conditions. These political activities attracted black women to the national capital who wanted "to provide professional services to the growing Black bourgeoisie of this racially segregated, southern city."[18] Black women who came to the federal city faced intense hostility and racism at the end of the nineteenth century. Widely accepted views of social theorists, like Herbert Spencer, provided justification for the power of whites over blacks and argued for social and racial stratification as natural and desirable. Others thought blacks to be inferior intellectually. Only a few institutions of higher education, such as Spelman Seminary and Howard and Fisk Universities, admitted blacks, and prominent white schools like Vassar declined to welcome them at all. American black institutions of higher education also refused to welcome black women. Twelve black women were enrolled at Fisk University and none were enrolled at Howard University in 1892. Only 0.3 percent of the female students in American colleges and universities by 1911 were black. Most black women had little hope of getting a higher education because racism was so predominant. Not until the third decade of the twentieth century did the number of black women enrolled in American institutions of higher education rise significantly. Worse yet, lynching had become common practice by the time Hearst acted on her plan to establish kindergartens for whites and blacks in Washington DC.[19]

Hearst's elite attitude toward blacks, by the early to mid-1890s, was a complicated, broadminded, but still patronizing one. Many white Americans believed in black intellectual inferiority, advocating segregation, as well as lynching. But Hearst, like settlement worker Jane Addams, held slavery responsible for black hardship and promoted equality through education and segregation. Most settlements, including Addams's Hull House, excluded blacks and instead organized "segregated activities" for whites and blacks. But Addams did join Ida B. Wells-Barnett in leading "a protest against discussions in Chicago to segregate the public schools." Wells-Barnett was a journalist, lecturer, and founder of anti-lynching groups and black women's clubs.[20]

Hearst, in common with other white women, possessed the ability to acknowledge "individual nonwhite women as" the "equals" of a white female. But it was difficult for her, and other white women, to see the "entire" black race as the equal of the white race because of her belief in white "racial superiority." Her actions, like those of many white American and British female feminists, supported "racial motherhood"—meaning that it was the responsibility of female parents to preserve the white race and "civilization itself," which placed restrictions on white women and blacks who sought to gain equality. Hearst and her kindergarten reform colleagues held concerns about race and the demise of the Republic. They thought blacks fell short of Anglo-Saxon standards and must be made "worthy representatives of American civilization. Not to achieve these standards would be the death knell of the Republic," according to Hearst's employees. Hearst's reform partners advocated dealing with the racial problem in the South by providing blacks with "education of the right *kind*, at the right time." What Hearst's staff meant was that they must teach blacks what they needed to know to reestablish family life destroyed by slavery so the race would "be able to rise to the full duties of American citizenship," as defined by whites, and so that "the two races may the sooner through *community* of interest live together in peace and harmony." Hearst believed that blacks possessed the intellectual capacity to receive the same kind of education as whites. Yet she and her compatriots assumed that the white race would "determine the place the colored race must occupy in the social whole."[21]

Although lacking the financial and material assets of the wealthy, black women had already been pushing for reform when Hearst established her Washington DC kindergartens to provide black children with the opportunity for self-support and self-esteem. But Hearst ignored the views and needs of black women before she opened her free public coeducation kindergartens for black girls and boys. She refused to consult them to determine black needs and desires. She assumed, instead, that she knew what was best for them. She rented "three buildings for the purpose she leased for a term of years, furnished and equipped completely and attractively, not only for school uses, but as comfortable homes for the teachers and helpers," according to Hearst's staff.

In 1897 Hearst opened the Phoebe A. Hearst Kindergarten College in Washington DC—a training school for white and black professional kindergarten teachers and administrators and "for young women who, though not intending to become teachers" wanted to learn and study Froebel's principles. Her kindergartens were "accepted as models, with the unexpected result of rather discouraging similar enterprises." That is, they were such good models and achieved such success that others gave little thought to opening similar institutions to compete with Hearst's. She set high standards for admission. She admitted only the most talented and deserving students with good character. Black women who set racial uplift as a priority over white women's respectability found it difficult to get in at first, so Hearst's kindergartens and training school set about to serve black women so they could resist discrimination, gain respectability, and, eventually, contribute to racial uplift and the advancement of all black women. Some black women enrolled, graduated, and became teachers, special supervisors, assistants, and directors. Others failed to complete the course.[22]

Hearst became so curious about the effectiveness of her kindergarten reform politics that she wrote to "the Superintendent [of Education in Washington DC] asking what proportion of kindergarten teachers in the Department had been trained in her post-graduate classes," according to Brooks. The *New York Times* confirmed later that "about 90 percent of the public school teachers there were graduates of her classes." Hearst's kindergarten activism placed her in the forefront of the professionalization of white and black kindergarten teachers. Her kindergartens were among the few places where black children could get a free kindergarten education; and her college was among a handful of places where white and black women could receive training for professional jobs.[23] No evidence is available to establish whether white and black women trained together or separately.

The ways Hearst used her money and resources, in the world of education, expressed her views and convictions, along with the values she wanted imposed on white and black women, girls and boys, and on the working class, immigrants, and the poor. While her methods reinforced traditional racial attitudes, her approach also held out hope that by providing free education and job training opportunities, prejudice and discrimination experienced by white and black women and students, and perhaps by any other disadvantaged groups, could be reduced, making it easier for them to climb social, economic, and political ladders. Her achievements in Washington DC made Hearst, one male reporter wrote, "the philanthropic *grande dame of the capital*."[24] Newspaper reports continued to offer Hearst public recognition, drawing attention to her effectiveness and her rise among the national elite, especially in kindergarten and political reform circles.

By the mid-1890s, a new direction, one that would complement her passion for educational reform, began to open up for Phoebe Hearst. Inspired by her European travels, as well as her visit to the 1893 World's Columbian Exposition, Hearst's enthusiasm for the potential of design and architecture to transform both personal and public spaces began to take shape in her mind. The Columbian Exposition was the first to have "a comprehensive plan for buildings and grounds on a single scale." As she walked about the exposition grounds, Hearst would have taken in the built architectural plan, or "White City," as the design was called, developed by the Chicago firms of Daniel Burnham and by McKim, Mead and White. Influenced by the style of architecture taught at the École des Beaux-Arts school in France, some observers saw Burnham's design as a model for "the city beautiful" or a distinct style of American architecture.

But the architectural design also sent several resounding messages to Hearst and the other visitors: the United States was culturally independent from Europe and promoted a white hegemonic vision of democracy and empire. White exposition officials and visitors alike displayed an elite entitlement, as well as "racial arrogance and nationalistic chauvinism," toward diverse ethnic and racial groups. Exposition elites referred to the design as the White City because of the building materials used. That label, though, also held intense racial overtones that reflected Hearst's and the common American belief in white racial superiority. It spoke to the dominance of whites in defining American civilization and spreading that vision to foreign nations. Nonetheless, Hearst's visit to the White City, exposed her to a stimulating mix of rich and poor men and women of varying ethnic, racial, and foreign ancestry. Issues of importance to the advancement of women were also evident at the exposition. An architectural competition was held for a Woman's Building to honor and promote women's home, labor, and reform activities. The contest was restricted to females "on the fringe of the profession" in architecture, a field based on science. The winner, Sophia G. Hayden, received $1000 plus expenses.[25] All told, Hearst's attendance at the exposition made a lasting impression.

Phoebe's son, William Randolph Hearst, prodded her to act on her interest in design and architecture, which had been aroused at the World's Columbian Exposition, sooner than she had planned. Will had entered the newspaper world after his father purchased the *San Francisco Examiner* in 1880—a publication that was the voice for the Democratic Party. Owning the *Examiner* brought George greater recognition and political power. George and Phoebe transferred the control of the Hearst newspaper enterprise to William in the late 1880s. Will issued the first edition of the *San Francisco Examiner* on March 4, 1887, the same day that George took his seat as a U.S. senator. Will worked hard in his newspaper business. But there were times when he wanted to take a break from his business endeavors to rest and relax, so he frequently spent time enjoying the ranchland his father had bought in Pleasanton, California, in the early 1880s. He began to act on his plans for the property during some of his visits while his mother was abroad. He arranged for a "five-ton stone wellhead from Italy" to be shipped from Europe to place in the yard outside the front door. He then hired a San Francisco architect, Albert C. Schweinfurth, to discuss the idea of building "a new and grander house" on the ranch that was part of his mother's estate and under her control.

Schweinfurth had made the largest contribution to the design of the California Building at the 1893 World's Columbian Exposition. He became a leading architect of the romantic, mythical Mission style—a distinctive Spanish-California style with a mixture of innovative and traditional elements that harmonized with the natural landscape and expressed the western regional environment. The Mission style became part of the academic movement in architecture. It was linked with the Arts and Crafts movement. Under Will's influence, his mother decided to hire Schweinfurth. Will, in the meantime, felt he needed to live in New York to run and make the newspaper successful after his mother gave him one million dollars to purchase the *New York Morning Journal*. This gave Phoebe the opportunity to reassert her control over the ranch property and act on her own plans. Several years before, she had written to a female friend that she was starting to think about building a new house to suit her. Phoebe agreed with Will's original plan to build a mansion in the Spanish-California Mission revival style. And she agreed to support his choice of architects. She probably knew of Schweinfurth's connection to the World's Columbian Exposition. So she asked him to design a mansion to honor California's Spanish American past and alter and give expression to the state's rural environment and her own values. Phoebe took this opportunity to build her dream home in the West because the region was a unique and wide open space that fostered a new society unfettered by entrenched East Coast traditions.[26]

Meanwhile, Schweinfurth faced controversy in accepting such a commission from Hearst. Critics in the 1890s charged architects with bowing to the demands of a handful of wealthy elite patrons while arrogantly showing no interest in planning homes for the average American. Architects under attack were finding it hard to get commissions in the wake of the Panic of 1893. Schweinfurth chose to ignore such criticisms and he accepted Phoebe A. Hearst's offer to design her mansion. But he downplayed the importance of meeting clients' needs and tastes. People in the West were not free of discriminatory views, especially toward women, and Hearst had to contend with Schweinfurth's overt prejudice toward her. He assumed, moreover, that Hearst lacked the intellectual ability to grasp his ideas. He preferred dealing directly with Edward H. Clark, Hearst's employee, rather than with Phoebe because he wanted to be assured his "ideas would be understood," he wrote Clark. Schweinfurth did not entirely get what he wanted.[27]

Hearst, a charming and imperious woman and very much her own person, forced Schweinfurth to work with her. Faced with the possibility of losing Hearst's commission, Schweinfurth capitulated to his employer's desires. It is unclear whether he ever dealt directly with her. But Schweinfurth solicited her views through Clark, did what she wanted, and sought and got her approval. Schweinfurth sent his client working drawings, including details of the mansion design with suggestions for the

5. Back of Hacienda del Pozo de Verona with terraces and road leading up to mansion, ca. 1910. BANCPIC 1905.11714–11715 a–b. Courtesy of the Bancroft Library, University of California, Berkeley.

furnishings, and asked for her response. Hearst's completed mansion—the Hacienda del Pozo de Verona—was located about thirty-five miles southeast of San Francisco. It stood "in an ideal spot . . . with no fog and no wind to disturb the pleasures of the country." It set new standards for size and luxury, following the trend established by rich tycoons living on New York's Fifth Avenue, on Chicago's Gold Coast, in Newport, Rhode Island, and other places.[28] The completion of Hearst's mansion advanced Schweinfurth's career as a professional architect. People associated Schweinfurth's reputation with Hearst's mansion and saw the structure as a stately home. One look at the new mansion encouraged a person to think of her as being on par with rich, elite, and male, industrial tycoons, especially in the East.[29] The Hacienda was a striking and permanent expression of Phoebe Apperson Hearst's beliefs, values, power, prominence, and status.

While the Hacienda was under construction, Hearst came up with an unprecedented idea for another architectural project—the National Cathedral School for Girls—which would serve to promote her good name as well as her political ideals and values in the field of education. She thought about building a school for "young daughters of her friends in official life" who were "sent away to distant schools for the kind of training that could not be obtained nearer home." She needed a place to construct a school that would express the reform convictions and issues she believed were important. During the years that George and Phoebe Hearst were living in Washington DC, Phoebe had, of course, noted that women were not allowed to walk the halls of, or represent Americans in, the United States Congress. So Hearst got as close as she could get to the center of power in Washington by helping to build a private Cathedral School for Girls. Reverend George William Douglas, rector of St. John's Church, Lafayette Square, and dean of the Cathedral Foundation in Washington DC, asked Hearst to become one of five donors to establish a private school next to what later was called the National Cathedral. Hearst probably sensed the advantages of accepting Douglas's proposal. She likely recognized that acting on it would give her a way to advance her political reform agenda and enhance her national esteem and renown.[30] Douglas's offer meshed nicely with her beliefs and values, including the traditional definition of femininity. Accepting his invitation provided Hearst with a way, through design and architecture, to build closer connections with the political elite in Washington, advancing herself as well as her goal of helping women achieve educational opportunities.

Hearst made clear from the start her ambition and desire to control the National Cathedral School project. As she put it to those interested in her plans, "One person can do this work better than five. The amount you name is insufficient. I will give $175,000 for the school"—the largest single donation. She also suggested an architectural competition "for which she assumed the entire expense." Expressing "the deepest interest in having the building [be] *a model of its kind*," she increased her gift to $220,000 to cover the costs for the architectural competition. The National Cathedral School Board of Trustees met to discuss her plans. They agreed on a location for the school. Hearst conveyed her strong disapproval of the site chosen by the board and wanted to alter their decision. So she acted like a banker would to secure a location that pleased her. She added another $24,000 to the amount she offered, including an interest-free loan of $8,000, to buy the land. She then secured board approval to purchase the site she favored.[31] As she became practiced at doing, Hearst ignored what men thought and pursued her goals.

As Hearst's National Cathedral plan unfolded, a controversy erupted regarding the architect chosen originally for the project—Ernest Flagg. Flagg's name had not been suggested for the architectural competition Hearst financed because his estimates of between $294,000 and $315, 000 were too high. He had also refused to make any suggestions for price reductions. Flagg's refusal delayed Hearst's architectural project for a year and a half. It became evident that another architect needed to be selected for the project. Hearst politely declined to suggest one. She possessed confidence in the competition jurors to offer names of architects while the haggling with Flagg continued. To return the favor, the board chose J. W. Gibson of New York by unanimous vote. Gibson did what Hearst wanted regarding the building design. He included the sculpture pieces she desired on the outside of the new building, ones that reflected her values and goals and those of the school: the development of the students' spiritual, moral, intellectual, and physical life, the inculcation of Christian principles and values, and the establishment of the highest intellectual standards.

The groundbreaking ceremony took place in April 1899. The laying of the cornerstone occurred about one month later on May 9. Hearst paid the salaries of one teacher, Miss Rowland, and one secretary. Her plans stipulated a modern school for young women with rooms for learning, living, sitting, cooking, eating, and exercising. She equipped the place with new appliances, heat, electricity, sanitary facilities, and fireproof construction.[32] Her deferential, conservative approach paid off. Men with the power over what was called the National Cathedral School for Girls, in turn, did what Hearst wanted.

The completion of her National Cathedral School for Girls added to Americans' growing recognition of Hearst as a wealthy and distinguished national philanthropist. The *Review of Reviews* had published an article six years earlier, in the February 1893 edition, titled "American Millionaires and Their Public Gifts," which featured a discussion of eighty-six female and male philanthropists. "Our social life, our political methods, and our democratic institutions are all profoundly affected by the existence among us to-day of a recognized class of great capitalists who command congeries of agencies and forces," the article stated. Men, including Andrew Carnegie, were mostly discussed in the article. But some women were included too—Hearst among them. These prominent philanthropists had possessed the good sense and integrity to use wealth in responsible social and political ways to serve the common good, for whites mostly. In contrast, the article ignored the success Hearst had achieved in assisting black women to become teachers.[33] Accomplishments and prominence in philanthropy on the national level were reserved for whites only, according to the *Review of Reviews*.

Having achieved such success with the National Cathedral School, a confident Hearst began to make plans and strategic decisions to attract and support more women to attend the University of California (uc) and, not long after, to address the need for a comprehensive architectural plan for its Berkeley campus. Once more, architecture and educational reform would come together in advancing Hearst's philanthropic ambitions. The university was a land-grand institution of higher education, which meant that it was designated by the state of California to receive funding by means of the Morrill Acts of 1862 and 1890. John W. Dwinelle presented "The Act to Create and Organize the University of California of 1868" to the California legislature. Governor Henry H. Haight signed the law in the third week of March 1868. The act declared that "any resident of California, of the age of fourteen years or upwards, of approved moral character, shall have the right to enter *himself* [emphasis added] in the University as a student at large." Women were ignored. Forty male students were enrolled in the autumn of 1869 on the Oakland campus.

Academic reformers after the Civil War, meanwhile, insisted "that they believed in gradual change and sought to balance the 'progressive' against the 'conservative.'"[34] Academically reform-minded officials of the university sought to advance that political balance as they considered how to attract more students to California for practical, economic reasons. And they wanted to compete with East Coast institutions of higher education. So in the autumn of 1870, "a very conservative Board of Regents" took a progressive position. They unanimously voted to admit women "into the University on equal terms, in all respects with young men," the *Register of the University of 1870* noted.

Eighty-two men and eight women entered the University of California in 1870, without discussion or controversy. The admittance of women placed the university in the vanguard of coeducational institutions of higher education. Classes were held at the Berkeley location in 1873. The California legislature by this time had constructed two buildings, North and South Halls, on campus. A few years later, in 1885, Hearst gave a gift of $3,500 to the university in support of her husband's interest in mining. Her donation established a Department of Mining machine shop, designed by Clinton Day. This was at about the same time that Phoebe was remodeling the Hearst's Washington DC mansion in the Richardson Romanesque style she favored. Henry Hobson Richardson would later play a key role in bringing about a shift from the Victorian to the academic worlds in American architecture as well.[35] Hearst's gift associated her name with political moderates at the university.

There were so many new UC students by the mid-1880s that campus structures could not accommodate them all, and American architecture had yet to direct its attention to the needs of the academic world. Hampered by limited state funds, the university was in desperate need of additional money to grow institutionally. Over seventy young women undergraduate coeds were attending the University of California in 1888 (there were no female graduate students), so university president Horace Davis invited "some woman, interested in the education of her sex," to come forward with financial support to construct a women's building so females would "have a hall of their own" intended for comfortable study and reception areas, a gymnasium, and "possibly a dining room and dormitories." He also called on "some large-hearted friend of education" to build an independently standing fireproof museum. Women undergraduate students numbered one hundred and graduate students numbered fifteen two years later. University president Martin Kellogg described their accommodations as "utterly inadequate" and asked "some generous friend of education in California to embalm *his* [emphasis added] memory by erecting a women's hall or a museum building."[36] But by 1890, no one had stepped forward to make donations for these projects.

In the fall of 1891, Hearst joined with other philanthropists and academic reformers interested in creating opportunities for more women to attend the University of California. Most Americans increasingly saw universities as the most important route to economic power, upward career and social mobility, professionalism, and success for women as well as men. But females after graduation struggled with the question "After College, What?"[37] And Hearst, by this time in her life, had a great deal of experience surmounting the difficulties involved in managing her new estate and trying to help females become teachers and physicians. So she knew the prejudices against women getting a higher education and how women, especially young ones, needed money, even small amounts, and additional support to get an education on equal terms with men. Hearst, after the acceptable six months' period of mourning for her husband, decided to get involved, tactfully and deferentially, in promoting coeducation at the University of California, significantly increasing her financial gifts to the university. By now, the university had been moving away from its evangelical roots and was evolving into a more secularized institution, eager to embrace the sciences, though still tolerant of religious views.[38]

Hearst's donations displayed what physician Mary Bennett Ritter later called her "deep and abiding" interest in higher coeducation for women. Ritter was a graduate of Cooper Medical College of San Francisco (taken over by Stanford University in 1908 and later moved to Palo Alto) and an intern at the Women's and Children's Hospital in 1886–87. She had married William E. Ritter, an instructor in the Biological Laboratory at the University of California, three months earlier. Hearst, in September 1891,began an annual contribution of $1,500 to the university to create in perpetuity, she wrote, "five three hundred dollar scholarships for worthy young women." She established qualifications for her scholarships: "noble character and higher aims, it being understood that without the assistance here given, a University course would in each case, be impossible." The Hearst scholarships may be the first scholarships in America based on economic need. Hearst's scholarships also encouraged others to think about and demand that financial support be made available for female students to get a university education. The time seemed right to create such scholarships for the University of California. Wealthy elite women were giving money to help their sex become professionals. A growing number of Americans, especially women participating in the movement for female advancement, were beginning to lay the foundation for defining economic self-sufficiency as a right and working for state regulation of the economy.[39]

By the time Hearst established her scholarships, the University of California was the core of the city of Berkeley. The university provided the main impetus in the city's growth from a small town—with small groups of wooden houses, gardens, and rough, loose earth roads—into a fast-growing metropolis. As the state institution outgrew its accommodations, however, "the magnificent possibilities of the site at Berkeley were still obscured by an inharmonious mingling of commonplace buildings neither individually suitable nor collectively impressive," according to Brooks. The underdeveloped campus gave a reformer like Hearst a great opportunity to integrate her philanthropic and architectural interests in transforming the state's coeducational institution of higher education—which was a microcosm of a democratic society, surrounded by rolling hills and engulfed by the physical beauty of the Bay Area—into a model community that would reflect her political agenda and values and represent a hopeful, though some would say an unattainable, ideal and organic vision of a whole city that others could emulate at the dawn of a new century in the Progressive Era.[40]

By the end of 1891, however, Hearst's attention to comprehensive architectural reform for the Berkeley campus would have to wait. The stress and strain produced by the hard work of developing and acting on her various other architectural projects, while also managing her business affairs and participating in a wide range of political activities, had weakened her physical stamina. Hearst suffered from an attack of grippe or fever influenza. Mary Kincaid was concerned about the load Hearst was carrying. "I worry ever lastingly to think that with the multitude you have to plan for & the awful load you carry that you should also bear me as an addition to the load." Phoebe was in need of a rest and relief from her cares and activities.[41] Despite her health, she was still taking on duties and political obligations as well as the responsibilities of supervising Kincaid. She knew it was futile to think about taking a break. Worse yet, trying to cope and keep up with her work and activities, including organizing and holding a cotillion for Florence (Bayard) Hilles some thought would be "the one event of the season," only aggravated her physical problems. The strain and stress was too much. She came down with rheumatic fever. She turned to Dr. William Pepper, her private physician, for medical advice.

Pepper was a member of one of the leading blue-blood elite families in Philadelphia. He was the intensely ambitious president of the Department of Archaeology and Paleontology. He also served as the provost of the University of Pennsylvania. Hearst's professional relationship with Dr. Pepper signaled her acceptance by men among the national elite— quite an accomplishment for a woman with an ordinary background from rural Missouri. Pepper diagnosed her with "a little valvular trouble" and impoverished blood in December 1891. He explained to Hearst that the problem would worsen. He warned her to take precautions. His advice: walk up and down stairs slowly, avoid heavy lifting. "You should not make straining exertions, as in moving any heavy object or lifting any weight," he explained. "You must insist upon having your rest regularly and in full quantity," he ordered. He added, "You must not overtax yourself with your duties; business, social, benevolent, combined."

As Hearst slowly recovered, though, she never lost sight of doing what she thought was expected of her. She did want to follow Dr. Pepper's advice so she could improve her health as well as escape her constant worries, at least for a time. Knowing it was acceptable for a woman of wealth to travel, Hearst planned another trip abroad with her niece, Annie Apperson, and Agnes Lane. Pepper was "convinced of the wisdom of" Hearst's plan to set sail for England on April 20, 1895, even though travel could be exhausting.[42] Hearst was eager to cross the Atlantic again to escape her burdens, to rest, and to restore her health. She wanted to be ready for the difficulties that surely lay ahead in working toward her architectural and political goals for the University of California. Pepper's approval strengthened her resolve to make the trip.

While she made her travel preparations, Hearst went to work to build on the strategic and systematic steps she had begun as early as 1894 to develop and carry out her innovative idea for a comprehensive architectural plan for the University of California. Her visit to the World's

Columbian Exposition in 1893 had first exposed her, via Daniel Burnham's creation of the White City, to the style of architecture taught at the École des Beaux-Arts in France. It was, at the time, a model school for those interested in using education to set professional standards for the design and construction of buildings in America. People interested in improving standards in American architecture admired the school's courses, well-thought-out theories of design, and support from national partisan politicians. California politicians, though, refused to follow the lead of their French counterparts. The California legislature, in fact, failed to provide adequate financial support and material assets for expansion of their land-grant university in an era of economic turmoil created by the Panic of 1893. So the budget allocation for the university suffered. The time was right for Phoebe Hearst to step forward. Contributing to the comprehensive design and funding of the state's flagship university would also permit advancement of her reform vision and agenda for women in education, though still limited primarily to white women. Her involvement also encouraged people to exert pressure on the state to advance the university in all directions. From a broader perspective, Hearst would be making a significant contribution to the continued process of defining the state of California, the western region of the country, and the nation-state.[43]

Hearst's vision included financing the construction of two "permanent and harmonious" buildings on the beautiful UC site and the promotion of an international architectural competition for an ideal university design with club houses, a library, a museum, and a gymnasium. One of the two buildings would be a memorial to her late husband, George Hearst. She left unspecified the function of the second building at the time she made her original proposal to the university's regents. The international architectural competition was meant to produce a winning design for the perfect model of a "City of Learning," a design that would promote a natural, harmonious order for the university in an environment ideally free of conflict and centered on cooperation between the sexes. Hearst anticipated that her architectural improvements would bolster the reputation of the campus, the state of California, and the country.[44] As well, her plan held the potential to advance her into the world of nonpartisan academic politics at the University of California.

But it would take more than her original idea and mere money for Hearst to get the university regents to accept and approve her comprehensive architectural plan. To accomplish this goal, she would need an even more delicate, strategic, and diplomatic approach than had worked for her in the past with other male professionals. Hearst would use her considerable knack for creating a network of allies to help achieve her aims. She decided first to discuss her ideas for a comprehensive architectural plan with Milicent Shinn, a resident of Washington DC, in the summer of 1894. Shinn was a University of California graduate, class of 1880, author, and editor. She had led the Public Reform Association during the 1888 San Francisco School Board election campaign while Hearst was president of the Century Club. Shinn also served as secretary of the California Branch of the Association of Collegiate Alumnae from 1893 to 1895. In January 1896 she would gratefully accept Hearst's generous offers to associate the Hearst name with hers and to pay for the publication of some of Shinn's academic work. Shinn, in late 1898, would become the first female, and the eleventh individual in the field of psychology, to receive a doctorate at the University of California at Berkeley.[45] Ultimately, Shinn was essential in getting the regents to accept Hearst's comprehensive architectural plan.

After she talked to Shinn, Hearst thought about the second building in her architectural plan. She later wrote to Caroline Severance, the founder of the first American women's club, that she had wanted "one other building in my own name" and that "it is not my intention to place a bust of myself in either of the [two] buildings." Because of her deep interest in middle-class, working-class, and poor female students, Hearst intended for women to use the second building for exercising, reading, and a place to eat lunch. After some contemplation, she began to move her idea for her architectural plan through her network. Shinn discussed Hearst's idea for her plan with University of California president Martin Kellogg,

William Carey Jones, professor of jurisprudence, and several others. She warned Hearst afterward that "there might be difficulty about a gymnasium combined with girls' reading and lunch rooms, as it was important that the gymnasium should be sufficiently isolated to set the girls perfectly free to 'make as much noise as they like.'" Subsequently, in discussing the architectural plan with male faculty and administrators, Hearst chose, strategically, not to mention her specific intentions for the second building.

Meanwhile, once President Kellogg learned of Hearst's comprehensive plan, he put her in touch with Bernard Maybeck, a geometry teacher who taught some drawing classes at the university. Thus, Maybeck became "identified with the idea of this plan from its inception," Hearst wrote. But some believed that Maybeck "lacked the power, the means, to carry out the ideas" of Hearst's comprehensive architectural plan, according to Professor Jones.[46] Hearst could see that it would be up to her to provide the economic means, authority, and connections to make the plan, including the construction of the two buildings, a reality at the University of California.

Hearst and Maybeck "liked each other and set fire to each other's ideas," according to Jacomena, the spouse of Maybeck's son, Wallen. Hearst and Maybeck were dramatic, dreamers, and big thinkers. Both possessed an interest in expanding the campus by means of a comprehensive plan and advancing their careers as professionals. Both displayed aspects of conventionality and unconventionality. Hearst was a dignified, rich woman. She was interested and involved in reform causes, especially the advancement of women. Maybeck was an urbane, bucolic, vegetarian and wild and expressionistic eccentric with twinkling eyes and full beard who wore a tam-o'-shanter, smock, and trousers high at the waist. Privately, Hearst discussed with Maybeck the details for the second building in her plan, and they agreed to an arrangement. Maybeck prepared a preliminary sketch for what was later called Hearst Hall. A rumor circulated that Maybeck had remarked on what "a miserable sketch it was." True or not, Hearst liked his drawing and approved it as a beginning. For now, though, she would still refuse to reveal to the board of regents what specific function the building would serve. The completed sketch helped Maybeck arouse interest among university officials in Hearst's offer to support and finance a comprehensive architectural plan. In April 1896, the regents voted to consult with Maybeck on developing a competition for, a newspaper reported, "a permanent comprehensive plan of the grounds and buildings." Five months later, however, "little or no progress" had been made to move Hearst's plan forward.[47] Hearst would have to broaden her political network yet again.

About a month after Hearst had moved into her Hacienda in the summer of 1896, Bernard Maybeck began to lobby Regent Jacob B. Reinstein to get Hearst's comprehensive architectural plan accepted and approved. Reinstein was a member of the university's first graduating class and a prominent San Francisco lawyer. Following Maybeck's lobbying, Hearst sat down in her Palace Hotel room in San Francisco, on October 22, 1896, to write a carefully worded letter to Reinstein. Having been warned that there might be problems in getting the regents to support her plan for a women's building, Hearst concluded that a careful yet savvy approach to avoid offending the male regents would be warranted. Her interactions with them would need to send a message that she would not overstep the bounds of propriety in getting what she wanted. The regents must not yet be told the real purpose she had in mind for the second building. The function of the building was "to be determined upon later," as she explained to Caroline Severance. Instead, because the university "had grown into poverty and straits," according to the *Berkeley Advocate*, a California newspaper, Hearst stepped forward to express her desire merely to build two structures on campus and "to contribute the funds necessary to obtain by international competition plans for the fitting architectural improvement of the University grounds at Berkeley."[48] Maybeck's lobbying had thus paved the way for Hearst to present her plan in writing to the board of regents.

Hearst employed a sophisticated, misleading strategy to move her plan forward. It was an approach that would demonstrate a subtle combination of generosity, deception, and deference. She decided to appear naïve about money in her fall 1896 letter to avoid antagonism and gain support from the regents. She wrote Regent Reinstein that she understood from his estimate that her plan could "be procured for about fifteen thousand ($15,000) dollars." That was an absurdly unrealistic sum. It was much less than what she spent on the architectural competition for the National Cathedral School for Girls. Hearst by this time knew more than most women about money, especially its value, as well as business and the law. It is possible she lacked enough financial expertise to calculate a more accurate estimate of the cost. Yet she knew that the design and construction of her plan would cost at least as much as she had given to complete her National Cathedral School for Girls project—over $200,000. She could have easily consulted, moreover, with several of her expert business managers and male friends and acquaintances in architecture to obtain a more realistic figure.

Hearst really wanted the regents to adopt her offer. So she presented them with a proposal they could not refuse. Included in her letter was the incredible statement: "the success of this enterprise shall not be hampered in any way by a money consideration." Hearst also suggested the formation of a special committee to "represent the several interests involved"— California's Democrat governor James H. Budd, Professor William Carey Jones, and Regent Jacob B. Reinstein. She suggested Maybeck be relieved of his teaching duties to promote her architectural plan and consult with architects in the East and abroad since she had a good working relationship with him. A rich woman and an advocate of reform ideals and values, Hearst's only "wish in this matter [is] that the plans adopted," she wrote, "should be worthy of the great University whose material home they are to provide for that they should harmonize with and even enhance the beauty of the site whereon this home is to be built and that they should redound to the glory of the State whose culture and civilization are to be nursed and developed as its University." Hearst insisted that whatever plans the board of regents adopted must express core values and principles she advocated and promoted. Her requirement signaled the emergence of the University of California as a symbol of progressive ambitions and, by the turn of the new century, "perhaps the most powerful and enduring symbol for" progressives and "their ideals."[49]

But Hearst ran into trouble almost immediately with the regents after she offered her comprehensive architectural plan. She received competition from another donor to build a mining department and building. While Hearst disdained overt traditional partisan politics, she was determined to accomplish her goal, so she made a practical decision. She set aside her feelings and threw herself into the rough-and-tumble world of male-dominated academic politics to gain control over the architectural competition. She knew she would have to get university leaders to side with her over her rival. It was quite a challenge because Americans, especially men, often felt uncomfortable with powerful women and refused to recognize and praise them publicly, so it would not do to appear too brash or confrontational. Many people would even assume that Hearst's ideas for a comprehensive architectural plan had originated with men. Others would lack an understanding, as had her husband, of the intelligence that went into coming up with the ideas for her plans and the hard work required to realize and achieve them.

To beat out the competition, then, Hearst would draw on her unique blend of intelligence, informal, interpersonal skills and economic clout to win over the administration. To this end, she decided to actively lobby on her own for the support of Regent Reinstein. Reinstein was known to be an ardent advocate of building a great state university. Such an enterprise would serve "to stir the people of this Commonwealth to patriotism and pride in their State, and to arouse a true California spirit, for out of this will grow loyalty and love for all her institutions," he would announce a bit later.[50] In cultivating Reinstein's support, Hearst's religious tolerance emerged to serve her own ends, as she had shown earlier in supporting Hannah Solomons, a Jewish immigrant, for president of the Women's Educational and Industrial Union. The university also was moving in the same direction toward religious tolerance and increased secularism. Knowing that Regent Reinstein was an admirer of both her and her comprehensive architectural plan, she moved without hesitation to cultivate Reinstein as a key ally in her quest to overcome the barriers she faced.

Reinstein acted quickly to present Hearst's plan. He gladly made the case to the board of regents that it would be better for the university to support her plan over that of a male competitor. Reinstein, at a regents' meeting, raised "the single main question" before the board: "Will the interests of the University of California be better served by her [Hearst's] donation for that purpose [the mining building], than by a larger donation for a singular purpose from a stranger to the University? I have no hesitation in saying that I believe the University would be benefitted by giving her gift a preference," he wrote to William Carey Jones. Reinstein saw the obvious financial, material, and cultural benefits of Hearst's architectural plan. Approval would help attract additional financial support to ease the university's economic woes. At the same time, Hearst's project would institute an ideal design that embraced and expressed symmetry, balance, and natural social harmony, and promote these values between the sexes on campus.

Reinstein made a point to rally others to support Hearst's plan because he hoped to "rival the dreams of the builders of the Columbian Exposition" and develop an institution of higher education on par with eastern and European colleges and universities. Hearst deferred to Reinstein. He touted her ideas and proposal as a key to the "Future Greatness of the University of California" and its local, state, and national influence. Making Hearst's plan a reality, according to Reinstein, held the potential for turning the university into a symbol of "Love of California as a Unifying Force" and a "representative of the western civilization as against the eastern."[51] Reinstein became Hearst's champion and unequivocally promoted her project.

Reinstein relied on several methods to convince the regents to support Hearst's proposal. He praised Hearst as "the pioneer patron of the 'Greater University of California.'" He also played on traditional male sensibilities toward women. And he exploited the regents' dreams to establish a university to rival those in the East. As he put it, "I do not think she [Hearst] should be forced to forego the fulfillment of that duty [celebrating the memory of her husband] merely because some stranger to the University can afford to donate more bare money than she can, especially where her gift is sufficient for an adequate mining department." Reinstein's argument was a subtle reminder that men eternally circumscribed Hearst's control and efforts to bring her plan to fruition. Reinstein, moreover, was keen to have Hearst sway Will Hearst and his *San Francisco Examiner* to support and promote the passage of a law in the California legislature to raise a one-cent tax on every one hundred dollars for new buildings and to improve the University. He explained that the mere mention of Hearst's plan had already brought the university worldwide renown as an institution representing reform ideals and values, and one that benefitted the nation-state. Reinstein, nonetheless, considered other important issues and benefits to the University and California besides money.[52]

Even with Reinstein's support and lobbying efforts, Hearst continued to face obstacles. Prominent architect Louis Sullivan complained that architectural competitions were utterly silly, pointless, and an unrealistic product of the imagination.[53] Some grumbled about Maybeck's involvement as well. Reinstein himself described Maybeck as "a freak," adding, "We don't any of us regard him seriously." But A. C. Schweinfurth conceded that Maybeck, like other Beaux-Arts–trained architects, appreciated "architecture as an art" and possessed talent. Others wondered if Hearst's architectural plan would even benefit the University and might cost too much money in any case. Among the detractors was the editor of the *University of California Magazine*. He criticized the board of regents for even considering Hearst's plan. Ultimately, though, the magazine editors retracted their criticism and hailed Hearst's "efforts for the welfare and advancement of the University" when they received the news that her plan had in fact originated outside the board of regents and would be paid for by private rather than public funds.

Opposition was dissolving, and public support continued to increase for Hearst's comprehensive architectural plan. Finally, the board of regents "adopted on a call of the ayes & naes" a resolution empowering Hearst "to act with and aid the trustees selected by her and appointed by the Regents" in realizing the Phoebe Apperson Hearst Architectural Plan.[54] Despite the challenges of presenting such a bold project during a time of tumultuous economic and political change and uncertainty, Hearst's sophisticated, diplomatic, and multipronged approach had succeeded. The University of California regents granted Hearst power over her comprehensive architectural plan.

Hearst, more than likely, understood the valuable role her comprehensive architectural plan could play in advancing her career. She had written to Sarah Cooper, a politically active San Francisco Golden Gate Kindergarten Association reformer and member of the state central committee of the California suffrage association in 1896, several years earlier, "that I was one of the first to aid the good work in San Francisco." She added that she did "not wish" Cooper, a member of the joint campaign committee of the state suffrage association, "to infer from" her letter "that I do my work from any such miserable motive as public notice." Hearst's statement spoke to the demure, respectable public image and persona she had crafted so carefully, and she downplayed her ambition. Yet she sent a strong message that she wanted to be recognized and given credit for her political reform efforts and accomplishments.

Hearst used a similar approach to gaining the support of the all-male board of regents. Her subtle political performance and skills, well-honed during her years in Washington DC, convinced university officials she was a paragon of modesty and virtue and not overly ambitious.[55] Comfortable with her approach and fearing that their dreams for an ideal university would never materialize unless they went ahead with her plan, the regents declined to criticize her approach as "unwomanly" or too ambitious. Instead, they approved her plan. Their approval meant that the regents had made a tacit agreement to support and recognize women on campus interested in getting a liberal, up-to-date education.[56] It was worth the wait. Hearst probably sensed that if Regent Reinstein's praise proved to be correct, there would be a time when the successful implementation of her comprehensive architectural plan would bring her and the University of California distinguished reputations and worldwide recognition.

Approval of Hearst's architectural plan coincided with the increasingly conservative National American Woman's Suffrage Association (NAWSA) leadership's preference for an elite strategy. NAWSA officials, among them Susan B. Anthony, had known that California suffragists had the "ability, energy, patriotism, and desire for political freedom, but up to this time they had no conception of the immense amount of money and work which would be required for a campaign," Ida Husted Harper explained. So Anthony recruited wealthy women for the cause. Hearst decided about one year before, in the fall of 1896, to respond to the fundraising campaign of California suffragists. She gave the largest single cash donation of $1,000 to the 1896 California amendment campaign (Hearst and suffrage will be discussed in greater detail in chapter 8).[57]

Hearst's offer to fund a comprehensive architectural plan happened to coincide with the lobbying efforts of the Pacific Association of Collegiate Alumnae (PACA)—an organization that wanted to flex its muscle and get university officials to appoint the first female to the University of California Board of Regents. The PACA consisted of young, college-educated, elite and prosperous reformers, and suffragists devoted, among other things, to helping women college graduates break down barriers that kept females out of the hallowed halls of institutions of higher education and from getting jobs. "The Collegiate Alumnae for years," president of the PACA, May Treat Morrison, wrote, "have been inspired by the hope that a woman would finally be placed on the Board of Regents and, for years, have worked industriously to accomplish this end." Prosperous PACA members circulated a petition on behalf of the appointment of a woman regent and lobbied the governor of California. It was time, they argued, to appoint a female regent; five hundred women students were attending the university and the number continued to rise. The California Constitution, ratified in 1879, had stated that the university "shall be entirely independent of all political or sectarian influence, and kept free therefrom in the appointment of its Regents."

But it was the state governor who appointed members of the board of regents. So in reality, they were political appointments of men who often engaged intensely in California partisan politics. May Treat Morrison, Milicent W. Shinn, Dr. Sarah I. Shuey, and a few other female graduates of the university, sent a letter to Governor James H. Budd requesting that he make the political appointment of Phoebe A. Hearst as a regent. Hearst was a natural, and the best, candidate for such a political position, one local reporter noted. The reason the governor eventually selected Hearst, according to the same reporter, was that she appeared to be "independent of all question of sex, eminently, pre-eminently, qualified for the post." Hearst stood out from all other candidates, both men and women, as the best selection for this exalted state office. The *Berkeley Advocate* claimed that Regent Hearst would be "a good fairy" with a magical touch to set her architectural plan in motion and give it life. "Hearst's pledge was surely a turning point in the fortunes of the University," the newspaper observed.[58] The PACA's lobbying efforts paid off. Women would be represented for the first time on the University of California Board of Regents.

Governor Budd signed the groundbreaking commission for the appointment of Phoebe A. Hearst on July 28, 1897 (she was to complete the term of deceased regent Charles F. Crocker).[59] With this appointment, however, Budd skirted any acknowledgment of the force of Hearst's ideas, economic power, or political abilities. He was, instead, rewarding this notable benefactor of the university and "one of the wealthiest women of America in her own right" (as one newspaper reported it) for her achievements in and gifts to education. As we have seen, Hearst relied on her ideas, sophisticated strategies, financial gifts, and connections to prominent people to make her the first female regent of the University of California. While some of her supporters might have made use of philosophical and moral arguments on her behalf, such discourses, intended to persuade, were out of Hearst's reach, given her ordinary upbringing, rudimentary education, and general knowledge. Nor did she use direct political methods to force the regents to do what she wanted. She used subtle persuasion and pressure. After her investiture as a regent, Hearst became one "of twenty-two members [of the board of regents], all of whom shall be citizens and permanent residents of the State of California," according to the Organic Act of 1868 to Create the University of California. University regents constitute "undoubtedly the most dignified and respectable public body in the State who represent par excellence, the intelligence of this State," according to A.C. Schweinfurth. In this capacity, at least, Hearst would now have the authority to advise and influence the university on equal terms with men.

White women in California, and white and black women in Illinois, had all paved the way for Hearst's appointment. Laura de Force Gordon and Clara Shortridge Foltz had lobbied successfully to include a section in the California Constitution of 1879 that guaranteed women equal access to the University of California. Gordon was a lecturer, journalist, lawyer, advocate for women's advancement, and Western suffragist. Foltz was an advocate for women's advancement, a western suffragist, and the first female attorney in California. The section in the state constitution they succeeded in getting legislators to pass stated, "No person shall on account of sex be disqualified from entering upon or pursuing any lawful business, vocation, or profession" in the state. Black and white women in Illinois appeared to support this California law when they voted with men in 1894 to elect Lucy Flower to the University of Illinois's Board of Trustees, a public institution of higher education, thereby setting a precedent for Hearst's appointment and election to the University of California Board of Regents.[60] As a regent, Hearst became a member of the California and national elite in higher education on equal terms with University of California male regents. All UC regents exercised formally recognized and equal political authority and legal powers on the board of regents. All members of the board were California citizens with the right to vote as regents. Hearst was the only citizen regent without the right to vote in local, state, and national elections.

Governor Budd's pioneering appointment, and the election of Hearst as a regent, received universal approval and was "unaccompanied by political squabbling," according to the *University of California Magazine*. Budd and the state, in making the appointment, lauded Hearst for arousing hope and promise for the future of the university. As the *University of California Magazine* explained: "It was only fitting—nay, it was the really necessary thing, that some marked recognition of her services be shown her." As a regent, Hearst now held formal, public, institutional power and authority over UC men and women. She had won nomination and election to serve at the state level as a regent at a university with a national purpose. And yet, to gain her seat as a regent, Hearst had been compelled to accept traditional sex, class, and racial subordination and hierarchies.[61]

Phoebe Apperson Hearst's accomplishments in the 1890s represented well her proven abilities to control and allocate her wealth and resources to achieve power by design. She conceived of creative ways to satisfy her ambition and her ardent passion for education. She rose to greater prominence and stature in Washington DC by participating in the kindergarten reform movement there, providing educational opportunities to white and black women and children. Building on the success of her Columbia Kindergarten Association classes and training school for white and black women in the nation's capital, she continued to pursue her interest in education through design and architecture as well. She returned to California after her visit to the Chicago World's Columbian Exposition.

Back in her home state, she gratified her rising ambition by coming up with an innovative architectural project and competition for the National Cathedral School for Girls in Washington. Her success on that project gave her the confidence to promote another original idea, through her network of prominent contacts in academia, for a comprehensive architectural plan for the University of California. Her achievement in advancing the comprehensive architectural plan in turn resulted in her appointment to the board of regents, and she would now be on equal terms with men in the world of academic politics at a time when other women in California and the nation-state did not have a constitutional right to citizenship and the ballot. It did not take Hearst long to see that serving on the board of regents would provide her with the opportunity to further advance her progressive reform agenda and to capitalize on her power and authority to benefit women on a much greater scale at the University of California.

5

Benefits for Women

Regent Hearst walked into the room at the Mark Hopkins Institute of Art in the second week of August 1897 for her first meeting as a member of the University of California Board of Regents. "Calm, dignified, graceful, Mrs. Hearst would charm everyone by her beauty and refinement of presence alone," a female reporter observed. Hearst, furthermore, impressed people with her "expression of deep thoughtfulness—the realization of the importance of the duties she was assuming." "To those who watched her," it appeared as though she felt it was "a great and holy privilege" to be a regent invested with "the same sacred trust [as the male regents] for its future citizens of both sexes," especially the power and authority to acquire "the education and advancement of the young women of the state," according to reporter Adelaide Marquand. Hearst was "the embodiment of the highest type of womanhood" and "pre-eminently the representative of her sex for the State of California," the same reporter wrote. Her presence was "a tribute to the equality of woman with man," another reporter declared. Surely her reception at this first meeting would have dispelled any hesitations she may have entertained about taking on this august position.

But this new venture had been a great challenge for Hearst. Although she never revealed what she thought were the main reasons prompting her appointment and election, she must have maintained at least a passing concern that it was due to her wealth and financial gifts alone. Her friend Mary Kincaid tried to put that idea to rest: Hearst was "being sought and urged to accept the regency . . . from men of character and influence, lots of them, too," she insisted. Hearst's nomination, furthermore, was "a right, just tribute to your mind and character, *not* to your money," Kincaid explained to her friend. But Hearst did not bring merely mind and character to the position; she was also a veteran of nonpartisan American voluntary association politics.[1] There can be little doubt that Hearst's well-deserved reputation for results in this arena would have persuaded the board that she would be serious about representing and meeting the needs of her constituents, especially women, at an institution of higher education that some saw as symbolic of progressive ideals.

Still, the pressure on her was enormous. What would it be like to serve, at the age of fifty-five, as the only woman regent surrounded by a sea of male regents, most of whom had extensive business experience and various academic credentials from elite universities such as Yale, Michigan, Cambridge University in England, the College of Braunschwig in Germany, and the like? Any mistakes she made could adversely affect her efforts to advance her career and achieve benefits for women, as well as men, on and off campus. Upon admittance to the board, she had expressed surprise at the "formidable document" sent to her by the secretary of state of California and "all the red tape" involved in making her a regent. She was startled by the unfamiliar world of university men and the processes and procedures of state government administration. Hearst had doubts about taking on the duties and obligations of a regent. Was she up to the job? Shortly after the board of regents approved her official nomination and election, she had remarked to Governor Budd, "I trust that you will never have cause, through any lack of judgment in my official relations to the Board of Regents, to regret making the courageous departure of appointing a woman."[2]

She need not have worried. Reports of her performance at this first regents' meeting had been stellar. It is true that the bar had been set very high for Hearst to serve and represent the interests and welfare of her constituents, particularly women, in the world of nonpartisan academic politics.[3] But although her experience in academic politics had been limited prior to this appointment, the concept and the practice of Regent Hearst's representation at this point had virtually nothing to do with traditional male partisan politics as practiced in other spheres of representative democracy. Hearst would represent the university and its students in the way that kings and queens represented "a nation." Officials at a public institution of higher education "can sometimes represent the state," according to one scholar. In Hearst's case, representation meant "popular representation . . . linked with the idea of self-government" embodied by the governing arm of the University of California—its board of regents. Hearst would do this very well. She was off to a good start. And her subsequent successes in university politics would help remedy the unequal political power relationship between women and men on campus as well as more broadly in American society.

After her investiture as a regent, Hearst would rely on an approach that struck the right tone and balance between deference and modesty on the one hand, and self-confidence and assertive use of her money and other resources on the other. Soon after she took her post, Hearst let it be known that she depended on and trusted President Martin Kellogg. "In anticipation of any difficulties that may come to me through the problems of a new position and relation to affairs," she wrote Kellogg, "I already find myself relying upon your kind assistance and experience." This was a ladylike approach, designed to put the president at ease and reinforce public perception of her as a dignified, respectable woman who understood the necessity of appearing submissive. But at the same time, Hearst was sending a subtle message about the pleasure she took in being invited to hold the position of regent on equal terms with her male colleagues. "Although my own cares are about all I ought to undertake," she explained, "still I accept the unsought office as a recognition of the expressed desire of many whose opinion I regard highly." Her modesty also gave way to a tactful expression of her aspirations. She ended her letter to Kellogg "with the hope and trust that my connection with the official side of University interests may help to its advancement in all directions."[4]

Hearst laced her conservative approach, honed over many years while she served as a high-society hostess, with her ardent desire for rank and power. She wasted no time in linking her ambition with that of university and its officials. She wanted, like her male colleagues, to turn the University of California into a great institution of higher education. University administrators and regents welcomed Hearst's balanced approach, especially her response to her formal appointment that alluded to her proprietary rights and authority as an official uc regent. But they also found her financial commitment to the university and innovative ideas greatly appealing.

President Kellogg, among others, believed that the addition of Hearst to the board of regents would assure the future of California's institution of higher education, particularly financially. Hearst's generous gift "will start a flow of endowments whose aggregate will more than quadruple the sum total of the past ten years," concluded an editorial in the University of California Magazine. Regent Jacob Reinstein saw the practical economic and political value of making Hearst a regent: placing Hearst on the board of regents would help the university get the California legislature to pass the one-cent law that would "double" the university's "income." But despite the enlightened view of Kellogg and Reinstein, other university officials maintained the sort of traditional views on femininity that devalued and ignored Regent Hearst's power, influence, and accomplishments. They refused to acknowledge publicly the power of her money, connections, and ideas, such as her groundbreaking comprehensive architectural plan. While these men did acknowledge that Hearst held influence to get the support of the Examiner, they refused to concede she possessed any real power and authority. Hearst chose to ignore these insults and refused to criticize her detractors publicly, maintaining instead an outwardly deferential manner that belied her power.

These same men, meanwhile, saw Will and his newspaper in terms of power and influence, and they wanted Phoebe Hearst's support in securing his. "We hope to have the powerful influence of the Examiner in favor of this legislation. But if we were doubly assured of such assistance by your influence & exertions" on Will and his newspaper, Reinstein explained to the new regent, "I should feel a little safer." Hearst typically downplayed the power and authority, economic or otherwise, she held over her son and his daily publications. She explained years later to Caroline Severance the nature of her power-working relationship with Will: "When my son first entered upon his newspaper work I made an agreement with him to interfere in no way in the management of his papers, and I have tried to keep to this agreement." She admitted at another time, nonetheless, that she and Will consulted "about important business." She had learned some time ago that it was hard to control her son. But she possessed power as well as influence over him because she controlled the vast Hearst estate. Will often asked for money from his mother. She usually, but not always, gave her son the money he asked for to help him grow and broaden his newspaper empire. She respected Will and his monetary requests, generally speaking. Yet Phoebe held significant economic leverage and control over her son, as well as others, including university officials, because she could deny their requests, especially for money.[5] Though perhaps unwilling to wield her power as aggressively in public as did the men of her time, Hearst had, nonetheless, mastered the art of knowing how, and when, to balance a deferential, subtle approach with an ambitious, risky, and assertive one in order to gain acceptance, achieve her goals, and be effective.

Money and politics were on the minds of many university officials while California struggled to strengthen its economy in the wake of the depression that followed the Panic of 1893. In response, the California legislature addressed a law to increase the university's economic fortunes by creating a one-cent tax on every one hundred dollars for new university buildings and improvements. Kellogg and Reinstein praised Hearst for the contributions she made in getting the legislation passed. Kellogg insisted to Hearst that the passage of the law was "a very remarkable fact, when we take into consideration the comparative newness and heterogeneous character of our population, the sectarian jealousies so easy to be aroused, and the hard times which have borne so heavily upon the State." He went on: "It gives me especial pleasure to note that your own generosity has contributed to this fortunate result." Reinstein thought Hearst's architectural plan and her service as a regent played an important role in securing the passage of the favorable tax legislation: "I do not think the average person, even if connected in some-wise with the University, will ever be able to appreciate how much influence in favor of the passage of this bill was brought to bear by yourself and your action of last October [a reference to Hearst's offer of a comprehensive architectural plan] and ever since in the University's interest."

But President Kellogg's and Regent Reinstein's tributes may have been a bit overblown. Some legislators possibly were swayed to vote for the tax, believing that the offer of Hearst's comprehensive architectural plan would give a big boost to the future of the university, but the truth was that by early 1897 Hearst's influence in the California legislature was slim, indirect, and from afar.[6] Such political power as Hearst possessed was largely kept within the confines of the university. She was not a member of the California legislature. Hearst must have been flattered by the praise, but she probably understood that leaders and politicians at the state level were the ones possessing the public political power, authority, and connections to steer the passage of the one-cent tax through the senate and assembly.

Shortly after Hearst's appointment to the board of regents, she was assigned to the Committee on Grounds and Buildings and other property as the strength of the state's economy improved. She would also begin her push for a comprehensive architectural plan to create an ideal "City of Learning" at the University of California's Berkeley campus. At about the same time, Leland Stanford "had sought the nation's best designers to create the campus that would bear his son's name." The idea was to create an overall architectural plan for Stanford University in Stanford, California, about forty miles south of San Francisco. Unlike the approach taken by the University of California, Stanford officials had refused to have architects submit designs to a jury to select a winner in an international architectural competition. Instead, they had selected Frederick Law Olmsted, a Beaux-Arts–trained architect to design the Stanford campus. No school of architecture existed at Stanford at the time that Olmsted received the commission.[7] Nonetheless, Hearst's international architectural competition aroused interest among Stanford's administration and faculty. Should Stanford hold a competition like Hearst's to benefit its university, especially since Olmsted's plan was unfinished?

The uc regents, meanwhile, approved the appointments suggested by Hearst to serve as the trustees of her international architectural competition: J. B. Reinstein, Governor James H. Budd, and William Carey Jones, a faculty member in the Department of Jurisprudence. The trustees also deposited fifty thousand dollars for the project received from Hearst. Having arranged to free Bernard Maybeck from his university duties to help with the architectural competition, Hearst then sent Maybeck and his wife, Annie, to Europe at her expense. The trip was a dream come true for the Maybecks. They sent Hearst the details of their expense account while abroad. Annie, in particular, felt concerned about the money spent and the results of the trip. She explained to Hearst: "If you feel that my expenses are not a legitimate part of the account—please tell us so frankly and we'll find some way of paying them ourselves or come home that much sooner." The Maybecks' activities abroad satisfied Hearst. They consulted with the heads of large institutions of higher education on the number and design of buildings for the ideal university. They talked with leading educators and "prominent architects, painters, sculptors, and landscape gardeners in England and Scotland, France, Germany,

Italy, Holland, Belgium, Austria, Hungary and Switzerland." Maybeck convinced distinguished architects to serve as jurors and submit design entries for Hearst's competition.[8] Hearst's decisions and actions showed the regents how serious she was about following through, in ways that would appear acceptable to both men and women, on her offer to realize her comprehensive architectural plan.

Hearst's typically balanced and deferential approach to promoting her plans for the UC campus at last convinced the board of regents to "unanimously adopt" a resolution in the spring of 1898 that officially granted Regent Hearst formal political and legal power over her comprehensive architectural plan. "Regent J. H. Budd moved that the thanks of the Board be tendered to Mrs. Hearst and that the whole matter be referred to her with power to act." Hearst now had full control over her plan and could act to construct the first building in her proposal—the George Hearst Memorial Mining Building. She was likewise granted the power to hold and supervise her international architectural competition.[9] The regents clearly possessed great confidence in Hearst, persuaded by the adept and sophisticated comportment she showed in pursing her goals that she knew what she was doing.

With the project firmly under her control and direction, Hearst began the difficult and time-consuming, but also energizing, work of bringing her entire architectural plan to life, one which she expected would help increase the enrollment of women students. The UC campus consisted of North and South Halls and a "square brick building occupied by the Engineering Departments," a library, art gallery, and Harmon Gymnasium as late as 1887. There were, in addition, several other buildings surrounded by "a straggling village clustered around the University" with "no public buildings, no paved streets, no sidewalks except rattling boards."[10] The number of women students enrolled in the 1896–97 academic year totaled 596 of the 1,498 that comprised the total student body. The total female enrollment jumped to 702 of 1,665 in 1897–98, Hearst's first academic year on the board of regents. Male students by this time were struggling with the confusion and flux they experienced in male and female roles and believed women threatened their dominance and control over the campus and beyond. This new generation of women—independent, self-reliant, confident, educated, reformers and suffragists, women involved in politics and with wage-earning jobs—seemed especially threatening.

Meanwhile, female coeds in general were outnumbered by their male counterparts, in a hostile environment controlled by men, and confronted with male animosity. As undergraduates, they also faced a body of campus laws and policies that underscored the importance of men. They confronted faculty and student conflict as well on the as yet crude and undeveloped university campus. Women students possessed no space to call their own. That meant they needed "to eat their paper-bag luncheons in a corner of the restroom in Old North Hall." Virtually no university programs, facilities, or extracurricular activities for women existed at the university before Hearst's appointment. This situation, furthermore, intensified class differences on campus. Most women found they were invisible and excluded from the mainstream of campus and American public life by the time Hearst became a regent. But with power in hand, Hearst began the work of transforming the university from a rustic, rugged appearance into a splendid and orderly university and "campus community" that included women and would rival Stanford and institutions of higher education in the East and elsewhere.[11]

The vote from Hearst's male colleagues to accept and approve her comprehensive architectural plan may have given her the confidence to reveal more broadly, and in public, the role she had in mind for the second single building in her plan, later called Hearst Hall. She was cautious and shrewd. She refused, at first, to divulge details about the second structure. But having successfully obtained the votes to give her official political and legal power over her plan, she must have felt more comfortable and at liberty to divulge to Maybeck what she really wanted to do with the second building.

She informed him of her desire to provide female students with a place to go and a space to call their own. Hearst put in place a stopgap measure to help female coeds while the second single building was under construction. She established a lounge in East Hall for them to use until Hearst Hall was completed and opened. Regent Hearst's innovative ideas would help rectify the strained, unbalanced, and unequal power relationships between female and male students on campus. But at the same time, the hall could serve to create tensions on campus because women coeds could use the building as a refuge to protect themselves and as a foundation from which to courageously challenge the dominance of men at the university.[12]

Hearst Hall, contained within the comprehensive architectural plan, was the heart of Hearst's "entering wedge" to assist uc women. The Association of Collegiate Alumnae (aca), formed in Boston in 1882 by just under twenty young female graduates from institutions of higher education, loved to use the label "an entering wedge" to describe plans to protect college and university women "from hostility and suspicions" and strengthen their position on campus. The aca was an early lobbying group. It supported "suitable and important project[s] . . . to act as an entering wedge to broaden opportunities for women everywhere." These projects could "prove to be a resoundingly successful kind of 'creative' (or coercive, depending on one's point of view) philanthropy."[13] Hearst's plan offered a dignified, respectable way to make university women visible and bring them gradually into the mainstream of campus and American life.

Hearst's strategy was designed to integrate women into the campus and then into the town of Berkeley, California, and by implication to make them a part of a new, more inclusive American social order. But it also set standards for the winning architectural design for the ideal University of California—a part of her plan that appealed to male university officials, students, and architectural critics. A reserved woman who preferred harmony over conflict, Hearst knew it was unacceptable, to men in particular, for her to appear ambitious and overly interested in power in public, so she expressed her interest in power, lofty ideals, and ambition indirectly by the standards she set for the design. It needed to be, Hearst wrote, "upon a scale commensurate with the power, the pride and the dignity of a great and glorious State." Americans, including Bernard Maybeck, anticipated that the winning design would erase, as one writer in Harper's Weekly noted, "the wretched crazy quilt of discordant buildings that disfigured the beautiful site" and "make the image of an ideal University—a noble architectural harmony." The architectural design would make the university a part of "the entire educational system of a mighty State co-ordinated into one harmonious organism." The ideal campus would consist of enough "buildings to form a small town," uplift culture, and improve the welfare of American citizens, including women, on and off campus. Hearst's criteria sent a message that a public university, of which she was a part, held the power to support and advocate progressive and egalitarian ideals and values on behalf of American citizens, particularly females, and the nation-state.[14]

Hearst's comprehensive architectural plan identified her with the state of California and reform ideals, particularly human equality, drawing attention to her, the university, and female coeds. Maybeck wrote to Hearst years later that Charles Mulford Robinson had declared that her comprehensive architectural plan started "the modern [American] movement in town planning." Robinson was a journalist, author, professor of civic design at the University of Illinois, an admired architectural critic, and a popular city planner.[15] Despite giving Hearst a prominent position in the town planning movement and highlighting the University of California, Robinson had lacked Hearst's devotion to assisting uc women and refused to acknowledge the inclusion of females in her plan. His view on her comprehensive architectural plan, nonetheless, bestowed national prominence upon Hearst and the university.

Press and university publications spread the news, laced with political overtones, around the world about Hearst's international architectural competition. One particular aspect of the contest drew a lot of attention:

architects need not be hampered by financial considerations. Designers held "absolute freedom to express their ideal of what a great University should embody" based on Regent Hearst's standards and guidelines. But not everyone was enthralled with Hearst's competition. Some argued that no prominent architects would enter because they would be working on better-paying projects. Others claimed the prizes were insufficient to induce architects to submit entries. Still others feared damage to their reputations and careers if they failed to win. Regardless of the criticism, Hearst was undaunted. She moved forward with her challenging, bold project. Harper's Weekly recognized her innovative contest as a reflection of her vaulting ambition: "There has never been anything in the history of education or of architecture quite like the competition which the University of California owes to the munificence of Mrs. Hearst."

People began to talk after the publication of the prospectus for the competition was printed in thirty-one languages. Ten thousand copies were sent, as the trustees recounted, "to every country in the world, and to every state in the Union" and "throughout the civilized world." People in places far away and unknown to her recognized the Hearst name and valued her comprehensive architectural plan, especially her international architectural competition. A student of mathematics wrote from Zurich, Switzerland, that he fielded questions repeatedly about the competition. Someone else wrote Hearst that her contest destroyed the "annoying misconception" that the University of California was Stanford University. Published reports of Hearst's activities, in addition, gave Berkeley the impetus to grow in 1900 from a small town of 13,000 inhabitants into an orderly metropolis of 40,000 by 1910.[16] The big publicity splash brought her and the university fame and prominence worldwide.

The International Competition for the Phoebe Hearst Architectural Plan centered on the male world of design and architecture. The preliminary contest opened in the United States "and all countries outside of Europe on January 1, 1898." The submissions were accepted in Europe on January 15, 1898, at noon and January 5, 1898, at noon for all other points around the world. The contest closed on July 1, 1898. Hearst traveled to Antwerp, Belgium, in the fall of 1898 for the first stage. To generate publicity, the Bürgermeister, Herr Jan Van Rijswijck, and his colleagues and their spouses, received Hearst and the international jurors—J. L. Pascal from Paris; Paul Wallott from Berlin; R. Norman Shaw from Hampstead, London; Walter Cook from New York; and J. B. Reinstein, from San Francisco, representing Hearst and the university—at City Hall. Ambitious and powerful, Van Rijswijck, made good use of Hearst's competition to build a national reputation and possibly propel himself into a better position in a larger city or into "state or imperial politics and administration." Hearst's contest generated town planning policies and civic pride. Van Rijswijck escorted Hearst to the Royal Museum of Fine Arts to look at the competition drawings on display guarded by police officers and soldiers. Hearst was present during the five days of jury deliberation. The jurors selected, deliberated, and announced eleven finalists from the one hundred and five entries received. Hearst then invited the final competitors to Berkeley, all expenses paid, to see the site before they submitted their final designs in the second stage of the competition to be held in San Francisco.

The day the drawings were open for inspection at the San Francisco Ferry Building, a newspaper reported the physical toll on Hearst: "Toward the end of the evening, the heat, the lights, the crowd, the fatigue and excitement of the culmination of her heart's desire proved too great a strain for her always frail health, and she fainted." Given American prejudices, some may have concluded that her seeming lack of stamina at this important event demonstrated that she was "unfit" for full citizenship rights, even though she sat as a voting citizen on the University of California Board of Regents. Defying the reporter's description, however, Hearst recovered quickly, in time to hold a reception and banquet in the Maple Room at the Palace Hotel in San Francisco. Attendees met and honored her jury of architects and waited eagerly for her to announce the awards of her international architectural competition.

Hearst was the only female at the event. Dressed appropriately for a woman with virtuous character and high standing, she sat at the front table with the rich Democratic San Francisco mayor James D. Phelan, Republican U.S. senator George Clement Perkins (1893–1915), and other male dignitaries. The room was filled with over ninety professional men, a reporter noted, "representing the scientific, judicial, literary and political life of the State." Mayor James Phelan presided and spoke on behalf of Phoebe A. Hearst. While the men raised their glasses to toast Hearst's international architectural competition and jurors, they also praised her personally, her health, and the Hearst scholarships to deserving young women at the University of California—surely a good sign that Hearst would be able to count on their support for other projects benefiting women, both on and off campus. After the tribute, Hearst was to announce the winner of the first prize, expected to "be a man of fame and artistic power."[17]

The competition prizes revealed how much it mattered to Hearst to raise the standards for American architecture, a field controlled by men, and how seriously she took her international competition. Prizes totaled $20,000 to encourage prestigious architects to enter her contest—a $10,000 first, $4,000 second, $3,000 third, $2,000 fourth, and $1,000 fifth prize. On the unanimous vote of her jurors, Hearst announced the first-prize winner—Henri Émile Bénard, an École des Beaux-Arts–trained architect, the winner of the 1867 Architectural Prix-de-Rome, and a prominent Parisian. His winning plan became a victory for formal architectural design. It stressed the established principles of unity, order, simplicity, and tradition over originality. His single, unified design was on a "grand scale" with "rich architectural detail." It included twenty-eight buildings harmonized with the topography. It solved the main architectural problem stemming from the difficulties posed by the natural geography of the site. His plan, moreover, reflected the harmonizing of design and nature to promote a romanticized university ideal as well as an institution of higher education national in purpose and scope.

Hearst probably continued to enjoy the celebration of the competition finale for a few more hours before segregating herself from the male crowd, as would be expected of her, and leaving at 11:00 p.m. The men would have lingered for several hours more, smoking cigars and bantering back and forth with each other, as if to emphasize that the nature of the field of architecture, political or otherwise, was still dominated by men.[18] But the social occasion in fact honored and celebrated the ideas and power that a woman, Phoebe A. Hearst, possessed to hold an international architectural competition that professionalized architecture in a field controlled by men.[19] This was no high-society affair, but an elaborate cultural and political event. Nonetheless, although notable local and state politicians, among others, were prompted to include women in their thoughts and comments for the occasion, they still refused to acknowledge Hearst's power publicly, probably because such pronouncements about women were rare and generally considered unacceptable. While Hearst graciously accepted what praise they offered for the successful conduct and execution of her design competition, her chance to enjoy the warm glow of satisfaction did not last long.

Scathing criticism of Hearst's competition came from the mouths and pens of prominent men in architecture. Louis Sullivan, father of the Chicago School of design, and local architects held unfavorable views. Sullivan mounted a blistering, bitter attack aimed at Hearst's contest. He announced that holding a fair university competition was "as false as it [was] specious and tempting." Max Junghaendel ("possibly a pseudonym for Willis Polk"), a German art critic trained at B. J. S. Cahill in England, praised Hearst as "thoroughly well-intentioned" but attacked her as "badly advised" and the winning design as "over influenced." Junghaendel reserved his strongest criticism for the scale of the design, calling it "gigantesque." He claimed the decoration was "overdone" and referred to the architectural style as "un-American." To add insult to injury, some practitioners of architecture in the surrounding area held a strong belief that local American architects should have been awarded the commissions for the university buildings. The chorus of criticism contained an international dimension too. Annoyed and dismayed with the outcome, the London Daily Mail reported that the Royal Institute of British Architects registered its disapproval because a British architect did not draw any of the architectural plans selected. The winner, after all, came from France. Despite the opposition, Hearst and her supporters relied on traditional male language, the kind used by Sullivan and Junghaendel and often published in newspapers, to respond to criticism and explain that her competition influenced the transformation of architecture into a profession in America and around the world.

Yet even Hearst held doubts about the jury's decision to award the first prize to Bénard, in part because he had refused to visit the university site before submitting his final design.[20] Lacking formal training and expertise in architecture and concerned about conducting herself properly, especially in public, Hearst had distanced herself from the internal politics of the competition and deferred to architectural experts on the jury to select the winner. And despite her initiation, guidance, and funding of the event, she kept to herself any criticism and doubts she may have had about the jury proceedings and their selection of the winner, Bénard, in an effort to be pleasing and harmonious.

Despite her efforts, harmony was difficult to achieve because Hearst was necessarily drawn into an international intellectual and political debate over the criticism directed at her competition and the selected winner. Junghaendel's unfavorable comments took direct aim at Hearst. He held her, rather than the male jurors, responsible for awarding the first prize to Bénard since her name was attached to the contest and she directed it. Most, though, were unaware of the control Hearst possessed over her competition, especially behind the scenes. Hearst considered Junghaendel's attacks to be unfair. Understanding the power of the press, she transformed her moral indignation into a cold-blooded exertion of power to persuade the critics of their misguided views. She gave a sharp, angry, and defensive reply, published in the Bulletin [San Francisco], rather than her son's newspaper, the San Francisco Examiner. The Bulletin reported that Hearst argued: "It is not hard to conceive that there are narrow critics who find more gratification, perhaps more pay in enlarging on petty defects rather than in dwelling on the vast aggregate or noble and quickening elements of a great work." She reminded those who found fault with her competition that the process had been fair and that professional architects and others had responded favorably to Bénard's design. She also pointed out that "the competition both in its general outline from start to finish and in the details has been conducted in accordance with the very best obtainable advice, the most just methods, the most intelligent suggestions, and I am entirely satisfied with the result."[21]

It is clear that Hearst felt confident enough in her knowledge to set aside propriety and insert herself into a public debate. Mindful of what might happen to her political agenda for university women, as well as the realization of Hearst Hall, if she neglected to defend her position, she threw herself into architectural competition politics to protect the Hearst name, reputation, and the competition itself. But she needed to tackle the problems with Bénard first, even as she handled international architectural politics.

Did Bénard have difficulty doing what such a powerful woman as Hearst wanted him to do? After he received the Hearst prize, he had offended Hearst because, as she wrote to Republican governor Henry T. Gage: "Monsieur Bénard's plans were made without his having visited the site, or being acquainted with the innumerable conditions affecting the intellectual and material growth of the University." Hearst and the architectural plan trustees invited Bénard, after the first prize had been announced, to visit the Berkeley site to "to confer with them and consider the necessary modification in his designs." He arrived in Berkeley and gathered the information he needed. He then "returned to Paris, there to elaborate on his plan" because he thought he could work better abroad with fewer "distractions," William Carey Jones wrote, rather than remain in Berkeley to alter his sketches to fit the sight and submit his final design.[22] Bénard's decisions and actions fell short of soothing Hearst's ruffled feathers.

Hearst made her unhappiness with Bénard known to J. L. Pascal, head of her competition jury. Upset at Bénard's refusal to do what she wanted, she focused her criticism on his character flaws, especially his penchant for irrationality, rather than his abilities as an architect, which she seemed to mention in passing. She thought Bénard to be "an extremely able architect, with much artistic feeling, but he is a very difficult man to deal with. Undoubtedly he is, as you remark embittered and irritable, and above all suspicious which has been the cause of much friction between him and the Trustees, whom moreover he insulted with his insinuations," she explained to Pascal. She added: "Mr. Bénard's chief idea seems to be that the Trustees of the University and I are trying to impose upon him; than which there is nothing further from our intentions, but this makes it extremely difficult if not impossible to work harmoniously together, which is the first condition necessary to bring our plans to successful issue." She doubted he could take on "the responsibility of such a task." Bénard got too excited, refused to "listen to argument and has on several occasions been unfair in relying upon . . . outsiders . . . instead of trusting in the good faith of the Regents, Trustees and myself," she explained. A nasty, unpleasant, and rigid man, from Hearst's perspective, Bénard "has always point blank refused to take up his residence in California, even if the execution of some of the buildings should be entrusted to him," she wrote. She thought "he might work serious injury to the . . . University," including women students. Hearst argued that "tact" and "genius" were needed to work together for the project to be completed successfully.

Pascal diplomatically defended Bénard and argued he should be hired to bring his design to life. The regents, meanwhile, decided to build the university president's house first and, "soon after," the construction of the George Hearst Memorial Mining Building could begin. The erection of the administration building, auditorium, library, and gymnasium would follow as soon as the money became available. People expected the entire university design to be completed "within twenty years."[23] But Hearst thought the construction of the first building in her comprehensive architectural plan, later called the George Hearst Memorial Mining Building, might not be finished unless she moved quickly to replace Bénard with an architect she liked and one who could do the job to her satisfaction. It would be almost impossible to construct Hearst Hall if she failed to complete the first building in her comprehensive architectural plan.

Hearst acted decisively and quickly to exert her power as a regent, hiring another architect—John Galen Howard of New York—to modify Bénard's design and construct the George Hearst Memorial Mining Building. University president Benjamin Ide Wheeler, who by then had replaced Martin Kellogg in the position, supported her decision. As Wheeler wrote her: "I received your telegram that you had arranged with Mr. Howard to plan your building. . . . Let me know your wishes in regard to him [Howard] and they shall be carried out." Wheeler continued: "So far as I know, there is no obligation, legal or moral, binding us to further regard Mr. Bénard in the matter." Hearst, as she contemplated what to do about Howard, tried to shield herself from criticism, especially regarding money matters. She clarified her economic commitment to fit the reality. She regretted the rumor abroad "that I would bear all charges of rebuilding the whole University, which as you know," she wrote Pascal, "is not the case, as I have only donated the plans and the mining building" (Hearst Hall was yet to be built).

Pascal and Bénard were "unable to understand" Hearst's decision to hire Howard. Bernard Maybeck, who had been an instructor of architecture at the university since late 1898, supported Hearst as well as Bénard to a point. "As I understand it, the U.C. has accepted Bénard's plan and the program then arranges between the University and the Architect it does not say Mrs. Hearst and the Architect. From this, I conclude that Mrs. Hearst is free to donate anything she wishes in any way she likes and the

6. George Hearst Memorial Mining Building, south façade, ca. 1914. UARCPIC 10S:11. Courtesy of the Bancroft Library, University of California, Berkeley.

University is free to choose Mr. Bénard for any building." Maybeck hoped that Bénard could be given "something to carry out, say the Gymnasium," he wrote Hearst. Hearst had other ideas. She had previously donated to the university prized books marked by unusual quality, merit, and appeal on architecture and antiquities. Now Hearst came up with another new idea, as early as December of 1898, of creating a school of architecture "as good as any in the world," according to Regent Reinstein. It was Hearst's "desire to establish at Berkeley a school of architecture" and her "thought that its direction might well be undertaken by the architect in charge of the execution of the buildings themselves," John Galen Howard wrote in the midst of discussions to hire him at the dawn of the new century. The fact that Hearst originated the idea raised expectations that a uc school of architecture would grow and expand.[24]

Hearst's original idea to create a uc school of architecture appealed to Howard for obvious reasons, while others wondered when the construction of the first buildings of the architectural plan would begin. Howard would have control over revising Bénard's original design to better fit the needs of Hearst and the university. He also would be able to design the George Hearst Memorial Mining Building at the same time that he assumed and held an academic position that would advance his professional career and status in the field of architecture. Hearst and President Wheeler arranged for Howard to get a double appointment as the supervising architect on Hearst's project and as a professor of architecture. Hearst paid Howard's salary. Pascal appealed to Wheeler to see the error of Hearst's ways in hiring Howard. But to no avail. Hearst's rhetorical power was up to the task. She possessed the argument she needed to handle Pascal. As she put it: "I never promised Mr. Bénard the supervision of my building and . . . could not promise anything to that effect."

Caroline Severance, meanwhile, wondered when the winning international architectural design, including the mining building, would be erected. Hearst lamented her situation. She responded, "I fear it will be many years before any of the more highly ornamented structures go up. The gymnasium is the building calling for the most decoration in sculpture, etc., but as it is also one of the costliest of the buildings, we have no idea when an offer will be received to erect it. With that of course I shall have nothing to do except that as a Regent I shall have one vote."[25] Used to getting what she wanted from others, especially employees, Hearst felt powerless with only one vote to move the project forward. She needed support from the other regents. So she waited patiently while moving ahead with her ideas for benefiting uc women.

First she would attend to gaining approval to build Hearst Hall. A rich woman with fifteen household employees, Hearst understood that "academic qualifications are to cultural capital what money is to economic capital." Controlling plenty of money had contributed to her self-assurance and her success in amassing cultural capital before she became a regent. But she grew up in a generation of women denied opportunities to get a higher education and so she lacked the academic qualifications possessed by her male colleagues on the board of regents. Hearst did the next best thing. She took the considerable resources that she had used to build cultural capital, and her political experiences in nonpartisan voluntary association politics, and turned them into academic capital by helping "young women" strive "for the higher education closed to her and which she so ardently desired," a San Francisco newspaper noted. She acquainted herself with and studied female coeds who were "far from home and struggling against adverse circumstances," the *San Francisco Chronicle* reported. Eventually, she felt ready to reveal to the general public, especially men, her specific thoughts about the second building in her plan—Hearst Hall.

She intended the hall to be a home away from home, and more, for women. She expected it to be a hospitable, comfortable environment and space for "rich and poor" female coeds to come together to enjoy a "social life" and a place they could call their own. While she had asked Howard to locate the mining building in "the exact site" she desired, she requested that Hearst Hall be built in parts so it could be moved elsewhere on campus, as needed. The completion of Hearst Hall, and the establishment of her scholarships explicitly to benefit university women, made Hearst the first person to respond to the calls of university presidents to construct buildings to address the needs of female students on campus. Hearst took these appeals one step further by taking into account specifically the moral, physical, and spiritual needs of uc women.[26] Hearst's plan to benefit female coeds, and the university at the same time, made sense to the regents. Had Hearst's approach focused only on benefits for women, it would likely have been more difficult, if not impossible, for her to persuade the regents to accept her comprehensive architectural plan.

Hearst's balanced plan, her patience, and her skill paid off. The board of trustees approved and accepted Hearst's architectural plan in late 1900. It included Hearst Hall. The regents officially hired Howard in December of 1901 to properly place "the mining building, but all other structures contemplated in said [Hearst architectural] plan, and to make necessary revisions and changes in said plan for those purposes." Julia Morgan, an 1895 graduate from the uc Engineering Department, "drafted for" the George Hearst Memorial Mining Building "during her first months with Howard." Howard, after the work was completed, was required to present "important modification of the Bénard plan" to the Hearst jury for approval. The cornerstone of the mining building was laid in November of 1902. The final price tag for the mining building reached $1,065,000. But Hearst believed she had made the right decision to hire Howard, and others agreed. Hearst knew clearly her top political priority—to gain acceptance and approval from uc regents for a plan that included benefits for women. The official power she exerted confidently opened "a new era for the University," a reporter declared, that made women a part of the order of things in the university and in America.[27]

Hearst borrowed from principles taught at L'École des Beaux-Arts to formulate guidelines for Maybeck in sketching a design for her hall. Maybeck claimed, according to one writer, that his original sketch was "miserable." But he produced an exciting, bold, and unorthodox design for Hearst's approval. Maybeck was assisted by Julia Morgan. The design that flowed from Maybeck's pencil, pen, and ink brimmed with the power of myth and symbolism—religious and practical. A dramatic, enchanting exterior arch on the front of the building was reminiscent of a European Gothic cathedral and reflected Hearst's devotion to universal religious principles. It conveyed a sense of Christian idealism and an inspirational quality that gave the stamp of religious approval to what Hearst wanted

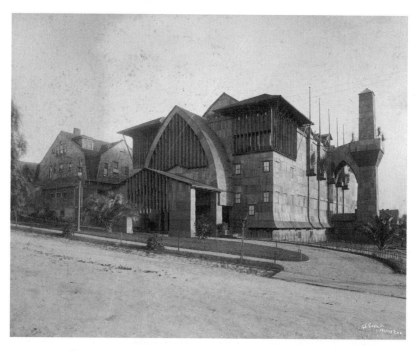

7. Hearst Hall, 1899, with buttress and chimney. UARCPIC 1000A:1. Courtesy of the Bancroft Library, University of California, Berkeley.

the building to convey. But the design also expressed Hearst's political values. The interior looked like one big tastefully furnished living room. It beckoned female students to enjoy the comforts of an orderly home, while the exterior was industrial looking and evoked thoughts of a factory.

The building communicated Hearst's conviction that women seeking independence, money, and economic power were not engaged in any kind of sacrilegious behavior or activity. Considered as a coherent whole, the hall suggested Hearst's personal interests in women's domestic and economic activities regardless of class, within or outside the home, or on or off campus. It expressed her conviction that women's work and activities were as valuable and as important as men's—valuable enough for Americans, particularly men of good moral character, to approve of

8. Inside Hearst Hall, 1899 (looks like a living room). UARCPIC 1000A:2(a). Courtesy of the Bancroft Library, University of California, Berkeley.

women's work, whether paid or unpaid. The completed structure reflected Hearst's understanding of the link between her innovative, progressive reform ideas and values, expressed by Maybeck's architectural design, and women's economic rights.[28] The entire hall represented Hearst's feminine, unaggressive way of putting people at ease about her assertiveness, her exercise of power, and especially her right to vote and her ability to lobby the regents. The hall was a shrewd way for Regent Hearst to convey her intention to help women advance socially, culturally, economically, and politically, as well as to make them visible on and off campus.

To better supervise construction of the hall, Hearst rented Pennoyer House on Piedmont Avenue and Channing Way. Pennoyer House was "one of the largest homes" in Berkeley and next door to the site. Living so near her construction project gave her the chance to get to know students, faculty, and the university better. Moving into the house also helped her be an efficient regent and supervisor. Being in close proximity, she could make sure the structure was built in accordance with her guidelines and specifications. Hearst never intended to use the house for purely social functions, but she and her sumptuous-looking home must have seemed rather intimidating at first to many of the young female students. If invited to visit Pennoyer House, said one young woman, "I'll send regrets and stay at home and regret that I had nothing to wear." Hearst responded, with "a grieved look" on her face, "If the girls think that I am coming for social functions and to give formal parties [at the Pennoyer House], they are much mistaken. The girl who has only one print dress will be the oftenest in my home," a reporter quoted Hearst as saying. Issues of class were on Hearst's mind. Hearst planned to bring women of lesser means to her home for more useful and meaningful purposes than social affairs. She intended the hall to be a place where all students could come together, men as well as women and students of all classes, while better preparing young women to involve themselves in university activities, including politics. "It will be those who need the most who will get the most," Hearst added.[29] Using her power to finish the project and carry out her political agenda was never far from her mind.

Phoebe Hearst also wanted Hearst Hall to be a place to help women, especially young ones of lesser means, become fit. Her objective was to have the hall built and then "moved to the University grounds" and "used as a temporary gymnasium for women." Only men could use the uc Harmon Gymnasium at the time. University policy allowed female coeds into the gym only three times a week at times when men were nowhere to be found. Hearst instructed Maybeck to include in the hall design a gymnasium for women—a fitting place for female coeds to breathe new spirit, energy, and courage into themselves and their campus life.

Hearst was fifty-nine years old when the dedication of Hearst Hall took place in the women's gymnasium upstairs in the three-story building, on

February 9, 1901. Helen P. Sanborn, the married daughter of Margaret Peck, spoke on Hearst's behalf at the ceremony because Hearst was in Washington DC holding a musicale for two hundred diplomatic and public officials. The construction of Hearst Hall cost almost twenty-nine thousand dollars—a much smaller sum than she spent on the George Hearst Memorial Mining Building to honor her deceased husband. Hearst had also spent eleven thousand dollars for the land on which to build the hall and five to six thousand dollars to move it to a location next to the University. The building became a space for coed "college affairs," meetings, musicales, dinner parties, cultural entertainments, and the center of life for women students. Women ate lunch there, met "committees, and . . . held meetings . . . and college affairs innumerable," a uc report declared.

As she had intended, the student activities in Hearst Hall brought female and male coeds together, strengthening connections between the Associated Students and the Associated Women Students of the University of California.[30] The small sum she spent on Hearst Hall, compared to what was spent on the mining building, appeared to send a message that her top priority was to construct the mining building rather than Hearst Hall. But spending more money on a memorial was an acceptable way for her to meet American expectations that widows should honor their deceased husbands and, at the same time, downplay her top political priority—to benefit female coeds, to gain acceptance for women on and off the campus, and garner acceptance and approval of the fact that she was a woman with considerable power.

Hearst used her hall to stand for and express, realistically and symbolically, what she would not or could not say in public about her power and progressive reform politics. Her building provided female coeds with a base on campus to challenge men for control of uc—a male bastion of higher coeducation. It showed Hearst's proven power as a uc regent to turn her money into symbolic academic capital—"a transformed and thereby disguised form of physical 'economic' capital." This form of capital "con-

9. Inside Hearst Hall gym, ca. 1902. UARCPIC 10A:2(a). Courtesy of the Bancroft Library, University of California, Berkeley.

ceals the fact that it originates in 'material' forms of capital," one scholar wrote. She used her symbolic academic capital, her status, "prestige, and renown attached to" her family name, for purposeful and meaningful political ends that produced effects, especially to benefit women, and serve as "the source of its effects."[31]

The money and resources put into Hearst Hall sent a message in a subtle and acceptable way that Hearst possessed and exerted substantial power, which she wielded to establish a strong foundation for women to become politically active and obtain their own power on or off campus. Her approach and accomplishments helped her bridge the gap between herself and women of a younger generation. Nonetheless, the practical and symbolic meaning of Hearst Hall fell short of giving other women, older or younger, much insight into just how she managed to obtain the support and approval of university men in accomplishing her goals.

Hearst told Maybeck to design, and the contractor to build, Hearst Hall in parts, to be reassembled on campus. Her directive was perhaps a recognition that people were living in a fragmented society in a new industrial age. Hearst moved the structure to College Avenue and onto the university grounds in the summer of 1901. It was reassembled there into a unified, whole structure. The building made "a silent but unremitting influence upon those who [passed] in and out their doors," an editorial in the University of California Magazine noted.

Hearst Hall inspired hope and raised expectations among women coeds who saw the building or walked through its portals. Female students loved the hall. As one put it: "Hearst Hall means so much to most of us college women. It is the one place that we may call our own; where our comforts as well as our needs are cared for, even to the smallest details." The hall, another wrote Hearst, "is another privilege which we owe to you. To many girls college life would mean nothing at all without it." The hall encouraged women to obtain a "college education," one female coed wrote, and gave them hope that they could survive the university experience and graduate, to make their dreams and ambitions, political or otherwise, come true. Once women gained admittance to the university, they visited the hall to get what they needed. In Hearst's home away from home, they learned how to build networks, support each other, and become fit enough to jump into campus social, cultural, and political activities that challenged the dominant power of men and helped make them a permanent part of the university.[32] The hall reflected Hearst's aspiration that a harmonious whole university and a new American order of society could be created that fully included women.

By the time the George Hearst Memorial Mining Building and Hearst Hall were completed, Regent Phoebe Hearst had overseen, managed, and spent more than $200,000 for her International Architectural Competition and then another $1,105,000, by 1899, for construction of the two buildings. She also paid for additional costs. Aware of the crucial role Hearst had played in making her architectural plan come to life, Jacob Reinstein showed respect for the University of California's major early benefactor. He lavished compliments on Hearst for her skillful use of power in public—a rare gesture for a man. She showed "a mastery of the innumerable details," he remarked. She also possessed "a complete knowledge of its status at every point" and the "wisdom and judgment" to make it successful, he noted.[33] Hearst's effective use of power showed men like Reinstein that she possessed enough academic capital to be awarded the same kind of recognition and praise the male regents received for their achievements in higher education.

Hearst's success brought her acclaim not only from male academics but from Charles Mulford Robinson. Robinson too praised Hearst in public. The City Beautiful "movement's first permanent conquest in the United States was probably in the University of California," according to Robinson.[34] Hearst's accomplishments placed her on the cusp of the City Beautiful movement from the design of single structures, such as the George Hearst Memorial Mining Building and Hearst Hall, to an overall conception of a comprehensive architectural plan.

Professional architects and city leaders from around the world credited Hearst with keen vision, creative genius, and wisdom. President Kellogg touted her as a savior of the University of California. "Honors were heaped upon" Hearst "when she reached Paris," Brooks wrote, on her way to Antwerp. Hearst's name was recognized in Zurich, London, and as far away as Egypt. She set new high standards and a model for future competitions. She made contests between architectural rivals popular. Her proud son, William, wrote her from Cairo that "everybody asks about you." Her triumphs led other institutions of higher education to mount architectural competitions to match her vision and plan for an ideal university. Harvard, Yale, Columbia, and Princeton Universities, the University of Pennsylvania, the United States Military Academy West Point, Washington University in St. Louis, Carnegie Technical Schools in Pittsburgh (now Carnegie Mellon University), the University of Minnesota, and Western University of Pennsylvania, as well as various cities, publicized the accomplishments of Hearst's architectural plan or held similar competitions that aroused excitement and support for civic art and cultural achievements. A photograph of Hearst was distributed widely. The competition designs were published and exhibited in various cities "much to the interest and benefit of the profession," the president of the Architectural League of America wrote. Ernest Flagg, the first architect chosen to design Hearst's National Cathedral School for Girls, wrote Hearst: "You have done much for the cause of American art and [for] that you deserve the thanks of the whole profession."

At a gathering of professional architects in Washington DC, in December 1900, to celebrate the one hundredth anniversary of the establishment of the nation's capital, Glenn Brown, secretary of the American Institute of Architects, displayed the Phoebe A. Hearst International Architectural Competition design entries to arouse strong support for a similar artistic comprehensive design for the federal city. The exhibit helped inspire federal government officials, two years later, to appoint Daniel H. Burnham; Charles F. McKim, a New York architect; Frederick Law Olmstead Jr., son of the "nation's foremost landscape architect"; and Augustus Saint-Gaudens, a prominent sculptor, to the Senate Park Commission headed by Senator James McMillan of Michigan, to create a general design for the city of Washington. The uc Board of Regents, meanwhile, formally adopted Hearst's completed, permanent architectural plan in 1908, after the construction of the first two buildings in her plan were finished.[35]

Hearst's influence as a powerful and capable woman at the University of California would soon be extended to the long overdue consideration of women as faculty members. University president Martin Kellogg noted that "the policy of the Board has been to appoint no women on the teaching staff. Since the coming of Mrs. Hearst into the Board of Regents, the question has been often asked, Why not allow women a representation in the Faculty?"[36] Men had been allowed to use the gymnasium for, and take physical education classes separately from, women for years. That situation had contributed to the development of mistrust and resentment between the sexes in the field of physical education, as well as on the campus in general. In 1888 university policy had prescribed "five half hours" per week of physical exercise for men. The director of the Physical Culture Department, Dr. Frank H. Payne, a physician, thoroughly examined every male undergraduate to determine if their physical condition was sufficient to engage in physical exercise in the Harmon Gymnasium. It was not recommended that women be authorized to use the gymnasium, according to physician Mary B. Ritter,—a reformer and member of the Pacific Coast branch of the national YWCA and the State Federation of Women's Clubs—because men thought it would damage women's happiness and physical health. As Ritter put it, "I sometimes felt as if the masculine powers-that-be thought that women were made of glass and might break to pieces if they fell down."

Hearst and UC women students challenged this view. They took steps to establish, develop, and control a female physical education program within the university environment but separate from the men's physical education program. They asked the gymnastics instructor if they could use the gymnasium on a permanent, regular basis. He responded, "Of course you have a right to part time in the gymnasium and I would be willing to give you one hour a week" but only after the boys left "at five o'clock." The gym instructor added, according to Ritter, "But I could not possibly admit anyone to the ["gym"] class without a medical examination and there is no money for that."[37] His view spoke to male fears about the increase in number of female college and university students.

Americans at the time, especially men, grew anxious about women demanding entrance into college and universities. Earlier, critics of female higher education had drawn on Dr. Edward H. Clarke's *Sex in Education*, published in 1873, to justify restricting the kind of education women could receive. Clarke was an emeritus professor of Harvard Medical School. He argued for "male" and "female" curricula to "educate a man for manhood, a woman for womanhood, both for humanity. In this lies the hope of the race," he wrote. In his popular book that went through over a dozen printings, he championed the notion that if women were to receive the same education as men, it would endanger their health and reproductive systems. Severe consequences would occur: "neuralgia, uterine disease, hysteria, and other derangements of the nervous system." Educating women in institutions of higher education, Clarke argued, would weaken women's ability to bear children and undermine national efforts to protect against a decline in marriage and birthrates.[38]

Hearst, University of California reformers, and female students and college graduates at the turn of the century all challenged Clarke's and traditional nineteenth-century medical and biological views. American intellectuals who promoted secularism to achieve moral improvement were speaking up, and opposition to female physicians was on the decline. This trend occurred at a time when Hearst and many other Americans were substituting science for religion. Views describing women as frail, delicate, physically inferior and, therefore, "unfit" and not entitled to the same education as men and full citizenship rights were becoming passé. To disprove cautionary advice that restricted girls and women, Hearst and other supporters allied themselves with social scientists who saw social problems as moral problems. These social science advocates promoted engaging in political reform activities to improve health and make society better. Hearst's alliance with these ideas and reform activities inspired uc women.

Familiar with what Hearst had already managed to accomplish for them, women students sought her advice in presenting a petition to the board of regents. A document was circulated demanding that the university hire a physician both to serve as a lecturer in the Physical Culture Department and to perform medical examinations so female coeds could use Harmon Gymnasium. If they passed the physical exam, enrolled women would be able to get athletic exercise and gain some autonomy while they proved their sex to be "fit" for, and worthy of, the same subject matter and knowledge men received in classes, and with full citizenship rights as well.[39] Men held rights and privileges to exercise and attend gym classes on a permanent, regular basis. So why not challenge traditional scientific views, especially about females, and allow women the same rights and privileges?

Hearst and uc female students joined medical societies and educational reformers, at the end of the nineteenth century and into the next, who were pushing officials at institutions of higher education to adopt physical culture as part of the curriculum. The establishment of a class in the Department of Physical Culture could become a way to educate students about sex, sexuality, and prostitution. Instruction would address fears that dancing led to "uncontrolled sexual activity" and to teach coeds about the dangers of venereal diseases. The university, though, would need someone on the faculty to teach these classes and to examine female students. The male instructor of gymnastics did not count "on feminine determination," according to Dr. Ritter. Knowing that a medical examination was required for male students before they could use the gym, sometime in 1888 or 1889 female students had contacted Ritter to ask "if I would be willing to make the medical examinations without pay," Ritter wrote. She agreed. The male gymnasium instructor granted Ritter the use of an examining room in the Harmon Gymnasium where students discussed with her "their ills of body, mind or 'hearts.'"

The Pacific Branch of the Association of Collegiate Alumnae and women students planned to seek Hearst's help in getting a permanent appointment for a woman physician as a medical examiner sometime during the first half of 1898. Ritter was the top candidate for the official job. But deciding that Hearst's involvement could be crucial to their cause, the association postponed further action until after she was due to return from a trip, sometime in the summer of 1899.[40] In their estimation, Hearst might be the only woman they could turn to for advice on how to lobby the male regents.

Hearst's trip in the summer of 1899 was not the only obstacle facing the students and women alumnae in their quest to have the university hire a female medical examiner. Presidential politics at the University of California would also delay the realization of their plans. Earlier that year, serving UC president Martin Kellogg had decided that it would be in the best interest of the institution that he resign so that a younger man could assume the reins of power and leadership. Kellogg's resignation announcement made most university matters even more complex because he added his name to what had become a quick succession of university presidents. The rapid series of resignations had contributed to the institution's instability and threatened its chances of survival. The selection of presidents also exacerbated tensions and conflict. Political and class struggle erupted over the role of the university and the board of regents. University officials argued about money, institutional autonomy, cheating and hazing, and the pranks and hostile behavior of male coeds. Faculty and administrators tried to control the university's decline in fortunes. The board of regents had created a committee on the selection of a university president about six months before, in the midst of the university crisis. Governor Budd named Hearst to the committee to select a new president, believing that she possessed the essential capital, academic or otherwise, for the job. He and other state officials relied on her to help stabilize the institution and its finances.

With Hearst on the new committee were the California governor, Henry Gage; the speaker of the assembly; President Martin Kellogg; and Regents Jacob B. Reinstein, Arthur Rodgers, James H. Budd, and Andrew Hallidie. The time it took for the regents to make a decision on a new president became "wearisome and wearing," according to William Carey Jones. To speed the process along, Jones and some of Hearst's female friends lobbied her to consider Professor Jones as well as Benjamin Ide Wheeler, the son of a minister, for the university presidency. Wheeler had received a doctorate from the University of Heidelberg in 1885, and taught Greek and Comparative Philology at Cornell University from 1888 to 1899.

Wheeler visited California at the invitation of the regents in March 1899. While Hearst was enjoying a visit to Paris, the board of regents voted eleven to three, on June 16, 1899, to replace Kellogg and make Wheeler the new university president with a salary of $10,000 per year.[41]

Wheeler informed the regents, as Hearst was traveling from Paris to New York, that he wanted certain conditions met before he accepted the presidency. He asked that the president "be in fact as in theory the sole organ of communication between Faculty & Regents" to unify the campus and move the university toward greater prominence. That meant he wanted "sole initiative in appointments and removals of professors and other teachers and in matters affecting salary."[42] Wheeler knew how important Hearst and her gifts, ideas, and activities were to improving and securing a bright future for the university. He thought "Hearst was the University's greatest benefactor" and "believed in the best things." She was "gifted not only with exquisite taste, but with a singularly clear and powerful mind," he wrote. Wheeler knew Hearst's architectural plan had aroused interest in the East as well as among university men. As he explained to Hearst in grandiose style: "You are doing one of the wisest and noblest things ever undertaken in the interest of human uplifting." Knowing it would be a tactical mistake politically to accept his new post without getting Hearst's support and approval, Wheeler took the first step in forging a power-working relationship with Regent Hearst. As he explained: "I shall first see Mrs. Hearst in New York if an interview can be arranged on her arrival from Europe and learn whether she cordially approves of my appointment and seek to gain a definite idea of her purposes regarding the endowment and equipment of the institution."

Wheeler met with Hearst in June of 1899 in New York. Hearst, who liked Wheeler, must have been flattered by his compliments and attention.[43] But she was faced with a fait accompli. Her fellow regents had already voted to approve the new president while she was gone. So how could she refuse Wheeler's request to support his appointment, or oppose it? Male university officials, it appeared, were happy to support Hearst's exercising considerable political power when she enhanced the university's reputation, helped the institution survive financially, and saved the university money and time in providing for women. But when she was not actively supplying resources that worked to the advantage of the regents, especially financially, some university officials, perhaps unsure whether Hearst would support or oppose Wheeler, had relegated her to a marginal role. On this occasion, Hearst accepted her peripheral role and refrained from criticizing university officials.

But Hearst's decision not to make a fuss gave some state politicians license to go even further and end the term of the only female regent. Three days after meeting Hearst in New York, Wheeler sent a written copy of a telegram to the regents: "Saw Mrs. Hearst. She agrees with me entirely desires acceptance." But California Republican governor Henry T. Gage, meanwhile, had withdrawn all of the regent appointments made by the previous governor, Democrat James H. Budd, including Hearst's. But other state officials were intent on rewarding Hearst for her accomplishments and for backing Wheeler as president. There was such an outcry from Democrats, some Republicans, and supporters of the university to the withdrawal of Hearst's name that Gage reappointed her to the unexpired term of J. West Martin, ending on March 1, 1914. Hearst's colleagues, with her in attendance, officially approved her reappointment at the same meeting as they adopted the conditions Wheeler set forth to accept the presidency. Wheeler assumed his new post on October 1, 1899. His official inauguration took place on October 25.[44] The new era for the university began formally and officially on the day of Wheeler's inauguration. Wheeler and Hearst shared and exerted power together, as well as independently, in academic politics for approximately the next twenty years. It was now up to the new president to take on the request from female students to hire a female medical examiner while Hearst began a new term as regent.

Talks with Hearst subsequent to her reappointment led to female coeds joining health reformers in an effort to take "responsibility for their own health" by presenting to the board of trustees their petition to hire a female medical examiner for the university. Wheeler responded favorably to the petition. He approved the permanent appointment of Dr. Mary B. Ritter as medical examiner for female coeds and as a lecturer in hygiene in the Department of Physical Culture on August 8, 1899. Ritter's appointment was made shortly after Hearst offered the newly elected university president her support and before his official inauguration as president. Hearst made possible "the permanent position of a woman medical examiner in the University," according to Ritter. She leveraged her power and supported the political maneuverings of female coeds to get Ritter hired. Ritter became the first female faculty member with an academic title and a salary, albeit a part-time job paid by Hearst, at the University of California.

Ritter's job eventually turned into a full-time appointment. Ritter examined female coeds so they could use the gymnasium in Hearst Hall. She also gave lectures on "home sanitation as well as personal hygiene, which was largely physiology," Dr. Ritter noted. Hearst, moreover, placed the supervision of the women's gymnasium in Ritter's hands and paid the salary of Ritter's assistant in hygiene, Dr. Alice Robertson. Ritter and Robertson taught a laboratory course. But Ritter struggled with being the first permanent woman faculty member: "I have always felt that I was considered a sort of pariah in the University," she wrote.[45] The timing of Hearst's proposal to hire Ritter was crucial in convincing President Wheeler to make the appointment at a time when the university was in financial straits and transition. Hearst's balanced strategy, which intertwined her typically deferential comportment with political aims that were both assertive and courageous, worked to her advantage and the benefit of uc women.

Regent Hearst and President Wheeler got along so well with each other that in early 1901 Wheeler announced that at the start of 1902 all women would be required to take physical culture and gymnastic classes five times per week. Why? Because, Wheeler wrote Hearst, "This is your intention and wish; and that is as it should be." Ritter's appointment, in essence, made her the "first Dean of Women in fact if not in title," President Robert

Gordon Sproul said in a tribute to Ritter upon "the conferring . . . [of] the Honorary Degree of ll.d" on Ritter some years later. Ritter's appointment set a precedent to hire, in 1904, the first full-fledged, tenure-track female faculty member, a lecturer in sociology, Jessica Blanche Peixotto. Two years later, the first dean of women, Lucy Sprague, was hired despite her being, as one scholar noted, "insecure about her lack of training."[46] Female coeds were so overjoyed with Hearst's accomplishments for women at uc that they thought the first female regent to be "the best friend the University women have ever had" and suggested that a permanent monument be erected to her.[47]

On yet another front, the number of poor and working-class women seeking admittance to colleges and universities had been steadily growing by the 1880s and 1890s. Educated female college and university graduates could expect to earn money after graduation to purchase products and services in the open marketplace, provided they were fortunate enough to gain admittance to college and survive the experience. Not all women, though, possessed the good fortune to come from families with the economic means to pay for their higher education. Amanda Hicks addressed this challenge, coming up with a way for young women to become self-supporting to pay for a university education. Hicks's approach meshed with Hearst's political agenda, and Hicks would need to collaborate with Hearst to make her idea to help college-bound women economically a reality.[48]

In June of 1900, Hearst offered financial backing to establish the Hearst Domestic Industries (HDI) to give young working-class and poor women the opportunity to earn money to put themselves through college. Sewing, in the industrial age, was one task women performed at home that could then shift to paid work outside the domestic realm, and it was "organized according to profit-making imperatives." HDI women learned to sew and sell embroidered needlework products to earn money to use for school. Hicks acted as Hearst's representative. Hearst gave Hicks the financial means to secure a house on Haste Street. Hearst wanted to create a hospitable, comfortable environment in which women could live and be protected and safe while they made profits to attend the university. Hearst set the qualifications for women who wanted admittance into HDI: "good moral character" and "need of self-help," particularly economic need.[49] The HDI may have been the first, and possibly the only, program in America to provide women without the economic means a way to earn money to pay for a university education.

The way Hearst exerted power over, and through, the HDI became a double-edged sword, however. Hearst paid HDI women twenty cents an hour to learn traditional domestic skills to make and sell products. But they were still dependent on Hearst for the finances they needed to survive and go to college. Women who fell short of Hearst's standards for admission found it difficult, even impossible, to get the money needed to obtain the rights and privileges of a university graduate with a bachelor's degree. Moreover, although most male inventors of new technologies "drew little distinction between labor performed by professionals and labor performed in the home," HDI women demonstrated a bridge between the two. Unfortunately, HDI workers experienced competition with other female seamstresses in the area and also with home sewers who made their own clothes. HDI needlework was at such a high level, some claimed, that they reduced the Berkeley dressmaker trade by half. Frightened by the competition that had "diminished" their "trade at least fifty per cent," as well as by the loss of their jobs, over a thousand Berkeley dressmakers organized a mass protest meeting to voice their displeasure with the HDI "upstart invaders of our rights." Emotions ran so high and feelings so deep that there was talk of a possible riot and raid on the HDI building.[50] While Hearst had indeed given college-bound women a chance to gain a measure of independence, self-support, and upward mobility, she had unwittingly created tension between ambitious working-class and poor female applicants and HDI needleworkers, who were themselves in competition with other sewers to make and sell products.

But what about other women who wanted to go to the university and the obstacles they faced? Even if they could afford to attend, how would they handle the daunting task of finding lodging? It would be almost impossible to attend classes, let alone graduate, if a student was unable to find a place to live. University administrators and faculty offered uc women virtually no aid. There were no dormitories at the university, and no places were available for females to live on campus. Men had solved the housing problem by organizing and using an "old boy network"—national fraternities and residence clubs—and by persuading so-called mixed boardinghouse owners, or managers of these houses near the university, to accept them. Boardinghouses, in reality, often rented only to men. Because of prejudice and exclusion, women who needed housing found it almost impossible to get a place to live close to campus.[51]

When Dr. Mary B. Ritter informed Hearst that young female students lived "in small attic rooms or sunless basements, with one small window in either case and all sorts of desolate conditions," Hearst acted to alleviate the problem. She paid Ritter to survey as many women's colleges as she could—about twelve in all. Ritter investigated institutions from Wellesley to Bryn Mawr and Smith, and coeducational institutions from the University of Chicago and the University of Wisconsin to Cornell University. She gathered, on Hearst's behalf, information and ideas about residences for women students. Armed with Ritter's survey of facts and her own ideas, Hearst established two respectable, comfortable homes, or boarding clubs, for women near campus—the Enewah and the Pie del Monte clubs. Each club consisted of fifteen to twenty young women "paying their own expenses pro rata, except as to room rent which varied according to size and location of the rooms," Ritter wrote. These became the first clubhouses, or women's clubs, in Berkeley. The clubs were entirely self-supporting but without the stuffy, elitist attitude of sororities, though each was furnished with a housemother.[52] Hearst's women's clubs helped break down the barriers that prevented women from attending the university at the same time that they reinforced traditional ideas about propriety and femininity.

Regent Phoebe A. Hearst made the most of her political and legal power and authority to benefit University of California women as the twentieth century unfolded. She took an astute, diplomatic approach early on. She moved quickly between 1897 and 1902, her time as a regent that might be called her honeymoon period, to take advantage of her power as a regent to gain benefits for university women and some men too. Hearst effectively used the force of her personality and her ideas and intelligence. But she also showed her ability to maintain a balance between deferential politics and her need to forcefully wield power to accomplish her goals. She displayed her skill in knowing when and when not to press male colleagues to advance women. She showed her sophisticated knack for using her networks and choosing key people to help her achieve her top political priority—to provide unprecedented opportunities for female students. A dignified, modest, but ambitious and courageous woman, Hearst took political risks and met challenges and conflict successfully that made uc women visible and moved them into the mainstream of campus life. Regent Hearst, undoubtedly, played an important role in bringing more women into the University of California. The ways she used power made female coeds, once admitted, a part of a whole university and a new American order. "There are today more women students in the University of California than in any other institution in the country which provides for the higher education of women, with the single exception of Smith," President Wheeler announced at the turn of the twentieth century. Hearst, indeed, was "the best friend the University ever had," especially for female students.[53] She achieved great benefits for the university and students in general and for the overall well-being of women coeds in particular. Having achieved such success, would it be harder or easier for Hearst to grapple with the limits of power while she tried to advance herself and the university further and in new directions?

6

Limits

As early as 1892, Phoebe Hearst began to realize that she could move in a new direction and make her mark in a modern way on American academic and public life. In that year, she began to think about the promise of public architecture and emulating "the great museum builders" to serve the general public.[1] The first concrete sign that Hearst, an amateur social scientist and anthropologist, was setting her sights on establishing a museum of culture in San Francisco devoted to the procurement, care, study, and display of objects of lasting interest emerged shortly after George's death that same year. She later abandoned that specific vision, but her interest in museums and anthropology deepened once again when she visited the World's Columbian Exposition in Chicago in 1893. It is possible, though unlikely, that Hearst made contacts at the exposition with prominent people in this new field of anthropology. She never commented on any such meetings. But her exposure to the subject at the exposition probably spurred her to think more about the study and science of human beings. She came up with the idea of creating a museum and department of archaeology (later anthropology) at the University of California about six years after her visit to Chicago in 1893 and after taking her seat on the UC Board of Regents. The center of power in anthropology, at the same time, was shifting, becoming "more evenly distributed," between New York, Boston, and Washington DC to new centers of academic work in Berkeley, Chicago, and Philadelphia.[2]

Hearst was a westerner, and she would make her mark in American academic and public life in a different way than did her East Coast counterparts. Many people considered elite, wealthy white men to be the great museum builders, not elite, wealthy white women. Women usually got involved in "museum development" rather than museum building. But Hearst understood that building a museum would be a good way to broaden her social and cultural influence and display her wealth, giving her an opportunity to alter public space as well. Following in the footsteps of rich male museum builders would provide her an opportunity to build a grand permanent expression of her power and status on equal terms with elite, wealthy white men.[3]

Hearst's University of California museum and department idea was influenced by her extensive travel abroad and what she had seen at the World's Columbian Exposition. She intended her museum to serve the general public—to help people gain a broader appreciation of other cultures, races, and nations through material objects like those on display in European museums. Hearst counted on her money and resources to bring her ideas and plans for anthropology to life. As it turned out, she would also embroil herself in philosophical and political debates with university officials and academics over the shape and direction of the museum, department, and new field of anthropology to reach her goal. Her efforts to obtain greater power and status as a regent would have an impact on the nascent field of anthropology and alter people's lives. But she discovered, along the way, that money and resources could only take her so far. She came face-to-face, in other words, with the limits of power at the University of California—a transformative experience that became a major turning point in her life.

Hearst's private physician and friend, Dr. William Pepper, had introduced her to museum building politics in the academic world in the late nineteenth century. Hearst and Pepper met through her extensive intellectual, social, and political networks. Pepper was a member of a prominent blue-blood Philadelphia family and an educational and medical reformer. He graduated with a medical degree from the University of Pennsylvania in 1864. Intensely ambitious, he served as medical director at the 1876 Philadelphia Centennial Exhibition and was a professor of clinical medicine. He became the provost of the University of Pennsylvania (UP) after 1880 and was instrumental in defining the modern research university during a period of profound social change. Pepper met Hearst when he worked for the UP Museum of Archaeology and Paleontology. The museum displayed exhibits based on evolutionary theory and functioned to "civilize" visitors. Pepper and the University of Pennsylvania took the lead in turning archaeology into anthropology by hiring Daniel Brinton in 1886 to serve as the first professor of anthropology on a university faculty in the United States. Highly ambitious, Pepper also cofounded the Commercial Museum in Pennsylvania that used exhibits to promote the benefits of American commercial expansion and empire without the disadvantages of colonialism.

Pepper also gave Hearst medical care and advice, which signaled acceptance of Hearst by the Philadelphia elite—quite an accomplishment for a woman with her modest upbringing. Hearst described Pepper as "the friend who saved my life, and whose wise council and judgment helped me to solve many serious problems." He played a key role in putting Hearst on the path to becoming a member of the old guard of museum builders—amateur, dedicated, and reasonably well-informed collectors of anthropological objects who wanted to establish museums for public learning. Hearst's friendship and association with Pepper became typical of her reliance generally on professional allies to broaden her power and advance her progressive agenda to solve American urban problems.[4] Hearst was an elite, wealthy white woman with a rudimentary, formal education. Pepper was an elite white man with a job in a formal institution of higher education. Hearst possessed a higher class standing than Pepper. Yet both were part of the elite. Hearst was among the elite in the nonpartisan political world of the wealthy and voluntary association politics. Pepper was nowhere near as wealthy as Hearst. But he was considered among the elite in the world of nonpartisan academic and museum politics.

Hearst and Pepper began a power-working relationship to build collections for the University of Pennsylvania at a time when museums represented "the late-nineteenth-century impulse to order and rationality." Pepper knew Hearst's support was essential for building the collections and reputation of the museum—a home for the new academic discipline of anthropology that consisted of the subfields of archaeology and ethnology. Anthropology combined science and art, investigating powerful idealistic and mythical aspects of diverse cultures, races, and nations. Hearst possessed a keen intellectual curiosity and a deep love of travel and museums that fed her strong interest in the field. That made it easier for Pepper to inspire and convince her to become among the first women to join the elite coterie of nineteenth-century American museum builders. Pepper intended to fill the museum not with curios but with meaningful material cultural objects collected in systematic and orderly ways. His aim appealed to Hearst. Hearst, a methodical woman, had enjoyed the orderly displays of objects and artifacts she saw in European museums and brought those pleasant experiences, visual images, and knowledge back to her homeland. Viewing museum exhibits, for Americans, including Hearst, was a tool for understanding themselves and their relation to the rest of the world.[5]

Hearst's health problems justified, in her mind, another trip abroad by the mid-1890s to absorb more European culture. Phoebe was so overburdened with responsibilities and so active in early 1895 that she suffered from a "serious attack of grippe [fever influenza]," Mary W. Kincaid wrote. She experienced some heart problems, too. So Dr. Pepper advised her to avoid the pressures of business matters, rest, and be careful. Hearst convinced herself she needed to take her physician's advice and relax in Europe. The excursion, of course, would give her another chance to learn more about museum exhibits so she could better understand herself and her place in the world. Hearst eagerly made plans to travel abroad. Pepper was delighted with the idea of Hearst getting a "charming rest," he wrote. "[I went] carefully over in my mind the detail of your proposed trip. I am more and more convinced of the wisdom of the plan," he explained. As she prepared for her journey across the Atlantic, Hearst grew concerned about issues of trust and privacy related to her business obligations and additional responsibilities. She relied increasingly on secrecy.[6] Keeping her personal affairs private might reduce the stress and strain that contributed to her poor health. Traveling to reduce pressures helped her stay physically strong, because she controlled her time and energy and improved her chances of promoting and protecting her public persona and image, even though travel could also be exhausting.

Hearst willingly, in the midst of making plans for another trip abroad, set aside secrecy and reserve to take bold, diplomatic public action to build a name and reputation for herself in a budding new academic field—anthropology. She added more to her growing University of Pennsylvania Museum collection of material cultural objects and artifacts. She created her first public expedition to support anthropological research—the Pepper-Hearst Expedition—while she was busy packing her bags for her trip abroad. She pursued her interest in anthropology through another patient of Dr. Pepper's, Smithsonian ethnologist Frank Hamilton Cushing. Cushing had discussed anthropology with Alice Fletcher and Zelia Nuttall at the World's Columbian Exposition. Hearst funded Cushing's 1895–96 archaeological diggings in Key Marco, Florida. She then procured a letter of introduction from the Department of State instructing the diplomatic consular officers of the United States to give her official courtesies in case she needed them to purchase items in foreign nations for her museum collection.[7] Hearst, in other words, used the letter from the Department of State as a tactful political and diplomatic tool to make it easier for her to consume material cultural objects and artifacts abroad.

Hearst sailed "for England [the] first week of May [of 1895]," she wrote, on the *Lucania* with her niece, Annie Apperson, and a female friend, Agnes

Lane. Phoebe was "evidently quite sad in leaving her relatives and home." She was "very tired and somewhat regretful." And she was unhappy that her brother, Eppy, and his wife, Lizzie Apperson, "were not in her party," according to Hosmer Parsons, one of Phoebe's business managers. It would have brought her comfort to have immediate family members accompany her. Before she sailed away from American shores, Hearst gave extensive instructions to Parsons to send her correspondence abroad so she could keep up with all her affairs. After a long and "rough voyage but feeling rested," she disembarked. She stayed in London with Thomas F. Bayard, the U.S. ambassador to Great Britain and the father of her friend Florence Bayard Hilles. The ambassador presented Hearst to Queen Victoria, an exhilarating experience. Phoebe left the Bayards and traveled on to Paris, Munich, Norway, Sweden, Denmark, Germany, and Russia to learn more about foreign culture and artifacts. Used to doing "the work of twenty women," one friend wrote, the trip became the tonic Phoebe needed. Her working vacation in Europe made her feel much better.

Yet her stay abroad was not enough to free her from care completely, according to Parsons.[8] Hearst's industrious nature had pushed her to travel abroad to learn more about material cultural objects and artifacts. And although when she was younger her evangelical principles had made her reluctant to spend money on personal pleasures, she had rid herself of that constraint long ago. She enjoyed spending money on buying materials to fill museums, and she shipped the objects and artifacts home by the caseloads. On this trip, however, Hearst was growing increasingly concerned about her son. Will's demand for more money to finance his newspaper business was making her anxious. Parsons agreed with his "boss" that "it would be an unkindness to give him [Will] the unrestrained control of a large fortune" because "he has no sound conception of the care and uses of money."[9] Phoebe's anxieties about Will's spending encouraged her to return home. Although she stayed there long enough to take care of her affairs, particularly those related to her son, she could not long resist the lure of travel.

She returned to Europe in late August 1895. Upon arrival, she took the opportunity once more to learn as much as she could, sailing back to America after staying abroad for a couple of months. She managed to avoid the unpleasant experience of becoming seasick. So the voyage was a good one. She arrived in Washington DC sometime in mid-to-late November. But Europe beckoned her yet again, and she returned in 1896. In that year, Hearst hired Zelia Magdalena Nuttall to work for her in Russia to collect information on a variety of rare objects for the University of Pennsylvania Museum collection. Nuttall was the daughter of a wealthy San Francisco banker. While in Dresden in the spring of 1896, Hearst met up with Nuttall and sent her to Moscow. Nuttall saw the president of the Imperial Archaeological Society of Moscow and arranged for the exchange of museum objects at Hearst's behest. Having carried out Hearst's instructions, Nuttall returned home with some useful knowledge about Russian material pieces. Hearst, not long after Nuttall's return, made her first purchases to preserve fragile and rare objects. She bought artifacts for the Russian department in the University of Pennsylvania Museum and a large archaeological collection that had been displayed and popularized at the 1876 Philadelphia Centennial Exposition—the Charles D. Hazzard Cliff Dweller ruins excavated in Mesa Verde, Colorado. Hearst was serving on the Executive and Building Committees of the Board of Managers of the University of Pennsylvania's Department of Archaeology, chaired by Pepper, at around the same time that she bought and filled their museum with a mountain of objects.[10] Hearst continuously juggled becoming increasingly informed about anthropology with performing, at a high level, her myriad of family duties and business obligations and responsibilities while abroad.

Pepper came to visit Hearst at the Hacienda del Pozo de Verona in the summer of 1898, probably quite pleased with her level of interest and competency in anthropology. But he died of angina pectoris unexpectedly at the Hacienda in late July at the relatively young age of fifty-five. Pepper's death was a real blow to Hearst. She had so many cares. And now, she wrote, "I have lost one of the best friends of my whole lifetime."[11] Hearst could no longer rely on Pepper's medical advice, guidance, and support. Who would advise her now on building collections of material objects and learning more about archaeology and ethnology?

Hearst turned to Sara Yorke Stevenson to fill Dr. Pepper's shoes. Pepper had introduced Hearst to Stevenson, his close friend and collaborator, before his visit to the Hacienda. Stevenson was a founding member of the University of Pennsylvania Archaeological Association. She suggested the group be renamed the Department of Archaeology, which later developed into the University of Pennsylvania Museum. Stevenson, like Hearst, was a wealthy woman who gave away money and was an advocate for the advancement of women. Stevenson became the secretary and president of the museum and the first curator of the Babylonian, Egyptian, and Mediterranean collections. Stevenson knew Frederic Ward Putnam. He was considered by men, in general, to be better informed than Hearst in the study and science of human beings. He attended Harvard University and "became assistant (1857–64) and friend to the naturalist Louis Agassiz" and was "listed among the S.B.'s of 1862," but he "never received an academic degree." Putnam had become an archaeologist, ethnologist, and the chief of the Department of Anthropology at the 1893 World's Columbian Exposition. He played a key role in getting Stevenson appointed to the Jury of Awards for Ethnology for the department once Congress had passed a special law to allow women to serve on the juries. Stevenson approved of Putnam's view on the importance of educating the public. She also became the first woman to be awarded an honorary doctorate from the University of Pennsylvania.

Pepper's and Stevenson's interests, moreover, largely complemented one another. While Stevenson, unlike Pepper, refused to define archaeology to include ethnology or to hire experts in archaeology or professional anthropologists, she did agree with him that the chief purpose of museums lay in collecting and exhibiting material cultural artifacts for public learning. Stevenson committed herself to doing all in her power to carry on Pepper's academic museum work and place it "upon a permanent basis . . . as a worthy monument to his foresight and courage," she explained to Hearst. Sensitive to Hearst's aspirations, and committed to building Pepper's legacy, she gently reminded Hearst, in August 1898, that what she did for the University of Pennsylvania Museum "will prove important and will do you credit."

Under Stevenson's tutelage, Hearst continued to make strategic purchases of material objects for the museum collections and projects that Pepper had been building. Hearst built the Italian Etruscan and Cliff Dwellers collections and bought the Tebtunis Papyri—a large collection of papyrus manuscripts on different topics that contained new information on the domestic history of Ptolemaic Egypt. She also familiarized herself with the study of objects and artifacts of human history and prehistory through the excavation of sites and the analysis of physical remains gathered by archaeologists for the museum.[12] Stevenson cultivated Hearst's friendship and acted as her mentor for her own ends as archaeology and ethnology turned into the new field of anthropology. Hearst, in turn, developed a friendship with Stevenson to help her accomplish her goals.

Pepper, before he died, had created an independent organization—the American Exploration Society (AES)—to raise funds to buy artifacts and collections for the museum and to sponsor archaeological work. Stevenson was interested in keeping Hearst involved in Pepper's museum projects and in developing the AES's work on a national scale, so she invited Hearst, in the fall of 1898, to run for election to be the AES honorary president. Hearst accepted the invitation because she realized the rewards of holding the office. As she explained, "Being officially connected with the Society would insure some advantages." Hearst "was unanimously elected," even though, as she put it, "I had no technical knowledge of archaeology, having only the enthusiasm acquired through general reading and visits to the world's greatest museums." The new field of anthropology was in an early stage of development, which gave both Hearst and Putnam the room to rise to a higher status without advanced academic degrees.

But Putnam's posts would have held higher value than Hearst's to many Americans because Hearst's position as AES president was honorary and voluntary, or unpaid, while he held paid positions.

Hearst's connections served her well, however. Hearst, while in office, played a diplomatic role when she represented the AES in Rome and Egypt. But at the same time she was "worried and annoyed with other peoples troubles" concerning financial aid and university and Hearst estate business, according to James C. Hooe, another Hearst business manager. Being the honorary president of the AES meant she could make a contribution to an organization that promoted her strong personal interest in archaeology (as it was turning into the field of anthropology) and her deceased friend's memory while she handled the burdens of wealth and her family and business obligations. Holding the AES office gave her another reason to travel and a chance to broaden further her knowledge and understanding of the world of museums while she addressed the problems of others.[13]

Hearst traveled to Europe again in the fall of 1898 to satisfy her curiosity and accumulate even more knowledge and experience. "Travel is," she wrote, "the most widening and deepening experience of my life." She added, "It's seeping down to my vitals and new interests greet me at every turn." Her schedule, as usual, was very full. She supervised her international architectural competition. She contemplated the inner workings of museum exhibitions such as organization and arrangement. While she was busy buying material cultural objects for her collections, she relied on her diplomatic role as an AES representative to smooth the way for her purchases. On previous trips abroad, she had walked through museums and galleries. She repeated more of these experiences on this trip. She visited "the Luxembourg and three times to the Louvre each day spending two hours. That is about as much as one can do without great fatigue," she wrote. She saw other museums and galleries too. She sailed the Nile and stopped in Cairo to study art and the kinds of material cultural objects that would form the building blocks and core of her museum collections.

Hearst refused to be stopped because of restrictions placed on women. Her wealth, reputation, and status helped her transcend the constraints of sex and class at the same time that she was bound by them. She methodically bought ancient objects and artifacts to build her understanding of cultures, races, and collections. She gathered technical knowledge and expertise about anthropology. She made new acquaintances in foreign lands. But, while she enjoyed the view along the Nile, she still kept up with her voluminous correspondence from America. The correspondents often asked for "some favor." She answered sixty letters during this trip, even though she felt herself to be "bothered with all kinds of requests."[14] While she continued to meet American expectations as to her philanthropic obligations and personal conduct, she was soaking up as much of the local customs, culture, and history of people's lives as she could to help inform her decisions about what objects and artifacts to buy. The amount of time, energy, and money she spent revealed Hearst's desire to be more than a dilettante in anthropology. This visit abroad provided her with the experience and knowledge necessary to give her AES elected honorary office substantive meaning and purpose.

Phoebe Hearst built a good reputation as a collector of antiquities in Egypt. She was intent on purchasing the best material objects and artifacts money could buy to add to her collections. She scoured Egypt for the most valuable ones in 1899. Will met his mother in Egypt that same year. Phoebe was Will's cultural mentor and guide. She became a valued client of Egyptian antiquity dealers while she helped her son develop his cultural knowledge and understanding. Because of his mother's good name and generosity, merchants, in the market to buy ancient material pieces, were eager to represent his mother. They besieged Will in Egypt. As he explained to Phoebe, "I am going to write a book about the conquest of Egypt by Mrs. P. A. Hearst." He added, "I am entertained with tales of the generosity of Mrs. P. A. Hearst and here at Luxor I am overwhelmed with antiquity dealers (guaranteed) who were the particular favorite of Mrs. P. A. Hearst." He went on: "Seriously you must have had a great time and everybody speaks of you with so much admiration and affection that I am very proud to be my Mother's son."[15] It took more than money, of course, for Phoebe to build a good name. She proved she possessed a discerning ability to select the right material objects to buy—objects that would distinguish, and get others to respect, her and her collections. She needed to be careful about what she selected. Her ability would be a crucial factor in making a reputation for herself as a serious collector of anthropological objects worthy of display in a reputable museum. Dr. Pepper, Sara Yorke Stevenson, and others, assisted her in making her choices. But she had the final say about which items to purchase.

After she returned from Egypt, praise from her son and others for her deft collecting of antiquities led Hearst to consider that it was time for the University of California to have a museum and department of anthropology. "By 1899, the concept of a great University Museum, serving not only the academic community but the people of California, had taken clear shape in her mind," President Benjamin Ide Wheeler noted. Hearst knew that America lacked the aristocratic family collections like those she saw in Europe. But she had no intention of developing her assembly of material objects merely to arouse "envy and hatred among" people. She planned to have a museum that would be an exposition of human physical and cultural evolution from across all times and places, Frederic W. Putnam explained. Making a contribution to uplifting American culture and "taste in civilized life," popular notions at the time, took precedence for Hearst. She made her move while archaeology was on its way to turning into anthropology and anthropology was on its way to becoming a full-fledged, professional academic discipline. Hearst knew an opportunity existed for her to manifest her power to match elite male museum builders, not in Europe, but in America.[16] So she took it.

Before traveling to Egypt, Hearst had sent Bernard Maybeck to solicit Stevenson's advice about organizing a new department of archaeology at the University of California. Enthused by Hearst's innovative idea, Stevenson wrote Hearst: "I will give you every bit of experience I possess and frame a plan for you upon which the thing can practically be carried out." After word got out that Hearst intended to bring her department and museum idea to life, the University of Pennsylvania and the University of California vied with each other for Hearst's support. The competition between the universities pressured her to decide where to focus her attention and gifts in anthropology. Elite University of California men began a campaign to flatter Hearst and exploit her ambition. The new university president, Benjamin Ide Wheeler—scheduled to travel east on business in early 1900—appointed Hearst acting president in his absence. His appointment was a testament to Regent Hearst's intellectual and practical abilities, social position, power, and reputation. Wheeler's decision prompted William Carey Jones to write Hearst: "Your duties will be increased, but some honor will be given you through your practical acting Presidency." Acting President Hearst possessed the authority "to sign the requisitions on behalf of the president." Hearst's experience while acting president would give her the opportunity to learn more about how the university operated and might help her in establishing the new department and museum.

Wheeler's decision to make Hearst's appointment worked. When she heard of her election in 1900 to the advisory board of managers for the University of Pennsylvania's Department of Archaeology and Paleontology, Hearst chose instead to step back from her involvement with their museum to focus on developing a department and museum of anthropology at Berkeley. She promptly resigned from the board of managers. Writing to Stewart Culin, curator of the General Ethnology and the American Section of the University of Pennsylvania Museum, about her decision, Hearst emphasized that she possessed a desire "to turn every effort to giving the people of California every education advantage in my power to secure." She wrote Culin requesting a redistribution to the University of California of part of the Hearst collections, "to which I have contributed, may I not say liberally?" Hearst's request complicated a conflict already underway between Culin and Stevenson at Pennsylvania. Culin resented Stevenson's power over areas of the museum and her different views. He also was envious of her support from the board of trustees and businessmen with a general interest in material culture and artifacts.[17]

Culin mounted an attack against Hearst that was intended to damage Stevenson's work and diminish Hearst's standing. He disclaimed Hearst's right to dispose of part of the University of Pennsylvania Museum collections in response to her redistribution request. Hearst hoped the board would beat back Culin's challenge and rectify the matter in her favor. They did. Hearst then acted to fulfill her pledge to advance the University of California "in all directions." She resigned as honorary president of the AES and declined to accept her reelection to the University of Pennsylvania Advisory Board of Managers. Those decisions gave her the freedom to accept the honorary presidency of the American Archaeological Association, giving her the opportunity to gain more useful knowledge to perform her anthropological and museum activities at the University of California.[18] The cooperation of University of California officials and Culin's challenge to Hearst's power, in effect, pushed Hearst to sever her ties with Stevenson and the University of Pennsylvania Museum.

Museums played a significant role in convincing Americans that culture mattered at the time that Hearst was shifting the focus of her anthropological and museum activities to the University of California. The academic and public arguments on the meaning and purpose of culture and museums were a strong force in shaping American identity and advancing a national political agenda. Hearst was influenced by these discussions. Lewis Henry Morgan, seen by some as the father of American anthropology, joined these debates in 1877 with the publication of *Ancient Society*. Morgan thought some races had evolved to higher stages of development than others. Morgan's thinking was built on Charles Darwin's evolutionary theories and shaped further by social Darwinism. His views presaged a deep disjuncture between the old guard of amateur anthropologists, which included Hearst, and the new guard—academics interested in profession-alizing anthropology.

Social Darwinists viewed human beings as being in a constant struggle for survival, trying to adapt to a changing, often hostile, environment. The "fittest" survived. Humans who failed to adapt were weak, inferior specimens and fell by the wayside. Morgan identified the process of human struggle and development through three stages—savagery, barbarism, and Western "civilization." Hearst too was interested, according to Brooks, in "how prehistoric man had lived his life [and] fought his way up from primal ignorance to civilizing knowledge." For Morgan and Hearst, Europe and the United States represented the highest standard of "civilization." This view justified American imperial ambitions, expansion, and domination over others. It was a perspective that some suffragists relied on to convince people at home and abroad to support their cause.[19] Hearst shared Morgan's racial and anthropological views, which in turn influenced her vision for the academic work to be done by faculty, and actions to be taken, at the new department and museum of anthropology she was hoping to establish.

The shape and structure of Hearst's vision for the new department and museum mixed traditional and dominant cultural values, classes, and hierarchies, based on Morgan's racial and anthropological perspective, with her commitment to helping the masses—seemingly contradictory views. But she was not unusual in this. Historians have likewise noted "two competing critical approaches to museum history—institutions created by and for America's wealthy, and museums as the site of hegemonic control." Hearst represented the contradictions in these two competing views. She knew that building a department and museum would give her a chance to show she possessed the same wealth and power of elite male museum builders. But while completion of this new project would display her power to promote dominant and traditional cultural values and entrenched hierarchies, just as the men had done, she knew, too, that museums served as places to house ideas that could bring "civilizing knowledge" to the masses, improving their lives.

She saw such philanthropy to be the responsibility of wealthy bene-factors like herself. Although believing herself to be an avid advocate of research in the new discipline of anthropology, she also saw universities and museums as places to promote her racial and class superiority and the dom-inant cultural values. She decided then to promote a public persona for her-self that centered on her deep interest in cataloguing and arranging material cultural objects so that visitors to the new museum and department could learn to appreciate more broadly diverse cultures, races, and nations. Her primary purpose in establishing a department and museum of anthropol-ogy, she argued publicly, was to provide all the educational advantages she could for the academic community and the general public in California.[20]

Hearst claimed that her "sole reward" in funding this new venture would be her "pleasure" at being able "to help in opening up these [anthropo-logical] records of the past and in placing them where our own people may study them." She would become known as "a great educator" to aca-demic scholars and to the community. Meanwhile, Hearst downplayed her wealth and the control she expected to exert over the new department and museum. She stressed public progressive education as the chief function of a museum. As she explained: "The true object in view in centralizing collections, as I take it, is the dissemination of knowledge among the many, not the pride of possession by the few." Nonetheless, Hearst had marveled at how aristocratic Europeans spent their money on art galler-ies, libraries, architecture, and museums as manifestations of power, and she identified with white men who, imaging themselves to represent the pinnacle of human evolution, saw "primitives" in descending order on down the ladder. She thought that housing, organizing, and classifying col-lections, in association with the University of California, would bring her validation from academic scientists of her racially superior views, status, and power as an elite and wealthy white woman.[21] How the department, museum, and Euro-American cultural values related to the academic field of anthropology, and how they fit together with her own values and class position, mattered to Hearst, personally, publicly, and politically.

Hearst's vision for the University of California's Department and Museum of Anthropology positioned her on the cusp of a new generation of cultural leaders who balanced conservatism with a measure of tolerance for diverse people, cultures, and races. These trailblazers accepted dominant American values and hierarchies while they crafted a progressive museum agenda to serve the academic community and the general public. The agenda included using museums to help the urban poor become worthy citizens.[22] Hearst's perspectives provided an opening for her to think about, and recognize, nonwhite races as equals at the same time that she was reinforcing traditional cultural values, entrenched hierarchies, and class and racial superiority in the name of improving the lives of and civilizing the masses. Hearst's good fortune to be wealthy, and in the right place at the right time, may have helped her weave together these competing visions of the purpose of museums. As she guided the establishment of academic anthropology at the University of California, she could expect to rise in prominence in the academic and museum worlds.

At the dawn of the twentieth century, an older era in anthropology came to a close when Frank Hamilton Cushing—who possessed "no formal training" in anthropology but who had aroused public interest in the field of anthropology at the World's Columbian Exposition in 1893—choked on a fish bone, suffocated, and died in 1900. Several years later, in 1902, a new era began after the passing of John Wesley Powell, a prominent anthropologist, geologist, explorer, and founder of the Bureau of American Ethnology, particularly "oriented toward Theory." Powell became a leader among Washington DC anthropologists. But "his early work fit" a "nonprofessional pattern" of a "gentleman amateur," according to one historian. The deaths of Cushing and Powell marked a shift in anthropology away from learning "through experience" to a focus on formal academic training and credentials and away from an emphasis on white racial dominance and support for existing hierarchies to grappling with racial differences that were highly contested.

Hearst set to work to create a new University of California Department and Museum of Anthropology at the start of this transition period. She announced to the regents, in March 1900, that she would place her collection of anthropological materials in a new museum she assumed would be built at the institution. More women had arisen to become prominent collectors of material objects by this time. Few, though, were involved in building, or shaping policies for, their own museums.[23] Hearst's announcement made clear her intention to establish a permanent collection and museum that would place her on an equal footing with the great male museum builders. The new field of anthropology, meanwhile, began to move deeper into its new stage of academic development.

Hearst, at this point, intended to move in a more modern direction from other female museum collectors of the 1870s and 1880s who celebrated decorative art objects from the home environment like "ceramics, laces, and fans." She devoted much of her money and resources instead to building a museum that centered on the importance of the academic research she was funding. She focused her gifts on excavations to collect artifacts from a broad range of cultures, races, and societies. She paid ten thousand dollars per year for five years to Dr. George A. Reisner to direct the Hearst Egyptian Expedition. Reisner served later as the Hearst Lecturer in Egyptology and field director of explorations in Egypt at the University of California.

Stevenson then informed Hearst that Dr. Max Uhle would no longer be under contract at the University of Pennsylvania. Uhle headed the Peruvian excavations for their museum. That gave Hearst an opening to hire him for $3,500 annually to conduct expeditions in South America and the Yucatán for the University of California. Uhle served as the Hearst Lecturer in Peruvian Archaeology and field director of explorations in South America. Hearst also paid six thousand dollars a year for Dr. Philip Mills Jones, a trained medical doctor. He performed multiple roles. He excavated Old Mexico, conducted research to establish the existence of California aborigines in prehistory, and acted as Hearst's agent to purchase collections. Hearst also provided ten thousand dollars a year, for two years, for Dr. Alfred Emerson's explorations and purchases of Greek, Roman, and Etruscan antiquities. Her expeditions and excavations collected a great mass of material cultural objects sent to the University of California and tested her skills in dealing with customs duties inspectors.[24] Hearst obviously understood the value of research. Her collections constituted a rich source of materials for academic archaeologists to study and analyze in the emerging new era of anthropology.

A self-taught, amateur anthropologist, Hearst hoped that building her permanent collection would get people, especially academic men, to classify her among professionals in anthropology in the modern age. Eager to see what the Hearst Egyptian Expedition was doing, she visited Dr. Reisner's dig years later. She described the excavation as "splendid." But the experience reminded her of what she had understood years earlier when she had come on to the board of regents. She was a woman who lacked the academic qualifications that other university officials and faculty possessed. Yet she knew she possessed the original ideas and wealth to mount and develop such an expedition. Present when the Reisner party opened an Egyptian tomb, she hung "over the edge of the place [a dig] looking down to see the figures as they were uncovered," she wrote later to Orrin Peck. She added: "You might have thought it right to class me with excavators."[25] Hearst thought that her devotion of considerable wealth to finance expeditions, excavations, and museum purchases and her ability to navigate and negotiate power, could persuade others to classify her with excavators in the field of anthropology. She convinced herself that her effective use of power over her university projects was a sufficient substitute for her lack of academic credentials. Hearst, in other words, wanted people, especially men at the University of California, to respect and see her as a professional anthropologist.

By this time, most Americans already accepted the fact that wealthy and prosperous male regents involved themselves in managing the day-to-day operations of the University, including the hiring and firing of faculty and presidents. But Hearst was deeply involved in her project to create a new academic department at a time of widely held prejudice against women involved in academic affairs and university politics. Some saw women like Hearst as meddlers. Others more than likely believed that Hearst's decisions and actions represented interference in university affairs. Yet as a member of the board of regents, she, too, possessed the power to supervise the daily operations of the university. She held the right to vote on faculty and administrative appointments. She voted to determine faculty salaries and policy.[26] Some university officials undoubtedly accepted Regent Hearst's involvement and right to control university affairs and politics. These men took her ideas and plans as a regent seriously. Others refused.

Hearst's first goal was to do everything she could to build permanent collections for a University of California museum. With "this object in mind," she bought a slew of objects and artifacts. She prepared herself to handle what a friend told her would be "customs regulations" that were "troublesome." She rose to the occasion and shipped the cultural items home successfully. Hearst knew, meanwhile, that "systematic and scientific explorations and researches were essential to enhance the value of the collections," according to Putnam. She had, by 1900, accumulated almost "one hundred cases of archaeological materials," in need of "a proper place for their unpacking and display." University buildings served as storage places for a heap of materials she sent home. The university also understood "that so long as these valuable and significant collections remain stored they will be well-nigh useless."

That realization hastened "the erection of a permanent museum building." The need "to have them properly supervised, cared for, and made useful as soon as possible" led President Wheeler to suggest that Hearst, himself, Frederic Putnam, Alice Cunningham Fletcher, and Zelia Nuttall get together to have a formal discussion about officially creating a department and museum of anthropology.[27] Hearst's subtle and deliberate approach—flooding the university with large amounts of objects and artifacts—pressured administrators, colleagues on the board of regents, and faculty into taking the first step toward the creation of the University of California Department and Museum of Anthropology.

Putnam agreed to serve as a member of the group President Wheeler convened. Putnam promoted museums as institutions that solved scientific problems through excavations and systematic scientific research and investigation. He had founded the Peabody Museum of American Archaeology and Ethnology at Harvard University and served as its curator since 1875. The Peabody Museum was the first museum dedicated to the science of anthropology. Putnam also established the Peabody professorship for anthropological research at Harvard. His work as chief of the Department of Ethnology and Archaeology at the World's Columbian Exposition, from 1891 to 1894, contributed to his prominent reputation in anthropology. His ethnological exposition exhibit promoted Henry Morgan's cultural views. Putnam and Hearst shared the view that American culture should accommodate diverse races. But neither viewed members of different races as social equals. Putnam's primary assistant at the Columbian Exposition had been Franz Boas. Putnam had accepted a position as part-time curator of anthropology at the American Museum of Natural History in New York City in 1894. He hired Boas, a faculty member at Clark University, as his chief assistant in physical anthropology and ethnology and took on Alfred L. Kroeber as a volunteer on his staff at the New York museum. Putnam, by the mid-1890s, was one of the primary architects of modern anthropology.[28]

Several prominent women in anthropology served on Wheeler's committee with Hearst and Putnam. Alice Cunningham Fletcher, a suffragist, had attended Brooklyn Female Academy. She knew Frank Hamilton Cushing. She had worked with Putnam as the first ethnologist at the Peabody Museum in 1882 and become loyal to him. Fletcher was one of the founding members and vice president of the Women's Anthropological

Society of America in 1885 and an official of the Women's National Indian Association. Matilda Coxe Stevenson (no relation to Sara Yorke Stevenson) established the organization because the Anthropological Society of Washington refused to admit women. Fletcher, while a member, supported "civilizing" Native Americans and played a key role in the passage of the Dawes Severalty Act of 1887. The act included a program that she truly believed would help Native Americans assimilate and become citizens. Fletcher's "civilizing work" led to her election victory, in 1890, as president of the Women's Anthropological Society. She began a life fellowship at the Peabody the next year, a gift from her wealthy woman friend in Pittsburgh, Mary Copley Thaw.

Fletcher lacked a PhD, so she had a position somewhere between that of an amateur and a full-fledged professional academic anthropologist. She firmly believed, by the time she arrived at Hearst's Hacienda to meet with Wheeler's California committee, that "Indians were the equals of whites in their capacity for civilization, a conviction that coexisted without any tension with her cultural ethnocentrism."[29] Hearst's kindergarten politics in Washington DC showed that she believed blacks were equal to whites in their power to learn and act. Fletcher saw Native Americans as equal to whites in their power to learn and act. Both Hearst and Fletcher thought whites held a responsibility to "civilize" Native Americans and blacks, believing that people of diverse races could be assimilated and learn to be citizens.[30] Hearst and Fletcher stopped short, however, of thinking non-white groups were equal to whites. Nonetheless, they supported efforts to provide opportunities for members of diverse races to advance themselves.

Fletcher became "a kind of scientific mother confessor to Zelia Nuttall" who was almost twenty years younger than Fletcher. Nuttall's work on ancient Mexicans first brought her to Putnam's attention. Putnam named Nuttall an honorary special assistant in Mexican archaeology at Harvard's Peabody Museum. Nuttall introduced Hearst to Fletcher. After reciprocal formal visits and attendance at social affairs, Hearst invited Fletcher, and her interpreter, clerk, and friend, Francis La Flesche, to a small, private dinner where they discussed, among other interests, Indian music. Nuttall served later as field director of the Crocker-Reid Researches in Mexico for the University of California's Department of Anthropology.[31] Hearst was on Wheeler's committee with some of the most distinguished archaeologists, ethnologists, and anthropologists in America.

Nuttall strongly advised Hearst and Wheeler to carefully consider the views of Franz Boas, "the most important single force in shaping American anthropology in the first half of the twentieth century," one historian noted. Boas was an expert on the ethnology and linguistics of the Pacific Coast tribes. He became the first anthropology professor at Columbia University. He was well known for his views on cultural relativism—the notion that all values and judgments are relative, differing according to cultures. Cultural relativism urged researchers, and others, to comprehend and appreciate "other cultures on their own terms." The chief task of anthropology for Boas turned out to be anthropological investigations rather than presenting material culture and objects for public learning. He wanted to use museums as a foundation for systematic academic training of specialists focused on field work, linguistics, and symbols instead of relying on museums to educate the masses and democratize taste.[32] Boas's notion of cultural relativism argued for moving beyond the constraints, bias, and prejudice of Western civilization and values and possessed the potential for dissolving entrenched hierarchies and notions of racial and class superiority. His perspective appealed to Hearst's interest, appreciation, and tolerance for diverse races and cultures but undermined her view that whites possessed higher racial and class status and should have more privileges than others.

Boas contacted Nuttall to explain his interest in, and need to raise money for, research on California "Indian tribes and languages about which we know practically nothing." He asked Nuttall to approach Hearst to arouse her interest in and support for his work. Hearst, in response, wanted from Boas "a detailed statement in regard to the investigations on the history of the aborigines of California." He complied. He also included a short description of the overall scope of work on the Native peoples of North America. He offered a suggestion as to how Hearst's money should be spent—to finance training fellowships in ethnology at Columbia and archaeology at Harvard and that these fellows should be transferred to the University of California for fieldwork. He made another suggestion: that he be named director of the work for about four or five years to build "a strong department" at the University of California. Having received and discussed Boas's information with Hearst, Nuttall asked him to consider leaving Columbia University to join Hearst in establishing a department and museum of anthropology at Berkeley.[33]

As she waited for a response from Boas, Charles Stetson Wheeler (no relation to Benjamin Ide Wheeler) invited Hearst in early 1900 to "The Bend," his "hunting lodge" and retreat on the McCloud River surrounded by the beauty of California's natural wonderland. Wheeler, a prominent San Francisco attorney and close friend of Hearst's, possessed characteristics and interests similar to hers. He was a brilliant University of California regent and an avid reader. Hearst was a dignified lady and devoted to high standards in public education. Wheeler too was a gentleman who promoted high standards in public education. He also worked against corruption, for municipal progressive reform, and collected fine art like Hearst. Hearst enjoyed her visit on the McCloud River in Siskiyou County between Mount Shasta and Mount Lassen near the Oregon border.[34]

Regent Hearst dreamed of building a mansion on the McCloud River. The natural beauty and pristine character surrounding "The Bend" so impressed Hearst that she asked Wheeler if he would be willing to sell her a parcel of his property along the river so she could build a modest summer house. Katherine Hamilton McLaughlin, the manager of Hearst's household from 1898 to 1919, recounted that since Wheeler expected Hearst, a Victorian woman of "good taste and judgment," to build a "bungalow," he agreed to lease seven miles of his river frontage land for ninety-nine years. But when he saw Hearst's plans, he was reportedly outraged. He miscalculated. He had failed to understand the complex personality of his determined colleague who "could be both charming and imperious," possessed vaulting ambition, and exerted power confidently.[35] Hearst knew what she wanted and approached Wheeler directly in private to get it.

Hearst relied on an indirect approach to communicate her ambition and love of power because it was inappropriate for a modest woman of her generation and wealth to speak of these issues in public. She commissioned Bernard Maybeck, three years after he designed Hearst Hall, to design and build a mountain lodge for a modern age that looked like a medieval castle on the McCloud River property that she leased from Wheeler. The Hearst family bought the property later. Hearst named her castle Wyntoon, after a peaceful tribe of California Indians who had previously inhabited the area. Maybeck, while working on Hearst's project, went from designing three-to-five-thousand-dollar houses in the Bay Area to "an unlimited budget" with "almost no restrictions" that eventually swelled to one hundred thousand dollars, an incredible sum in that day and age. The five-story massive, impressive, and luxurious castle, or mansion, became Hearst's and Maybeck's most fabulous project to date.[36]

Wyntoon expressed Hearst's desire to make people think of her as a medieval queen with the secularized divine power and right to rule.[37] Her mansion's dramatic, bold design symbolized and represented "a host of" Hearst's "dreams about what a medieval castle should be" and the considerable power, reminiscent of a dignified, stately imperial head of a nation-state, the occupant possessed. The interior design was rustic and evocative of Gothic castles. It held "allusions to both a medieval church and a baronial hall." Strong, massive blue-gray stone, the color of Phoebe's eyes, comprised the "Gothic" living room. A massive, free-standing stone fireplace that was "as high as a man" stood at one end of the room. The initials PAH were carved on a large-scaled keystone above the fireplace. One of two "massive, rough, stone fireplaces," it stood below a stone arch and in front of a leaded and stained-glass cathedral window with

10. Departing Wyntoon aboard horse and cart. UARCPIC 1980.7.5–A. Courtesy of the Bancroft Library, University of California, Berkeley.

"deep blues, reds, and yellows" that reminded one of a Roman basilica or royal palace.[38]

Hearst's castle was far greater in size and more magnificent and extravagant than her Hacienda del Pozo de Verona and Wheeler's hunting lodge and retreat. Maybeck's design spoke to myths contained in "popular tales and superstitions" that interested lots of Victorians at the end of the nineteenth century. The castle was located in a private, secluded, and enchanted spot 6,300 feet above sea level and nestled in a beautiful, virgin forest of pine, fir, incense cedar, poplar, and black oak trees, some of which stood two hundred feet tall. A female friend understood why Hearst selected the site because she thought "the wilderness and crudeness" appealed to Hearst.[39]

Wyntoon merged the power expressed by the building itself—embodying Hearst's devotion to nondenominational Protestant religion—with the power of nature's organic environment, which religious devotees believed was controlled by God. The structure conveyed the idea that religion sanctioned the power she possessed to rule and lead over her "subjects" or constituents. It expressed Hearst's desire to be recognized and legitimized as having the power, prominence, and status that surpassed almost all other Americans and was commensurate with the queens and kings of Europe. The design encouraged people to think of her as a woman with considerable control over money and resources as well as a representative of the nation-state.[40] Gazing upon Wyntoon left little doubt about Hearst's craving to be viewed and treated like a queen. Regent Hearst's decisions and actions to promote the new discipline of anthropology in California occurred against the backdrop of the construction of Wyntoon. Her medieval castle voiced her strong sense of class superiority, her limitless ambition, and her appetite for and pleasure in wielding power. It was a short intellectual leap to conclude that Hearst believed she possessed the power to rule over the new University of California Department and Museum of Anthropology.

Hearst's affection for power, and desire to establish and control a department and museum for general learning, came into direct conflict with the Putnam and Boas's campaign to professionalize anthropology and make it into an academic discipline based on science and, in the case of Boas, the theory of cultural relativism. Putnam held prejudicial views common for his day, especially on race. Although he believed in the teaching of archaeology, his support for "formal classroom teaching came slowly." Still he "saw early the need for organization, communication, and publication outlets for science" and refused to side with any "particular theory" in anthropology. Putnam and Boas wanted to get rid of "vulgar popularizers from anthropology." Boas, in particular, worked to "rid anthropology of its amateurs and armchair specialists." He urged those discussing Hearst's project to concentrate on rigorous standards in research, especially in ethnographic and linguistic fieldwork, and on symbols to train cultural anthropologists as the sine qua non of professional status. Nuttall, toward this end, asked Hearst to "carefully" consider Boas's recommendation, "in the interest of science alone," to hire Alfred L. Kroeber, the first student under Boas's direction to receive a PhD in anthropology at Columbia University.

Hearst intended to wield power over her plan and vision for the department and museum. But she lacked deep knowledge and experience in matters of academic anthropology and sophisticated academic politics. She trusted Nuttall. And she held high regard and respect for Boas. So she relied on their advice and offered Kroeber a position in the new department. Hearst cautioned that she "could not reply with definiteness [about her offer] without consulting with President Wheeler, and this I have, as yet, been unable to do." Wheeler was interested in building not only a professional reputation for the new department but a national one. He knew Hearst would pay Kroeber's salary and fund the department's expeditions and excavations. So he understood the advantage of ceding to Hearst's wishes in the matter and must have respected and valued the recommendation of Boas. He agreed to hire Kroeber. Hearst was pleased that Kroeber accepted her offer and would come to California.[41] But she would come to regret the decision.

Hearst's ideas and resources, especially financial, helped anthropology come into its own as an academic discipline. Hearst, Wheeler, Putnam, Fletcher, and Nuttall met for the first time at the Hacienda del Pozo de Verona on September 7, 1901, to establish a department and museum of anthropology to encourage both anthropological research and build a useful museum at the university to educate the public. The university's official stamp of approval occurred three days later. The committee also decided that Hearst and Wheeler should approach the board of regents to consider the appointment of an advisory committee to get the new department and museum up and running. Wheeler recommended that the advisory committee consist of Hearst, himself, Putnam, Boas, Nuttall, Fletcher, and John C. Merriam, a researcher in paleontology. Merriam later became an assistant professor of paleontology and historical geology and field director of geological explorations. Putnam headed the committee.

The committee resolved to accept Hearst's gift for ethnological, linguistic, and "mythological research among the Indians of California." Hearst paid Kroeber's salary of $1,200 per year and set his budget. Hearst provided Pliny E. Goddard a $900 a year salary to do research on California Indians and set a ceiling on his expenses. Hearst gave $2,000 a year, in addition, for geological and paleontological research of California gravel formations under the direction of Putnam and Merriam. She also gave financial support for the maintenance of the large amounts of material received by the university.[42] Hearst's innovative thoughts and monetary support provided the bedrock foundation for the establishment and operations of the new department and museum. Her decisions and actions encouraged others to see her as an expert in the new field of anthropology.

The formation of the University of California's Department and Museum of Anthropology triggered a philosophical and political battle between the university's early major benefactor, university officials, and scholars over the shape and direction of the new field of academic inquiry in anthropology. Would the new department focus on teaching and would the museum that housed material objects from other cultures, races, and nations mount exhibits for visitors to see like the ones Hearst saw and appreciated in European museums? Or would anthropologists, like Putnam and Boas, interested in science, professionalizing the field, and cultural relativism, develop a link between the new department and museum and the university that centered on research, including ethnographic and linguistic fieldwork, symbols, cultural relativism, and the academic training of cultural anthropologists?[43] An intense theoretical and nonpartisan battle between Hearst and others involved in the creation of the new department and museum would determine the answer.

Hearst acted quickly to shape the department and museum of anthropology along the lines she favored. A hurdle for anthropology that had loomed large, since the end of the 1880s, was securing adequate funding from institutions of higher education. "After 1900 the existence of anthropology as a profession was taken more for granted and *either* a museum *or* a university department could provide sufficient institutional backing for anthropological research" that included expensive fieldwork. Putnam realized how crucial Hearst's support, financial and otherwise, was to the new department and museum. He acknowledged her innovative idea to create and unify them with the university as a whole. As he explained Hearst's original plan a few years later: "When the Department of Anthropology was established in 1901 its first purpose was to co-operate in the broad plans of Mrs. Phoebe A. Hearst and to carry out her views it was made an integral part of the University." Putnam was loyal to Hearst's views and priorities associated with the museum. "I should have nothing to do with the establishment of a museum anywhere that did not meet with the approval of Mrs. Hearst," he wrote, "for I should consider it disloyal to her when she has given the start to the whole matter." Putnam "planned to have a museum which should be an exposition of the life of man from his beginning in geological time, through savagery and barbarism to the periods of his civilization as shown by the life of the different people distributed over the earth," he explained.[44] Putnam, at this point, refused to take cultural relativism into account. He intended to organize the exhibits in such a way as to meet with Hearst's approval.

Putnam's loyalty to Hearst, though, had its limits. He wanted to draw a line when it came to Hearst's direct involvement in the department, implying that the academic power of the male faculty over the department would take precedence over Hearst's. Putnam attempted to clarify that the expedition finds had been turned over specifically to the department: "The results of the several archaeological and ethnological expeditions maintained by Mrs. Hearst were turned over to the Department and generous provision was made for exploration and research." These results came from Hearst's archaeological and ethnological expeditions, which unearthed material cultural objects to form her collections from Egypt, Greece, Italy, Peru, parts of North America, the Philippines, Pacific Islands, northern Europe, China, and Japan. When Hearst handed over the material, according to Putnam, they became the foundation for the museum and the department plan that Hearst approved, which focused on achieving desirable academic goals: to conduct research, preserve "materials and facts secured," diffuse "knowledge by publications and lectures," and establish "courses of instruction and research in the University" to provide students a liberal arts education.

But Putnam gave license to other men involved in the establishment of the department and museum to place restrictions on Hearst's involvement in accomplishing these academic aims. When Hearst refused to consider furnishing the future museum, the secretary of the committee wanted permission from Putnam to abandon her wishes if they interfered with the department.[45] Hearst, then, could have control over the museum but not the department—a view that would have a profound impact on the conflict between Hearst and anthropologists interested in making the field into a professional academic discipline.

Hearst continued to experience a growing divide between herself and academic anthropologists over the form and direction of the new department and museum during the first year of departmental operations. The newly formed advisory committee announced, in that year, that regular teaching would not be given, inasmuch as the whole university was moving toward secularism and the field of anthropology was challenging religious orthodoxy. When the department was ready to offer anthropology classes, then a chair would be chosen to head the department. Until that time, the committee decided to appoint instructors and assistants who would, on occasion, present lectures on their research.[46] These decisions, in effect, meant that research trumped teaching as the top priority in the new department. But Hearst's grand vision for the department and museum centered on using anthropology as a tool for teaching the general public to appreciate diverse races, cultures, and societies.

Almost immediately after he came onto the University of California faculty, Kroeber began to challenge Hearst's vision for the department and museum, along with the traditional cultural values she espoused related to entrenched hierarchies and racial and class superiority. Kroeber was a shy, serious, and mischievous young man with black beard who walked around with bulging pockets filled with pipes, a tobacco pouch, pencils, and paper. He contended that the university, and not the museum, was the primary tool for promoting true knowledge. For academic anthropologists, like Boas and Kroeber, "only 'science' constituted true knowledge." Both Boas and Kroeber advocated for theories supported by concrete scientific evidence. Kroeber also promoted cultural relativism by arguing that little evidence existed to support racial, and by implication, class inferiority. Kroeber's anthropology, all in all, promoted linguistic investigation through fieldwork as the main vehicle of study.[47] He encouraged appreciation and respect for diversity, especially in languages. So Kroeber backed Boas's theories and commitment to research based on fieldwork and his devotion to professionalizing anthropology.

Boas eventually received the news, in early 1902, that the university's advisory committee had rejected his specific plans to professionalize the new department. He had suggested the establishment of fellowships in ethnology and archaeology at Columbia University that gave the fellows a chance to do fieldwork for the University of California. He recommended, moreover, that he be given "the opportunity to direct the operations, in order to establish them on a definite systematic basis" to form "a strong department in the University of California . . . entirely independently of any further co-operation on our [Columbia University's] part." Nuttall encouraged Hearst and Wheeler to "carefully" consider Boas's view. But instead of bringing Boas onto the faculty, the advisory committee vetoed his proposal but kept him on the advisory committee "apparently . . .

without his prior approval." He remained at Columbia University, where he directed the Department of Anthropology. The shifting academic politics at the University of California mirrored the upheavals in the social sciences at other universities during the transition from older models to modern ideas of scientific, objective research.

Putnam, at about the same time, planted a thought in Hearst's mind that was self-serving. He suggested that if she "would like" he would "give a good part of my time to the University. I should like to be instrumental in the work of another great centre of anthropology and California is the place for it." But he wanted her to keep this suggestion "strictly confidential & only between us," he wrote. Putnam argued, further, he could make the department a "great success," especially since his previous work had helped him develop national connections.[48] By refusing to put Boas's detailed plan and theories of cultural relativism in place, and by promoting himself to head the new department, it would appear that harmony had prevailed on the committee, which appealed to Hearst. Further, Putnam implied that he would maintain cooperation in departmental operations, which also was to Hearst's liking. But the harmony was short lived. Boas became a leader, and the University of California's major competitor, in advancing anthropology as a profession after the advisory committee overruled his detailed proposal.

The power struggle between Hearst and academics interested in professionalizing anthropology and promoting modern ideas grew quickly and "reached a crisis," according to Fletcher. Hearst, looking out after her own interests and used to getting her way, moved to solidify her control over the advisory committee. She believed the committee was too cumbersome and unwieldy to do business. So she recommended that the committee be reduced to three members—herself, Wheeler, and Putnam. She excluded Fletcher and Nuttall. In this instance, it appeared that Hearst was abandoning her personal interest in the advancement of women to get what she wanted—control over the new department and museum. Hearst's suggestion, in effect, raised her power and stature above theirs. Hearst mostly got what she wanted. The committee, headed by Putnam, and renamed the executive committee, was reconstituted to include the three members she wanted, with Merriam added. The executive committee, in the fall of 1901, agreed that the department would generally disseminate knowledge through lectures.

Regent Hearst understood the value of academic research and explorations, but clearly expressed her dissatisfaction with the lecture classes the department offered during its first year. She wanted the department to give popular lectures. But when Putnam and Kroeber visited with each other during one of the executive committee meetings at the Hacienda, Kroeber told Putnam that Wheeler had given him a choice—he could teach a class in anthropology or give popular lectures. Giving popular lectures "would take from fieldwork," Kroeber explained to Putnam. So Kroeber decided he "could give a course better than popular lectures." The benefit: he could use the classes to analyze, study, and present material collected from his research. The heart of the battle to form the department by this point was wrapped up in the question of to what purpose Hearst's money be used—professional university-level classes or popular lectures in anthropology? Kroeber developed his own interpretation of what Hearst was doing without asking her. His understanding was that Hearst was paying him to do anthropological research and investigations and present his findings in his academic lectures. Kroeber's decision to give a course opposed and challenged Hearst's power to impose her grand vision on the department and increase and broaden her power at the university to bolster her racial and class status and privileges. In the end, Kroeber taught the first departmental course in North American ethnology in the spring of 1901 and pursued ethnological research influenced by Boas's cultural relativism.[49] The crisis, then, reached a boiling point.

Hearst now challenged Kroeber, but indirectly. Self-confident and knowing full well the power she possessed, Hearst chose a subtle, practical and political approach. She selected Fletcher to act as her power broker and as her representative in her dealings with university officials and academics regarding the day-to-day running of the department. Her choice may have eased any animosity Fletcher still held against Hearst for removing her from the original committee. Hearst raised her concerns, through Fletcher, to President Wheeler. Seeing a continual increase in departmental issues that were left unattended, she demanded that someone be chosen to look after the quotidian procedures in the department. Putnam, in the meantime, was running the new department from the Peabody Museum, some three thousand miles away. The fact that Kroeber became the de facto head of the daily operations, since Putnam was so far way, precipitated the decisive moment in the political battle over anthropology at the University of California.[50] Hearst could not sit still for what Kroeber was doing.

Hearst criticized the daily operations in the new department rather than mount a direct attack on the cultural relativism that Kroeber and Boas advocated. Hearst objected to Kroeber serving as the de facto head of the department. George Pepper (no relation to Dr. William Pepper) explained the crux of the problem. Pepper was assembling a pueblo pottery collection for Hearst while he worked for the American Museum of Natural History in New York City. Hearst was "very frank with" Pepper about "her views on many plans of the University work," Pepper wrote to Putnam. The trouble "was the man in charge is not the man for the place (You of course know who I mean)." Pepper explained further to Putnam that his and Kroeber's "work has been stamped with her [Hearst's] seal of disapproval." Dissatisfied with the situation, Hearst had pressed university officials and faculty to appoint "a resident head to the Dept. of Anthropology at the University and President Wheeler agrees with her," Fletcher wrote Putnam. Hearst wanted someone "to draw the thought & interest of the public to this Dept. of the University in order to infuse for it proper support," Fletcher wrote. She wanted a head of the department who would "devote his whole time & thought to this branch of science"—"a man who commands the respect of the scientific men of the country & who is filled to take an honorable place with the other Professors of the University,"[51] Fletcher added. Executive committee members, meanwhile, jockeyed for power. Wheeler backed Hearst's desire to get someone to head the department who shared her approach and vision—a focus on teaching the general public to appreciate various cultures, races, and nations through popular lectures and material objects and artifacts like those she had seen in Europe.

Hearst broached the issue of the philosophical and political battle lines clearly drawn to form the new department and museum of anthropology. She raised the subject of what kind of classes Kroeber should be teaching. Kroeber's response: a fit of anger. George Pepper wrote to Putnam: "Mrs. Hearst told me that when certain work was suggested, and moreover, work that was distinctly mentioned in the rule and regulations adopted by the board last year," Kroeber "flew into a rage and insisted that he was not paid to do such work and that he would write to you without delay." Hearst's response did not bode well for Kroeber. She argued that there were problems "continually arising when some one who is responsible for the Dept. should be on hand to look after its affairs." Hearst thought that "there is no one here fitted for this place," Fletcher wrote Putnam. Fletcher, then, clarified Hearst's position: "Mr. Kroeber is unsatisfactory" and should be "freed from the Department and allowed to seek employment else where."[52] It was nothing new for Hearst to fire and replace professional men. The regents, moreover, were the real managers of, and held power over, the university. She was, furthermore, a democratically elected regent. But Hearst assumed that her official position, work, and major gifts to the University of California entitled her to have control over the department and museum. She expected Kroeber to do what she wanted. If Kroeber refused, Hearst thought she possessed not only the power but the right to fire him.

Hearst promoted Dr. William T. Brigham, director of the Bishop Museum of Honolulu, Hawaii, as the perfect man for Kroeber's job. Brigham was older than Kroeber. He shared Hearst's approach that emphasized the value of teaching the public through lectures and museum exhibits rather than focus on university academic programs and cultural relativism. Charles Reed Bishop, banker and husband of Princess Pauahi, of the Kamehamehas, established the Bishop Museum in 1889 to honor and house material cultural objects, mostly of the royal Kamehameha family lineage. Bishop, like Hearst, wanted to create a museum to rival the great ones he and his wife had seen while traveling abroad. Brigham became the first "curator-scientist" of the Hawaiian museum. Bishop and Brigham filled the museum with material cultural objects "of the people of Hawai'i whatever their ethnic background." Wheeler explained to Putnam about Hearst's and Fletcher's support for hiring Brigham to head the department for about three to five years. President Wheeler thought Brigham was "advanced in years, and naturally could not serve us long, but he might bridge over from the present time to that time when we can secure a young well-trained man," Wheeler wrote Putnam.[53] Wheeler walked a fine line to avoid alienating Hearst, Putnam, and Kroeber. He knew Hearst's wealth kept the new department and museum afloat, but his professional allegiance was to Putnam, Kroeber, and Boas rather than to Hearst and Brigham.

Hearst sent Fletcher to the Hawaiian Islands to see Brigham. She instructed Fletcher to keep Putnam informed about discussions with Brigham before Nuttall was told about what was going on. Hearst, then, was taking another step to solidify her control over the department and advance her agenda and vision. Fletcher reported to Putnam, by early September 1902, that Hearst was "fast losing her patience over the matters here. She said that her 'patience was almost exhausted' & she might wash her hands of every thing," according to Fletcher. Fletcher reminded Putnam that Hearst provided "all the capital & she also is practical & often has to set things straight." If something was not done soon, Hearst would "surely give it all up"; the dream of a department and museum of anthropology would go up in smoke. Fletcher explained her deepest fear: "If Mrs. Hearst stops the work, this will be a loss to science that ought not to be allowed to occur."[54] Fletcher fully backed Hearst's choice of Brigham to save the department and museum project.

Putnam was in a difficult position. He tried to sooth Hearst's ruffled feathers. "Do not, I beg of you, get discouraged by the annoyances that have arisen," he wrote her. He then got to the heart of the matter. "The suggestion of securing Mr. Brigham, as head of the department, places me in an embarrassing position, but I beg of you to believe that I have only your best interests at heart and that not a personal feeling has entered my mind," he said a bit disingenuously. Putnam tactfully conceded that Brigham "would be a good man to make a collection of Pacific Island material." But "I feel sure it would be a great loss to the department to give him [Kroeber] up, unless there are reasons of which I am entirely ignorant." He believed the department needed Kroeber to establish its credentials and a national reputation in anthropology as a professional academic discipline.[55] Rather than please Hearst to retain her financial support, Putnam decided to challenge her power.

The executive committee, chaired by Wheeler, addressed Kroeber's fate in the fall of 1902. Hearst moved, and Merriam seconded, that Kroeber be informed that "his services will not be required by the department after the termination of the period for which he is officially appointed." The committee resolved that Kroeber would "be released from all obligations to the department after October 1st." That meant Hearst would stop paying for his fieldwork in about a week. A telegram from Putnam was read at the meeting of September 29, asking to postpone pending action on Kroeber. Responding favorably to Putnam's request, Hearst moved that "further action concern the resignation of Dr. A.L. Kroeber be postponed until the arrival of F. W. Putnam" from the East Coast. The committee agreed to take up the Kroeber issue at their next meeting. Putnam had yet to arrive.[56] The committee waited for Putnam because they knew he would play a key role in the determination of Kroeber's future.

Hearst moved, at the September 29 meeting, that the discussion of the Kroeber issue be postponed again. Putnam, though, wrote a penciled note that he initialed on a copy of the minutes of this meeting that indicated he had advised the committee to keep Kroeber in spite of the fact they had gone on record to relieve him of his duties. Rather than support Hearst, Putnam allied himself with Kroeber. But why would Putnam add his note to the minutes, and when did he do so? Since the minutes were produced after the meeting, is it possible that the committee met after the September 29 without Hearst and made the decision on Kroeber without her knowledge? It is difficult to tell exactly what happened because committee discussion and reaction are omitted from the minutes. The date that Putnam penciled in his comments is also lacking. Generally speaking, it appears Putnam refused to take Hearst's position seriously. It seems the committee members, with Putnam's support, outmaneuvered her behind the scenes, forcing her to go along with the committee's decision to retain Kroeber.[57]

Hearst was accustomed to getting her way, particularly at the University of California. She expected that her wealth, class position, and contributions to the university would be enough to win the philosophical and political battle with the university and academic men. But she lacked breadth and depth of knowledge and experience in academic anthropology. She failed to understand fully how sophisticated university politics worked. Considering Wheeler's, Putnam's, and Kroeber's commitment to science and the professionalization of anthropology and building a national reputation for the new department, the direction in which Hearst wanted to take the department became untenable. Academic men decided to offer the kind of anthropology classes that Kroeber wanted. Kroeber's work and theories represented the modern wave of the future in the new field of anthropology. The organization of the department and museum was complete by 1904. Putnam became professor of anthropology, the director of the museum and the head of the department, "the first of its kind west of Chicago." He remained as head until he retired in 1909.[58] This time, Hearst's money and resources had failed her. Her battle with university men and experts in anthropology undermined her efforts to be seen as more than a dilettante in anthropology and potentially set the stage for an erosion of her sense of racial and class superiority. Although she had challenged the dominant power of academic men, she fell short miserably of her goal to increase and expand her power at the university.

Hearst needed to face up to the fact she had lost her battle with academic anthropologists. The department and museum of anthropology would not be focusing on educating the general public and validating her privileged status and white race. From the perspective of those interested in museum activities, this meant she had failed in making a contribution to the democratization of taste and helping Americans become better citizens and overcome American cultural inferiority. University men and academic anthropologists, meanwhile, moved on. But it took Hearst time to adjust to her significant loss in academic politics.

Phoebe received news during her bruising battle with professional university men that added to her difficulties. Her mother, Drusilla Apperson, manifested the "bronchial trouble she had a year ago" that had now become tuberculosis. Drusilla was "a woman of phenomenal vigor and strong personality," according to Will Hearst's newspaper the *San Francisco Examiner*. But she was "very feeble" and would "continuously grow weaker until the end comes which will not be very many weeks," Drusilla's private physician observed.[59] Drusilla thought about how rarely she had shown her daughter fondness as her health took a turn for the worse. Her guilt finally got the best of her. She wanted to talk with Phoebe. "Whatever she may have said or done before or since to mask her affection for you," another private physician and surgeon wrote Phoebe, "she did say again and again, 'I wish I could just see Phoebe once more.'" Drusilla's magnificent and imposing physical and mental state kept her alive, her doctor reported. Phoebe granted her mother's dying wish. She visited Drusilla before traveling to Europe again.[60] Drusilla must have been pleased.

The battle at the university and her mother's illness had taken such an emotional, psychological, and physical toll on Hearst that she decided to focus more attention on herself. "For a change—I shall think of myself a little," she wrote, an exaggeration perhaps to gain sympathy. She began to organize a trip to relieve her stress, restore her energy and vitality, and more than likely rebuild her confidence in her racial and class beliefs and standing after her defeat. The excursion would be one that only the very wealthy in America and Europe could afford—an around-the-world tour. Hearst was up almost all night, the day before she set sail, taking care of correspondence and business. She was in her early sixties. But still she struggled with the tension between dependence and independence. She knew it was unacceptable "for a woman to travel in India without a man in the party," she wrote. Yet she wanted to be on her own this trip. So she developed a plan that would be acceptable. It consisted of traveling with Henry Rogers and his wife "but not be dependent upon each other." They could go their separate ways if they desired. They boarded the steamship *Doric* to sail from San Francisco on October 7, 1903, bound for India and Ceylon by way of the Hawaiian Islands, Japan, the Philippines, and China.[61] She was so weary on board that after the vessel left the dock she slept the entire day and night. She rested, relaxed, and recuperated with her friends during the "delightful" voyage of about "three weeks" to Yokohama, Japan, with a stop in Honolulu.[62] Hearst gave virtually no thought at that time to the corrosive and corrupt influence of wealth as she spent a large amount of money on travel to heal the wounds inflicted during her bruising battle in academic politics.

Phoebe A. Hearst arrived at Agra, India, in late 1903 or early 1904. She then traveled to Paris, the City of Lights. There she learned of her mother's death in January 1904. Phoebe had experienced a similar family tragedy several years earlier when her father passed away.[63] The news of her mother's death made her cut short her travels. She returned to America, Benjamin Ide Wheeler explained, "earlier than" she "had planned" to take care of her mother's affairs. Phoebe dreaded going home. She felt stressed and emotionally strained. On board the RMS *Oceanic*, she wrote Janet Peck, daughter of Margaret Peck, Phoebe's lifelong friend whom she had met on board the steamer to San Francisco in 1862: "I try to keep my so-called mind so *busy* that I cannot think of all the cares that await me. They will have to be met all too soon."[64] Phoebe's self-deprecating humor gave her temporary relief from, and acted as a defense against, her deepest feelings of pain. Once the laughter subsided, the suffering came through. She was "unhappy and distressed," according to James Cecil Hooe, one of her business managers, about her family affairs, her failure at the University of California, and business problems that would face her once she returned home. She relieved her stress thinking about returning to England "at the latest the middle of April," she wrote Janet Peck.[65] Going abroad, after her mother's passing, would give her an opportunity to relax and restore her energy to handle future political battles.

Phoebe's physician supported her decision to return to Europe. He advised her to reduce her responsibilities and obligations and travel again to make herself feel better. She found "a long rest absolutely necessary at this time," she remarked, and planned at her earliest opportunity "to run away and shirk all." "I am making many changes in my business in order to lessen my responsibilities and obligations as far as possible, so I may leave my business for another year or two spending the time in travel," she wrote the directors of the San Francisco Settlement Association.[66] Hearst had provided financial backing and support for the establishment of the association. "I want to go to some quiet place that will not be expensive." She felt better in Marienbad. "How thankful I feel to be here where I can be quiet and control my time," she explained to Janet Peck a bit later.[67] She wanted "to stay longer [than a year] but may not be able to do so," she noted.[68] Her goal, as she explained about a year later from Cairo to Orrin Peck, son of Margaret Peck, was "to be at a safe distance from the U.S. at least half of every year for the next three and get rid of as many burdens as possible."[69] Her defeat at the University of California had pushed her to take care of herself and think a little less about handling other people's problems. But a trip abroad could never free her entirely from what Americans expected a wealthy woman, with her good name and reputation, to do, especially if she wanted to remind people of her racial and class privileges and status.

Hearst, then, continued to wrestle, as did many Americans, with the paradox of morality and materialism while she made preparations to sail to Europe. She wanted to enjoy a lavish lifestyle abroad. But the attacks of moral critics on the wealthy, for being corrupted by materialism in an age of "rising inequalities" in the Progressive Era, bothered her.[70] Phoebe's parents had raised her to be a Christian "lady" and instilled in her a desire to work for reform and political issues that evangelicals deemed important. For some well-intentioned female evangelical reformers that issue was temperance. Not for Phoebe. She was not a "'lady tippler'—a woman of good family and comfortable circumstances who publicly quaffed spirits" like women in Chicago at the turn of the new century. She was "opposed to intemperance." Yet she was not a teetotaler either. "I am not and never have been in favor of Prohibition," a newspaper quoted her years later. Phoebe served champagne to friends in private, tolerated "a moderate use of wine," and owned "considerable acreage in wine grapes." She provided alcohol for guests but never drank in public. "In this wine-producing State especially, I think it would be a mistake and do much more harm than good to establish prohibition," she remarked. Some of the reform issues the supported by the Women's Christian Temperance Union, like improved health standards, appealed to Hearst. Even so, she never became an active member in the WCTU. But she understood that since she was a very rich woman, she risked damage to her name and reputation when she had sixty-one cases of wine and her furniture shipped overseas so she could imbibe occasionally, with friends and guests, and live in Europe surrounded by amenities. She knew that transporting these goods might invite criticism that she would live in the lap of luxury in Paris and was morally decadent, self-indulgent, and corrupt.[71]

Phoebe could recall feeling anxious and angry when moral critics had attacked her, in April 1895, for what they considered an ostentatious ball she organized and held for several hundred, at the end of the social season in Washington DC, to honor Florence Bayard Hilles. Guests were dressed in colonial era gowns, and servants wore the costumes of "Moorish slaves, gorgeous in crimson velvet suits, embroidered in gold," and heads crowned with "fantastic turbans of rich silken stuffs," one newspaper noted. Hearst "wore a Colonial dress of gray striped satin, brocaded in roses," and trimmed in "rich old lace." Diamonds and rubies were draped around her neck. Hearst was castigated for "the requisite costumes" being "so costly as to preclude the attendance of none but millionaires" and for spending "the considerable sum of $15,000" on one of her musicales in her Washington DC home. She vigorously defended herself, arguing that "both" figures were "far from the truth," she wrote the editor of the *Chicago Herald*. "I greatly regret to have such inaccuracies given newspaper currency. While the Musicale was, according to the expressions of those who attended, an enjoyable affair, its cost was not unduly great and not nearly as much as the sum mentioned in your paper. Our efforts were directed more towards making it harmonious and appropriate than a costly display," Hearst explained. She refused to reveal the exact amount of money she spent on her parties. She wanted, moreover, "the false impression" the newspaper gave to be corrected.

She could not let the criticisms go unanswered for fear of being labeled a philistine. She was not a philistine. She spent hundreds of thousands of dollars, for example, to demonstrate her sophisticated cultural tastes. Her ideas, as well as money, after all, had created a department and museum of anthropology that contained cultural artifacts for herself and others to enjoy. From her perspective, she was not lacking in, nor indifferent to, cultural and aesthetic values. She held such lavish high-society affairs because it was the proper thing to do for a woman of her wealth and class and a means to build connections and networks. But Hearst set aside, in 1905, any fear of being attacked by moral critics. She had gotten caught up in the shift taking place, at the turn of the new century, "from self-control to self-realization." Self-control was based on "the values of self-denial and achievement." Now Americans were looking to a "consumer culture" centered on gratification and indulgence to achieve self-fulfillment.[72] In such a changed cultural environment, Hearst believed that by this point she possessed such a good name and reputation that there could be little risk that moral critics would condemn her for shipping her creature comforts abroad. So she did.

Phoebe looked forward to living a "royal life" in her Paris apartment on the Place de l'Alma, a life that would center on cultural matters, international relations, and enjoying a whirlwind of social affairs. It was difficult, though, for her still to feel at ease about living the luxurious lifestyle of women like Caroline Schermerhorn Astor. Astor was a wealthy New York high-society woman with "aristocratic" pretensions who was wallowing in luxury and conspicuous consumption by the 1890s.[73] Hearst refused to mimic Astor's life entirely. She needed to have a specific reason in her own mind to justify spending such a large amount of money on the trappings of wealth during her extended stay in Paris if she was to feel comfortable.[74] Deep down, Phoebe felt "bound to do what I am able for those whose needs are *vital*," she wrote a bit later.[75]

She persuaded herself it was the right thing to do to spend money abroad to build her physical strength and endurance so she could be very active in high society *and* progressive reform circles when she returned home. As she put it: "I hope to recharge my batteries and gain the necessary strength to resume my work at home a year or two years later." For all the burdens she tolerated as a rich woman, Hearst's political activism in nonpartisan voluntary associations and academic politics made her life meaningful and worthwhile.[76] Hearst used the language of self-sacrifice and altruism and participation in acceptable political arenas, rather than militant protest, to protect herself from the harsh censure of moral critics. It made her, and the public, feel comfortable with her wealth, ambition, and politics. The material, moral, social, cultural, ethical, and political mattered to Hearst.

Hearst convinced herself she was justified in spending money to go abroad this time to live like a queen who possessed the conscience of a political progressive reformer. She decided not to go to California after she took care of her mother's affairs and business, as well as her own social responsibilities and obligations. She stayed in Washington DC instead. A powerful regent and representative of the West in a developing nation-state, while in the nation's capital, she asked for a leave of absence from the board of regents meetings at the University of California. She cited unsatisfactory health and doctor's orders to rest and relax. She sailed from American shores on May 18, 1904, for an extensive stay in Paris and other places far away.[77] Hearst left her burdens and responsibilities in America behind to rest, relax, and really enjoy the benefits of her wealth in Europe.

Hearst possessed the time to think about what she had learned from her experiences in academic politics while she enjoyed her trip across the Atlantic. She was upset and deeply hurt that academic men refused to take her seriously, ignored her, and failed to do what she wanted. To complicate matters, she was at a loss to understand fully what was going on academically in the field of anthropology and university politics. Once she arrived on European soil, she decided to do what Alice Fletcher feared most. Hearst announced, in late May 1904, that she would withdraw her financial support from the University of California, including the department and museum of anthropology.[78] Hearst became clearheaded while abroad about Putnam's decision to oppose and reject her vision and goals. Putnam's decision turned out to be a perilous one.

Hearst directly and confidently explained to Putnam why she was thinking of withdrawing some portion of her aid. She justified her actions in financial terms men could understand: "As I told you, a very large investment consumed twice the amount I expected to put in it and very costly improvements in another very valuable property necessitated a reduction in my income which obliged me to retrench in every way possible." Putnam concluded that "her income is reduced some $16,000 a month for the next two years." He thought, though, that Hearst regarded this withdrawal as "simply a temporary suspension" of her active work.

Hearst disagreed and had other ideas. The university needed "to secure help for the department from others, and to do this, of course it will have to be known that I will no longer maintain it," she wrote Putnam. That meant that the department "had to stop all field work and get along with as few helpers in museum work as possible." The department, furthermore, needed to end its ongoing archaeological and ethnological investigations and any future studies.[79] Hearst, by this point in her life, was a mature, older woman with extensive skills and knowledge in the sophisticated use of her intellect and considerable economic power. Her life experiences had generated a strong consciousness about the powers she possessed. So she made no bones about expressing her utter dissatisfaction to Putnam.

In command of a voice of authority, Hearst issued a new directive that set limits on university men, faculty, and the department and museum of anthropology. Because Hearst knew that her continued association with the University of California was essential if she wanted to exert any power over its officials and academic men, she refused to withdraw herself, or her financial support, completely. She wrote to inform Putnam that "as to the future of the department, I am not prepared yet to say what I can do." That made Putnam even more anxious. "Even now I am not entirely clear as to just what the department will be able to do for the next two years," he explained in a draft letter to Wheeler. Hearst, then, softened her original blow slightly. If Putnam raised "half the amount by subscription" needed to keep the department going in the 1904–5 academic year, she would provide "the other half." In keeping with her principles and values, in essence, she required the department and museum to stand on its own two feet and gain "public and institutional financing."[80] Her command included specific criteria that set constraints on university officials and professors in the department and museum, at least insofar as the funding and museum were concerned. By withdrawing some of her financial backing, she made it clear that she wanted to remain involved with the institution but refused to consent to the opposition university men had mounted to her plans and vision. The limits she set established Hearst as a crucial policymaker for the department and museum.

Regent Hearst's directives took Putnam by surprise. It was "a Terrible Shock," one newspaper reported. "It is a sad blow to me to have this curtailment," Putnam revealed in a draft letter to Wheeler. Faced with the unanticipated consequences of Hearst's decision, Putnam wrote Edward Hardy Clark to make sure he understood Hearst correctly. Her order "was not his [Putnam's] understanding," Clark explained to Hearst. Putnam contended that Hearst had committed herself to funding the department for five years. "People, including himself, have been engaged on that basis," he explained. Putnam conceded that he would "make some other arrangement," if necessary, "but that it was embarrassing to do so." Hearst protected and distanced herself from Putnam. She responded through Clark that her "work had gone to such an extent that" she "did not feel justified in keeping up such an expense as" Putnam "had been under for the last few years."[81] Hearst placed the responsibility for the funding squarely on the shoulders of the head of the department and museum—Frederic W. Putnam.

Stunned and desperate to get Hearst's financial support, Putnam did the best he could to get Hearst to change her mind. He gave her the "most kind letter giving one such a full account of everything connected with the museum and the Department of Anthropology generally" and went so far as to suggest the museum be named after her. Hearst rejected the idea. Replying to Putnam in her characteristically direct manner, she explained: "Your kind suggestion to call the museum the Hearst Museum of the U.C. would never do for California" because of the animosity many Americans directed toward rich families like the Hearsts, especially toward her son, a wealthy newspaper tycoon and self-promoter who had thrown his hat into the presidential ring a few months earlier. Phoebe held a realistic view, based on extensive experience, about the problems of the wealthy and famous. As she replied: "If the museum were named for the Hearst family, other people would not contribute to it." The Hearsts' wealth, power, and social position, in other words, would discourage people from giving to the museum because the Hearst family had enemies. Hearst displayed her characteristic modesty and reserve that belied her ambition when she explained further: "It is most kind of you to wish to have the museum bear my name; but I do not care especially about that." When people "[understand] that I am no longer maintaining it, I think others may be interested in the work." What she really cared about was "that the museum receive the help it needs."[82] Hearst refused to budge, and Putnam failed to get Hearst to alter her policy. The irony was that in weaning the state institution from its dependence on her active financial support, Hearst forced the university to get more deeply involved in state politics to seek public financing. Meanwhile, Hearst's policies made it more challenging for Putnam and the department and museum to get the help it needed.

Hearst felt slighted by Putnam and the men of the university and unappreciated and neglected by other recipients of her largesse. She thought they were taking advantage of her in general. At the same time she reduced her contributions to the university, a newspaper announced that Hearst mysteriously "has withdrawn her active support from several educational, religious, and charitable institutions" in San Francisco and Washington DC. But the secret reasons behind her withdrawal were revealed one way or another. She "felt that she was being imposed upon by certain charitable institutions, and as she had withdrawn her support from some she felt compelled to treat all alike." Treating all institutions that received her donations the same meant she withdrew funds from all of them. "As a business woman she is very methodical and painstaking" in her investigations of the requests she received for help. It was "a matter of principal to investigate the appeals for aid," a reporter noted. Her goal: to avoid indiscriminate giving or "foster idleness and vice rather than relieve real need."

A believer in women doing work well and "preparing themselves to render excellent service," she stopped giving to those she determined unworthy, that is, "where the work accomplished," her employee Josephine

Egan explained, "did not correspond with the outlay." Hearst ended her aid to the Hearst Domestic Industries because it had failed to become self-supporting. She withdrew her aid for Hearst Hall, the Pie Del Monte and Enewah clubs, and the Young Women's Christian Association affiliated with the university located near the campus. She reduced her gifts to the Golden Gate Kindergarten Association, the West Berkeley College Settlement, established in 1895, which she supported and equipped, and abandoned support for her Washington DC kindergarten and Kindergarten College—San Francisco, Berkeley, and DC organizations that aided the working class, poor, immigrants, and white and black women and children. She backed away from support for California kindergartens, even though she had "understood the value of kindergarten work and contributed more to it than anyone else in California." She felt, nevertheless, that her activities and gifts were undervalued, and her support for Washington DC kindergartens was withdrawn because she "had no faith in the success of the plan adopted by the teachers and the alumnae." On the heels of Hearst's announcement, the *Chicago-Record Herald* reported that the "Good Fairy" was "in Eclipse" and cleaning house.[83] Intensely offended by not being taken seriously and feeling devalued, Hearst set her own personal boundaries and limits on men and women in American academic and voluntary association politics. She was tired of being seen and treated as an easy mark—as a money machine. She was fed up with not getting the grateful recognition she thought she deserved. People, in her eyes, owed her a certain measure of respect and deference. Her withdrawal of aid sent a loud message that she would no longer consent to such treatment and would continue to exert her considerable power over academic men, and others, as she saw fit.

Setting her own limits, especially on men, did little, if anything, to protect her from the pain and anxieties produced by the criticisms aimed at her for withdrawing her aid. Keenly aware of how effective her decisions and allocation of resources were, she believed she "had done for others all in my power," Hearst explained. So when "such [critical] comments were made and such attacks upon myself and my family, I felt very much hurt," she wrote. She thought such condemnations were unjust. She was concerned, moreover, about the great "deal of gossip . . . in barrooms and barbershops, on street cars, and on sidewalks." Showing a side of herself that was rather self-centered, but rarely revealed in private or in public, she tried to figure out what she had done to get such reactions. She agreed with her attorney that people had grown "accustomed" to her gift-giving. Her sense of duty, obligation, and responsibility, which often masked her ambition, drove her to do all she could. She then revealed her drive to establish her legacy, which now had fallen just short of an obsession. "My reason for attempting so much was that I was anxious to do all I could during my lifetime," she remarked to Putnam, "and not leave it on paper only when I passed away."

She admitted, though, that her ambition had gotten the best of her. She had taken on too much. "It was my great desire to do which carried me a little too far," she lamented. "Reports were so grossly exaggerated, so many unkind things said, and I was so severely criticized for doing what I believed I had the right to do," she wrote, "that I really felt I never wanted to do anything for others again." Taking a mature approach, though, she quickly added: "But of course I know it is not right to entertain such feelings and I have ceased to feel that way." Her anxiety about the impact of the criticism was unwarranted as well. Josephine Egan reported to Hearst that Edward Hardy Clark told her "that the publicity given your affairs had done no harm whatever among business circles." In general, then, Clark did not think any harm had "been done by the published gossip," rumors, and speculation.[84] One of the richest and most powerful women in America, Hearst had learned a valuable lesson. She learned she could make decisions, without male approval, to protect herself and avoid serious damage to her name, reputation, or public image if she took responsibility for her actions.

Hearst now decided to test all university men by submitting her resignation to the board of regents. She offered several reasons for her action.

The first was her health. Sara Y. Stevenson, years earlier, had "seriously contemplate[d] . . . invalidism as a means of escaping . . . [her] burdens." Hearst followed suit. Relying on the language of self-sacrifice and martyrdom rather than active public protest, she explained she suffered from "neuralgia in the face, teeth, and eyes"—a claim perhaps to gain sympathy and provide a rationale to explain why she was still abroad. The second was her announcement that she had rented an apartment in Paris "for the greater part of . . . the next three years." That meant she would not attend regents' meetings for three years and would not be able to discuss her ideas and plans with colleagues nor be able to do her "share of the work." Hearst held strong convictions. She valued industriousness and preferred being very active as a regent. She was unwilling to be a regent in name only. So, in accordance with the bylaws of the board of regents, she resigned. She suggested "some good, capable man should be appointed in" her "place"—a rather conservative position. A reserved, shy, and deferential woman in public, when it helped her accomplish her goals—but not necessarily in private, where she ruled over her own home, estate, and employees—she was unwilling to use her considerable economic and political power to pressure her male colleagues into naming another woman to fill her position as a regent. She made it clear, though, that her resignation would not mean she would "lose interest in the University."[85] She understood the value, especially to her career, in remaining associated with the university.

Hearst had now turned the tables on university officials and men, forcing them to be deferential to her. Governor George C. Pardee and the board of regents unanimously opposed Regent Hearst's resignation. They wanted her to rescind it. The governor, and others, were concerned about the possibility that Hearst might completely sever her ties to, and withdraw her financial support from, the university. Pardee gushed with grateful appreciation when he argued that renouncing her position "would be very detrimental to the interests of the University if you should insist upon resigning, and I know that all the people of California, remembering the great things you have done for the University of California, would desire to see you continue to be a member of the Board of Regents." He implored her to stay in office and give "wise counsel and advice." He understood that she might not be able to be an active regent but no matter. State and university officials knew that the success of the university, and to some extent the state and nation, depended upon the continued association of the Hearst name and wealth with California's premier institution of higher education.

Pardee asked Wheeler to request Hearst to take back her resignation. Wheeler wrote informing her that the regents spoke with one voice on this issue: she should not resign. Wheeler tailored his argument to appeal to Hearst's desire to travel. He acknowledged she wanted "to be out of the State for some time to come; but that should not make any difference, and I do not think that any friend of the University would think so either." He also spoke to her personal need for grateful appreciation. He suggested she could serve three months of the year when she was in California. As he put it, "I honestly think you can do more work and be of more service to the University during the three months of your presence here, joined with the touch with University affairs you are able to maintain at a distance, than most of the Regents are able to render."[86] University officials sent a strong message that they were willing to bow to Hearst and accommodate her needs.

Hearst was highly intelligent. She knew the benefits she derived from her association and active work with the university. She recognized how satisfying it was to be able to discuss her ideas and plans and be effective performing meaningful and purposeful academic work and politics. So she complied with the board of regents' request. Hearst, in the process, forced the California governor and university men to be deferential to her and accept the limits she placed on them. They faced the distinct possibly that Hearst's name and resources would no longer be available to benefit California's premier institution of higher education if they chose to ignore her policies. To get to that point and remain on the job, though, Hearst made a series of messy compromises and decided to accept certain limits.

Regent Hearst, from this point on, served the University of California at a greater distance and apart from university and academic politics. The pain and suffering she had experienced over her battle to establish the department and museum of anthropology ran deep. University men, in exchange, particularly Kroeber, accepted the obvious—Hearst's money gave her power to keep the department and museum going. Kroeber was secure in the knowledge that Putnam and the executive committee now supported him after the fierce political conflict over the shape and direction of the department and museum. He moved to solidify his control over the kind of research that would build the department's professional reputation and standing. He was uncertain, at first, of Hearst's wishes and unwilling to confront her. He wrote to Putnam to ask if Regent Hearst "really wants to keep me or whether she would be relieved if I should go." Kroeber sent her "copies of two papers published at the University" on research she had funded—a gesture of reconciliation. He trusted "that the results may in some degree meet your expectations," he explained to Hearst. Time healed Hearst's wounds to an extent. As she remarked to Kroeber, she "was glad" to have knowledge of this first paper on his California work, was eager to see "his report when it is issued." Pleased with Hearst's response, President Wheeler kept her informed about university affairs. Hearst, meanwhile, tried to restore friendly relations in her own way. After she received Kroeber's papers, she wrote him: "As you say, it [anthropological information] may be technical, but I shall understand enough—knowing what I do now of your work—to appreciate it." She came to understand, value, and respect Kroeber's academic anthropological expertise to the point where she resumed funding his scholarly work, increasing the chances that cultural relativism would find acceptance among intellectuals and the public even though, in effect, her failure to win her political battle in the academic world meant she had lost a measure of status and privilege at the university.

Kroeber was relieved that Hearst wanted him to stay. He, in turn, became even more secure and comfortable in his faculty and departmental position.

As his confidence grew, he treated Hearst with respect. He wrote Putnam: "I shall do first according to Mrs. Hearst's wishes and then according to yours." Kroeber kept Hearst abreast of what was going on in the museum and departmental research. He told her how her gifts were spent and informed her when Putnam came to the museum so she could meet with him. He also reassured Hearst: "Whenever you advise me what you wish us to do, I shall immediately proceed according to your instructions." Kroeber and other university officials did her bidding where her artifacts and the museum were concerned. They also kept her up-to-date on departmental activities, research, and explorations. But Hearst no longer held the power to hire and fire faculty and determine the direction of the department or faculty research and theory.[87] The forces to professionalize anthropology, which also embraced Kroeber's modern theories, had triumphed over Hearst's focus on teaching. Showing Hearst that the university valued her erased to some extent any wounded pride and real annoyance and pain she might have felt from her bruising battle with, and her exclusion from, the world of academic professionals. Hearst came to accept her new relationship with Kroeber, the museum, and the department after Kroeber's conciliatory acts. She may have believed she was as powerful as a queen. But she learned a great deal about the restrictions placed on her power, especially those produced by constraints on her sex and class, in academic politics and in the field of anthropology, and how to set limits on the power of men.

Regent Hearst experienced some deeply painful lessons about the limits of power at the University of California. Her lack of a higher education and professional expertise in anthropology led university officials and academic men, interested in professionalizing the discipline, to challenge her power and vision. These factors, coupled with her assumptions about the power she possessed over the department and practical university politics, made it impossible for her to transcend the boundaries set by men at the University of California. She did hold economic power over the department and museum. She spent $111,088.78 for explorations, expenses for the

11. Charter Day ceremonies with Phoebe Apperson Hearst, Benjamin Ide Wheeler, and Theodore Roosevelt at Greek Theater, 1911. UARCPIC 1:81. Courtesy of the Bancroft Library, University of California, Berkeley.

museum, and salaries to keep the department and museum going by the end of June 1902.[88] But lacking in-depth knowledge of anthropology and the persuasive skills her university colleagues held, she failed to convince professional academic anthropologists that the direction in which she wanted to take the new department and museum was in the best interests of the university and its students. Nor did she persuade university men that she possessed the academic qualifications to be considered a professional in anthropology. So political support—especially from Wheeler, Putnam, and Fletcher, to some degree—to move the department in the overall direction she favored never materialized.

Wheeler, Putnam, Kroeber, and Fletcher understood that Hearst lacked expertise as an academic anthropologist. To build anthropology into a legitimate, professional scientific discipline and the new department into an academically prestigious one, they believed students needed to receive the proper scientific training from academically trained scholars with knowledge about the latest theories in anthropology and with advanced degrees from accredited, distinguished institutions of higher education. Only those with advanced scholarly degrees in the field held the power and authority to be honored and treated with respect as professionals. There were exceptions, of course. Hearst, like Putnam, lacked a degree in anthropology from a reputable college or university. But different academic standards applied to Putnam who, unlike Hearst, had attended Harvard University. Like Hearst, Putnam did not possess a degree from a higher institution of education, but he still received praise and honors for his work in anthropology. University officials and academics accepted Putnam's views and knowledge in the field of anthropology. But they dismissed Hearst's criticism of Kroeber's work and philosophically and politically battled with her for power over the department and museum. Hearst only got so far with her money and dignified, modest, feminine approach. She had, in effect, fooled herself into thinking that her money and resources gave her enough power to get what she wanted.

Phoebe Apperson Hearst failed to bring to life her idea and plan to build an empire at the University of California by establishing a department and museum of anthropology, at a time when the United States was also on a mission to build an empire. She experienced her first serious political defeat. History passed her by. She had been unable to wield her considerable power effectively to achieve her goal of building a museum to educate the masses to appreciate diverse races, cultures, and nations.[89] Her failure became a major turning point in her life, however. On the one hand, it gave her confidence to continue exerting power to set limits on men. On the other, it forced her to accept the fact that she would never be considered a professional in the field of anthropology. But what now? Would she make a mark ever again on American academic politics and in public life? Was her career as a powerful, progressive woman in American voluntary association reform and academic politics at an end?

7

National Politics

The allure of world travel to unfamiliar places and learning about different cultures, races, and nations was once again just the tonic for Phoebe Apperson Hearst as the pain she had experienced from her defeat at the University of California slowly subsided and faded away.[1] Constantly on the go, she sailed "upon the Nile" to Egypt in early 1905 to view the expedition she was funding under the supervision of anthropologist George A. Reisner. Adventuresome as ever, she rode a "camel and donkey" to visit the pyramids and her University of California Egyptian excavations. She put up with the forces of nature at the diggings. "The wind blew night and day, and the sand was everywhere, in our rooms and in our eyes," she wrote. The challenges of the trip made her thankful for what she had. "It is good for me no doubt to be without conveniences and then I appreciate my blessings" and "home more than ever," she explained. Enthralled with the fruits of her "splendid" anthropological research expedition, she took delight in the intellectual stimulation and cultural knowledge she gathered at the site. She had a wonderful time on her trip to Palestine and Jericho as well. Eventually she returned to Paris to absorb more French culture and take in the Parisian way of life.[2] Phoebe was willing to endure the problems of travel to enjoy the intellectual and cultural blessings her wealth provided.

Phoebe's conscience pulled and pushed her in opposite directions as she struggled with her old internal nemesis—the paradox between materialism and morality. She received disturbing news, when in Paris, about the destruction to San Francisco from the 1906 earthquake and fire. "San Francisco is a dreadful sight. There is nothing left of it but heaps of burnt bricks and piles of twisted iron," Millicent Veronica Willson Hearst, William Randolph Hearst's spouse, wrote her mother-in-law. The stories Hearst heard about the earthquake and fire got her thinking. She started to grasp, she explained, "the enormity and horror of the destruction and suffering." But Edward H. Clark, her employee and cousin, informed her that there was no reason why she should sail back to America because her properties had suffered little damage. "It is certainly not sufficient to make any difference in your affairs," he wrote, "except it will be necessary to keep expenses as low as possible until we get things adjusted." Hearst paid attention to Clark's advice. She decided it was best to stay in Paris. "At first I felt as if I must go home at once but reasoned the matter out that I could do little if there. I would give all I could to the destitute anyway," she explained a bit disingenuously.[3] At this point in her internal struggle, materialism seemed to take precedence over obligation and responsibility to those in need as a justification for doing what made her happy. Phoebe enjoyed her life in Paris.

But her sense of what she needed to do as a businesswoman and a parent, triggered by the news about Will's financial problems, stemming from his newspaper business and his 1906 New York gubernatorial campaign, tugged at her conscience. Bound to keep the Hearst estate strong and on a healthy financial footing, she grew worried when Millicent informed her that the *San Francisco Examiner* was losing forty thousand dollars of income per month. Phoebe was no stranger to difficult economic times. When she thought the Hearst family was in danger, especially financially, she had always mixed the careful supervision of her businesses and academic affairs with the conscientious supervision of her home and family. Once again, she felt the need to tighten her economic belt, watch her pennies, and help her son. Phoebe saw the debt incurred by the *San Francisco Examiner* as a significant drain on her estate income at a time when she wanted to keep expenses low. "As my resources had been diminished it seemed best to stay in my little apartment [in Paris] and spend as little as possible," she explained. Her desire to economize surfaced several months before the earthquake and fire when she sent word that she would fund the department and museum of anthropology for three more years but would not add to the collections.[4] Her sense of moral duty to her son and her business obligations was so strong that Will's financial problems intensified her desire to economize.

At times, Phoebe's sense of personal and political obligation to moral progressive reform pushed her in the opposite direction. When "Mrs. Whitelaw Reid sent me her box for the opera [when] 'Siegfreid' [*sic*] was given, I could not enjoy it," she wrote. "As I looked over the house and saw such gorgeous jewels on many women who appeared to live only for pleasure," she added, "my thoughts went far away to the destroyed city and suffering anxious people in what was S.F. and I felt that things were strangely wrong in many ways. my heart ached so that I wished I had stayed at home."[5] Her sense of loyalty and commitment to improving the lives of her constituents got her thinking about going back to San Francisco to set things right.

Phoebe's devotion to her family, business, and those she had a duty to serve, finally got the best of her. Stories of Will's political failure and deepening economic crisis weighed heavily on her mind. Will had enjoyed a visit to the White House to see President Theodore Roosevelt while Phoebe was abroad. But his unsuccessful 1906 New York campaign for governor as a Democrat was not as pleasurable. He endured blistering criticism from male moral reformers who "fear[ed] him . . . because while he spoke about restoring democracy, he wasn't really a democrat," according to one historian. He was "dedicated to securing power to do as he thought best and subordinating every means to that end. Will Hearst personified 'the old spirit' that the political reformers were trying to change." He held up under the attacks. But it was difficult. Thinking that being with his mother would bring him comfort, he felt sad that he was unable to see more of her. "It seems as if we were fated never to be with each other and some of these days we will die without having had more than a speaking acquaintance—or rather a writing acquaintance," Will wrote Phoebe in the summer of 1906.[6]

Phoebe received news then from Edward Clark that Will was teetering on the brink of financial disaster. "He owes nearly $2,000,000 . . . but from $100,000 to $250,000 may have to be paid before long," Clark explained. Clark also told his boss about Will's plan to replace the *Examiner* building, which was destroyed in the San Francisco earthquake and fire. Will wanted to erect "a 12 story building with a six story tower on top of it." Clark was troubled by Will's plan. He explained to Hearst that construction of the building would not be to her financial advantage because it would cost too much to build the tower. Clark asked for her advice and told her he would support any decision she made. "If you feel you would like to accommodate him in the style of building he wants, of course I will be glad to carry out your instructions," Clark wrote.

Phoebe enjoyed her special interest in buildings. They were financial and personal assets that increased the value of the Hearst estate. They also drew attention to the family name and expressed her convictions, values, and station in life. But she refused to give Will the money he requested, and finally, the combination of material and moral political factors dictated that she "must go home to stay." Hearst sailed from Europe for the last time on January 8, 1907, aboard the ss *Kaiser Wilhelm II* to New York.[7] Phoebe set foot on American soil in New York City. She said goodbye, eventually, to New York City and returned to her Hacienda in California—a state in the vanguard "of social welfare legislation for women during the Progressive Era."[8]

Never one to adhere strictly to the constraints of womanhood and class, Hearst could not remain idle or sit on her laurels for very long. Getting involved again in departmental and museum academic politics at the University of California was out of the question because of her past experiences. So her only choice, practically speaking, was to throw herself back into the exhilarating world of nonpartisan voluntary association politics. She would need to manage her resources skillfully, though, to jog people's memories about the Phoebe Apperson Hearst name and her past reform and political activities as a University of California regent and a suffragist. She had to remind people about her accomplishments in voluntary organizations, especially those that helped the downtrodden. It was necessary, in essence, to refashion her past political identity and role to fit a modern age of mass consumption and progressive reform politics if she was to exert power and advance her political agenda in voluntary association politics further, especially at the national level.[9]

The Panama-Pacific International Exposition (PPIE), "a gigantic enterprise of voluntary service," similar to the 1893 World's Columbian Exposition in Chicago and the 1904 Louisiana Purchase Exposition in Saint Louis, gave Hearst the chance to resurrect and revitalize her career on a national political stage.[10] San Francisco's Dream City of 1915 would cost millions to build, would be visited by 18.9 million attendees, would cover 635 acres, and would hold a massive number of exhibits in "sixty-eight buildings" and "eleven major exhibit halls" or departments.[11] The PPIE opened the door for Hearst to resolve her internal conflict between materialism and moral principle and became the culminating event of national nonpartisan voluntary association politics in the Progressive Era.

Charles C. Moore, a businessman and health reformer, issued a call for subscriptions for the Panama-Pacific International Exposition Company—a nonpartisan, chartered commercial organization that included men involved in traditional partisan politics—to fund the exposition. Male capitalists and moral reformers responded quickly to Moore's request. It took only several hours for PPIE Company subscriptions to climb to $4,089,000.[12] The first unsettled question PPIE businessmen and progressive reformers faced, after the subscriptions came pouring in, was how to use partisan political methods to get the federal government to approve San Francisco as the official site of the exposition. PPIE men began to lobby Congress to hold the exposition on the Pacific Coast.[13] While it was meant primarily to celebrate the completion of the Panama Canal, the exposition was also widely seen by Bay Area residents as an opportunity to parade its recovery from the 1906 earthquake. From the start, elements of partisan and moral nonpartisan politics were woven into the plans for the exposition.

Women, initially, took no part in the partisan and moral progressive politics of the PPIE. "In the beginning, when everything connected with the Exposition was a problem, there was nothing definite for women to do" while men lobbied, according to Anna Pratt Simpson, a PPIE historian. Prosperous and wealthy women interested in doing "constructive work" at the exposition believed "that the time would come in the affairs of the great project when women must take their 'turn at the wheel.'" So they prepared for that time and took the initiative. Bettie Lowenberg, without delay, called Laura Lovell White. Both were clubwomen and progressive moral reformers. Lowenberg was a philanthropist, president of the Philomath Club of Jewish women in San Francisco, and a suffragist. She also was an advocate for uniform marriage and divorce laws across the country. White was the founder of the California Club of San Francisco, president of the Political Equality Club, and married to a banker. White offered the resources of the California Club to help women who were interested in getting involved in the PPIE. Lowenberg suggested a meeting be held of competent women to discuss how clubwomen, reformers, and other interested females, could take part in exposition politics to promote their personal and shared interests with men and represent their constituents.[14]

The women agreed to meet in early January 1910 to organize "a campaign to secure votes in Congress" to hold the exposition in San Francisco. The Panama-Pacific Exposition Company initiated a postcard campaign "to flood the country with pleas for congressional endorsement of San Francisco as the official site for the Panama Exposition in 1915," White wrote. The postcard campaign was associated with the holding of San Francisco Woman's Day. White, chair of the San Francisco Women's Post Card Day Committee, recruited Hearst for the postcard campaign. Hearst agreed to send postcards. As White wrote to Hearst: "I shall see that you receive all [the postcards] that you think you can send out."[15] Women lobbyists for the PPIE from the committee traveled to Washington DC as the postcard campaign unfolded to see California Republican senator George C. Perkins and California Republican congressman Julius Kahn to enlist their support and lobby men in Congress.[16] By early 1911, PPIE women understood that both their economic and political roles were important and went hand-in-hand if they were to successfully promote progressive reform goals and represent their constituents on a national political stage at the exposition.

Hearst felt comfortable participating in lobbying efforts traditionally used by partisan politicians, but not directly or in person. Lobbying members of the U.S. Congress openly in public was unacceptable to Hearst. But she felt at home in "a female dominion in the mostly male empire of policymaking" that included the political world of nonpartisan voluntary reform associations. She understood that women were to be nonpartisan and stay out of partisan American party politics. Hearst's political involvements reflected the belief that women were to be "viewed" and "present . . . themselves as motivated by issues not elections and by principles not a search for power." Americans identified men, though, "as inherently partisan."[17] Hearst, a businesswoman, endorsed a conventional line of thinking on partisanship expressed a few years later by Democrats in the *Suffragist* newspaper. Democrats advised readers to "remain non-partisan," by which they meant "taking no active part in the Presidential campaign."

The definition of nonpartisan and partisan, though, varied depending on one's perspective. Hearst took the position that women should exhibit "ladylike" behavior to find a place in the female and male political worlds. Yet she knew that women and men "continually negotiated . . . with one another for power, influence, and place in American political life." Up to this point, she had refused to take on roles that men traditionally performed in Democratic or Republican Party politics. Hearst, unlike Jane Addams, who was eighteen years younger, believed women should refrain from participating in the major American political parties. But she thought it was acceptable for her sex to engage in activism with men in nonpartisan voluntary reform and political associations on issues of shared interest such as improving health standards, kindergartens, academic, industrial, and educational reform, including moral protective labor legislation, and votes for women, among other issues.[18] Even so, she supported the practice of lobbying by both men and women—a method used extensively in conventional partisan politics.

Hearst's involvement in the postcard campaign helped the PPIE lobbyists win the fight in Washington DC to get Congress to hold the exposition in San Francisco. Will Hearst was "One of the Great Factors," the *Los Angeles Examiner* reported, in getting members of Congress to vote for San Francisco as the site of the Panama-Pacific International Exposition. "With energy characteristic of California, Mr. Hearst plunged into the fight and placed at our disposal [according to the chairman of the congressional committee] his entire [newspaper] service East and West."[19] Will frequently employed the power of the press in partisan politics for political causes in which he and his mother held shared interests.

PPIE women got together at the St. Francis Hotel to discuss their political "plans for forming a Women's Panama-Pacific International Exposition Association" in April 1911 soon after Will Hearst began to use his newspapers on behalf of PPIE lobbyists.[20] Laura Lovell White was elected president of the Women's Panama-Pacific International Exposition Association or the Panama-Pacific International Exposition Association of Women (PPIEAW). White knew that women who wanted to get involved in the PPIE would need to be prominent in California, have the time and physical constitution to participate in the process, and demonstrate the leadership abilities, economic means, and political connections, especially national ones, to make the PPIEAW contributions to the exposition an overall success. Plenty of women who were married to wealthy industrial tycoons in San Francisco and the Bay Area might be interested in getting involved: these could include Ellis Spreckels, wife of Claude Spreckels, a wealthy sugar manufacturer; Mary S. Merrill, married to John Merrill, a prominent businessman and philanthropist; and prosperous public-spirited women like White, among others.[21] Which wealthy and prosperous women would be interested in taking part in PPIE politics? Which ones would have the ideas, reputation, skills, know-how, and connections with the right people to garner an invitation to serve officially? Would all prominent, rich women accept such a huge challenge and the responsibilities, obligations, and duties associated with nonpartisan political participation in the PPIE?

Phoebe A. Hearst was experiencing an active life from 1907 to 1911; her hands were full just taking care of her social, cultural, economic, political, and legal affairs. She was so hardworking and active that she became more discerning about how she spent her time. "My life is a very busy one and I am left no time for attendance at clubs," she wrote. She still possessed a general interest in women's clubs but had resigned from many because she lacked the time to attend. She traveled east, attended University of California regents' meetings, and handled Department and Museum of Anthropology matters. She made more discriminating decisions about the financial and emotional support she gave to female friends and others in need. She struggled with her health and tried a rest cure. She kept up with her voluminous correspondence and held social gatherings from time to time, but none that garnered the extensive press attention she had received in the late nineteenth century.[22] She seemed to be biding her time, waiting for the right opportunity to once again advance her career and political agenda.

The PPIE provided Hearst with the right opportunity to resurrect and revitalize her career in nonpartisan voluntary association politics as the summer of 1911 approached. Her first step was to convince PPIE women and men of her "willingness to serve the city with the best" she "had to give" at the PPIE—a national patriotic, cultural, economic, and nonpartisan voluntary reform organization event.[23]

Hearst relied on her home near Pleasanton, the Hacienda del Pozo de Verona, as a foundation for launching her political campaign. Hearst's "dwelling within a mansion" had grown, by the second decade of the twentieth century, to ninety-two rooms! Sizeable additions had been designed by Julia Morgan. Morgan had graduated from the University of California, Berkeley with a degree in engineering. The additions she designed included a banquet room, heated indoor swimming pool, music room "with a 30-foot ceiling and windows," and "ballroom with sunken gardens." Servant's quarters, garages, buildings for leisure activities, and places to keep horses existed on the hill behind. Travelers could get to the Hacienda by "a special boat and train" Hearst provided. To get to Hearst's mansion from Oakland, Morgan and other guests needed to "go down to First and Broadway" and take the train "on to Niles and" slowly climb "up the Niles Canyon," a guest recalled. Passengers enjoyed "two hours of sheer delight, riding through one of the most beautiful sections of California" to visit "a citizen of the world, albeit California claims her heart and first love"—the "first woman of California," an early twentieth-century female storyteller of the PPIE wrote.

Travelers were met at Hearst's private Southern Pacific or Western Pacific Railroad Hacienda stops by carriages and tally-hos (coaches with four smartly drawn horses that emulated the famous English coach, the *Tally-Ho*, imported to the United States in 1876) with the "initials— PAH—in a rather elaborate monogram on the . . . doors of the carriages." Or they were greeted by "uniformed chauffeurs in a Packard and white Stanley Steamer"—just several of the eight automobiles Hearst owned between 1906 and 1913 that included one electric car. The cars ranged from forty to sixty horsepower. Hearst's employees drove people up a long winding road lined with palms and flowers through the lower Hacienda gates to the white-walled, Mission-styled—or as some described it, "Hispano-Moresque"—stately mansion with tiled roof and window awnings surrounded by picnic grounds and tables, great swings, and live oaks. People stepped out of the carriage, or automobile, and were greeted by Hearst's employees at the front door.

Inside, Hearst's extensive, exquisite "notable objects of art" covered the walls and dotted room interiors. Hearst was a charming, modest woman, tastefully dressed, never overdressed or laden with too many jewels. She met her guests and presided over her "self-contained little domain," or "principality," "in a rather royal way," a son of one of Hearst's employees observed.[24] Adelaide Johnson, sculptress of suffragists Lucretia Mott, Elizabeth Cady Stanton, and Isabella Beecher Hooker, remarked that the mansion was a "masterpiece in achievement." Having passed through the front portal, people entered a structure that represented and expressed, symbolically, concretely, and realistically, Hearst's social, cultural, economic, and political worlds.[25] Hearst now orchestrated a series of high-society affairs at her Hacienda del Pozo de Verona to impress upon others her interest in taking part in PPIE politics. She timed her decisions perfectly to give more and more guests the pleasure of experiencing her elaborate, extravagant Hacienda parties to coincide with the early stage of exposition planning.

Hearst and her political entertainments represented the transition between the past and the modern age for those interested in the Panama-Pacific International Exposition. She entertained, "during the preparatory years" of the PPIE, from April 1911 through early 1915, "every week-end at her home in Pleasanton, companies of distinguished men and women who came in connection with the building of the Exposition, those who participated in its activities, and its honored guests," PPIE historian Anna Pratt Simpson remarked. Hearst's Hacienda activities took place while a major shift was underway in the first decades of the twentieth century from older nineteenth-century American ideas and values on selfhood and culture—the importance of worthy, or moral, character, hard work, self-denial, and sacrifice—to a new emphasis on personality, pleasure, good health, self-fulfillment, and abundance and consumption.[26] Her events established an environment in which she hoped to shape a new political identity and role that appealed to modern Americans interested in both consumption and progressive reform.

Hearst put on quite a display of the force of her personality, wealth, and ability to consume at her Hacienda political parties for a huge number of guests connected or involved with the Panama-Pacific International Exposition. She brought together up to six hundred at a time before and during the exposition. One of the first entertainments of significance she held was in the summer of 1911. She wrote to a friend, Frances Lummis, about her "busy summer" and taking care of all her house guests. "I had thought my house full, but this year exceeded all previous records," she explained. Hearst rubbed elbows at her social and political affairs with the Marquis and Marchioness (or Count and Countess) Aberdeen, of Ireland. The Countess was "one of the world's greatest living women philanthropists," according to one newspaper. She represented the Federated Women's Club of Great Britain, Ireland, and the Netherlands and would preside at the International Congress of Women's Congresses.

Hearst conversed at her parties with PPIE officials Charles C. Moore, president of the board of directors and his wife; PPIE vice presidents and their spouses; as well as Judge Lamar, representative of the federal government at the PPIE; state regents; and other elite and honorable people interested in the exposition.[27] In 1911 alone, the number of Hearst's guests went "from ten to 15 & sometimes 20, though the difficulties of domestic service was at times very trying," Hearst wrote, reminding herself and others of her class superiority.[28] She hosted 1,490 guests for barbeques and garden parties and 1,750 for weekends, luncheons, and dinners through the end of 1911 and over the next several years. By 1915 she had entertained and served "not less than 4,000 guests at the Exposition," and hosted "6,000 more" at the Hacienda! Of these, 1,840 stayed overnight, spent the day or weekend, or had lunch. This figure excluded people who stayed for an hour or who made courtesy calls.[29] Holding political affairs was not new for Hearst, but the size and scale of her latest political events were unprecedented.

Hearst crafted her guest lists carefully and organized her affairs down to the last detail. Her mind drifted to thinking about partisan politics while she organized her parties. She contemplated going to a smoker at the University of California Faculty Club to honor Theodore Roosevelt, a progressive moral reformer, the epitome of manliness, and an advocate for American imperialism in the early twentieth century. She was tempted to go. But in the end she declined the invitation. "How surprised they would be if I should attend," she remarked.[30] The personification of femininity and a supporter of American imperial expansion, Hearst's evangelical upbringing and Victorian reserve told her it would be unacceptable for a woman of her generation to appear. So she did the next best thing. She held high-society political parties and displayed her varied powers in the congenial, comfortable atmosphere of her own home or mansion. She brought together diverse political elements of a divided society and shaped them into a harmonious, organic whole—at least while guests were at the Hacienda. Hearst's skillful management and masterly display of her wealth and consummate skills and talents captivated virtually all who stayed at the Hacienda. She cast such a spell over the place—aiming to get others to pay attention to her and the Hearst name—that people gushed with joy when recounting the experience attending Hearst's lavish events. Some referred to her as a "Queen" or "Fairy Queen waving" her "enchanted wand over the enchanted Hacienda."[31]

Hearst moved around the Hacienda to converse with old acquaintances and meet new people, usually socially and politically active nonpartisan and partisan women and men who were wealthy, public-spirited, and who shared her reform views and other interests and had distinguished reputations in San Francisco, California, and beyond. She turned her Hacienda high on a hill, in essence, into her political campaign headquarters to draw attention to herself and convince people interested in the Panama-Pacific International Exposition of her willingness to participate and serve.[32]

Hearst's Hacienda visitors fell under the spell of a woman "representative of California herself" who furthered, an admirer believed, "every good cause for the welfare of California" and by implication the nation-state and federal government.[33] Hearst's high-society entertainments mimicked the political events held by men running for partisan elective offices in search of votes, as well as the larger meet-and-greet events for candidates hosted by rich people participating in traditional partisan politics today.

Hearst spared no expense in using the Hacienda as her main office or center to promote the reform issues, like health, near and dear to her heart and the heart of other progressive reformers. Because Hearst knew the importance of taking proper care of herself, especially to get rest, relax, and eat homegrown, healthy foods, she turned her place into a kind of health spa and resort. She made it possible for guests to take pleasure in the "Hacienda state of health with none of the New York disabilities," as one female guest wrote. Another woman described to a female friend a visit to Hearst to take "the 'Hacienda Cure.'" She explained to Hearst that she told her friend that it "will do her more good than any doctor's regime—I speak from experience."

Hearst served healthy, sumptuous meals to help strengthen guests' physical well-being. She took pride in meals made mostly from local agricultural products. Elizabeth W. Allston Pringle, a South Carolina rice plantation manager and author of her diary excerpts titled *A Woman Rice Planter*, published in 1913, recounted the pleasure she experienced eating an extremely costly and magnificent meal during an extensive stay at Hearst's mansion. Guests took a break from their busy worlds and enjoyed each other's company in Hearst's home, a place surrounded by the bucolic beauty of the rolling hills in Pleasanton. They discussed issues of personal interest related to the exposition such as health, art, literature, business, politics, and how to make people's lives better.[34] Hearst seduced PPIE people with her wealth to convince them of her serious interest in good health, serving the exposition, and becoming very active again in progressive, nonpartisan voluntary reform politics.

Hearst's political campaign worked. The "three hundred representative women of the city" in the Panama-Pacific International Exposition Association of Women, "a very large body," took steps to form a PPIE Woman's Board. They invited Hearst, among other women, to become a stockholder in the PPIE Corporation. The money raised from women purchasing stocks would be used to establish a separate, legally chartered and incorporated woman's board to "secure the interest, attendance and participation of women" in, and promote, the PPIE. Most members of the PPIE Woman's Board Directorate, which consisted of the thirty-two original stockholders, were prominent Protestant westerners (a few were Jewish) with wealth. They "represented the greatest variety of activities and interests," according to Anna Simpson. Most, including Hearst, were high-society women and progressive reformers listed in the *San Francisco Blue Book*. A few were socialites only. Many were married to businessmen and some to University of California regents. Two were single, female physicians. Another was a newspaper writer.

These female stockholders signed "The Articles of Incorporation of the Woman's Board of the Panama-Pacific International Exposition and World's Fair" in the third week in August 1911, several months before the passage of California suffrage. The total "amount of the Capital Stock of said [Woman's Board] Corporation" was "Twenty-five Thousand Dollars ($25,000)," a far cry from the almost $5 million in stock subscriptions raised by the men who became members of the exposition's board of directors. "Directors of the Woman's Board . . . were elected from the stockholders." A majority of the female stockholders were, like the board of directors, "citizens and residents of the State of California." Female directors were "to take charge of the affairs of said corporation for the first six (6) months, and until their successors are elected and qualified." Hearst's campaign made her one of the original female stockholders and directors of the woman's board.[35] Sitting on the woman's board and engaging in PPIE politics became yet another of Hearst's ways of resolving successfully her inner conflict between materialism and moral principle.

Hearst used a subtle and skillful gift-giving plan to impress and distinguish herself from other wealthy women members once she was elected a director of the woman's board. Her strategy was based on the concept of a new morality that made gift-giving more consumer-oriented and political and could help shape "the destinies of her time," one reporter wrote. As one gentleman explained to Hearst: "You have the God given talent to give right."[36] One of the most typical and dramatic ways Hearst carried out her plan to remind people of her wealth and power was to wave her "magic wand" just before the Christmas holidays, her favorite season.[37]

Hearst made a habit of shopping throughout the PPIE preparatory years for Christmas gifts. One year, the manager of a San Francisco store kept the place open just for her until she completed spending money on the gifts she desired. The Christmas of 1911 was a particularly memorable one in the annals of Hearst's gift-giving. As Christmas approached, Hearst stood in the midst of two rooms packed floor to ceiling with "a succession of shelves and drawers filled with 'stuff' enough to start a department store," a *Santa Cruz Surf* reporter wrote. Amid the hustle and bustle were, the reporter continued, "several women around a long center table, wrapping and addressing packages, [and] Mrs. Hearst dictating and directing" to send gifts according to the recipient's station in life. Hearst's largesse benefited over a thousand family members, friends, janitors and men at the University of California Department of Anthropology Museum. Other recipients were South Dakota mine and San Simeon employees, ranch hands on her Babícora estate in Mexico who worked for the Babícora Development Corporation, Mexican schoolchildren, and people in Asia, Europe, and Africa.

Folks became dazzled by Hearst's generosity and benefited from her gifts. The press took notice too. The huge amounts of money she spent brought her publicity in western and eastern newspapers in America and as far away as Asia, Europe, and Africa.[38] The attention the press gave Hearst made her stand out from other rich women of substance and privilege on the PPIE Woman's Board, such as Mary S. Merrill—a social worker, clubwoman, member of the board of directors of the Children's Hospital, Young Women's Christian Association (YWCA), and Red Cross official—or Laura Lovell White, among others.[39] Few, if any, women with lots of money matched or surpassed Hearst in using political gift-giving to draw attention to her name and get people to think of her generosity and past accomplishments.

Hearst's wealth, ideas, abilities, connections, reputation, physical endurance, and veteran experience in progressive reform politics so impressed PPIE women that the exposition directorate invited her to run unopposed for the elected office of honorary president of the woman's board. PPIE women turned to a rich, high-society woman with enough economic and political clout and talent, the right associates, and access to the press to convince themselves, and others, they could succeed. Hearst filled the bill. She came up with innovative ideas. Her abilities and say-so could move mountains. She got things done. She possessed good tact and judgment. She had extensive experience and commanded a stellar reputation in social and political circles. As Charlotte Anita Whitney wrote, Hearst's reputation in "progressive movements in the State" was well known. She possessed a good reputation in Washington DC as well. Hearst's networks were vast. She had access to many famous, powerful people and important connections to the newspaper world.[40] Hearst accepted the invitation to run unopposed in a nonpartisan election for office that mimicked some, but not all, aspects of partisan electoral politics. Voluntary association politics focused on candidates with abilities and means, the use of political events to attract press attention to the candidate and political support, and the process of voting, among other elements.

Hearst parlayed her earned reputation for distinguishing herself from other rich women, through her Christmas gift-giving and parties, into a political victory. She stood for the election to the post of honorary president of the woman's board in the second week of September 1911. The vote took place while she organized her annual 1911 Christmas gift-giving, several weeks after the board was officially formed and about three weeks before women won the right to vote in California. Hearst won for several reasons, according to published and private sources. She was seen "as the First Lady of the State." Her "generosity seemed boundless." She brought together at her Hacienda "those who participated in [PPIE] activities, and its honored guests" and attended "all important deliberations" leading up to the exposition. Her "hospitality, princely in every way, brought people from every part of the globe to one of the most interesting houses in the entire country," Anna Simpson explained. And Hearst had long been identified with progressive moral reform issues and was a veteran in progressive movements.

All these factors coalesced and led to Hearst's official installment as the head of the PPIE Woman's Board on November 12, 1911. The bylaws of the woman's board stated that the office of honorary president was a ceremonial office "free of all obligations of office or dues, in recognition of . . . [Hearst's] eminence in woman's work."[41] Will's *San Francisco Examiner* reported on his mother's election success immediately. The report drew attention to Hearst's and the woman's board's victory in getting the all-male board of directors of the PPIE to accept them as part of the exposition's national power and political structure.[42] Hearst got ready for the challenges that lay ahead after her election victory. But she had a wealth of experience in nonpartisan voluntary association politics to draw on to guide her through her term.

Hearst threw herself into PPIE politics even though the office of honorary president was a ceremonial position. From the start, she had every intention of being more than a titular president of the woman's board. She set conditions before she formally accepted her election victory and the office. Because of Hearst's age and the demands on her of work already underway, she wanted a young, energetic woman to handle the day-to-day responsibilities, obligations, and duties of the board. "If they would appoint a perfectly fit and proper person with whom she could work, she would accept the honorary presidency and work to the extent of her power [she understood her limits], but she would not undertake the actual active running of the whole thing," biographer Adele Brooks noted. The PPIE Woman's Board complied with Hearst's wishes. They selected Helen P. Sanborn from among the candidates on the directorate and asked her to run unopposed in an election for "acting president."[43] Hearst and Sanborn worked as a political team from the start.

Sanborn was the daughter of Margaret Peck. She "was as like Mrs. Hearst as her own daughter might have been," Brooks observed. She "had really formed herself on Mrs. Hearst's ideals—she was as much an imitation of Mrs. Hearst as anyone could be"—energetic, "very competent," and "really a wonderful executive" with "tact and good judgment" and good ideas. She also served as president of the Sorosis and Century Clubs and the Protestant Orphan's Asylum. She was a former executive officer of the California Red Cross and a YWCA supporter. Hearst was fond of Sanborn.[44] Sanborn was devoted to Hearst and worked closely with her. Both Hearst and Sanborn contributed ideas and talents. But Sanborn sought Hearst's approval, in general, and did what she wanted rather than the other way around.

Honorary president Hearst and the other woman's board voting members were expected to work with and represent active, voting members of PPIE voluntary associations from across the country.[45] In a relatively short period of time, then—from 1907 to 1911—Hearst had resurrected and revitalized her career by being elected to head a board of a legally chartered and incorporated nonpartisan voluntary reform organization that oversaw female social, cultural, and political activities at the exposition.

While Hearst was an honorary president in name only, according to the bylaws of the woman's board, she was committed, privately, to being an active, powerful head of the board and doing a good job—carrying out, behind the scenes, what she believed were the social, cultural, economic, political responsibilities, and legal obligations and duties of her office that contributed to the advancement of issues of concern to her colleagues and constituents. She had to be an effective and qualified head of the woman's board to feed her soul. That meant she had to turn the honorary presidency into an office with power and political meaning and purpose and place it on par with the head of the PPIE Board of Directors.

Hearst faced challenges and came up against the limits of power as she tried to make the office of honorary president into something more than a ceremonial position. Problems arose that tested Hearst's skills even before she accepted her official election victory. Hearst and other board officials were expected to advance elite interests, inspire confidence, and contribute financially to the exposition. But Moore and his colleagues were concerned from the beginning about the financial obligations and responsibilities they had assigned to the woman's board. Previous American expositions had "had financial aid from the Federal Government." The PPIE in "San Francisco, backed by the State of California, handled all its own problems," Simpson wrote, especially financial. That meant that the all-male board of directors expected the woman's board to "finance . . . all its own undertakings as well as those undertakings which it cheerfully assumed at the request of the Exposition [male] directorate."[46] The woman's board faced limits on financing the exposition from the start because most PPIE women lacked access to, and control over, the large amount of money many men possessed.

Hearst and her board aspired to turn her office into a position with real power and authority over all women's work and activities, including financial, in the original contract that created the woman's board. The initial "outline of a proposed contract between the Panama Pacific International Exposition Company and the Woman's Board of the Panama Pacific International Exposition and World's Fair" gave Hearst and her board "an absolute monopoly, by the legal contract, of all women's affairs," according to PPIE director Gavin McNab, making the woman's board a truly separate and independent deliberative body from the board of directors. In addition, Hearst's board made "no promises whatever to discharge any duties, and [the contract] gives the Exposition Company no recourse whatever, if it should be dissatisfied with work, or if the work should be a complete failure," according to the proposed contract. The woman's board also assumed, according to McNab, "no responsibilities, financial or otherwise" under the auspices of the board of directors. Frightened that "the Exposition [Company] might cease to have the power, in the event of this corporation [the woman's board] failing to accomplish results" and "would be powerless to change the situation," McNab argued that the proposed contract would not be in the best interests of the board of directors. Helen P. Sanborn told Hearst she would "try to get them to drop this business." The contract was then cancelled.[47] Hearst had failed to turn the honorary Presidency into the kind of position of power and substance that would have given it meaning as defined by women.

Faced with this disappointing situation, Hearst capitulated and reached agreement on a new contract that set greater limits on the power and politics of Hearst and the woman's board. Hearst and her female colleagues appeased the board of directors by taking full responsibility to "finance their own affairs" in order to hold a successful exposition. In exchange, contract provisions were made for Hearst and the woman's board to have, as did the board of directors, "full power and authority to appoint its own heads of departments and select its executive and administrative staff."[48] The woman's board, like the board of directors, would also have the legal right and privilege to vote and "to conduct, manage, and control the affairs and business of the Corporation [in the case of the woman's board, this included the associate membership] and to make rules and regulations not inconsistent with the laws of the State of California" and federal legislation.[49]

The woman's board "had an absolutely separate existence" from the board of directors and was "independent and responsible," according to Simpson.[50] Hearst's board made its own decisions and exerted its own official public power and authority like the board of directors. The board of directors officially accepted the legal incorporation of the woman's board with membership voting rights and elected male board of directors' officers several months before Hearst's official election. In so doing, "no more forceful body of women has ever been gathered together in organization," according to the male Panama-Pacific Press Association editor and compiler of an exposition history.[51] The new binding legal agreement avoided embarrassing the board of directors and created a complicated PPIE power and political organizational arrangement. The success of Hearst and members of the woman's board in securing a contract showed how far the honorary president's deft handling of money and resources in had taken white women interested in the PPIE.[52] Yet Hearst and her board members had come only so far because they continued to accept the constraints of sex and class as defined by dominant male power.

Both Hearst and Moore and their boards had power and authority, political and otherwise. But PPIE men still set boundaries for women within the complex national PPIE power and political structure. Hearst—a supporter of California suffrage, which passed in October 1911—and her female colleagues on the woman's board saw the legal rights and privileges they possessed as part of "the first fruits of woman's emancipation in a state newly made politically free, a practical thank-offering of woman's pride and woman's patriotism," according to Simpson, hardly a dispassionate observer. But private PPIE politics told a different, more complicated story. The all-male board of directors knew of the recent election victory on women's suffrage in the state of California. Even so, they refused to take the recent enfranchisement of California women "into consideration . . . in making a contract with the Woman's Board."

For all the power Hearst and her colleagues possessed on paper, in reality they fell short of having enough to force the board of directors to give them the same rights as, and treat them on equal terms with, men. Since California women now had the ballot, the board of directors felt compelled to explain why they refused to treat Hearst and her board on equal terms with men. The reason: they concluded that the PPIE Exposition Corporation addressed "itself more to public policy than to law." This was a distortion of fact. All the activities of the woman's board and

12. Phoebe Apperson Hearst signing the constitution of the Panama-Pacific International Exposition Woman's Board. POR 12. Courtesy of the Bancroft Library, University of California, Berkeley.

13. Older Phoebe Apperson Hearst with pearl brooch on dress, ca. 1916. BANCPIC 1991.064–AX, box 1:02. Courtesy of the Bancroft Library, University of California, Berkeley.

board of directors were guided, and validated, by the state of California as legally incorporated public bodies and publicly chartered organizations that operated separately from, but were associated and intertwined with, the PPIE Corporation. John A. Britton, a member of the board of directors, claimed he spoke for Hearst and her board when he wrote that the woman's board wanted "to receive recognition at the hands of this [PPIE] company as an *auxiliary* [emphasis added] organization." PPIE men argued they saw "no reason why the 'Woman's Board' . . . should not be officially recognized as a body auxiliary to the Panama-Pacific International Exposition Company" and be made "a sub-committee of the Exposition directorate" subject to its "control through the Women's Affairs Committee" chaired by Britton.[53]

Hearst and PPIE women remained silent on the issue after they failed to secure the original proposed contract. They accepted the constraints on sex and class established by PPIE men in the subsequent contract. They allowed the board of directors to speak for them rather than pressure them to carry out the principle of equality to its full extent. Hearst and the woman's board, in the final contract, needed to seek the approval of the board of directors on "exposition activities as may properly justify or require the participation of women."[54] So Hearst, a practical politician in progressive, nonpartisan voluntary reform circles, found it necessary to make messy compromises from the start that undermined her own power and authority, as honorary president, and that of the woman's board in order to get Moore and the board of directors to give refined, wealthy, white women a place in the complicated PPIE political and power structure.

Hearst and the woman's board did what was expected of genteel American middle- and upper-class white women. They took on the generally approved role of "official hostesses of the Exposition," cordially and hospitably welcoming people from around the world to San Francisco.[55] Hearst thought it was to her benefit to act dignified and cautious in public so as not to offend men, and the board of directors specifically. Her approach must have worked because a male chronicler of the PPIE declared: "There was never a hint of a policy on the part of the Woman's Board that might tend to embarrass the Exposition management or any of the Exposition officials." But Hearst had allowed her nonpartisan PPIE male counterparts and opponents to define her and her colleagues without challenge or protest, even though she believed privately that women should have the latitude to define themselves as they saw fit.[56] The board of directors entertained at all male social events and held events with the woman's board, according to Brooks. Thus, although both men and women entertained, the woman's board was officially assigned the role of social hostesses. The board of directors was not. The board of directors also allowed the woman's board to control "general Exposition activities" from their headquarters in the California Building, giving them authority over a wide range of activities, within limits, at the exposition.[57]

Hearst became overwhelmed with work and responsibilities as the opening day of the PPIE approached. She tried to keep track of everything she had to do. Sanborn kept her informed about exposition business and affairs. Hearst and Sanborn also conferred on presenting "the right names" for appointments to the nominating committee as Hearst traveled back and forth between the Hacienda and San Francisco every week to meet with PPIE women between 1912 and 1915 before the exposition opened. The board of directors took Hearst's and Sanborn's recommendations for appointments seriously. They selected women as assistants in the Departments of Mines and Metallurgy, Social Economy, Manufacturers, Live Stock, Fine Arts, Horticulture, and the Division of Exploitation based upon the recommendation of Hearst and Sanborn. Shortly thereafter, Hearst took on Sanborn's duties and obligations, too, when Sanborn fell ill. The work "pretty nearly killed her." She "barely" survived it. But she "went right on working . . . she never gave it up," Brooks wrote. Her work ethic and "pride would not have permitted it."[58]

To give the office of honorary president greater political meaning and purpose, Hearst knew she needed to shape it into a position that advocated for and promoted progressive reform. That way she could effectively represent the interests and needs of women, and some men, she believed were her constituents and she thought she had a responsibility, obligation, and duty to serve.[59] For Hearst that meant she needed to move herself into a formal position of power that was aligned with her progressive reform politics and could fit relatively easily and comfortably into the national PPIE power and political structure.

The Young Women's Christian Association gave Hearst just this opportunity. Hearst's election victory to head the woman's board had triggered discussions on the YWCA field committee about "definite plans" to carry out "national work" at the PPIE. Plans for the exposition were "too large an undertaking to be handled locally." So regional Y members "began correspondence with the National Board to discuss how to proceed."[60] Grace H. Dodge headed the YWCA's national board. Dodge was a philanthropist, teacher, social-service worker, and a politician. She was the first woman appointed, in 1886, to the New York City Board of Education. She also considered herself to be a wage earner. As she thought about the upcoming PPIE, she announced in 1911 that Phoebe A. Hearst had extended an invitation to entertain the Y 1912 summer leadership conference in the West and use the meeting fees to "be the nucleus of a fund to purchase a permanent site for" a conference and training center, or base of power, for the YWCA on the Pacific Coast. The YWCA intended to use the conference and training center for, among other things, the association's meetings and conferences during the exposition. The organization would need to raise thousands of dollars in donations to construct the center.

Hearst first became aware of, and grew interested in, the YWCA and the power of organized Christianity in early 1866. As a young twenty-two-year-old mother raising a three-year-old son, she had heard Dr. Wadsworth "deliver a course of lectures to the 'Young Men's Christian Association.'" Hearst began to contribute fifty dollars a month to the

San Francisco Davis Street Branch as early as 1892 to keep the lunch and reading rooms open to help shield girls and young women from the dangers of prostitution and corruption, among other urban vices, often associated with American fears about immigrants. Hearst funded and supported the Pacific Coast Students' YWCA Conference at Capitola in 1900 and became the largest individual donor to the San Francisco YWCA in early 1904.[61] Hearst's gifts to the YWCA thus opened the door for her years later to make the ceremonial post of honorary president into a meaningful, privileged position with real political power.

Hearst must have realized she had a chance to make her office into something meaningful and powerful when the association turned to her for help in achieving the YWCA national board's political goals. In the fall of 1911, physician Mary Ritter, a member of the Pacific Coast Branch of the YWCA as well as the board of the State Federation of Women's Clubs, suggested that the YWCA's national board follow up on Hearst's interest in the YWCA. Had it not been for Hearst, it would have been highly unlikely that Mary Ritter would have become the first female faculty member with an academic title and salary at the University of California. Ritter was convinced that Hearst "surely has a magic wand which can accomplish anything." So at the behest of the national YWCA officers, Ritter wrote Hearst to solicit a yearly donation of one hundred dollars to the Territorial Committee of the national board for California, Arizona, and Nevada. This was a paltry sum compared to Hearst's donations to other voluntary organizations and the University of California.[62] A positive response from Hearst, though, would send a signal to the national board that she might be interested in building stronger, deeper ties with the association and represent and promote its brand of politics.

Not one to let opportunities slip by, Hearst responded positively to the YWCA. She knew, as one of her female protégés wrote her, that "religion is a great stumbling block for" her and women universally. But she refused to let that hold her back or defeat her. She accepted the constraints of sex and class, particularly those shaped by general Christian principles. But she wanted to find a way to use religion to her advantage. She figured the best way to put Christianity to good use was to exploit conventional notions and principles of evangelical religion while yet remaining true to herself. An old-fashioned evangelical in some ways, she adhered to the convictions and sense of religious and familial duty instilled in her by her parents. In one respect, she agreed with Harriet Taylor, executive secretary of the foreign department of the YWCA's national board. As Taylor explained to Hearst: "I was deeply touched to hear you say that you thought the Young Women's Christian Association was to you, the best illustration of the power of Christianity."

Yet Hearst was not a traditional evangelical. A thread of broad-mindedness ran through her political views and positions. The YWCA appealed to her because it was a cross-denominationally Protestant group allied with no specific institution of religion and interested in moderate progressive reform. As one Y member explained, the YWCA generated "inevitable conflict between conversatism [sic] and progress." Moreover, the Y usually refused to "risk a revolution." The association's brand of moderate progressive reform politics was aimed at providing training for YWCA secretaries, including "special lectures" on a variety of topics, and moral protection in cities for women in danger from predatory and unethical men. The Y also supported a living wage (or minimum wage) for "necessities food, clothing, rent, health, savings, and a small miscellaneous fund," as well as low-cost food, lodging, and jobs for married or unmarried women who wanted to be self-supporting. The organization helped women "adrift," females living in American cities separate from immediate family members and relatives, and people of different races as well as boys and men.[63] The YWCA brand of politics was the kind of politics that fed Hearst's soul.

Getting more deeply involved in YWCA politics would be a comfortable fit for Hearst and would give her something more important to do than holding a ceremonial PPIE office and being an official exposition hostess. It could meet her own political needs and those of her constituents. So

Hearst took advantage of Ritter's request to give a yearly donation of one hundred dollars to the YWCA. But she had other things in mind and offered more. "Yes. 100 for each yr. for 2 yrs. May possibly renew for 2 more years," her note to Ritter declared.[64] Hearst's gifts to the San Francisco YWCA and the national board became one way for her to indicate she was "interested still in our Association movement," according to Dodge.[65]

Hearst's political strategy focused on her offer to finance and organize a ten-day YWCA Pacific Coast Conference at her Hacienda del Pozo de Verona in 1912. Instead of using "retail and commercial spaces, commercial places of entertainments, and the streets," like other 1911 suffragists, Hearst planned to hold a YWCA conference that would turn the private power and authority she had over her Hacienda mansion into public power and authority, transforming its surrounding property into social, economic, cultural, and political spaces to advance women's causes. Dodge and the YWCA's executive committee accepted Hearst's "very timely" idea and offer in the fall of 1911. They dubbed the meeting the Hacienda Conference. The Hacienda Conference would be held from May 17 through 27. Hearst made arrangements for, and expected, about three hundred delegates to attend—including Japanese, Chinese, and Native American representatives, many of whom were college students. Each would pay a ten-dollar attendance fee that would be used to help purchase land for a permanent conference site on the Pacific Coast as a conference and training center. The local San Francisco YWCA honored Hearst at a reception after the YWCA's national board accepted her conference plan.[66] Hearst's idea and plan put her in the good graces of Dodge and the national board to the point where Dodge was eager to discuss "the spiritual power" of the YWCA with Hearst.[67]

Will's *San Francisco Examiner* immediately publicized his mother's Hacienda Conference idea and offer, helping to spread her and the YWCA's name and reputation from coast-to-coast and worldwide.[68] The YWCA's vote to hold the Hacienda Conference repeated a pattern long established by Hearst of moving herself into the power and political structures of nonpartisan voluntary associations through skilled use of her abilities, innovative ideas, money, contacts, and other resources. Hearst showed off, once again, her knack for selecting the best people and organizations to work with to get what she wanted. But this time, she developed her network with a national organization whose officers were deeply interested in the same political issues shared with her and some men.

Hearst's Hacienda Conference plan appealed to the YWCA's interest in "finding ways of generating more power," particularly moral and spiritual, to help people, especially women, address festering social problems in cities from coast-to-coast. Anglo-Protestant, New England male leaders had worked years ago to transpose the coherence of East Coast morality onto the West in the nineteenth century. Old School Presbyterians, Northern Methodists, Baptists, and Episcopalians waged a campaign for the souls of new Euro-American settlers in California during the gold rush era. But the state was politically, economically, and socially unstable. Male religious leaders in California and elsewhere wanted to create a "spiritual example" for the whole nation and the entire world "to follow." They saw Christ as a civilizing, stabilizing influence and wanted to bring the Social Gospel movement to the West to reform society, especially to achieve democratic and egalitarian change and preserve national virtue. The fate of the civilized world, they believed rested on their success.[69] Hearst's conference would establish a Y presence in the West and would be a way to spread the "civilizing" influence of the association as well as influence male Anglo-Protestant religious leaders in the West and East.

Eastern morality, though, created problems for western Anglo-Protestant leaders who wanted to establish religious dominance in California. The problem was that Anglo-Protestantism in California was more tolerant than elsewhere in the nation. Immigrants from western Europe with diverse religious backgrounds flooded into California in search of riches and great opportunities in the late nineteenth and early twentieth centuries. This religious diversity helped the San Francisco Bay Area and region cultivate a cosmopolitan flavor, "a remarkable spirit of openness," and "something of a 'different civilization.'"[70] Over time, Anglo-Protestants, especially evangelicals, found it difficult to achieve dominance because they were a minority among many ethnic groups in competition for support in the state. The YWCA could help Anglo-Protestant men win their struggle for dominance in California by putting down roots and building a permanent base of political power in the West to advance the YWCA's mission of promoting Christian morality to reform society in a modern age.

Hearst engaged in several months of methodical, practical preparation to complete the conference plan that would make her a part of the YWCA's formal national power and political structure. She hired a contractor and worked with him to develop a detailed, definite plan for the Hacienda Conference that provided "for the comfort and pleasure of her" conference attendees. She sketched a campsite located "on the hill about a couple of hundred feet above the Hacienda" surrounded by hundred-year-old oak trees and a gorgeous view of the Livermore valley. The sketch resembled the general appearance and physical structure of evangelical tent camp-meeting sites where religious believers heard exhortations from ministers about reform. Her design included a tent large enough to handle about 350 attendees for the general assembly. There were seventy-three smaller tents to house delegates and serve as committee and meeting rooms. Comfortable, modern accommodations were provided. A kitchen and dining room, along with installed new conveniences and facilities, such as hot and cold water and piping for toilets and showers, completed the design. Workers cleared space on her property and built the conference accommodations. Hearst hired a female physician to take care of representative delegates. She employed the Bohemian Club steward to cater the event. (The Bohemian Club was an exclusive private men's club on Taylor Street in San Francisco.) Hearst directed her staff to make meals from local farms products and orchards and to hire workers "from the surrounding farms and villages."[71] Hearst's preparations to rise into national YWCA politics began at the local level.

The YWCA made plans to "generate power" and announce "national work," or national political goals, at the Hacienda Conference. The aims of the YWCA's national board consisted of an exposition building campaign, getting women work at the PPIE and after, and acquiring a commission to do Travelers' Aid work at the PPIE. National YWCA officials also wanted the Hacienda "conference to result in the securing of a permanent location for future conferences." Harriet Taylor, Pacific Coast organizer and executive secretary of the foreign department of the YWCA's national board, proposed that "it would be well to have three of the national workers and three of the Territorial Committee in . . . [Hearst's] house" during the conference to answer questions about the Y. Taylor thought it would be wise to have Mrs. Baldwin stay in the mansion, she wrote Hearst, "so that you could become personally acquainted with her and judge whether she could render you assistance at the time of the Panama Exposition."[72] The YWCA definitely made known at the Hacienda Conference that they planned for Hearst to advance the national YWCA political agenda and represent its interests and members at the PPIE.

Publicity was one of Hearst's main objectives during the Hacienda Conference to promote herself and the YWCA's brand of politics. Relying on the same mass entertainment and marketing techniques that suffragists had used to sell votes for women, Hearst invited newspaper reporters to attend. She understood the power of the press. She greeted the correspondents in a kind, friendly way. She made them comfortable and provided "special facilities for accurate reporting on the part of all newspapers," according to Brooks. Newspapers published daily articles about Hearst, the Hacienda Conference, and the YWCA political agenda. Hearst and the YWCA also used the conference to promote their interest in, and encourage debate on, progressive reform issues of personal interest associated with "the public good," such as public service, or civic work, and Travelers' Aid. The Hacienda Conference gave Hearst an opportunity to discuss with the YWCA's national board and delegates how she would represent and advance the Y's progressive reform politics at the exposition. Hearst, moreover, sought to demonstrate her and the Y's moderate reform politics and promote respectable political methods that would not embarrass women or men.

Hearst knew that national YWCA officials wanted to develop "the ways and means of enlarging the work of Travelers' Aid & of securing the cooperation of interested organizations & individuals, & of planning the machinery to carry on the work at the time of the Panama Pacific Exposition." So steps were taken at the conference to construct the first conference grounds and permanent conference and training center owned and controlled by the YWCA where "conferences and conventions . . . could be held," including those for the PPIE. Gatherings could be held at the center "almost every ten months or the year round if the Association could get the financial backing for adequate equipment and development of the place," according to Ella Schooley, secretary of the YWCA Field Work Department.[73] National YWCA officials arranged to meet with a representative of the Pacific Improvement Company (PIC), while the Hacienda Conference was in session, to discuss the location of the "most desirable" land for the YWCA first permanent Pacific Coast center and a place from which to "organize a campaign to interest and inform people as to" the YWCA's plans.[74] Carrying out Hearst's design and plan meant that the Hacienda Conference served as the foundation of power for her and the Y staff to publicize and recruit new YWCA members and mobilize delegates to represent the YWCA and act on its national agenda at the exposition and around the world.[75] Hearst understood how to use the press to advocate and promote the YWCA's brand of politics.

The Hacienda Conference gave city association board officials, members, and delegates an opportunity to come together to educate, encourage, and train diverse women to be a potent force. The Hacienda proceedings prepared attendees for "leading positions in the Association" and to become conscious of themselves as "person(s) of power" so they could "make a very real and definite contribution to the progress of the world," according to Jessie Woodrow Wilson, daughter of the president of the United States.

Hacienda delegates saw San Francisco YWCA exhibits, attended leaders' sectional conferences, platform addresses, regular public and delegation meetings, lectures, religious and prayer gatherings, and dinners. They learned how to make choices and "to be more efficient, to earn more, to be healthier, to have a better time and to realize the ever-present love of God," Wilson explained. The YWCA representative delegates aimed "to be, not a follower and imitator, but one who, with vision of the fundamental needs of the nation and of her community, initiates and executes suitable plans to meet those needs."

Until the Y's plans for a conference and training center in the West were complete, Hearst's Hacienda Conference served as the association's base to teach and inspire delegates to become members, get involved in the exposition, and learn how to acquire power and authority to challenge dominant male power in subtle, dignified ways. Attendees also learned how to perform public service to better the lives of people and to help themselves and others, mostly women, move up social, economic, and political ladders in the society and the nation-state.[76] Hearst and the YWCA, in other words, used the Hacienda Conference to make it acceptable for women to seek and acquire power, especially to promote and advance political issues of shared interest with some progressive reform men.

Hearst's display of power and authority over the Hacienda Conference captivated and left an indelible impression on YWCA representative delegates. For some, "it was little short of a fairy tale!" and surpassed the magnificent entertainments of Queen Elizabeth. Others experienced "all the joy and profit it has brought . . . to each individual girl" and the YWCA. It was "a high water mark in conferences" not only because of Hearst's conference idea and overall plan but also because of the personal touches Hearst used, especially those that helped women become physically fit. "The little details of thoughtfulness. The dainty tent trimmings, the rubbers and umbrellas, and the wonderful food! We will never forget those pickles! The tent life, the milk and eggs and abundance of everything did much for the health of many," a young University of California doctoral candidate remarked. Still others enjoyed the "chance . . . to gain some experience & knowledge of the 'Feminist Movement' in the United States in all its branches and aspects!" A Jewish salesgirl from a Philadelphia department store joyfully told her employer "that life would never be the same to her after those two weeks." Being exposed to the power of networks thrilled her because most women did not attend conferences of any kind, certainly not ones that taught them about power. This young wage earner gushed: "The personal contact which is possible for the force of volunteer workers to have with the girls [at the conference] is most desirable. . . . It helps them to understand each other and gives them a new insight into life." This young woman was inspired to think about and reach out for new, daring aspirations, to serve others, and get involved in political arenas and issues of interest to the YWCA and its members. The Hacienda Conference impressed men too. The meeting presented the gift of the strength of Hearst's personality, as one man explained. "For that reason even more than any other" benefit, "it will be a turning point for many in life," he wrote.[77] Hearst's Hacienda Conference provided YWCA representative delegates valuable lessons on how to become powerful and be active in progressive political campaigns centered on the YWCA's reform issues and goals supported by their constituents.

The Pacific Improvement Company played a key role in helping Hearst move into the YWCA's national power and political structure while the Hacienda Conference convened. The PIC was a construction and real estate development company controlled by Southern Pacific Railway tycoons, or the "Big Four"—Leland Stanford, Charles Crocker, Mark Hopkins, and Collis P. Huntington. The Big Four supervised the PIC business empire. The PIC wanted to establish towns near the Southern Pacific railroad tracks and develop Monterey land. The National YWCA secretaries went "over every inch of the . . . 9000 acres" that the PIC owned on Monterey peninsula as the 1912 Hacienda Conference proceedings took place. Hearst and Mary Merrill, an exposition woman's board member and head of the YWCA's exposition committee, also visited the site during the conference.

YWCA officials, after seeing the property, "had a very remarkable interview with the general manager of the Pacific Improvement Company," A. D. Shepard. Shepard met the Y board members at Pacific Grove and "entertained" them at the Del Monte Hotel on the Monterey peninsula. A magnificent place built by the PIC in the early 1880s, the hotel served "for decades [as] a major watering place for the world's elite," especially those traveling in California.[78]

The PIC, after a long discussion, made an offer to the YWCA that included the Moss Beach land. Shepard then made a concentrated effort and argument to promote the deal. He pointed out that a "spur" of the Southern Pacific railroad "runs almost to the beach." To get the YWCA to accept his offer, he insisted that the Southern Pacific "would undoubtedly" run special trains for the Y conferences. He also recommended to the PIC board that they sign a ten-year contract with the YWCA that stipulated that once the Y made $35,000 worth of improvements on the thirty-five acres of the Moss Beach site, the property would be deeded to the Y.[79]

Hearst had a variety of resources at her disposal, including her modest financial gifts, to help get the Moss Beach project off the ground and completed. Y board officials understood the challenges and the unusual amount of stress and strain that would result from being involved in the project. Harriet Taylor explained to Hearst that Ella Schooley felt "the future of the work on the Coast depends on you but we hope that you will not undertake so much that you will break down. We cannot spare you."[80] The association of Hearst's name alone with the project was worth its weight in gold. Hearst and her parents had battled the environment to survive during her childhood. But now she was in a position to help the YWCA take control of the land and exert power to change the public space and surroundings to benefit women. The YWCA's national board possessed "every confidence" in Hearst's judgment about the "selection of the location" and that "the price to be paid will be right." Board members discussed the PIC negotiations with Hearst before they did anything. Hearst told Y officials that the PIC offer "was away beyond what she expected.

She advised" the YWCA "by all means to accept it." YWCA board members assured Hearst that "after the [PPIE] Exposition is over," they would mount "a regular campaign to interest people and secure the money that would be necessary for permanent buildings."[81]

Hearst agreed to head the YWCA's advisory committee to do fundraising for the PPIE-YWCA building and make discreet calls on Californians living in New York to raise money. She allowed the YWCA to use her name to secure $35,000 to improve the grounds and buildings on the Moss Beach land. She also "made a loan of $8200 at 'a most critical point' . . . and later forgave the loan." She handed over the dues collected at the Hacienda Conference to help purchase the land and finance the project. The YWCA's field committee, moreover, appointed Hearst to the conference grounds committee "for the development and management of the grounds." The YWCA signed the contract with the PIC in spring 1913.[82] Hearst and the association refused to concern themselves with any disgrace that might occur as a result of making a deal with a company deemed by many Americans to be corrupt. The practical economic, political, social, and publicity benefits that came from the PIC land deal, which would be used to establish a YWCA base in the West, trumped any moral concerns that Hearst or the YWCA may have had.

Hearst's ideas also were important. She came up with an ingenious notion to help recruit and mobilize younger women for the YWCA, especially potential professionals. Mabel Cratty, general secretary of the national YWCA, asked whether, after the property negotiations ended, Hearst would like to name the West Coast YWCA center "the Hacienda." Hearst suggested, instead, that a contest be held to name the Y site. Helen Salisbury, a Stanford student, submitted the winning name, Asilomar—a Spanish term that means refuge by the sea.[83]

Hearst sent word that she "would make some finance calls on Californians living in New York," as she promised, following the announcement of the contest winner. She also commissioned architect Julia Morgan to design the first building—later called the Phoebe A. Hearst Administration Building. Morgan had been the first woman admitted to the Paris architectural school, École des Beaux-Arts.[84] Morgan spared "no pains to give" the YWCA "the greatest possible result for the least expenditure," according to Schooley. "The builder, in looking over her [Morgan's] plan for the administration building, said, 'There is nothing like it in these parts.' I said, 'Do you think it compares favorably with Pebble Beach Lodge?' His reply was, 'It has it skinned a mile,'" Schooley added.

The Asilomar commission helped set Morgan's professional career on fire and led to a whole host of jobs for her, including the additions to the Hacienda and the design and construction of William Randolph Hearst's ostentatious, dazzling castle in San Simeon, California. Morgan commented to Hearst, years later, about how happy she was "to see the little 'general plan'" for Asilomar "you went over and approved gradually take form." The Y used Hearst's 1912 Hacienda Conference as a model for the activities, including conference proceedings, at Asilomar once the first building opened. The outline, structure, and organization of Asilomar training and events mimicked those at the Hacienda Conference.[85] The YWCA's Pacific Coast center of power shifted from Hearst's Hacienda to Asilomar after the Y's conference and training center was finished. Asilomar became the YWCA's base of operations for the Panama-Pacific International Exposition, once its doors opened for operations in 1913, and an important branch in the national and international association.[86] Hearst was without equal in assisting the YWCA to achieve its political goals in the West.

The success of the Hacienda Conference and the completion of Asilomar made Hearst a candidate for regional and national elective offices in the YWCA. The YWCA's national board rewarded Hearst's financial savvy, connections, instincts in choosing the right people, and experience to transform the once "vague" YWCA dreams "into organized action." National YWCA officials voted to elect Hearst a member of the Pacific Coast field committee and unanimously elected her to head the executive committee on the national board. The national board wanted Hearst to accept her election victories so badly that they elected her to the field committee with the understanding that she need not go to any meetings "(except when you might find it perfectly convenient so to do) or to perform any additional regular duties." It was much more important for the YWCA to use the Hearst name and for Hearst to serve as "a master hand at the helm" of the national board's executive committee than on a regional committee, according to Schooley. National YWCA officials believed the association needed Hearst to lead Y fundraising efforts for a YWCA building, to "bring about better conditions for young women," and to represent the association's brand of politics on a national political stage at the PPIE.[87]

Hearst, in turn, needed the national YWCA so that she might be more than a figurehead. She wanted to do an effective, competent job as head of the woman's board. So she accepted the election victories that made her a YWCA elected officer. By 1913, Hearst had succeeded in making the office of honorary president into a position focused on meaningful progressive reform politics. Her rise to the national level in the YWCA established her as a member of the American female ruling elite—a small group of powerful women who stood on the top tier of nonpartisan voluntary organizational or federal government politics in the female dominion within a larger male political world.

Hearst likely wanted to bring YWCA political agenda items of personal interest into national PPIE politics as soon as possible. She and the woman's board possessed the opportunity to appear cooperative, at least in public, by choosing to leave their progressive reform "convictions at home in the closet." But Hearst and her board were too political for that. Acting on her and the YWCA's reform convictions and values became Hearst's obligation if she were to represent the association and her constituents effectively and competently. As Helen A. Davis, national YWCA executive of the department of field work wrote to Grace Dodge: "Mrs. Hearst and others felt that they did not want to give their time and money to just the social side of the Exposition." They "really wanted to do work that counted." Organized, nonpartisan voluntary Travelers' Aid Society (TAS) work "came to . . . mind," Davis wrote, "as a [public] service that needed to be rendered, and rendered in a big and broad way." A top political priority for Hearst and the YWCA in the early stages of exposition planning, then, was to establish a role for the Travelers' Aid Society at the PPIE.[88]

The Boston YWCA established the first Travelers' Aid Society in 1866. The San Francisco YWCA had a "distinct department . . . in charge of a Travelers' Aid Committee" as early as 1906. So the groundwork had already been laid, by late 1913, for Hearst and Merrill to spend "much time and thought to the launching of Travelers' Aid Work under the woman's board of the Exposition." They wanted to establish a Travelers' Aid Society at the exposition to deal with the pernicious, hazardous forces that preyed on urban dwellers, especially young women. By the time Merrill headed the YWCA's California, Arizona, and Nevada territorial committee and the YWCA's exposition committee, Travelers' Aid was "no longer classified as a religious organization" but as "a moral protective and preventive agency" that helped "all in need," especially "the innocent and inexperienced." Its members were "agents of the society," used social casework methods, and "became a factor in modern social work."

The society claimed it was "a non-sectarian, non-commercial, non-political," and nonpartisan group that through investigation shielded, assisted, and helped assimilate travelers, including immigrants, "without regard to age, race, creed, class or sex, and without fee or gratuity." But, in reality, the society also addressed issues of political interest to its members. It connected travelers "with religious and social organizations of their own choice for their proper development and assimilation in the community." Agents of both sexes kept people, especially women, safe from urban danger, and such vices as white slavery, and homelessness, by meeting travelers at railroad stations. In part to help reduce American fear toward immigrants, the Travelers' Aid Society worked to intervene before problems could occur; it also offered help to old and young white men with employment and lodging and prepared citizens of the future.[89]

The shared moral and material interests and political obligations of the woman's board and the board of directors opened the door for Hearst to bring Travelers' Aid into the complicated web of formal national PPIE-YWCA nonpartisan voluntary association reform politics. The members of the two boards were interested in moral protection and in holding a financially successful exposition during a period of success for protectionist legislation. Both boards, on the surface of it, publicly accepted the serious responsibility of "the welfare of the young." Both boards wanted to make sure the Panama-Pacific International Exposition was "one of the safest of places for the inexperienced traveler," in part to attract as many paying visitors as possible. Charles C. Moore, early on, appointed an all-male Committee on Moral Protection to see that exposition attendees were "properly cared for," a PPIE male chronicler wrote. The Committee on Moral Protection saw the welfare of the young, in public, as a grave responsibility and held an official obligation to provide for moral protection at the PPIE. Most PPIE men were Protestants interested in projecting and promoting a moral persona. But Moore, in reality, absolved men of their obligation to provide moral protection. He eagerly placed the task squarely on the shoulders of the respectable head of the woman's board and her colleagues instead.

Unsurprisingly, PPIE men saw moral protection as "peculiarly woman's work." Moore, by shifting the obligation, moved the balance of power toward Hearst and her board, who many people saw as possessing, as one man put it, "influence and moral persuasion." Hearst and the woman's board now had the ability, power, and authority to decide which women's organization was the most appropriate to handle moral protection and to manage PPIE policies and plans to shield exposition visitors from moral hazards and help improve life in San Francisco.[90] Hearst, at this point, saw the chance to make at least one national YWCA agenda item, possibly more, part of PPIE politics. By wielding power and authority wisely and effectively, Hearst and her board could make a contribution, at the same time, toward the financial success of the exposition—a result that would please both the woman's board and the board of directors.

Hearst knew she would have to sort through the competition among women's organizations for the PPIE commission to provide moral protection. Helen A. Davis, contrary to public calls for the woman's board to bring people together at the PPIE, explained privately that "the state Catholic and Jewish associations and all kinds of welfare workers" would compete against each other for the commission. Davis understood, nonetheless, that the Y held quite an advantage because Hearst also headed the national YWCA's executive committee. The association, according to Davis, had high hopes that Hearst could convince the board of directors to award the commission to the YWCA Travelers' Aid Society because association members believed that Hearst and the woman's board could "command the attention" of PPIE officials.

Hearst understood that she should appear to keep her political reform convictions to herself and cooperate with PPIE men in public. Hearst and her female colleagues promoted a public image and persona of themselves as lively, public-spirited, patriotic social hostesses with pleasant, benevolent, and kind natures. But Davis privately pressured Hearst to exert her official public power and authority to help the YWCA Travelers' Aid Society beat out other women's organizations vying to do moral protection.[91] Because of her rudimentary education, Phoebe shied away from using the power of persuasion with men or making speeches in public. She never discussed in public the pressure she received from, or the intense competition that existed, between women's organizations. She appeared "ladylike," as American society would expect of her, including most men. Hearst, as she had most of her life, relied heavily on Victorian notions of womanhood, her good personality, name, and reputation, her personal connections and networks, as well as her money and class status, to negotiate and navigate power with others, especially men, in public.

But how Hearst exerted control over her male employees and women in private was a different matter. She was hardly apologetic or demure when she forced the male and female employees of her estate, or the recipients of her largesse, to do what she wanted. In private, she used diplomatic, and sometimes deceptive, businesslike methods to negotiate and navigate power with men. She also made no bones about abandoning her cautious, demure public approach when necessary to control and dominate women on her board. She loved wielding raw power and self-consciously exerted political power and authority directly over women in private without constraint or regret as head of the woman's board.[92] She rarely, if ever, expressed her love of power directly or openly to the opposite sex in public or in private. The ways Hearst wielded her magic wand and cultivated and promoted her public image and persona created false impressions. She was dignified in public and at home with guests. But she was willing to abandon her reserve and speak her mind in private if it was necessary to get her way. She was much more reluctant to do so beyond the confines of her home for fear of embarrassing men or tarnishing her persona and image. She also gave virtually no indication in public that she maintained her control and sway over others with the assistance and support of other talented men and women like Helen P. Sanborn.

Hearst, the woman's board, and the San Francisco YWCA, an early organizer of the Travelers' Aid Society across the nation, supported Sanborn's efforts to establish the society in San Francisco to provide moral protection for exposition visitors. PPIE-YWCA women called a joint meeting to discuss the pay, estimated at $120 a month for three months or $40 per month, for Travelers' Aid workers at the exposition. The standard of pay was too low, according to members who attended the meeting. So they decided to increase the wages to $50 per month, or $560 a year, per worker—enough, they thought, to provide a decent living as defined by the YWCA: "a minimum wage which shall permit a woman to earn enough to sustain her health, buy decent food, clothes and lodging, and secure a little recreation." Sanborn announced "that the Woman's Board of the Panama-Pacific Exposition would assume the responsibility . . . [to pay the] two new workers." A resolution passed, at the same meeting, that the YWCA and the woman's board would ask Orin C. Baker—general secretary of the Travelers' Aid of New York—to come to San Francisco, in January 1914, to organize a Travelers' Aid Society there. Sanborn visited representatives of an array of religious denominations and large interest groups in the city to recruit people of any religious persuasion to join Travelers' Aid. Once Baker arrived, criticism for coming to California "from Eastern organizations stampeded" and overwhelmed him, according to Sanborn. Baker then balked "at going on with Travelers' Aid formation & responsibilities unless we can get the Exposition & the Municipality to come to terms," Sanborn explained to Hearst. Baker was afraid that moral protection by Travelers' Aid would fail at the exposition and in San Francisco without a commitment from exposition and local political officials.

Sanborn, like Hearst, had "mighty little faith in . . . municipal" partisan politicians, and the board of directors, to adequately address the "rotten," dangerous "political conditions of the City," especially vices. Sanborn further explained to Hearst: "We are not authorized by the Expo. to assume the work of moral protection [PPIE men had the official authorization] for the Expo. & consequently cannot be responsible for it. I think one Committee & Mr. Moore & Mr. Burt [directors of concessions and admissions] & all of them had better understand it. A nice time we should have trying to regulate moral conditions. We are willing to help in all ways possible, but *the responsibility is not ours.* Am I right? I do not propose that the Woman's Board shall be made the goat of the Expo. if things are not right." Sanborn knew that Hearst and the woman's board lacked power on equal terms with the board of directors and partisan politicians to address the social ills, evils, and urban dangers that could arise at the exposition and in San Francisco. So PPIE president Helen Sanborn recommended to Hearst that PPIE-YWCA women take control of the situation and establish a California branch of Travelers' Aid. "It is for us [the woman's board] to decide whether this [Travelers' Aid] work shall go on" at the PPIE, Sanborn wrote. Hearst and the woman's board, from Sanborn's perspective, needed to "go to work on our own job—finance & organize our own work."[93]

A permanent California branch of the Travelers' Aid Society was established in San Francisco in the spring of 1914 with the support and approval
of Hearst, Sanborn, the woman's board, and the San Francisco YWCA.
There would be an "equal representation with the Woman's Board,"
selected by the San Francisco YWCA, on the board of the California Travelers' Aid Society. The branch claimed publicly to be "non-political" so
as not to offend people, particularly men. But the real aim of Travelers'
Aid activities was political in nature: "to protect the innocent" and to
improve the lives of, as the *San Francisco Examiner* noted, "good men and
women of the State of California," especially girls. Once the California
branch of Travelers' Aid opened its doors, members became active in
"the largest organization of women in the world," according to the *San
Francisco Chronicle*, and a "world-wide movement," a female PPIE historian
wrote.[94] Sanborn played a pivotal role in the formation of a long-lasting
California branch of the Travelers' Aid Society. She provided Hearst with
crucial guidance and support, shielded her superior from any unwelcome
political consequences, such as criticism from the board of directors or
the public, if things went wrong, and aided Hearst in keeping her distance
from people of lesser social, economic, and political stature and power.

In addition to her position on the woman's board, Hearst was now a
"unanimously elected" honorary president of the California branch of the
Travelers' Aid Society and attended regular meetings. She served with two
other female honorary vice presidents and with several male honorary vice
presidents. Helen Sanborn was elected to the board of directors. Hearst
and Sanborn also worked with other women and men on the executive
committee headed by Milton H. Esberg, who submitted an M.A. Gunst
and Company application for a cigar concession at the PPIE.

The early twentieth century was a time when most progressives agreed
"that government should rely on *expertise*." Hearst, an amateur social
scientist, knew the value of the studies the YWCA had conducted of social
and economic conditions of women, including wage earners. Hearst and
the woman's board supported the Travelers' Aid Society because they

possessed "character and standing and commanded the services of experts." They conducted sociological investigations and completed studies on the rotten conditions in San Francisco, especially among wage-earning women, a male PPIE chronicler observed.[95] So it came as little surprise that Hearst endorsed the YWCA's Travelers' Aid Society as the best women's organization to handle moral protection at the exposition. Moore and the board of directors accepted Hearst's recommendation and seal of approval. Hearst and the woman's board, in other words, legitimized and made acceptable their power and authority by relying on experts—a standard also followed by the federal government in the Progressive Era.

A "very active" Hearst approached her seventy-second birthday with "good," "general health." She refused to let her age get her down and was as active as ever. She put to good use her "Napoleonic executive ability" to advance the YWCA's national progressive reform agenda. That meant, among other things, addressing the YWCA board's national goal of constructing a building to house their "headquarters for the use of men and women" at the exposition.[96]

Rather than construct a separate woman's building, as had been the case at the 1893 World's Columbian Exposition in Chicago, PPIE-YWCA women planned to build a YWCA building that would serve as the woman's building and aid all female *and* male PPIE visitors. It would be built by PPIE-YWCA women with the YWCA's name on it. Dora M. Thurston, a YWCA secretary, contacted Hearst about the project. Hearst was excited by and deeply interested in the construction of a YWCA building. She instructed her employee: "Send a note immediately with special delivery stamp. Say that I will be very glad to see her on Wed. after the meetings, or that p.m. . . . Make the note nice." YWCA officials were pleased. They believed that "whatever success we shall have . . . will be because of [Hearst's] great generosity of time and strength and influence." Hearst, of course, needed support from, and to work with, both sexes as the project unfolded. Schooley looked forward to inviting "men whom we are wanting on our various committees" to help the YWCA achieve their goals, including the building project.

But many PPIE-YWCA women had little experience and confidence in dealing with men. They grew anxious when Hearst's expertise and support were absent. Evelyn B. Keck, general secretary of the San Francisco YWCA, for example, wrote Hearst about how distressed she became trying to deal with the problem of Mr. Wilcox's salary: "Lo, I am to face all the men without you to uphold me! Mr. Wilcox will be here tomorrow and the others later. I am holding myself in readiness for whatever is before me. I do trust that success will crown all our efforts. You know New York and its people so well . . . and we will do our best without you."[97] PPIE-YWCA women relied on Hearst for her experience and guidance in handling exposition affairs, especially financial and political, and meeting the challenge to exert power and authority over, and with, men.

Hearst and PPIE-YWCA women engaged in a battle over space as soon as they started to haggle with the board of directors over the construction of a woman's club building or YWCA building.[98] The board of directors' position on the building was not to the liking of Hearst and the PPIE-YWCA women: "no space allotted for Woman's Club Building, but it is possible if sufficient financial responsibility guaranteed space may be allotted," a PPIE male official wrote. The board of directors kept Hearst and her board in limbo about how much space females would receive at the exposition because they possessed little confidence women would raise enough money to carry out their plans. Hearst and the woman's board, meanwhile, grappled with constituent pressure. "The plans for the California building seem to be about completed, & we must know just what amt. of space will be given the women," Sanborn wrote Hearst. She explained further: "The organized bodies of women in this country have always had adequate space for headquarters in former Expositions, & I am being absolutely bedeviled by women's associations for headquarters. If we are not to have adequate space at our disposal for this, we must have a building [of our own] for the purpose," Sanborn wrote. Hearst's involvement was crucial. PPIE-YWCA women believed in her forceful talents and charms when it came to handling men. Mary Ritter reasoned "that if the 'powers that be' could meet" Hearst, "more could be accomplished in ten minutes than local persuasion could do in ten weeks, if ever." Ritter added: "No mere man" could "resist Phoebe" Apperson Hearst.

PPIE-YWCA women asked Hearst to push for their demands. She pressed the board of directors quietly and gently. Hearst's methods worked to a point. She got the board of directors to agree to give exposition women some space in the California Building that would assure the status and visibility of PPIE-YWCA females at the exposition. But that space was not enough to accommodate all her constituents. So PPIE-YWCA women needed to arrange for a site to construct a building of their own. The problem was that they wanted a piece of land "which the government of Hawaii had expressed a preference for." Hearst and the woman's board insisted the board of directors give them the site. PPIE men denied the demand.[99] Hearst accepted the board of directors' decision without disagreement and let the matter drop, possibly fearing that they could reduce, or eliminate, their control over PPIE-YWCA exposition activities. In refusing to fight for the entire space and the building they wanted, however, Hearst had gone some way toward undermining the power and authority of PPIE-YWCA women, economic, political, or otherwise.

There was yet a bigger problem lurking in the background that bedeviled Hearst and the woman's board, upending the efforts of PPIE-YWCA women to secure the space they needed. Hearst and PPIE-YWCA women were battling the board of directors over the very issue that unsettled the male official leaders in the first place—finances. The woman's board publicly announced, as early as the summer of 1913, "that there was no hope of the Young Women's Christian Association doing the [concession] work." "It has almost amounted to personal insult when it came to discussing whether or not we were to have work on the Exposition ground," according to Helen A. Davis. Women needed to get the space to do the concession work. But the board of directors refused to give them the legal right to use the land or property for noncommercial or commercial activities. PPIE-YWCA women would be unable to get the space if they could not secure the temporary property rights. Without the property rights, they could not get the space. Without the space, they could not construct the building. Money was the problem. PPIE-YWCA women lacked access to and control over the large amounts of money men had at their disposal. The YWCA, initially, fell short of what they needed to make the board of directors confident that the woman's board could complete the building project.

Worse yet, the PPIE-YWCA women battled with the board of directors over high "food prices" and the amount the association intended to pay the board of directors. PPIE-YWCA women, meanwhile, needed to come to grips with additional money problems. Mary S. Merrill suggested she and Hearst meet to discuss what to do about paying a pile of bills. The board of directors then gave women some hope by requiring the YWCA field committee to contribute twenty-five thousand dollars to get the right of concessions. This was an amount outside the financial reach of the local Y field committee. Davis solicited Hearst's advice. She asked Hearst to intervene to resolve the conflict. Hearst seemed "to thrive best on work and difficulties to be overcome," according to one male friend. Hearst responded to Davis's request. She came up with a plan. She suggested a businesslike way "to break this apparent deadlock," according to Davis: the YWCA's national board would make a loan to the field committee. Seeing dollar signs when she thought of Hearst's idea, Davis suggested a way for it to work. Have "the National Board, invest twenty-five thousand dollars which might be raised from a few friends [such as Hearst] with the expectation of having it paid back entirely or in part" from the YWCA lunch rooms at the exposition.[100] Davis, in essence, hoped to borrow the bulk of the money from Hearst. Hearst's political guidance, connections, and financial support were essential if PPIE-YWCA women were to win their battles with the board of directors to secure the exposition site and construct the YWCA Building.

Looking for a way to resolve these financial problems and tensions, the board of directors next suggested that the PPIE-YWCA women construct a smaller, more utilitarian building, which would reduce the amount of money to not "more than a fifty thousand [dollar] investment, equipment and all." PPIE-YWCA women agreed to the idea of a smaller building that would stand independently from other PPIE structures, and Hearst backed the plan as well. The Y's national board celebrated the news, a day before Hearst's seventieth birthday, that she would provide the twenty-five thousand dollars to the field committee to construct the exposition's YWCA Building. The YWCA would use money from Hearst's local fund-raising efforts and the profits from the YWCA lunchrooms to pay back the loan. The money saved from building a smaller structure and a reduction from the board of directors on a 10 percent waiver on the gross receipts would help too.

Mary S. Merrill eagerly awaited receiving Hearst's pledge. No architectural contest was held to select a woman architect to design the building, possibly to save money. Nor did the Architectural Advisory Committee select a female architect. PPIE officials, instead, appointed Edward F. Champney, an École des Beaux-Arts–trained architect, to design the exterior of the YWCA Building and the Press Building. Hearst probably relied on her network of personal friends, associations, and political connections to help Julia Morgan get the commission to design the interior of the YWCA Building located, finally, "between the main entrance gate and the Court of the Moon and Stars." Hearst was invited to "turn the first spadeful of earth" at the groundbreaking ceremony in the summer of 1914. The structure was "the largest ever erected by a State or Nation participating in an exposition," according to the YWCA. The national board erected and equipped the building "at a cost of $43,000." The commission advanced Morgan's reputation as a professional architect and enhanced her class position.[101] But Hearst and the YWCA had made messy compromises in working toward this structure. They had settled for less from the board of directors in order to get the land and space needed to construct the YWCA Building. Champney's contribution, in the process, took precedence over Morgan's architectural contribution, which was relegated to a less visible and significant position. Although Hearst and her colleagues managed to resolve the concession and building issues, they were unable to entirely meet their original goals.

The completed YWCA Building, or the "Social Service Power Plant," as one visitor called it, symbolically and concretely expressed and represented Hearst's and the YWCA's abilities to control money and resources and use them effectively to promote, advocate, and advance the YWCA's moderate progressive reform agenda, especially protective and social welfare legislation, and make their brand of politics a part of the PPIE national power and political structure. The YWCA Building was constructed "to provide comfort and rest to the visitors at the Exposition" and "to afford protection, friendliness and a many-sided service for the hundreds of girls employed on the Fair ground," a male PPIE chronicler declared (a rather limited view considering the myriad of other activities and goals of PPIE-YWCA women at the exposition). The YWCA provided "guests representing thirty-two different national organizations" hospitality. The YWCA Building served "actively" as "headquarters for all women," not just California women. People—women and men—used the many and "varied activities" inside the YWCA Building that were "not purely social." Julia Morgan designed every nook and cranny of the interior as a safe, comfortable, congenial space for all respectable women to come together to read, discuss, and listen to lectures on a broad range of economic, political, cultural, and social issues that Hearst and PPIE-YWCA women supported. "Speakers and visiting delegates of religious, educational, and social congresses came as guests of" the YWCA and were provided with a chance to "exchange . . . ideas and discuss . . . methods" relating to political issues.

Before 1913 there had been virtually no legislative protection for women workers, so PPIE-YWCA women took charge. They used the building to advocate protecting working-class females from prostitution and preserving their morality by helping them get jobs to earn enough wages so they could avoid sin and vice. Moral protection politics, for Hearst, was one

14. Phoebe Apperson Hearst standing on podium in front of California Building sign at the Panama-Pacific International Exposition, May 7, 1914. BANCPIC 1939.006, vol. 13, pt. 58, p. 477, photo 2259. Courtesy of the Bancroft Library, University of California, Berkeley.

means to a finer womanhood—one that reflected her Victorian notion of what it meant to be a feminine, moral, and a self-supporting white female citizen with an ardent desire to move up the economic, social, and political ladders. But support for a minimum wage "held open the door of ambition only to a meagre independence." "In practice, survival was the best, not the worst, that the wage embodied" because "estimates made by well-intentioned reformers and the efforts of the most well-meaning women were compromised by the refusal of most employers to concede a woman's need even to support herself," one historian noted, or even contribute to the survival of her family. One-third of the women "employed at the Exposition" possessed "absolutely no resources and have others dependent upon them," Merrill explained.

At the same time, the YWCA made "a careful survey of possibilities in the Bay Region for employment in various trades and offices and department

15. Phoebe Apperson Hearst at groundbreaking ceremony at the Panama-Pacific International Exposition, June 7, 1914. PPIE. BANCPIC 1991.064–AX, box 1:2, photo 2259. Courtesy of the Bancroft Library, University of California, Berkeley.

stores." Hearst, over the arc of her life, advocated and promoted self-support for women who wanted it, married or unmarried. She backed the YWCA's progressive reform agenda by giving advice and financial support to help women find employment at the exposition as demonstrators, saleswomen, waitresses, stenographers, and bookkeepers. But she did so without consulting the female constituents that Hearst and PPIE-YWCA women tried to protect and represent.[102] Hearst was unwilling to speak out or take direct political action in public for minimum-wage legislation. She refused to fight in the streets for jobs or against employers to improve working conditions or for the vote. She relied on a national nonpartisan political approach to help her constituents.

Unwilling to engage in direct political action, Hearst and other PPIE-YWCA women believed that helping women find employment and constructing the YWCA Building would still address the needs of women of diverse races and classes. Their approach altered the city structure to advance the woman's board's and the YWCA's brand of politics. They also lobbied for the passage of legislation to help close the gaps between classes, and they helped women find employment after the exposition. The YWCA provided working and wage-earning women, who saw themselves as breadwinners entitled to full citizenship rights, the tools and implicit support they needed to improve their lives. Nonetheless, YWCA policies and actions for improving the lives of women, before and after the PPIE, were still less than adequate, especially for black women.[103]

Enthusiastic women and men of all ages—white, black, Chinese, and Japanese, from California and around the nation and from foreign lands—came in droves to see the exposition and the YWCA Building. As the sun rose on February 20, all the church bells in the city rang continuously for an hour to herald and celebrate the Panama-Pacific International Exposition. Fire department whistles and automobile horns joined in. President Woodrow Wilson, at 9:00 a.m., "pressed a golden key . . . attached by wire to the 835-foot aerial tower at Tuckerton, New Jersey, and radio waves were sent 3,000 miles to the top of the Tower of Jewels," a PPIE chronicler wrote. Engines hummed, the main door of the Machinery Palace opened, banners unfurled, and water burst from the Fountain of Energy. General admission for adults was fifty cents and children under twelve paid twenty-five cents, ten cents less on Saturday and Monday.

People poured into the exposition grounds to view the Dream City and its exhibits once the gates swung open for business. Rave reviews filled newspapers the next day. Extensive press coverage declared that the first day's attendance of over two hundred thousand had exceeded first-day visitors to the 1893 World's Columbian Exposition in Chicago. PPIE visitors saw a world shaped by powerful reformers, feminists, professional, wage-earning, and wealthy, elite women and men set in a "veritable fairyland." Opening day was not entirely without controversy, however. Newspaper

16. YWCA Building, outside. Smith Collection. Courtesy of the Sophia Smith Collection, Smith College.

stories reported that women had walked around the grounds and talked to complete strangers without being properly introduced. They engaged in unladylike behavior by shouting or screaming their excitement, behavior certainly unacceptable and unbecoming generally to those with Victorian sensibilities and a traditional nineteenth-century view of femininity. The singing of the "Star-Spangled Banner," meanwhile, acted as a patriotic bond to bring people together.[104]

A female chronicler went so far as to declare, after the exposition opened, that "everything was always well at the California Host Building"—where the woman's board office was located—which suggested that the people inside were working together in harmony.[105] But problems still needed to be solved even as millions enjoyed the buildings, grounds, and exhibits. Hearst grappled constantly with tensions and conflicts that arose over space. She dealt with "many unofficial but threatening protests made to

17. YWCA Building, inside. Smith Collection. Courtesy of the Sophia Smith Collection, Smith College.

its [the woman's board's] members." In particular, she handled complaints about the Joy Zone, the amusement space named to celebrate the Panama Canal Zone that contained a typical variety of concessions.[106]

When accusations of immorality and corruption in San Francisco and the Joy Zone caused distress among male and female exposition visitors, Hearst and her board acted. The Zone stretched across seventy acres and contained exhibits of diverse people in "in their so-called ethnic villages." These displays emphasized racial and class hierarchy, particularly the beliefs of social Darwinists. The exposition's board of directors, of course, had made the decisions about which exhibits to accept for the Zone without consulting Hearst and the woman's board. Exposition officials had known that San Francisco possessed a reputation as a city filled with tolerant cosmopolitan residents. Many also saw it as a place where thousands of saloons and brothels existed and vice activity abounded, especially in the Barbary Coast area. Male and female moral reformers, however, especially PPIE-YWCA women, were concerned about issues of sexuality, vice, and morality in the city and at the exposition. Many members of the woman's board had joined moral reformers in opposition to prostitution or white slavery. The YWCA, the Women's Christian Temperance Union, the General Federation of Women's Clubs, the American Purity Alliance, and other women's organizations and some men, like Anthony Comstock, a member of the Young Men's Christian Association, had supported the Mann White Slave Traffic Act passed by the United States Congress in 1910. The Mann Act made it a crime "to transport or facilitate the transport of any woman or girl over state lines, or within a territory and the District of Columbia" for immoral purposes such as debauchery and prostitution. PPIE-YWCA women supported the Mann Act because they believed it protected "women and girls from forced prostitution and sex trafficking."[107]

Believing that young girls and women were vulnerable to danger at the hands of immoral and unethical men, PPIE-YWCA women began repeatedly to protest the "Turkish smoke" and the maids "in the harem-like parlors" in the Cairo Café on the Zone. Others complained to male exposition officials about the vulgar and obscene shows on the Zone. Julia George, first vice president of the California Civic League, wrote to object to "the indecency of the dances given" at the "Streets of Cairo." Businessmen protested too. An owner of a real estate firm wrote Moore that he would refuse to bring his family to the exposition if he felt his children would not "be safe from solicitation and the usual temptation from the vice interest." Other men and women opposed the gambling, high consumption of alcohol, "the snake dance," and "muscle dances." Albert Palmer, minister of the Plymouth (Congregational) Church in Oakland, insisted that Moore and the board of directors do what they promised: provide for moral protection and observe the "decency" Moore had pledged to Hearst, Helen P. Sanborn, the woman's board, and others.[108]

Merrill issued a written demand—on behalf of Hearst, the woman's board, and PPIE-YWCA women in general—that increased the pressure on

Moore and the board of directors to provide decency and guard against sin and vice. Merrill wrote Moore that the YWCA "Exposition Committee, composed of 150 influential women of the whole Bay Region, have discussed the present situation and are unanimous in feeling that immediate action should be taken by the Exposition Management to safeguard the morals both of employees and visitors." Moore responded that "there will be no cause whatever for uneasiness on the part" of anyone "as to the moral tone of any concession in the Exposition." He argued that "several members of the Board of Directors" had helped establish a branch of the Travelers' Aid Society and that "these members [of Travelers' Aid] constitute in part the authority in charge of the work," implying that the board of directors held authority over the work as well. Moore spoke to the individual traits of the members of the board of directors and the woman's board with a special focus on Hearst's character. Hearst's involvement was "surely a sufficient guarantee to any high-minded person that the moral tone of the Exposition will be vigorously safeguarded," Moore wrote.[109] Moore hoped that Hearst's service as honorary president of the woman's board would take care of the problems Merrill was raising.

But Hearst, PPIE-YWCA women, and others needed more from Charles C. Moore and his board of directors than mere words about the moral character of the honorary president of the woman's board. They demanded deeds. The YWCA was a leading organization in policing sexuality. It had worked to eradicate the sexual double standard and vigorously supported the Mann Act to protect women. Representing Hearst and PPIE-YWCA women, Sanborn requested "that four police matrons, two for day & two for night—and un-uniformed police women for special duty, be appointed during the entire term of the Exposition," with the approval of the woman's board and the Travelers' Aid Society. Moore explained that he was "by no means [yet] a convert to the suggestions" Sanborn made. He knew of the PPIE-YWCA women's advice and "the necessity for providing protection of the character" they recommended. He considered seriously the requests and suggestions of PPIE-YWCA women and the Travelers' Aid Society. He would adopt them if appropriate. Merrill, a colleague and representative of Hearst and the woman's board and chair of the exposition committee of the YWCA's national board, with Hearst's approval, became more forceful with Moore. She insisted that the board of directors deal with the conditions on the Zone and regulate it "to the satisfaction of our Association" and "others interested in the welfare of our young people."[110]

Hearst and her supporters wanted, at the very least, for the board of directors to close down the Cairo Café concession. Male religious leaders backed Hearst's and PPIE-YWCA women's efforts to remove any exhibits that fell short of the standards of sexual morality, as advocated by Hearst, PPIE-YWCA women, and their supporters, including evangelical and concerned men. Hearst and these followers held a shared interest. They supported policing the Zone to protect vulnerable women. But Hearst and the woman's board also held shared financial and political interests with the board of directors, and both bodies needed to do something about the immorality on the Zone in order to continue to draw large crowds and make the exposition a financial triumph. So the board of directors closed down the Streets of Cairo and the Cairo Café in early August 1915 for moral, financial, and political reasons. The board next reopened the Café ten days later "under strict behavioral guidelines" that met the moral standards of Hearst and male religious leaders and concerned women and men. Other concessions on the Zone were shut down for financial as well as legal reasons.

Frank Burt (the exposition's director of concessions and admissions) concerned himself primarily with exposition finances. Recognizing the impact of progressive politics on the Panama-Pacific International Exposition, he lamented, at the end of the exposition, that prohibiting Moore from helping "concessionaries to finance their concessions in the earlier part [had been] a mistake." Many PPIE concessionaires got off to a rocky financial start because they were in debt from the first day the exposition opened. In addition, Burt claimed, "the pressure brought to bear upon the Directorate [to do something about the crude shows in the Zone] was of such a nature that they were eliminated, to the financial detriment of the concessionaire and the Exposition." He argued that the "reform wave which swept over" California and that had "put the state in the national vanguard of" progressivism during the administration of progressive Republican governor Hiram Johnson (1911–17) had "cost" his concession division "many thousands of dollars and extracted that carnival feature from the Zone which is so necessary" to making money. Burt was essentially blaming these financial losses on the woman's board, progressives interested in reform issues, and their supporters. He pointed to PPIE-YWCA efforts to promote and enforce their progressive agenda as the main culprit for the exposition's financial difficulties.[111] In the end, however, it was Hearst and the woman's board who had resolved the Joy Zone and financial problems created by the board of directors.

The woman's board and their supporters, who were interested in protecting women and the exposition's proceeds, had "forced the men to take a stand in order to protect their profits." Burt had relied on a selective memory when he wrote his report. He failed to take into account what would have happened if the board of directors had refused to take care of public concerns about depraved sexual behavior on the Zone. The board of directors could not afford to appear to be immoral men. That could lead to financial ruin for the exposition. Many on the board were businessmen and a few were attorneys. They may not have possessed a basic devotion to the standards of morality held by PPIE-YWCA women, but Moore, at the very least, recognized that the board of directors needed to assuage the moral concerns of those who objected so strongly to what they saw as the abhorrent and despicable activities on the Zone. Burt conveniently omitted the fact that members of both PPIE boards had recognized that moral standards played an important role if the exposition was to turn a profit.

Burt also neglected to acknowledge that the board of directors and Hearst and the woman's board were in agreement that the exposition be a financial success. Hearst and the woman's board proved their commitment to this goal by financing their own affairs and ending the exposition without debt. Their account contained over $13,000 cash on hand when the national event closed. Hearst and the persuasive, forceful lobbying of her PPIE-YWCA colleagues had prevailed.[112] But they had also paid a significant price to achieve a limited victory. Their success continued to reinforce traditional constraints of sex and class and also undermined PPIE-YWCA women's efforts to help white women and women from diverse races become self-supporting. Hearst's and the woman's board's approach had left little room for women to define themselves, even though Hearst believed that only women should determine what it meant to be a woman.

Phoebe Apperson Hearst had achieved great success by the time Americans and people around the world saw "the lights go out forever" at the PPIE on December 4, 1915. She showed that she had mastered the art of PPIE-YWCA power and politics on a national stage even before women possessed the constitutional right to vote. Most females involved in the exposition agreed that the huge accomplishments of PPIE-YWCA women occurred because of Hearst's competent, skillful participation.[113] But while she exercised power over some PPIE-YWCA men, Hearst had also ceded control and say-so to them on some important issues. She had been cautious and restrained. She had relied on behavior, conduct, and methods that would not embarrass the board of directors, herself, or other women and men. Those decisions, in turn, had restricted and weakened significantly the power and authority of Hearst and PPIE-YWCA women.[114] Hearst and women on the woman's board had possessed power and authority like Moore and men on the board of directors. But her decisions and actions had made it difficult for her and the woman's board to wield power on equal terms with Moore and his board and other male PPIE officials.

Hearst, nevertheless, had been effective in revitalizing her career and promoting issues near and dear to her heart and the heart of PPIE-YWCA female and male progressives on a national political stage. She had played a key role in advocating and realizing national PPIE-YWCA progressive reform goals. But her ability to rule over PPIE-YWCA women and men was only temporary. It vanished when the exposition gates closed, although the California Branch of the Travelers' Aid Society lived on as an enduring organization without Hearst's active participation. The U.S. Congress needed to pass a constitutional suffrage amendment if Hearst and other women were to exercise power in national American politics on a permanent and wider basis. But how much of her money and resources would Hearst spend in the campaign for national constitutional votes for women, considering that she was a woman who had typically accepted and often relied on "ladylike," deferential diplomacy in nonpartisan voluntary association politics?[115]

8

The Vote

Phoebe Apperson Hearst did not take the path followed by radical suffragists in supporting and advocating for a constitutional right for women to vote. She chose "a different way."[1] Susan B. Anthony had been a dearly loved, impressive, and aging radical suffrage leader when her term as National American Woman's Suffrage Association president ended in 1900. Anthony backed "a movement controlled and defined by women." She took radical positions, moreover, "on marriage and domestic reform." She criticized "the absolute control husbands had over their wives" and tried to educate NAWSA members to support "the liberalization of divorce laws."[2]

Hearst lacked the devotion and commitment to the suffrage cause that Anthony and Elizabeth Cady Stanton possessed. They had sought the ballot after the Civil War "by any means, regardless of the personal and political costs." Hearst refused to publicly back Anthony's criticism of the control husbands had over their wives and Anthony's radical positions on marriage and liberalization of divorce laws. "Aunt Susan's" strategy focused on the vote as a tool of political power, as narrowly defined by men, and on the state and federal political actions that had contributed to four suffrage victories in the West, a particularly wide-open society unfettered by entrenched traditions shaped by the old elite in the East:

territorial suffrage in Wyoming in 1869 and in Utah in 1870 and state suffrage in Colorado in 1893 and Idaho in 1896.

Suffrage politicians were hard at work in the 1890s to achieve the California ballot for women, and suffrage politics in the Golden State centered on the San Francisco Bay Area, making the state and Hearst part of the national suffrage movement. The politics of women at this time had been undergoing a transition from a voluntarist style of moral reform and pressure-group politics, prevalent throughout the late nineteenth century, to a modern style that influenced the substance of political action and methods. Hearst willingly used her home for political meetings and participated in parades and nonpartisan politics.[3] But she was dignified, cautious, and careful in her support for suffrage. It was not her way to adopt aggressive, confrontational tactics to advocate for votes for women. The distinctive ways Hearst backed and promoted the ballot put her in a different position in the suffrage camp from radical suffragists.

The first sign that Hearst was choosing a different way to support and advocate for suffrage emerged in 1895 when she joined the advisory council of the Woman's Congress Association of the Pacific Coast (WCAPC). Women's congresses had become popular after a woman's congress had gathered at the 1893 World's Columbian Exposition, with Hearst in attendance. In May 1894, in a hall in San Francisco, a "public space used cautiously" at the time by suffragists, women met to organize an 1895 congress. The 1895 Woman's Congress met from May 20 to 26 to form the WCAPC, an active lobbying group and "a permanent statewide organization" that launched and built a political movement across the state. The association was designed to discuss "the leading questions of the day, and to awaken the thought and urge the action of women in the issues affecting humanity," especially the use of the ballot, among other tools, to ameliorate the adverse conditions produced by wealthy industrial tycoons in the wake of the Panic of 1893.[4] Hearst signaled her backing and promotion of the national ballot as a tool of reform when she became a member of the WCAPC advisory council.

Hearst was drawn to the WCAPC's advisory council because of the association's support for political reform issues of personal interest to her and because she knew many of the prominent women involved. At the 1895 Congress women delegates came together from Northern and Southern California along with "representative women from all parts of the Pacific Coast, [and] with distinguished visitors from the East." The program was "devoted to the study and discussions of The Home, and its deepest and widest relations." The congress officers included Sarah Brown Ingersoll Cooper, president of the Golden Gate Kindergarten and Women's Press Associations, and Louise Sorbier, president and treasurer of the Women's Educational and Industrial Union. Charlotte Perkins Stetson Gilman, a rising intellectual, served on the executive board. Gilman was a feminist, author of the soon-to-published *Women and Economics* (1898) and also *The Home*, published in 1903. The 1894 and 1895 Woman's Congresses advanced Cooper's career and helped launch Gilman's nationally. Hearst served on the advisory council with Mary W. Kincaid, Caroline Severance, Milicent Shinn, Laura Lovell White, and Ellen Sargent, a California suffragist, among other prominent, politically active women.[5] Having worked over the years with quite a few of the well-known nonpartisan reform WCAPC officers and advisory council members who shared her political interests, Hearst felt comfortable lending her name to the WCAPC.

Hearst allied herself with an array of political reform issues in a wide-ranging agenda, which included suffrage as a tool to improve lives, addressed by the 1895 Woman's Congress. The delegates focused on issues related to women's domestic role to help quiet suffrage critics who argued that if women got the vote "they would neglect homes and families in favor of politics." Elite NAWSA officials Susan B. Anthony and British-born Dr. Anna Howard Shaw, a physician and ordained Methodist minister who was NAWSA's vice president, were in the West to build support for the national suffrage movement, especially a constitutional suffrage amendment. Shaw and Anthony attracted "unprecedented crowds of 2,500" and publicity to the 1895 Congress. Shaw spoke at the congress. She took the position that women needed the ballot to protect "homes and children" and purify the home and society to "protect the nation," and especially San Francisco, from the "degradation caused by the foreign vote" (i.e., naturalized immigrant men) while "concern over corrupt political machines controlling government" was on the rise. Anthony spoke on the question: "Influence or Power—Which?"[6] Anthony's view, of course, focused on the vote as a tool of political power equal to men's rather than as a tool of influence—a radical view when compared to Shaw's more conservative perspective.

Unlike Anthony, men rarely used the word *power* in a positive way in public in the same breath with the word *women*. They liked to refer to women with power as having "influence and moral persuasion"—a more conservative way to define the control of resources women possessed and one that fit Shaw's perspective more closely. Influence and moral persuasion harkened back to "the fervor that characterized northern Protestant benevolence in the 1830s, the hope that 'moral suasion' would redeem the world." But women were more often unapologetic and direct in using the term power in private correspondence to describe Hearst's ability to exert her power and authority. As one woman who was involved in creating a Pioneer Mothers' monument for the Panama-Pacific International Exposition wrote to Hearst: "That first day of our organization meeting, at the Exposition rooms, many arose and greeted you because of your power." Hearst missed Anthony's speech at the 1895 Congress because she was in London to get "a much needed rest" and recuperate after suffering heart problems.[7] Had she heard the speech and had someone asked her in public if she supported Anthony's radical view about power, more than likely a demure Hearst would have remained silent and would have staked out a position that emphasized suffrage as a tool of reform rather than a radical device for obtaining power.

While Hearst was abroad, the delegates of the 1895 Woman's Congress voted unanimously to support a suffrage amendment that broadened the emphasis on reform and women's rights to include a constitutional suffrage amendment. Anthony helped organize "an independent California

Suffrage Constitutional Amendment Campaign Association (CSCACA), chaired by Sarah B. Cooper," after the resolution passed. The CSCACA consisted mostly of San Francisco white women (there is no mentioned of black women at the congresses) interested in a variety of political reforms, including the passage of a federal suffrage amendment. Hearst was not a member, although her association with the WCAPC implied her support.[8] A privileged, rich, white businesswoman and reformer who believed in her class and racial superiority, Hearst backed the 1895 Congress suffrage resolution but from a distance and quietly. Since she accepted the constraints of sex and class as defined by the conventions of her day, Hearst refused to speak out publicly for a state or federal women's ballot or in opposition to nativist, antiminority, and antilabor views while abroad or at home.

Hearst attended the 1896 Woman's Congress, which convened in Native Sons Hall on Mason Street with some of San Francisco's skilled progressive females. She sat on the WCAPC advisory council through at least 1897. The 1896 Congress focused on "Woman and Government"—a subject of "especial value to both men and women," according to the congress program. The congress agenda noted that "California will presently be called upon to decide whether she will give to her women their share in the rights and duties, the privileges and obligations of government; and the decision should rest upon a clear and full knowledge of the matter in hand." Attendees at the 1896 Congress intended to get educated about their rights, moral duties, and obligations regarding the ballot for women, and those present shared with each other the history of women in political positions of control and authority.

Meanwhile, as the 1896 Congress met, Anthony struggled with the economic and political climate in a state that continued to suffer from a weak and unstable economy in the aftermath of the Panic of 1893. The 1896 suffrage campaign desperately needed funds. "Often" there were times when "there was not enough money on hand at headquarters to buy a postage stamp," a suffrage historian wrote. The campaign also needed publicity if a state referendum on the ballot for California women was to have any chance of success. Working with several experienced political organizers from the East Coast, Anthony set out to recruit wealthy, respected women like Jane L. Stanford, Sarah Knox-Goodridge, Ellen Sargent, Mary Sperry, and Phoebe Hearst to support California women's suffrage. While Hearst was learning from the discussions and debates at the 1896 Woman's Congress, and Anthony engaged in her recruiting efforts, Carrie Chapman Catt arrived in California from Idaho in September 1896 to help get the California suffrage amendment passed.[9]

Hearst unexpectedly ran into Anthony one day in late September of 1896 on the ferry that brought people back and forth between San Francisco and the East Bay. Hearst explained to Anthony that she was going to her Hacienda del Pozo de Verona and that she "had invited a large number of friends to go out with her to spend Sunday." Hearst invited Anthony to join her guests. Anthony accepted Hearst's offer. The two disembarked from the ferry after it docked across the bay and boarded Hearst's "special car attached to her train." Hearst, traveling in imperial style, talked openly and freely to Anthony about women's political and economic rights. Anthony explained afterward, in a letter to Jane L. Stanford, that Hearst straddled the suffrage issue. Hearst did not "quite believe in suffrage—and yet acknowledges that the great freedom and equality which women enjoy today is the result of our agitation," Anthony explained. Anthony added that Hearst's "many experiences since she became manager of her estates have done much toward making her see and feel the need of woman's possessing political *power* as well as financial freedom."

Speaking about political power and financial freedom in the same breath helped bridge the gap between classes in Phoebe's mind. But Hearst's statements to Anthony were a far cry from a public endorsement of Anthony's views on women possessing political power as traditionally defined by partisan politicians. Anthony went on to explain that her Hacienda visit convinced her that Hearst would eventually "grow into the full realization of the importance of woman's enfranchisement." The famous suffrage leader had sized up Hearst correctly—sort of. Not long after

Anthony and Hearst met, Hearst gave the largest single cash donation of one thousand dollars to the 1896 California suffrage campaign, a measly amount when compared to Hearst's donations to the University of California and education in general.[10] Hearst knew about the importance of the ballot. But unlike Anthony, by 1896, Hearst had yet to become clear about, and develop a full understanding of, the significance of state and national suffrage.

The significance of suffrage gradually became clearer to Hearst after her conversations with Anthony. The level and growth of her understanding and commitment to the ballot for women was reflected in the amount of money and resources, or her "wonderful power for good," as one of her female friends called it, that she devoted to the 1896 California suffrage campaign. Hearst and her son were interested in making money and in politics, particularly the 1896 presidential election, while ordinary Americans remained captivated by them both: with Phoebe A. Hearst and the ways in which she dispensed her large fortune, and with Will, who was in control of a newspaper empire that brought him great wealth and which gave him the opportunity to expect "to play a role in New York politics in 1896," as one historian observed. Phoebe was interested in keeping her estate on a sound financial footing. Her son, moreover, was interested in growing his newspaper business and in making money while he tried to figure out exactly what political role to play. Women used education and advertising, meanwhile, to promote their political views as their purchasing power rose. Will understood that appealing to women readers, especially on suffrage, would help sell more newspapers.[11]

Having a newspaper tycoon for a son and having used the educational and advertising techniques of suffragists and partisan politicians, Phoebe understood the power of the press. She realized "that a small percentage of the people are informed on political questions, and very few make an effort to become enlightened . . . by attending public meetings or otherwise, but a paper devoted to the facts might reach many," she wrote years later. An advocate of the importance of an educated citizenry, she thought it "an excellent" plan to distribute to "every voter a campaign edition of some paper devoted exclusively to giving people the facts in an attractive form," she explained in the same letter. Will's newspapers, from her perspective, were a valuable tool to inform readers and champion worthy causes. But Will's deep involvement in partisan electoral politics only served to undermine the power of his newspapers to advocate for the right causes, Phoebe wrote, after her son ran for governor in New York. When someone suggested Will as a candidate for the presidency, Phoebe replied: "I am very sorry that there is any thought, on the part of any one" about this suggestion "for I think he can do more good in his fearless efforts to stand by and champion the cause of right through his newspapers than would be possible in any public office." She appreciated the suggestion that Will run for president, "but I sincerely hope he will never accept the nomination for any office again, for the moment his name is mentioned as candidate for office, his papers lose their influence for good and are accused of being used solely to further his own personal desires," she explained.[12] Since she had little faith in partisan politicians, Phoebe thought her son possessed more power to advance political reform as a newspaper owner than as a partisan electoral politician (even though she had raised him to be a power in partisan electoral politics).

Will, for his part, refused to be on the wrong side of suffrage. His Democratic *San Francisco Examiner* appeared "friendly" to the 1896 suffrage campaign. The paper asked Susan B. Anthony to write editorials for the Sunday editions with several conditions, including "that she herself would write and sign her articles." Anthony accepted. Every Sunday for seven months her 1,600-word articles appeared. The articles helped sell newspapers and suffrage in homes and on the streets. But having Anthony write articles on suffrage for the newspaper was one thing. Getting the *Examiner* to make an official endorsement publicly for suffrage was quite another. Anthony was savvy about the power of newspapers to publicize and attract support for the women's ballot. She also was well aware that

Will Hearst owned the *Examiner*. Anthony believed it would benefit the suffrage campaign if she could get Will's paper to "lead" the Democrats in public support to pass the ballot for California women. A shrewd political operative, Anthony, as the 1896 suffrage campaign unfolded, pleaded with Will to have the *Examiner* express support for suffrage out of love and social fairness, the virtuous name and reputation of his mother, and for the state. As she wrote to him, "So, I pray you for the love of justice, for the love of your noble mother, and for the sake of California," have the paper's editorials endorse the 1896 suffrage amendment.[13]

Electoral party politics, as traditionally understood, made it difficult for Anthony to get the public endorsement of Will's *Examiner*. Voters were distracted by presidential election politics in 1896—Republican William McKinley was running against Democrat William Jennings Bryan—which diverted the attention of voters away from suffrage "and created strange political bedfellows in California," according to one historian. Populists and Democrats established a "fusion" of the Democratic-Populist-Silver parties to campaign together in 1896. Republicans, "pressured by the liquor interests and by the power of the Populist-Democratic alliance," dropped active support for suffrage even though the Republican Party state platform in California listed the issue as its first priority.

To complicate matters, people thought a lot of Democrats were "neutral" on suffrage. Some factions of the Democratic Party supported it. Yet Democrats refused to include suffrage in their party platform. Populists "were forced to virtually abandon the woman suffrage plank in their platform" because of their alliance with the Democrats. Anthony, meanwhile, pushed hard to get the endorsement of Will and his *Examiner*. But her plea fell on deaf ears. The paper "remained silent" on suffrage. On the other hand, it "did not . . . contain a line in opposition," which could be read as tacit approval of the cause. Phoebe could influence her son, but only so far, and she refused to pressure him. Will did work behind the scenes to support suffrage, but the *Examiner* still refused to make an official public endorsement. His newspaper, nevertheless, printed and distributed, at the Democratic Party's state convention, several thousand leaflets urging Democrats to support the ballot for women.[14]

Although willing to provide some financial support for suffrage from her own funds, Hearst did not recruit other wealthy women to the movement. Donating money to the 1896 campaign seemed to be on her mind more than devoting herself to deep, personal involvement in the movement. Because of her conservative temperament and inability to see completely the value of suffrage, for now she supported suffrage from a distance, did not press her son on the issue, and stayed out of his newspaper affairs. These decisions and actions contributed, in part, to the defeat of the 1896 California suffrage amendment.

The suffrage amendment was defeated in part because supporters failed to get enough socially prominent and wealthy women like Hearst to back the cause publicly. There was stiff opposition from those at the bottom of the social ladder, machine politicians, and liquor interests as well. The disheartening 1896 defeat moved Jane L. Stanford to declare publicly that she was a suffragist. Hearst refused to follow Stanford's lead. She wrote Anthony a delicately phrased explanation, instead, of her position on suffrage: "While I have never been an advocate of woman suffrage," an approximate statement at best, "I regard with deep respect your heroic life and entire devotion to the cause you have consecrated it to."[15] Hearst, unlike Anthony, was unwilling to support the cause regardless of the personal cost. From Hearst's perspective, her reserved approach to suffrage protected her name, reputation, and public image from criticism. She cautiously expressed admiration for Anthony without yet labeling herself a suffragist or endorsing the cause publicly.

It took Hearst quite a while to commit herself and her resources to the votes-for-women campaign after the turn of the new century.[16] Suffragists, including Anthony, had stayed active in the state after the 1896 campaign.

But a new generation of NAWSA leaders emerged after Elizabeth Cady Stanton and Susan B. Anthony passed away, in 1902 and 1906 respectively. Carrie Chapman Catt assumed the NAWSA presidency in 1900. She resigned from office in 1904. Dr. Anna Howard Shaw was president of NAWSA from 1904 until 1915. Hearst had pledged money, but not her ideas, talents, and energy to the California suffrage campaign in 1896. Between 1896 and 1910, she refused to pledge her ideas, skills, effort, and finances directly to the 1911 California or national suffrage campaign. Hearst clearly stated her unwillingness to devote herself to the suffrage cause while the 1911 California votes for women campaign was well underway. As she stated unequivocally in the spring of that year: "I am not a suffragist."[17]

It was not until after Hearst began her campaign to draw attention to herself and express her interest in participating in the Panama-Pacific International Exposition that she recognized publicly the vote for women as being inevitable; yet she was reluctant to support the aggressive, con- frontational methods used by radicals in the movement. As she stated in late August 1911, the day after Panama-Pacific International Exposition women met to discuss how they would participate in exposition politics: "I feel that the day when woman will vote is sure to come." The 1911 California suffrage campaign, during the period when the plans for the exposition unfolded, "was the largest and broadest waged in the United States to that date and borrowed some strategies from the radical suffragettes in England." But Phoebe was bothered by the strategies of radical suffragists. As she explained to one supporter who requested to use her name in the campaign: "I have always held myself apart from the organizations that were working for suffrage because the methods did not appeal to me." She made a fine distinction between her personal interest in, and support for, the cause and what she believed were the unpleasant, unattractive, and sensational methods used by militants. She was uncomfortable with what she saw as their daring, unconventional, and male-like hostile ways. Yet she personally allied herself and her name with Susan B. Anthony and believed that women were entitled to economic freedom and equal political rights.

Although she declined to go so far as to divorce herself entirely from the suffrage cause, in response to a request for her to make a public endorsement for the ballot, Hearst explained delicately: "While I have not been willing to join the forces of those who were and are working for suffrage, neither have I wished to take any active part however small on either side." Making no mention of having served on the WCAPA advisory council, she added: "I prefer to take *no* part for or against this struggle and for that reason I do not wish to allow my name to be used as you suggest." Nonetheless, Hearst held out the hope that down the road she might bestow her imprimatur upon the 1911 California campaign. "This is my attitude now," she wrote. "I will not say that I may not favor one or the other side later on."[18] Hearst's position encouraged Anthony and other suffragists to keep tabs on her politics and pressure her to make a public endorsement. For now, however, she withheld her public support and made contradictory statements to protect herself and give herself leverage, particularly with antisuffragists.

Because of the way Hearst was positioning herself on suffrage, a "dispute" erupted "between suffragists and antis," a newspaper reported. Which side of the political fence was Hearst on? Both sides claimed her as one of their own. One correspondent from the Massachusetts Woman Suffrage Association wrote Hearst about a year later, asking her to clarify her position on votes for women during the 1911 campaign. "Several times lately, anti-Suffragists, when speaking at meetings where both sides of the question were being presented, have declared that in California you had opposed suffrage, and that the claim some suffragist had made that you had given your moral and financial support to suffrage because you had learned that the vice interest were supporting the opposition was absolutely false. Now we suffragists have understood that you did help California win her fight and that when you learned of the sums of money the corrupt interests were giving the antis you helped our cause financially. . . . Will you send me in reply a few lines stating your attitude towards suffrage at the time of the California campaign?"[19] But Hearst was still waiting quietly to see which way the political winds were blowing so she could figure out the most effective and comfortable way to position herself on the ballot while avoiding harm and criticism. Her public position appeared contradictory. But, in reality, the dedicated single-minded militancy of Anthony, and Hearst's temperamental dislike of radical methods and style, served to determine exactly if, how, when, or where she would publicly endorse the ballot. Suffragists and antisuffragists alike kept a close eye on Hearst to see which way she would go.[20]

While Hearst procrastinated, powerful male moneyed interests mounted immense opposition to, and pounded California progressives on, the ballot for women; and the Southern Pacific Railroad—called the "Octopus"— was dominating California state politics.[21] Suffragists were well aware that Hearst was an elite, white businesswoman with real power in her own right and connections to prominent, wealthy female and male reformers and businessmen. If suffragists could get Hearst to come out publicly in favor of votes for women, would that provide an antidote to the over- whelming opposition of moneyed men and help infuse more femininity and respectability into the ballot campaign? A public endorsement from Hearst might lead to convincing conservative, wealthy political opponents to drop their opposition and switch sides. It might even lead to Hearst increasing her financial support for the campaign.

While Hearst bided her time regarding a public endorsement of votes for women, Dr. Anna Shaw was serving as NAWSA president and the suffrage movement took "a conservative turn." During Shaw's term, race and class came to the forefront and a general direction in America developed "toward support for qualified suffrage." This trend was fre- quently associated with "anti-Black and anti-immigration sentiments, and in the South, to states' rights advocacy, opposition to any federal voting amendment, and efforts to guarantee white supremacy," according to one historian. NAWSA had developed a suffrage movement in the 1890s that emphasized a "'Southern Strategy' and the courting of southern white suffragists." The national suffrage organization had, in essence, decided to "[abandon] controversial positions" and to set aside the needs of blacks in order to attract broad-based and deeper support, particularly among Southern whites. NAWSA, under Shaw's leadership in the first decade of the twentieth century, was led by "a self-conscious elite advocating a narrow political philosophy and exercising increased control over the movement as a whole."[22] The conservative direction of the NAWSA appealed to Hearst's reserved temperament and sensibilities.

Under Anna Shaw's leadership, the NAWSA was becoming more conservative, while radical suffragists, such as Harriot Stanton Blatch and other elite suffrage officials, were busy recruiting wealthy, high-society women to the movement. Mary McHenry Keith took the lead in approaching Hearst. Keith had been the first woman to get a degree from Hastings Law School and was the spouse of William Keith, California landscape painter and beneficiary of Hearst's largesse. An organizer for the College Equal Suffrage League (CESL), she had helped establish the group in 1907 as an affiliate of the NAWSA. She also assisted the Berkeley Political Equality League in its efforts to begin operations and was a prominent leader of a younger generation of suffragists. In 1908 Keith had used a subtle approach with Hearst, hoping to persuade her to endorse votes for women publicly: she had offered Hearst an honorary position on the board of trustees of the Susan B. Anthony Memorial Fund as a representative of the Pacific Coast. But Hearst declined.

Some two years on, members from institutions of higher education in the Northeast were in control of the College Equal Suffrage League as the political momentum began to build toward the 1910 suffrage victory in Washington State. Anna Shaw, meanwhile, "concentrated her efforts" on states in the East in 1911, to the exclusion, some suffragists believed, of other regions in the nation. The College Equal Suffrage League, now led by Charlotte Anita Whitney, became the most active suffrage organization in the Bay Area. Whitney was a member of a distinguished Northern California family and a social worker. She was also a socialist, pacifist, and tepid communist. Whitney increased the pressure on Hearst in 1911 to make an endorsement as young, white advocates of votes for women thought about the benefits of getting Hearst's public support. Flattering Hearst, Whitney reminded the First Lady of California that her name had "always been associated with the progressive movements of the State and for those things that make for the ennobling of womanhood." Constance Lawrence Dean of the CESL pandered to Hearst's ego by writing to Phoebe: "You are recognized as the First Woman of the West." CESL members also appealed to Hearst's understanding of political reform in the Progressive Era, arguing that her endorsement would attract "hundreds—more probably thousands of votes" to the suffrage campaign.[23] Hearst's open endorsement would strengthen public perception of suffragists as tempered, respectable women and might diminish the role of radical suffragists, an appealing prospect to Shaw.

For now, however, the subtle approaches crafted to appeal to Hearst's ego and fit her politics failed to work. Hearst found it too difficult to break away from the pull of convention and risk subjecting herself to public condemnation and attacks if she associated herself with militants. She could have donated much larger amounts of money and could have made a public announcement earlier. But she chose not to do so. She held back and limited her financial contributions. She was very careful not to speak out publicly or associate herself with selling paraphernalia that raised money for the cause, even though by this time it was more acceptable for suffragists to use public space to claim women's full citizenship rights in the name of political reform. Hearst played it very safe in the fall of 1911 as compared to militant suffragists. She refused to commit herself publicly to votes for women. Nor did she place herself in any "formalized political public sphere" associated with the 1911 California campaign.[24] Since she felt uncomfortable with militancy, Hearst kept her distance from the CESL and refused to reveal her position on the national ballot until the very last minute.

Hearst had led people to believe she was on the side of both the pro- and antisuffrage campaigns as a wave of progressivism swept over California. But in 1911, as her campaign unfolded to win election as honorary president of the woman's board of the Panama-Pacific International Exposition, she decided to eliminate any ambiguity and come out clearly in favor of California suffrage. The CESL helped get Hearst to budge on suffrage during the administration of progressive Republican governor Hiram Johnson. Johnson supported the ballot for women. The CESL "sent telegrams" and "night letters" to get the California Senate Judiciary Committee to support votes for women during Johnson's gubernatorial campaign. The principle of equality stood out in the campaign literature that advertised the cause, especially to state legislators. "Equal suffrage for Men and Women Why? Women Need it. Men Need it. The State Needs it," CESL literature stated. All women needed the vote to protect wage-earning women, mothers, housekeepers, taxpayers, philanthropists, and teachers too: "85 per cent of the public school teachers in California are women. Is it fair to ask disfranchised individuals to teach citizenship?" the published CESL literature proclaimed.

Striking a progressive reform chord often played by women's clubs, the CESL took the position that women, or "HOME keepers," many of whom taught citizenship, needed the ballot to properly take care of home issues in society: "Pure Food," "Pure Water," "Clean Milk," "Clean Streets," an "Adequate Garbage System," and "Good Schools"—issues traditional partisan politicians controlled but failed to address adequately. The ballot for women, from the CESL's perspective, was a tool of progressive reform to teach people how to be good citizens and improve lives in society and the nation-state as a whole. These progressive views attracted support from Hearst and other female and male reform suffragists, feminists, club women, YWCA supporters, and labor activists.[25]

Hearst finally declared she was a suffragist in the summer of 1911, just months before her victorious election to head the woman's board of the Panama-Pacific International Exposition. She later clarified in a newspaper article, after the California suffrage referendum passed, why she supported the ballot for women in California. A letter written by Hearst, on January 2, 1913, and published in a newspaper, quoted her as saying: "I was not in favor of suffrage until the campaign in California was well on, and then certain information came to me which convinced me that the time had come—here, at any rate—when women should have the right to vote." Hearst's views as a reformer and her dissatisfaction with men shaped her perspective. She added, "I felt convinced then that women would unite in favoring certain work tending towards the betterment of conditions affecting women and children particularly which men heretofore could never be relied upon to favor when it came to the test of the ballot." Hearst wrote Caroline Severance: "I share your feeling about the benefit our State will receive through the right of its women to the ballot." She added, "I decided to unite with those who were working to obtain it after considerable thought, and have great hopes that the results will justify all our expectations." Then Hearst clearly stated her position: "I am a suffragist."

She had had to think about it for some time before making her declaration. When she did make it, she clearly separated herself from the improper confrontational, aggressive methods of suffrage militants. She adamantly announced in her letter of January 2: "I have no sympathy whatever with the tactics of the militant suffragette."[26] Hearst refused to support suffragettes (a slang term of derision first used by opponents to scorn British militants) who engaged in what she considered too strong or emphatic, unfeminine and excessive actions such as "speaking from automobiles." Suffragists with conservative temperaments supported domesticity and considered such militant methods to be "sensational," unladylike, and a way to lose votes.[27]

Hearst had now established herself as a "moderate" suffragist, in the same camp as Katherine Duer Mackay, a high-society "beauty" married to a wealthy businessman, who had founded the Equal Franchise Society in New York. The organization had been designed to recruit rich, elite women—like militant Alva Belmont, divorced wife of William Vanderbilt and wife of the railroad tycoon O. P. Belmont—to get involved in the votes-for-women movement. Hearst was, by the second decade of the twentieth century, an elite, white, wealthy woman and reform suffragist who used dignified, respectable, and tactically conservative political ways—such as proper public behavior, education, advertising, publicity, and lobbying—to support and achieve votes for women.[28] Hearst's reserved position on suffrage contributed to her successful election to head the woman's board of the Panama-Pacific International Exposition. It would have been highly unlikely for a radical suffragist to have been elected to the post.

Once she decided that she could support women's suffrage publicly, Hearst arranged for a surprise announcement of her endorsement to ring out at a suffrage rally that was to take place in San Francisco's Dreamland Rink (the "largest auditorium in the city") at eight o'clock in the evening of October 5, 1911, five days before the special election on votes for women on October 10. Hearst had in fact already taken a step toward participation when she requested that a delegate to the Woman Suffrage Party of San Francisco "respect" her "wish in not mentioning her name as a suffrage supporter" earlier in the 1911 campaign. Hearst had chosen instead to establish her new political reform identity as a moderate in the women's suffrage camp by making a masterful, careful, and strategically timed public endorsement through a CESL surrogate at the Dreamland Rink rally, just days before the votes-for-women election.[29] She had planned and orchestrated her diplomatic announcement down to the last detail.

The College Equal Suffrage League had invited representatives from all suffrage organizations to the Dreamland Rink rally. The league had developed their plans thoughtfully, adopting methods of labor reformers battling for power and using modern advertising and mass entertainment techniques to arouse interest in the event. While Hearst accepted the CESL's use of modern publicity and mass amusement techniques, she would have no association with the league's organized rallies and public speaking on city streets. Nor did she have any interest in personally helping the CESL post flyers all over San Francisco or join a band the league had hired to march up and down the city streets to arouse interest.

Perhaps of greater concern to the rally organizers was that class tensions had been boiling over that summer and labor violence was on the rise in San Francisco and Los Angeles. CESL workers were "terrified" that the worst might happen at the rally—violence might break out. Yet they "felt we must risk it," the league reported. All of this made Phoebe's own physical presence at Dreamland Rink unthinkable and risky as well. In addition to worry over her physical safety, she could not afford to place herself in a political situation in public where she might be criticized for associating with militant suffragists. Neither was she willing to risk having her respectability and distinguished reputation tarnished or her political capital diminished.

To great fanfare, the rally took place on October 5, as planned, and Will Hearst's *Examiner* reported on the Dreamland Rink event (which had been chaired by George A. Knight) the very next day. The newspaper described a huge "overflow street crowd" jammed into the rink that spilled out the door while hordes of people waited for the speakers at one of the largest public meetings of the California suffrage movement. When a CESL representative announced that Hearst "had sent word to the mass meeting she endorsed the proposition of equal suffrage," about ten thousand exuberant people inside and outside the hall erupted in applause, a reporter wrote.[30] There was no outrage. Hearst must have been pleased. The last thing she had wanted was to appear as though she was a rabble-rouser. She had made her public endorsement in an adroit, delicate, and tactful way from afar since she was unwilling to promote the suffrage cause at just any personal or political cost. Her approach helped to define femininity and its relationship to voting rights from the perspective of a white, elite, wealthy woman supporter, rather than a working-class advocate, of California suffrage. Even as she rejected the traditional, old-fashioned view that opposed the constitutional ballot for women, however, Hearst continued to rely on a cautious and reserved approach to making her position known.

Suffragists argued that Hearst's endorsement had made quite an impact and helped create momentum for the campaign. According to Ernestine Black, head of the CESL, Hearst gave "impetus . . . not only to the suffrage movement here in California but in America" and possibly abroad. The endorsement enhanced Hearst's reputation, displayed her savvy political skills, and sent a message that she was in a class by herself on the vote for women in California. Other wealthy women had become advocates of the ballot for women. But it appears that virtually none got the attention Hearst received from the press, probably because other rich women lacked a son who was a newspaper tycoon. The tactics Hearst used to make her public endorsement cast her in the best possible light among pro-suffragists and the uncommitted. It added respectability, interest, and excitement to the campaign, arousing greater enthusiasm and support for votes for women. No suffragist commented publicly on Hearst's reluctance to provide financial support for the campaign. They were just pleased she had made her public endorsement. Shortly after the election, the final tally on votes for women came to light: 125,037 for and 121,450 against. California suffrage won by a slim margin—3,587 votes.

Hearst drew attention to herself and the campaign and may have gotten some voters to vote yes on election day. But the political reality was that the victory came "because [the] urban working class combined with the rural vote to overcome the generally negative influence of large cities." In San Francisco, 40 to 42 percent of working-class men voted for the ballot. In the professional and middle-class neighborhoods, only about 37 percent cast their votes for women. It appeared that Hearst had timed her public endorsement specifically to have the most impact on the opposition. One male admirer was so taken with Hearst's endorsement that he urged her to run for governor of California. Hearst, as she approached her seventieth birthday, politely rejected the suggestion as beyond the realm of her ambition and reality.[31]

Hearst now turned her attention to the 1912 presidential election and the federal votes-for-women amendment. Many considered William Randolph Hearst "to be a strong possibility for the" 1912 Democratic Party nomination. Will's mother had never wanted him to be a contender for the presidential nomination. Hearst backed Champ Clark and the Champ Clark Women's League. Clark was a homegrown Missouri boy and was an old political ally of Will Hearst. Clark opposed the Democratic Party presidential nomination of Woodrow Wilson, and the Champ Clark Women's League eagerly sought Hearst's support for Clark's 1912 presidential bid. The Women's League was affiliated with the Champ Clark League—a group that became the Wilson-Marshall Progressive Democratic League of San Francisco after the Democratic Party chose its presidential nominee.

Phoebe Apperson Hearst, a registered Democrat, offered her name, social position, and money to benefit Clark's candidacy as women's involvement in partisan electoral politics became more acceptable. The executive committee of the Champ Clark Women's League elected her the honorary president at large, with Hearst's consent. But the decision to associate her resources with Clark's presidential ambitions drew outrage from some who cast aspersions on the public image she had so cleverly and carefully crafted and promoted as a dignified representative of American womanhood. Hearst was worried. There was no cause, ultimately, for alarm. Withering criticism from a great many never materialized. There was not enough disapproval of her backing of Clark to warrant her resignation from the Champ Clark Women's League because she was "not very active," as R. A. Clark, one of Hearst's employees, wrote to her. It was inevitable, Clark concluded, that the more active Hearst became on issues of political interest, the greater the chance for public scrutiny and criticism.

Part of an older generation of women reluctant to get deeply involved in male partisan electoral politics, Hearst refused to support Champ Clark's campaign actively and in public. Her contribution, nevertheless, helped the Clark campaign win the California primary (although it was insufficient for him to win the national Democratic Party nomination). The coveted nomination prize went to Woodrow Wilson on the forty-sixth ballot at the convention. Wilson, in 1912, supported state suffrage but not a federal suffrage amendment.[32]

After dabbling in the waters of partisan party politics without damage to her reputation, Hearst now felt comfortable supporting Woodrow Wilson against Republican William Howard Taft and Progressive Party candidate Theodore Roosevelt. Wilson was "perhaps the most elusive on" suffrage. He sidestepped questions from reporters and women heavily involved in American politics about the "contentious suffrage issue." He claimed it was an inappropriate issue for presidential contenders to talk about and devalued the subject of the ballot during his campaign. As he put it: "Suffrage is not a national issue." He argued, instead, that it was a state issue. Wilson calculated that if he backed the federal amendment he would lose the support of loyal white-supremacist voters in the South, where blacks were disfranchised, as well as the Democratic Party nomination.[33]

Although Hearst shared an interest in a constitutional amendment on the ballot for women with one of Wilson's presidential election opponents, Theodore Roosevelt, she remained loyal personally and publicly to the Democratic Party in 1912. The Democratic Party recognized her "vast wealth" and "great power," as one correspondent described her, by electing her vice president for a party reception to be held to honor delegates from the Baltimore Convention, which had nominated Woodrow Wilson and his vice-presidential running mate, Thomas R. Marshall.[34] She thought better of getting involved in either Democratic or Republican Party electoral politics, remained true to her definition of nonpartisanship, and kept her distance. She refused an invitation to attend either a smoker and reception to honor Roosevelt or the Democratic Party gathering.

Phoebe stuck to what she thought was proper and acceptable. She made financial contributions of $50 to the state Democratic Women's Committee and $250 for Woodrow Wilson's campaign at about the same time that Alice Paul, a radical NAWSA member, arrived in Washington DC to organize a drive for a constitutional suffrage amendment and revitalize the votes-for-women movement.[35] Hearst's paltry contributions hardly signaled a robust endorsement of Wilson or his position on votes for women. But it was a safe political approach because her contributions went unreported in newspapers and were hidden from public view. Hearst felt at ease backing Wilson as long as she stuck to giving small monetary donations to progressive male politicians behind the scenes and avoided making a public spectacle of herself in the streets. But her shared political interests with, and quiet support for, partisan politicians provide an incomplete picture of Hearst's complex suffrage reform politics.

Hearst had first decided to place her good name and reputation on the line to support a constitutional amendment on women's right to vote during the same period in 1911 when she was turning her ceremonial position as honorary president of the Panama-Pacific International Exposition into a position with real power and authority. While head of the PPIE Woman's Board, she supported the Congressional Union for Woman Suffrage's booth at the exposition. Anna Howard Shaw, now president of the NAWSA, and Alice Paul, a radical member of the NAWSA, wanted a constitutional suffrage amendment. But they disagreed significantly on tactics. The NAWSA, under Shaw's leadership, backed using nonpartisan, nonmilitant political tactics, which pleased wealthy women with conservative sensibilities like Hearst. In 1914, Paul started to hold the national political party in power—at the time, the Democrats—responsible for blocking the passage of a constitutional suffrage amendment, and she advocated the use of militant tactics to defeat Wilson and the Democrats—tactics that ran counter to what Shaw and Hearst supported.[36]

Paul became chair of the Congressional Committee within the NAWSA. Earlier Paul had established a separate organization, the Congressional Union (CU), "on paper," with the aim of assisting the NAWSA's Congressional Committee. But when the NAWSA removed her as head of its Congressional Committee, Paul decided to reform the Congressional Union into "a genuine alternative to the NAWSA." She requested that the

Congressional Union be granted an affiliate status with the NAWSA. But the relationship between the NAWSA and Congressional Union took a turn for the worse because it competed with NAWSA officials, activities, and fund-raising and was too independent and militant, according to Shaw. Shaw and NAWSA officers offered to accept the Congressional Union's request for affiliate status with conditions: the NAWSA officers would control the CU. But Paul refused to relinquish control of the Congressional Union. Consequently, NAWSA president Shaw disavowed the CU in December 1913 because she thought the group was too dangerous. The Congressional Union's top priority in 1914, meanwhile, was to get the U.S. Congress to pass a national suffrage amendment.[37]

Paul, who was without equal when it came to getting wealthy women to finance the suffrage movement, organized a Congressional Union advisory council of rich, elite women to help advocate for and finance the national votes-for-women campaign. Most of the advisory council women shunned involvement in the Congressional Union's day-to-day organizational operations. But they did provide the respectability and financial backing to keep the radical, or militant, wing of the votes-for-women movement going. Alva Belmont's support for the Congressional Union, especially financial, was essential. Belmont was an unapologetic radical suffragist, a member of the CU executive committee, and a divorcée. She had an open disregard for convention and law that shocked or horrified some. She also spoke out strongly and aggressively in support of a constitutional amend-ment. Her decisions and actions drastically eroded traditional norms and helped generate vital publicity for the cause by defying convention.[38] Hearst could identify with Belmont's class status. But she rejected Belmont's "unladylike," unconventional behavior, which included participating in suffrage protest marches. At the time, one of Hearst's female friends was assisting Paul in her recruiting efforts.

But when Hearst joined the advisory council of the Congressional Union in late 1914 or early 1915, through Florence Bayard Hilles of Delaware (a trusted friend and CU council member, who picketed the White House in 1917), she had little to no understanding of the internal politics of the Congressional Union while the organization was transforming itself, in 1916, into the National Woman's Party under the leadership of militant suffragist Alice Paul. The NWP was a party controlled and operated by white, mostly militant women involved in partisan electoral politics with one goal—to get Congress to pass a federal amendment on votes for women. Paul sent CU organizers to western suffrage states, at about the same time Hearst joined the CU's advisory council "to urge women to vote against Democratic congressional candidates." Hearst, while serving on the advisory council in 1916, was a veteran of voluntary association and academic politics. She was not a political insider with knowledge of the inner workings of organizational politics in the NAWSA, the CU, and the NWP. She was unaware of the political tensions and divisions between Shaw's NAWSA, Paul's Congressional Union, and later, the National Woman's Party. She had virtually no experience, moreover, in traditional partisan electoral politics. Nor did she fully understand the complexities of the militant political tactics Paul advocated and used.

Shaw's conservative temperament and political positions appealed to her. She liked that the Congressional Union was an organization aligned with Shaw's dignified, reserved ways and that it supported Wilson's efforts for national defense. By agreeing to serve on the advisory council, Hearst linked her name with those of other rich female militants like Alva Vanderbilt Belmont, another council member.[39] Even so, not all wealthy and prosperous women progressive reformers on the Congressional Union's advisory council accepted and supported militancy. Hearst was among those rich women who refused to back militant methods while she was very busy being the honorary president of the PPIE Woman's Board.[40] It would take time for Hearst to unravel the complex differentiations between NAWSA and NWP politics.

Hearst's dignity and reputation played a role, while she sat on the Congressional Union's advisory council, in getting the board of directors of the PPIE to respond positively to suffragists' request for a votes-for-women's booth at the exposition. Elizabeth Kent, head of the Congressional Committee of the NAWSA, after Paul was ousted, had the responsibility of seeing to it that votes-for-women legislation was introduced to Congress. She was supposed to arrange two committee hearings in the U.S. Congress before the Panama-Pacific International Exposition opened. Kent also was a "member of the Exposition Committee in charge of the Social Economy Building" and the spouse of Congressman William Kent, a millionaire, socialist, and California representative in the U.S. Congress. Kent, with Hearst's blessing, arranged for a votes-for-women booth in the Palace of Education and Social Economy where the Travelers' Aid Society had general headquarters.[41]

Hearst and the woman's board did their part in making the PPIE "the first exposition" to approve a woman suffrage exhibit. Hearst's support for the ballot, by this time, encouraged partisan electoral politicians to invoke her name to convince people to support the cause for a constitutional suffrage amendment. When he made a public plea for the national suffrage amendment, Governor Cary of Wyoming invoked Hearst's good name, reputation, class, and race when he asked: "Is it right that Phoebe Hearst is denied the ballot while the man who grooms her horse is permitted to exercise that privilege?" The mention of Hearst's name jogged people's memories about her past accomplishments, reputation, and privileged status. That, in turn, helped the PPIE board of directors to justify, in their own minds, support for national suffrage, increasing the likelihood that they would officially approve the Congressional Union booth. Feminine, dignified suffragists made it easier for PPIE men to make good on their promise to administer the exposition along "general lines with reference to equal rights," helping to shield the board of directors from public attacks and criticism.[42] Had unconventional radical suffragists like Belmont asked the board of directors to approve the booth, the board members probably would have felt threatened, making it more likely for them to deny the request. The board of directors was publicly endorsing a constitutional ballot for women when they voted to allow the suffrage booth at the exposition.

The Congressional Union booth "contained every argument that could be presented visually for" a constitutional vote-for-women amendment. A large picture of Susan B. Anthony, flags, and a "banner bearing the words of the Susan B. Anthony Amendment, which demanded that the right of citizens of the United States to vote should not be denied by the United States or by any State" hung on the wall. Visitors saw snapshots of suffrage campaign events and copies of the *Suffragist* that were available for people to read. Votes-for-women conferences convened in the booth three times a week. Kent was hostess at a reception to honor Hearst and other prominent western female suffragists after the board of directors approved the booth.[43]

Alva Vanderbilt Belmont believed that if distinguished wealthy women, like Bertha Honoré Palmer, were to receive "representative women from the west," like Phoebe Hearst, "it would have a tremendous political significance."[44] Being accepted by wealthy women east of California was one way to encourage women like Hearst to do their part in making the suffrage movement important and respectable to attract more support. Hearst did her part. She provided "beautiful flowers" for the exhibit, organized by Doris Stevens, a Congressional Union activist. She attended the dedication ceremony for the CU booth, led by Charlotte Anita Whitney, and held in the auditorium of the YWCA Building. The YWCA never officially endorsed the ballot. But it never opposed it either, and it allowed suffragists to use YWCA space and buildings. The audience listened closely, at the ceremony, to speeches on suffrage that rang throughout the hall. Hearst listened intently but remained silent. She presided, though, over the reception that followed the dedication ceremony.[45]

Hearst's participation in the celebration sent a clear message that she would conduct herself with decorum and propriety while she backed, and acted on behalf of, the votes-for-women campaign. Her support also helped convince throngs of exposition attendees to visit the suffrage booth and examine the voting record of each representative in the Sixty-Third Congress. They were encouraged to sign a petition to Congress to pass a woman's constitutional suffrage amendment. The petition, with five hundred thousand signatures, was 18,333 feet long. Female "envoys" prepared, as visitors stopped by the Congressional Union booth, to drive across the country to deliver the votes-for-women petition to politicians in Washington DC.[46] Hearst was not one of the envoys. She considered being an envoy an audacious act for a wealthy, elite suffragist. But she participated in the Congressional Union for Woman Suffrage Voters' Convention that Paul held in the Palace of Education at the PPIE in mid-September 1915. Only delegates from states where women had the right to vote would attend in Chicago to launch a campaign to establish a National Woman's Party "with branches in different States."[47]

Alva Belmont tried to get the honorary president of the PPIE Woman's Board more involved in the Congressional Union while plans unfolded, during the exposition, to hold the Chicago convention to launch the NWP. Belmont knew how beneficial it would be if the Congressional Union could use Hearst's name to attract support for and promote votes for women. She was sensitive to Hearst's cautious and conciliatory politics. And she recognized that Hearst was incredibly busy as head of the woman's board. So Belmont tailored her efforts to fit Hearst's needs. As she explained to Hearst: "I quite understand that it will be impossible for you to take an active part or do any personal work on the Committee, and did not expect to ask you to give us your valuable time. What we want more than all is your name" to "appear on our membership list, but I am going to beg of you to reconsider your decision in regard to letting us use it as a vice-chairman." Belmont went on: "I pledge my word to you that if you comply with my request, it will involve no work for you at all, but will be a great help to us and will stimulate others to do likewise." Hearst must have been flattered by a request from a woman of her class who was committed to national suffrage. She responded positively. She instructed her secretary to "send a very nice note. I grant her request. Don't make note too brief but say yes in good *style*." As the acceptance of women's involvement in electoral party politics increased, Phoebe A. Hearst allowed the Congressional Union to use her name as vice chair of California at the Woman Voters' Convention. Hearst felt comfortable enough, while in her own PPIE political backyard, to make a brief welcoming address to delegates on the first day of the September CU-PPIE convention.[48] But her limited participation in the Chicago gathering expressed her remaining reserve as a suffrage supporter.

Using Hearst's name would help convince other wealthy women who might be as reserved and conservative as Hearst to join the campaign planned at the Chicago meeting. It might also influence Will Hearst to make an offer like the one he had made to get the U.S. Congress to choose San Francisco as the site of the exposition; that is, to offer his newspaper services to the campaign to get a federal ballot. It might also sway businessmen to support the votes-for-women campaign. The honorary president of the woman's board consented to Belmont's request because she assumed correctly that as long as she stood for and represented the PPIE-YWCA national political agenda and would not get involved with militant maneuvers, she would be all right and no damage would come to her reputation or standing overall.

As we have seen, Hearst was not an adamant nor outspoken supporter of a constitutional votes-for-women amendment. She flirted only briefly with another militant organization when she sent a small private donation to Blatch's Women's Political Union (WPU) in New York. The WPU challenged "the existing standards of femininity"—ladylike helplessness and pleasing behavior—by using sensational, rebellious, and dangerous methods.[49] As long as Hearst's donation to the WPU was small and unknown to the public at large, she felt safe. Hearst believed she needed to be especially careful and avoid controversy while she headed the woman's board of the exposition. Otherwise, she might fail to effectively represent her constituents and negotiate and navigate power with the board of directors.

The Congressional Union, nonetheless, tried to get Hearst more deeply involved in partisan electoral politics. Florence Brewer Boeckel, press chairman of the Congressional Union, followed up on Belmont's success in the spring of 1916. Boeckel wrote to Paul: "The only way you are going to get real support from the press is to have some group of papers make your case." She added: "But couldn't you through Mrs. Hearst get the support of the Hearst papers and news service? There could surely be no better move—whether you like [William Randolph] Hearst as a backer or not, he has backed mighty good causes." The newspapers of Phoebe's son reached the masses around the nation. The issues he addressed were ones "other papers cannot ignore," Boeckel concluded. The only way suffragists could get "serious consideration in the papers," Boeckel thought, was to secure the backing of the Hearst newspapers through Phoebe Apperson Hearst.[50]

Hearst understood the importance of the press but also of spending money on the Congressional Union for lobbying and women's space to claim power and demand political rights. She knew that donating money for buildings was considered acceptable behavior for a wealthy woman and could help make possible the passage of a constitutional amendment. So she gave $500 to the Congressional Union for organizers and then $750 to rent the Blackstone Theatre for the union's convention in Chicago, to be held June 5–7, 1916, to help Paul and her supporters establish the National Woman's Party. Theaters were a commercial public space, by the 1910s, where rich women increasingly could go, accompanied by friends and family members, without a male escort. Hearst's gifts, earmarked for specific purposes, helped transform the theater from a place of entertainment into a place where women formally claimed, publicized, and mobilized for power and political equality. She hoped her contribution would lead to success, but she was unsure. She declared in a letter that acknowledged her financial contribution: "We may not succeed but it will not be owing to lack of effort."

While Hearst's contributions benefited the young party's ability to get a constitutional suffrage amendment, her money had a limited effect on the decisions and plans of NWP officials. Hearst's financial gifts and direct participation were never significant enough to shape the overall strategies and tactics of the National Woman's Party. Her donations, unlike the much larger amount of money and resources Belmont provided to the NWP, fell far short of being sizable enough to determine major policy decisions and plans in the two organizations. Paul, moreover, had firm power over the National Woman's Party to the point that some, like Charlotte Anita Whitney, claimed that the partisan political organization was autocratic because it was controlled by a single woman, namely Paul. Paul's firm control created tension with the advisory council.[51] Hearst, nonetheless, backed the party from afar and avoided getting deeply involved in the organization's internal and electoral politics.

As was typical, Hearst was tactful and dignified as she resisted deeper, more public involvement in the National Woman's Party. Anne Martin, "elected permanent" head of the new party, had requested to see Hearst in Washington DC shortly after Hearst sent them a donation. Hearst explained she was "so hurried with other matters . . . that not even a five minute interview could be managed." Hearst lacked the passion and will to try to force Paul and the women's organizations to make decisions and fashion policies, even as she believed the ballot for women was a good cause. Nonetheless, she refused to see Martin. She sent a short statement to her, instead, to "express at once my protest against the continued obstruction of the National Suffrage Amendment by the Judiciary Committee of the House of Representatives." Hearst explained her reasons: "I believe in the interests of justice and freedom, that the Committee should make an immediate report of the Susan B. Anthony Amendment to the House of Representatives." Her brief written protest appeared in the *Washington*

Post a few days later. She made her declaration from a safe distance rather than out on the streets. William Randolph Hearst's *San Examiner* joined many California newspapers in their endorsement of a constitutional amendment for votes for women after his mother's statement appeared in the *Washington Post*. Will also "telegraphed" the *Los Angeles Examiner* and the *Chicago Examiner* "asking them to be particularly alert" to providing "assistance and encouragement" to the ballot campaign.[52]

Although Hearst had been reluctant to commit herself fully to the National Woman's Party, the party had found a way to appeal to Hearst's conservative temperament and accommodate her cautious, nonconfrontational political style, as well as her positions on important policy issues. In so doing, they exploited her shared political interests with her son and the power of his press to attract support nationally to achieve victory on a constitutional suffrage amendment. Setting pen to paper in protest revealed how far Hearst had come in seeing the value of coming out more forcefully in support of a constitutional suffrage amendment. Nonetheless, her published written protest could in no way be seen as an endorsement of militant methods to achieve votes for women. In fact, Hearst continued to demonstrate in public her commitment to methods and issues that reflected her conservative temperament and sensibilities.

By 1916 Hearst also came to see the value of support for war preparedness and national defense in staking a claim "to citizenship" while she was involved with the National Woman's Party. In that year an invitation came her way to participate in a formal preparedness parade in support of Wilson's official policy position on national defense. "For the propertied" and powerful, parades had become a political act that accomplished or advocated "respectability." The preparedness movement was dominated by conservative white men, and it was by then common practice for large numbers of women to march publicly as well. But if Hearst decided to march, although she would not be marching in a suffragist parade, she would have to contend with criticism from people, particularly antisuf-fragists, who thought it inappropriate for a respectable woman to march and who had a history of criticizing "parades and mass meetings staged by suffragists as 'spectacular and unwomanly.'"[53]

Hearst heeded the call to march for Wilson's policies in support of preparedness and national defense as the possibility of the United States entering World War I loomed large in 1916. But the Woman's Peace Party opposed preparedness. Some charter members of the party belonged to organizations Hearst had supported and in which she had been active in the past, as well as groups she had recently joined: "The WCTU, the Daughters of the American Revolution (Hearst's application for membership was approved in 1914), the National Federation of Settlements, the General Federation of Women's Clubs . . . and even the International Kindergarten Union."[54] But Hearst's politics on Wilson's war policies went in a different direction from these women's organizations.

Hearst backed Wilson's supporters in San Francisco who were plan-ning a nonmilitant Preparedness Day parade for July 22, 1916. Parade officials accepted female participation as a means to focus on nationalism, patriotism, motherhood, and broadening democracy. The right to enter, paradoxically, was "limited by wealth, opinion, custom, and everyday practice, and served interests that can be described as particular and pri-vate," which meant they were "inaccessible to less-powerful citizens" as a resource. Thornwell Mullally was grand marshal of the parade. Mullally had served on the concessions and admissions committee of the Panama-Pacific International Exposition, and on other exposition committees, when Hearst served as head of the woman's board. Mullally appointed Elizabeth [Bessie] Kittle Taylor the "grand marshal of the woman's division." She had served as the third vice president on Hearst's woman's board. Taylor, like Hearst, was a Southerner living in the West, "a woman of gentlest breeding," and a "society matron." She also was active in the Ladies' Protective and Relief Society of Oakland, a founder of the Francesca Club, and a member of the Woman's Athletic Club. She had "a grave

18. Phoebe Hearst marching in the Preparedness Day parade in San Francisco on July 22, 1916. BANCPIC 1991.064–AX, box 1:02. Courtesy of the Bancroft Library, University of California, Berkeley.

delusion," like most women, according to Paul, that females had to show they deserved to get the vote. So Taylor invited women to take part who had proven themselves to be respectable, worthy forces. She asked Hearst to march in the parade.[55]

Hearst accepted Taylor's invitation to march. She would march as a representative of moderates in the suffrage camp. That meant marching as an advocate and promoter for the vote as a tool of progressive reform, for the use of dignified, respectable, nonmilitant political tactics, and for Wilson's national preparedness and defense policies. Hearst, as the day of the march approached, "had been ill and her physician forbade her" to participate, "saying it might prove fatal," a woman friend of Hearst's recalled years later. It had become more acceptable for women to march by the second decade of the twentieth century, but there were reasons not to march, too. Americans categorized men like Tom Mooney—a socialist and anarchist who backed the use of violence—as militant, or radical, and outside the law. Mooney had been targeting the preparedness parades because they reflected popular support for America entering a war he opposed—World War I. The parade, as one of Phoebe's friends explained, "was greatly denounced and opposed by the lawless element who threatened that those who took part in it would do so at the risk of their lives." Paul's suffrage militants refused to support or advocate violence.[56] But that alone would not stop Americans from associating militants who backed Paul with Mooney, British suffragettes, and anarchists who used violent tactics. By accepting Taylor's invitation, Hearst risked placing her good name and reputation as a moderate in the suffrage camp in jeopardy.

American concern about militancy and violent methods aroused concern about threats to the lives of Hearst and other females if they marched. Some tried to get them to stop. But to no avail. Hearst would not listen. A Los Angeles newspaper quoted Hearst years later as saying on the day of the march: "It was rather warm this morning. I had almost decided not to come out today, but when the mail came, it contained seven letters of threat that, if I marched I would be killed. So, of course, there is nothing else for me to do but march on." A patriotic, imperious, courageous, deceptively frail-looking woman who battled diseases but possessed a strong constitution overall, Hearst set aside health considerations and threats to life and limb. She refused to be intimidated. She "announced that she was going in the parade, and that she was going on foot and no one could stop her," as Elizabeth Allston Pringle later recalled. "We all tried . . . to get her [not] to march—but it made no impression," one woman wrote.[57]

Hearst disagreed with Alice Paul, who was a pacifist opposed to Wilson's positions on World War I and state suffrage. Hearst felt comfortable enough to take to the streets to support Wilson's views but not on votes for women. Raised to be an evangelical reformer and patriot, it would have been scurrilous in Hearst's eyes not to march in a dignified, respectable way to back Wilson. When Hearst and her female compatriots decided to march, they challenged the view that men protected women. For Hearst, marching meant carrying out the obligations and duties of American citizenship and being loyal to and protecting the nation-state without any guarantee of male protection. She refused, moreover, to support or advocate extremes of behavior. She would march to promote respectable, cautious, conciliatory, safe politics that showed that "the influence of woman over man is not gained by kicking, scratching and biting and never has been."

Hearst would walk along Market Street the embodiment, practically and symbolically, of an elite wealthy woman, holding a ceremonial position in the parade that had political meaning. She would be a flesh-and-blood female marcher who represented past activities and accomplishments that addressed a variety of interests and concerns of the constituents she served. She would walk as a physical symbol to advocate indirectly for moderate strategies and tactics as a suffragist in negotiating power for herself and women with men in American politics. She was "sufficiently like" moderates in the suffrage camp that she felt a responsibility to march to represent the best interests of her constituents, the American people, women, and the nation-state.[58]

Hearst knew the preparedness parade was not the kind of protest march Alice Paul would organize. Hearst's march for preparedness and national defense gave her the chance to represent her patriotism, nationalism, and support for motherhood in a way that would not endorse Paul's militant tactics.[59] Her participation helped to recast the meaning of citizenship and femininity. It also was a way for her to make it respectable for women, especially mothers of her age and generation, to support the United States military. Hearst felt comfortable marching in a preparedness parade. She was never comfortable enough, though, to march in one of Paul's suffrage protest spectacles. So she never did. Hearst's decision was made easier by the fact that "no suffrage parades" were held "in San Francisco (although one was held in Oakland in 1908.)"[60]

Taylor structured the women's division in the Preparedness Day parade to express and clearly delineate the power, authority, and status that Phoebe Apperson Hearst had as a chief representative, or standard bearer, for her progressive constituents, that included moderates in the suffrage camp.[61] Taylor accorded Hearst "the place of honor in the line, leading the division of the woman's board of the Panama-Pacific International Exposition." Hearst walked by herself at the head of an "imposing line" that marched with "military precision." The marchers evoked an image of women as powerful beings in command of their lives. Hearst represented "home women of all classes," elite, white American women; professional, and working women citizens; those with political convictions; and generations who supported females taking their place "among thousands of their fellow citizens."[62]

Hearst was dressed from head to toe in white, as if to emphasize her virtuous, unassailable personality, reputation, and status. She walked along Market Street among "an army of men and women," "two thousand strong," as a citizen who claimed the political space to prove women were worthy of, and entitled to, the vote. She held an American flag in her right hand, an expression of her nationalism and patriotism. But she held the flag dipped almost parallel to the ground. Was holding the American flag as she did a delicate, sophisticated way of objecting to the Wilson administration's support for state suffrage without offending or appearing as though she was desecrating the flag? Hearst defiantly and bravely walked "immediately behind" Taylor as if to signal the passing of the baton of power and authority to a younger generation of white women in American politics. Hearst gave, a reporter noted, "a scintillating effect to the parade as a whole." She and Taylor received "a continuous ovation," like ones given to major political party candidates, marching past over fifty-one thousand cheering spectators and thousands of American flags lining Market Street.[63] Hearst was the epitome of a loyal patriot who was also a progressive reform suffragist.

Hearst's participation challenged the views of anyone who still thought of women as being dependent, frail, weak, or disorderly and critics of Wilson's war policies. This view had given men license to justify opposition to and violence against women, especially marchers and suffragists. Most antisuffragists claimed that women marchers lacked self-respect and worthiness. Hearst helped put these views to rest once and for all. With her female compatriots, Hearst "showed little sign of fatigue" and "refused the aid of automobile, or even to lean on another's arm," a reporter noted. Her womanly good health and endurance might have been seen as refuting those social Darwinists who held that women did not have the physical stamina or courage to compete equally with men, and thus were not worthy to vote, either. She walked the entire parade route "as fearlessly and nobly as the men," starting at the Crocker Building and ending at the Masonic Building.[64]

She refused to throw all caution to the wind nor did she abandon entirely any pretense of the ladylike behavior for which she was most commonly known. She marched to help quell criticism against women marchers and convince people that it was time to give them the national ballot so they could support Wilson's policies on preparedness and national defense. Hearst's pro-Wilson position put her at odds with Paul and the NWP, Jane Addams, the Woman's Peace Party, settlement house residents and workers, social workers, officials of the Women's Trade Union League, presidents of women's clubs, and experienced female suffrage workers who feared that if the federal government prepared for war, money would be diverted to war preparations from social programs and from those opposed to U.S. entrance into the Great War.[65] Her participation in the march, then, was also meant to challenge those women's organizations that were in opposition to Wilson's war efforts.

Hearst took lively, rhythmic steps along Market Street while onlookers enjoyed the patriotic and nationalist spirit wafting through the air. What many warned would happen, then did. Shortly past 2:00 p.m., a newspaper reported, "Pipe, Filled with Dynamite, Surrounded by Slugs of Jagged Metal and Bullets, More Deadly Than Shrapnel Used in Grim Work of War, Strikes Down Innocent and Peaceful Citizens, Among Them Mothers with Babes in Arms." The blast killed six spectators—an Alameda woman, a seventy-two-year-old veteran, a male bystander, a lumber salesman, a commissary clerk, and a physician.[66] Other "bodies of men, women, and children lay scattered about the street" among the injured.[67] Some Americans hurled charges that, according to the *New York Times*, "Emma Goldman, who has been lecturing in San Francisco for a week," had moved anarchists to plant the bomb. Goldman "denied that the anarchists—at least as an organization—could have been responsible" for the bomb blast.[68] In any case, the dastardly deed had been done. Hearst had witnessed women in active duty being killed or injured by militants while serving the nation-state.

Agreement among the sexes prevailed after the smoke cleared. People refused to describe the female marchers as "disorderly," "unmotherly," scurrilous, or "incapable of true citizenship." All agreed that Hearst and her compatriots had proven women and men to be citizens cut from the same cloth. When the bomb went off, a reporter noted, "not a woman faltered in her idea of courage."[69] Newspapers made a point of the "special effort . . . to stop the women" but reported the females as being as fearless and noble as any male. Both sexes carried out the responsibilities and obligations expected of loyal American citizens.[70] Writing about the courage, determination, and patriotism of Hearst and her fellow citizens despite the danger of marching, Grand Marshall Thornwell Mullally declared: "Not even threats and the explosion of a bomb that killed nine [there was disagreement on the exact number killed] and wounded scores affected them in any way," he observed. He added: "It was a patriotic cause and the women responded most heroically. It was due largely, therefore, to the women that the event was in the opinion of army officers and others qualified to judge the greatest of its kind, in numbers, personnel and in the way it passed off, in the history of the city."[71]

Hearst had survived the blast without male protection. The irony and unintended consequence for her was that the violent actions taken by the opposition had served to strengthen the suffragists' argument that women were fit to vote. Hearst's prominence as a respectable, wealthy woman was so well established and legendary by this time that people accepted her support for preparedness and national defense and her credentials as a moderate in the suffrage camp. Although she had marched publicly in the preparedness parade, she was no militant, and her good name and reputation remained untarnished. Others were now reinforced in their view of Hearst as the equal of patriotic and progressive reform men.

Phoebe Apperson Hearst, acting as a political symbol and representative, "evoked feelings or attitudes" from her constituents that echoed the same emotions and views Americans expressed for partisan electoral politicians. Women, particularly, felt great happiness seeing her march. For some it was a joy and thrill to see her walk along Market Street. "It was wonderful to see her—with head up—with a long *swinging gait* and so rapidly—Everybody about cheered their heads off," a female spectator wrote. Others felt inspired by the fact that Hearst had survived the explosion and showed their appreciation for her. A woman who had been a recipient of Hearst's material assistance exclaimed: "What an example you set us! You are a continual inspiration and I am thankful every day for the privilege of knowing and loving you and for the glimpses that affords of the richness and resources of your nature which seems to acknowledge no law of limitation on any plane."[72] Hearst's participation in the parade brought increased respect and admiration for women and support for suffrage and Wilson's policies. But her presence on Market Street would also lead some women to believe, falsely, that there were no limits to what a woman of her resources and political persuasion could accomplish.

Hearst was fooling herself and others if she thought that her participation in the Preparedness Day parade would bring her the same kind of national recognition and appreciation that men of her race, class, and stature received, especially politicians. Some men did praise Hearst and the women marchers. Mullally was one who thought Hearst and women played a key role in making the Preparedness Day parade a success. He held Hearst in high esteem for her courage despite the threats to life and limb. But marching to represent moderates in the suffrage camp did little to dispel the notion of Hearst as a Fairy Godmother—a title that spoke to an imagined character rather than a flesh-and-blood woman with real power and authority. People still thought of Hearst as "the fairy godmother of the [PPIE woman's] board"—a view touted by her son's newspaper and that contributed to his mother's ability to attract support and receive praise, particularly from men.[73] Others saw the title of Fairy Godmother as a badge of honor. The Fairy Godmother was "the embodiment of the highest type of womanhood," and as such stood "pre-eminently [as] the representative of her sex for the State of California" as one newspaper reported when men first coined the term Fairy Godmother and assigned it to Hearst at the end of the nineteenth century.

The Fairy Godmother represented a rich, patriotic, and nationalistic mother to many women and men.[74] Yet there were men who knew what it was like to be on the receiving end of Hearst's power, whether in public or private. Nonetheless, when Hearst marched at the head of the PPIE Woman's Board division, people still thought of her as the Fairy Godmother.[75] She was an emotionally charged symbol of wealth, motherhood, patriotism, and the nation-state rather than a flesh-and-blood human being asserting the rights and privileges of a citizen and a claim to real public economic, social, cultural, and political power.[76]

A woman who preferred ladylike behavior, harmony, and order to militant tactics, conflict, and disorder, Hearst refused to flaunt the Fairy Godmother image in a crass sort of way. Nor she did she challenge the designation publicly. Her silence encouraged people to think of her as the symbol of a mythical, childlike woman, constrained by sex and class, with ephemeral, temporary power. Privately, though, Hearst mocked the Fairy Godmother label. As one of her female friends put it sarcastically: "You certainly merit the name Fairy Godmother even if you do scout [scoff] it when applied to you, for you know you just look around and lo! changes take place trunks *don't* fly out of windows but old carpets come up, curtains come down, and behold there is a wondrous change!"[77] Phoebe's friend knew Hearst controlled a vast amount of money and resources and used them to create change. But she explained Hearst's Fairy Godmother image and role using familiar domestic terms that Americans could understand and accept but which masked Hearst's ability to exert the various forms of power she had, especially for reform.

Hearst's reserve, meanwhile, made it difficult for her to speak out against the depiction of her as a Fairy Godmother—a title which in fact devalued her—while pointed, sharp debates over "what [it] meant to be a loyal American" and the meaning of citizenship played out around the nation-state. In refusing to reveal publicly her contempt for the Fairy Godmother title, Hearst left the impression that she supported the characterization, encouraging others to do the same. There were few men, in private or in public, with the exception of a small group of close family members and relatives and her male employees, who took Hearst and her power seriously. But her willingness to allow men to define her as having symbolic rather than real power made it less likely for anyone, particularly a broader array of men, to accept and recognize publicly her efforts to assert her clout, whether in nonpartisan voluntary reform associations, academic politics, or partisan electoral politics.[78] Yet she had cultivated the gracious Fairy Godmother image in public to reduce sex and class tensions and promoted the designation to persuade others, men especially, to advance her career. Since she accepted and upheld the conventional standards of femininity, it was acceptable for men, in particular, to give her some latitude to command and rule in her own right in public to accomplish her goals as long as she remained within the constraints of sex and class.

Did Hearst ever entertain the thought that rejecting the Fairy Godmother image openly and turning herself in public into a militant suffragist in the National Woman's Party might get men to give her the recognition, respect, and appreciation in public she thought she deserved? It is doubtful. Hearst helped distribute NWP leaflets, in early 1916, that said "in strong militant terms, 'Vote against the man who has blocked the Freedom of American Women—Defeat Pres. Wilson.'" It was one thing for Hearst to send leaflets that contained militant words. But it was quite another for her to use militant tactics outside for all to see. Hearst increasingly relied on nonmilitant, nonthreatening ways to support the federal ballot campaign as time passed. When two thousand women and some men met at a convention at the Blackstone Theatre in June 1916, Hearst and Belmont attended a reception to welcome attendees to the convention. Elizabeth Kent "chair of the nominations committee, presented as the report of her committee the following nominations: Anne Martin for permanent NWP president, both Phoebe A. Hearst from California and Judge Mary A. Bartelme of Illinois as vice chairman, and Mabel Vernon of Nevada for secretary. This report was accepted by a unanimous vote." Kent's husband held two terms in Congress from California and led Independents for Wilson. Hearst also made a $2,655 contribution to the National Woman's Party for the constitutional amendment campaign. Her nomination was one way to reward her for the financial gifts and resources she gave to the suffrage campaign and was an attempt by the Woman's Party (soon to be renamed the National Woman's Party) to get Hearst to make a stronger commitment to the votes-for-women campaign.[79]

Lending her name and giving money to the National Woman's Party, as well as being elected as a vice chairman, were appropriate tactics for Hearst to draw public attention to herself and exert power in the ballot campaign after the Panama-Pacific International Exposition had closed. But these activities hardly indicate that Hearst took strong, vigorous, and aggressive actions in the suffrage movement. Hearst's relatively small monetary contributions, restrained written public protest, willingness to distribute NWP leaflets, attendance at NWP receptions, and her decision to allow her name to be placed in nomination as a NWP vice chair, were as forceful, adamant, or militant, as she ever got in the Woman's Party and during the campaign for a constitutional amendment.

Hearst judged that becoming an ardent supporter of NWP militancy would make her uncomfortable and not bring her the respect, appreciation, and recognition she thought she deserved. So she stuck to her careful, restrained ways. She gave a luncheon for the Congressional Union in the spring of 1916. She "acted as chairman" for another luncheon in the St. Francis Hotel fit for high society in mid-September 1916. This was the "first California state conference of the Congressional Union." The name of the California branch of the Congressional Union "was formally changed to 'The National Woman's Party of California,'" a constitution adopted, and "officers and a central committee were selected, and a campaign fund raised" at this event. Hearst's participation, and donation of one thousand dollars to the anti-Wilson 1916 reelection campaign, helped establish a California National Woman's Party branch that pledged to defeat President Wilson in November. A reporter noted, "The setting and the event were paradoxical. The pretty, doll-like ladies of the Colonial tapestries

in the Colonial ballroom surrounded a gathering in which a commanding grasp of issues of the day was characterized."[80] The suffrage event
promoted Hearst and the power women held to defeat Wilson, because
of his opposition to a constitutional suffrage amendment, in ways that
made Hearst comfortable.

Hearst, by this time, had a clearer, better understanding of the true
political nature of the National Woman's Party and its involvement in
partisan electoral politics. Feeling uncomfortable generally with radical politics, she involved herself in the Woman's Party only in limited,
conservative ways and never sought, or campaigned for, a party office.
Hearst, in fact, expressed her regret at being "selected as one of the [NWP]
Executive Committee for I cannot possibly do any active work," shortly
after she agreed to distribute NWP leaflets and several months before Paul
and the NWP picketed the White House. She added: "Therefore can be of
no assistance to the committee," she wrote Doris Stevens, NWP organizer
in the West. Stevens was Alva Vanderbilt Belmont's "ghostwriter and
sometime amanuensis" and NWP California campaign manager who liked
to incite unrest. Three days before her appointment as manager, Stevens
wrote Hearst to ask if she wished "to serve on the Executive Committee
of Woman's Party for one year?"[81]

Being an active NWP officer on the executive committee when the party
picketed the White House was more of a commitment to the passage of
the constitutional suffrage amendment than Hearst was willing to make.
Serving on the executive committee meant Hearst's good name, reputation, and status would be forever associated in people's minds with the
NWP pickets and opposition to Woodrow Wilson and Democratic Party
partisan politics—an offense to her sensibilities and those women of her
generation in general, especially conservatives. Hearst, from time to time,
flirted with partisan electoral politics. But most of her political career had
been spent in the world of nonpartisanship. To be nonpartisan meant to her
that she was to refrain from participating in Democratic and Republican
partisan electoral politics, especially picketing.

Hearst, moreover, was at a point in her life when she wanted to spend her time enjoying being with her grandchildren. She had been happy with her son's children at the Hacienda several months before Stevens wrote to ask her if she was willing to serve on the executive committee. Hearst explained her resignation to Stevens in a diplomatic way: "I think it very important that every member of that committee be active so please accept my resignation and elect some one who can attend all meetings and assume her full share of the work and responsibility." Hearst's participation in the National Woman's Party no longer meshed with her values. She was unable to fathom being on the executive committee without being very active and involved in discussions about her political positions that were at odds with Paul's policies on preparedness and national defense. She also was unable to grasp being on the executive committee of an organization that by this time was involved deeply in American political party electoral politics and had a strong commitment to militancy, particularly picketing, so she resigned her post as an NWP vice president.[82]

A complicated, contradictory woman, Hearst refused to divorce herself entirely, though, from NWP partisan politics. She wanted Wilson to fail in his 1916 reelection bid because he was opposed to the passage of a federal suffrage amendment. As long as she was not personally or directly involved with or used militant methods, she felt at ease and turned her attention to the defeat of Wilson in 1916. But her heart was not in the effort; nor was she very active. Her efforts to defeat Wilson consisted mainly of giving a thousand dollars to prevent his reelection and lending her name to the Charles Evans Hughes campaign. She protested Wilson's 1916 reelection bid subtly by registering as a Republican. Wilson, nonetheless, won reelection. His victory disturbed Hearst. She lamented: "The greatest fault I have to find with California just now is that they elected Wilson."

Hearst, from this point on, distanced herself further from the National Woman's Party. Margaret Wittenmore, an NWP lobbyist, wrote Hearst in early May 1917 that the party was "in an excellent strategic position—but we do need money, very much." Hearst responded that "I gave liberally to the cause of suffrage when I could, but am not able to continue my support at the present time."[83] Hearst had accepted Paul's view that Wilson should be thrown out of office, even though she had always been a Democrat, like her father. Alice Paul asked Hearst, then, on the heels of Wilson's reelection victory, to renew her last financial contribution of $2,655 she made to the National Woman's Party a year earlier. In a note on the back of Paul's letter, Hearst wrote: "*No*. Impossible, can't consider it."[84] Hearst's decision indicated her unofficial and official involvement with the party was at an end. She was almost seventy-four years old.

The amount of money and resources Hearst had poured into the NWP votes-for-women campaign, by the time the United States entered World War I, was small when compared to the financial contributions of Belmont. Accurate estimates of the money and resources Belmont contributed to the suffrage movement are difficult to come by. Belmont's financial gifts to the cause between 1909 and 1919 totaled $419, 602, according to one historian. Hearst's monetary donations, by comparison, totaled less than $10,000. Hearst never donated anywhere near the amount of money, time, energy, or additional resources toward setting the "priorities, strategies, and ultimately the success of" the Congressional Union, the National Woman's Party, and the woman's rights movement that Belmont did.[85]

Hearst's contributions were not such that she would be considered a feminist but not a radical suffragist, even though, like Belmont, she had little faith in male politicians to get things right, especially when it came to women. Given her core personality traits and values, she accepted the limits of sex and class circumscribed by men, and although she challenged men, she refused to work to dismantle, male-dominated hierarchies. Nor did she throw herself wholeheartedly into the votes-for-women campaign as did Belmont. Hearst was interested more in respectable progressive reform issues traditionally associated with her personal interests and the concerns of other women: children, education, design and architecture, economic self-support, moral protection, and working with men to help advance women within the existing system defined and controlled by men. She consciously exerted power and was involved in activities to get women the national vote. But she was never much of a public protestor or strong, vigorous advocate for a constitutional suffrage amendment. She felt most comfortable as a moderate, keeping her distance from militant methods while making limited contributions, financial and otherwise, to the National Woman's Party to achieve a federal suffrage amendment.

Phoebe Apperson Hearst turned seventy-five years old in early December of 1917. She supported and dispensed business and legal advice and become less active. She cut back on the money, time, effort, and energy she devoted to high-society affairs. And when she did entertain at the Hacienda, she sat on a low dais in the music room, "before a Gobelin tapestry, her old friends grouped about her." She was no longer active publicly in the worlds of nonpartisan voluntary association and academic politics. Nor was she active in the votes-for-women campaign. She hired a social worker, instead, to investigate and determine the worthiness of people requesting financial assistance. She considerably reduced her financial gifts. She contributed small amounts of money to the University of California and, from time to time, lent her name to organizations that supported issues of personal interest.[86]

It seemed as though Phoebe Apperson Hearst became somewhat of an anachronism the older she got. She appeared to be chronologically out of place as a moderate in the suffrage camp when compared to National Woman's Party militants like Alva Belmont and a younger generation of female supporters of votes for women. Hearst must have realized on some level, as she approached her seventy-sixth birthday, that if women were ever going to get permanent political power and economic freedom on equal terms with men, a constitutional suffrage amendment had to be passed and ratified. But when would that happen? Would she live long enough to see it?

Epilogue

Phoebe Apperson Hearst lived long enough to see the U.S. House of Representatives pass a constitutional amendment for votes for women in January 1918.[1] She remained a voting member of the University of California Board of Regents and the Mount Vernon Ladies Association but was not very active throughout 1918 and early 1919, a situation that ran counter to her busy adult life of power and politics.

Hearst focused her attention, instead, on her personal life while the U.S. Senate debated the constitutional amendment. She worked independently on design and architectural projects of personal interest that in years past had brought her prominent positions of power, authority, and fame. As she explained to Carl Oscar Borg, a Swedish-born artist known for paintings that stressed Southwestern themes and who was a recipient of Hearst's largesse, "Building is one of the most interesting things anyone can do," a metaphor perhaps for her love of power and the pleasure she took in acquiring and exerting it. She commissioned Bernard Maybeck to design "a general plan" for Mills College, a women's college in the San Francisco Bay Area, but Hearst never mustered the passion, drive, and energy to make her plan a reality. She also contended with guests and requests for assistance. As Elizabeth Pringle wrote in the fall of 1918, Hearst was "tormented by visitors and people applying for things and has no peace." She tried as best she could to get some peace.[2] She retreated into her private world to focus on her own interests. This very public woman, in other words, became more private.

President Wilson, meanwhile, bowed to political realities and shifted his position on a constitutional suffrage amendment in 1918. Wilson argued to U.S. senators: "I regard the concurrence of the Senate in the constitutional amendment essential to the successful prosecution of the great war of humanity in which we are now engaged." Americans needed, he continued, "as we have never needed them before, the sympathy and insight and clear moral instinct of women of the world."[3] Wilson conceded, in late 1918, that women were crucial economically, politically, and morally to the United States winning World War I.

The year Wilson shifted his position to support a constitutional amendment on votes for women proved to be a difficult year for Phoebe Apperson Hearst. She was concerned about World War I and experienced hardships, including financial. She seemed to pay more attention to finances than to the other resources she controlled. Making money on munitions during the war was beyond her personal interest. But she cared about the rise in workers' wages, and the high cost of living, as well as the scarcity of labor. She still played the role of consumer. Her consumption, though, was aimed primarily at her immediate personal and business needs rather than economic, cultural, and political gift-giving to help others advance. She kept abreast of Hacienda production by reading over monthly pig, hog, vegetable, and poultry reports as she enjoyed a "royal" lifestyle at her mansion in rural Pleasanton, California.[4] She seemed to be reconnecting with her rural roots to handle the disruptions, particularly economic, caused by World War I.

But there was something in her bag of personal interests that often took precedence over her finances and her business and social affairs—her family: William and Millicent Wilson Hearst and their children. Phoebe spent and enjoyed time with her grandchildren who came to visit her from New York. She took pleasure in helping them grow and mature.

When Will was young, she had thought carefully about his education and took responsibility for it. Now she advised her son about where to send his children to school. She took pleasure especially in assisting her grandson, George. Will credited his mother for George's development.[5] The peripatetic Phoebe Apperson Hearst still possessed enough stamina and endurance to travel, so she set aside her traditional Christmas political gift-giving projects and went east to visit her son and grandchildren.[6] Hearst's life had come full circle as she centered her attention on her family in New York.

The influenza epidemic hit during her visit and reached its peak in New York City in late October of 1918. Hearst lived in fear of getting influenza. She burned a letter from a woman with children who had measles, whooping cough, and scarlet fever. She made sure she disinfected her hands to protect herself. To no avail. Her health failed again. She came down with the flu anyway. The disease was killing thirty million, a conservative estimate, around the world. The flu epidemic spread so fast that the U.S. Public Health Service "wasn't ready for danger of this magnitude." They were unprepared for the harsh reality of it. Oddly, for a woman so concerned with good health and health reform, she neglected getting inoculated with a vaccine (although an effective cure for the flu was not yet developed). Nor did she wear a mask to protect herself. She hated "to be bothered with" taking precautions, according to biographer Adele Brooks.[7] Hearst's response to the flu epidemic showed her to be somewhat out of step with modern medicine. It appeared she was more in step with nineteenth-century than early twentieth-century American medical practices and society.

When she was sick with the flu, Hearst found herself in a position that strengthened nineteenth-century attitudes, pervasive at the time of her birth, of women as dependent, vulnerable, and physically weak, frail, and in need of male protection. Yet she had a long history of challenging and disproving the myth of male protection of women. Although she had not been one to take precautions, Hearst now tried to do as much as she could to protect herself while she suffered from the flu. Besides burning letters and disinfecting her hands, she slowed down more and reduced carrying out what she saw as her moral and political obligations. She contemplated her resignation from positions she held on boards in American nonpartisan, voluntary academic, reform, and political associations while she battled her illness. She instructed an employee, in January 1919, to inform Mayor James Rolph on her behalf that "I have had to resign from a number of things in which I am very much interested because I am absolutely unable to work and that unless my health improves I will have to send in my resignation." Rolph had appointed her to a committee to raise funds for a memorial to commemorate the involvement of women and men from San Francisco in World War I. She recovered enough to travel back to the Hacienda. But she was in "delicate health" as spring of 1919 approached. She took pleasure at home in knowing that her close friend, Helen Elizabeth Sanborn, held the reins of power as president of the San Francisco Board of Education.[8] But Hearst's usually strong physical condition was fading away even as the possibility rose in the United States Senate for the passage of a constitutional suffrage amendment.

Hearst's ability to shake the flu to restore and strengthen her physical constitution were wanting. American sailors who experienced influenza displayed fierce symptoms, such as blood that came from the nose or ears, violent coughs, writhing "in agony or delirium," headaches so severe that people felt like their skulls were splitting open behind their eyes, "body aches so intense that they felt like bones breaking," vomiting, and odd skin color. The 1918–19 influenza was different from most flu in that it had a proclivity to turn into pneumonia. Hearst refused to think she would die since her parents had lived long lives—her mother to eighty-six and her father to ninety-two. The thought of long-lived parents probably pushed her to stay active. She got partially dressed every day and dictated business and social correspondence to her employees. She walked about and received and talked to numerous visitors—members of her extensive networks. She was cheerful and planning for the future. She discussed holding a

Christmas party at Wyntoon for young people the next year. She talked about her plans for different projects at the University of California and the condition of her personal physician's patients. Ray Lyman Wilbur, president of Stanford University, served as her private doctor. She felt so anxious about her own health, though, that she asked Dr. Wilbur, to tell her if she was going to die. In brutal, honest fashion, he told her: yes. Phoebe refrained from expressing her emotions, just as her mother had trained her to do when she was a child. She remained cheerful and made plans to establish a health center for her Babícora employees.[9] But the time and energy she devoted to these activities declined quickly because her health now took a turn for the worse.

Hearst found herself at the mercy of forces beyond her control and powerless to do anything about it. William Randolph Hearst, accompanied by Millicent and their children, left New York and traveled to California to be with his mother as Phoebe's condition grew dangerous. His mother's health improved briefly after he arrived. The bodily power, then, that had served Phoebe so well over the years began to weaken significantly. Her condition became much worse. One of her blood vessels broke. She became "seriously ill," according to the *New York Times*. Her illness became "critical" on April 4, 1919. The "tubercular lesion of very long standing opened up and brought about complications." Phoebe became alarmed for the first time about her ailment. Scientists had been working feverishly, during the crisis, to produce a cure for influenza. But they possessed no weapons that worked effectively. Deaths of Americans, many in their twenties and thirties, meanwhile, climbed to almost 250,000. The deaths produced an undetermined impact on families, especially on the working poor, that included the loss of children's parents and household income.[10] Days before, three physicians had attended to Phoebe. But they were unable to cure her.

Phoebe Apperson Hearst took her last breath on April 13, 1919, at 4:30 p.m. She died from pneumonia at her beloved Hacienda del Pozo de Verona at the age of seventy-six, with William Randolph and Millicent Hearst, and

19. Phoebe Apperson Hearst's funeral. BANCPIC 1905.6788. Courtesy of the Bancroft Library, University of California, Berkeley.

her grandchildren, and the three physicians in attendance. Phoebe Apperson Hearst's "great reserve of power" vanished forever at the moment of her passing.[11] Neither she nor her male physicians had possessed the ability, money, or resources to protect her against the further weakening of her once sound physical constitution. The real power that Hearst had amassed over her lifetime was no help either.

"Condolences Poured in from All Over" the state of California and the nation, a newspaper announced during the mourning period for Hearst. An overwhelming majority of people, in speeches, eulogies, telegrams, and newspaper articles, spoke and wrote about Phoebe A. Hearst as the epitome of womanhood. The Alameda County Auxiliary's praise was typical. They referred to Phoebe Hearst as the "Fairy Godmother of the Exposition." Senator Hiram Johnson and Governor William D. Stephens paid tribute to Hearst's feminine traits. Woodrow Wilson's vice president, Thomas Marshall, and his wife, did the same.[12] Condolences came from all levels of government. But the day after her death, virtually every newspaper reported that she was best known for her philanthropic, charitable, and educational work and was one of the leaders in social life in Washington DC. The accolades were understandable. They recognized the rise to fame and prominence of a woman with an ordinary background. This would have satisfied Hearst's desire to receive acknowledgement for her work. But most held a narrow, biased view and understanding of Hearst's life and her skills and talent to accomplish what she did as she built on the foundation she was given at birth. Virtually no one, in the public condolences after her passing, associated Hearst with holding and exerting political power and financial freedom on equal terms with men. Hardly anyone discussed the power and influence Hearst had exerted over women and men, within and outside her home. The primary focus, instead, was on Hearst's feminine qualities and traditional domestic roles—those traits that people used, especially men, to disqualify women from securing full citizenship rights.

Hearst's acceptance of the limits of power, circumscribed by men and her social and economic class, warranted symbolic tributes by men after her death much like those received by rich, powerful, and prominent male businessmen and politicians. Hearst was seen by some as the "Best Citizen State Ever Had," but only symbolically for the most part. Nonetheless, she was admired in public through representative acts that honored her on equal terms with wealthy, powerful men.[13] The San Francisco Board of Education adjourned out of respect for Hearst. The California State Legislature suspended sessions "as a Mark of Respect." For what was "said to be the first time a woman was so honored" in San Francisco, Judge W. W. Morrow adjourned the U.S. Circuit Court. The University of California and the city of Berkeley ordered all flags to fly at half-mast. "For the first time in its history the flag on the Federal building and post office yesterday floated at half-mast in honor of a woman." The secretary of the treasury in Washington DC gave the order. Such an honor was accorded by the U.S. Flag Code to "'principle figures' of the federal and state governments and for deaths of notable private citizens." The federal government had determined that Hearst deserved the tribute.[14] Rarely, though, did anyone, especially men, praise Hearst directly and openly in public as a powerful, wealthy woman on equal terms with powerful, wealthy men, although Will Hearst tried to compensate for the oversight to some extent.

Phoebe Apperson Hearst's body lay in state at the Hacienda (a decision probably made by her son) like that of a queen or prominent male politician. Her casket was set in her beloved music room. In those early years of the twentieth century, it would have been unacceptable to even think of taking the coffin of a woman, even a famous and powerful one, to Washington to lie in state under the U.S. Capitol rotunda. Beautiful flowers in her favorite color, lilac, draped and engulfed the coffin.[15] Family members and friends held three separate, simple funeral services. One took place at Grace Cathedral in San Francisco with municipal, California, and federal officials, and University of California professors and Academic Senate in attendance. Senator James D. Phelan, Governor William D. Stephens, President Benjamin Ide Wheeler of the University of California, President Ray Lyman Wilbur of Stanford University, and Mayor James Rolph Jr., among others, were honorary pallbearers. The University of California declared an academic holiday, stopped all exercises, and canceled classes so that faculty and students could attend the cathedral funeral. All Hearst plants stopped for five minutes, all "industry was suspended," and city cars halted at the hour of the Grace Cathedral funeral, at 2:00 p.m.

University of California faculty and students, in cap and gown, and others packed into the church to see the casket "smothered in orchids and wisteria." Thousands stood outside unable to get in as the choir sang. Church bells rang and bells pealed from the Civic Auditorium during a public memorial service. The second service consisted of a private cere-mony at the Hacienda. The last funeral service took place at Cypress Lawn Cemetery in Colma, California, about fifteen miles south of San Francisco. Phoebe Apperson Hearst was laid to rest at Cypress Lawn Cemetery "in the family mausoleum" next to her husband, George Hearst. The body of Mary W. Kincaid, Phoebe's dear, close friend, was placed in the tomb later. Nine days after this funeral service, the university paid tribute in the Hearst Greek Theater to "the most generous benefactress of the University" and to the soldiers who had represented the United States in World War I and were fortunate enough to return. The ceremony linked Hearst, a battle-tested woman in American politics, with the heroic and courageous patriotism of battled-tested men. Next, a University of Cali-fornia graduate, class of 1873, eulogized Phoebe Apperson Hearst as "the FIRST Lady of California, the FIRST Lady of the United States, and . . . the FIRST Lady of the world."[16] It fell to younger generations, especially of women, to learn as much as they could about exactly how Hearst had acquired and exercised power. The reading of the last will and testament of the head of the Hearst estate came after her casket was taken to the burial grounds and the sound of the peeling bells at her funeral had faded.

The will expressed Phoebe Hearst's lack of confidence in her son, Wil-liam Randolph Hearst, to exercise sole control over such a vast estate with so many intricate parts. Phoebe instead assigned three executors—her son, Edward H. Clark, and Frederick G. Sanborn—the power "to sell at public or private sale" her assets not bequeathed and "to carry on any and all business ventures" until they were in order.[17] Hearst saw providing her son one-half of her estate, out of love for him, as the moral obligation of a dutiful parent, so the remainder, or bulk of her estate, was left to Will. A methodical woman, her assets were to be handed over to her son only after all was in order. Concerned about her family and business obligations, she was a first-rate businesswoman until the end of her life.

But the actual value of Phoebe Apperson Hearst's estate when she died is unclear. The *New York Times* estimated it to be worth "between

$15,000,000 and $20,000,000, principally in mines, stock, and ranches."[18] A 1924 California Superior Court Case document indicated Hearst left $91,336.51 in cash and $8,490,310. 96 in property. "Inheritance tax due was $1,056,845.20."[19] Phoebe had given William Randolph Hearst over $8 million, between 1895 and 1902, to buy two newspapers: the *New York Journal* and the *Chicago American*. She had provided her brother, Elbert Clark Apperson, a monthly income derived from a $50,000 trust for the rest of his natural life. Elizabeth S. Apperson, Eppy's wife, received a monthly income from Eppy's trust after her his death. Hearst allocated "title and interest in" Wyntoon and $250,000 in cash to Anne D. Apperson Flint, her niece; $100,000 to Edward H. Clark, her employee; $25,000 to Richard A. Clark; and $5,000 each to Mary W. Kincaid and Kate McLaughlin and friends and staff employees. She willed smaller amounts to various other relatives, friends, and staff. The only institution to which Hearst bequeathed money was the University of California at Berkeley. She gave $60,000 to maintain in perpetuity her scholarships for women and "pictures, bronzes, and other personal property" to the regents for the university museum.[20]

Hearst's greatest permanent legacy overall, which lives on today, is what her life teaches us about how she acquired and controlled money and resources that brought her the power she exerted in nonpartisan voluntary association and University of California politics in order to assist those less fortunate, and especially to benefit women. Hearst's most important legacy—paying tribute to how a young girl from rural Missouri with an ordinary upbringing had turned into such a distinguished force in American politics—are her ideas and political activities associated with the University of California, beginning with the scholarships for women students she endowed in September of 1891. Phoebe A. Hearst Scholarships are offered still at the University of California, where thousands of undergraduate women have benefited from Hearst's program. No application per se is required. Any woman student is considered who submits the Free Application for Federal Student Aid, an application that students must complete to receive financial assistance. Female students must meet the GPA requirements, which are 4.10 and above for entering high school students, and 3.5 and above for continuing students or entering community college transfer students. Applicants must show they have financial need to be awarded a Hearst scholarship.[21]

Hearst's legacy at the University of California also lives on in the fields of design and architecture. Her International Architectural Competition was indispensable in making the University of California the state's premier teaching and research institution of higher education, bringing the school a worldwide reputation and status that lives on today. The Berkeley Art Museum and Pacific Film Archive mounted an exhibition, at the turn of the twenty-first century, called "Roma Pacific: The Phoebe Hearst International Architectural Competition and the Berkeley Campus, 1896–1930." The University of California presented a symposium during this exhibition on "Designing the Campus of Tomorrow: The Legacy of the Hearst Architectural Plan, Present and Future." University officials at the symposium praised Hearst and Henri Émil Bénard's design as a monumental and inspiring plan for the City Beautiful movement in the Progressive Era. Presenters celebrated Hearst's architectural competition and discussed the outgrowth of Regent Hearst's contributions, financial and otherwise, to the university—the New Century Plan—the effects of which will be felt well beyond the University of California in Berkeley and into the future. The plan is "a strategic vision for its facilities and space, both for the central campus and for auxiliary sites throughout the region." The university's vision of renewal to retrofit buildings and develop new facilities and space for the twenty-first century is moving forward. Another part of Hearst's legacy is her idea to establish a school of architecture at the university. The university's undergraduate program in architecture is among the best in American and international institutions of higher education.[22]

The field of anthropology reaped benefits from Hearst's academic politics as well. She originated the idea and plan to establish the Department and Museum of Anthropology and funded it. She hired Alfred L. Kroeber, who became a distinguished faculty member and "is regarded as something of a founding saint" in the department. The Museum of Anthropology, though, has had a vexed history. The university named the museum after Robert H. Lowie, a professor of anthropology from 1917 to 1950 and chair of the department for fourteen years. Because of later developments in the field, museum curators decided in the spring of 1992 to rename the museum to honor Phoebe Apperson Hearst. Changing the museum name was a move to help get the University of California out of political difficulties during the Lowie years that surrounded Kroeber's work on Ishi, the last surviving member of the Yahi (a group of the Yana people of Northern California). Many faculty and students in the department protested the museum name change. The *Daily Californian* reported it was "the first time a building named after a university professor has been renamed for a benefactor, and critics say the move is a shameless appeal for funds."

James Deetz, the head of the Lowie Museum in the 1980s, candidly explained how "horribly expensive" it is to conserve the collections of Hearst and other collectors, which "were decaying due to neglect." Hearst donated the "most important collections" to the museum, according to Burton Benedict, the museum director in 1992. He pointed out that Lowie "had never shown any interest in the museum" and had "never even set foot in the place." Hearst, of course, never wanted the museum named after her. She thought it would create too much "bad publicity." Her assessment stands as correct over a hundred years later. The museum, nonetheless, is now named for her. It contains about 3.8 million artifacts. The University of California Department of Anthropology undergraduate program is considered in the top tier of American and international university anthropology departments.[23]

The ideas, plans, and organizations Hearst used to help girls and women, and some men, are alive, operating, and strong. The Golden Gate Kindergarten Association's Phoebe A. Hearst Preschool Learning Center is the oldest preschool in San Francisco and continues to employ teachers and educate children. It serves a multicultural, multiethnic, and multiracial student population. The Century Club of California, founded in 1888, with Hearst as its first president, is a private women's club that honors the nineteenth century, the "Woman's Century." It provides spaces for education, recreation, and social functions. The Century Club building was designed by Julia Morgan and built in 1905. It is located today on Franklin Street in San Francisco.[24]

The results of Hearst's nonpartisan political reform activities—which continue to change people's lives today—now exist and operate in the world of partisan politics. The National Congress of Mothers in 1897 (now the Parent and Teacher Association), cofounded by Hearst and Alice Birney, is a large child-advocacy organization throughout the United States. It organizes and mobilizes the public to lobby legislators, government bodies, and other organizations to propose and support legislation on behalf of all children and youth, especially on education issues like prayer and religion in public schools, bullying, national health reform, federal budget policies, high school graduation, college preparation and access, libraries, mass media, segregation, citizenship, and equality. It also provides effective state and national leadership training that includes minorities. Hearst's National Cathedral School for Girls (now called the National Cathedral School) is open and thriving in Washington DC. The daughters and sons of national government politicians are enrolled.[25]

The fruits of Hearst's involvement with the Young Women's Christian Association are with us too. Asilomar is still an ideal location to host conferences and train women and others for power, politics, and leadership. It is a beautiful place to have group meetings, corporate retreats, weddings, and family gatherings. There is a university YWCA located across the street from the University of California campus on Bancroft Way. It provides a foundation of power for women students and assists them in the acquisition and development of knowledge, skills, growth experiences, and training for participation in social, cultural, economic, and political affairs at the university and in Berkeley, California, the United States, and around the world.[26] Hearst's power and politics is ever present years after her passing.

Phoebe Apperson Hearst's spirit lives on in this biography as well. Her story is a call to take as a serious field of study the power that women and others have painstakingly acquired and exerted throughout American history, understood here in terms beyond those narrowly defined by men. A scholar has written that nineteenth-century feminists believed "the vote to be the ultimate repository of social and economic power in a democratic society," implying that women possessed real power only when they held and exercised the vote in partisan politics dominated by men. But women, especially elite, rich women like Hearst, held and exerted real power before state and constitutional suffrage was passed. A study and analysis of Hearst and her daily existence shows that her abilities and other resources, and what she did with them, brought her power to accomplish individual and group goals that altered the lives of women and men in specific ways. The investigation and examination of Hearst's life encourages us to devote the same kind of attention and in-depth analysis to women that has been given to the study of the money and resources that men have long controlled and used. We need to research and scrutinize the considerable power, politics, and leadership of white women, as well as the power and advances that have been made, political and otherwise, by multicultural, multiethnic, and multiracial women in America.[27] More research and study on rich and diverse groups of women, including wealthy women, with a focus on the ways they acquired and handled power, can enrich our understanding of how women have shaped American politics.

Phoebe Apperson Hearst had more faith in nonpartisan and partisan female politicians, than in their male counterparts, to get things right, especially when it came to women.[28] Although Hearst passed away before the enactment of the constitutional amendment by the United States Senate in June 1919, Dr. Anna Howard Shaw lived long enough to see the passage of the federal suffrage amendment, having died several months after Hearst.

But neither Hearst nor Shaw witnessed its ratification in August 1920.[29] The loss of Hearst's bodily power with her passing did not foretell failure to ratify the Nineteenth Amendment. Other women and men labored on to secure its passage and ratification. Had Hearst lived long enough, she would have been pleased that the U.S. Senate went on to ratify the constitutional suffrage amendment after its passage by the House.

But at the end of her life of power and politics, she would have not been so naive as to think that the support of male politicians for national suffrage would make further acquisition and exertion of power and independent political action, on behalf of women in American politics, unnecessary. The young girl from rural Missouri with an ordinary upbringing, but with vaulting ambition to rise in the world, had spent much of her adult life exerting power to promote and advocate for a progressive reform agenda that made her nationally and international renowned. But for all her power and accomplishments, Hearst died before women received their full citizenship rights and before she saw women achieve political power and economic freedom on equal terms with men. The women of Phoebe Apperson Hearst's day, and the next generations of younger women, started to make things right. But complete sexual equality was still a long way off.

Notes

NSDAR	National Society of the Daughters of the American Revolution
NWPP	National Woman's Party Papers
NYWCA	National Young Women's Christian Association Archives
OPC	Orrin Peck Correspondence
PAHAPC	Phoebe Apperson Hearst Architectural Plan Correspondence
PAHD	Phoebe Apperson Hearst Diary
PC	Peck Collection
PPIER	Panama-Pacific International Exposition Records
PPIEWB	Panama-Pacific International Exposition Woman's Board
RCHIR	Register of the California Homeopathic Institutions Records
RGA	Ralph Gregory Archives
SBCP	Sarah B. Cooper Papers
SCP	Sada Cornwall Papers
TAS	Travelers' Aid Society Records
TBD	Thomas Barry Diary
TMP	Thomas Mooney Papers
UCAPR	University of California Academic Personnel Records
UCARCH	University of California Archives
UCBIO	University of California Biography Forms
UCROP	University of California Records of the Office of the President
UCRR	University of California Records of the Regents
UPMAA	University of Pennsylvania Museum of Archaeology and Anthropology Archives
WRH	William Randolph Hearst Papers

1. "Woman's Party Formed Here," *San Francisco Examiner*, September 16, 1916, 4. Brooks, "Phoebe Apperson Hearst," part 1, chap. 1; "Advisory Council," *Suffragist*, January 30, 1915, 2; "Rival Suffragists Will Demand Recognition," *Los Angeles Times*, June 7, 1916, ProQuest, 13; "Women Urge Plank Favoring Suffrage," *New York Times*, June 7, 1916, ProQuest, 6; "Voting Women Launch a Woman's Party," *Suffragist*, June 10, 1916, 6; Lebsock, "Women and American Politics," 35–62. See below for citations that define American politics. Carol Ellen DuBois states that "it makes more sense to characterize an unmarried woman with an independent income who was not under financial compulsion to work for her living as 'elite,' rather than 'middle class.'" See DuBois, "Working Women, Class Relations," 36. But what about married or widowed women with an independent income who were not under financial compulsion to work for a living? Are they elite women? A distinction can be made between the wealthy and the top tier, or elite, among the wealthy. Mary S. Merrill, for example, was married and became a prominent wealthy San Francisco widow, like Hearst, but was neither as rich nor as prominent as Hearst. Although Merrill was politically active in nonpartisan voluntary associations, as was Hearst, the estimated value of Merrill's estate when she passed away was "in excess of $500,000." It is difficult to determine the exact value of Hearst's estate when she died. The value exceeded $500,000 by far. It was estimated in the millions, according to contemporaries. Merrill fell short of reaching the status and prominence of Hearst in nonpartisan voluntary association or academic politics too. See "John Merrill, Noted Merchant, Is Dead," *San Francisco Examiner*, September 10, 1912. People—married, unmarried, widowed, and with or without children—can be members of the religious, educational, and political elite, for example, without having a fortune. See Baltzell, *Philadelphia Gentlemen*. Further, are we to classify both Hearst, who was married, and then a widow, and Mary W. Kincaid, who was unmarried, as elite women? It is possible that prosperous but not rich widows inherited or possessed enough money to have a sufficient independent income so they were not compelled financially to work for a living. Unmarried women, like Kincaid, saved and/or invested money earned from the sale of assets and lived off the interest. As Kincaid wrote to Hearst: "I

shall at once put the money on long term deposit in the Hibernia Bank, & as soon as my property is sold, put that amount also there, & for the rest of my life live on the combined interest for my habits are simple & inexpensive, & I can be comfortable, & without business anxiety the rest of my life." See Kincaid to PAH, May 2, 1896, GPAHP. Both Hearst and Kincaid possessed independent incomes. Both were able to survive without working for a living. It would make more sense, in the broad scheme of class categories, to classify Hearst as a wealthy woman in the top tier, or in the elite, of American rich women, married, unmarried, widowed, or with or without children; and Kincaid, married with children, as an elite, prosperous woman in the next lower class. For a discussion on "why women appear so infrequently in the ranks of elites," see Epstein, "Women and Elites," 3.

2. "Woman's Party Formed Here," *San Francisco Examiner*, September 16, 1916, 4; Zahniser and Fry, *Alice Paul*, 500–2. Doris Stevens was known for her radicalism and beauty and, years later, married Dudley Field Malone, former adviser to President Wilson. See "Congressional Union Plans for Chicago Announced," *San Francisco Chronicle*, May 21, 1916, 9; Lundardini, *From Equal Suffrage to Equal Rights*, 63, 166.

3. Nickliss, "Phoebe Apperson Hearst"; Nickliss, "Phoebe Apperson Hearst's 'Gospel of Wealth.'" For an analysis of the "constructions of meaning and relationships of power" and the debate on equality-versus-difference, see J. W. Scott, "Deconstructing Equality-Versus-Difference," 33. On the need for a feminist notion of power, see Miller, "Women and Power," 240–48. For a discussion pertaining to theories on power that "explain the immersion of human beings in nets of power relations that constrain their possibilities while simultaneously uncovering the means by which human beings have the ability to resist and challenge those relations," see Wartenberg, introduction to *Rethinking Power*, xiii–xiv, xix, xiv, xix, xxiv, xix. On the "four independent factors that assure control" for those with political power, see Roty, "Power and Powers." On women and men constantly discussing and bargaining over issues of power, authority, and knowledge, see Gramsci, *Selections from the Prison Notebooks*, and Foucault, *Power/Knowledge*. On the power of persuasion, see Sandra Gustafson, *Eloquence Is Power*. On power and powerlessness, see Janeway, "On the Power of the Weak," 103–9.

For a rejection of the essentialist definition of women and the positioning of females that does not fall into essentialism, see Alcoff, "Cultural Feminism," 405–36. On gender and historical analysis, see Scott, "Gender," 1053–75. On gender and power, see Davis, Leijenaar, and Oldersma, *Gender of Power*. Research shows that inherited mental traits, from ancestors, mothers, and fathers, and lessons learned from parents, such as beliefs and values, and from others in and out of the family, all contribute to shaping individual personality, and so I explore the life of Phoebe Hearst from this point of view. As Leta Stetter Hollingworth, a psychologist in the early twentieth century, remarked: "So far as we know, daughters inherit mental traits from fathers as well as from mothers, and sons inherit them from mothers as well as from fathers." See Russett, *Sexual Science*, 159. The genetic traits and lessons learned are elements of, and interact with, the shifting multifaceted parts of individual personality influenced by culture. For a contemporary study conducted by the University of Minnesota from 1979 to 1986 that provides evidence to support the position that certain genetic traits are mostly inherited but some are learned, see Daniel Goleman, "Major Personality Study Finds that Traits Are Mostly Inherited," *New York Times*, December 2, 1986, http://www.nytimes .com/1986/12/02/science/major-personality-study-finds-that-traits-are -mostly-inherited.html?pagewanted=all. On the impact of medical science on the mind and body, influenced by culture, and how it helps people understand themselves, see Fellman and Fellman, *Making Sense of Self*.

Phoebe A. Hearst's life becomes clearer and takes on deeper meaning and significance when we look at it through a "thick description" of culture. This understanding of culture takes into account the beliefs and values, especially those learned from ancestors and parents, as well as feelings, behavior, actions, organizations, and institutions in which Hearst and women like her, as well as men, participated. These were set in complicated "webs of significance" that people spun in the public sphere or the "sphere between civil society and the state"—keeping in mind that "in concrete reality, civil society and State are one and the same," one scholar has written. There is much to examine and contemplate regarding women's lives, such as Hearst's, and the complicated relationship between females, and other women and men, and power in culture, civil society, or the state. See Rosaldo and Lamphere, introduction to

Women, Culture, and Society, 1–15; Rosaldo, "Woman, Culture, and Society," 17–42; Ortner, "Is Female to Male," 67–87; Geertz, "Thick Description," esp. 3, 5; Ryan, *Cradle of the Middle-Class*, and Bledstein and Johnston, *Middling Sorts*. Also see Habermas, *Structural Transformation*, xi; Gramsci, *Selections from the Prison Notebooks*, 208.

The shifting, complex, complicated parts of individual personality influenced by culture produce "unsuspected fissures," contradictions, and conflict that women, like Hearst, experienced and exploited "over time," especially through the individual decision-making process, which subverted and challenged "prevailing gendered notions" in private and in public. Women maintained enough of an acceptable traditional female or "feminine" role, public persona, and image that they could acquire power over women and men and on equal terms with men. See Banner, "AHR Roundtable," 579–86, esp. 581–82; Butler, *Gender Trouble*, esp. xi–xii; Margadant, *New Biography*, 2, 3, 7. On complementary sexual equality, see Nickliss, "Phoebe Apperson Hearst's 'Gospel of Wealth.'" For an investigation of women's biography, see DuBois and Gordon, "Daughters Writing," 80–102. On the challenges of writing a feminist biography, see Alpern et al., *Challenge of Feminist Biography*.

On ambition in women as an inherited mental trait and possibly a learned lesson as well, see Scott, "Almira Lincoln Phelps," 89–106. On ambitious women and progressive reform, see Muncy, *Creating a Female Dominion*. On ambition in men as an inherited mental trait as well as a learned lesson, see Hilkey, *Character Is Capital*. For an investigation of the changing concepts of manhood influenced by culture, see Carnes and Griffen, *Meanings of Manhood*; Rotundo, *American Manhood*; and Bederman, *Manliness and Civilization*.

For studies of sexual power, feminism, and family, see Smith, "Family Limitation," 40–57; Johnston, *Sexual Power*. On women's control of material resources, see Gamber, *Female Economy*; Lebsock, *Free Women*, esp. chap. 5; Sparks, *Capital Intentions*; Robb, "Enterprising Women," 166–71. On how women used material resources to alter public space for their own political purposes, see Deutsch, *Women and the City*; Sewell, *Women and the Everyday City*. On women as consumers and citizens, see Cohen, "Citizens and Consumers," 145–61. On cultural capital, see Bourdieu, *Distinction*. On symbolic capital, see Bourdieu, "Structures, Habitus, Power," 155–99; Dirks, Eley, and

Ortner, introduction to *Culture/Power/History*, 3–45; Fox and Lears, *Power of Culture*, 1–10. On women's and men's use of money and other resources, such as time and energy, in philanthropy, see Horowitz, *Culture and the City*; McCarthy, *Lady Bountiful Revisited*, *Noblesse Oblige*, and *Women's Culture*; Crocker, *Mrs. Russell Sage*; Sander, *Mary Elizabeth Garrett*; Hoffert, *Alva Vanderbilt Belmont*; Adam, *Buying Respectability*; Wall, *Andrew Carnegie*; and Nasaw, *Andrew Carnegie*. On the need for a new national synthesis of American history that argues for a complex, deeper meaning of "political" history, see Bender, "Wholes and Parts," 120–36. On the close connection and interconnection between private and public arenas, see Habermas, *Structural Transformation*. On women's position within society in general, see Kelly, "Doubled Vision," 216–27.

On separate spheres as a trope that masks the dynamic interrelationship between women and men and the society, see Kerber, "Separate Spheres," 9–39. On the relationship of women to the state, see Kerber, *Women of the Republic*. On feminism in the public arena, see Ryan, "Gender and Public Access," 259–88. On women's political culture, see DuBois et al., "Politics and Culture," 26–64. On the emergence of women's political culture, see Sklar, *Florence Kelley*. On the blurred, shifting notions of "public" and "private" and their porous boundaries, see Boylan, "Claiming Visibility," 17–40; Cohen, "Citizens and Consumers," 145–61; and Finnegan, *Selling Suffrage*.

On the dual role of women's religious organizations that gave women a chance to grow at the same time that they constrained them, see Cott, *Bonds of Womanhood*," 155–59. On the establishment of nonpartisan voluntary organizations in which women created networks of communication and support, see Scott, "What, Then, Is the American," 679–703. On all-female nonpartisan voluntary associations, see Scott, *Natural Allies*. Regarding a brief discussion on women and power in organizations, pressure-group tactics, and petitioning, see Lerner, "New Approaches," 354. On the power of female moral reformers' networks, see Ryan, "The Power of Women's Networks," 66–85. For an analysis of women's benevolent organizations, see Boylan, "Women in Groups," 497–523. For an investigation of moral authority in women's home mission organizations in the West, see Pascoe, *Relations of Rescue*.

For a study of the entrance of women into the world of male political parties and electoral actions, events, and politics in the late eighteenth and early nineteenth centuries, see Zagarri, *Revolutionary Backlash*. On the female members of families in politics who drew on the unofficial arena to build essential connections to make politics work, see Allgor, *Parlor Politics*. On women and the duties and obligations of citizenship, see Kerber, "A Constitutional Right to Be Treated Like Ladies," 17–35. On the notion of ability, power, and communication in groups, see Habermas, "Hannah Arendt's Communications," 3–24. On clubwoman as feminist, see Blair, *Clubwoman as Feminist*. On including diverse races and ethnic groups of women in U.S. women's history, see Armitage, "Revisiting 'The Gentle Tamers Revisited.'" For a study of early nineteenth-century nonpartisan women's organizations and the impact of race, religion, and class on unifying and dividing women, see Boylan, *Origins of Women's Activism*. On nonpartisan voluntary associations and democracy, see Skocpol, *Diminished Democracy*. On economic power and authority in organizations, see Parsons, *Max Weber*.

For an analysis of women as political strategists and how they use resources to advocate politically for issues of personal interest, see Collier, "Women in Politics," 89–96. On the impact of domesticity on politics, see Epstein, *Politics of Domesticity*. For an analysis of the impact of domesticity in politics and a definition of politics, see Baker, "Domestication of Politics," 620–47. For an investigation of separatism as a political strategy, see E. Freedman, "Separatism as Strategy," 512–29. For an analysis of three political networks of women in Rochester, New York, see Hewitt, *Women's Activism*. On women, politics, and social activism in the 1850s, see Ginzberg, "Moral Suasion," 601–22. On the shift from moral suasion to politics, and from gender to class, in women's world of benevolence, see Ginzberg, *Women and the Work of Benevolence*, esp. 5. On feminists who recognized the complexities and diverse unswerving allegiances among females who wanted to replace the notion of "woman" with the idea that females were a "human sex" between 1910 and 1930, see Cott, *Grounding*, book jacket.

For a definition, and overview, of politics and its dimensions and points of fissure that political females, especially ambitious ones, exploited in the United States, see Tilly and Gurin, *Women, Politics, and Change*. For a study of women's participation in nonpartisan voluntary associations before 1848, see Boylan, "Women and Politics Before Seneca Falls," 363–82. On philanthropy as women's politics, see Lebsock, "Women and American Politics," 35–62. On racial thinking and white women's rights in American politics, see Newman, *White Women's Rights*. On the relationship between women's political arenas and the larger male world of politics, especially progressive reform, in the late nineteenth and early twentieth centuries, see Muncy, *Creating a Female Dominion*. On progressive reform politics, see Muncy and also Rodgers, *Atlantic Crossings*. On black women using the church as a power tool for social and political change in black communities, see Higginbotham, *Righteous Discontent*. On black women and philanthropy, see Hine, "We Specialize in the Wholly Impossible," 70–93, and Hine, King, and Reed, *We Specialize in the Wholly Impossible*, esp. parts 5 and 6. For a discussion of blacks and the American settlement house movement, see Quinn, *Black Neighbors*. For an analysis of various notions, and the symbolic meaning, of representation, see Pitkin, *Concept of Representation*.

For a study of parades as "dramatic representations" and "political acts," see Davis, *Parades and Power*, 5, and Ryan, "American Parade," 131–53, *Women in Public*, and *Civic Wars*. For a study of electoral activism, see Monoson, "Lady and the Tiger," 200–35. On the interplay between partisan electoral and nonelectoral politics as traditionally defined by men, see Gilmore, *Gender and Jim Crow*. Gilmore examines "women's political culture" and its interrelationship with "men's politics" to redefine the meaning of "political" or the "'interactions between electoral and *non*-electoral politics [emphasis added].'" See Gilmore, xvi and the blurb by an academic on the back cover of the paperback. On women and partisan and nonpartisan politics, see Gustafson, "Partisan and Nonpartisan"; Gustafson, "Partisan Women," 8–30; and Gustafson, *Women and the Republican Party*. On feminism, power, and politics, see Lloyd, *Beyond Identity Politics*. On lobbying methods, see Odegard, *Pressure Politics*. On the shared political interests of women and men, see Lansing, *Insurgent Democracy*. On the emergence and growth of a California women's movement, see Gullett, *Becoming Citizens*. On California progressivism, see Deverell and Sitton, *California Progressivism Revisited*.

For a study of racial and gender groups challenging restrictions, unjust exercise of power and authority, and abuse in the arenas of citizenship and labor, see Glenn, *Unequal Freedom*. On black women and electoral politics, see Materson, *For the Freedom of Her Race*. Among the significant analyses of efforts to acquire political power, or the vote as narrowly defined by men, and the suffrage movement are Gillmore, *Story of the Woman's Party*; DuBois, *Feminism and Suffrage*; DuBois, "Working Women, Class Relations," 34–58; DuBois, *Harriot Stanton Blatch*; DuBois, *Woman Suffrage*; Thurner, "Better Citizens Without the Ballot," 33–60; Graham, *Woman Suffrage*; A. Gordon, *African American Women*; Beeton, *Women Vote*; Terborg-Penn, *African American Women*; Tetrault, *Myth of Seneca Falls*; Franzen, *Anna Howard Shaw*; Lundardini, *From Equal Suffrage*; Marilley, *Woman Suffrage*; Mead, *How the Vote Was Won*; Baker, "Getting Right With Women's Suffrage," 7–17; Sneider, *Suffragists in an Imperial Age*; Zahniser and Fry, *Alice Paul*; M. Wheeler, *New Women*; M. Wheeler, *One Woman*; M. Wheeler, *Votes for Women!*; Finnegan, *Selling Suffrage*; Goodier, *No Votes for Women*; Pfeffer, *Southern Ladies*; Johnson, "Following the Money," 62–87. For suggestions about "the persistence of women's contributions to social reform" and the important role "voluntary associations . . . continued to play in sustaining progressive reform" after the passage of the Nineteenth Amendment, see E. Freedman, "Separatism Revisited," 38.

4. Boris, "Class Returns,"74.

5. On feminist biography, see Alpern et al., *Challenge of Feminist Biography*; Kathleen Barry, "New Historical Synthesis," 75–105; Margadant, *New Biography*; Banner, "AHR Roundtable," 579–86; Harris, "Why Biography?" 625–30, esp. 626; Booth and Burton, "Editors' Note," 8–12. For studies that address implicitly the power women possessed, see Bordin, *Women and Temperance*; Hewitt, *Women's Activism and Social Change*; McCarthy, *Lady Bountiful Revisited*; Muncy, *Creating a Female Dominion*; Boylan, *Origins of Women's Activism*; Lyons, *Sex Among the Rabble*; Block, *Rape and Sexual Power*; Deutsch, *Women and the City*; García, *Negotiating Conquest*.

6. Rosaldo and Lamphere, introduction to *Woman, Culture, and Society*, 1–15; Rosaldo, "Woman, Culture, and Society, 17–42; Ortner, "Is Female to Male," 67–87; Geertz, "Thick Description," 3–30; Ryan, *Cradle of the Middle-Class*;

Habermas, *Structural Transformation*; Gramsci, *Selections From the Prison Notebooks*.

7. See introduction note 3 of this volume. On gendered power, see Norton, *Founding Mothers and Fathers*, esp. 3–24; Sklar and Dublin, *Women and Power*; Smith, *We Have Raised All of You*; McGerr, "Political Style," 864–85. Also Davis, Leijenaar, and Oldersma, introduction to *Gender of Power*, 1–18. Power is not gendered. But "gender is tied to power." Komter, "Gender, Power, and Feminist Theory," 61; Davis, "Critical Sociology and Gender Relations," 73; Matthews, *Rise of Public Woman*," esp. chaps. 4–10; K. Anderson, "Work, Gender, and Power"; Sklar, "Historical Foundations," 43–93; Fischer and Davis, introduction to *Negotiating at the Margins*, 3–20; Blackwell and Oertel, *Frontier Feminist*; Batzell, "Labor of Social Reproduction," 310–30. Women possessed the right in some states to vote in municipal elections on tax and bond issues before the passage of state suffrage and the Nineteenth Amendment. See Keyssar, *Right to Vote*, 400. Miller, "Women and Power."

8. Hoffert, *Alva Vanderbilt Belmont*, 123; Davis, Leijenaar, and Oldersma, *Gender of Power*, 1–18.

9. PAH to George Hearst, June 29, 1873, GPAHP; Ada Butterfield Jones to PAH, February 1891, GPAHP. On women and American politics, see Tilly and Gurin, introduction to *Women, Politics, and Change*, 3–32; Lebsock, "Women and American Politics," 35–62; Baker, "Domestication of Politics"; Scott, "Gender," 1069–70; Muncy, *Creating a Female Dominion*; Lloyd, *Beyond Identity Politics*, 3–7; Sklar, "Organized Womanhood," 176; Cott, *Bonds of Womanhood*, 153; Pitkin, *Concept of Representation*; Boylan, "Claiming Visibility"; Boylan, "Women in Groups," 497–523; Boylan, "Timid Girls," 779–97; Boylan, *Origins of Women's Activism*; DuBois et al., "Politics and Culture," 26–64; Ginzberg, *Women and the Work of Benevolence*; Epstein, *Politics of Domesticity*; Scott, "Almira Lincoln Phelps," 89–106; Scott, *Natural Allies*; Hewitt, *Women's Activism*; Lerner, "New Approaches," 354; Lerner, "Reconceptualizing Differences Among Women," 106–22; Gilmore, *Gender and Jim Crow*, especially xvi; Waugh, *Unsentimental Reformer*; Materson, *For the Freedom of Her Race*.

10. Hearst used her "'creative'" or "coercive" power often as an "entering wedge." See Rossiter, *Women Scientists*, 39; Fellman and Fellman, *Making*

Sense of Self; Jessie W. Wilson, "What Girls Can Do For Girls," *Good House-keeping* 56 (April 1913): 436–45. Also Golden Gate Kindergarten Association Reports; RCHIR; CCC; Minutes of the General Federation of Women's Clubs, GFWC; Columbian Kindergarten Association Files; GPAHP; UCARCH; National Congress of Mothers, Minutes, NCM; Mount Vernon Ladies' Association, MVLA; YWCA Records.

11. Rossiter, *Women Scientists*, 39; GPAHP; Panama-Pacific International Exposition, PPIER; YWCA, National YWCA Board Records.

12. Rossiter, *Women Scientists*, 39. See GPAHP and later chapters on Hearst's involvement in nonpartisan voluntary associations.

13. Cronon, Miles, and Gitlin, "Becoming West," 7, 21; Brooks, "Phoebe Apperson Hearst," part 1, chap. 1, 1–5; Armitage, "Women and Men," 381–95; Starr, *Americans and the California Dream*; Jeffrey, *Frontier Women*; Jameson, "Women as Workers," 1–8; Paula Petrik, *No Step Backward*. For an investigation of new approaches to studying women's pasts in the American West, see Jensen and Miller, "Gentle Tamers Revisited," 173–213. For an examination of the experiences of women who came West, see Myres, *Westering Women*. On including women in western history, see Armitage, "Women and Men in Western History," 381–95. On western women as workers and civilizers, see Jameson, "Women as Workers," 1–8. On class, race, ethnic, regional, religious, and other classifications of differences between women, see Lerner, "Reconceptualizing Differences among Women," 106–22. On work, gender, and power in the American West, see Anderson, "Work, Gender, and Power," 481–99. On including diverse races and ethnic groups of females in U.S. women's history, see Armitage, "Revisiting 'The Gentle Tamers Revisited,'" 459–62. On the politics of western women's history, see Scharff, "Else Surely We Shall All Hang Separately," 535–55.

For studies that help us understand how individuals shape regional and national identities and, in turn, how those identities form individuals, see Ridge, "American West," 125–41; Barth, *Instant City*; Hyde, *An American Vision*; Wrobel, "Beyond the Frontier-Region Dichotomy," 401–29; Wrobel and Steiner, *Many Wests*; Matthews, "Forging a Cosmopolitan Civic Culture," 211–34; Bergland, *Making San Francisco America*. On the American West and its formation by Indians, Europeans, Asians, and Africans, see White, *"It's Your Misfortune and None of My Own."* On process and place in the West, see Cronon, Miles, and Gitlin, *Under the Open Sky*. On power and place in the North American West, see White and Findlay, *Power and Place*.

There is only a handful of scholarship on wealthy women in the West. See R. Peterson, "Philanthropic Phoebe," 284–315; R. Peterson, "The Philanthropist and the Artist," 278–85, 316–18; Scharlach, *Big Alma*; Nickliss, "Phoebe Apperson Hearst's 'Gospel of Wealth,'" 575–605. On wealthy men in the West, see Barth, "Metropolitan and Urban Elites," 158–87; R. Peterson, *Bonanza Kings, Bonanza Rich*, and "Spirit of Giving," 309–36.

14. Brooks, "Phoebe Apperson Hearst," part 1, chap. 1 and chap. 5, 36.

15. Mattie Wynn to PAH, April 27, 1883, GPAHP; Wynn to PAH, August 9, 1883, GPAHP.

16. Ada Butterfield Jones to PAH, August 17, 1886, GPAHP.

17. Brooks, "Phoebe Apperson Hearst," part 1, chap. 1, 1–5; Mattie Wynn to PAH, August 9, 1883, GPAHP. See also letters from Emily Wynn to PAH in GPAHP; Emily (Wynn) Elias, *Benezit Dictionary of Artists*. Oxford Art Online, http://www.oxfordartonline.com/subscriber/article/benezit/b00058354; Ada Butterfield Jones to PAH, August 17, 1886, GPAHP.

18. Lebsock, "Women and American Politics," 35–62, esp. 37, 35; Baker, "Domestication of Politics," 620–47.

19. For historical studies on philanthropy, see McCarthy, ed., *Lady Bountiful Revisited*; McCarthy, *Women's Culture*; McCarthy, *Noblesse Oblige*; Ginzberg, *Women and the Work of Benevolence*; Bremner, "Scientific Philanthropy," 168–73; Waugh, *Unsentimental Reformer*; Crocker, *Mrs. Russell Sage*; Himmelfarb, *Poverty and Compassion*; Quataert, *Staging Philanthropy*; Sander, *Mary Elizabeth Garrett*; Adam, *Buying Respectability*; Hoffert, *Alva Vanderbilt Belmont*. On the recent popular interest in philanthropy, see Associated Press, "Zuckerberg Tops Philanthropist List in U.S. in '13," *San Francisco Chronicle*, February 10, 2014; Stephanie Strom, "40 Who Committed Half of Their Wealth for the Pledge," *New York Times*, November 11, 2010; Strom, "What's Wrong with Profit," *New York Times*, December 13, 2006, Special Section; Patrick Cole, "40 Top Execs Join Buffett's Aid Drive," *San Fran-*

cisco Chronicle, August 5, 2010; Stanley N. Katz, "Philanthropy's New Math," *Chronicle of Higher Education*, February 2, 2007; Kelly Field, "Philanthropist Calls on Colleges to Inspire Students to Give," *Chronicle of Higher Education*, June 22, 2007; "American Millionaires and Their Public Gifts," *Review of Reviews* 7 (February 1893), 48–60.

20. Bremner, "Scientific Philanthropy," 168.

21. Brooks, "Phoebe Apperson Hearst," part 1, chap. 1, esp. 1–5; Phoebe Apperson Hearst, January 1, 1866, PAHD; PAH to Eliza Pike, September 15, 1867, GPAHP; Florence Bayard Hilles to PAH, September 1890, incomplete, GPAHP.

22. Brooks, "Phoebe Apperson Hearst," part 1, chap. 1, 5; George Hearst and Phoebe E. Apperson Marriage Record, June 15, 1862, Missouri State Archives, Records Management and Archives Service, a Division of the Office of the Secretary of State, Jefferson City MO; George Hearst and Phoebe E. Apperson Pre-Nuptial Contract, June 14, 1862, Joint Collection, University of Missouri, Western Historical Manuscript Collection, Columbia and State Historical Society of Missouri Manuscripts; PAH, January 1, 1866, PAHD; PAH to Eliza Pike, July 21, 1867, GPAHP; PAH to Eliza Pike, February 8, 1873, GPAHP; PAH to George Hearst, May 11, 1873, GPAHP; PAH to George Hearst, June 29, 1873, GPAHP.

23. Ahlstrom, *A Religious History*, 444–45; Cossitt, *Life and Times of Rev. Finis Ewing*; Homberger, *Mrs. Astor's New York*, 4; Mrs. Madeleine Vinton Dahlgren, *Etiquette of Social Life*, 50–51.

24. Juliette M. Babbitt, "Mrs. Phoebe A. Hearst: Prominent Women in Washington's Social World," no magazine title, ca. 1895, original newspaper clipping in author's possession.

25. Juliette M. Babbitt, "Mrs. Phoebe A. Hearst," no magazine title, ca. 1895.

1. ABILITY

1. Pringle, "In Memoriam: Phoebe Apperson Hearst," Minutes of the Council of the Mount Vernon Ladies' Association of the Union, 1, MVLA.

2. Owens and Owens, *Sons of Frontiersmen*, 45; Hinman, "Biographical Sketch of Mrs. Hearst," 72, GPAHP; George Hearst, *Autobiography*, 1890, 3, 4, UCARCH; Jameson, "Women as Workers," 1–8; University of California, "Phoebe Apperson Hearst Biography Form," Biographies, Inactive, E-H, Secretary of

the Chief of Staff of the Regents of the University of California, Office of the President of the University of California, Oakland, California; Welter, "Cult of True Womanhood, 1820–1840," 151–74; Kerber, "Separate Spheres," 9–39.

3. Jameson, "Women as Workers," 1–8; Owens, *Sons of Frontiersmen*, 47, 50; Col. Robert J. Owens, *Whitmires of Whitmire SC and Kin*, 1:3, 55, 229; Brooks, "Phoebe Apperson Hearst," part 1, chap. 1; A. Scott, *Southern Lady*, 1–10; Kerber, *Women of the Republic*, 231, 283, 189; Cronon, Miles, and Gitlin, "Becoming West," 8, 10; Cronon, *Changes in the Land*. There are different spellings used for Phoebe's mother in family sources. I've chosen to use Drusilla because it is the spelling Phoebe used. See National Society of Daughters of the American Revolution, "Application for Membership," March 6, 1914, 2, NSDAR.

4. Brooks, "Phoebe Apperson Hearst," 1–5; Ryan, *Cradle of the Middle-Class*. On the intricate and complex interrelationship between the female and male attributes of human identity, see Butler, *Gender Trouble*. Also Hewitt, *Women's Activism and Social Change*, 20.

5. "Phoebe Apperson Hearst Biography Form"; Brooks, "Phoebe Apperson Hearst," part 1, chap. 1, p. 3. For the proper spelling of the first name of Randolph's mother, see National Society of the Daughters of the American Revolution, "Application for Membership," 2–3, NSDAR; Owens and Owens, *Sons of Frontiersmen*, 45, 61–2, 90; Owens, *Whitmires of Whitmire*, 1:229; Appleby, *Inheriting the Revolution*, chap. 3, 11; Forte, "Biographical Sketches," 443–44; Fischer and. Kelly, *Bound Away*, xiii. Forty thousand seven hundred and seventy-seven Virginia emigrants settled in Missouri. See Fischer and Kelly, *Bound Away*, 140.

6. Hatch, *Democratization of American Christianity*, chap. 4, 184; Forte, "Biographical Sketches," 443–44; Ahlstrom, *Religious History of the American People*, 444, 445; Cronon, Miles, and Gitlin, "Becoming West," 10; Smith to PAH, GPAHP; March, *History of Missouri*, 1:309, 341; Vander, *Presbyterian Churches and the Federal Union*, 406; Cossitt, *Life and Times of Rev. Finis Ewing*, 43.

7. Appleby, *Inheriting the Revolution*, 21; Brooks, "Phoebe Apperson Hearst," part 1, chap. 1, 1–5; Owens, *Whitmires*, 229; Forte, "Biographical Sketches," 444.

8. Myres, *Westering Women*, 67; A. Scott, *Southern Lady*; Welter, "Cult of True Womanhood"; Young, "Hearst Ancestors From S.C.," *South Carolina News-*

paper, November–December 1971, p. 20; Appleby, *Relentless Revolution,* chap. 6; Lewis, *Whitmires of South Carolina.* Reprinted from the *Atlanta Sunday American,* December 22, 1935, copy, pamphlet, South Caroliniana Library, South Carolina.

9. Bledstein and Johnston, introduction to *Middling Sorts,* 5, 6, 29; Appleby, "Social Consequences of American Revolutionary Ideals," 38, 39, 48; Cronon, Miles, and Gitlin, "Becoming West," 14; Lewis, *Whitmires of South Carolina,* 1; Appleby, *Inheriting the Revolution,* 73. Also Owens, *Sons of Frontiersmen,* 61–62, 90, 45, 47, 52; Brooks, "Phoebe Apperson Hearst," part 1, chap. 1, 1. Brooks reported Drusilla was six years old rather than two years old when her parents left the South. See Brooks, "Phoebe Apperson Hearst." Also *Marriage Book,* vol. "A," microfilm reel c2388, p. 180, Missouri State Archives, Jefferson City MO.

10. Forte, "Biographical Sketches," 443–44; Smith, *History of the Christian Church,* 517; Hatch, *Democratization of American Christianity,* 3, 106; Appleby, *Inheriting the Revolution,* chap. 4.

11. Owens and Owens, *Sons of Frontiersmen,* 61–62; Owens, *Whitmires of Whitmire,* 1:231; Brooks, "Phoebe Apperson Hearst," part 1, chap. 1, 1–3. Typewritten and handwritten rough drafts of Brooks's unpublished biography exist in the GPAHP archive at the Bancroft Library, University of California, Berkeley. Drafts cited in these notes are from the typewritten version unless otherwise indicated. Also George Hearst, *Autobiography,* 3, 4, UCARCH; Brooks, "Made from a Conversation with Mrs. Hearst in May 12, 1896" and "Phoebe Apperson Hearst"; Myres, *Westering Women,* 2, 167–68, 167.

12. Myers, *Westering Women;* Riley, *Female Frontier,* 95–96; Homberger, *Mrs. Astor's New York,* 1.

13. Brooks, "Phoebe Apperson Hearst," part 1, chap. 1; A. Scott, "Almira Lincoln Phelps," 91.

14. A. Scott, "Almira Lincoln Phelps," 91; Brooks, "Phoebe Apperson Hearst," part 1, chap. 1; Kelley, *Learning to Stand and Speak,* 107; Fox, "Nice Girl," 807. Brooks's characterization of Drusilla and Phoebe is corroborated by written descriptions of them in letters and newspaper articles contained in the GPAHP archives and elsewhere. Also A. Scott, *Southern Lady,* 7.

15. Brooks, "Phoebe Apperson Hearst," part 1, chap. 1, p. 2; Guinn, "Annie Wittenmyer," 351–77, esp. 351–53, 364, 371, 373; Horowitz, *Morality of Spending*, xxii, xxix, 1–3, 10; Blair, *Clubwoman as Feminist*, 2; Fox, "Nice Girl," 806; Aron, *Working at Play*, 6, 7, 9; Welter, "Cult of True Womanhood," 152; Boylan, "Evangelical Womanhood," 62–80; Boylan, *Origins of Women's Activism*, 27; Boylan, "Evangelical Womanhood," 66; Bancroft, *Biography of George Hearst*, 2:379.

16. Brooks, "Phoebe Apperson Hearst," part 1, chap. 1, p. 2; Fox, "Nice Girl," 806; Banner, "AHR: Roundtable," 581; Kessler-Harris, "Why Biography?" 626.

17. Pringle, "In Memoriam: Phoebe Apperson Hearst," 2, MVLA; Brooks, "Phoebe Apperson Hearst," part 1, chap. 1, pp. 3–4; Parsons, *Max Weber*, 56–77; Childs, "Elizabeth Waties Allston Pringle," 3:100–101; Hatch, *Democratization of American Christianity*, 195–96; Boylan, *Sunday School*, 4, 60, 133, 169, 134; Rosaldo and Lamphere, *Woman, Culture, and Society*, 21; Aron, *Working at Play*, 18.

18. Brooks, "Phoebe Apperson Hearst," part 1, chap. 1, pp. 3, 4; Randolph W. R. Apperson, Edwin L. E. Apperson, and Nancy N. Apperson to Vonnie V. Eastham, typewritten copy, RGA; Forte, *Pen Pictures*, 444.

19. R. Peterson, *Bonanza Kings*, xi; Pringle, "In Memoriam: Phoebe Apperson Hearst," 2, MVLA; Rotundo, *American Manhood*, chaps. 1–5.

20. Banner, "AHR Roundtable," 581.

21. Kelley, *Learning to Stand and Speak*, 65, 275–76, 91, 1; Kerber, *Women of the Republic*; Suzanne Hill, "In Memory of Phoebe Apperson Hearst," *Washington Missourian*, November 12–13, 1988; Ralph Gregory, "Founders Day Address," February 14, 1964, RGA; Tyack and Hansot, *Learning Together*, 28, 73.

22. Hoffman, *Women's 'True' Profession*, 11; Tyack and Hansot, *Learning Together*, 45. Some scholars argue that the beginning of the women's rights movement occurred before the 1848 Seneca Falls Convention. See Ginzberg, *Untidy Origins*; Tetrault, *Myth of Seneca Falls*; Newman, "Reflections on Aileen Kraditor's Legacy: 291–316, esp. 291n7.

23. Tyack and Hansot, *Learning Together*, 28, 30; Kerber, *Women of the Republic*; Suzanne Hill, "In Memory of Phoebe Apperson Hearst," *Washington Missourian*, November 12–13, 1988; Ralph Gregory, "Founders Day Address," Feb. 14, 1964, RGA; Davis, "Education of Southern Girls," 53–57; Brooks,

"Phoebe Apperson Hearst," part 1, chap. 1, p. 4; Glauert, "Education and Society in Antebellum Missouri."

24. The 1860 United States Census listed 16,484 free people: 8,854 white males, 7,611 white females, 6 free colored men, 13 free colored females, and 1,601 slaves in the county, 824 male slaves, 777 female slaves, for a total population of 18,085. See Joseph C. G Kennedy, Superintendent of Census, comp., *Population of the United States in 1860; Compiled From the Original Returns of the Eighth Census Under the Direction of the Secretary of the Interior* (Washington DC: Government Printing Office, 1864), accessed Aug. 1, 2015, http://babel.hathitrust.org, digitized by Internet Archive, original from the University of California, 275, 279, 281, 286; Myres, *Westering Women*, 13, 14; Bremner, *From the Depths*, 4; Riley, *Female Frontier*, 45–46; PAH to Eliza Pike, July 5, 1868, GPAHP.

25. Bancroft, *Biography of George Hearst*, 375.

26. Bonfils, *Life and Personality of Phoebe Apperson Hearst*, 5; Myres, *Westering Women*, 2; Brooks, "Phoebe Apperson Hearst," part 1, chap. 1, p. 4; Scharff, "Lighting Out for the Territory," 292–93; introduction to *Middling Sorts*, 2; Starr, *Americans and the California Dream*, viii, 46.

27. Kaufman, *Women Teachers on the Frontier*, xxii; Kelley, *Learning to Stand and Speak*; Botting, *Vindication of the Rights of Woman*, 47; Sapiro, *Vindication of Political Virtue*, 104. On the feminization of public school teaching, see Strober and Lanford, "Feminization of Public School Teaching," 212–35. Also Swager, "Educating Women in America," 333–61; Kerber, *Women of the Republic*; A. Scott, "The Ever Widening Circle," 3–25; Woody, *History of Women's Education*, 1:379; Brooks, "Phoebe Apperson Hearst," part 1, chap. 1, 5; Crawford County History Book Committee, "Steelville Presbyterian," 59.

28. Brooks, "Phoebe Apperson Hearst," part 1, chap. 1, p. 5; Hoffman, *Women's 'True' Profession*, 11; James Foundation, *Lucy Wortham James*, 18, 17; C. V. Mann, "Story of Dunmoor," 2–3, JCUM; Vogel, *Maramec Iron Works, 1825–1876*, 12; Norris, *Story of Maramec Iron Works*, 15–16, 18, 22, 114, 115, 116, 120. Upper class, in this context, refers to a group of *families*, whose members are "descendants of successful individuals (elite members) of one, two, three or more generations ago." Upper-class families stand "at the top of

the *social class* hierarchy." Members of upper-class families have childhoods, friendships, and marriages that intertwine with one another. See Baltzell, *Philadelphia Gentlemen*, 6, 7. Studies and analyses centered on women and class, especially on wealthy, elite women, are needed.

29. C. V. Mann, "Story of Dunmoor," 3–4, JCUM; Fox, "Nice Girl," 809; James Foundation, *Lucy Wortham James*, 21–22; Hemphill, *Bowing to Necessities*, 6–7.

30. C. V. Mann, "Story of Dunmoor," 2, JCUM; Morgan, *Women and Patriotism in Jim Crow America*, 21; Waldstreicher, *In the Midst of Perpetual Fetes*, chaps. 1–2, p. 3; Norris, *Story of Maramec Iron Works*, 41, 57; *A History of Maramec Iron Works*, by Robert G. Van Nostrand, a thesis submitted to the New York Community Trust Trustees of the Lucy Wortham James Estate in fulfillment of a request from Mr. Ralph Hayes, May 10, 1941, 50, 51, 53, 56; James Foundation, *Lucy Wortham James*, 18, 21, 19; Brooks, "Phoebe Apperson Hearst," part 1, chap. 1, p. 5; Aron, *Working at Play*, 24–26; Norris, *Story of Maramec Iron Works*, v; Igler, "Industrial Far West," 159–92.

31. Norris, *Story of Maramec Iron Works*, 21–22, 147–49. Vogel listed 1848 as the first year Phoebe taught at Maramec. The year was 1861. See Vogel, *Maramec Iron Works, 1825–1876*. Also Mann, *Story of Dunmoor*, 4; Tyack and Hansot, *Learning Together*, 63.

32. PAH to Mr. Long, collection no. 1, February 17, 1862, folder 2020, LWJC; Ralph Gregory, "To Dedicate Memorial to Famous Franklin County Woman Sunday," *Washington (County) Missourian*, August 1, 1963, RGA; James Foundation, *Lucy Wortham James*, 14, 18, 22; Kelley, *Learning to Stand and Speak*, 78; Wrobel, "Beyond the Frontier-Region Dichotomy," 401–29; Wade, *Urban Frontier*; Brooks, "Phoebe Apperson Hearst," part 1, chap. 1, p. 5. Elite, in this context, refers to "the most successful" family in the area—a family that stood "at the top of the *functional* class hierarchy." See Baltzell, *Philadelphia Gentlemen*, 6, 7.

33. Brooks, "Phoebe Apperson Hearst," part 1, chap. 1, p. 5; Strober and Lanford, "Feminization of Public School Teaching"; Warren Randolph Burgess, *Trends of School Costs* (New York: Russell Sage, 1920), 32. The average weekly pay, in 1861, for male city teachers was $18.07 and for female city teachers was $6.91. Also PAH to Mr. Long, February 17, 1862, folder 2020, LWJC; Lucy Ann Dun and William James, November 15, 1861, January 27, and March

13, 1862, Cash Books, v. 83, collection no. 1, LWJC; May, *Protestant Churches and Industrial America*, 21; Lucy Ann Dun and William James's Cash Book, May 5, 1862, v. 84, collection no. 1, LWJC; *A History of Maramec Iron Works*, by Robert G. Van Nostrand, a thesis submitted to the New York Community Trust Trustees of the Lucy Wortham James Estate in fulfillment of a request from Mr. Ralph Hayes, May 10, 1941, 44, 49.

34. Brooks, "Phoebe Apperson Hearst," typewritten copy, part 1, chap. 1, 4–5; Ralph Gregory, "To Dedicate Memorial to Famous Franklin County Woman Sunday," *Washington (County) Missourian*, August 1, 1963, RGA; Kerber, *No Constitutional Rights to Be Ladies*; Kaufman, *Women Teachers on the Frontier*, xxi–xxii; Finkelstein, "Pedagogy as Intrusion," 349–78; Finkelstein, "Moral Dimensions of Pedagogy," 81–89; Field, *Struggle for Equal Adulthood*, prologue, chaps. 1–2; PAH, January 1, 1866, PAHD; Tyack and Hansot, *Learning Together*, 46–47, 59, 73, 58; Riley, *Inventing the American Woman*, 1:95; Rankin, "Teaching: Opportunity and Limitation," 148.

35. Scott, "Almira Lincoln Phelps," 91; Brooks, "Phoebe Apperson Hearst," chap. 1, p. 5; *St. Clair (MO) Chronicle*, August 1, 1963, PAH Historical Society, 1.

36. George Hearst, *Autobiography*, 4, 7; Bancroft, *Biography of George Hearst*, 357; Gregory, "George Hearst in Missouri," 76–77, 81.

37. Gregory, "George Hearst in Missouri," 75–79; Mr. and Mrs. Older, *Life of George Hearst, California Pioneer*, 13; George Hearst, *Autobiography*, 2–5; Butler, *Gender Trouble*; Rotundo, *American Manhood*, 33, 46; Banner, *American Beauty*, 76; Kastner, *Hearst Ranch*, 22.

38. George Hearst, *Autobiography*, 15, 34; Jung, "Capitalism Comes to the Diggings," 68–69, 52; Smith, "Mother Lode for the West," 149; R. Peterson, *Bonanza Kings*, xi–xiv.

39. R. Peterson, *Bonanza Rich*; Jaher, *Urban Establishment*, 2–3; Decker, *Fortune and Failures*, 231–36; Baltzell, *Philadelphia Gentleman*, 6, 7; U.S. Congress, "Address of Mr. Stewart, of Nevada," *Memorial Addresses on the Life and Character of George Hearst*, 27, 28; George Hearst, *Autobiography*, 36.

40. Paul, *Mining Frontiers of the Far West*, 63–64; George Hearst, *Autobiography*, 17, 38; George Hearst to PAH, January 10, 1874, GPAHP; Hoffert, *Alva Vanderbilt Belmont*, 39; Rotundo, *American Manhood*, 157–63; Gregory, "George Hearst

in Missouri," 83–84; Robinson, *The Hearsts*, 51–53; Brooks, "Phoebe Apperson Hearst," part 1, chap. 1, p. 6; Banner, *American Beauty*, 13.

41. George Hearst, *Autobiography*, 17, 38; U.S. Congress, "Address of Mr. Bate, of Tennessee," *Memorial Addresses on the Life and Character of George Hearst*, 34; "Mrs. Hearst 'Goes In' for Society," *Commercial Advertiser*, March 1, 1890, GPAHP; Brooks, "Phoebe Apperson Hearst," part 1, chap. 1, p. 6.

42. Brooks, "Phoebe Apperson Hearst," part 1, chap. 1, 1–5, and chap. 2, 11–12; Passport for Europe and Russia, July 18, 1889, oversize box, GPAHP; Banner, *American Beauty*, chap. 3; Clark, "Reminiscences of the Hearst Family," 2.

43. George Hearst, *Autobiography*, 1, 37; PAH, February 4, 1866, PAHD; [Peter Toft] to Editor of the *New York World*, May 23, 1886, GPAHP; "He Envied Titled Ones," *New York Times*, June 25, 1886; Swanberg, *Citizen Hearst*, 11; Clark, "Reminiscences of the Hearst Family," 2.

44. Massey with Berlin, *Women in the Civil War*, 255–56; Brooks, "Phoebe Apperson Hearst," part 1, chap. 1, 5–6; Charles H. Hardin, commissioner appointed by the Missouri Legislature, *The Revised Statutes of the State of Missouri, Revised and Digested by the Eighteenth General Assembly, During the Session of One Thousand Eight Hundred and Fifty-Four and One Thousand Eight Hundred and Fifty-Five*, vol. 2 (City of Jefferson, 1856), 1059; A.F. Denny, commissioner appointed by the Missouri governor, *The General Statutes of the State of Missouri, Revised by Committee Appointed by the Twenty-Third General Assembly, Under a Joint Resolution of February 20, 1865, Amended by the Legislature, and Passed March 20, 1866* (City of Jefferson, 1866), iii–iv, 658. The revised 1866 statute, section 1 stated: "Marriage is considered, in law, as a civil contract, to which the consent of the parties capable, in law, of contracting, is essential." The revised statute makes no mention of having parental consent.

45. A. Hearst, *Horses of San Simeon*, 83.

46. March, *History of Missouri*, vol. 2, chap. 21; Bonfils, *Life and Personality of Phoebe Apperson Hearst*, 10; Crawford County Courthouse, Marriage Record, 4–6; Crawford County Courthouse, Marriage Record, 139; Crawford County History Book Committee, "Steelville Presbyterian," 59; Gregory, "George Hearst in Missouri," 84.

47. Crawford County Courthouse, Marriage Record, Book 1, June 14, 1862, 4; Crawford County, Marriage Record, 139; Lebsock, *Free Women of Petersburg*,

57–59; Gregory, "George Hearst in Missouri," 84; Lord, *Comstock Mining and Miners*, 128.

48. "Civics Library of the Missouri Bar," http://members.mobar.org/civics /women.htm, copyright 2006, accessed Aug. 13, 2012; Missouri State Legislature, Fifteenth General Assembly, "Marriage Contracts" and "Married Women," *Laws of the State of Missouri* (City of Jefferson, 1849), 67–68, http:// heinonline.org, accessed Aug. 13, 2012; Shammas, "Re-Assessing the Married Women's Property Acts," 13, 14.

49. Lebsock, *Free Women of Petersburg*, 57–59; Cott, *Public Vows*, 55.

50. Gregory, "George Hearst in Missouri," 85; Ralph Gregory, "To Dedicate Memorial to Famous Franklin County Woman Sunday," *Washington (County) Missourian*, August 1, 1963, RGA; Wright, "Making of Cosmopolitan California," part 1, 65; Kemble, *Panama Route, 1848–1869*, 37, 95, 96, 110, 111, 113, 139, 140, 146–65, 238–39, 247; Brooks, "Phoebe Apperson Hearst," part 1, chap. 2, 7–8, 11.

51. Brooks, "Phoebe Apperson Hearst," part 1, chap. 2, p. 7; Morantz, "Making Women Modern," 490; Duffin, "Conspicuous Consumptive"; Delamont and Duffin, *Nineteenth-Century Women*, 26, 29; Pitts, "Disability, Scientific Authority, and Women's Political Participation," 38. On "Biography" and family tree, Janet M. Peck Papers, 1860–1956, Manuscript Department, California Historical Society, San Francisco CA; on female friendships, see Rosenberg, "Female World of Love and Ritual," 1–29.

52. Fischer, "Women in California in the Early 1850s," 231–53; Wright, "Making of Cosmopolitan California—Part 2," 74; Older, *George Hearst*, 119–20; Bonfils, *Life and Personality of Phoebe Apperson Hearst*, 13; Kemble, *Panama Route, 1848–1869*, 152.

53. Berglund, Making San Francisco America, as quoted on 3; Barth, *Instant City*, xxvii–xxviii; Wright, "Making of Cosmopolitan California—Part 2," 73–74. Females were only 37 percent of California's entire population by 1870. See Wright, "Making of Cosmopolitan California," 74.

54. Berglund, *Making San Francisco America*, 5, 2, 8; Wrobel and Steiner, *Many Wests*, 214; Older, *Life of George Hearst*, 52; Older, *George Hearst, California Pioneer*, 124; Bonfils, *Life and Personality of Phoebe Apperson Hearst*, chap. 2; Issel and Cherny, *San Francisco, 1865–1932*, 19, 119.

55. Myres, *Westering Women*, chap. 7; Berglund, *Making San Francisco America*, 40; Brooks, "Phoebe Apperson Hearst," part 1, chap. 2, pp. 11–12, and chap. 3, p. 13; Berglund, *Making San Francisco America*, 32, 40, 42–44; Riley, *Female Frontier*, 88; Bonfils, *Life and Personality of Phoebe Apperson Hearst*, 14; deFord, *They Were San Franciscans*, 65, 66; Cocks *Doing the Town*, 26, 165; Brooks, "Phoebe Apperson Hearst," part 1, chap. 2, p. 11.

56. George Hearst to PAH, April 14, 1864, GPAHP; PAH, January 2, 1866, PAHD; PAH to Eliza Pike, June 16, 17, 1864, GPAHP; PAH to Eliza Pike, June 25, 1864, GPAHP; Swanberg, *Citizen Hearst*, 11.

57. PAH to Eliza Pike and Willie, June 16, 1864, GPAHP; Golden, *Social History of Wet Nursing in America*, 6, 39, 41; PAH, February 4, 1866, PAHD.

58. PAH to Eliza Pike, June 25, 1864, GPAHP.

59. Nash, *State Government and Economic Development*, 29–30; State of California, *Journal of the Assembly during the Sixteenth Session of the Legislature of California, 1865–66* (Sacramento: O. M. Clayes, 1866), 34; Chief Clerk of the Assembly, *Journal of the Assembly during the Sixteenth Session of the Legislature of California, 1865–66* (Sacramento, 1866), http://www.clerk .assembly.ca.gov, accessed February 3, 2016, 111; U.S. Congress, "Address of Mr. Stanford, of California," 22; Brooks, "Phoebe Apperson Hearst," part 1, chap. 3, p. 15.

60. PAH, January 2, 1866, PAHD; PAH to Eliza Pike, February 20, 1867, GPAHP.

61. PAH, January 1, 1866, PAHD; PAH, January 2, 1866, PAHD; Brooks, "Phoebe Apperson Hearst," part 1, chap. 3, p. 16; PAH to Eliza Pike, September 1866, GPAHP; Homberger, *Mrs. Astor's New York*, 148; PAH to Eliza Pike, July 2, 1865, GPAHP; PAH to Eliza Pike, February 20, 1867, GPAHP; PAH to Eliza Pike, December 8, 1867, GPAHP; PAH to Eliza Pike, July 2, 1865, GPAHP.

62. PAH to Eliza Pike, July 2, 1865, GPAHP; PAH to Eliza Pike, September 1866, GPAHP; PAH to Eliza Pike, June 19, 1867, GPAHP; Brooks, "Phoebe Apperson Hearst," part 1, chap. 3, pp. 13, 14, 17–18.

63. George Hearst to PAH, April 14, 1864, GPAHP; George Hearst to PAH, August 29, 1867, GPAHP; Brooks, "Phoebe Apperson Hearst," part 1, chap. 3, p. 13; Older, *Life of George Hearst*, 124–25.

64. Older, *Life of George Hearst*, 138; Paul, *Mining Frontier of the Far West*, 69, 194; Limbaugh, "Making Old Tools Work Better," 24–51; Jung, "Capitalism

Comes to the Diggings," 69–70; PAH, January 1, 1866, PAHD; PAH to Eliza Pike, June 19, 1867, GPAHP.

65. PAH, January 1, 1866, PAHD; PAH, January 2, 1866, PAHD; PAH, January 18, 1866, PAHD; PAH to Eliza Pike, November 18, 1866, GPAHP; Lynch-Brannan, *Irish Bridget*, 68–69. On family economy, see Ryan, *Cradle of the Middle Class*, chap. 5 and conclusion.

66. Veblen, *Theory of the Leisure Class*, 155, 149, chaps. 3–4, 36–37, 40, 41, 149; Appleby, *Inheriting the Revolution*, 148, 184; PAH, January 4, 1866, PAHD; PAH to Eliza Pike, February 20, 1867, GPAHP; PAH to George Hearst, August 19, 1868, GPAHP; PAH to Eliza Pike, November 18, 1866, GPAHP.

67. PAH, February 4, 1866, PAHD; PAH, March 14, 1866, PAHD; Kelley, *Learning to Stand and Speak*; PAH, February 25, 1866, PAHD; PAH, January 14, 1866, PAHD; PAH, January 21, 1866, PAHD; PAH, January 17, 1866, PAHD; PAH to Eliza Pike, November 16, 1866, GPAHP; PAH to Eliza Pike, February 20, 1867, GPAHP; PAH to Eliza Pike, March 29, 1867, GPAHP; PAH to Eliza Pike, September 15, 1867, GPAHP; PAH to Eliza Pike, July 21, 1867, GPAHP; Clara Anthony (Reed) to PAH, June 9, no year, GPAHP; PAH, January 2, 1866, PAHD; PAH, January 7, 1866, PAHD.

68. PAH to Eliza Pike, September 15, 1867, GPAHP; PAH to Eliza Pike, June 19, 1867, GPAHP; Herndl, *Invalid Women*, 37; Sears, *Sacred Places*, 6; PAH to Eliza Pike, July 21, 1867, GPAHP; PAH to Eliza Pike, November 18, 1866, GPAHP.

69. PAH to George Hearst, June 29, 1873, GPAHP; Ryan, *Cradle of the Middle Class*; Smith, "Feminism in Victorian America," 40; Golden, *Social History of Wet Nursing in America*, 39, 41; PAH to Eliza Pike, February 20, 1867, GPAHP; Dye and Smith, "Mother Love and Infant Death," 333, 343.

70. Herndl, *Invalid Women*, 25; PAH to Eliza Pike, February 20, 1867, GPAHP; PAH to Eliza Pike, September 15, 1867, GPAHP; PAH to Eliza Pike, July 5, 1868, GPAHP; PAH to Eliza Pike, January 8, 1869, GPAHP; PAH to Eliza Pike, June 19, 1867, GPAHP.

71. PAH to Eliza Pike, September 1866, GPAHP; Johnston, *Feminism and the Family in America*; George Hearst to PAH, December 11, 1867, GPAHP; PAH to George Hearst, July 5, 1868, GPAHP; PAH to Eliza Pike, January 26, 1870, GPAHP; PAH to Eliza Pike, August 8, 1870, GPAHP; PAH to Eliza Pike, May 8, 1870, GPAHP; PAH to Eliza Pike, August 8, 1870, GPAHP; PAH to Eliza

Pike, May 22, 1871, GPAHP; PAH to Eliza Pike, May 26, 1871(?), GPAHP; PAH to Eliza Pike, January 8, 1871, GPAHP; PAH to George Hearst, July 28, 1873, GPAHP; PAH to George Hearst, June 29, 1873, GPAHP; PAH to George Hearst, November 21, 1873, GPAHP; Riley, *Female Frontier*, 82, 51.

72. PAH to George Hearst, June 29, 1873, GPAHP; PAH to Eliza Pike, December 27, 1875, GPAHP; PAH to Eliza Pike, January 26, 1870, GPAHP; PAH to Eliza Pike, May 8, 1870, GPAHP; PAH to Eliza Pike, August 8, 1870, GPAHP; PAH to Eliza Pike, September 1866, GPAHP; PAH to Eliza Pike, May 22, 1871, GPAHP.

73. PAH to Eliza Pike, September 15, 1867, GPAHP; PAH to Eliza Pike, May 8, 1870, GPAHP; PAH to George Hearst, n.d., GPAHP.

2. MONEY

1. Bourdieu, *Distinction*, 53–54. Editor Randal Johnson states: "Bourdrieu defines cultural capital as a form of knowledge, an internalized code or a cognitive acquisition which equips the social agent with empathy toward, appreciation for or competence in deciphering cultural relations and cultural artefacts." See Bourdieu, *Field of Cultural Production*, 7.

2. PAH to Eliza Pike, August 28, 1871, GPAHP; George Hearst to PAH, December 18, 1871, GPAHP; Hilkey, *Character Is Capital*, 5, 164; PAH to Eliza Pike, November 18, 1866, GPAHP; PAH to Eliza Pike, November 13, 1870, GPAHP; PAH to Eliza Pike, August 28, 1871, GPAHP.

3. George Hearst to PAH, December 18, 1871, GPAHP; Issel and Cherny, *San Francisco, 1865–1932*, 23–24; Bonfils, *Life and Personality of Phoebe Apperson Hearst*, 20; Brooks, "Phoebe Apperson Hearst," part 1, chap. 3, p. 14.

4. PAH to Eliza Pike, August 10, 1872, GPAHP.

5. PAH to Eliza Pike, August 10, 1872, GPAHP; Watson, *San Francisco Society*, 9–11, 23–26.

6. Watson, *San Francisco Society*, 9–11, 23–26; Brooks, "Phoebe Apperson Hearst," part 1, chap. 3, p. 16; Bonfils, *Life and Personality of Phoebe Apperson Hearst*, 22; Hemphill, *Bowing to Necessities*, 152, 151; PAH to Eliza Pike, January 8, 1869, GPAHP; PAH to Eliza Pike, June 20, 1869, GPAHP; PAH to Eliza Pike, January 26, 1870, GPAHP.

7. PAH to Eliza Pike, August 28, 1871, GPAHP; PAH to Eliza, August 10, 1872, GPAHP; Phoebe Apperson Hearst, PAHD; Allgor, *Parlor Politics*; Berglund, *Making San Francisco*, 31–32; Watson, *San Francisco Society*, 10, 25. Also invitations and guest lists in GPAHP; PAH to Eliza Pike, June 20, 1869, GPAHP; PAH to Eliza Pike, September 15, 1867, GPAHP; PAH to Eliza Pike, January 8, 1869, GPAHP.

8. PAH to Eliza Pike, September 15, 1867, GPAHP; PAH to Eliza Pike, August 10, 1872, GPAHP.

9. PAH to Eliza Pike, September 15, 1867, GPAHP.

10. PAH to Eliza Pike, August 10, 1872, GPAHP; PAH to Eliza Pike, February 8, 1873, GPAHP.

11. PAH to Eliza Pike, August 10, 1872, GPAHP; PAH to Eliza Pike, February 8, 1873, GPAHP; PAH to Eliza Pike, September 26, 1873, GPAHP; Gustafson, *Eloquence Is Power*, xiii–xxv.

12. PAH to Eliza Pike, August 10, 1872, December 10, 1873, GPAHP; PAH to Eliza Pike, February 8, 1873, GPAHP; PAH to George Hearst, June 5, 1873, GPAHP; Kelley, *Learning to Stand and Speak*, 109.

13. Brooks, "Phoebe Apperson Hearst," part 1, chap. 3, 20–21; Sears, *Sacred Places*, 4–5; PAH to George Hearst, July 14, 1868, GPAHP; PAH to Eliza Pike, August 10, 1872, GPAHP; Peter Toft to George Hearst, June 9(?) 1873, GPAHP; PAH to Eliza Pike, February 8, 1873, GPAHP; PAH to Eliza Pike, September 26, 1873, GPAHP.

14. Sewell, *Women and the Everyday City*, 60; Sparks, *Capital Intentions*, 9, 172–73, 174, 205; Hilkey, *Character Is Capital*, 5; PAH to George Hearst, July 14, 1868, GPAHP; PAH to Eliza Pike, February 10, 1869, GPAHP; PAH to George Hearst, July 14, 1868, GPAHP; PAH to Eliza Pike, February 10, 1869, GPAHP; PAH to Eliza Pike, August 10, 1872, GPAHP; PAH to George Hearst, June 29, 1873, GPAHP.

15. George Hearst to PAH, March 31, 1873, GPAHP; Burkhardt et al., *Concise Dictionary of American Biography*, 382, 1052–53; PAH to George Hearst, ca. 1873, GPAHP.

16. PAH to George Hearst, July 28, 1873, GPAHP; Scott, "Almira Lincoln Phelps," 91; PAH to George Hearst, ca. 1873, GPAHP; Heilbrun, *Writing a Woman's Life*, 13.

17. PAH to George Hearst, July 28, 1873, GPAHP; PAH to George Hearst, June 29, 1873, GPAHP; George Hearst, *Autobiography*, 6.

18. PAH to Eliza Pike, February 8, 1873, GPAHP; PAH to George Hearst, March 23, 1873, GPAHP; PAH to George Hearst, n.d., attached to April 15, 1873, GPAHP.

19. PAH to George Hearst, March 25, 1873, GPAHP; PAH to Eliza Pike, March 17, 1873, GPAHP; PAH to Eliza Pike, April 13, 1873, GPAHP; Rodgers, *Atlantic Crossings*, 3, 108; Hyde, *American Vision*, 107–10, 10, 15; MacCannell, *New Theory of the Leisure Class*, 5; PAH to George Hearst, ca. 1873, GPAHP; PAH to George Hearst, June 29, 1873, GPAHP; Aron, *Working at Play*, 49, 134, 136, 140.

20. Brooks, "Phoebe Apperson Hearst," part 1, chap. 4, p. 22, GPAHP; PAH to Eliza Pike, April 13, 1873, GPAHP; PAH to George Hearst, April 1, 1873, GPAHP; Levine, *Highbrow/Lowbrow*; PAH to George Hearst, April 15, 1873, GPAHP; PAH to George Hearst, n.d., ca. 1873, GPAHP.

21. Aron, *Working at Play*, 53; Levenstein, *Seductive Journey*, 125.

22. PAH, January 1, 1866, PAHD; Ratner, Kaufman, and Teeter Jr., *Paradoxes of Prosperity*, 1, 2, 69; Horowitz, *Morality of Spending*, xxvi, xi; PAH to Eliza Pike, July 2, 1865, GPAHP; PAH to Eliza Pike, January 26, 1870, GPAHP; W. E. Vaughan to Millicent Hearst, September 29, 1916, PAH note on back, GPAHP.

23. PAH to George Hearst, May 11, 1873, June 15, 1873, and August 16, 1873, GPAHP.

24. PAH to George Hearst, June 15, 1873, GPAHP; Ratner, Kaufman, and Teeter Jr., *Paradoxes of Prosperity*, 1.

25. PAH to George Hearst, June 5, 1873, May 17, 1873, June 15, 1873, and July 28, 1879, GPAHP.

26. PAH to Eliza Pike, December 10, 1873, GPAHP. On the difficulties Americans have in facing up to class, see Benjamin DeMott, *Imperial Middle*.

27. PAH to George Hearst, September 2, 1873, GPAHP; PAH to Eliza Pike, September 26, 1873, GPAHP. On 2014 terms of purchasing power, see www .measuringworth.com/uscompare/relativevalue.php.

28. PAH to George Hearst, May 11, 1873, GPAHP.

29. PAH to George Hearst, June 5, 1873, GPAHP; PAH to Eliza Pike, June 29, 1873, GPAHP.

30. PAH to George Hearst, August 16, 1873, GPAHP; PAH to George Hearst, June 29, 1873, GPAHP.

31. Horowitz, *Morality of Spending*, xvii, 10; PAH to Eliza Pike, December 10, 1873, GPAHP; PAH to George Hearst, June 15, 1873, GPAHP; Brooks, "Phoebe Apperson Hearst," part 1, chap. 4, p. 24, GPAHP; Stowe, *Going Abroad*, xii, 29, 34; Trease, *Grand Tour*, 3, 5; Richards, "Introduction: Culture and Tourism in Europe," 5; Aron, *Working at Play*, 128, 130.

32. PAH to George Hearst, June 5, 1873, GPAHP.

33. Kelley, *Stand and Speak*; PAH to George Hearst, June 15, 1873, GPAHP; PAH to George Hearst, June 29, 1873, GPAHP; PAH to George Hearst, June 30, 1873, GPAHP; PAH to George Hearst, July 13, 1873, GPAHP; PAH to George Hearst, September 26, 1873, GPAHP; Horowitz, "Nous Autres," 68–95, esp. 69, 95.

34. PAH to George Hearst, June 5, 1873, GPAHP; PAH to Eliza Pike, September 26, 1873, GPAHP; PAH to George Hearst, August 16, 1873, GPAHP; PAH to George Hearst, June 29, 1873, GPAHP; PAH to George Hearst, July 13, 1873, GPAHP; PAH to George Hearst, December 3, 1873, GPAHP; Stowe, *Going Abroad*, 29, xi. Bourdieu, *Distinction*, 53–54; Bourdieu, *Field of Cultural Production*, 7. Also Aron, *Working at Play*, 2, 6, 9.

35. PAH to George Hearst, July 28, 1873, GPAHP; PAH to Eliza Pike, September 26, 1873, GPAHP; PAH to George Hearst, December 3, 1873, GPAHP.

36. Adam, *Buying Respectability*, 14; PAH to George Hearst, May 11, 1873, June 15, 1873, June 29, 1873, August 16, 1873, September 26, 1873, May 11, 1873, and May 17, 1873, GPAHP.

37. PAH to George Hearst, June 5, 1873, GPAHP.

38. PAH to George Hearst, August 16, 1873, GPAHP.

39. PAH to George Hearst, June 5, 1873, GPAHP.

40. PAH to George Hearst, August 16, 1873, GPAHP.

41. PAH to George Hearst, May 11, 1873, and August 16, 1873, GPAHP.

42. PAH to George Hearst, June 29, 1873, and August 23, 1873, GPAHP.

43. PAH to Eliza Pike, September 26, 1873, GPAHP; PAH to George Hearst, June 5, 1873, GPAHP; George Hearst to PAH, October 4, 1873, GPAHP; PAH

to Eliza Pike, December 10, 1873, GPAHP; PAH to Eliza Pike, February 10, 1874, GPAHP; George Hearst to PAH, February 28, 1874, and March 23, 1874, GPAHP; PAH to Eliza Pike, September 1, 1874, GPAHP; PAH to Eliza Pike, September 26, 1874, GPAHP; PAH to George Hearst, October 25, 1874, GPAHP; PAH to Eliza Pike, October 26, 1874, GPAHP; PAH to Eliza Pike, December 27, 1875, GPAHP.

44. Rydell, *All the World's a Fair*, 17, 11, 35–36; Aron, *Working at Play*, 150.

45. PAH to George Hearst, September 30, 1876, GPAHP; Rydell, *All the World's a Fair*, 2–8, 10, chap. 1, 3; Beers, "Centennial City," 466, 467, 470.

46. PAH to George Hearst, September 30, 1876, GPAHP; Boisseau and Markwyn, *Gendering the Fair*, 4, 8; Darney, "Women and World's Fairs," 14–22, 38, 46; Bourdieu, *Distinction*, 2, 53–54.

47. PAH to George Hearst, September 30, 1876, GPAHP; Rydell, *All the World's a Fair*, 2–8, chap. 1, 3; Markwyn, *Gendering the Fair*, 4, 8; Darney, "Women and World's Fairs," 14–22, 38, 46; Bourdieu, *Distinction*, 2, 53–54; Beers, "Centennial City," 466, 467, 470; "Nation's Centennial," *New York Times*, May 11, 1876, 1; Matthews, "Forging a Cosmopolitan Civic Culture," 211–34, 214; Weimann, *Fair Women*, 1–4; Shapiro, *Child's Garden*, 65, 66; Fletcher and Welton, *Froebel's Chief Writings*, 1–30; Dr. Silas Reed to PAH, March 24, 1886, RGA; PAH to Eliza Pike, September 24, 1876, GPAHP.

48. "Mail Steamers Saloon," September 11, 1878, *Personalia*, Miscellaneous, GPAHP; Bonfils, *Life and Personality of Phoebe Apperson Hearst*, 51; Albert Shumate, *A Visit to Rincon Hill and South Park: San Francisco's Early Fashionable Neighborhood*, pamphlet, San Francisco, 1963, 3; Brooks, "Phoebe Apperson Hearst," part 1, chap. 5, p. 31; University of California, *Commencement Programs, 1862–1903*, July 22, 1874, UCARCH.

49. Bremner, "Scientific Philanthropy," 172, 168, 169; Himmelfarb, *Poverty and Compassion*, 4–5, books 3, 4; PAH to George Hearst, GPAHP; Thomas Barry Diary, TBD.

50. From Thomas Barry's diary, May 1879, and May 31, June 2, June 3, June 6, June 7, June 9, June 12, June 15, June 18, June 23, June 25–July 2, July 7, July 12, August 12, 1879, TBD; PAH to George Hearst, August 23, 1873, GPAHP; Matthews, "Forging a Cosmopolitan Civic Culture."

51. Brooks, "Phoebe Apperson Hearst," part 1, chap. 5, pp. 31, 32; PAH, January 20, 1882, Pocket Diary, GPAHP; from Thomas Barry's diary, June 5, 1879, TBD; Mackaman, *Leisure Settings*, esp. 1, 2, 6, 127, 133, 134.

52. Bonfils, *Life and Personality of Phoebe Apperson Hearst*, 53; Jensen and Lothrop, *California Women*, 45, 46.

53. Brooks, "Phoebe Apperson Hearst," handwritten copy, chap. 1, p. 13; PAH letter on her employees, n.d., GPAHP.

54. Baltzell, *Protestant Establishment*, 127; Kit and Frederica Konolige, *Power of Their Glory*, 9; William Randolph Hearst to PAH, ca. 1879 WRH 131, Letters and Telegrams to His Parents, 1878–79, WRH; Baltzell, *Philadelphia Gentleman*; *Elite Directory for San Francisco and Oakland*, 47; Decker, *Fortunes and Failures*, 232–33.

55. Brooks, "Phoebe Apperson Hearst," part 1, chap. 5, p. 36. People like Peter Toft, a European artist, wrote to P. A. Hearst, rather than George, for money and about philanthropic work after June 1873. See Peter [Peterson] Toft, June 3, 1873, and additional letters in GPAHP.

56. In "incomplete Letters-Correspondence unidentified"—"is full of fizz," fragments of letters, n.d., GPAHP; PAH, January 1, 2, 9, 11, 12, 14, 18, 20, 1882, Pocket Diary, 1882, GPAHP; Swanberg, *Citizen Hearst*, 10.

57. William R. Hearst to PAH, August 29, 1899, WRH Letters, fifteen letters and telegrams to his mother, 1898–99, WRH Papers.

58. Tilly and Gurin, introduction to *Women, Politics, and Change*, 7, 28; Lebsock, "Women and American Politics," 35–62, esp. 37. Also E. Freedman, "Separatism as Strategy," 512–29; Kelley, *Stand and Speak*, 8; Muncy, *Creating a Female Dominion*, esp. chap. 1; Lloyd, *Beyond Identity Politics*, 4; Cronon, Miles, and Gitlin, *Under an Open Sky*, 7.

59. Watson, *San Francisco Society*, 28–9; Maffly-Kipp, *Religion and Society in Frontier California*, chap. 6; Pascoe, *Relations of Rescue*, chaps. 1–2; Bordin, *Woman and Temperance*, 102; PAH to George Hearst, August 23, 1873, GPAHP; PAH to Ada Butterfield, August 17, 1886, GPAHP; PAH to Eliza Pike, December 10, 1873, GPAHP; Thomas Barry, June 11, 1879, 25, 26, TBD; Tyack and Hansot, *Learning Together*, 95–96. On the shared nonpartisan political interests of women and men in voluntary associations, see Lansing, "'Women Are Voluntarily Organizing Themselves.'"

60. Brooks, "Phoebe Apperson Hearst," handwritten copy, part 1, chap. 1, pp. 4–5, GPAHP; Ralph Gregory, "Founders Day Address," February 14, 1964, RGA. A replica of the log cabin school Phoebe E. Apperson attended is located at the Phoebe Apperson Hearst Historical Society in St. Clair, Missouri. Also E. Freedman, "Separatism as Strategy"; Tyack and Hansot, *Learning Together*.

61. De Cos, *History and Development of Kindergarten in California*, 7, 8, 9, 51n10; Hopkins, *Concise Dictionary of American Biography*, 921–22; *Pioneers of the Kindergarten Movement in America*, 8–10, 271–72, 285–86, 288.

62. *Pioneers of the Kindergarten Movement in America*, 8–10, 271–72, 275, 285–86, 288; Sarah B. Cooper to PAH, June 3, 1889, GPAHP; Jackson Street Kindergarten, "Constitution, Article II," 45; Sarah B. Cooper, "The Kindergarten as a Child-Saving Work," in Golden Gate Kindergarten Association, *Fifth Annual Report*, Phoebe Apperson Hearst Preschool Learning Center Archives, San Francisco CA, 7, 18–19, 20, 21, 23; Ward, "Phoebe Apperson Hearst's Influence on the Kindergarten Movement," 50–54; "The Kindergarten," *Union Signal*, March 27, 1890, 8; Golden Gate Kindergarten Association, "Constitution and By-Laws of the Golden Gate Kindergarten Association," *Golden Gate Kindergarten Association Annual Reports*, Phoebe Apperson Hearst Preschool Learning Center Archives, San Francisco CA, 1; Ross, *Kindergarten Crusade*, 26, 35.

63. Jacklin, "Sarah Brown Ingersoll Cooper," 1:380–82; de Cos, *History and Development of Kindergarten in California*, 9; Golden Gate Kindergarten Association, *Fifth Annual Report*, 23; Allen, "Spiritual Motherhood," 323, 319, 327, 335; Nickliss, "Phoebe Apperson Hearst's 'Gospel of Wealth,'" 575–605; Feinstein, "Kindergartens, Feminism, and the Professionalization of Motherhood," 28–38; Sarah B. Cooper, "The Kindergarten," February 18, 1893, Huntington Library, San Marino CA.

64. Bordin, *Frances Willard*, chaps. 9, 11; Bordin, *Woman and Temperance*, 3, 179n2.

65. Golden Gate Kindergarten Association, *Eleventh Annual Report*, 34; Golden Gate Kindergarten Association, *Fifth Annual Report*, 4, 69; Kerber, "Constitutional Right To Be Treated Like Ladies," 20, 24; Hayden, *Grand Domestic Revolution*; Deutsch, *Women and the City*, esp. 22, 24; Sarah B. Cooper to PAH, October 28, 1889, GPAHP.

66. PAH to Sarah B. Cooper, July 6, 1891, GPAHP; Edward H. Clark to Sarah B. Cooper, December 16, 1895, GPAHP; Sarah B. Cooper to PAH, June 3, 1889, GPAHP; Sarah B. Cooper to PAH, April 2, 1890, GPAHP; letters to and from Sarah B. Cooper and PAH, SBCP; Golden Gate Kindergarten Association, *Fifth Annual Report*, 4; Golden Gate Kindergarten Association, *Decade Report*, 42, 164–65; Sarah B. Cooper to PAH, February 8, 1890, GPAHP; Sarah B. Cooper to PAH, August 21, 1889, GPAHP.

67. PAH to Ada Butterfield, August 17, 1886, GPAHP; PAH to Sarah B. Cooper, July 6, 1891, SBCP; PAH to Sarah B. Cooper, December 16, 1895, SBCP; Allen, "Spiritual Motherhood," 327, 323; Bancroft, *Chronicles of the Builders*, 2:378, 379; Glenn, *Unequal Freedom*, 59; Bancroft, *Chronicles of the Builders*. By 1906 Hearst's gifts to the GGKA exceeded eighty thousand dollars. See the Golden Gate Kindergarten Association *Annual Reports*, 1884–1906, PAH Preschool Learning Center Archives, San Francisco. Also Roland, "California Kindergarten Movement"; Feinstein, "Kindergartens, Feminism, and the Professionalization of Motherhood," 30; "Rules for the Phoebe A. Hearst Kindergartens by P. A. Hearst," GPAHP, 1–7.

68. Sarah B. Cooper to PAH, August 21, 1889, GPAHP; Sarah B. Cooper to PAH, October 28, 1889, GPAHP; Sarah B. Cooper to PAH, April 4, 1893, GPAHP; Sarah B. Cooper to PAH, March 24, 1896, GPAHP; Emma Marwedel to PAH, December 17, 1889, GPAHP; Tyack and Hansot, *Learning Together*, 95–110, 112; GGKA, "Golden Gate Kindergarten Association Constitution and By-Laws, Article I," *GGKA Annual Reports*, 1:1; "Constitution and By-Laws, Article VII," *GGKA Annual Reports*, 1:4; Roland, "California Kindergarten Movement," 13; Kipp, *Religion and Society in Frontier California*, chap. 6; Lerner, "New Approaches to the Study of Women," 354; GGKA, "Constitution and By-Laws of the Golden Gate Kindergarten Association," *Annual Reports*, vol. 1; GGKA, *Fifth Annual Report*; P. Baker, "Domestication of Politics," 620–47; PAH to George Hearst, September 16, 1889, GPAHP; Golden Gate Kindergarten Association, *Decade Report*; Ross, *Kindergarten Crusade*, chap. 2, 52; Vandewalker, *Kindergarten in American Education*, 48.

69. Bancroft, *Biography of George Hearst*, 379; de Cos, *History and Development of Kindergarten in California*, 15; "A Noble Charity," *Daily Evening Post*, December 24, 1883, original newspaper clipping in author's possession; Sarah

B. Cooper to PAH, July 23, 1888, GPAHP; Jaher, *Urban Establishment*, 5; Jane Lathrop Stanford to PAH, January 4, 1893, GPAHP; Blow, "Kindergarten Education," 3; Ross, "Susan Blow," 1:181–82.

70. Bordin, *Frances Willard*, 126; Frances F. Cleveland to PAH, March 13, 1888, GPAHP; Allen, "Gender, Professionalization," 119; Westbrook, *John Dewey and American Democracy*, 9, 24–27, 93–111.

71. Boylan, "Claiming Visibility," 20; Deutsch, *Women and the City*, 20, 22, 24; Hayden, *Grand Domestic Revolution*, 11, 129, 156, 165; Gullett, *Becoming Citizens*, 30. Hearst contributed about $80,000 by 1906 to the GGKA. See Roland, "California Kindergarten Movement," 97.

72. PAH (Ada Butterfield writing for Phoebe) to William R. Hearst, April, 23, 1884, GPAHP; PAH to [George Hearst], GPAHP; Duffin, "Conspicuous Consumptive," 26–55; Veblen, *Theory of the Leisure Class*, chap. 3, esp. 36; Herndl, *Invalid Women*, 25; Morantz, "Making Women Modern," 491–507, esp. 494–95; Jefferis and Nichols, *Search Lights on Health*, 7, 9, 18.

73. Haber, *Quest for Authority and Honor*.

74. Morantz-Sanchez, *Sympathy and Science*, 90–100; Walsh, *"Doctors Wanted,"* xvi.

75. Haller, *History of American Homeopathy*, xi; Kaufman, *Homeopathy in America*, 23–24, 27; Register of the California Homeopathic Institutions Records, 1884–1984, RCHIR, 2, 3; California Homeopathic Institutions, "Schedule of Lectures of the Hahnemann Medical College," carton 2, RCHIR; Vogel, *Invention of the Modern Hospital*, 1.

76. Burrow, *Organized Medicine in the Progressive Era*, 72, 73, 87; M. Kaufman, *Homeopathy in America*, 9, x, chap. 2, 23–27, 30, chap. 5, 62, 64; Haller, *History of American Homeopathy*, 69.

77. Sara A. D. McKee to Dr. G. M. Pease, October 10, 1882, GPAHP; *Langley's San Francisco Directory Year Commencing 1883* (San Francisco: Francis, Valentine, 1883); 207, San Francisco History Center, San Francisco Public Library, http://archive.org/stream/langleyssanfranc1883sanf, accessed September 4, 2015; Morantz-Sanchez, *Sympathy and Science*, chap. 4. A central philosophy of homeopaths was "'like cures like'; the theory that each disease may be cured by the application of a drug which causes in a healthy person symptoms similar to those of the disease." Homeopaths opposed the bleeding and purging methods of medical school–trained physicians and supported the

balanced, ordered structure of nature and preventative and medical reform. They also promoted "the healing power of nature and the non-intervention of physicians." See Rogers, "Proper Place of Homeopathy," 181n3; California Homeopathic Institutions, "Facts Figures and Faces; Hahnemann Medical College of the Pacific," carton 2, RCHIR; Sara A. D. McKee to Dr. G. M. Pease, October 10, 1882, GPAHP; Register of the California Homeopathic Institutions Records, 1884–1984, RCHIR, 3; Sara A. D. McKee to Dr. Currier, copy of letter written in March 1883, GPAHP; Walsh, *"Doctors Wanted,"* 148; M. Kaufmann, *Homeopathy in America*, 110, 143, 145; Sander, *Mary Elizabeth Garrett*, 154, 153.

78. Sara A. D. McKee to Dr. Currier, copy of letter written in March 1883, GPAHP; *Langley's San Francisco Directory for the Year Commencing April 1883* (San Francisco: Francis, Valentine, 1883), 207, San Francisco History Center, San Francisco Public Library, accessed August 8, 2011, http://archive.org/stream/langleyssanfranc1883sanf; Register of California Homeopathic Institutions Records, 1884, 2; Leach, *True Love and Perfect Union*, 3, 4.

79. Sara A. D. McKee to Dr. Currier, copy of letter written in March 1883, GPAHP; John Gilbert Follansbee to PAH, January 2, 1883, GPAHP; Lida Nordhoff to PAH, n.d., GPAHP.

80. Sara A. D. McKee to Dr. Currier, copy of letter written in March 1883, GPAHP; California Homeopathic Institutions, "Schedule of Lectures of the Hahnemann Medical College," carton 2, RCHIR.

81. PAH to Drs. Eckel, Pease, Ledyard, Davis, Schreck, Canner, Palmer, Albertson, Currier, French, Worthy, Peterson, and Curtis, November 10, 1883, GPAHP; Sara A. D. McKee to Dr. Currier, copy of letter written in March 1883, GPAHP; Taber and Prindle, "College Physicians and Surgeons of San Francisco," 67; PAH to Dr. J. N. Eckel, n.d., GPAHP.

82. Sara A. D. McKee to Dr. Currier, copy of letter written in March 1883, GPAHP; PAH to Drs. Eckel, Pease, Ledyard, Davis, Schreck, Canner, Palmer, Albertson, Currier, French, Worthy, Peterson, and Curtis, November 10, 1883, GPAHP; Taber and Prindle, "College Physicians and Surgeons of San Francisco," 67; PAH to Dr. J.N. Eckel, n.d., GPAHP; Sara A. D. McKee, August 6, 1883, Minutes of the Board of Directors Meeting of the Homeopathic Hospital, GPAHP.

83. Nasaw, *Life of William Randolph Hearst*, 58; John Gilbert Follansbee to PAH, January 14, 1884, GPAHP; Follansbee to PAH, January 22, 1884, GPAHP; Follansbee to PAH, February 2, 1884, GPAHP; PAH to William R. Hearst, April 20, 1884, GPAHP; PAH to William R. Hearst, April 23, 1884, GPAHP.

84. Williams, *Democratic Party and California Politics 1880–1896*, 24–25.

85. PAH to William R. Hearst, March 14, 1889, GPAHP; Swanberg, *Citizen Hearst*, 30–32, 39; Robinson, *Hearsts: An American Dynasty*, 190; William R. Hearst to PAH, May 5, 1884, GPAHP; Lady Waterlow to Peter Toft, May 14, 1884, GPAHP. There is disagreement over exactly what pranks Will engaged in that antagonized Harvard's administration and faculty. Swanberg indicated Will sent a messenger to "the home of each of his instructors, leaving a large package which, when opened, proved to contain a chamber pot with the recipient's name lettered on the inside bottom." Edward Hardy Clark, a family relative and one of Phoebe Hearst's business managers, recounted Will was thrown out of Harvard for squirting professors with soda water. See Swanberg, *Citizen Hearst*, 39, and Clark, *Reminiscences of the Hearst Family*, 7.

86. PAH to Will (in Ada Butterfield's writing), April 23, 1884, GPAHP; PAH to Will (in Ada Butterfield's writing), April 30, 1884, GPAHP; PAH to William R. Hearst, May 5, 1884, GPAHP; PAH to Will, November 10, 1884, GPAHP; Will to PAH, October 4, 1885, GPAHP; PAH to George Hearst, January 4, 1885, GPAHP; PAH to George Hearst, October 22, 1885, GPAHP; William R. Hearst to PAH, 1885, GPAHP; PAH to George Hearst, October 28, 1885, GPAHP; PAH to George Hearst, November 12, 1885, GPAHP; William R. Hearst to PAH, 1885, GPAHP; Nasaw, *Life of William Randolph Hearst*, 43, 57.

87. PAH to Jennie (Peck?), April 15, 1885, PC; Morantz, "Making Women Modern," 491–507; PAH (Ada Butterfield writing for Hearst) to William R. Hearst, April 23, 1884, GPAHP; PAH to William R. Hearst, May 5, 1884, GPAHP; PAH to William R. Hearst, May 12, 1884, GPAHP; University of California, Organic Act of 1868, "Prospectus of the University of California," 5–34; Hall, *Organization of American Culture*, 1; Stadtman, *Centennial Record of the University of California*, 52.

88. Williams, *Democratic Party and California Politics*, 97–98; Robinson, *Hearsts*, 185–86; California Legislature, *Senate; Twenty-Seventh Session*, in Senate, Senate Chambers, January 18, 1887, GPAHP.

89. Mitchell, "Backward Art of Spending Money," 269–81; Zunz, *Philanthropy in America*, 1.

90. "How to Spend Money; Mrs. Hearst of California," From the *Illustrated American*, n.d.

3. POLITICAL AGENDA

1. PAH to George Hearst, October 22, 1885, GPAHP; PAH to Hannah, List and Special List, November 29, 1893, GPAHP.

2. Nickliss, "Phoebe Apperson Hearst's 'Gospel of Wealth,'" 575–605; Ryan, "Power of Women's Networks," 66–85.

3. PAH to Orrin Peck, December 22, 1886, PC; PAH to George Hearst, September 28, 1889, GPAHP; Nasaw, *Life of William Randolph Hearst*, 56; Swanberg, *Citizen Hearst*, 37–38. Swanberg stated that Phoebe Hearst provided a financial incentive to get Calhoun to go away. Swanberg relied on Annie Apperson Flint, Phoebe's niece, for this information. One historian has implied that Flint had an axe to grind where Phoebe Hearst was concerned. See Robinson, *Hearsts*, 385. Also PAH to Margaret Peck, n.d., PC.

4. Yeo, *Contest for Social Science*, 184, 185; Fellman and Fellman, *Making Sense of Self*, 10.

5. Jacob, *Capital Elites*, 125; Mary W. Kincaid to PAH, n.d., GPAHP; PAH to Orrin Peck, December 22, 1886, PC.

6. Dahlgren, *Etiquette of Social Life in Washington*, 53; Carpenter, *Carp's Washington*, chap. 10; Jacob, *Capital Elites*, 125, 177, 178.

7. Flack, *Desideratum in Washington*, vii. On scandals, political corruption, competitive elections, and the "spoils system" in Washington DC, see Lessoff, *Nation and Its City*, esp. chap. 6. Also PAH to Orrin Peck, December 22, 1886, PC.

8. PAH to Orrin Peck, December 22, 1886, PC; Mary W. Kincaid to PAH, n.d., GPAHP; PAH to Will, May 5 and May 12, 1884, GPAHP.

9. PAH to Orrin Peck, December 22, 1886, PC; Bremner, *From the Depths*, chaps. 2–4.

10. PAH to Orrin Peck, December 22, 1886, PC; Yeo, *Contest for Social Science*, 142; Bremner, *From the Depths*, chap. 2.

11. PAH to Orrin Peck, December 22, 1886, PC; Bremner, *From the Depths*, chaps. 2–4; Yeo, *Contest for Social Science*, 142; PAH to Mrs. Hester Holden, September 7, 1892, GPAHP; Elizabeth A. Apperson to PAH, July 14, 1895, GPAHP.

12. PAH to Orrin Peck, December 22, 1886, PC; PAH to Margaret Peck, n.d., PC.

13. Phoebe Hearst, January 21, 1866, PAHD; "A Californian in Washington," *New York Sun*, February 23, 1890; Morantz, "Making Women Modern," 490. Also "A Californian in Washington," *New York Sun*, February 23, 1890, original newspaper clipping in author's possession, GPAHP.

14. Fellman and Fellman, *Making Sense of Self*, 10–11; Wiebe, *Search for Order*; PAH to Orrin Peck, December 22, 1886, PC.

15. Orrin Peck to Other Mother [PAH], January 9, 1885, GPAHP; PAH to Orrin Peck, December 22, 1886, PC; Carpenter, *Carp's Washington*, 92, 93; Dahlgren, *Etiquette of Social Life in Washington*, 3, 50; "A Californian in Washington," *New York Sun*, February 23, 1890.

16. PAH to Orrin Peck, December 22, 1886, PC; Dahlgren, *Etiquette of Social Life in Washington*, 50–54; Carpenter, *Carp's Washington*, 92; Jacob, *Capital Elites*, 125, 129, 73–74.

17. Carpenter, *Carp's Washington*, 93; "Dinners and Dinner-Givers," *New York World*, January 31, 1889, GPAHP; Jacob, *Capital Elites*, 173, 147. See GPAHP correspondence and guest lists for information on Hearst's high-society affairs.

18. Frances Benjamin Johnston, "Some Homes Under the Administration," *Demorest's Family Magazine* 26 (October 1890): 714–20; Goode, *Capital Losses*, 95; Gowans, *Styles and Types of North American Architecture*, xiv, xii; PAH to George Hearst, March 15, 1889, GPAHP; *Baltimore Sun*, May 9, 1890, GPAHP. The relative value in 1889 of $300,000, in terms of historic standard of living value in 2015 terms, is $7,970,000. See www.measuringworth.com.

19. Jacob, *Capital Elites*, 115; Dr. Silas Reed to PAH, March 24, 1886, RGA; Wright, *Moralism and the Model Home*, 12–13; Carpenter, *Carp's Washington*; Goode, *Capital Losses*, 96.

20. Gowans, *Styles and Types of North American Architecture*, 202; Longstreth, *On the Edge of the World*, 16–7.

21. R. Peterson, *Bonanza Rich*, chap. 3, esp. 73; "A Californian in Washington," *New York Sun*, February 23, 1890; PAH to Sarah B. Cooper, February 20,

1890, SBCP; "Dinners and Dinner-Givers," *New York World*, January 31, 1889, GPAHP; additional newspaper clippings in GPAHP.

22. "Society Events in Washington," *New York World*, February 20, 1889, GPAHP; Dahlgren, *Etiquette of Social Life in Washington*, 50, 51; "Dinners and Dinner-Givers," *New York World*, January 31, 1889, GPAHP; Carpenter, *Carp's Washington*, 87; Jacob, *Capital Elites*, 129.

23. Jacob, *Capital Elites*, 177–78; Dahlgren, *Etiquette of Social Life in Washington*, 13; "The Capital's Gay Gown," *New York World*, January 5, 1890; PAH to Orrin Peck, December 22, 1886, PC.

24. "Another Thursday House," *Free Press* (Burlington VT), February 7, 1889, GPAHP; Goode, *Capital Losses*, 114. Randal Johnson, ed. and introduction to Bourdieu, *Field of Cultural Production*, 7; Bourdieu, *Distinction*, 2, 53–54.

25. Berch, *Woman Behind the Lens*, 4, 143–49; Frances Benjamin Johnston, "Some Homes Under the Administration," *Demorest's Family Magazine* 36 (October 1890): 713–20.

26. "The Boston Advertiser Says," *Journal* (New Bedford MA), January 5, 1895; "Dinners and Dinner-Givers," *New York World*, January 31, 1889, GPAHP; *Illustrated American*, December 29, 1890, GPAHP; no author, no title, May 3, 1890, *Denver Union*, GPAHP; R. Peterson, *Bonanza Rich*, chap. 3; "A Californian in Washington," *New York Sun*, February 23, 1890, GPAHP.

27. Juliette M. Babbitt, "Mrs. Phoebe A. Hearst: Prominent Women in Washington's Social World," no magazine title, ca. 1895, original newspaper clipping in author's possession; Goode, *Capital Losses*, 114; Margaret Peck to PAH, January 9, 1888, GPAHP.

28. PAH to Orrin Peck, December 22, 1886, GPAHP; PAH to George Hearst, incomplete, n.d., GPAHP.

29. PAH to Sarah B. Cooper, June 17, 1889, SBCP.

30. PAH to Eliza Pike, June 25, 1864, GPAHP; PAH to Eliza Pike, September 1866, GPAHP; PAH to Eliza Pike, August 10, 1872, GPAHP; PAH to Eliza Pike, February 8, 1873, GPAHP; Issel and Cherny, *San Francisco, 1865–1932*, 81, 103–4; Ethington, *Public City*, 27; Bonfils, *Life and Personality of Phoebe Apperson Hearst*, 52–53; Lessoff, *Nation and Its City*.

31. Wiebe, *Search for Order*; Dahlgren, *Etiquette of Social Life in Washington*, 53–54; Goode, *Capital Losses*, 95; Mary W. Kincaid to PAH, January 23, 1888,

GPAHP; PAH to Sarah B. Cooper, June 17, 1889, SBCP; Aron, *Working at Play*; PAH to George Hearst, August 27, 1889, GPAHP; Chandler, *Biography of San Francisco State University*, 27.

32. Mary W. Kincaid to PAH, January 23, 1888, GPAHP; Mary W. Kincaid to PAH, February 23, 1890, GPAHP; Ethington, *Public City*, 342–43; Orrin Peck to PAH, n.d., ca. 1885, GPAHP; PAH to George Hearst, August 2, 1889, GPAHP; Margaret Peck to PAH, August 30, 1891, GPAHP; Mary W. Kincaid to PAH, October 13, 1891, GPAHP.

33. Mary W. Kincaid to PAH, April 15, 1886, GPAHP; PAH to George Hearst, August 6, 1889, GPAHP; PAH to Orrin Peck, April 8, 1896, PC.

34. Mary W. Kincaid to PAH, April 8, 1893, GPAHP; Mary W. Kincaid to George Hearst, August 28, 1889, GPAHP; Mary W. Kincaid to PAH, February 23, 1890, GPAHP; Mary W. Kincaid to PAH, February 7, 1886, GPAHP; Gettleman, "Charity and Social Classes," 313–14; San Francisco Board of Supervisors, "In Memoriam: Mary W. Kincaid," 949. Later, San Francisco mayor James D. Phelan appointed Kincaid a member of the San Francisco Board of Education in 1900. Mayor Edward R. Taylor reappointed her.

35. PAH to George Hearst, August 2, 1889, GPAHP; PAH to George Hearst, August 27, 1889, GPAHP; PAH to George Hearst, September 16, 1889, GPAHP; PAH to Mrs. Butterfield, August 17, 1886, GPAHP; PAH to Orrin Peck, December 22, 1886, GPAHP; PAH to Sarah B. Cooper, June 17, 1889, SBCP; Mary W. Kincaid to PAH, May 23, 1889, incomplete, GPAHP; Kincaid to PAH, July 2, 1889, incomplete, GPAHP; Aron, *Working at Play*, 3; Orrin Peck to PAH, n.d., ca. 1885, folder 3, GPAHP; Kincaid to PAH, n.d., GPAHP; PAH to Mrs. Holden, September 7, 1892, Letters to Members of the Holden Family, September 7, 1892–January 5, 1907, and n.d., GPAHP; Kincaid to PAH, January 12, 1889, incomplete, GPAHP.

36. Mary W. Kincaid to PAH, April 8, 1889, GPAHP; Kincaid to PAH, July 2, 1889, GPAHP; PAH to Sarah B. Cooper, June 17, 1889, SBCP; Cooper to PAH, July 29, 1889, GPAHP; Levenstein, *Seductive Journey*, 185; Virginia Knox Maddox to her mother, June 28, 1889, Knox Family Papers, California Historical Society, San Francisco.

37. PAH to Mrs. Holden, September 7, 1892, Letters to Members of the Holden Family, September 7, 1892, GPAHP; PAH to George Hearst, August 2, 1889,

GPAHP; Mary W. Kincaid to PAH, April 8, 1889, GPAHP; Mary Kincaid to PAH, May 23, 1889, GPAHP; Mary Kincaid to PAH, August 28, 1889, GPAHP; Mary Kincaid to PAH, July 2, 1889, incomplete, GPAHP; Orrin Peck to PAH, n.d., ca. 1885, folder 3, GPAHP; Lebsock, "Women and American Politics"; Ryan, "Power of Women's Networks," 66–85; PAH to Sarah B. Cooper, July 29, 1889, SBCP; Yeo, *Contest for Social Science*; Orrin Peck to PAH, n.d., ca. 1885, GPAHP; Rodgers, *Atlantic Crossings*.

38. PAH to Sarah B. Cooper, July 29, 1889, SBCP; Cremin, *American Education*, 278; Allen, "Spiritual Motherhood," 319–39.

39. PAH to Sara B. Cooper, July 29, 1889, SBCP; Allen, "Spiritual Motherhood," 325–26, 330; Allen, "Gender, Professionalization," 118.

40. PAH to Sarah B. Cooper, July 29, 1889, SBCP; Mary W. Kincaid to PAH, May 23, 1889, incomplete, SBCP; PAH to George Hearst, August 6, 1889, GPAHP; PAH to George Hearst, August 18, 1889, GPAHP; Mary W. Kincaid to PAH, July 2, 1889, incomplete, GPAHP. Also Cremin, *American Education*, 279; Mary W. Kincaid to PAH, July 2, 1889, incomplete, GPAHP; PAH to George Hearst, September 16, 1889, GPAHP; PAH to George Hearst, August 2, 1889, GPAHP; PAH to Mrs. Holden, September 7, 1892, Letters to Members of the Holden Family, September 7, 1892, GPAHP.

41. PAH to George Hearst, August 2, 1889, GPAHP; PAH to George Hearst, August 6, 1889, GPAHP; PAH to George Hearst, August 18, 1889, GPAHP.

42. Kunzel, *Fallen Women, Problem Girls*, 3; Sklar, "Historical Foundations of Women's Power," 43–93.

43. Mary W. Kincaid to PAH, April 8, 1889, GPAHP; Orrin Peck to PAH, undated letters, ca. 1885, folder 3, GPAHP; Kincaid to PAH, May 23, 1889, GPAHP. Both Hearst and Kincaid served the Century Club of California, San Francisco, and the GGKA. After Kincaid died on July 18, 1914, her remains were placed next to Phoebe A. Hearst's in the Hearst mausoleum in Cypress Lawn Cemetery in Colma, California. See San Francisco Board of Supervisors, "In Memoriam: Mary W. Kincaid," 949.

44. PAH to George Hearst, September 16, 1889, GPAHP; PAH to George Hearst, August 27, 1889, GPAHP; Kincaid to George Hearst, August 28, 1889, GPAHP; PAH to George Hearst, September 28, 1889, GPAHP.

45. Mary W. Kincaid to George Hearst, August 28, 1889, GPAHP; Mary W. Kincaid to PAH, September 23, 1889, GPAHP; DuBois, *Harriot Stanton Blatch*, 107.

46. Mary W. Kincaid to PAH, September 23, 1889, GPAHP; Veblen, *Theory of the Leisure Class*; Homberger, *Mrs. Astor's New York*, chap. 6; Davies, "Caroline Webster Schermerhorn Astor," 1:62–64.

47. PAH to George Hearst, August 27, 1889, GPAHP; PAH to George Hearst, September 16, 1889, GPAHP; Mary W. Kincaid to George Hearst, August 28, 1889, GPAHP; Kincaid to PAH, September 23, 1889, GPAHP.

48. Boylan, "Claiming Visibility," 17–40, esp. 19; Ryan, "Civil Society as Democratic Practice," 560; Ryan, "Gender and Public Access," 259–88, esp. 262; Habermas, *Structural Transformation of the Public Sphere*, 20; Habermas, "Hannah Arendt's Communications," 3, 4.

49. James, "Emma Jacobina Christiana Marwedel," 2:506–8; Emma Marwedel to PAH, December 17, 1889, GPAHP; PAH to Ada Butterfield, August 17, 1886, GPAHP; PAH to Sarah B. Cooper, January 31, 1890, GPAHP; Mary W. Kincaid to PAH, January 24, 1891, GPAHP; Orrin Peck to PAH, undated letters, ca. 1885, folder 3, GPAHP; Swift, *Emma Marwedel*; Ginzberg, "Moral Suasion Is Moral Balderdash," 601–22; Kincaid to PAH, January 24, 1891, GPAHP.

50. "A Noble Charity," *Daily Evening Post*, December 24, 1883; Sarah B. Cooper to PAH, July 23, 1888, GPAHP; Westbrook, *John Dewey and American Democracy*, ix, 24, 27, 93–111; Allen, "Gender, Professionalization," 119, 120; Roland, "California Kindergarten Movement," 24; Blow, "Kindergarten Education," 3, 4; Ross, "Susan Blow," 1:181–82. At the height of the GGKA's success in the 1880s and early 1890s, the association operated forty-one kindergartens, educated over thirty-one thousand students, and published more than eighty thousand annual reports. See Blow, "Kindergarten Education," 5.

51. Jane Lathrop Stanford to PAH, January 4, 1893, GPAHP; Roland, "California Kindergarten Movement," 97; Frances F. Cleveland to PAH, March 13, 1888, GPAHP; Bordin, *Frances Willard*, 126; Allen, "Spiritual Motherhood"; Boylan, *Origins of Women's Activism*, 54.

52. Woloch, *Class By Herself*, 1; Buhle, *Women and American Socialism*, 58–59; Newman, *White Women's Rights*, 86–87.

53. WEIU, *Report for Year Ending May 7, 1879*, 8; Women's Education Industrial Union, *First Annual Report, 1888–1889*, 25, 34–40, 9, 5; Tetrault, *Myth of Seneca Falls*, 92; Blair, *Clubwoman as Feminist*, 74, 79.

54. "A Business Woman: Lessons for Young Women from the Life of Mrs. Hearst," *New York Herald*, ca. January 16, 1895. See back of newspaper clipping for an estimated date of the newspaper. Also Newman, *White Women's Rights*, 86; Women's Educational and Industrial Union, *First Annual Report, 1888–1889*, 7, 10, 25, 31, 6.

55. Kessler-Harris, *Out to Work*, chap. 4, esp. 94–95; Murolo, *Common Ground of Womanhood*, 3; Newman, *White Women's Rights*, 98; WEIU, *First Annual Report, 1888–1889*, 5–10, 33; Anderson, "Work, Gender, and Power," 481–99; Bancroft, *Chronicle of the Builders*, 2:378–79.

56. Mary W. Kincaid to PAH, April 29, 1886, GPAHP; Pitkin, *Concept of Representation*.

57. WEIU, *First Annual Report of San Francisco* 9, 31; WEIU, *Second Annual Report, 1890–1891*, 17; WEIU, "Officers for 1891–92," *Third Annual Report, 1890–1892*, 16; Mme. Louise Sorbier, "Women's Work for Women in San Francisco," *San Francisco Call*, December 25, 1895, newspaper clipping, Louise Sorbier, Scrapbook, vol. 1 (San Francisco, 1897), California Historical Society; Gullett, *Becoming Citizens*, 47, 80; WEIU, *Fourth Annual Report, 1893*, 13, 15, 18.

58. WEIU, *First Annual Report, 1888–1889*, 33; WEIU, *Second Annual Report, 1891*, 10; Gullett, *Becoming Citizens*, 50; "The Ladies Kiss; War Is All Over at the Women's Union," *San Francisco Call*, May 9, 1893, 4; "Warring Women; The Old Administration Withdraws," *San Francisco Call*, May 10, 1893, 2; WEIU, *Sixth Annual Report, 1894*, 16; WEIU, *Seventh Annual Report, 1895*, 4; WEIU, *Tenth Annual Report, 1898*, 2.

59. Muncy, *Creating a Female Dominion*, xv. Muncy pointed out that at the dawn of the twentieth century "female professionals could succeed in satisfying their need for respect, autonomy, and effectiveness only at the expense of other women."

60. WEIU, *Sixth Annual Report, 1894*, 16; WEIU, *Seventh Annual Report, 1895*, 7; WEIU, *Tenth Annual Report, 1898*, 2.

61. Croly, *History of the Woman's Club Movement*, 250; Century Club of California, "Historical Sketch, List of Officers, etc.," GPAHP; Gullett, *Becoming Citizens*,

40; Brooks, "List to (A.S.B.) by Mrs. Clara R. Anthony of Boston, Made from a Conversation with Mrs. Hearst in May 12, 1896," "Phoebe Apperson Hearst," pp. 1–2; "Four years' Work, Constitution, and By Laws," Century Club of California, 1893, quotations on 3, 23, 25, 26, ccc.

62. Century Club of California, "Historical Sketch," 4, 5; Century Club of California, "Century Club of California," "List of Officers from September 22, 1888, to September 1, 1889," 9, 10, GPAHP; Century Club of San Francisco, Minutes of Members' Meetings, December 5, 1888, ccc, n.d., 1; Peter Toft to PAH, June 7, 1887, GPAHP; Century Club of California, "Report of First Vice-President, Fanny W. Bancroft," *Annual Reports for 1889–1890*, 8, ccc; Virginia S. Gibbons, "Phoebe Apperson Hearst," 1, ccc; Mary I. Wood, *History of the General Federation of Women's Clubs*; Houde, *Reaching Out*, chap. 1.

63. Virginia S. Gibbons, "Phoebe Apperson Hearst," 1, ccc.

64. Century Club of California, "Historical Sketch," GPAHP, 1, 5, 7; Virginia S. Gibbons, "Phoebe Apperson Hearst," 1, ccc; Croly, *History of the Woman's Club Movement*, 250; Mary Folger to PAH, May 3, 1909, GPAHP; Gullett, *Becoming Citizens*, 40. Hearst and Mary W. Kincaid were charter members. See Century Club of San Francisco, *Twenty-Fourth Annual Report*, 60, 62.

65. Mary McHenry Keith to President Benjamin Ide Wheeler, September 29, 1905, box 31, folder 34, UCROP; Gullett, *Becoming Citizens*, 45–46, 36–37; Mead, *How the Vote Was Won*, 25, 85; Rice, Bullough, and Orsi, *Elusive Eden*, as quoted on 301; Nickliss, "Phoebe Apperson Hearst's 'Gospel of Wealth,'" 581.

66. California, *An Act to make women eligible to educational offices*, *The Statues of California Passed at the Twentieth Session of the Legislature 1873–74*, Sacramento: G. H. Springer, State Printer, 1874, http://192.234.213.35 /clerkarchive/, 356, quotation sec. 1, accessed September 12, 2013; Buechler, *Transformation of the Woman Suffrage Movement*, 7; Materson, *For the Freedom of Her Race*, 3, 4, 7, 11.

67. Monoson, "The Lady and the Tiger," 100–135; Gullett, *Becoming Citizens*, 37–40, 47.

68. Cohen, *Reconstruction of American Liberalism*, 5.

69. Gullett, *Becoming Citizens*, 41; "'School Directors: Campaign of the Female Candidates," *San Francisco Chronicle*, October 18, 1888, 6; "School Reform,"

San Francisco Chronicle, October 19, 1888, 8; "Political Forces: Campaign of the Women School Directors," *San Francisco Chronicle*, October 19, 1888, 8; "Three Ladies Nominated," *San Francisco Chronicle*, October 16, 1888, 8; "Women on San Francisco School Board," *Woman's Journal* 19 (December 8, 1888): 392; Blair, *Clubwoman As Feminist*.

70. "School Directors: Campaign of the Female Candidates," *San Francisco Chronicle*, October 18, 1888, 6; "School Reform," *San Francisco Chronicle*, October 18, 1888, 8; "Political Forces: Campaign of the Women School Directors," *San Francisco Chronicle*, October 19, 1888, 8; "The Lady Candidates: The Committee of One Hundred Meets," *San Francisco Chronicle*, October 20, 1888, 8; "Fair School Directors," *San Francisco Chronicle*, October 26, 1888, 8; "The Ladies Nominated," *San Francisco Chronicle*, October 16, 1888, 8; Gullett, *Becoming Citizens*, 42–47; "Women on San Francisco School Board," *Woman's Journal* 19 (December 8, 1888): 392.

71. PAH to Ellen Davis Conway, October 30, 1888, in W. A. Swanberg envelope, EDCC; Hopkins, *Concise Dictionary of American Biography*, 185; Fisher, "Wandering in the Wilderness," 212–13, 217.

72. PAH to Ellen Davis Conway, October 30, 1888, EDCC; Gullett, *Becoming Citizens*, 44–45, 46.

73. Edelman, "Red Hot Suffrage Campaign," 53.

74. Century Club of California, San Francisco, "Historical Sketch," 6, 7, CCC. For an examination of women's clubs and education, see Martin, *The Sound of Our Own Voices*; Gere, *Intimate Practices*; Croly, *History of the Woman's Club Movement*; Blair, *Clubwoman as Feminist*.

75. Century Club of California, San Francisco, "Historical Sketch," bylaws, sec. 7, GPAHP; Mary McHenry Keith to President Benjamin Ide Wheeler, September 29, 1905, box 31, folder 34, UCROP; Sada D. Cornwall to unknown, January 20, 1909, box 1, folder 12, SCP. Cornwall became the president of the Century Club in 1896.

76. Cordelia Kirkland to PAH, February 2, 1889(?), GPAHP; Kirkland to PAH, March 8, 1889(?), GPAHP; Blair, *Clubwoman as Feminist*, 93; Skocpol, *Diminished Democracy*, 50, 58; Houde, *Reaching Out*, chaps. 1–2, esp. 19, 30–31; GFWC, Minutes, 3 vols. (Washington DC: GFWC, 1891).

77. Blair, *Clubwoman as Feminist*, 98, 93; "Not a Man Was Present," *Chicago Tribune*, April 24, 1890; General Federation of Women's Clubs, "Draft of Constitution Adopted by the Advisory Board," October 22, 1889, article 3, sec. 1, 4, GPAHP; Houde, *Reaching Out*, chaps. 1–2, esp. 13–14, 33; Minutes of the General Federation of Women's Clubs, 1891, GFWC; Glenn, *Unequal Freedom*, 46; Gittell and Shtob, "Changing Women's Roles in Political Volunteerism," s69; Mary Wood, *History of the General Federation of Women's Clubs*, chap. 4, 7. The GFWC consisted of 495 affiliates and 100,000 members in 1892. See Mary Wood, introduction to *History of the General Federation of Women's Clubs*.

78. Charlotte Emerson Brown to PAH, April 26, 1890, GPAHP; Adele S. Brooks, "Phoebe Apperson Hearst: List of Donations," GPAHP; "List of Mrs. Hearst's Activities Sent to Adele S. Brooks by Mrs. Clara Anthony of Boston Made From a Conversation with Mrs. Hearst on May 12, 1896, GPAHP; "Not a Man Was Present," *Chicago Tribune*, April 24, 1890; Minutes of the General Federation of Women's Clubs, 1892–1893, GFWC; Blair, *Clubwoman as Feminist*, 114, 95; Mary Wood, *History of the General Federation of Women's Clubs*, 28, 3; Keller, *Affairs of State*, chap. 5; Pitkin, *Concept of Representation*, 2, 38–39, 40–45, chap. 4, esp. 61, chaps. 5–6.

79. Helen M. Barker, "The Industrial Department and the Women's Dormitories," GFWC Minutes, May 12, 1892, 3:67–68, GFWC; Charlotte Emerson Brown, Presidential Address, May 11, 1892, GFWC, 3:27, 29; Marcia L. Gould, "State Work," May 12, 1892, GFWC, 3:61–63; Frances Willard's Address, May 12, 11892, GFWC, 3:72–82; Dr. Lelia G. Bedell, "Helps and Hindrances in the Organized Work of Women," GFWC, 3:83–101; Mrs. June Cunningham Croly, GFWC, 3:102–9; Celia Parker Woolley, "Results of Club-Life on the Character and Work of Women: The Club as a Means of Intellectual Growth," May 18, 1893, GFWC, 3:110–14; Mrs. J. H. Lozier, "Educational Influence of Women's Clubs," May 13, 1892, GFWC, 3:115–20; Mrs. J. A. Crouse, "Kindergarten Work," GFWC, 3:121–35; Miss May Rogers, "The New Social Force," May 10, 1894, GFWC, 3:224–28; Croly, *History of the Woman's Club Movement*; Watson, "Carnegie Ladies, Lady Carnegies: Women and the Building of Libraries," 160–61; Nickliss, "Phoebe Apperson Hearst's 'Gospel of Wealth,'" 585–86;

A. Scott, *Natural Allies*; Blair, *Clubwoman as Feminist*, 108–9; Blair, "General Federation of Women's Clubs," 242; Houde, *Reaching Out*, 6, 15–16, 55–56.

80. Russett, *Sexual Science*, 11–12; Butler, *Gender Trouble*; Leach, *True Love and Perfect Union*; Charlotte Emerson Brown to PAH, April 27, 1890, General Federation of Women's Clubs, GPAHP; Clara Anthony to Miss Ramirez, 1896, GPAHP; "Phoebe Apperson Hearst: List of Donations"; "List of Mrs. Hearst's Activities Sent to Adele S. Brooks by Mrs. Clara Anthony of Boston Made From a Conversation with Mrs. Hearst on May 12, 1896, GPAHP; Charlotte Emerson Brown, Presidential Address, May 11, 1892, GFWC Minutes, GFWC 3:27.

81. "Not a Man Was Present," *Chicago Tribune*, April 24, 1890; Butler, *Gender Trouble*; Leach, *True Love and Perfect Union*; Blair, *Clubwoman as Feminist*; Minutes of the General Federation of Women's Clubs, 1892–1893, GFWC; Mary Wood, *History of the General Federation of Women's Clubs*, 3, 28–30; Keller, *Affairs of State*, chap. 5; Pitkin, *Concept of Representation*, 45; Coker, *Organismic Theories of the State*, 9; Bedell, "Help and Hindrances in the Organized Work of Women," May 12, 1892, GFWC Minutes, GFWC 3:87–88.

82. Florence Bayard Hilles to PAH, September 1890, GPAHP; PAH to Orrin Peck, December 22, 1886, PC; Hopkins, *Concise Dictionary of American Biography*, 57.

83. Florence Bayard Hilles to PAH, September 1890, GPAHP; "Senator Hearst Dying," *New York Press*, January 12, 1891, GPAHP; "Worried About Hearst," *New Orleans States*, January 5, 1891, GPAHP; "Senator Hearst's Case Hopeless," *Baltimore Sun*, January 14, 1891, GPAHP; Ada Butterfield Jones to PAH, February 1891, GPAHP; PAH to Orrin Peck, December 22, 1886, PC; Ada Butterfield Jones to Phoebe A. Hearst, February 13, 1893, GPAHP; William Carey Jones, Biographical Forms of Academic Personnel, UCBIO; Ada Butterfield Jones to PAH, February 1891, GPAHP; PAH to (probably Janet Peck), February 6, 1891, GPAHP; Mary W. Kincaid to PAH, January 24, 1891, GPAHP. Smith-Rosenberg, "The Female World of Love and Ritual," 1–29.

84. Mary W. Kincaid to PAH, September 23, 1889, GPAHP; Kincaid to PAH, January 24, 1891, GPAHP; PAH to My Dear [a member of the Peck family], February 18, 1891, PC.

85. PAH to Janet Peck, March 1, 1891, telegram, PC; "Senator Hearst Dead," *San Francisco Examiner*, March 1, 1891; "George Hearst Is Dead," *Anaconda Standard*, March 1, 1891; U.S. Congress, *Memorial Addresses on the Life and*

Character of George Hearst, 11, 16; Brooks, "Phoebe Apperson Hearst," part 1, chap. 5, p. 37.

86. Mary W. Kincaid to PAH, January 24, 1891, GPAHP; Habenstein and Lamers, "Pattern of Late Nineteenth-Century Funerals," 93; Brooks, "Phoebe Apperson Hearst," part 2, chap. 1, p. 2.

4. POWER BY DESIGN

1. Schuele, "None Could Deny the Eloquence of This Lady," 170; Brooks, "Phoebe Apperson Hearst," part 1, chap. 1, pp. 2–3; Prager, "Persistence of Separate Property Concepts in California's Community Property System," 46–47; *Chicago Inter Ocean*, February 4, 1891, newspaper clipping, GPAHP; Boutelle, *Julia Morgan*, 171; "Mrs. Phoebe Hearst Dies in California," *New York Times*, April 14, 1919, 13.

2. PAH to George Hearst, July 14, 1868, GPAHP; Florence (Bayard) Hilles to PAH, August, 1891, GPAHP; Hilles to Hearst, April 3, 1891, GPAHP.

3. Hilles to Hearst, April 3, 1891, GPAHP; PAH to Sarah B. Cooper, July 6, 1891, SBCP.

4. Brooks, "Phoebe Apperson Hearst," handwritten copy, chap. 1, 13, GPAHP; PAH to Mr. Green, ca. 1891, GPAHP; PAH to Irwin C. Stump, ca. 1891, GPAHP; Wyatt-Brown, *Southern Honor*, 132.

5. PAH to Irwin C. Stump, July 3, 1892, GPAHP; Clark, "Reminiscences of the Hearst Family," 6; Brooks, "Phoebe Apperson Hearst," part 1, chap. 1, pp. 2–4. Brooks's statement on Hearst's desire to know all the details about her affairs and have all matters referred to her are corroborated in the George and Phoebe Apperson Hearst Papers.

6. PAH to Mr. Green, 1893, GPAHP; Edward Hardy Clark to PAH, August 1, 1895, GPAHP; Clark, "Reminiscences," 6. Stump worked for Hearst as a business manager by fall of 1891. See PAH to the Board of Regents of the University of California, September 28, 1891, box 26, folder 4, UCRR.

7. PAH to George Hearst, July 28, 1873, GPAHP; PAH to Eliza Pike, December 10, 1873, GPAHP; PAH to George Hearst, May 11, 1873, June 5, 1873, July 28, 1873, December 3, 1873, June 29, 1873, GPAHP. Sutcliffe, *Towards the Planned City*, 56–57; Rodgers, *Atlantic Crossings*, chaps. 4–5.

8. Sutcliffe, *Towards the Planned City*, 23–24, 18; PAH to George Hearst, August 2, 1889, GPAHP; PAH to Mrs. Holden, September 7, 1892, Letters to Members of the Holden Family, September 7, 1892–January 5, 1907, GPAHP; Ryan, "A Laudable Pride in the Whole of Us," 1132–34.

9. Brooks, "Phoebe Apperson Hearst," part 2, chap. 3, pp. 15–16 (4 crossed out and 3 written in faint blue pencil), GPAHP; Columbian Kindergarten Association, *First Statement of the Columbian Kindergarten Association*; Sklar, "Hull House in the 1890s," 658–77.

10. Vandewalker, *Kindergarten in American Education*, 70; Ross, *Kindergarten Crusade*, 88; Columbian Kindergarten Association, *First Statement of the Columbian Kindergarten Association*, 5, 10, 11; Sarah E. Stevens, CKA corresponding secretary, "The Columbian Kindergarten Association," B. Mann '93 December 6 [1893] written on top of page, CKA Files; Skocpol, *Diminished Democracy*, 106; de Cos, *History and Development of Kindergarten in California*, 7; George S. Mann, *Genealogy of the Descendants of Richard Man of Scituate, Mass*, 28, 27; Leiby, *Carroll Wright and Labor Reform*, vii, 107; Hopkins, *Concise Dictionary of American Biography*, 1255; Olive E. Weston, "Free Kindergarten Associations," *The Kindergarten News*, n.d., copy in author's possession, 149–50, quotation from B. Pickman Mann's report, 149.

11. Cremin, *American Education*, 154; Green, *Washington: A History of the Capital*, 2:viii–ix, 55–56, 57, 61–62; Bremner, "Scientific Philanthropy," 168.

12. Columbian Kindergarten Association, *First Statement of the Columbian Kindergarten Association*, 5–13; Russett, *Sexual Science*, 57–63; Allen, "Gender, Professionalization," 119; Brooks, "Phoebe Apperson Hearst," part 2, chap. 4 (IV crossed out and 3 written in faint blue pencil), 16–17; "National Kindergarten Training School Incorporated," Requests for Help in Securing Employment, n.d., 2–17, GPAHP; John Belcher, "A Journey to California," John Belcher Collection, College of Environmental Design Archives, University of California, Berkeley, 1999–98, 63; "A Business Woman: Lessons for Young Women from the Life of Mrs. Hearst," *New York Herald*, January 16, 1895. For an example of a receipt, see Lucy S. Doolittle, "Washington DC, $227.00 Receipt for Furniture and Apparatus for Model School of Columbia Kindergarten Association," November 11, 1893, GPAHP. Also PAH to Harriet Niel, "PAH Kindergarten College," April 1, 1897, GPAHP; Ross, *Origins of*

American Social Science, 162–71. Robyn Muncy argues in *Creating a Female Dominion in American Reform* (p. xiv) that "within the history of the social sciences, scholars have detected a tension that pitted professionalization (with its requirement of objectivity) against the expression of political convictions." Hearst's kindergarten work integrated professionalization and politics.

13. Columbian Kindergarten Association, *First Statement of the Columbian Kindergarten Association*, 5–7, 11, 13; PAH to M. E. Baker, April 10, 1896, GPAHP; Nunis Jr., PAH to Benjamin Pickman Mann, March 20, 1896, CKA Files; PAH, "The Phebe [*sic*] A. Hearst Kindergarten No. 1; List of Washington DC Kindergartens," CKA Files; Nunis, "Kate Douglas Smith Wiggin," 3:605–7; "Questionnaire Sent Out," March 23, 1896, CKA Files; PAH to Harriet A. Niel, Salary List for April 1897, PAH Kindergarten College, Washington DC, GPAHP; PAH to Harriet Neil, December 1899, PAH Kindergarten College, Washington DC, GPAHP; Benjamin Pickman Mann, "At the meeting of the Columbia Kindergarten Association held February 27, 1896," March 16, 1896, Antiochiana, Antioch College, Yellow Springs, Ohio. See the CKA files for additional information on CKA investigations.

14. Allen, "Gender, Professionalization," 112, 119–20.

15. Allen, "Gender, Professionalization," 119; Muncy, *Creating a Female Dominion*, xii, xiii, xv; PAH to Orrin Peck, December 22, 1886, PC; "Questionnaire Sent Out," March 23, 1896," CKA Files; "Lists of Washington DC Kindergartens," CKA Files; B. Pickman Mann Report, March 16, 1896, CKA Files; U.S. Congress, Senate. "Columbian Kindergarten Association, Washington DC, March 5, 1898," 55th Congress, 2d Session, S. Doc. 177; United States Congress, Senate. "For kindergarten instruction, twelve thousand dollars," Washington DC, 1898, 55th Congress, 2d Session, chap. 540; Ross, *Kindergarten Crusade*, 83.

16. Hinsley and Wilcox, "Introduction: The Chicago Fair and American Anthropology in 1893," xix; William J. Shaw to PAH, 1893, GPAHP; John J. Flinn, Official Guide to the World's Columbian Exposition in the City of Chicago, State of Illinois, May 1 to October 26, 1893 (Chicago, 1983), 6; John Gilbert Follansbee to PAH, November 1, 1893, GPAHP; Green, *Washington*, 2:62; Ross, *Origins of American Social Science*, 24, 63; Rydell, *All the World's a Fair*, 40; Wiebe, *Search for Order*; Cremin, *American Education*, 154; Aron,

Working at Play, 153; Weimann, *Fair Women*, 7–9, 22, 25, 27–32, chap. 3, 241; Buhle, *Women and American Socialism*, chap. 2; Frank Hamilton Cushing, "Document E. Excerpts from the Diary of Frank Hamilton Cushing at the World's Fair (June 16–September 12, 1893)," in Hinsley and Wilcox, eds., *Coming of Age in Chicago*, 186, 149n12, 190.

17. PAH to the Columbian Kindergarten Association, Washington DC, October 4, 1895, CKA Files; Richard Hollinger, Robert Turner Biography, draft of an article for the Bahá'í Encyclopedia project, July 1, 1997, copy in author's possession. Hollinger used the following sources for his draft: Louis Gregory, "Robert Turner," *World Order* 12 (April 1946); and census records, city directories, and Turner's death certificate in the GPAHP. Part of this information was provided by Roger Dahl. There is also a typescript of a tablet to Robert Turner in the Emogene Hoagg Collection in the Washington DC Bahá'í Archives. See the Helen Hillyer Brown and Ella Goodall Cooper collections in the National Bahá'í Archives, Wilmette, Illinois. Also Robert Turner to PAH, October 26, 1895, box 8, HFA; Hogeland, "The Female Appendage," 101–14, especially 103; "National Kindergarten Training School Incorporated," Requests for Help in Securing Employment, ca. 1895, 2–17, GPAHP; Brooks, "Phoebe Apperson Hearst," part 2, chap. 3, p. 16; Phoebe A. Hearst to Janet Peck, October 13, 1892, PC; A. Scott, *The Southern Lady*, 7; Hogeland, "'The Female Appendage,'" 101–14, especially 103; Clara Anthony to PAH, May 10, 1895, GPAHP; Rodgers, *Atlantic Crossings*, 3.

18. Brooks, "Phoebe Apperson Hearst," part 2, chap. 3, p. 16; Green, *Washington*, vol. 2, chap. 6; Green, *Secret City*, 137; Penn, *African American Women in the Struggle for the Vote*, 62.

19. Altschuler, *Race, Ethnicity, and Class*, 83; Southern, *Progressive Era and Race*, 29; Higginbotham, *Righteous Discontent*, 22–23; Solomon, *In the Company of Educated Women*, 76; Gordon, *Gender and Higher Education in the Progressive Era*, 6, 46–47; Royster, *Southern Horrors and Other Writings*.

20. National Kindergarten Training School Incorporated, Requests for Help in Securing Employment, ca. 1895, GPAHP, 7; Stromquist, *Reinventing "The People,"* 150; Flanagan, *Seeing With Their Hearts*, 49; Quinn, *Black Neighbors*, 3, 14–17.

21. Newman, "Reflections on Aileen Kraditor's Legacy," 291–316; Newman, *White Women's Rights*; Burton, *Burdens of History*, chap. 5, 48; National Kindergarten Training School Incorporated, Requests for Help in Securing Employment, ca. 1895, 2–16, GPAHP.

22. Hine, "We Specialize in the Wholly Impossible," 70–93; Berkeley, "Colored Ladies Also Contributed," 181–203; PAH to Harriet A. Niel, Salary List, April 1897, Phoebe A. Hearst Kindergarten College, Washington DC, GPAHP; Phoebe A. Hearst Kindergarten Training School, Announcement, 1901 (Washington DC), GPAHP; Phoebe A. Hearst Kindergarten College, Enrollment Blank Statement March 1904, GPAHP; Phoebe A. Hearst Kindergarten College, Records of Colored Students, Statement March 1904, GPAHP; Brooks, "Phoebe Apperson Hearst," part 2, chap. 4, p. 16; Washington Public School Kindergartens, Students and Graduates of Phebe [*sic*] A. Hearst Kindergarten College holding positions, Phoebe A. Hearst Kindergarten Training School, GPAHP; Higginbotham, *Righteous Discontent*, 14–18.

23. Brooks, "Phoebe Apperson Hearst," part 2, chap. 4, p. 21; "Mrs. Phoebe Hearst Dies in California," *New York Times*, April 14, 1919, 13; Nickliss, "Phoebe Apperson Hearst's 'Gospel of Wealth.'"

24. *Sunday Republic*, June 18, no year, newspaper clipping, GPAHP.

25. Wilson, *City Beautiful Movement*, 48; Elizabeth Brown and Alan Fern, introduction to *Revisiting the White City*, organizers Carolyn Kinder Carr and George Gurney (Washington DC, 1993), 11, 12, 13; Rydell, "Rediscovering the 1893 Chicago World's Columbian Exposition," 55; Reed, *"All the World Is Here!"*, xxv; Weimann, *Fair Women*, 147; Gullett, "Our Great Opportunity," 264; Wright, "On the Fringe of the Profession," 280; Hayden, *Grand Domestic Revolution*; Elizabeth W. Allston Pringle, "In Memoriam: Phoebe Apperson Hearst," *Minutes of the Mount Vernon Ladies' Association of the Union*, 5, MVLA; Brooks, "Phoebe Apperson Hearst," part 3, chap. 1, 1–2; Brooks, "Notes for Mrs. Hearst's Biography, Mrs. Wickersham's Notes Taken From Halting and Very Imperfect Dictation, February 1927," GPAHP, second 1.

26. Swanberg, *Citizen Hearst*, 79; Brooks, "Notes for Mrs. Hearst's Biography, Mrs. Wickersham's Notes Taken From Halting and Very Imperfect Dictation, February 1927," GPAHP; Hosmer B. Parsons to PAH, January 20, 1896,

GPAHP; Gebhard and Von Breton, *Architecture in California, 1868–1968*, 16; Longstreth, *On the Edge of the World*, 258–66, 281–86; Nasaw, *Life of William Randolph Hearst*, 40, 63; PAH to Hannah, November 29, 1893, GPAHP; A. C. Schweinfurth to Edward H. Clark, December 20, 1895(?), GPAHP.

27. On professionalizing architects and the École des Beaux-Arts as a model, see Kristof, *The Architect*, chaps. 8, 10, 11. Also Wright, *Moralism and the Model Home*, 46–48, 201–2; A. C. Schweinfurth to Edward H. Clark, December 20, 1895(?), GPAHP.

28. A. C. Schweinfurth to PAH, March 23, 1896, GPAHP; Jean Andrews, "Wyntoon, Dappled Fantasyland: Hearst Castle: Symbol of Success in a Bygone Era," *Chico (CA) Enterprise-Record*, June 10, 1977, 12A; Boutelle, *Julian Morgan*, 172; Lewis, *Here Lived the Californians*, 229.

29. Garnet, *Stately Homes of California*; Wright, "On the Fringe of the Profession," 280.

30. Brooks, "Phoebe Apperson Hearst," part 2, chap. 3, pp. 8(1), 9(2); "History of the Cathedral of St. Peter and St. Paul; Private Record of Henry Y. Satterlee," CLE Clergy/National Cathedral School, connected box 1, NCSGA, 7.

31. "History of the Cathedral of St. Peter and St. Paul," 7, 8–18, 32, NCSGA; "School for Girls," *Washington Evening Star*, January 18, 1896, newspaper clipping, BLD Hearst Hall: 1895–1903, box 2, NCSGA; Brooks, "Phoebe Apperson Hearst," part 2, chap. 3, p. 10(3); A. T. Britton and John M. Wilson, Building Committee to the Trustees of the Protestant Episcopal Cathedral Foundation of the District of Columbia, Agreement dated April 19, 1896, to provide $175,000 for National Cathedral Girl's School Building Contingent on the architect, Ernest Flagg's, plans, copy dated August 8, 1896, GPAHP.

32. A. T. Britton and John M. Wilson to Right Reverend H. Y. Satterlee, December 14, 1896, BLD Hearst Hall: June–December 1896, BLD Hearst Hall: 1895–1903, box 2, National Cathedral School for Girls, 1–3, NCSGA; "History of the Cathedral of St. Peter and St. Paul; Private Records of Henry Y. Satterlee," National Cathedral School for Girls CLE Clergy/National Cathedral School, box 1, 7, NCSGA; A. T. Britton to Colonel John M. Wilson, December 14, 1896, BLD Hearst Hall: June–December 1896, 1, NCSGA; "School for Girls," *Washington Evening Star*, January 18, 1896, newspaper clipping, BLD Hearst Hall, January–May, 1896, National Cathedral School for Girls, box 2, NCSGA;

W. E. Speir to Ernest Flagg, December 19, 1896, copy, BLD Hearst Hall: 1895–1903, BLD Hearst Hall: June–December 1896, box 2, NCSGA; Building Committee to PAH, May 1, 1897, BLD Hearst Hall: 1895–1903, BLD Hearst Hall: January–May 1897, box 2, NCSGA; Lois A. Bangs to Henry Y. Satterlee, HDS Bangs-Whiton: 1900–1906: Letters Regarding Hiring–1899, Easter 1900, Bangs to Satterlee, box 1, National Cathedral School for Girls, NCSGA; A. T. Britton to Brigadier-General John M. Wilson, July 5, 1899, NCSGA; "Extract from the opening address of the Bishop of Washington," October 1, 1900, copy, CLE Satterlee Biography, CLE Clergy/NCS connected box 1, p. 1, NCSGA.

33. "American Millionaires and Their Public Gifts," *Review of Reviews* 7 (February 1893): 48–60.

34. University of California, "Organic Act to Create the University of California," 20–21; Vesey, *Emergence of the American University*, 1; Geiger, *History of American Higher Education*.

35. "The University Created by Statute," *Prospectus* (San Francisco, 1868), 18. The creation of the University of California was "the first time that an Agricultural College has been expanded into a University, and that any University has combined Colleges of Instruction with Colleges of Examination for Degrees." See "Note to" paragraph 47, *Prospectus* (San Francisco, 1868), 18. Also Moss, *Bright Epoch*, especially 1–7; "An Act to Create and Organize the University of California," *Prospectus*, 19–33; Nerad, "Situation of Women at Berkeley Between 1870 and 1915," 68; Stadtman, comp. and ed., *Centennial Record of the University of California*, 211–12, 52; Martin Kellogg, "Salient Points in Retrospect," *Blue and Gold 1900* (Berkeley: Junior Class of the University of California, Press of Louis Roesch Company, 1899), 6–7; Gordon, *Gender and Higher Education in the Progressive Era*, 6; Longstreth, *On the Edge of the World*, 16–17.

36. Stadtman, *Centennial Record of the University of California*, 214; University of California, *Biennial Report of the President on Behalf of the Regents, 1888*, 17 (hereafter *Biennial Report*); University of California, *Biennial Report, 1890*, 16.

37. Vesey, *Emergence of the American University*, 2, 3; Muncy, *Creating a Female Dominion*, xiv; Fitzpatrick, *Endless Crusade*; Bledstein, *Culture of Professionalism*, 34, 277–79; Solomon, *In the Company of Educated Women*, chap. 8.

38. Marsden, *Soul of the American University*, chap. 8.

39. Ritter, *More than Gold in California*, 158, 167–69, 173, 203; GFWC Minutes, September 29, 1891, GFWC 2:29, 30; Marsden, *Soul of the American University*, part 2, esp. chap. 8; biography card for William E. Ritter, April 14, 1891, box 78, folder 34, UCBIO; biography card for Mary Bennett Ritter, UCBIO; Muncy, *Creating a Female Dominion*, 20; PAH to the Board of Regents of the University of California, September 28, 1891, University of California Regents, 1899, box 26, folder 4, UCRR. For an examination of feminists redefining "satisfaction of social and economic needs as rights," see Lipschultz, "Hours and Wages," 115. On the infiltration of women into universities and innovative philanthropy, see Rossiter, *Women Scientists in America*, chap. 2.

40. Longstreth, *On the Edge of the World*, 313; Leon Richardson, "Berkeley Culture," interview by Amelia R. Fry; Brooks, "Phoebe Apperson Hearst," part 3, chap. 1, p. 1; Rodgers, *Atlantic Crossings*, 160; Douglass, *California Idea and American Higher Education*, 83.

41. "A Business Woman: Lessons for Young Women from the Life of Mrs. Hearst," *New York Herald*, January 16, 1895, GPAHP. See back of newspaper clipping to ascertain the approximate date of publication. Also Mary W. Kincaid to PAH, February 4, 1895, and May 30, 1895, GPAHP.

42. "Society," *Times*, (New York), February 10, 1895, GPAHP; E. Digby Baltzell, *Philadelphia Gentlemen*, 74, 168–69; Sarah B. Dean to PAH, February 25, 1895, GPAHP; University of Pennsylvania, *A Guide to the University Museum Archives*, 12, UPMAA; William Pepper to PAH, February 25, 1895, and April 15, 1895, GPAHP; PAH to [William Randolph Hearst], ca. August 1895, GPAHP; Hosmer B. Parsons to Mrs. E[lbert] C. Apperson, April 20, 1895, GPAHP.

43. Draper, "École des Beaux-Arts and the Architectural Profession in the United States," 209; Brooks, "Phoebe Apperson Hearst," part 3, chap. 1, p. 1; Douglass, *California Idea*, 69–70; Nickliss, "Phoebe Apperson Hearst's 'Gospel of Wealth,'" 590; Steinmetz, *State/Culture*, 9.

44. Brooks, "Phoebe Apperson Hearst," part 3, chap. 1; Albert M. Oppenheimer to Madame [PAH], December 11, 1895, GPAHP; Milicent Shinn to PAH, January 14, 1896, GPAHP; PAH to Regent J. B. Reinstein, October 22, 1896, PAHAPC; J. R. K. Kantor, *The Best Friend the University Ever Had*, pamphlet, UCARCH; University of California, *Programme For An International Competition for*

the Phoebe Hearst Architectural Plan of the University of California (Berkeley, December 3, 1897), 19, 21; University of California, *Biennial Report, 1896–1898*, 7; William Carey Jones, "California's City of the Intellect," *Daily Berkeley Advocate*, Special University Edition, October 31, 1896, Records of the Office of President, Regents' Material, series 1, box 2, folder 22, PAHAPC; J. B. Reinstein, "The Western Acropolis of Learning," Records of the Office of President, Regents' Material, series 1, box 2, folder 22, PAHAPC, 2.

45. Milicent Shinn to PAH, January 14, 1896, GPAHP; Albert M. Oppenheimer to Madame [PAH], December 11, 1895, GPAHP; Gullett, *Becoming Citizens*, 38; Burnham, "Milicent Washburn Shinn," 3:285–88; PAH to Secretary of the Interior, August 30, 1894, GPAHP. Thank you to Kathleen Nutter, archivist of the Sophia Smith Collection, Smith College, Northampton MA, for the information that Shinn was secretary of the California Branch of the Association of Collegiate Alumnae, 1893–95.

46. Milicent Shinn to PAH, January 14, 1896, GPAHP; PAH to Regent J. B. Reinstein, October 22, 1896, GPAHP; PAH to Caroline Severance, December 17, 1899, CSC; Maybeck, *Maybeck*, 7; Brooks, "Phoebe Apperson Hearst," part 3, chap. 1; Cardwell and Hayes, "Fifty Years From Now," 20–21; "The Jury of Architects Were Special Guests," *San Francisco Examiner*, September 1, 1899, newspaper clipping, University of California "Press Notices," vol. 1.

47. Jordy, *American Buildings and Their Architects*, 275–76, 313; Gebhard and Von Breton, *Architecture in California, 1868–1968*, 12–13; PAH to Regent J. B. Reinstein, October 22, 1896, GPAHP; Maybeck, *Maybeck*, 7, 8; Woodbridge, *Maybeck: Visionary Architect*; Longstreth, *On the Edge of the World*; McCoy, *Five California Architects*; Hays, "Some Interesting Buildings at the University of California," 71–75; Cardwell and Hays, "Fifty Years From Now," 21. Also Jean Murray Bangs, *Maybeck*, Miscellaneous Clip File, CED Documents Collection, College of Environmental Design, n.d., University of California, Berkeley; Brooks, "Phoebe Apperson Hearst," part 3, chap. 1, p. 2; "49. Plan of Grounds," University of California "Press Notices."

48. Brooks, "Phoebe Apperson Hearst," handwritten copy, part 2, chap. 7, p. 4; H. Thornburgh to PAH, August 11, 1896, GPAHP; University of California "Press Notices," 1; H. S. Allen, "Phoebe Hearst Architectural Competition," 434; PAH to Jacob B. Reinstein, October 22, 1896, PAHAPC; Milicent Shinn to

PAH, January 14, 1896, GPAHP; "Mrs. Hearst's Reception," *Berkeley Advocate*, October 11, 1897, newspaper clipping, *Personalia*, volume bound by the University of California, UCARCH; PAH to Caroline Severance, December 17, 1899, CSC; University of California, PAH to Regent J. B. Reinstein, October 22, 1896, *Biennial Report, 1896–1898*, 8.

49. PAH to Jacob B. Reinstein, October 22, 1896, PAHAPC; Brooks, "Phoebe Apperson Hearst," part 2, chap. 5, p. 26; "Mrs. Hearst's Wise Use of Her Fortune," newspaper clipping, n.d., GPAHP; Douglass, *California Idea and American Higher Education*, 83.

50. PAH to Jacob B. Reinstein, October 22, 1896, PAHAPC; Jacob B. Reinstein to William Carey Jones, September 4, 1897, PAHAPC; PAH note on *Evening Post*, August 20, no year, newspapers clippings about W. R. Hearst Esq. and His Publications, GPAHP; Walsh, "Regent Peter C. Yorke and the University of California," 100; J. B. Reinstein, "Address of Regent J. B. Reinstein at the Special Meeting of the Regents of the University of California 'For the purpose of suggesting and discussing matters necessary to the prosperity of the University,' January 15, 1898," UCARCH, 1898, p. 2.

51. PAH to Jacob B. Reinstein, October 22, 1896, PAHAPC; Jacob B. Reinstein to William Cary Jones, September 4, 1897, GPAHP; J. B. Reinstein, no article title (but possibly "Criticism of Architectural Competition"), *The California Architecture and Building News*, January 1896, University of California "Press Notices," 1:2; Reinstein, "Address at the Special Meeting of the Regents," UCARCH, 9–11.

52. Jacob B. Reinstein to William Carey Jones, September 4, 1897, GPAHP; Reinstein, "Address at the Special Meeting of the Regents," esp. 9–10, UCARCH; Jacob B. Reinstein to PAH, January 9, 1897, folder 1, PAHAPC.

53. J. B. Reinstein, "Criticism of Architectural Competition," *California Architecture and Building News*, January 1896, University of California "Press Notices," chap. 1, pp. 1–2.

54. J. B. Reinstein, "Criticism of Architectural Competition," *California Architecture and Building News*, January 1896, University of California "Press Notices," chap. 1, p. 2; A. C. Schweinfurth, "Communication," *Wave*, November 28, 1896, 3; Jacob B. Reinstein to William Carey Jones, September 4,

1897, GPAHP; University of California, *University of California Magazine* 4 (February 1898): 382, 383; University of California, Resolution, October 24, 1896, box 20, folder 11, UCRR.

55. PAH to Sarah B. Cooper, December 1, 1895, SBCP; PAH to Orrin Peck, December 22, 1886, PC; Harper, *Life and Work of Susan B Anthony*, 2:863.

56. Solomon, *In the Company of Educated Women*, chap. 6.

57. Susan B. Anthony to Jane L. Stanford, September 18, 21, 1896, box 4, folder 18, JLSP; Mead, *How The Vote Was Won*, 8; Harper, *Life and Work of Susan B Anthony*, 2:864, 888.

58. Gullett, *Becoming Citizens*, 34; May Treat Morrison to PAH, September 11, 1897, GPAHP; "Mrs. Hearst for Regent," no newspaper title, 1897, *Personalia*, volume bound by the University of California, newspaper clipping, UCARCH; California Legislature, *Constitution of the State of California* (Sacramento, 1879), sec. 9, xxxiv; Walsh, "Regent Peter C. Yorke and the University of California," 100; "Mrs. Hearst as Regent," *Berkeley Advocate*, October 11, 1897, newspaper clipping, *Personalia*, volume bound by the University of California, UCARCH; "Mrs. Hearst's Reception," *Berkeley Advocate*, October 11, 1897, newspaper clipping, UCARCH.

59. "Mrs. Hearst, widow . . . ," *Christian Advocate* (New York, City), January 12, 1893, GPAHP; Mowry, *California Progressives*; Brooks, "Phoebe Apperson Hearst," handwritten copy, part 2, chap. 8, p. 18; Roll Call and Votes of Regents of the University, August 10, 1897, Regents, 1895–97, box 25, folder 24, UCRR.

60. University of California, "Organic Act to Create the University of California," 24; A. C. Schweinfurth, "Communication," *Wave*, November 28, 1896, 3; Gilb, "Laura de Force Gordon," 2:68–9; Gilb, "Clara Shortridge Foltz," 1:641–43; Bryce, *American Commonwealth*, appendix: The Constitutions of California, Article IX and Article XX, sec. 18, respectively, 2:663, 680; Ethington, *Public City*, 299–300; Babcock, "Essay: Clara Shortridge Foltz," 673–717; Babcock, "Clara Shortridge Foltz: Constitution-Maker," 849–940; Materson, *For the Freedom of Her Race*, 25.

61. Editor, *University of California Magazine* 3 (September 1897): 214–15; Nickliss, "Phoebe Apperson Hearst's 'Gospel of Wealth,'" 596; Glenn, *Unequal Freedom*; Hall, *Organization of American Culture*.

1. Adelaide Marquand, "Mrs. Hearst's First Session," *Berkeley Advocate* (?), August 11, 1897, original newspaper clipping in author's possession; "Mrs. Hearst As Regent," *Berkeley Advocate*, October 11, 1897, newspaper clipping, *Personalia*, volume bound by the University of California, UCARCH; Pitkin, *Concept of Representation*, 1–13; Lebsock, "Women and American Politics," 35–62; Mary W. Kincaid to PAH, July 1897, gpahp; PAH to Martin Kellogg, 1897, GPAHP.

2. University of California, *Annual Report of the Secretary to the Board of Regents of the University of California for the Year Ending June 30, 1897*, 3; Stadtman, *Centennial Record of the University of California*, 410–28; PAH to Clara Anthony, 1897, GPAHP; PAH to James H Budd, 1897, GPAHP; biography card for Phoebe Apperson Hearst, UCBIO; PAH to Martin Kellogg, 1897, GPAHP.

3. Pitkin, *Concept of Representation*, 1–13; Lebsock, "Women and American Politics," 35–62.

4. PAH to President Martin Kellogg, 1897, GPAHP; Pitkin, *Concept of Representation*, 2, 3.

5. President Martin Kellogg to PAH, October 25, 1896, GPAHP; University of California, editorial, *University of California Magazine* 2 (November 1896): 302; Jacob B. Reinstein to PAH, January 9, 1897, PAHAPC; PAH to Caroline Severance, September 19, 1907, box 26, CSC; Mary E. Gilmer to PAH, January 29, 1896, PAH note, GPAHP; Sarah Brown Cooper to PAH, July 6, 1891, SBCP.

6. Martin Kellogg to PAH, February 19, 1897, GPAHP; Jacob B. Reinstein to PAH, February 21, 1897, PAHAPC.

7. William Carey Jones, "California's City of the Intellect," *Berkeley Daily Advocate*, October 31, 1896, special edition, Records of the Office of President, Regents' Material, series 1, box 2, folder 22, 1, PAHAPC; University of California, September 21, 1897, Regents Minutes, box 25, folder 24, 3, UCRR; Longstreth, *On the Edge of the World*, 245; Paul V. Turner, "Rethinking the First University of California Campus at Berkeley and Designing the Tenth at Merced," paper presented at the Designing the Campus of Tomorrow: The Legacy of the Hearst Architectural Plan, Present and Future symposium held at the Berkeley Art Museum, organized by the Center for Studies in Higher Education, University of California, Berkeley, February 10, 2000; Turner,

"The Phoebe Hearst Architectural Plan in Context," Designing the Campus of Tomorrow, symposium; Turner, *Campus*, 180.

8. University of California, *Programme for an International Competition for the Phoebe Hearst Architectural Plan of the University of California* (Berkeley, December 3, 1897), 1–23; Annie Maybeck to PAH, September 9, 1897, pp. 32–33, GPAHP.

9. University of California, April 12, 1898, Regents Minutes, box 25, folder 25, 6, ucrr.

10. J. R. K. Kantor, *The Best Friend the University Ever Had*, pamphlet, ucarch; Janette Howard Wallace, *Reminiscences of Janette Howard Wallace: Daughter of John Galen Howard and Mary Robertson Howard*, Bancroft Library, University of California, Berkeley, 1986, 9; Ritter, *More than Gold in California*, 174, 173.

11. Ritter, *More than Gold in California*, 203; Stadtman, *Centennial Record of the University of California*, 216; Gordon, *Gender and Higher Education in the Progressive Era*, 11, 52–55; Prytanean Alumnae, vol. 1. An oral history, interviewer Jill Porter (Berkeley, 19uu), 1:47; Gordon, "Co-Education on Two Campuses"; Solomon, *In the Company of Educated Women*, chap. 7; Horowitz, *Campus Life*, 13, 41, 42.

12. E. V. Matignon, "What Mrs. Hearst Will Do in 1900, *San Francisco Chronicle*, December 31, 1899, 31; Associated Women Students, Resolution Expressing Appreciation for Phoebe Apperson Hearst gift of the Women's Lounge in East Hall, Committee on Resolutions, September 6, 1898, box 44, folder 23, GPAHP; Gertrude Maxwell Jewett, President of the Associated Women Students, University of California, *Biennial Report of the President 1898–1900*, 91–92; Hays, "Some Interesting Buildings at the University of California," 71–75; Cardwell, *Bernard Maybeck*, 45–46.

13. Rossiter, *Women Scientists in America*, 39.

14. PAH to Regent Jacob B. Reinstein, October 22, 1896, PAHAPC; Samuel E. Moffett, "A Western City of Learning," *Harper's Weekly*, September 11, 1897, pamphlets, Descriptive of the University of California, vol. 1, ucarch; Robinson, *Improvement of Towns and Cities*, 209; Jacob B. Reinstein, "The Western Acropolis of Learning," *Berkeley Advocate*, October 31, 1896, special edition, Records of the Office of President, Regents' Material, series 1, box 2,

folder 22, PAHAPC; Douglass, *California Idea and American Higher Education*, 83; Hall, *Organization of American Culture*, 1–4.

15. Robinson, *Modern Civic Art*, 275; Bernard Maybeck to PAH, December 9, 1913, GPAHP; Hopkins, *Concise Dictionary of American Biography*, 873.

16. Brooks, "Phoebe Apperson Hearst," part 3, chap. 1, p. 4; Charles S. Green, "The Hearst Architectural Competition," 66, 67; Samuel E. Moffett, "A Western City of Learning," *Harper's Weekly*, September 11, 1897, pamphlets, Descriptive of the University of California, vol. 1, ucarch; "A Model Architectural Competition," *Harper's Weekly*, October 7, 1899, University of California "Press Notices," vol. 1; Jacob B. Reinstein to the uc Regents, "Report of the Trustees for the Phoebe Hearst Architectural Plan of the University of California at Berkeley," Regents Correspondence and Papers, December 14, 1900, box 34, folder 13, 3, PAHAPC; Mary W. Kincaid to PAH, November 23, 1898, GPAHP; Newel Perry to PAH, November 17, 1900, GPAHP; Professor E. Bichat to PAH, December 25, 1897, PAHAPC; Longstreth, *On the Edge of the World*, 313.

17. University of California, *Programme for an International Competition*, 6; Jan Van Reijswijck to PAH, October 8, 1898, PAHAPC; Melendy, *Governors of California*, 259–71; H. S. Allen, "The Phoebe Hearst Architectural Competition for the University of California," 435–38; Brooks, "Phoebe Apperson Hearst," part 3, chap. 1, pp. 6–8; "Select Plans for University of California, *San Francisco Examiner*, October 5, 1898, University of California "Press Notices"; Sutcliffe, *Towards the Planned City*, 25; "Mrs. Hearst's University Plans," no newspaper title, June 1899, newspaper clipping, GPAHP; "Genius Honors Genius at the Banquet Table," *San Francisco Call*, September 1, 1899, newspaper clipping, University of California "Press Notices," vol. 1; "The Jury of Architects Were Special Guests," *San Francisco Examiner*, September 1, 1899, newspaper clipping, GPAHP. It was almost as if the depiction of Hearst's face hidden behind a floral arrangement on the front table in the September 1, 1899, article in the *San Francisco Examiner* appeared to be drawn in such a way to satisfy men who refused to acknowledge Hearst's power and authority. Also "Architects Honored By Compatriots," *San Francisco Examiner*, September 12, 1899, newspaper clipping, University of California "Press Notices," vol.

1; Hopkins, *Concise Dictionary of American Biography*, 787; "Interview with Mrs. Hearst Regarding UC plans—for publication," n.d., GPAHP.

18. University of California, *Programme for an International Competition*, 12; "Interview with Mrs. Hearst Regarding UC plans—for publication," n.d., GPAHP; "A Model Architectural Competition," *Harper's Weekly*, October 7, 1899, University of California "Press Notices"; Draper, "École des Beaux-Arts and the Architectural Profession," 209, 210, 214; Turner, *Campus*, 180; Cardwell, *Bernard Maybeck*, 44; William Carey Jones, "Phoebe Hearst Architectural Plan," *University of California Magazine* 5 (October 1899): 282, 284; "To the Trustees of the Phoebe Hearst Architectural Plan of the University of California," Report of the Jurors on the Final Competition, September 7, 1899, 4, 8, PAHARC; "The Jury of Architects Were Special Guests," *San Francisco Examiner*, September 1, 1899, newspaper clipping, University of California "Press Notices," vol. 1; "Genius Honors Genius at the Banquet Table," *San Francisco Call*, September 1, 1899, University of California "Press Notices," vol. 1.

19. John M. Carrere to Edward H. Clark, Esq., copy, PAH Architectural Competition, n.d., GPAHP.

20. Willis Polk, "The University Competition," *Wave* 15 (November 7, 1896): 3; Reinstein, "University of California Competition"; Cardwell, *Bernard Maybeck*, 44; "The Lady and the Architect," *Bulletin* (San Francisco), October 22, 1899, newspaper clipping, Material Regarding Phoebe A. Hearst Competition, William Carey Jones Correspondence and Papers, Bancroft Library, University of California; Miriam Michelson, "Controversy Between Junghaendel and Mrs. Phoebe Hearst," *Bulletin* (San Francisco), October 22, 1899, newspaper clipping, William Carey Jones Correspondence and Papers; *London Daily Mail*, October 8, 1898, GPAHP; "Interview with Mrs. Hearst Regarding UC plans—for publication," n.d., GPAHP; Architectural League of America, *Architectural Annual, 1900* (Philadelphia, 1900), 53–59, 90; "The Jury of Architects Were Special Guests," *San Francisco Examiner*, September 1, 1899, University of California "Press Notices," vol. 1.

21. University of California, *Programme for an International Competition*; J. B. Reinstein, *Report of the Trustees for the Phebe [sic] Hearst Architectural Plan of the University of California*, series 1, box 34, folder 13, 4, California Uni-

versity Regents Correspondence and Papers, PAHAPC; Miriam Michelson, "Controversy between Junghaendel and Mrs. Phoebe Hearst," *Bulletin*, October 22, 1899, newspaper clipping, Material Regarding Phoebe A. Hearst Competition, William Carey Jones Correspondence and Papers.

22. PAH to Governor Gage, 1899, incomplete, GPAHP; William Carey Jones to [Benjamin Ide Wheeler], January 18, 1900, box 4, folder 45, UCROP.

23. PAH to J. L. Pascal, March 1900, translation, GPAHP; PAH to J. L. Pascal, June 19, 1901, personal, translation, GPAHP; G. J. M. E. d'Aquin to PAH, July 3, 1901, GPAHP; "Interview with Mrs. Hearst Regarding UC plans—for publication," n.d., GPAHP; "The Greater University," *Berkeley Advocate*, February 21, 1900, vol. 1, University of California "Press Notices."

24. Benjamin Ide Wheeler to PAH, February 18, 1901, box 8, folder 17, HFA; Fred Clark to PAH, February 15, 1901, box 8, folder 17, HFA; PAH to J. L. Pascal, June 19, 1901, personal, translation, GPAHP; University of California, Minute Book, vol. 12, June 1898–February 1900, 108, 212, UCARCH; Bernard Maybeck to PAH, February 19, 1901, box 12, folder 17, HFA; "New Plan of Mrs. Hearst," December 4, 1898, *San Francisco Chronicle*, newspaper clipping, San Francisco Public Library, accessed January 19, 2016; "The Greater University," *Berkeley Advocate*, February 21, 1900, vol. 1, University of California "Press Notices"; John Galen Howard to PAH, January 17, 1901, box 12, folder 17, HFA; "A New San Francisco to Rival All Cities," *San Francisco Chronicle*, December 4, 1898, University of California "Press Notices," vol. 1; "Mrs. Hearst's Acceptance of Hearst Architectural Plans," in Board, December 14, 1900, series 1, box 34, folder 13, PAHAPC.

25. John Galen Howard to PAH, January 17, 1901, box 12, folder 17, HFA; J. L. Pascal to Benjamin Ide Wheeler, September 26, 1901, translation, series 1, box 8, folder 187, 1 UCROP; John Galen Howard to Benjamin Ide Wheeler, June 12, 1901, morning letter, series 1, box 8, folder 15, UCROP; John Galen Howard to Benjamin Ide Wheeler, June 12, 1901, afternoon letter, UCROP; Benjamin Ide Wheeler to Phoebe A. Hearst, January 12, 1901, GPAHP; PAH to Theodore A. Lescher, Esq., May 20, 1901, translation, GPAHP; Boutelle, *Julia Morgan*, 52; "Donations to the University by Mrs. Phoebe A. Hearst, 1897 to 1918," figures furnished by the kindness of Mr. C. J. Stuble, assistant comptroller, University of California, 1, 3, 6, 7, 8, 9, GPAHP; John Galen

Howard, "Architectural Plans for the Greater University of California," 273–91; "Interview with Mrs. Hearst Regarding UC plans—for publication," n.d., GPAHP; PAH to Caroline Severance, December 17, 1899, GPAHP.

26. Bourdieu, "Structures, Habitus, Power," 155–99; E. V. Matignon, "What Mrs. Hearst Will Do in 1900," *San Francisco Chronicle*, December 31, 1899, 31; Benjamin Ide Wheeler to R. A. Clark, April 12, 1901, series 1, box 7, folder 168, UCROP; Mary Bell, "Hearst Hall," *University of California Magazine* 6 (February 1900): 10, 13; Gordon, *Gender and Higher Education in the Progressive Era*, 54; editorial, *University of California Magazine* 6 (February 1900): 36–38; Ritter, *More than Gold in California*, 203. Bourdieu, *Field of Cultural Production*, 7; Bourdieu, *Distinction*, 2, 53–54.

27. "Mrs. Hearst's Acceptance of Hearst Architectural Plans," December 14, 1900, series 1, box 34, folder 13, Regents Correspondence and Papers, PAHAPC; "Resolution to Employ J. G. Howard," December 21, 1901, PAHAPC; Boutelle, *Julia Morgan*, 47, 52; "Laying of the Corner-Stone of the Hearst Memorial Mining Building," *University Chronicle* 5 (January 1903): 292–300; Stadtman, *Centennial Records of the University of California*, 60, 59; Robinson, *Modern Civic Art*, 275; "A New Era for the University of California," *Berkeley Daily Advocate*, October 31, 1896, special edition, Records of the Office of the President, Regents' Material, series 1, box 2, folder 15, 1, PAHAPC.

28. Prytanean Alumnae, *The Prytaneans*, 11–12; Cardwell and Hays, "Fifty Years from Now," 21; Hays, "Some Interesting Buildings at the University of California," 73–75; Boutelle, *Julia Morgan*, 48, 60; Cardwell, *Bernard Maybeck*, 17–19, 46–51; Hearst Hall and chimney attached, Channing Way near College Avenue, 1899, G. E. Gould photographer, College of Environmental Design Archives; Wright, *Moralism and the Model Home*; Ritter, *More than Gold in California*, 203.

29. University of California, "University Chronicle," *University of California Magazine* 6 (October 1899): 346; E.V. Matignon, "What Mrs. Hearst Will Do in 1900," *San Francisco Chronicle*, December 31, 1899, 31; Ritter, *More than Gold in California*, 203.

30. E. V. Matignon, "What Mrs. Hearst Will Do in 1900," *San Francisco Chronicle*, December 31, 1899, 31; "Formal Opening of Hearst Hall," *San Francisco Call*, February 9, 1901; "Hearst Hall Formally Dedicated," *Gazette* (Berkeley),

February 9, 1901; *Washington (DC) Times*, February 5, 1901, newspaper clippings, GPAHP; University of California *Biennial Report of the President, 1898–1900*, 54; University of California, *Biennial Report of the President 1900–02*, 63; Gertrude Maxwell Jewett, president of the Associated Women Students, University of California, *Biennial Report of the President 1898–1900*, 91–92.

31. Deutsch, *Women and the City*; Bourdieu, "Structures, Habitus, Power," 174, 178.

32. Wiebe, *Segmented Society*; Stadtman, *Centennial Records of the University of California*, 60; Donald H. McLaughlin, "Careers in Mining Geology," oral history interview, 2; editorial, *University of California Magazine* 6 (February 1900), 36, 37; Anna Herkner to PAH, October 6, 1903, Hearst Domestic Industries Students, GPAHP; Adelaide Grace Smith to PAH, October 6, 1903, Hearst Domestic Industries Students, GPAHP; Laura Mundy to PAH, October 5, 1903, GPAHP; Marion Schneider to PAH, October 7, 1903, GPAHP; J. R. K. Kantor, *The Best Friend the University Ever Had*, pamphlet, ucarch; University of California, *Biennial Report of the President, 1900–1902*, 63. Hearst Hall was destroyed by fire in 1922. See Stadtman, *Centennial Records of the University of California*, 60.

33. University of California, *Clip Sheet*, vol. 35, no. 2, July 14, 1959, Bancroft Library, University of California, Berkeley; University of California, *Biennial Report of the President, 1896–1898*, 9; Jacob B. Reinstein to the UC Regents, "Report of the Trustees for the Phebe [*sic*] Hearst Architectural Plan of the University of California at Berkeley," December 14, 1900, series 1, box 34, folder 13, Regents Correspondence and Papers, 3, PAHAPC.

34. Wilson, *City Beautiful Movement*; Bernard Maybeck to Phoebe A. Hearst, December 2, 1913, GPAHP; Robinson, *Modern Civic Art*, 275.

35. Martin Kellogg to PAH, October 25, 1896, GPAHP; Brooks, "Phoebe Apperson Hearst," part 3, chap. 2, pp. 1, 2; Newel Perry to PAH, November 17, 1900, GPAHP; William Randolph Hearst to PAH, 1899–1901, GPAHP; Robinson, *Improvement of Town and Cities*, 209; Robinson, *Modern Civic Art*, 275–77; Turner, *Campus*, 177, 180, 186; Albert Kelsey, president of the Architectural League of America, to PAH, January 11, 1900, microfilm reel 67, box 43, folder 2, PAHAPC; Ernest Flagg to PAH, January 2, 1900, GPAHP; Scott, *American City Planning*, 49–50; J. A. Peterson, "Hidden Origins of the McMillan Plan

for Washington DC," 3–18; University of California, Regents Meetings, May 12, 1908, series 1, box 67, folder 13, 2, UCRR.

36. University of California, *Biennial Report of the President, 1896–1898*, 20.

37. Kennard, "Review Essay: The History of Physical Education," 835–36; E.V. Matignon, "What Mrs. Hearst Will Do in 1900," *San Francisco Chronicle*, December 31, 1899, 31; University of California, *Annual Announcement of Courses of Instruction in the Colleges of Berkeley for the Academic Year 1889–1890* (Berkeley: Published by the University, 1889), 42–43; University of California, *Register of the University of California, 1888–1889* (Berkeley, 1889), 16, 54–55; Ritter, *More than Gold in California*, 191, 201–2.

38. Clarke, *Sex in Education*, 15, 16–19; Solomon, *In the Company of Educated Women*, 56.

39. Walsh, *"Doctors Wanted: No Women Need Apply,"* 178; Reuben, *Making of the Modern University*, chap. 5; Sarah J. Shuey to PAH, February 27, 1899, GPAHP.

40. University of California, *Annual Announcement of Courses of Instruction in the Colleges of Berkeley for the Academic Year 1889–1890* (Berkeley: published by the University, 1889), 43; University of California, *Register of the University of California, 1888–1889* (Berkeley, 1889), 54; Ritter, *More than Gold in California*, 202–3, 186, 202–4; biography form for William Emerson Ritter, box 78, folder 34, UCAPR; Solomon, *In the Company of Educated Women*, 102; Park, "A Gym of Their Own," 24–26; Kennard, "Review Essay: The History of Physical Education," 835–42; biography form for Mary Bennett Ritter, box 78, folder 34, UCAPR; University of California, *Annual Announcement of Courses of Instruction in the Colleges at Berkeley for the Academic Year 1897–1898* (Berkeley: published by the University, 1897), 94; "President's Report," June 16, 1899, President Kellogg, 1897–1899, box 25, folder 16, UCRR; University of California, Minute Book, June 16, 1899, vol. 12 June 1898–February 1900, 281, 287, UCARCH.

41. Otten, *University Authority and the Student*, 18–20; Ferrier, *Origin and Development of the University of California*, 405–6, 408–10; December 13, 1898, box 25, folder 25, 8, UCRR; W. A. McKowen to PAH, December 15, 1898, *Regents, 1891–1910*, box 8, folder 1, GPAHP; Ada Butterfield Jones to PAH, January 10, 1899, GPAHP; Melendy, *Governors of California*; William Cary Jones to PAH,

March 19, 1899, GPAHP; "Biography of Benjamin Ide Wheeler," box 95, folder 66, UCAPR; biography form for William Carey Jones, box 48, folder 21, UCBIO; Jones, *Illustrated History of the University of California*, 203; University of California, June 16, 1899, Minute Book, vol. 12, June 1898–February 1900, 281, 287, 292–93, UCARCH; University of California, Roll Call of the Regents of the University, June 16, 1899, box 26, folder 1, UCRR; University of California, Notes of the Board Meeting, June 16, 1899, box 26, folder 1, 4, UCRR; Benjamin Ide Wheeler to Dr. Martin Kellogg et al., June 24, 1899, in Board, July 1 and 18, 1899, box 25, folder 17, UCRR; PAH to Clara Anthony, June 6, 1899, GPAHP.

42. Benjamin Ide Wheeler to Dr. Martin Kellogg et al., June 24, 1899, box 25, folder 17, UCRR; biography form for Benjamin Ide Wheeler, box 95, folder 66, UCAPR.

43. Wheeler, *Abundant Life*, 335, 336; Wheeler to PAH, September 19, 1899, GPAHP; Benjamin Ide Wheeler to Dr. Martin Kellogg et al., June 24, 1899, GPAHP; Minnie [T.] Cropper to PAH, August 26, 1899, GPAHP.

44. Benjamin Ide Wheeler to Dr. Martin Kellogg et al., June 24, 1899, Records of the Regents, handwritten copy of telegram, note handwritten in pencil, July 1, 1899, attached to typewritten copy of letter from Wheeler to Martin Kellogg, July 24, 1899, GPAHP; Andrew M. Lawrence to Edward H. Clark, April 29, 1899, GPAHP; University of California, Minutes, July 18, 1899, Regents, 1899, series 1, box 26, folder 1, UCRR; University of California, Minute Book, July 18, 1899, vol. 7 (June 1898–February 1900), 304–5, ucarch; Jones, *Illustrated History of the University of California*, 203; biography form for Benjamin Ide Wheeler, box 95, folder 66, UCAPR.

45. Sarah J. Shuey to PAH, February 27, 1899, Letters from Women Students, 1898–1917, GPAHP; Morantz, "Making Women Modern," 490; President's Report, June 13, 1899, Board of Regents, June 16, 1899, series 1, box 25, folder 16, 1, 2, UCRR; University of California, Minutes of the Board of Regents, August 8, 1899, series 1, box 26, folder 1, 3, UCRR; Ritter, *More than Gold in California*, 202–6; University of California, *Biennial Report of the President 1900–1902*, 63.

46. University of California, *Minutes of Academic Council*, February 8, 1901, UCARCH, 384; Benjamin Ide Wheeler to PAH, January 29, 1901, box 7, folder 168, UCROP; PAH to Benjamin Ide Wheeler, February 16, 1901, GPAHP;

biographical cards for Jessica Blanche Peixotto, 1869–1958, box 73, folder 28, UCAPR; Ruyle, "Dean Lucy Sprague, The Partheneia, and the Arts," 65–74; Antler, "Lucy Sprague Mitchell," 484–87; Mary Bennett Ritter, "After Five Years," November 19, 1939, San Francisco Biography Collection, San Francisco History Center, San Francisco Public Library.

47. Mabel Clare Craft, "The Phebe [sic] Hearst Fountain." *University of California Magazine* 5 (October 1899): 329. Today a monument to Phoebe Apperson Hearst sits on the Music Concourse in Golden Gate Park across from the Academy of Sciences.

48. Kessler-Harris, *Out to Work*, 112, 113; Vapnek, *Breadwinners*, 120–21.

49. Vapnek, *Breadwinners*, 120; University of California, "The Hearst Domestic Industries," *Blue and Gold* (Berkeley, 1902), 203.

50. Gamber, *Female Economy*, 134; Hearst Domestic Industry Students, *Haps and Mishaps*, 28–30, GPAHP. "Workers at one Boston dressmaking shop started at fifty cents a week" in the early twentieth century. See Gamber, *Female Economy*, 70.

51. Gordon, *Gender and Higher Education in the Progressive Era*, 54.

52. University of California, *President's Biennial Report 1900–1902*, 64; Ritter, *More than Gold in California*, 209; J. R. K. Kantor, *The Best Friend the University Ever Had*, pamphlet, ucarch.

53. J. R. K. Kantor, *The Best Friend the University Ever Had*, pamphlet, ucarch; University of California, editorial, *University of California Magazine* 6 (February 1900): 37–8; University of California, *Biennial Report of the President, 1900–1902*, 63.

6. LIMITS

1. Conn, *Museums*, 9; Jacknis, "Patrons, Potters, and Painters," 141.

2. "I am informed that Mrs. Hearst . . . proposes giving to this city a museum," *Wave* 8 (February 6, 1892), 6; Hinsley and Wilcox, introduction to *Coming of Age in Chicago*, x–xvi, 11; D. R. Wilcox, "Essay Seven: Going National," in *Coming of Age in Chicago*, 430; Sara Y. Stevenson to PAH, January 18, 1899, GPAHP; Brooks, "Phoebe Apperson Hearst," part 2, chap. 5, 22–23.

3. McCarthy, *Women's Culture*, 71; Adam, *Buying Respectability*, 8, 14.

4. PAH to Mrs. Pepper, ca. August 2, 1898, GPAHP; Baltzell, *Philadelphia Gentleman*, 74; Burkhardt et al., *Dictionary of American Biography*, 453–56; Thoresen, "Paying the Piper and Calling the Tune," 258; Darnell, "Emergence of Academic Anthropology at the University of Pennsylvania,"81; Conn, *Museums*, 6, 10, 11, 27, 82. On egalitarianism in friendships between elite women and men in the early American republic, see Good, *Founding Friendships*.

5. Conn, *Museums*, 9, 82–83; Jacknis, "Patrons, Potters, and Painters," 142–43; Brooks, "Phoebe Apperson Hearst," part 2, chap. 5, p. 22; Adam, *Buying Respectability*, 14.

6. Mary W. Kincaid to PAH, February 4, 1895, GPAHP; "A Business Woman: Lessons for Young Women from the Life of Mrs. Hearst," *New York Herald*, ca. January 16, 1895, newspaper clippings, GPAHP; Hosmer B. Parsons to PAH, January 15,1895, GPAHP; William Pepper to PAH, February 24, 1895, GPAHP; William Pepper to PAH, April 15, 1895, GPAHP; Sarah B. Dean to PAH, February 25, 1895, GPAHP; PAH to editor of the *Chicago Herald*, April 1, 1895, GPAHP; Parsons to PAH, April 5, 1895, GPAHP; Parsons to PAH, April 18, 1895, GPAHP; Parsons to PAH, June 21, 1895, GPAHP.

7. Hosmer B. Parsons to PAH, January 15, 1895, GPAHP; Mary W. Kincaid to PAH, February 4, 1895, and July 4, 1895, GPAHP; William Pepper to PAH, February 24, 1895, GPAHP; Jacknis, "Patrons, Potters, and Painters," 143–44; Jacknis, "A Museum Prehistory,"50; W. Q. Gresham of the Department of State to Diplomatic and Consular Officers of the United States, April 19, 1895, GPAHP.

8. Parsons to PAH, March 29, 1895, April 5, 1895, and April 18, 1895, GPAHP; Parsons to W. R. Hearst, April 26, 1895, GPAHP; PAH to Clara Anthony, August 28, 1895, GPAHP; Parsons to PAH, April 20, 1895, GPAHP; Parsons to Mrs. E. C. Apperson, April 20, 1895, GPAHP; Parsons to William Randolph Hearst, April 20, 1895, and April 26, 1895, GPAHP; Parsons to PAH, June 21, 1895, GPAHP; Parsons to Union Bank of London, April 24, 1895, GPAHP; Margaret J. M. Sweat to PAH, n.d., GPAHP; PAH to Clara Anthony, May 21, 1895, GPAHP; Brooks, "Phoebe Apperson Hearst," typewritten copy, part 2, chap. 6, 33–34, GPAHP; PAH to Mrs. Doolittle, September 30, 1895, GPAHP; Parsons to PAH, August 1, 1895, GPAHP.

9. Eives and Allen to PAH, October 12, 1895, box 8, HFA; PAH to Clara Anthony, May 21, 1895, GPAHP; Hugh I. Gibson to Margaret Collier Graham, box 13, ca. 1895, MGP; Edward H. Clark to PAH, June 25, 1895, GPAHP; Hosmer B. Parsons to PAH, June 27, 1895, August 1895, and June 28, 1895, GPAHP.

10. Edward H. Clark to PAH, June 25, 1895, GPAHP; Hosmer B. Parsons to PAH, June 27, 1895, August 15, 1895, and June 28, 1895, GPAHP; A. T. Britten to PAH, June 26, 1895, GPAHP; PAH to Mrs. Doolittle, September 30, 1895, written by Josephine Egan, GPAHP; Laura Osborne Talbott, November 18, 1895, GPAHP; University of Pennsylvania, Executive Committee Minutes, January 15, 1897, 29, UPMAA; PAH to Clara Anthony, November 10, 1895, GPAHP; Thoresen, "Paying the Piper and Calling the Tune," 258; Parmenter, "Zelia Maria Magdalena Nuttall," 2:640; Zelia Magdalena Nuttall to PAH, April 16, 1896, GPAHP; Sara Yorke (Mrs. Cornelius) Stevenson to PAH, May 19, 1896, copy of Nuttall report, GPAHP; Francis Newton Thorpe, *A Remarkable Man: Dr. William Pepper*, GPAHP, 579–81; Jacknis, "Patrons, Potters, and Painters," 142–44.

11. "Dr. Pepper Dies Suddenly in California," *Philadelphia Record*, July 30, 1898, newspaper clipping, UPMAA; PAH to Mr. Leonard, August 17, 1898, vol. 9, William Pepper Manuscripts, Van Pelt Library, University of Pennsylvania, Philadelphia.

12. Thoresen, "Paying the Piper and Calling the Tune," 257–75, 259; Darnell, "Emergence of Academic Anthropology at the University of Pennsylvania," 81; Wister, *Sara Yorke Stevenson*, 8–16; Hinsley and Wilcox, introduction to *Coming of Age in Chicago*, 3; Hinsley, "Essay 1. Anthropology as Education and Entertainment," 11; "Biographical Note, Papers of Frederick Ward Putnam: An Inventory," Harvard University, http://oasis.harvard,edu/html/hua/15003.htm/, accessed June 3, 2017; Sara Y. Stevenson to PAH, January 15, 1899, GPAHP; Sara Y. Stevenson to PAH, August 29, 1898, GPAHP.

13. Sara Y. Stevenson to PAH, October 10, 1898, GPAHP; Stevenson to PAH, November 4, 1898, GPAHP; Stevenson to PAH, November 30, 1898, GPAHP; Minutes of the American Exploration Society, November 10, 1898, GPAHP; Cornelius Stevenson to PAH, December 1, 1898, UPMAA; PAH to Stewart Culin, July 24, 1900, Administrative Records, Director's Office, PAH, box 8,

UPMAA; James C. Hooe to PAH, December 21, 1898, GPAHP; Conn, *Museums*, 14, 22; Adam, *Buying Respectability*, 14.

14. Phoebe Apperson Hearst "is full of fizz," "incomplete letters–correspondents unidentified; fragments of letters," n.d., GPAHP; Hugh I. Gibson to Margaret Collier Graham, box 13, ca. 1895, MGP; Thomas Barry, May–August, June 9, 15, 23, 1879, TBD; PAH to Mrs. Holden, September 2, 1892, GPAHP; PAH to George Hearst, August 2, 1889, GPAHP; PAH to Janet Peck, May 30, 1899, PAH to Janet Peck, October 13, 1892, PC; James Cecil Hooe to PAH, March 12, 1898, GPAHP; Pitkin, *Concept of Representation*.

15. PAH to the Holden Girls, January 15, 1899, GPAHP; William Randolph Hearst to PAH, 1899–1900, GPAHP.

16. Sara Y. Stevenson to PAH, January 15, 1899, GPAHP; Fox, *Engines of Culture*, 3; University of California, *Department of Anthropology*, 3; University of California, *President's Biennial Report, 1906–1908*, 89; Kroeber, ed., *Phoebe Apperson Hearst Memorial Volume*, xiii, ix; Jacknis, "Patrons, Potters, and Painters," 141.

17. Sara Y. Stevenson to PAH, January 18, 1899, GPAHP; PAH to the Secretary of the American Exploration Society, ca. 1899–1900, GPAHP; University of California, Minutes, Notices of the Board of Regents, January 25, 1900, box 39, folder 9, UCRR; William Carey Jones to PAH, January 26, 1900, GPAHP; PAH to the Secretary of the American Exploration Society, December 28, 1899, Administrative Records—Early Administration History, box 2, UPMAA; PAH to Stewart Culin, July 24, 1900, Administrative Records, Director's Office, Phoebe Hearst, box 8, UPMAA; PAH to Stewart Culin, January 24, 1901, GPAHP.

18. Stewart Culin to PAH, January 30, 1899, GPAHP; Darnell, "Emergence of Academic Anthropology," 82; PAH to Stewart Culin, July 24, 1900, Administrative Records, Director's Office, Phoebe Hearst, box 8, UPMAA; Phoebe A. Hearst to Martin Kellogg, 1897, GPAHP; Conn, *Museums*, 83; Jacknis, "Patrons, Potters, and Painters," 142–43; Brooks, "Phoebe Apperson Hearst," part 2, chap. 5, 22–27; Jesse Y. Burk to PAH, February 27, 1899, GPAHP; Sara Y. Stevenson to PAH, January 16, 1900, GPAHP; PAH to Mrs. Cornelius (Sarah Y.) Stevenson, January 24, 1901, GPAHP.

19. Michael Kammen, *Mystic Chords of Memory*, 154–56; Conn, *Museums*, 12–13, 89–90; Kaplan, *Museums and the Making of "Ourselves*," 1–2; Degler, *In Search of Human Nature*, 245; Himmelfarb, *Darwin*, chap. 7; Brooks, "Phoebe Apperson Hearst," part 2, chap. 5, 22; Sneider, *Suffragists in An Imperial Age*; Burton, *Burden of History*.

20. Conn, *Museums*, 12, 20, 5, 19; PAH to [Stewart] Culin, July 24, 1900, Administrative Records, Director's Office, PAH, box 8, UPMAA.

21. PAH to Steward Culin, July 24, 1900, Administrative Records, Director's Office, box 8, UPMAA; Brooks, "Phoebe Apperson Hearst," part 2, chap. 5, p. 22; Phoebe Apperson Hearst "is full of fizz," "incomplete letters–correspondence, unidentified, fragments of letters," GPAHP; PAH to George Hearst, May 11, June 5, August 16, November 21, and December 3, 1873, GPAHP.

22. Foucault, *Power/Knowledge*; Task, *Things American*, 1–2.

23. PAH to Henry E. McBride, April 4, 1900, GPAHP; Mark, *Stranger in Her Native Land*, 281; Murray, *American Anthropology and Company*, xxxv, 9; Wilcox, "Essay 3. Anthropology in a Changing America," 125; University of California, "Phoebe Hearst Archaeological Explorations," *University Chronicle* 4 (February 1901): 49–50; PAH to Stewart Culin, July 24, 1900, Administrative Records, Director's Office, Phoebe Hearst, box 8, UPMAA; Philip Mills Jones to PAH, February 11, 1901, GPAHP; Brooks, "Phoebe Apperson Hearst," part 3, chap. 2, p. 5; Sara Y. Stevenson to PAH, October 10, 1898, GPAHP; Stevenson to PAH, November 4, 1898, GPAHP; Kroeber, *Phoebe Apperson Hearst Memorial Volume*, ix; University of California, Mrs. Hearst's Donation for the Department of Anthropology, 1898–1900, Regents' Files, carton 55, folder 36, UCRR; McCarthy, *Women's Culture*, 27–34, 75.

24. McCarthy, *Women's Culture*, 112; PAH to Henry E. McBride, April 4, 1900, GPAHP; Kroeber, *Phoebe Apperson Hearst Memorial Volume*, ix; University of California, *Department of Anthropology*, 5; Sara Y. Stevenson to PAH, October 10, November 4, 1898, GPAHP; Mrs. Hearst's Donation for the Department of Anthropology, 1898–1900, Regent's Files, carton 55, folder 36, UCRR; University of California, "Phoebe Hearst Archaeological Explorations," *University Chronicle* 4 (February 1901): 49–56; Jacknis, "A Museum Pre-

history," 50; Jacknis, "Patrons, Potters, and Painters," 143–44, 147; PAH to Orrin Peck, June 22–24, 1896, OPC.

25. PAH to Orrin Peck, February 9, 1905, PC; Pierre Bourdieu, "Structures, Habitus, Power," 181.

26. Otten, *University Authority and the Student*, 3, 36, 63n39; Stadtman, *Centennial Record of the University of California*, 85.

27. University of California, *Department of Anthropology*, 3; Kroeber, ed., *Phoebe Apperson Hearst Memorial Volume*, ix–xiv, ix; PAH to [Orrin?] Peck, May 3, 1899, PC; University of California, "Suggestions for the Organization of a Department of Anthropology," d'Aquin-Merriam, Putnam Correspondence; Hallowell, "Beginnings of Anthropology in America," 83; University of California, "Phoebe Hearst Archaeological Explorations," *University Chronicle* 4 (February 1901): 49–50; University of California, Mrs. Hearst's Donation for the Department of Anthropology, 1898–1900, Regents' Files, carton 55, folder 36, UCRR; PAH to Orrin Peck, June 22–24, 1896, incomplete, OPC; University of California, *Biennial Report of the President of the University, 1898–1900*, 55 (hereafter *Biennial Report*); University of California, "New Department of Anthropology," *University Chronicle* 4 (October 1901): 282.

28. Kroeber, "Frederic Ward Putnam," 714; Jacknis, "Patrons, Potters, and Painters," 144; Dexter, "Role of F. W. Putnam in Developing Anthropology at the American Museum of Natural History," 303, 304; Dexter, "Frederic Ward Putnam and the Development of Museums of Natural History and Anthropology," 153–54; Dexter, "Putnam-Kroeber Relations in the Development of American Anthropology," 91; Cole, *Franz Boas*, chap. 12; McCaughey, *Stand, Columbia*, 199.

29. Mark, *Stranger in Her Native Land*, 34–36, 281, 4, 119, 208; Thoresen, "Paying the Piper," 262; Newman, *White Women's Rights*, 26, 129; Wilkins, "Alice Cunningham Fletcher," 1:631–33.

30. Mark, *Stranger in Her Native Land*, 77; Newman, *White Women's Rights*, 129.

31. Zelia Magdelena Nuttall to PAH, April 16, 1896, GPAHP; Mark, *Stranger in Her Native Land*, 281–83, 147, 235, 240, 243; Thoresen, "Paying the Piper," 258; Parmenter, "Zelia Maria Magdalena Nuttall," 2:640–42; William Pepper

to PAH, March 1896, GPAHP; Alice Fletcher Diary, April 4, 1901, box 6, AFP; University of California, *Department of Anthropology*, 5.

32. Stocking Jr., *Franz Boas Reader*, 16; Gilkeson, *Anthropologists and the Rediscovery of America*, 7; Cole, *Franz Boas*, 132; McCaughey, *Stand, Columbia*, 199; Thoresen, "Paying the Piper," 267, 268.

33. Franz Boas to Zelia Nuttall, April 11, 1901, series 1, box 6, folder 97, UCROP; Franz Boas to PAH, May 11, 1901, series 1, box 6, folder 97, UCROP; Franz Boas to John C. Merriam, Copy Book, November 19, 1901, G. J. M. E. d'Aquin, Series 2, Department and Museum of Anthropology, box 2, Correspondence and Papers Report, 1901–1904, Correspondence, 1901–1905, Department of Anthropology, 1901–1902, UCARCH (hereafter Copy Book, Department of Anthropology, 1901–1902); University of California, "New Department of Anthropology," *University Chronicle* 4 (October 1901): 280–81; Franz Boas to Zelia Nuttall, May 18, 1901, GPAHP.

34. Jean Andrews, "Wyntoon Dappled Fantasyland Hearst Castle: Symbol of Success in a Bygone Era," *Chico (California) Enterprise-Record*, June 10, 1977, Bancroft Information Files, Bancroft Library, University of California, Berkeley, 12A; W. W. Murray, "Wyntoon," 13; Longstreth, *On the Edge of the World*, 171–76; University of California, box 95, folder 67, UCBIO. Stetson was the maiden name of Wheeler's mother.

35. Clark, "Reminiscences of the Hearst Family," 9; Longstreth, *On the Edge of the World*, 379n20; Jean Andrews, "Wyntoon Dappled Fantasyland Hearst Castle: Symbol of Success in a Bygone Era," *Chico (California) Enterprise-Record*, June 10, 1977, 12A.

36. Hester Holden to Phoebe A. Hearst, n.d., GPAHP; Longstreth, *On the Edge of the World*, 344–46. Wyntoon burned in 1933. See Longstreth, *On the Edge of the World*, 344. Also Jean Andrews, "Wyntoon Dappled Fantasyland Hearst Castle: Symbol of Success in Bygone Era," *Chico (California) Enterprise-Record*, June 10, 1977, 12A; Eugene W. Kower, "Wyntoon; Realm of Beauty, Sunlight, and Snow," December 19, 1940, HFP; McCoy, *Five California Architects*, 18; Jacomena Maybeck, *Maybeck*, 16; "Cost of Mrs. Hearst's McCloud Place," 1902, Miscellaneous Accounts, GPAHP. Also Cardwell, *Bernard Maybeck*, 53.

37. Markus, *Buildings and Power*; Steinmetz, *State/Culture*, 1–49.

38. Longstreth, *On the Edge of the World*, 345; Maybeck and White, architects, San Francisco, "House of Mrs. Phoebe A. Hearst in Siskiyou, Co., Cal.," *Architectural Review* (Boston), 11 (January 1904): 66.

39. Lears, *No Place for Grace*, 168; Longstreth, *On the Edge of the World*, 344–46; Cardwell, *Bernard Maybeck*, 226; Elizabeth Kincaid to Phoebe A. Hearst, n.d., GPAHP; W. W. Murray, "Wyntoon,"12–20, 15; "Wyntoon-Bavarian Fairyland in the Cascades," *Goodyear Chemical Review* (Winter 1963): 8, HFP; "To Build Summer Residence," June 14, 1901, no newspaper name, re University of California; WRH (papers, etc.), GPAHP.

40. Lowenthal, "Identity, Heritage, and History," 49; Longstreth, *On the Edge of the World*, 345; Maybeck and White, architects, San Francisco, "House of Mrs. Phoebe A. Hearst in Siskiyou, Co., Cal.," *Architectural Review* (Boston), 11 (January 1904): 66; McCoy, *Five California Architects*, 18; Woodbridge, *Maybeck*, 84; Nickliss, "Phoebe Apperson Hearst's 'Gospel of Wealth,'"; Mitchell, "Society, Economy, and the State Effect,"81.

41. Darnell, "Emergence of Academic Anthropology at the University of Pennsylvania," 84; Hinsley and Wilcox, *Coming of Age in Chicago*, 8, 9; McVicker, "Essay 6. Patrons, Popularizers, and Professionals," 377; Marvin Harris, *Rise of Anthropological Theory*, 250; Zelia Magdalena Nuttall to PAH, May 19, 1901, GPAHP; biography form for Alfred L. Kroeber, box 51, folder 64, card 1, UCBIO; PAH to Alfred Kroeber, July 30, 1901, box 17, ALKCP; PAH to Alfred L. Kroeber, July 20, 1901, telegram, box 17, ALKCP; Alfred L. Kroeber to PAH, July 22, 1901, box 1, ALKCP.

42. Summary, n.d., d'Aquin-Merriam, Department of Anthropology Records, Putnam Correspondence; accessed May 24, 2015; University of California, *Department of Anthropology*, 3, 7–8; Kroeber, ed., *Phoebe Apperson Hearst Memorial Volume*, x, xi; G. J. M. E. d'Aquin to PAH, November 23, 1901, Copy Book, Department of Anthropology, 1901–1902, UCARCH; biography card for Alfred L. Kroeber, box 51, folder 64, card 1, UCBIO.

43. Frederic W. Putnam to Zelia Nuttall, November 19, 1901, copy, University of California Department of Anthropology, d'Aquin-Merriam, Putnam Correspondence. The author's understanding of the battle to professionalize the academic field of anthropology comes from: Cole, *Franz Boas*;

Darnell, "Emergence of Academic Anthropology"; Freeman, "University Anthropology: Early Departments in the United States," 78–90; Hallowell, "Beginnings of Anthropology in America," 83–90; Lowie, "Reminiscences of Anthropological Currents in America," 995–1016; Mark, *Stranger in Her Native Land*; Steward, *Alfred Kroeber*.

44. Darnell, "Emergence of Academic Anthropology," 91; Frederic W. Putnam to Benjamin Ide Wheeler, June 25, 1908, Department and Museum of Anthropology Records, box 17, folder 12, UCARCH; Frederic W. Putnam to Zelia Nuttall, November 19, 1901, copy, University of California Department of Anthropology, Putnam Correspondence; G. J. M. E. d'Aquin to F. W. Putnam, January 15, 1902, Copy Book, Department of Anthropology, 1901–1902, UCARCH.

45. Frederic W. Putnam to Benjamin Ide Wheeler, June 25, 1908, Department and Museum of Anthropology Records, box 17, folder 12, UCARCH; "Suggestions for the Organization of a Department of Anthropology," University of California Department of Anthropology, d'Aquin-Merriam, n.d., Putnam Correspondence; G. J. M. E. to F. W. Putnam, December 31, 1901, Copy Book, Department of Anthropology, 1901–1902, UCARCH.

46. Marsden, *Soul of the American University*, chap. 8, 134; University of California, "Suggestions for the Organization," d'Aquin-Merriam, Putnam Correspondence.

47. Reuben, *Making of the Modern University*, 2; T. Kroeber, *Alfred Kroeber*, 2, 43, 45; Hymes, "Alfred Louis Kroeber," 13–14, 4.

48. Thoresen, "Paying the Piper," 267; G. J. M. E. d'Aquin, "Extract From the Minutes of a meeting held by the Department of Anthropology on January 16, 1902, at 3:45 p.m., Mills Building, room 19, San Francisco, California," Copy Book, series 2, box 2, Department of Anthropology, 1901–1902, UCARCH; Zelia Magdalena Nuttall to PAH, May 18, 1901, GPAHP; Nuttall to PAH, May 19, 1901, GPAHP; Frederic Ward Putnam to PAH, May 2, 1901, GPAHP; Putnam to PAH, July 20, 1902, GPAHP; McCaughey, *Stand, Columbia*, 199; Ross, *Origins of American Social Science*, parts 2 and 3; Reuben, *Making of the Modern University*.

49. Alice Fletcher to F. W. Putnam, August 31, 1902, Department of Anthropology and Museum, Miscellaneous, Museum Matters Chiefly Mrs. Hearst, 1901–1910,

folder 2, Putnam Correspondence; University of California, "Suggestions for the Organization of a Department of Anthropology," d'Aquin-Merriam, Putnam Correspondence, 2; Benjamin I. Wheeler to F.W. Putnam, August 25, 1902, Department of Anthropology and Museum, Miscellaneous, folder 2, Putnam Correspondence; Kroeber, *Phoebe Apperson Hearst Memorial Volume*, x; Alfred L. Kroeber to F. W. Putnam, November 14, 1901, Department of Anthropology, Miscellaneous, folder 2, Putnam Correspondence; PAH to Frederic W. Putnam, December 31, 1904, Department of Anthropology, Miscellaneous, Museum Matters Chiefly Mrs. Hearst, 1901–1910, Putnam Correspondence.

50. Alice Fletcher to Frederic W. Putnam, August 31, 1902, Department of Anthropology, Miscellaneous, Museum Matters Chiefly Mrs. Hearst, 1901–1910, Putnam Correspondence; PAH to Frederic W. Putnam, December 31, 1904, Department of Anthropology, Miscellaneous, Museum Matters Chiefly Mrs. Hearst, 1901–1910, Putnam Correspondence.

51. George Pepper to PAH, September 15, 1902, Department of Anthropology, Miscellaneous, Putnam Correspondence; Jacknis, "Patrons, Potters, and Painters," 146; Alfred L. Kroeber to Frederic W. Putnam, November 14, 1901, Department of Anthropology, Miscellaneous, folder 2, Putnam Correspondence; Alice Fletcher to Frederic W. Putnam, August 31, 1902, Putnam Correspondence.

52. George Pepper to PAH, September 15, 1902, Department of Anthropology, Miscellaneous, Putnam Correspondence; University of California, "Suggestions for the Organization," d'Aquin-Merriam, Putnam Correspondence; Alfred L. Kroeber to Frederic W. Putnam, November 14, 1901, Department of Anthropology, Miscellaneous, folder 2, Putnam Correspondence; Alice Fletcher to Frederic W. Putnam, August 31, 1902, Department of Anthropology, Miscellaneous, Museum Matters Chiefly Mrs. Hearst, 1901–1910, Putnam Correspondence.

53. Alice C. Fletcher to F. W. Putnam, August 31, 1902, Department of Anthropology, Miscellaneous, Museum Matters Chiefly Mrs. Hearst, 1901–1910, Putnam Correspondence; Kaeppler, "Paradise Regained," 22, 23; Benjamin Ide Wheeler to F. W. Putnam, August 25, 1902, Miscellaneous, University of California Department of Anthropology and Museum, 1901–1909, Putnam Correspondence.

54. Benjamin Ide Wheeler to F.W. Putnam, August 25, 1902, Miscellaneous, Department of Anthropology and Museum, 1901–1909, Putnam Correspondence; Alice Fletcher to Frederic W. Putnam, August 31, 1902, Department of Anthropology, Miscellaneous, Department of Anthropology and Museum Matters, Chiefly Mrs. Hearst 1901–1910, Putnam Correspondence; Alice Fletcher to Frederic W. Putnam, September 9, 1902, Putnam Correspondence.

55. F. W. Putnam to PAH, September 17, 1902, copy, Department of Anthropology, Miscellaneous, Department of Anthropology and Museum Matters Chiefly Mrs. Hearst, 1901–1910, Putnam Correspondence.

56. G. J. M. E. d'Aquin, Minutes of Advisory Committee of the Department of Anthropology, September 22, 1902, copy, d'Aquin-Merriam, Department of Anthropology and Museum, 1901–1909, Putnam Correspondence; G. J. M. E. d'Aquin, Minutes of the Advisory Committee of the Department of Anthropology, September 29, 1902, copy, Putnam Correspondence.

57. G. J. M. E. d'Aquin, Minutes of the Advisory Committee of the Department of Anthropology, September 29, 1902, copy, d'Aquin-Merriam, Department of Anthropology and Museum, 1901–1909, Putnam Correspondence.

58. Kroeber, *Phoebe Apperson Hearst Memorial Volume*, x, xiii; Long, "The 'Kingdom Must Come Soon,'" 15.

59. J. W. Paul to PAH, February 13, 1903, GPAHP; "Death of Well-Known California Woman," *San Francisco Examiner*, January 23, 1904, 3.

60. Ethan H. Smith to PAH, January 13, 1900, GPAHP; Ethan H. Smith to PAH, Feb 5, 1903, GPAHP; PAH to Orrin Peck, July 9, 1903, PC; PAH to Mrs. Meyer, May 15, 1904, GPAHP.

61. PAH's "Itinerary," October 7, 1901, to December 11, 1902, Miscellaneous, University of California Department of Anthropology and Museum Matters Chiefly Mrs. Hearst, 1901–1910, Putnam Correspondence; PAH to Orrin Peck, July 9, 1903, PC.

62. Brooks, "Phoebe Apperson Hearst," part 4 (For Mrs. Brooks), 1–3, GPAHP.

63. Brooks, "Phoebe Apperson Hearst," part 4 (For Mrs. Brooks), 3–4, GPAHP; PAH note, November 14, 1900, Miscellaneous Notes, Addresses, etc., GPAHP.

64. PAH to Benjamin Ide Wheeler, January 11, 1904, carbon copy, California University President Correspondence and Papers, series 1, box 18, folder

85, UCROP; PAH to Janet Peck, February 28, 1904, PC; G. W. Brockhurst, Singleton, Benda and Co., Ltd. in Yokohama, Japan to PAH, March 5, 1904, GPAHP; PAH to Mrs. Meyer, May 15, 1904, GPAHP.

65. James C. Hooe to PAH, May 29, 1904, GPAHP; PAH to Mrs. Meyer, May 15, 1904, GPAHP; PAH to directors of the San Francisco Settlement Association, May 15, 1904, GPAHP; PAH to Janet Peck, February 28, 1904, PC.

66. PAH to the directors of the San Francisco Settlement Association, May 15, 1904, GPAHP; PAH to Janet Peck, February 28, 1904, PC; Eaves, "University Settlements and Trade Unions," 1.

67. PAH to Mrs. Meyer, May 15, 1904, GPAHP; PAH to the directors of the San Francisco Settlement Association, May 15, 1904, GPAHP; PAH to Janet Peck, February 28, 1904, PC; PAH to Janet Peck, August 1, 1904, PC.

68. PAH to Janet Peck, February 28, 1904, PC.

69. PAH to Janet Peck, February 28, 1904, PC; PAH to Mr. D. M. Sharp, March 27, 1904, GPAHP; Alice Cunningham Fletcher to PAH, February 29, 1904, GPAHP; PAH to Mrs. Meyer, May 15, 1904, GPAHP; PAH to Orrin Peck, February 28, 1905, OPC.

70. Rodgers, "Capitalism and Politics," 381, 384.

71. PAH to George Hearst, August 16, 1873, GPAHP; Brooks, "Phoebe Apperson Hearst," part 1, chap. 1, 1–5; Remus, "Tippling Ladies," 751–77; "Mrs. Hearst Considers Prohibition a Mistake," *San Francisco Examiner*, July 27, 1914, San Francisco History Center, San Francisco Public Library, San Francisco; Thomas Barry Diary, June 11, 12, 1879, transcript, May–August, 1879, TBD; Arthur George to PAH, Labor Day, no year, GPAHP; Gerard d'Aquin to PAH, January 23, 1906, GPAHP; PAH to Orrin Peck, February 28, 1905, OPC; Hoganson, "Cosmopolitan Domesticity," 55–83; Kloppenberg, *Uncertain Victory*, 5. While abroad, Hearst had 480 bottles of wine "shipped from Rotterdam" to Pleasanton, California, via Panama. See Richard A. Clark to PAH, October 21, 1905, box 6, folder Post 1900, HFA.

72. "Mrs. Hearst's Colonial Ball will end social season in D.C., *Vanity*, New York City, February 14, 1895, original newspaper clipping in author's possession; "Rococo Concert," *Boston Herald*, February 27, 1895; "All in Colonial Dress," *Philadelphia Telegram*, February 27, 1895; PAH to *Chicago Herald* editor, April 1, 1895, GPAHP; Horowitz, *Morality of Spending*, xxvii. Phoebe

Hearst never revealed the total amount of money she spent on social events. She, or her employees, kept meticulous records. It is possible to examine these records closely and add the total costs she spent on each event. But it is unclear if an accurate total of what Hearst spent on social entertainments could be obtained. See Charles H. Babbitt in account will Mrs. P. A. Hearst, From February 1, 1895 (date of last statement), to December 1, 1895, box 8, HFA. Account sheets and business receipts are contained in the Hearst Family Archive—Phoebe A. Hearst, Hearst Corporation, San Francisco.

73. PAH to George Hearst, May 11 and June 5, 1873, GPAHP; Nickliss, "Phoebe Apperson Hearst's 'Gospel of Wealth'"; Homberger, *Mrs. Astor's New York*, 4, 237, 242, 244, 246, 250, 252.

74. Paris Apartment Map, box 77, folder 3, GPAHP; PAH to Eliza Pike, Sept, 15, 1867, GPAHP.

75. PAH to Mrs. Wright, January 30, 1909, GPAHP.

76. PAH to Mrs. Meyer, May 15, 1904, GPAHP; PAH note attached to application to be included in the *San Francisco Blue Book*, 1906, GPAHP; Arthur T. Goldsborough to PAH, February 28, 1906, GPAHP; Horowitz, *Morality of Spending*, 30–33; Rodgers, *Atlantic Crossings*, 3.

77. Cronon, Miles, and Gitlin, "Becoming West," 3–27; Pitkin, *Concept of Representation*; University of California, PAH Request for Leave of Absence from Board of Regents' Meetings, May 16, 1904, box 37, folder 5, UCARCH; PAH to Janet Peck, February 28, 1904, PC; PAH to Mr. D. M. Sharp, March 27, 1904, GPAHP; Alice Cunningham Fletcher to PAH, February 29, 1904, GPAHP; PAH to Mrs. Meyer, May 15, 1904, GPAHP; PAH to Miss Egan, January 10, 1906, GPAHP.

78. PAH to Mrs. Meyer, May 15, 1904, GPAHP; "Mrs. Phoebe Hearst, who is famous for her philanthropies, has given notice to the University of California," from the *Pittsburg (Pa.) Leader*, May 29, 1904; "Mrs. Hearst Withdraws Support," *Silver State*, May 30, 1904, GPAHP; "Loses Support of Mrs. Hearst," *San Francisco Call*, May 28, 1904; "Mrs. Hearst Withdraws Aid," *New York Times*, May 28, 1904; F. W. Putnam to A.L. Kroeber, May 31, 1904, Re Department of Anthropology, A. L. Kroeber 1902–1903, including Reports of the Department of Anthropology, Re UC Department of Anthropology,

d'Aquin, Department of Anthropology and Museum, 1901–1909, Putnam Correspondence.

79. F. W. Putnam to A.L. Kroeber, May 31, 1904, Re Department of Anthropology, A.L. Kroeber 1902–1903, including Reports of the Department of Anthropology, Re UC Department of Anthropology, d'Aquin, Department of Anthropology and Museum, 1901–1909, Putnam Correspondence; F. W. Putnam to Max Uhle, October 8, 1904, Re University of California Department of Anthropology, Putnam Correspondence; PAH to F. W. Putnam, December 31, 1904, Re UC Department of Anthropology, Miscellaneous, Putnam Correspondence.

80. F. W. Putnam to A. L. Kroeber, May 31, 1904, Re Department of Anthropology, A. L. Kroeber 1902–1903, including Reports of the Department of Anthropology, Re Department of Anthropology, d'Aquin, Department of Anthropology and Museum, 1901–1909, Putnam Correspondence; F. W. Putnam to Benjamin I. Wheeler, May 30, 1904, draft, personal and confidential, Re Department of Anthropology, d'Aquin, Department of Anthropology and Museum, 1901–1909, Putnam Correspondence; PAH to F. W. Putnam, December 31, 1904, Re Department of Anthropology, Miscellaneous, Putnam Correspondence; Edward Hardy Clark to PAH, May 19, 1904, GPAHP; University of California, *Department of Anthropology*, 8–35; Edward Hardy Clark to PAH, May 19, 1904, GPAHP; Thoresen, "Paying the Piper," 257, 272–73.

81. F. W. Putnam to Benjamin I. Wheeler, May 30, 1904, draft, personal and confidential, Re Department of Anthropology, d'Aquin, Department of Anthropology and Museum, 1901–1909, Putnam Correspondence; "Mrs. Hearst withdraws Support," *Silver State*, Winnemucca NV, May 30, 1904; Edward Hardy Clark to PAH, May 19, 1904, GPAHP.

82. PAH to F. W. Putnam, December 31, 1904, Re Department of Anthropology, Department of Anthropology and Museum Matters Chiefly Mrs. Hearst, 1901–1910, folder 1, Putnam Correspondence; Nasaw, *Life of William Randolph Hearst*, 172–73.

83. "Mrs. Phoebe Hearst and Her Work," *The Record*, Stockton CA, June 2, 1904; "Mrs. Hearst Makes an Explanation," *The Bulletin*, San Francisco, June 4, 1904, GPAHP; "A Business Woman," *New York Herald*, ca. 1895; Josephine R. Egan to PAH, 1904, GPAHP; "Mrs. Hearst Withdraws Aid," *New York*

Times, May 28, 1904; "Benefactions Will Not End," *San Francisco Call*, May 29, 1904; "Drops College Settlement," *San Francisco Chronicle*, June 1, 1904; West Berkeley College Settlement, Special Report, 1904, GPAHP; PAH to Mrs. Grace Gallander Kendall, April 3, 1905, GPAHP; "Good Fairy in Eclipse," *Chicago-Record Herald*, November 4, 1904, Miscellaneous Clippings, GPAHP.

84. PAH to Benjamin Ide Wheeler, February 10, 1905, GPAHP; Josephine R. Egan to PAH, 1904, GPAHP; PAH to Frederic W. Putnam, December 31, 1904, Re Department of Anthropology, Museum Matters Chiefly Mrs. Hearst, 1901–1910, Putnam Correspondence; Josephine R. Egan to PAH, June 11, 1904, GPAHP.

85. Sara Y. Stevenson to PAH, January 29, 1897, GPAHP; PAH to F. W. Putnam, December 31, 1904, Re Department of Anthropology, Department of Anthropology and Museum Matters Chiefly Mrs. Hearst, 1901–1910, folder 1, Putnam Correspondence, 5; University of California, *By-Laws of the Board of Regents of the University of California* (Sacramento: J. D. Young, 1880), 5; PAH to Board of Regents, February 8, 1905, Regents Records, series 1, box 37, folder 5, UCARCH; PAH to Benjamin Ide Wheeler, February 10, 1905, GPAHP.

86. George C. Pardee to PAH, April 17, 1905, GPAHP; Benjamin I. Wheeler to PAH, April 20, 1905, Regents: P. A. Hearst, 1905–1911, Records of the Regents, carton 66, folder 16, UCARCH.

87. A. L. Kroeber to Frederic W. Putnam, May 15, 1904, Re Department of Anthropology, Putnam Correspondence; Alfred L. Kroeber to PAH, July 26, 1904, GPAHP; PAH to Alfred L. Kroeber, May 5, 1903, GPAHP; Alfred L. Kroeber to PAH, n.d., GPAHP; PAH to Benjamin Ide Wheeler, February 26, 1907, series 1, box 7, folder 168, UCROP; Alfred L. Kroeber to PAH, February 27, and March 28, 1911, series 1, box 7, folder 168, UCROP; University of California, Regents Records, Secretary's Office, Secretary's Reports, 1908, series 1, box 68, folder 24, UCROP; University of California, Anthropology: 1907–1909, Regents Records, series 1, box 55, folder 36, UCROP.

88. G. J. M. E. d'Aquin, "Last(est) Quarterly Report of the Department of Anthropology of the University of California, September 30, 1902, University of California Department of Anthropology, Putnam Correspondence 1901–1910, 3. Phoebe Hearst provided this figure.

89. Bourdieu, "Structures, Habitus, Power," 181.

1. Phoebe Hearst "is full of fizz," "incomplete letters–correspondents unidentified; fragments of letters," GPAHP.

2. PAH to Janet Peck, February 7, 1905, PC; Julia Sommer, "Women Who
Built Berkeley: Phoebe Apperson Hearst," *Cal Report*, Fall 1992, Phoebe
Apperson Hearst Biography Collection, San Francisco History Center, San
Francisco Public Library, 1, 14; PAH to Orrin Peck, February 9, 1905, PC;
PAH to Orrin Peck, February 28, 1905, OPC.

3. Millicent Willson Hearst to PAH, 1906, GPAHP; Benjamin Ide Wheeler to
PAH, April 23, 1906, GPAHP; Edward Clark to PAH, April 23, April 24, and
April 28, 1906, GPAHP; PAH to Alice, June 1, 1906, GPAHP.

4. Millicent was a sixteen-year-old chorus girl and dancer at Herald Square
Theatre in New York before she met Will. See Nasaw, *Life of William Ran-
dolph Hearst*, 252, 205–14. See also Sigmund Beel to PAH, September 28,
1906, GPAHP; Sparks, *Capital Intentions*, 11, 148; Millicent Veronica Willson
Hearst to PAH, 1906, GPAHP; PAH to Alice, June 1, 1906, GPAHP; PAH to
Josephine R. Egan, January 26, 1906, GPAHP.

5. PAH to Alice, June 1, 1906, GPAHP; PAH to Miss Egan, January 26, 1906,
GPAHP; Edward H. Clark to PAH, April 28, 1906, GPAHP.

6. Sigmund Beel to PAH, September 28, 1906, GPAHP; William Randolph
Hearst to PAH, 1905, GPAHP; William Randolph Hearst to PAH, early
1905, GPAHP; Nasaw, *Life of William Randolph Hearst*, 205–14; William
Randolph Hearst to PAH, 1906, GPAHP; William Randolph Hearst to PAH,
Summer 1906, GPAHP.

7. Edward H. Clark to PAH, April 28, 1906, GPAHP; William Randolph Hearst
to PAH, ca. 1893, GPAHP; William Randolph Hearst Letters and Telegrams to
his Parents, William Randolph Hearst Papers, Bancroft Library, University of
California, Berkeley; PAH to Orrin Peck, January 14, 1907, PC; Nasaw, *Life
of William Randolph Hearst*, 205–17; PAH to Mrs. Holden, January 5, 1907,
copied from original in possession of Charles S. Pope, GPAHP. The repaired
Hearst Building, without a high-rise tower, stands today at the corner of
Market and Third Streets in San Francisco.

8. Letter from Robert Ingersoll Aitken, July 14, 1907, GPAHP; Katz, "Socialist
Women and Progressive Reform," 118.

9. Sparks, *Capital Intentions*; Kessler-Harris, "Wages of Patriarchy," 7–21; Butsch, *For Fun and Profit*; Finnegan, *Selling Suffrage*, 3; Cohen, "Citizens and Consumers," 145–61. There is a vast literature on female and male progressive reform. For example, see Gordon, *Gender and Higher Education*; Fitzpatrick, *Endless Crusade*; Muncy, *Creating A Female Dominion*; Frankel and Dye, *Gender, Class, Race, and Reform*; Rodgers, *Atlantic Crossings*; Rodgers, "In Search of Progressivism," 113–32; Flanagan, *American Reformed*; Kloppenberg, *Uncertain Victory*; Quinn *Black Neighbors*; Lessoff, Rodgers, Stock, Postel, and Johnston, "Forum: Populists and Progressives, Capitalism and Democracy," 377–43.

10. Simpson, *Problems Women Solved*; Tilly and Gurin, "Women, Politics, and Change," 3–31; Lebsock, "Women and American Politics," 35–62; Markwyn, "Encountering 'Woman' on the Fairgrounds," 169–86; Boisseau and Markwyn, "World's Fairs in Feminist Historical Perspective," 4; Rydell, *All the World's a Fair*, 214, chap. 8; Benedict, *Anthropology of World's Fairs*, 6; Todd, *Story of the Exposition*, 1:2, 35–37, 41, xiii; Muncy, *Creating a Female Dominion*, chap. 2, 38; Ewald and Clute, *San Francisco Invites the World*, 5; D. Anderson, "Through Fire and Fair by the Golden Gate," part 1, 246–50.

11. Rydell, *All the World's a Fair*, 209, chap. 8; Todd, *Story of the Exposition*, 1:xiii, xiv; Ewald and Clute, *San Francisco Invites the World*, 16, 7; Adams and Keene, *Alice Paul and the American Suffrage Campaign*, 104.

12. Buchanan and Stuart, eds., *History of the Panama-Pacific International Exposition*, 29, 30; Rydell, *All the World's a Fair*, 213; Todd, *Story of the Exposition*, 1:41, 126–27; Sparks, *Capital Intentions*, 189.

13. PPIE, "Voting Trust Panama-Pacific International Exposition Company," March 24, 1910, PPIE Records, 1893–1929, Panama-Pacific International Exposition Company pamphlet, carton 15, folder 23; Buchanan and Stuart, *History of the Panama-Pacific International Exposition*, 31.

14. Buchanan and Stuart, *History of the Panama-Pacific International Exposition*, 31; Simpson, *Problems Women Solved*, 12; "San Francisco Clubwoman, Philanthropist, Dies Suddenly," *San Francisco Examiner*, January 1, 1925, Mrs. I. Lowenberg envelope, *San Francisco Examiner* Newspaper Clipping Morgue, San Francisco History Center, San Francisco Public Library, San Francisco (hereafter San Francisco History Center); Gullett, *Becoming Citizens*, 116, 121,

133; "Many Laws Bad for People," *San Francisco Call*, September 24, 1913, *San Francisco Examiner* Newspaper Clipping Morgue, San Francisco History Center; "Death Takes Mrs. Lovell White," *San Francisco Examiner*, January 19, 1916, Mrs. Lovell White envelope, *San Francisco Examiner* Newspaper Clipping Morgue, San Francisco History Center; note that White, Lowenberg, and Hearst are listed in the *San Francisco Blue Book, Season 1910–1911* (San Francisco, 1911), 104, 80, 71, accessed August 6, 2014. For detailed information on PPIE women and men, see the *San Francisco Examiner* Newspaper Clipping Morgue, San Francisco History Center; Pitkin, *Concept of Representation*.

15. Simpson, *Problems Women Solved*, 5–6, 12; "San Francisco Welfare Worker Dies," *San Francisco Examiner*, October 31, 1925, *San Francisco Examiner* Newspaper Clipping Morgue, John F. Merrill and Wife envelope, San Francisco History Center; "Woman Leader Dies At Home," March 21, 1921, *San Francisco Examiner*, Mrs. Aylett Raine Cotton envelope, *San Francisco Examiner*, Newspaper Clipping Morgue, San Francisco History Center; Laura Lovell White to PAH, September 28, 1910, GPAHP; White to PAH, October 3, 1910, GPAHP; White to PAH, October 8, 1910, GPAHP.

16. Simpson, *Problems Women Solved*, 5; Hopkins, *Concise Dictionary of American Biography*, 514, 787.

17. Phoebe Apperson Hearst, PAHD; Brooks, "Phoebe Apperson Hearst," part 1, chap. 1, pp. 1–5; PAH to Orrin Peck, December 22, 1886, PC; Gustafson, "Partisan Women in the Progressive Era," 11; Muncy, *Creating a Female Dominion*, xii; Gustafson, Miller, and Perry, introduction to *We Have Come to Stay*, ix–xiv; Gustafson, "Partisan and Nonpartisan," 1–12; Gustafson, *Women and the Republican Party*.

18. Gustafson, *Women and the Republican Party*, chaps. 3–6; "Women Must Remain Non-Partisan," *Suffragist*, October 7, 1916, 6; Arthur MacArthur to PAH, March 27, 1888, GPAHP; PAH to Ellen Davis Conway, October 30, 1888, EDCC; Letters to and from PAH and Sarah B. Cooper, SBCP; Women's Educational and Industrial Union, *Women's Educational and Industrial Union*, 17; Gustafson, Miller, and Perry, introduction to *We Have Come to Stay*, xiii; Gustafson, "Partisan and Nonpartisan," 1; Lansing, "Women Are Voluntarily Organizing Themselves."

19. "San Francisco Sure of Fair; Wins in House; Senate Safe," *Los Angeles Herald*, February 1, 1911, PPIE Records, 1893–1929, v. 11, newspaper clippings, 344;

"1915 Bay City Fair Bill Quickly Passes Senate," *Los Angeles Examiner*, February 12, 1911, PPIE Records, 1893–1929, 361; "Exposition for 'Frisco Is Certain," *Times*, Rochester NY, February 11, 1911, v. 18, PPIE Records, 1893–1929, 130; Joseph Scott, "Mr. Hearst Was One of the Great Factors in Our Success," *Los Angeles Examiner*, February 1, 1911, PPIE Records, 1893–1929, v. 11, newspaper clippings, 348; "New Orleans Is Depressed, But Keeps in Fight," *Los Angeles Examiner*, February 2, 1911, PPIE Records, 1893–1929, 346; Pfeffer, *Southern Ladies and Suffragists*, 18.

20. PPIE, "Chronological History of the Panama-Pacific International Exposition," PPIE Records, 1893–1929, April 27, 1911, carton 15, folder 7, p. 24.

21. Simpson, *Problems Women Solved*, 5, 6; Todd, *Story of the Exhibition*, 1:110, 266–71, 135; Social Register Association, *Social Register, San Francisco including Oakland, 1912*, vol. 26 (New York, November 1911), 74; "First Contracts Let on Carolan Gardens," *San Francisco Examiner*, August 1, 1914, *San Francisco Examiner* Newspaper Clipping Morgue, Francis J. Carolan and Wife Harriet envelope, San Francisco History Center; "John Merrill, Noted Merchant, Is Dead," *San Francisco Examiner*, September 10, 1912, John F. Merrill and wife envelope, *San Francisco Examiner* Newspaper Clipping Morgue, San Francisco History Center.

22. PAH to Mrs. Wright, January 30, 1909, GPAHP; University of California, Regents Meeting, Regents Records, October 8, 1907, series 1, box 67, folder 6, UCARCH; PAH to Benjamin Ide Wheeler, November 7, 1907, Regents Records, series 1, box 66, folder 16, UCARCH; Susan Lincoln Mills to PAH, April 30, ca. 1909, PAH note, GPAHP; F. Von Lindner to PAH, October 13, 1909, PAH note, GPAHP; PAH to Frances Douglas Lummis, January 14, 1909, FDLP; M. E. Vanderbilt to PAH, July 17, 1910, PAH note, GPAHP; Jeanne Elizabeth Wier to PAH, July 23, 1910, PAH note, GPAHP; Clara R. Merrill to PAH, August 9, 1910, PAH note, GPAHP; PAH to Benjamin Ide Wheeler, Regents Records, July 3, 1911, series 1, carton 66, folder 16, UCARCH.

23. Simpson, *Problems Women Solved*, 4; Markwyn, *Empress of San Francisco*, chap. 7; Rydell, *All the World's a Fair*, chap. 8.

24. Boutelle, *Julia Morgan*, 172–73; Simpson, *Problems Women Solved*, 9, 110; Garnett, "Stately Homes of California," 844; Garnett, *Stately Homes of California*, 26; Donald Hamilton McLaughlin, "Careers in Mining Geology and

Management, University Governance and Teaching," interview by Harriet Nathan, 20, 14, 18; Hayes, "Weekend in the Country," 25; Harriet Bradford Talks about Mrs. Phoebe Apperson Hearst, June 26, 1964, HBT, copy in author's possession; R. G. Cholmeley-Jones to PAH, August 1, 1913, Motor Service Bureau of the *American Review of Reviews*, GPAHP.

25. Harriet Bradford Talks About Mrs. Phoebe Apperson Hearst, June 26, 1964, HBT; Homberger, *Mrs. Astor's New York*, 152; Harriet Bradford to Edward H. Clark, July 27, 1964, GPAHP; Adelaide Johnson to Phoebe A. Hearst, October 22, 1913, GPAHP; Handler, "Review Essays: Cultural Theory in History Today," 1520; Scott, *Only Paradoxes to Offer*, chap. 2.

26. Simpson, *Problems Women Solved*, 4, 8; Susman, *Culture as History*, xx–xxx.

27. Simpson, *Problems Women Solved*, 9; Susman, *Culture As History*, 276, 281; PAH to Frances Douglas Lummis, September 9, 1911, FDLP; Hayes, "Weekend in the Country," 25; Brooks, "Phoebe Apperson Hearst," "Mrs. Wickersham's Notes, Taken from Halting and Very Imperfect Diction, February 1927," GPAHP, second 1, second 2; Guest Lists, 1914, Guest Lists, 1915, and Guest Lists, GPAHP; Guest Book (bound in velvet with metal clasps), April 25, 1916, GPAHP; "Countess Aberdeen Here To-Day," *San Francisco Examiner*, October 31, 1915, PPIER 1893–1929, vol. 47, newspaper clippings, 234; "British Noblewoman Open International Congress," *San Francisco Chronicle*, November 2, 1915, PPIER 1893–1929, vol. 47, newspaper clippings; Todd, *Story of the Exposition*, vol. 2; PPIE, *An Announcement: Congresses, Conferences, and Conventions; Panama-Pacific International Exposition* (San Francisco, 1915), booklet, box 32, 5, HFA; PAH to Mrs. Lynch, 1915, GPAHP.

See GPAHP for lists of PAH invited guests who represented diverse fields and organizations. Visitors included notable businessmen, architects, artists, professionals, like members of the historical association, scientists, such as Thomas Edison, and feminists and suffragists like Katherine Philips Edson and Sara Bard Field. Prominent national and state politicians and organizations were well represented too. Guests talked to members of the Association of Prison Directors, former president William Howard Taft, Taft's vice president Thomas Marshall, Speaker of the House of Representatives from 1911 to 1919, and soon-to-be Democratic Party presidential candidate Champ Clark, the former governor of New York, Martin Glynn, and other prominent and aspiring individuals. Members of the General Federation of Women's Clubs, the National Child Labor Committee, the National Suffrage Headquarters, and the Lux School of Industrial Training were there too. See citations above in this footnote.

28. PAH to Frances Douglas Lummis, September 9, 1911, FDLP; Alex O. Richard to PAH, July 20, 1911, PAH note on back of page 2, GPAHP.

29. Guest Lists, 1914, Guest Lists, 1915, GPAHP; Elizabeth W. Pringle to unknown, 1915, EWAP; Guest Book, April 25, 1916, GPAHP; PPIE Woman's Board, "Story of Women's Activities at the PPIE, The Woman's Board," typed copy, p. 7, PPIEWB.

30. University of California Faculty Club, March 17, 1911, GPAHP; Moore, "Manliness and the New American Empire," 75–94.

31. Susman, *Culture as History*, 271–85; William J. Monroe to PAH, April 14, 1895, GPAHP; Mary Hooper to PAH, ca. February 1911, GPAHP; Hooper to PAH, September 12, 1911, GPAHP; Mary Meares Galt to PAH, July 26, 1911, GPAHP; Charlotte Frances Kett to PAH, May 29, 1912, GPAHP; Murray F. Taylor to PAH, December 18, 1908, GPAHP.

32. Mary W. Kincaid to PAH, March 31, 1911, GPAHP; Alex O. Richards to PAH, July 20, 1911, GPAHP; PAH to Frances Lummis, September 9, 1911,FDLP; Ada Butterfield Jones to PAH, February 1891, GPAHP; Simpson, *Problems Women Solved*, 1–5, 8; Chronological History of the PPIE, PPIER 1893–1929, carton 15, 24; Deutsch, *Women and the City*, 289–90.

33. Margaret E. Schallenberger to PAH, April 14, 1914, GPAHP.

34. PAH to Orrin Peck, May 26, 1896, PC; Ada (Butterfield) Jones, October 18,1907, GPAHP; PAH note on Edna Hallouquist to PAH, February 19, 1911, GPAHP; Mary Hooper to PAH, September 12, 1911, GPAHP; Louba Landfeld Loubanoff-Rastovsky to PAH, June 13, 1909, GPAHP; "House Party at Pleasanton Hills," no newspaper title, c. 1915–1916; Childs, "Elizabeth Waties Allston Pringle," 3:100–101; Elizabeth W. Allston Pringle to Mrs. C. A. Hill, July 19, 1915, EWAP.

35. PPIE, "Chronological History of the PPIE," PPIER 1893–1929, carton 15, folder 7, 24. Markwyn states that "three hundred local women soon chartered the Panama-Pacific International Association of Women, which later became the Woman's Board." There were thirty-two members of the Woman's Board

Directorate, according to "The Articles of Incorporation." See Markwyn, *Empress of San Francisco*, 19; "Articles of Incorporation of the Woman's Board of the Panama-Pacific International Exposition and World's Fair," PPIER 1893–1929, carton 146, folder 11; Brooks, "Phoebe Apperson Hearst," Mrs. Brooks, February 28, 1927, p. 3, GPAHP. Also PPIE, "Articles of Incorporation of the Panama-Pacific International Exposition Company. Incorporated under the Laws of the State of California. March 22nd, 1910," PPIER 1893–1929, box 24, folder 6, 61; PPIE, "Articles of Incorporation of the Woman's Board of the Panama-Pacific International Exposition and World's Fair," PPIER 1893–1929, carton 146, folder 11, 1, 2; Simpson, *Problems Women Solved*, 2; *San Francisco Blue Book Season 1910–1911*; W. J. Metson to Rudolph J. Taussig, October 24, 1911, PPIER 1893–1929, carton 11, folder 4, p. 1. See *San Francisco Examiner* Newspaper Clipping Morgue, San Francisco History Center for information on members of the Woman's Board. On the incorporation of the board of directors and the election of members, see Todd, *Story of the Exposition*, vol. 1, chaps. 9, 14, 22.

36. Litwicki, "From the 'ornamental and evanescent' to 'good, useful things'"; Frederick Bechmann to PAH, December 27, 1910, GPAHP; Finnegan, *Selling Suffrage*; Mollie Conners, "Mrs. Phoebe Hearst: An Appreciation," no newspaper name, December 25, ca. 1911, GPAHP.

37. Ada Butterfield Jones to PAH, October 10, 1890, GPAHP; Robinson, *Hearsts*, 28.

38. Katherine to PAH, June 27, no year, GPAHP; William Randolph Hearst Jr. with Jack Casserly, *Hearsts: Father and Son*, 19–20; "At Hacienda del Pozo de Verona," *Santa Cruz Surf*, November 21 or 22, 1911, newspaper clippings, GPAHP; PAH to Alfred Kroeber, December 13, 1911, GPAHP. See GPAHP for additional Christmas lists.

39. "Mrs. Merrill's Will Is Filed," *San Francisco Examiner*, November 5, 1925, *San Francisco Examiner* Newspaper Clipping Morgue, John F. Merrill and wife envelope, San Francisco History Center; "John Merrill, Noted Merchant, Is Dead," *San Francisco Examiner*, September 10, 1912, *San Francisco Examiner* Newspaper Clipping Morgue.

40. Simpson, *Problems Women Solved*, 16, 6; Charlotte Anita Whitney to PAH, June 24, 1911, GPAHP; "Chronological History," PPIER 1893–1929, March 6, 1912, carton 15, folder 7, 53.

41. Katherine E. Cerf to PAH, September 15, 1911, GPAHP; "Chronological History," PPIER 1893–1929, March 6, 1912, carton 15, folder 7, 53; Simpson, *Problems Women Solved*, 6, 8–9; editorial, *California Magazine* (July 1915), 372; "By-Laws of the Woman's Board of the Panama-Pacific International Exposition," PPIER 1893–1929, carton 146, folder 11, 3.

42. PPIE, "Chronological History of the PPIE," May 12, 1911, PPIER 1893–1929, carton 15, folder 7, 24, 61; "Women Organize as Auxiliary to World's Fair Directors," *San Francisco Examiner*, November 13, 1911, 3; Markwyn, *Empress of San Francisco*; Todd, *Story of the Exposition*, 2:324–29.

43. "Phoebe Apperson Hearst President of the Panama-Pacific International Exposition," ca. 1911, newspaper clippings, GPAHP; Brooks, "Phoebe Apperson Hearst," Mrs. Brooks, February 28, 1927, pp. 1–2, GPAHP.

44. Brooks, "Phoebe Apperson Hearst," Mrs. Brooks, part 5, typewritten copy, GPAHP; Brooks, "Phoebe Apperson Hearst," Mrs. Brooks, February 28, 1927, p. 2, GPAHP; M. E. Vanderbilt to PAH, July 19, 1914, GPAHP; Simpson, *Problems Women Solved*, 6, 9–11.

45. Simpson, *Problems Women Solved*, xi–xiii, 6; "An Uncrowned Queen," *New American Woman*, n.d., ca. 1915, 17, magazine clipping in author's possession; Hannah Cushing to PAH, August 9, 1913, GPAHP; Rydell, *All the World's a Fair*, 214; Pitkin, *Concept of Representation*, 2, 3, 4, 38–41, chaps. 4–9.

46. Simpson, *Problems Women Solved*, 2, ix. On the limits of power, see Nickliss, "Phoebe Apperson Hearst," chaps. 4 and above.

47. Gavin McNab to Board of Directors of the PPIE Corporation, PPIE Records, 1893–1929, October 24, 1911, carton 11, folder 4, 1–2, 7; Helen Sanborn to PAH, n.d., GPAHP.

48. Gavin McNab to Board of Directors of the PPIE Corporation, PPIER 1893–1929, October 24, 1911, carton 11, folder 4, 4; PPIE, "Voting Trust," March 24, 1910, PPIER 1893–1929, Panama-Pacific International Exposition Company pamphlet, carton 15, folder 23, 1–16.

49. PPIE, "By-Laws of the Woman's Board of the Panama-Pacific International Exposition," PPIER 1893–1929, pamphlet, carton 146, folder 11, 2.

50. "The Articles of Incorporation of the Woman's Board of the Panama-Pacific International Exposition and World's Fair," PPIER 1893–1929, carton 146, folder 11; Simpson, *Problems Women Solved*, 1, 13.

51. Buchanan and Stuart, *History of the Panama-Pacific International Exposition*, 64.

52. Hearst was a member of the finance committee. See "Story of the Women's Activities at the PPIE," 8, PPIEWB. The PPIE Corporation was not organized for financial profit. But the PPIE male and female directors were expected to hold a financially successful exposition that was not in debt when it opened. Todd, *Story of the Exposition*, 1:134.

53. Simpson, *Problems Women Solved*, x; Gavin McNab to Board of Directors of the PPIE Company, PPIER October 24, 1911, carton 11, folder 4, 6, 7; W. J. Metson to Rudolph J. Taussig, October 24, 1911, copy, PPIER 1893–1929, Carton 11, folder 4; Todd, *Story of the Exposition*, 1:100; John Britton to Board of Directors of the PPIE Company, Minutes of the Board of Directors of the PPIE Company, vol. 129, no. 2, PPIER 1893–1929, October 11, 1911, 125; Charles C. Moore to Board of Directors of the PPIE, PPIER November 9, 1911, carton 11, folder 4, 2.

54. PPIE, Minutes of the Executive Committee of the PPIE Company, 1910–1916, vol. 124, PPIER 1893–1929, April 14, 1912, 86.

55. Simpson, *Problems Women Solved*, xi.

56. Phoebe Hearst, January 1, 1866, PAHD; Brooks, "Phoebe Apperson Hearst," part 1, chap. 1, pp. 1–5; Brooks, "Notes on Mrs. Hearst's Biography: Mrs. Brooks, February 28, 1927," p. 7, GPAHP; Rodgers, *Atlantic Crossings*, chap. 5, 160; PAH to Ada Butterfield, August 17, 1886, GPAHP; Todd, *Story of the Exposition*, 2:325.

57. Brooks, "Phoebe Apperson Hearst," Mrs. Brooks, February 28, 1927, p. 7, GPAHP; Todd, *Story of the Exposition*, 2:226–27, 2:327.

58. Helen Sanborn to PAH, October 5, 1914, GPAHP; Helen Sanborn to PAH, December 28, 1912, GPAHP; Brooks, "Phoebe Apperson Hearst," Mrs. Brooks, February 28, 1927, 7, 8, 3, GPAHP; "List of Women Appointed as Assistants to Various Departments," PPIER 1893–1929, n.d., carton 11, folder 4.

59. Simpson, *Problems Women Solved*, 12; PAH to Eliza Pike, September 15, 1867, GPAHP; Ada Butterfield Jones to PAH, February 1891, GPAHP.

60. Mary McLean Olney to Mrs. Keck, June 29, 1913, GPAHP.

61. Cross, "Grace Hoadley Dodge," 1:489–92; National Board of the YWCA of the USA, October 19, 1911, National Board Minutes, 1910–1912, 1–2, NYWCA; Phoebe Hearst, February 4, 1866, PAHD; Phoebe Hearst, March 4, 1866,

PAHD; San Francisco YWCA, Eighteenth Annual Report, January 3, 1896, San Francisco YWCA Archives, 28, 34; Florence M. Romaine, "History of the YWCA in San Francisco 1878–1930, *YWCA Program*, Florence M. Romaine for 1932, Program Planning Study, San Francisco YWCA Archives, 13, 16; Young Women's Christian Association, *San Francisco Young Women's Christian Association Twenty-Sixth Annual Report*, January 8, 1904, San Francisco YWCA Archives, 37; National Board of the YWCA of the USA, December 6, 1911, National YWCA Board Minutes, 1910–1912, 2–3, 26, NYWCA; Clemens, *Standing Ground*, 41; Mary G. Welch, chairman and Rose F. Smith, secretary, State Committee of California, YWCA, May 25, 1900, GPAHP; Brooks, "Phoebe Apperson Hearst," part 4 (Mrs. Brooks), 2, 10, GPAHP.

62. Mary B. Ritter to PAH, October 9(?), 1911, GPAHP; PAH to Ritter, October 5, 1910, PAH note, GPAHP; National Board of the YWCA of the USA, National YWCA Board Minutes, 1910–1912, October 19, 1911, 2, NYWCA.

63. Margaret Rowan to PAH, February 22, 1905, GPAHP; Harriet Taylor, executive secretary of the Foreign Department of the YWCA, to PAH, October 27, 1911, GPAHP; Mary (McLean) Olney to PAH, August 22, 1912, GPAHP; Olney to PAH, August 7, 1912, GPAHP. Olney was head of the Pacific Coast Field Committee, vice chair of the Pacific Coast Territorial Committee of the National Board, the YWCA board president (1905–6), and the wife of Judge Warren Olney. Also Marion E. Hopkins, "The Lunch Room of the Young Women's Christian Association," *Association Monthly* 4 (March 1910): 52–54; Walter Mabie Wood, "Successful Secretarial Administration," *Association Monthly* 4 (November 1910): 404–5; YWCA, Editorial Department, "The Short Term of the Training School," *Association Monthly* 4 (April 1911): 119–20; Kessler-Harris, *Woman's Wage*, 11–13; Mary S. Sims, "For Working Girls—A Living Wage," *Association Monthly* 9 (June 1915): 219–21.

64. PAH to Ritter, October 5, 1910, PAH note, GPAHP.

65. Grace H. Dodge to PAH, April 5, 1911, GPAHP.

66. Sewell, *Women and the Everyday City*, 127, 128, 135, 130, 133; Cross, "Grace Hoadley Dodge, 1:489–92; Harriet Taylor, executive secretary of the Foreign Department of the National Board of the YWCA, to PAH, October 27, 1911, GPAHP; National Board of the YWCA of the USA, December 6, 1911, National Board Minutes, 1910–1912, 2–3, 26, NYWCA; "Mrs. Hearst Invites

Y.W.C.A. Convention," *San Francisco Examiner*, December 7, 1911, *San Francisco Examiner* Newspaper Clipping Morgue, 1907–1988, envelope 1, San Francisco History Center; Clemens, *Standing Ground*, 59; Brooks, "Phoebe Apperson Hearst," part 4 (Mrs. Brooks), 1, 2, 6, 10, GPAHP; Donaldina Cameron to PAH, n.d., PAH answered July 9, 1913, GPAHP; Mrs. Phoebe Hearst Honored By Y.W.C.A.," *San Francisco Examiner*, January 17, 1912, *San Francisco Examiner* Newspaper Clipping Morgue, 1907–1988, envelope 1, San Francisco History Center.

67. Grace H. Dodge to PAH, April 5, 1911, GPAHP.

68. "Women Hear Tribute to Mrs. Phoebe Hearst," *San Francisco Examiner*, February 18, 1912, *San Francisco Examiner* Newspaper Clipping Morgue, 1907–1988, envelope 1, San Francisco History Center.

69. YWCA, General Secretary's Report, October 1, 1913, 2, NYWCA; Douglas Firth Anderson uses the term Anglo-Protestant "as shorthand for Anglo-American Protestant." He defines Anglo-Protestant as the "community of British- and Northern European–derived theological traditions bound together in the United States by transdenominational organizations, revivalistic experience, republican ideology, and hegemonic aspirations." See Anderson, "We Have Here a Different Civilization," 200; Kipp, *Religion and Society in Frontier California*, 14, 37, 46, 27, 43; McDonald, "Presbyterian Church and the Social Gospel," 241–52.

70. Mathews, "Forging a Cosmopolitan Civic Culture, 214; Matthews defines cosmopolitan as "composed of elements gathered from all various parts of the world." See also Anderson, "We Have Here a Different Civilization," 203.

71. PAH to Frances Douglas Lummis, July 6, 1912, FDLP; Brooks, "Phoebe Apperson Hearst," part 4 (Mrs. Brooks), 1–6, 10, GPAHP.

72. YWCA of the USA, Pacific Coast Territorial Committee Minutes, August 19, 1912, NYWCA; Mabel Cratty of New York, General Secretary for the National Board, "Interpretation of the Biennial Report of the National Board presented by Grace H. Dodge of New York," Fourth Biennial Convention of the Young Women's Christian Associations of the United States of America, Richmond VA, April 9–15, 1913, 15, NYWCA; Ella Schooley, "Plans for Young Women's Christian Association work at the Panama-Pacific Exposition were presented

by Miss Ella Schooley of San Francisco," 15–16, NYWCA; Harriet Taylor to PAH, October 27, 1911, GPAHP; Harriet Taylor to PAH, March 2, 1912, GPAHP; Harriet Taylor to PAH, May 9, 1912, GPAHP; Julia Tolman Lee of San Francisco YWCA, *Report for May 1912*, June 7, 1912, 1, 2, GPAHP; YWCA of the USA, *YWCA Building PPIE 1915*, YWCA History–Expositions folder, PPIE pamphlet 1915, NYWCA; Ella Schooley, "Field Work Department Report," November 13–December 12, 1912, NYWCA; Mary (McLean) Olney to Evelyn Brown Keck, June 29, 1913, GPAHP; Young Women's Christian Association, National Board Minutes, May 29, 1912, 21–22, NYWCA.

73. San Francisco YWCA, *Report for May 1912*, June 7, 1912, 2, GPAHP; Sewell, *Women and the Everyday City*, 127, 128, 135, 130, 133; Harriet Taylor, Pacific Coast Territorial Committee of the National YWCA Board, May 9, 1912, GPAHP; Brooks, "Phoebe Apperson Hearst," part 4 (Mrs. Brooks), 1–10, GPAHP; YWCA of the USA, National Board Minutes, December 6, 1911, 2–3, NYWCA; YWCA of the USA, *Report of General Secretary for April 1912*, May 3, 1912, 2, GPAHP; YWCA of the USA, Ella Schooley, "Field Work Department," December 11, 1912, to January 8, 1913, 1555, NYWCA.

74. YWCA of the USA, Field Committee Minutes, August 19, 1912, NYWCA; Mary McL. Olney to Mrs. Keck, June 29, 1912, GPAHP.

75. Sklar, "Hull House in the 1890s," 658–77. The YWCA held PPIE meetings at Asilomar in May and August of 1915. See San Francisco Labor Council Reports, and PPIE, *An Announcement: Congresses, Conferences, Conventions; Panama-Pacific International Exposition, San Francisco 1915* (San Francisco, 1915), booklet, box 32, 5, HFA.

76. Jessie Woodrow Wilson, "What Girls Can Do for Girls," *Good Housekeeping* 56 (April 1913): 437–45; Harriet Taylor to PAH, May 69, 1912, GPAHP; Julia Tolman Lee of the San Francisco YWCA, *Report for May 1912*, June 7, 1912, 1, 2, GPAHP; Brooks, "Phoebe Apperson Hearst," part 4 (Mrs. Brooks), 2–3, 5–7, GPAHP; Lerner, "Placing Women in History," 358.

77. Charlotte Frances Kett to PAH, May 29, 1912, GPAHP. Kett received her PhD from the University of California in 1913. Her thesis is titled: "The Problem of the Individual: Certain Doctrines of Thomas Aquinas and Their Bearing on the Problem of the Individual." Also Emily (Wynn) Elias to PAH, June

16, 1912, GPAHP; (Mrs. Samuel J.) M. H. Broadwell to PAH, March 25, 1913, GPAHP; Mary B. Ritter to PAH, ca. 1912, GPAHP; William Horace Day to PAH, May 30, 1912, GPAHP.

78. Rice, Bullough, and Orsi, *Elusive Eden*, 278; Clemens, *Standing Ground*, 59; YWCA of the USA, Ella Schooley, "Field Work Department," December 11, 1912 to January 8 1913, 1555, NYWCA; YWCA of the USA, National Board Minutes, May 29, 1912, 21–22, NYWCA; Orsi, *Sunset Limited*, 114–23.

79. YWCA of the USA, National Board Minutes, May 29, 1912, 21–22, NYWCA; Southern Pacific Railroad, *California Resorts Along the Coast Line and in the Santa Cruz Mountains*, pamphlet, San Francisco, 1901.

80. Harriet Taylor to PAH, May 19, 1913, GPAHP.

81. YWCA of the USA, National Board Minutes, May 29, 1912, 21, 22 NYWCA; Helen A. Davis, Field Work Department, one month ending December 18, 1912, 1565, NYWCA; Almeda A. Ford to PAH, February 25, 1913, GPAHP; Harriet Taylor to PAH, May 19, 1913, GPAHP.

82. Mary S. Merrill to William R. Hearst, April 2, 1914, GPAHP; Ella Schooley to PAH, October 7, 1914, GPAHP; Clemens, *Standing Ground*, 60; YWCA of the USA, Minutes of Pacific Coast Field Committee of the National Board of the YWCA, May 25, 1914, 3, GPAHP. Hearst gave the association everything from the Hacienda Conference, after it closed, that was movable, including beds, bedding, and towels. This contribution was valued at $11, 574. The value of these monetary gifts to the YWCA was meager when compared to the worth of the gifts Hearst provided to the University of California. See "Young Women's Christian Associations," March, no year, GPAHP; and YWCA of the USA, National Board Minutes, May 29, 1912, 22, NYWCA. Also Eleanor W. Wood, Minutes of Pacific Coast Field Committee Meeting, May 26, 1913, 2–3, GPAHP.

83. Mabel Cratty to PAH, February 25, 1913, GPAHP; Ella Schooley to PAH, July 16, 1913, and March 8, 1913, GPAHP.

84. Mabel Cratty to PAH, February 25, 1913, GPAHP; Ella Schooley to PAH, May 19, 1913, and July 16, 1913, GPAHP; Hazel-Ann Hunt, *Asilomar, the First Fifty Years, 1913–1963* and "Asilomar at Sixty," compiled as a ten-year supplement to the *First Fifty Years 1913–1963*, Bancroft Library, University of California, Berkeley; YWCA of the USA, Pacific Coast Field Committee

Minutes, April 28, 1913, 2, GPAHP; Boutelle, *Julia Morgan*, 23–24, 88; YWCA of the USA, Pacific Coast Field Committee Minutes, May 25, 1914, GPAHP; Chair of the Conference Grounds Committee to Mrs. F. E. Shine, March 14, 1917, GPAHP. The name of the Phoebe A. Hearst Administration Building was changed to the Phoebe Apperson Hearst Social Hall in the summer of 2014, which, in this historian's view, neglects to represent and encapsulate adequately the variety and breadth of the YWCA activities and events that were held there, especially during the PPIE, as well as today. See California State Parks, "YWCA Builds Asilomar," *Asilomar State Beach and Conference Grounds*, Visitor Guide Issue no. 12 (2014): 8. My thanks to Michael J. Meloy, historian of the Asilomar State Beach and Conference Grounds for providing a copy of the visitor guide. See also *Asilomar Conference Grounds*, November 2016, http://www.VisitAsilomar.com.

85. Ella Schooley to PAH, March 8, 1913, GPAHP; Schooley to National YWCA Board, May 19, 1913, GPAHP; Boutelle, *Julia Morgan*, chaps. 2, 5, 7, 8; Julia Morgan to PAH, March 26, 1919, GPAHP; Jessie Woodrow Wilson, "What Girls Can Do For Girls," *Good Housekeeping* 56 (April 1913): 436–45.

86. YWCA of the USA, National Board Minutes, May 29, 1912, 1–23, NYWCA; Evelyn Brown Keck, General Secretary of the San Francisco YWCA, to PAH, April 29, 1913, GPAHP; Sewell, *Women and the Everyday City*, 127; Deutsch, *Women and the City*; San Francisco Labor Council Reports, and PPIE, *An Announcement: Congresses, Conferences, Conventions;* Panama-Pacific International Exposition, San Francisco 1915 (San Francisco, 1915), booklet, box 32, HFA, 24, 50.

87. Elsie Robinson, "My Hopes Are Voice for You: She Dried the Babies Tears," *Los Angeles Examiner*, May 8, 1938, newspaper clipping, FDLP; National Congress of Mothers, Minutes, NCM; Mrs. John F. (Mary S.) Merrill to PAH, March 19, 1913, GPAHP; Mary Olney to PAH, March 27, 1913, GPAHP; Ella Schooley to PAH, March 28, 1913, GPAHP; Mary McL. Olney to Evelyn Brown Keck, June 29, 1913, GPAHP.

88. YWCA of the USA, National Board Minutes, General Secretary's Report, October 1, 1913, NYWCA Records, 2; Helen Davis to Grace Dodge, November 11, 1913, NYWCA; YWCA of the USA, Report of the General Secretary for April, 1912, May 3, 1912, 2, GPAHP.

89. San Francisco YWCA, *Historical Sketch, 1893–1914; Travelers Aid Department Young Women's Christian Association*, Historical Sketch pamphlet, San Francisco, ca. 1914, Travelers' Aid Society records of San Francisco photos, box 5, folder 2, p. 2, TAS; Helen A. Davis, "Department of Field Work Report," October 10–November 13, 1913, 1487, NYWCA; Orin C. Baker, *Travelers' Aid Society in America*, 11, 19, 22–24, 30, 31, 35–37, 43, 46, 78, 82–85, 132; Kimble, *Social Work with Travelers and Transients*, 2, chap. 7, 90; YWCA, "History–Expositions," Expositions folder, PPIE pamphlet 1915, NYWCA; McGovern, "American Woman's Pre–World War I Freedom in Manners and Morals," 315–33; Muncy, *Creating a Female Dominion*, xii–xiii.

90. Simpson, *What Women Are Doing for the Panama Pacific International Exposition*, pamphlet, PPIE Woman's Board, 1, PPIEWB, San Francisco Ephemera Collection, San Francisco Public Library, San Francisco History Center, 1; Todd, *Story of the Exposition*, 1:112–17, 5:122–24; Charles N. Lathrop to Charles C. Moore, January 15, 1915, PPIER 1893–1929, carton 33, folder 28; Douglass, *California Idea and American Higher Education*, 83; Simpson, *Problems Women Solved*, xii, 2; Markwyn, *Empress of San Francisco*, 5; Ella Sterling (Clark) Mighels to PAH, August 26, 1913, GPAHP; James Montgomery to PAH, May 17, 1913, GPAHP; Woloch, *Class By Herself*, 84. On the West leading the way in defining the shared nonpartisan political interests of women and men, see Lansing, "The Women Are Voluntarily Organizing Themselves" and Lansing, *Insurgent Democracy*.

91. See letters from Helen V. Wheeler to PAH, March 1913, GPAHP; Simpson, *Problems Women Solved*; Todd, *Story of the Exposition*, 2:324–29; Helen A. Davis to Grace Dodge, November 11, 1913, GPAHP; Nickliss, "Phoebe Apperson Hearst," 561–65.

92. See letters from Helen V. Wheeler to PAH, March 1913, GPAHP; Simpson, *Problems Women Solved*; Todd, *Story of the Exposition*; Helen A. Davis to Grace Dodge, November 11, 1913, GPAHP; Nickliss, "Phoebe Apperson Hearst," 561–65; Buchanan and Stuart, *History of the Panama-Pacific International Exposition*, 75.

93. Evelyn B. Keck, secretary pro tem, "A joint meeting of representatives of the Woman's Board of the Panama-Pacific Exposition and the Young Wom-

en's Christian Association was held on the 21st of October, 1913," Minutes and Annual Reports, Board Minutes, 1914–1929, no title, TAS Records, series 1, box 1, folder 1, 15; Mary S. Sims, "For Working Girls—A Living Wage," *Association Monthly* 9 (June 1915), 221; SFYWCA, Minutes and Annual Reports, Board Minutes, 1914–1929, "Meeting of the Travelers' Aid Committee," October 31, 1913, TAS Records series 1, box 1, folder 1, 16, TAS; "How Other Folks Live," *Ladies Home Journal* 29 (September 1912): 17; Helen Davis to Grace Dodge, November 11, 1913, NYWCA; Simpson, *Problems Women Solved*, 70–71; Helen Sanborn to PAH, October 5, 1914, GPAHP; Sanborn to PAH, Woman's Board, sub-committee Exposition Building, n.d., PPIE, San Francisco, GPAHP; Sanborn to PAH, n.d., GPAHP; Todd, *Story of the Exposition*, 5:123; Travelers' Aid Society of California, *Protecting Traveling Public, Especially Girls*, pamphlet, San Francisco, ca. 1918, Bancroft Library, University of California, Berkeley.

94. C. D. Hitchcock, Meeting of the Board of Directors, April 9, 1914, TAS Records, series 1, box 1, folder 1, TAS; C. A. Whitney, acting secretary, "Travelers' Aid Committee," Minutes and Annual Reports, Board Minutes, 1914–1929, "Travelers' Aid Committee, January 10, 1914," TAS Records series 1, box 1, folder 1, 17, TAS; "Plans Made to Protect Women Visitors to Fair," *San Francisco Examiner*, December 5, 1913, accessed January 12, 2016, 5; "YWCA Will Exhibit Results At the Exposition," *San Francisco Chronicle*, January 1915, PPIER 1893–1929, vol. 10, newspaper clippings, 145.

95. C. D. Hitchcock, Secretary, Minutes and Annual Reports, Board Minutes, 1914–1929, April 9, 1914, series 1, box 2, folder 1, 22, TAS; Charles C. Moore to Orin C. Baker, September 29, 1914, PPIER 1893–1929, carton 140, folder 17; Helen Davis to Grace Dodge, November 11, 1913, NYWCA; secretary pro tem, Minutes of the Annual Meeting of the Travelers' Aid Society Held at the Hotel Fairmont, February 15, 1915, TAS; C. D. Hitchcock, Minutes of the Board of Directors of the Travelers' Aid Society of California, May 30, 1915, TAS; C. D. Hitchcock, Minutes of the Board of Directors of the Travelers' Aid Society, July 23, 1915, TAS; PPIE, Executive Committee Minutes, PPIER 1893–1929, November 13, 1911, box 18, folder 11, 1; Gordon, "If the Progressives Were Advising Us Today," 111; Todd, *Story of the Exposition*,

1:114, 5:123; Travelers' Aid Society of California, *Protecting Traveling Public* pamphlet, San Francisco, ca. 1918, Bancroft Library, University of California, Berkeley; YWCA, "The Most Pressing Need" and "Unique Features," n.d., pamphlet, YWCA folders, GPAHP.

96. Luther Burbank Society to PAH, December 23, 1913, GPAHP; Martha White to PAH, August 12, 1914, PAH note, GPAHP; YWCA folders in GPAHP; Mary S. Merrill to Charles C. Moore, September 9, 1915, PPIER 1893–1929, carton 48, folder 17, 1.

97. Ella Schooley, Field Work Department Report, November 12–December 10, 1912, 1565–66, NYWCA; Dora M. Thurston to Phoebe A. Hearst, early 1913, PAH note, GPAHP; Ella Schooley, Field Work Department Report, December 11, 1912, to January 8, 1913, 1555–56, NYWCA; Ella Schooley to PAH, March 28, 1913, GPAHP; Helen A. Davis, Department of Field Work Report, month ending December 18, 1912, 1563–66, NYWCA; Davis, Department of Field Work Report, month ending November 13, 1913, 1485–87, NYWCA; Schooley, Special Worker, Department of Field Work Secretaries, National YWCA, April 23, 1914, GPAHP; Evelyn B. Keck to PAH, April 29, 1913, GPAHP; Keck to PAH, October 27, 1913, GPAHP.

98. See Markwyn, *Empress of San Francisco*, for information and analysis on other political battles and power struggles between the woman's board and the all-male board of directors.

99. Joseph M. Cumming to Helen Sanborn, January 7 and January 8, 1913, telegrams, PPIER 1893–1929, carton 10, folder 20; Simpson, *Problems Women Solved*, 105–6; Todd, *Story of the Exposition*, 1:120, 266–67, 2:322, 324; Sanborn to Charles C. Moore, January 7, 1913, GPAHP; Helen Sanborn to PAH, February 24, 1913, GPAHP; Mary B. Ritter to PAH, April 14, 1916, GPAHP; Executive Secretary of YWCA Exposition Committee to H. D. H. Connick, PPIE Director of Works, December 19, 1913, GPAHP; Spain, *Gendered Spaces*, xv, 28–29; Deutsch, *Women and the City*, 24; Helen Sanborn to R. B. Hale, PPIER 1893–1929, April 19, 1915, carton 11, folder 4.

100. Helen A. Davis, Department of Field Work Report, month ending November 13, 1913, 1484, 1485, NYWCA; Putnam Griswold to PAH, July 5, 1913, GPAHP; Harriet Taylor to PAH, July 15, 1913, GPAHP; Ella Schooley to PAH, November 26, 1913, GPAHP; Mary S. Merrill, September 12, and December

2, 1913, GPAHP; Schooley to Helen Sanborn, April 9, 1915, PPIER 1893–1929, carton 48, folder 17; Mary S. Merrill to Charles C. Moore, September 27, 1915, PPIER 1893–1929; Mary S. Merrill to Charles C. Moore, September 9, 1915, PPIER 1893–1929; PPIE, Minutes of the Executive Council of the Finance Committee of the PPIÉ Company, PPIER 1893–1929, vol. 117, November 16, 1915, 270.

101. Helen A. Davis, Department of Field Work Report, month ending November 13, 1914, 1484–86, NYWCA; Putnam Griswold to PAH, May 28, 1913, GPAHP; Mary S. Merrill to PAH, December 2, 1913, GPAHP; Helen Sanford to PAH, August 21, 1913, GPAHP; Mary S. Merrill to Charles C. Moore, September 9, 1915, PPIER 1893–1929, carton 48, folder 17; Boutelle, *Julia Morgan*, 101, 102, 104–5; Helen Dare, "YWCA Will Exhibit Results at the Exposition," *San Francisco Chronicle*, PPIER 1893–1929, January 1915, vol. 10, newspaper clippings; "YWCA Will Break Ground at Fair Site," *San Francisco Examiner*, August 21, 1914, PPIER 1893–1929, vol. 49, newspaper clipping, 417; Julia T. Lee, comp., "Three Days at the Exposition Compliments of the National Young Women's Christian Association," PPIE Women, no place of publication, n.d., San Francisco History Center, 6, 27.

102. Buchanan and Stuart, *History of the PPIE*, 453–57; Markus, *Buildings and Power*; Rodgers, *Atlantic Crossings*, chap. 5; Ella Schooley to PAH, March 6, 1915, GPAHP; Boutelle, *Julia Morgan*, 101–5; YWCA of the USA, Fourth Biennial Convention of the Young Women's Christian Association of the United States of America, Richmond, Virginia, April 9–15, 1913, National YWCA Board, 15–16, NYWCA; Mary S. Sims, "For Working Girls—A Living Wage," *Association Monthly* 9 (June 1915): 219–21; Kessler-Harris, *Woman's Wage*, 20, 14–15; Natalie Coffin Green, "The YWCA and the San Francisco Exposition," *Women's International Quarterly* 1 (July 1915), 239–40; Frances A. Groff, "A Lovely Woman at the Exposition," *Sunset*, May 1915, 876–89; Mary S. Merrill to PAH, October 5, 1915, GPAHP; YWCA, National Board Minutes, January 28, 1916, 14, NYWCA; Ella Schooley, "The Association and the Exposition," *Association Monthly* 9 (May 1915): 181–83; YWCA, "Housewarming at the Exposition," *Association Monthly* 9 (May 1915): 260–65; Rydell, *All the World's a Fair*, 209; YWCA of the USA, "Statistical Material; Figure for Young Women's Christian Association Work Done at the Panama

Pacific International Exposition, San Francisco CA, February 20–December 4, 1915," *Year Book 1915–1916,* 49. Backing a minimum wage "simultaneously threw out a challenge to preserve morality." It "was not necessarily an invitation to raise wages. Since many imagined an unattached woman who did not live within a family to be immoral, they construed the wage as a contribution to family life. A higher wage might logically contribute to morality." See Kessler-Harris, *Woman's Wage,* 20.

103. Ella Schooley to PAH, April 15, 1915, GPAHP; Vapnek, *Breadwinners,* 1–7; Simpson, *Problems Women Solved,* 90–1; Deutsch, *Women and the City,* 15.

104. C. A. Horne, "People Open the Greatest of Expositions; Imposing Ceremony Marks Starting of the Wheels," *San Francisco Chronicle,* February 21, 1915, 48; Ewald and Clute, *San Francisco Invites the World,* 25, 26; "San Francisco Fair Will Open Today," *New York Times,* February 20, 1915, 7; Grace Armistead Boyle, "Opening Day Is Joyful Event for Women," *San Francisco Chronicle,* February 21, 1915, 50; Markwyn, "Constructing 'an epitome of civilization,'" 43; Markwyn, *Empress of San Francisco.*

105. Simpson, *Problems Women Solved,* chap. 5, 100.

106. Martha White to PAH, August 12, 1914, PAH note, GPAHP; Helen Sanborn to Rueben B. Hall, April 19, 1915, PPIER 1893–1929, carton 11, folder 4; Markwyn, *Empress of San Francisco,* 31.

107. Markwyn, *Empress of San Francisco,* 55, 56, 174–78, 111; "Biff! Goes the Lid on This Oriental Joy Zone Concession," August 20, 1915, *San Francisco Chronicle,* ProQuest, accessed August 15, 2014, 11; Pliley, *Policing Sexuality,* 71, 67, 1.

108. "Biff! Goes the Lid on This Oriental Joy Zone Concession," August 20, 1915, *San Francisco Chronicle,* ProQuest, accessed August 15, 2014, 11; Julia George to Charles E. Moore, PPIER 1893–1929, July 16, 1915, carton 33, folder 37; Frederic E. Elmendorf to Charles C. Moore, December 3, 1914, PPIER 1893–1929, July 16, 1915; Albert W. Palmer to Charles C. Moore, PPIER 1893–1929, October 6, 1915, carton 33, folder 37, 1, 3. Some of the various concessionaires on the Zone were the Russian Ballet, Cairo Café, Diving Girls, Mysterious Orient, Somali Village, Alligator Farm, Hawaiian Village, and Dixie Land. See PPIE, Minutes of the Executive Council of the

Finance Committee of the PPIE Company, PPIER 1893–1929, vol. 117, April 20, 1915, 148; PPIER 1893–1929, August 9, 1915, carton 24, folder 17, 2. A Club House also existed on the Zone. It was a "comfortable summer cottage" where people had lunch, relaxed, and used the services of a trained nurse. See Buchanan and Stuart, *History of the PPIE*, 456; Hearst never joined the Women's Christian Temperance Union and refused to endorse prohibition. See "Mrs. Hearst Considers Prohibition a Mistake," *San Francisco Examiner*, July 27, 1914, *San Francisco Examiner* Newspaper Clipping Morgue, envelope 2, San Francisco History Center. But she sent a private donation of $1,000 to the San Francisco County WCTU. See PAH to Florence J. S. Hartell, May 11, 1912, GPAHP.

109. Mary S. Merrill to Charles C. Moore, PPIER 1893–1929, July 23, 1915, carton 33, folder 37; Charles N. Lathrop to Charles C. Moore, PPIER 1893–1929, January 15, 1915, carton 33, folder 28; Moore to Lathrop, PPIER January 25, 1915 ; Matt Sullivan to Charles C. Moore et al., PPIER 1893–1929, September 21, 1915, carton 33, folder 37; Markwyn, *Empress San Francisco*, 25, 174–78, 31.

110. Pliley, *Policing Sexuality*, 71; Helen Sanborn to R.B. Hale, PPIER 1893–1929, October 4, 1914, carton 11, folder 4; Markwyn, *Empress of San Francisco*, 194–97, 294n96; Charles C. Moore to Orin G. Baker, PPIER 1893–1929, September 28, 1914, carton 140, folder 17; Mary S. Merrill to C. C. Moore, PPIER 1893–1929, July 23, 1915, carton 33, folder 37; PPIE, Mary S. Merrill to Joseph Cumming, PPIER 1893–1929, August 9, 1915, Cairo Café Concession, carton 33, folder 37.

111. PPIE, Minutes of the Committee on Concessions and Admissions, PPIER 1893–1929, vol. 123, August 9, 1915, 159; PPIE, Minutes of the Committee on Concessions and Admissions, PPIER 1893–1929, vol. 123, August 30, 1915, 165; PPIE, Minutes of the Executive Council of the Finance Committee of the PPIE Company, PPIER 1893–1929, vol. 117, April 20, 1915, 148; PPIER 1893–1929, August 9, 1915, carton 24, folder 17, 2; Albert Palmer to C.C. Moore, PPIER 1893–1929, October 6, 1915, carton 33, folder 37; Frank Burt to President and Executive Sub-Committee, PPIER 1893–1929, August 2, 1915, carton 20, folder 18; Frank Burt to Charles C. Moore, Report of the

Director of Concessions and Admissions, December 28, 1915, San Francisco Ephemera Collection, San Francisco History Center, 1, 10, 11–12; PPIER 1893–1929; Markwyn, "Queen of the Joy Zone," 67; Simpson, *Problems Women Solved*, 182–83; Putnam, *Modern California Politics*, 1; Todd, *Story of the Exposition*, 1:111–18, 127, 328, 113, 116.

112. Markwyn, *Empress of San Francisco*, 178; Todd, *Story of the Exposition*, 1:111–18; Pliley, *Policing Sexuality*, 71; Simpson, *Problems Women Solved*, 175, 182–83; Putnam, *Modern California Politics*, 1.

113. Simpson, *Problems Women Solved*, 189–91; Macleod, *Enchanted Lives, Enchanted Objects*, 127; Todd, *Story of the Exposition*, dedication before the Table of Contents.

114. Gavin McNab to the Board of Directors of the PPIE Company, PPIER 1893–1929,October 24, 1911, carton 11, folder 4; Todd, *Story of the Exhibition*, 2:325.

115. C. D. Hitchcock, Meeting of the Board of Directors of the Travelers' Aid Society of California, July 13, 1914, TAS Records, series 1, box 1, folder 1, 27, TAS; Travelers' Aid Society of California, *Protecting Traveling Public*, pamphlet, San Francisco, ca. 1918, Bancroft Library, University of California, Berkeley; Susan B. Anthony to Jane L. Stanford, September 21, 1896, box 4, folder 18, JLSP.

8. THE VOTE

1. Mary Wood Swift to PAH, October 18, 1910, GPAHP.

2. DuBois, *Feminism and Suffrage*, 190, 192. Although black women were allowed to join the NAWSA and invited to NAWSA conventions on rare occasions, they supported women's right to vote but opposed suffrage rhetoric laced with racism. Mary Church Terrell, for example, was a member of the wealthy black elite in Memphis, Tennessee, an educator, a suffragist, and a devoted clubwoman. She spoke at the NAWSA convention in 1898. See Marilley, *Woman Suffrage and the Origins of Liberal Feminism*, 14; Alexander, "Adella Hunt Logan, the Tuskegee Woman's Club, and African Americans in the Suffrage Movement," 75, 71. Also Terrell, "The Justice of Woman Suffrage," 151.

3. Free, "Money Changes Everything," 468; Zahniser and Fry, *Alice Paul*, 106; Mead, *How the Vote Was Won*, 19, 1; McGerr, "Political Style and Women's Power," 864–65; Sewell, *Women and the Everyday City*; Buecheler, "Elizabeth Boynton Harbert and the Woman Suffrage Movement," 78–97.

4. The Woman's Congress of the Pacific Coast, Second Annual Meeting of the Woman's Congress of the Pacific Coast, San Francisco, May 20 to 26, 1895, "Woman's Congress Association of the Pacific Coast, 1896–97," folder 4, CPGP, 3, 5–13, 7; Sewell, *Women and the Everyday City*, xxxiii; Gullett, *Becoming Citizens*, 74, 78; Mead, *How the Vote Was Won*, chap. 1, 76–77.

5. The Woman's Congress of the Pacific Coast, Second Annual Meeting of the Woman's Congress of the Pacific Coast, San Francisco, May 20 to 26, 1895, "Women's Congress Association of the Pacific Coast, 1896–97," folder 4, CPGP, 3, 9, 10–15, 6, 7; Mead, *How the Vote Was Won*, 76–77; Gullett, *Becoming Citizens*, 74; Sarah Brown Ingersoll Cooper and her daughter Harriet "appeared to have agreed to end their lives" on December 12, 1896. See Franzen, *Anna Howard Shaw*, 86. See letters to and from PAH and Sarah B. Cooper and Cooper to PAH, SBCP and GPAHP. See GPAHP for letters to and from PAH and Charlotte Perkins Stetson Gilman to PAH. Also Degler, "Charlotte Anna Perkins Stetson Gilman," 2:40–41.

6. See chapters 3 through 5 in this volume. Also Edelman, "Red Hot Suffrage Campaign," 80, 82–83, 81, 56, 57; Woman's Congress of the Pacific Coast, Second Annual Meeting of the Woman's Congress of the Pacific Coast, Program of the Woman's Congress of 1895, CPGP 13.

7. Ginzberg, "Moral Suasion Is Moral Balderdash," 601–22; James Montgomery to PAH, May 17, 1913, GPAHP; Ella Sterling (Clark) Mighels to PAH, August 26, 1913, GPAHP; Hosmer B. Parsons to Mrs. E. Imogine Hall, May 25, 1895, GPAHP; William Pepper to PAH, February 24, 1895, GPAHP.

8. Gullett, *Becoming Citizens*, 88; Woman's Congress of the Pacific Coast, Fourth Annual Meeting of the Woman's Congress of the Pacific Coast, San Francisco, April 26 to May 1, inclusive, 1897, CPGP; Mead, *How the Vote Was Won*, 80–82; W. H. Davis to Louise Sorbier, May 28, 1895, box 1, folder 3, LSC; Edelman, "Red Hot Suffrage Campaign," 57.

9. Woman's Congress of the Pacific Coast, Third Annual Meeting of the Woman's Congress of the Pacific Coast, May 4 to 11, 1896, folder 4, CPGP, 1895,

pp. 11–16, 9; "A Gathering of Prominent Women: Success Predicted for Next Week's Congress," *Evening Post*, May 2, 1896, newspaper clipping, Louise Sorbier, Scrapbook, vol. 1, California Historical Society, San Francisco; Woman's Congress of the Pacific Coast, Fourth Annual Meeting of the Woman's Congress of the Pacific Coast, San Francisco, April 26 to May 1, inclusive, 1897, CPGP; Mead, *How the Vote Was Won*, 82–83; Harper, *Life and Work of Susan B. Anthony*, 2:889; Edelman, "Red Hot Suffrage Campaign," 71.

10. Susan B. Anthony to Jane L. Stanford, September 18, 21, 1896, box 4, folder 18, JLSP; Mead, *How The Vote Was Won*, 8; Harper, *Life and Work of Susan B. Anthony*, 2:888.

11. PAH to Orrin Peck, June 24, 1896, OPC; "How Mrs. Hearst Dispenses Her Immense Fortune in Charities," *New London Day* (CT), July 11, 1896, newspaper clipping, GPAHP; Clara Anthony Reed to PAH, August 21, 1896, GPAHP; Nasaw, *Life of William Randolph Hearst*, 117.

12. PAH to Daniel O'Connell, October 26, 1916, GPAHP; Clara Anthony Reed to PAH, February 10, 1896, GPAHP; PAH to Orrin Peck, June 24, 1896, OPC; "How Mrs. Hearst Dispenses Her Immense Fortune in Charities," *New London Day* (CT), July 11, 1896, newspaper clipping, GPAHP; Clara Anthony to PAH, August 1896, incomplete, GPAHP; Clara Anthony Reed to PAH, August 21, 1896, GPAHP; Susan B. Anthony to Jane L. Stanford, September 18, 21, 1896, box 4, folder 18, JLSP; William Randolph Hearst to PAH, 1884, GPAHP; PAH to Orrin Peck, December 22, 1886, PC.

13. Harper, *Life and Work of Susan B. Anthony*, 2:867; Edelman, "Red Hot Suffrage Campaign," 98, 108.

14. Edelman, "Red Hot Suffrage Campaign," 98, 100, 108, 109; Mead, *How the Vote Was Won*, 87. A majority of California newspapers, with the exception of the *San Francisco Chronicle*, the *Sacramento Record-Union*, and the *Los Angeles Times*, supported the ballot for women or were "at least receptive to suffrage material." See also Harper, *Life and Work of Susan B. Anthony*, 2:867.

15. PAH to Susan B. Anthony, April 7, 1898, GPAHP; Harper, *Life and Work of Susan B. Anthony*, 2:867, 888–89; Mead, *How the Vote Was Won*, 83, 91; Susan B. Anthony to Jane L. Stanford, September 18, 1896, box 4, folder 18, JLSP; Stanton, Anthony, Harper, and Gage, *History of Woman Suffrage*, 6:28–29;

Gordon, *Selected Papers of Elizabeth Cady Stanton and Susan B. Anthony*. It appears Hearst was influenced by the commemorative celebrations Anthony held to "lay out an alternative memory of the Civil War, a hitherto unrecognized *suffragist memory* of Seneca Falls" or "the *myth* of Seneca Falls," as one historian observed. See Tetrault, *Myth of Seneca Falls*, 16–17.

16. "A new generation of suffrage leaders . . . rejected the outdated nineteenth-century term 'woman suffrage' in favor of a more contemporary-sounding slogan, 'votes for women'" in the twentieth century." See DuBois, *Through Women's Eyes*, 423.

17. PAH to Frances Douglas Lummis, April 28, 1911, FDLP.

18. PAH to Mrs. Wattles, August 28, 1911, GPAHP; Sewell, *Women and the Everyday City*, 130. While in England, Alice Paul made the distinction in 1909 "between suffragists and suffragettes ('the latter have pursed militant methods')." See Zahniser and Fry, *Alice Paul*, 62.

19. Anna Louise Stearns to PAH, December 20, 1912, GPAHP; "Mrs. Hearst is for Suffrage," January 2, 1913, original newspaper clipping in author's possession, GPAHP.

20. On antisuffragists, see Goodier, *No Votes for Women*.

21. Mead, *How the Vote Was Won*, 126.

22. Franzen, *Anna Howard Shaw*, 95, 11.

23. DuBois, *Harriot Stanton Blatch*, 4, 106–7; Mary McHenry Keith to PAH, July 22, 1907, GPAHP; Mead, *How the Vote Was Won*, 25, 122, 133; Franzen, *Anna Howard Shaw*, 111, 120, 132; Letters of Mary McHenry and William Keith to PAH, GPAHP; Constance Lawrence Dean to PAH, n.d., GPAHP; Charlotte Anita Whitney to PAH, June 24, 1911, GPAHP.

24. Mead, *How the Vote Was Won*, chap. 6; Sewell, *Women and the Everyday City*, 127–30, 128.

25. College Equal Suffrage League of Northern California (CESL), *Winning Equal Suffrage in California*, 25.

26. "Mrs. Hearst Is for Suffrage," January 2, 1913, original newspaper clipping in author's possession; PAH to Caroline Severance, July 9, 1912, CSC.

27. DuBois, *Harriot Stanton Blatch*, 101; Sewell, *Women and the Everyday City*, 157.

28. DuBois, *Harriot Stanton Blatch*, 3–4, 107–11.

29. Finnegan, *Selling Suffrage*; College Equal Suffrage League, *Winning Equal Suffrage in California*, 40; DuBois, *Harriot Stanton Blatch*, 102; Burkhardt et al., *Concise Dictionary of American Biography*, 883; Davis, *Parades and Power*, 33, 45; Mead, *How the Vote Was Won*, 123–25, 132, 144–45; Ella Costillo Bennett to PAH, October 11, 1911, GPAHP; Sewell, *Women and the Everyday City*, 161.

30. Finnegan, *Selling Suffrage*; "5,500 Attend Women's Suffrage Meeting at Dreamland," *San Francisco Examiner*, October 6, 1911, 1; CESL, *Winning Equal Suffrage in California*, 36; Mead, *How the Vote Was Won*, 144–45.

31. Ernestine Black to PAH, November 8, 1911, GPAHP; Ella Costillo Bennett to PAH, October 11, 1911, GPAHP; Mead, *How the Vote Was Won*, 144–45, 149, 147; Anny Bray to PAH, PAH note, November 12, 1911, GPAHP.

32. Josephine Monohan to PAH, March 16 and March 25, 1912, GPAHP; J. McCormick to PAH, July 12, 1912, GPAHP; California Voter Registrations 1900–1968, 1912, roll 10, San Francisco County, California State Library, Sacramento, ancestry.com, accessed February 22, 2016; Nasaw, *The Life of William Randolph Hearst*, 177, 187, 227; "Clark Declares for Suffrage," *New York Times*, June 28, 1914, ProQuest, accessed June 28, 1914, 10; Elizabeth W. McKinley to PAH, May 10, 1912, R. A. Clark notes, GPAHP; Cooper, *Warrior and the Priest*, 185.

33. Susan B. Anthony to Jane L. Stanford, September 21, 1896, box 4, folder 18, JLSP; Tichenor, "Presidency, Social Movements, and Contentious Change," 16; Irwin, *Story of the Woman's Party*, 60; Cooper, *Warrior and the Priest*, 186.

34. Gustafson, *Women and the Republican Party*, 117; Faculty Club Invitation for a Smoker and Reception to Colonel Theodore Roosevelt, March 17, 1911, PAH note on back, GPAHP; Forte, *Pen Pictures*, 444; Charles Adams to PAH, December 27, 1912, GPAHP; J. McCormick to PAH, July 12, 1912, GPAHP.

35. Charles Adams to PAH, December 27, 1912, GPAHP; P.J. McCormick to PAH, July 12, 1912, GPAHP; R. A. Clark to James D. Phelan, October 11, 1912, James D. Phelan Correspondence and Papers, Bancroft Library, University of California, Berkeley; Lundardini and Knock, "Woodrow Wilson and Woman Suffrage," 658.

36. DuBois, *Harriot Stanton Blatch*, 186–88, 184; Zahniser and Fry, *Alice Paul*, 168, 124; Franzen, *Anna Howard Shaw*, 146–48; Adams and Keene, *Alice Paul and the American Suffrage Campaign*, 32.

37. DuBois, *Harriot Stanton Blatch*, 187, 188; Zahniser and Fry, *Alice Paul*, 168–91; Franzen, *Anna Howard Shaw*, 146–49; Adams and Keene, *Alice Paul and the American Suffrage Campaign*, 100, 144.

38. Susan Ware, "Book I Couldn't Write," 16; Congressional Union, "Advisory Council," *Suffragist*, January 30, 1915, 2; Hoffert, *Alva Vanderbilt Belmont*, 40, 49; Lasch, "Alva Erskine Smith Vanderbilt Belmont," 1:126; DuBois, *Harriot Stanton Blatch*, 187–88.

39. PAH to Doris Stevens, September 29, 1916, microfilm reel 32, NWPP; Western Berkeley College Settlement, New York Congressional Union for Woman Suffrage circular, March 4, 1914, GPAHP; DuBois, *Harriot Stanton Blatch*, 192; Congressional Union, "Advisory Council," *Suffragist*, January 30, 1915, 2; Franzen, *Anna Howard Shaw*, 146–48.

40. I am grateful to Kimberly S. Jensen for providing the information that not all wealthy women who sat on the Congressional Union's Advisory Council supported militancy.

41. "Campaign Through the Country," *Suffragist*, December 12, 1914, 7; Adams and Keene, *Alice Paul and the American Suffrage Campaign*, 182; Frances A. Groff, "A Lovely Woman at the Exposition," *Sunset*, May 1915, 885; Irwin, *Story of the Woman's Party*, 18, 99–100.

42. Ewald and Clute, *San Francisco Invites the World*, 72; "Show City Wonders to Eight Governors," *New York Times*, December 12, 1911, ProQuest, 7, accessed July 8, 2015; "Gavin McNab to the Board of Directors of the PPIE Company, October 24, 1911, PPIER 1893–1929, carton 11, folder 4, 7.

43. Todd, *Story of the Exposition*, 4: 41–42; Adams and Keene, *Alice Paul and the American Suffrage Campaign*, 104; "Exhibitors Education and Social Economy, Palace of Education," Congressional Union for Women Suffrage, PPIER 1893–1929, n.d., carton 109, folder 22, 1, 6; "Mrs. John Temple Graves Hostess at Dinner for Mrs. Phoebe Hearst; Mrs. William Kent Hostess," *Washington Post*, May 18, 1916, ProQuest Historical Newspapers, accessed July 7, 2015, 7.

44. Alva Belmont to Bertha Honoré Palmer, May 1, 1916, reel 27, NWPP.

45. "Booth in Exposition Building Is Dedicated By Suffragists of the Congressional Union," *San Francisco Examiner*, March 5, 1915, 11; "California," *Suffragist*, March 6, 1915, 7; "Campaign Throughout the Country," *Suffragist*, March 13,

1915, 7; DuBois, *Harriot Stanton Blatch*, 196. I am grateful to Maida Goodwin, a librarian at Smith College, where the National YWCA Board Archives are housed, for the information on the YWCA and suffrage.

46. "Booth in Exposition Building Is Dedicated By Suffragists of the Congressional Union," *San Francisco Examiner*, March 5, 1915, 11; Adams and Keene, *Alice Paul and the American Suffrage Campaign*, 106; "Suffrage Envoys Welcomed to California," *Suffragist*, Mary 6, 1916, 4.

47. Congressional Union, "To The Woman Voters of America," circular, 1915, PPIE Women, San Francisco History Center; Todd, *Story of the Exposition*, 4:41–42; Congressional Union, Congressional Union for Woman Suffrage Woman Voters' Convention September 14, 15, and 16, 1915, Program, PPIE Women, San Francisco History Center; Bessie Beatty, "Suffrage Leaders to Launch Campaign for Woman's Party," no newspaper title, (April 26?), no year, reel 27, NWPP; Irwin, *Story of the Woman's Party*, 149.

48. Christmas Checks, 1914 and 1915, Elizabeth Cady Stanton Centennial (New York) paid to Woman's Political Union 20 (September 29), Christmas Lists; Gift Lists, etc., prepared by Miss Harriet Bradford when she was secretary to Mrs. Hearst, 1914–15, GPAHP; Alva E. Belmont to PAH, May 3, 1915, GPAHP, PAH note on back of 2; Congressional Union, Congressional Union for Woman Suffrage Woman Voters' Convention, September 14, 15, 16, 1915, Program, PPIE Women, San Francisco History Center.

49. DuBois, *Harriot Stanton Blatch*, 101, 149; Christmas Checks, 1914 and 1915, Elizabeth Cady Stanton Centennial (New York) paid to Woman's Political Union $20 (September 29), Christmas Lists; Gift Lists, etc., prepared by Miss Harriet Bradford when she was secretary to Mrs. Hearst, 1914–1915, GPAHP.

50. Florence Brewer Boeckel to Alice Paul, May 26, 1916, microfilm reel 28, NWPP.

51. Anne H. Martin, Legislative Chairman, Congressional Union for Woman Suffrage, May 27, 1916, GPAHP; Joy L. Webster to PAH, May 29, 1916, GPAHP; Sewell, *Woman and the Everyday City*, 127–29, 140, 107. Hearst sent another five hundred dollars to the NWP in late 1916. See Joy L. Webster to PAH, September 18, 1916, GPAHP. Also PAH to Dear Madam, May 27, 1916, reel 28, quotation 4, NWPP; Lunardini, *From Equal Suffrage to Equal Rights*, 52–53. For the argument that wealthy women "wielded the power to shape strat-

egy and decisions" and "their experience with the power of money (and its limitations) helped" make "the passage and ratification of the Nineteenth Amendment possible in 1920," see Johnson, "Following the Money," 62–87.

52. "Suffragists Sure Victory Is Near," *New York Times*, June 6, 1916, ProQuest, accessed June 26, 2014, 9; PAH to Anne Martin, May 22, 1915, reel 28, NWPP; "Protest by Mrs. Hearst," *Washington Post*, May 26, 1916, NWPP; PAH to Anne Martin's secretary, May 27, 1916, microfilm reel 28, NWPP; William Randolph Hearst to Mrs. O. H. Belmont, November 5, 1916, copy of letter received from Mr. Hearst to be sent to Miss Paul, microfilm reel 35, NWPP.

53. McGerr, "Political Style and Women's Power, 865; Kennedy, *Disloyal Mothers and Scurrilous Citizens*, 12, 11; Sewell, *Women and the Everyday City*, 115, 116; Davis, *Parades and Power*, 5–6, 136, 137, 139, 141, 162; Adams and Keene, *Alice Paul and the American Suffrage Campaign*, 171, 125; Marshall, *Splintered Sisterhood*, 53.

54. Finnegan, *Against the Specter of a Dragon*; Marchand, *American Peace Movement and Social Reform*, 206, 239–40; National Society of the Daughters of the American Revolution, "Application for Membership," NSDAR.

55. Kennedy, *Disloyal Mothers and Scurrilous Citizens*, 12; Davis, *Parades and Power*, 149, 166; "Bomb Threat Is Handed to Mrs. Taylor," *San Francisco Examiner*, July 23, 1916, bundle 2, p. 3, TMP; "Scenes in Great S.F. Defense Parade," *San Francisco Examiner*, July 22, 1916, TMP, 5; "Mullally Puts Blame for Bomb Upon Speeches, *San Francisco Examiner*, July 23, 1916, 2; Todd, *Story of the Exhibition*, 1:117; Simpson, *Problems Women Solved*, xv; Adams and Keene, *Alice Paul and the American Suffrage Campaign*, 36–37; "Mrs. Taylor Leaves $15,000 to Servants," Bessie Taylor envelope, *San Francisco Examiner*, March 14, 1931, *San Francisco Examiner* Newspaper Clipping Morgue, San Francisco History Center; "Garden Club's Founder Dead," *San Francisco Chronicle*, March 4, 1931, News Bank and/or the American Antiquarian Society, 2004, accessed June 11, 2015, on San Francisco Public Library site, 13.

56. DuBois, *Harriot Stanton Blatch*, 107; Pringle, "In Memoriam: Phoebe Apperson Hearst,"63–64, MVLA; Adams and Keene, *Alice Paul and the American Suffrage Campaign*, 32; Fernanda Pratt to PAH, July 31, 1916, GPAHP; from the Thomas Mooney Papers, bundle 2, TMP.

57. "6 Killed and 44 Wounded By Bomb Exploded in Preparedness Parade, *San Francisco Examiner*, July 23, 1916, 1; Dashiell, "California Golden Woman, Phoebe Apperson Hearst," *Los Angeles Herald-Examiner*, September 26, 1976, 1–3; Ellis Black Hayes to unknown, 1916, incomplete, GPAHP.

58. Jensen, *Mobilizing Minerva*, ix, 9; Kennedy, *Disloyal Mothers and Scurrilous Citizens*, xv, xvii, 1, 3; Sewell, *Women and the Everyday City*, 116, 124–25, 143–44, 168, 170; Pitkin, *Concept of Representation*, chaps. 4–6, 80.

59. By this time, Hearst was a member of the Mount Vernon Ladies' Association and the Daughters of the American Revolution. See Regents' Files, MVLA, and National Society of the Daughters of the American Revolution, "Application for Membership," NSDAR.

60. Sewell, *Women and the Everyday City*, 163.

61. "50,000 In Line Begin Defense March," no newspaper name, bundle 2, TMP; Davis, *Parades and Power*, 123; Morgan, *Women and Patriotism in Jim Crow America*, 5.

62. "Greatest Civilian Parade in History of San Francisco," *San Francisco Examiner*, July 23, 1916, 9; "Women Take Active part in Making Big Parade a Success," *San Francisco Chronicle*, July 23, 1916, 31; Genevieve Yoell Parkhurst, "Girls March Beside Men: Nobility of Women in Feminine Ranks," no newspaper name, July 22, 1916, newspaper clipping, bundle 2, TMP; "World Shown S.F. Spirit of Knowing How," *San Francisco Examiner*, July 23, 1916, 11; "51,000 Marchers Carry Flags in Imposing Parade, *San Francisco Chronicle*, July 23, 1916, 1; Sewell, *Women and the Everyday City*, 116; Pitkin, *Concept of Representation*.

63. "Women Take Active part in Making Big Parade a Success," *San Francisco Chronicle*, July 23, 1916, 31; "Greatest Civilian Parade in the History of San Francisco," *San Francisco Examiner*, July 23, 1916, 9; "Women By Thousands Respond to Defense Call; Reviewing Stand Overwhelmed by Display; Notables Cheer as 51, 329 Swing Past," *San Francisco Examiner*, July 23, 1916, 11; "Bomb Threat Is Handed to Mrs. Taylor," *San Francisco Examiner*, July 23, 1916, 3; "World Shown S.F. Spirit of Knowing How," *San Francisco Examiner*, July 23, 1916, 11.

64. "6 Killed and 44 Wounded by Bomb Exploded in Preparedness Parade," *San Francisco Examiner*, July 23, 1916, 1; "Women Take Active part in Making Big Parade a Success," *San Francisco Chronicle*, July 23, 1916, 31; Ellis Black

Hayes to unknown, incomplete, 1916, GPAHP; Russett, *Sexual Science*; Adams and Keene, *Alice Paul and the American Suffrage Campaign*, 36–37.

65. Marchand, *American Peace Movement and Social Reforms*, 208, 224, 183.

66. "Bomb Explosion Kills 6 and Maims 40 Preparedness Parade Spectators," *San Francisco Chronicle*, July 23, 1916, 1.

67. "Bomb Kills Six, Injures Scores in Defense Parade," *New York Times*, July 23, 1916, 1.

68. "Bomb Kills Six, Injures Scores in Defense Parade," *New York Times*, July 23, 1916, 1, 5.

69. Jensen, *Mobilizing Minerva*, 8, ix; Kennedy, *Disloyal Mothers*; "Women Take Active part in Making Parade a Success," *San Francisco Chronicle*, July 23, 1916, 31; Sewell, *Women and the Everyday City*, 124.

70. "6 Killed and 44 Wounded by Bomb Exploded in Preparedness Parade," *San Francisco Examiner*, July 23, 1916, 1.

71. Thurnwell Mullally to Phoebe A. Hearst, August 1, 1916, GPAHP.

72. Pitkin, *Concept of Representation*, 97; Ellis Black Hayes to unknown, incomplete,1916, GPAHP; Fernanda Pratt to Phoebe A. Hearst, July 31, 1916, GPAHP.

73. Thurnwell Mullally to PAH, August 1, 1916, GPAHP; Pitkin, *Concept of Representation*, 61; "Fair Sex Plays Bounteous Hostess for Whole State," *San Francisco Examiner*, February 21, 1915, 12.

74. Alice Stinson to PAH, February 24, 1897, GPAHP; "Mrs. Hearst's Reception, *Berkeley [Daily] Advocate*, October 11, 1897, University of California, *Personalia*, volume bound by the University of California, newspaper clipping, UCARCH; Adelaide Marquand, "Mrs. Hearst's First Session," August 11, 1897, original newspaper clipping in author's possession, no title, GPAHP; "Luncheon for Mrs. Hearst," *San Francisco Examiner*, February 9, 1915, 3; "Reviewing Stand Overwhelmed by Display; Notables Cheer as 51,329 Swing Past," *San Francisco Examiner*, July 23, 1916, 11; Pitkin, *Concept of Representation*, chaps. 4, 5.

75. "Luncheon for Mrs. Hearst," *San Francisco Examiner*, February 9, 1915, 3; Pitkin, *Concept of Representation*, chaps. 4, 5.

76. "Reviewing Stand Overwhelmed by Display; Notables Cheer as 51,329 Swing Past," *San Francisco Examiner*, July 23, 1916, 11; Pitkin, *Concept of Representation*, chaps. 4, 5.

77. Katherine Hamilton McLaughlin to PAH, November 10, 1913, GPAHP.

78. O'Leary, *To Die For*, quotation inside book jacket cover.

79. Doris Stevens to PAH, September 4, 1916, GPAHP; PAH to Anne Martin's secretary, May 27, 1916, microfilm reel 28, NWPP; "Protest by Mrs. Hearst," *Washington Post*, May 26, 1916, NWPP; PAH to Anne Martin, May 22, 1916, GPAHP; Zahniser and Fry, *Alice Paul*, 240; Anne Martin to PAH, May 27, 1916, GPAHP; Joy L. Webster to PAH, Mary 29, 1916, GPAHP; Cott, *Grounding of Modern Feminism*, 58–59; Sewell, *Women and the Everyday City*, 107, 127–28; Congressional Union, "Voting Women Launch a Woman's Party," *Suffragist*, June 10, 1916, 6–8. The gathering held in the Blackstone Theater was titled the "Woman's Party Convention." See Congressional Union, *Suffragist*, June 3, 1916, 3. Also Alice Paul to PAH, January 27, 1917, PAH note on back, GPAHP.

80. PAH to Clara S. Wolfe, April 13, 1916, microfilm reel 26, NWPP; "Congressional Union Plans for Chicago Announced," *San Francisco Chronicle*, May 21, 1916, ProQuest, accessed June 26, 2014, 9; "California Woman's Party Organizes for Defeat of Democrats," *Suffragist*, September 23, 1916, 7; "Woman's Party Formed Here; Wars on Wilson," *San Francisco Examiner*, September 16, 1916, 4.

81. Cott, *Grounding of Modern Feminism*, 58; Doris Stevens to PAH, September 26, 1916, note on back, GPAHP.

82. Emmie Wynn Elias to PAH, September 24, 1916, GPAHP; PAH to Doris Stevens, September 29, 1916, microfilm reel 32, NWPP.

83. Zahniser and Fry, *Alice Paul*, 192; DuBois, *Harriot Stanton Blatch*, 201, 199; PAH to Daniel O'Connell, October 26, 1916, GPAHP; Catt and Shuler, *Woman Suffrage and Politics*, 264; Daniel O'Connell to PAH, December 1, 1916, PAH note, GPAHP, quotation on back of 2; California Voter Registrations 1900–1968, San Francisco County, 1916, roll 17, July 1916, California State Library, Sacramentoancestry.com, accessed February 22, 2016; Margaret Whittenmore, May 8, 1917, GPAHP; PAH to Margaret Whittenmore, May 11, 1917, microfilm reel 42, NWPP; Congressional Union, *Suffragist*, January 2, 1915, 6.

84. Alice Paul to PAH, January 27, 1917, PAH note, GPAHP.

85. Hoffert, *Alva Vanderbilt Belmont*, Belmont's Financial Contributions to the Suffrage Campaign (1909–1919), appendix, 202; Johnson, "Following the Money Wealthy Women, Feminism, and the American Suffrage Movement," 62.

86. Charles J. Kelly to PAH, January 2, 1917, GPAHP; Ellen Hill to PAH, September 8, 1917, GPAHP; Ellen Hill to PAH, October 23, 1917, GPAHP; Letters from Sophia W. Rader Who Acted as Mrs. Hearst's Social Worker, GPAHP; Hayes, "Weekend in the Country," 25; Richard A. Clark to Benjamin Ide Wheeler, October 19, 1917, GPAHP; William Gus Smith to PAH, January 20, 1917, PAH note on back of page, GPAHP.

EPILOGUE

1. Florence (Bayard) Hilles to PAH, January 29, 1918, GPAHP; Benjamin Ide Wheeler to PAH, March 14, 1918, GPAHP; Harrison H. Dodge to PAH, June 10, 1918, GPAHP; Harrison H. Dodge to PAH, December 25, 1918, GPAHP.

2. Carl Oscar Borg to PAH, July 17, 1918, GPAHP, as quoted by Borg to PAH from a letter she wrote to him; Cardwell, *Bernard Maybeck*, 197; Elizabeth W. Allston Pringle to Mrs. C.A. Hill, October 15, 1918, EWAP; William Randolph Hearst to PAH, September 6, 1918, GPAHP.

3. Baker, *Woodrow Wilson*, 8:436.

4. PAH letter on brown paper, 1918(?), Miscellany, Notes, Addresses, etc., GPAHP. The following reports from George F. Kincaid prepared for Phoebe Hearst may all be found in the George F. Kincaid Papers at the University of California Archives in the Bancroft Library: "Monthly Pig Report for Mrs. P.A. Hearst"; "Summary of Hog Report for January, February, and March, 1918"; "Monthly Dairy Report for Mrs. P.A. Hearst"; "Monthly Dairy Report for February, 1918"; "Monthly Vegetable Garden for the Month of March, 1918"; "Monthly Report of Poultry Plant for December 1918."

5. William Randolph Hearst to PAH, September 5, 1918, GPAHP; William Randolph Hearst and Millicent Wilson Hearst to PAH, September 6, 1918, GPAHP; William Randolph Hearst to PAH, August 6 and September 16, 1918, GPAHP.

6. Caroline L. Morgan to PAH, February 4, 1919, PAH not per H. M., GPAHP; Mabel Grovitch to PAH, January 23, 1919, GPAHP.

7. PAH to Margaret Peck(?) per H.M. (1918, 1919?), GPAHP; Crosby, *America's Forgotten Pandemic*, xii, 5, 60–61, 78, chap. 7, 49; Mrs. Simmons to Phoebe A. Hearst, PAH note, ca. 1918, Miscellaneous Notes, Addresses, etc., GPAHP; Barry, *Great Influenza*, part 7; Adele S. Brooks to PAH, January 19, 1919, GPAHP.

8. Ralph McLaren to PAH, January 2, 1919, note on back page written by H.M. on behalf of PAH, GPAHP; PAH to Margaret Peck(?) per H. M. (1918, 1919?), GPAHP; PAH to James Rolph Jr., ca. December 30, 1918, GPAHP; "Mrs. Hearst Dies at Home in Pleasanton," *San Francisco Chronicle*, April 14, 1919, 11; Charles Stetson Wheeler, *In the Matter of the Estate of Phoebe A. Hearst*, 7.

9. Barry, *Great Influenza*, 2; "Mrs. Phoebe A. Hearst Seriously Ill," *New York Times*, March 27, 1919, 6; Elizabeth A. Apperson to PAH, December 26, 1918, GPAHP; PAH to James Rolph Jr., ca. December 30, 1918, GPAHP; Charles Stetson Wheeler, *In the Matter of the Estate of Phoebe A. Hearst*, 58, 59–60, 65, 68–70, 72, 74, 84, 86, 101.

10. Charles Wheeler, *In the Matter of the Estate of Phoebe A. Hearst*, 77, 60; "Mrs. Phoebe A. Hearst Seriously Ill," *New York Times*, March 27, 1919, 6; "Mrs. Phoebe A. Hearst Is Better," *New York Times*, March 28, 1919; Helen Adelaide Brown to unknown, April 4, 1919, GPAHP; Crosby, *America's Forgotten Pandemic*, 5, 60–61, chap. 7; Fanning, *Influenza and Inequality*; Bristow, *American Pandemic*; Opdycke, *Flu Epidemic of 1918*. The *San Francisco Chronicle* reported in 2001 on "a new highly controversial theory that the Spanish flu was triggered when a gene segment from pig influenza somehow swapped with a gene segment in a flu virus infecting humans—an event called recombination." See Sabin Russell, "Genetic Study Links 1918, '97 Flu Outbreaks," *San Francisco Chronicle*, September 7, 2001.

11. "Mrs. Phoebe Hearst Dies in California," *New York Times*, April 14, 1919; "Mother of Hearst Dies of Pneumonia," April 14, 1919, *Washington (DC) Times*, Vonnie Eastham folder, copy of newspaper clipping, RGA; "Mrs. Hearst Dies at Home in Pleasanton," *San Francisco Chronicle*, April 14, 1919, 11; Clara Anthony Reed to Miss Ramirez, 1896, GPAHP; "Nation, State and Cities Pay Tribute to Mrs. Hearst; Body Laid by that of Her Husband," April 17, 1919, 3, GPAHP; "Her Name Blessed Throughout Land," *San Francisco Examiner*, April 16, 1919; Clara Anthony (Reed) to Miss Ramirez, 1896, GPAHP.

12. "Services to Be Held Here Wednesday," *San Francisco Examiner*, April 14, 1919, 2; "Mrs. Hearst Dies at Home in Pleasanton," April 14, 1919, *San Francisco Chronicle*; "Whole State Mourns Loss, Says Johnson," *San Francisco Examiner*, April 14, 1919, 3; "'Godmother of Exposition,' Was Her Title," *San Francisco Examiner*, 3; "Girls' School Honors Donor," *San Francisco Examiner*, April 16, 1919, 7; "Early Ideals of Teacher Always Kept," *San Francisco Examiner*, April 16, 1919, 7; "Her Memory Will Live Forever, Says Governor," *San Francisco Examiner*, April 14, 1919, 2; Victor Matson, New York American to William Randolph Hearst, April 14, 1919, Family Archive—Phoebe A. Hearst, box 6, folder 5, Hearst Sympathy Telegrams, HFA.

13. "Was Best Citizen State Ever Had," *San Francisco Examiner*, April 14, 1919, 2; "Nation, State and Cities Pay Tribute to Mrs. Hearst," *San Francisco Chronicle*, April 17, 1919, 3.

14. "Her Name Blessed Throughout Land," *San Francisco Examiner*, April 16, 1919, 6; "Legislature Adjourns As Mark of Respect," *San Francisco Examiner*, April 15, 1919, 6; "Court Pays Rare Honor to Mrs. Hearst," *San Francisco Examiner*, April 16, 1919, 6; "Mrs. Hearst's Funeral," *New York Times*, April 17, 1919, 11; "Hearst Plants All to Stop for 5 Min. Today," *San Francisco Examiner*, April 16, 1919, 1; "U.S. Lowers Colors for Mrs. Hearst," *San Francisco Examiner*, April 17, 1919, 13; "Whole Nation Joins in Tributes to Mrs. Phoebe Hearst," *San Francisco Examiner*, April 15, 1919, 1, 6; "Fellow Regents of U.C. Deeply Grieved at News," *San Francisco Examiner*, April 14, 1919, 3; Leepson, *Flag*, 305, as quoted in footnote 259; "U.S. Lowers Colors for Mrs. Hearst," *San Francisco Examiner*, April 17, 1919, 13.

15. Eleanor (Stanley) Smallwood, *Reminiscences of Phoebe Apperson Hearst*, 4; photocopy of her recollections of Mrs. Hearst, by a member of the class of 1902. Photocopied by courtesy of her daughter, Mrs. Donald Fraser, July 1974.

16. Millie Robbins, "Phoebe Hearst and Her Hacienda," *San Francisco Chronicle*, September 1, 1969, copy of newspaper clipping, RGA; Jackie Dashiell, "California's Golden Women, Phoebe Apperson Hearst," *Los Angeles Herald-Examiner*, September 26, 1976, 2; "Entire University to Pay Final Tribute to the Memory of Mrs. Phoebe Apperson Hearst," April 15, 1919, *Daily California*; "Last Honors to Mrs. Hearst, *San Francisco Examiner*, April 17, 1919, newspaper clipping, Mrs. George Hearst, Vice Regent for California,

Archives, Vice Regents' Files, Mount Vernon Library, Virginia; "Entire University Is Dismissed in Honor of Mrs. Hearst and To Welcome Returning Soldiers," April 22, 1919, *Daily Californian*; "Mrs. Hearst's Funeral: State and San Francisco Officials at Services in Grace Cathedral," *New York Times*, April 17, 1919, *New York Times*, online archives, accessed January 2, 2016; "Thousands Unable to Get in Church," *San Francisco Examiner*, April 17, 1919, 13, 14; Pringle, "In Memoriam: Phoebe Apperson Hearst," Minutes of the Council of the MVLA, 1919, 66; "Mrs. Phoebe Hearst Dies in California," April 14, 1919, *New York Times*, 13; "Mrs. Hearst Passes Away at Pleasanton," *San Francisco Examiner*, April 14, 1919; San Francisco Board of Supervisors, "In Memoriam: Mary W. Kincaid," 949; "Stephens and Mrs. Hearst Eulogized," *Daily Californian*, April 18, 1919, 2.

17. Typed copy of Phoebe Apperson Hearst's will from Los Angeles Museum of Natural History provided by Burton Benedict when he headed the Lowie Museum, University of California, Berkeley, 1995, which is now called the Phoebe Apperson Hearst Museum; Charles Wheeler, *In the Matter of the Estate of Phoebe A. Hearst*, 49–51.

18. William F. Patton, transcribed information from California State Supreme Court Case, San Francisco, no. 11378, filed November 10, 1924, copy, RGA; "Mrs. Phoebe Hearst Dies in California," *New York Times*, April 14, 1919, 13.

19. William F. Patton, transcribed information from California State Supreme Court Case, San Francisco, no. 11378, filed November 10, 1924, copy, RGA.

20. Typed copy of Phoebe Apperson Hearst's will from Los Angeles Museum of Natural History provided by Burton Benedict, 1995; Charles Wheeler, *In the Matter of the Estate of Phebe A. Hearst*, 29.

21. Judith M. Frank, administrator of Phoebe Apperson Hearst Scholarships, oral interview by Alexandra M. Nickliss, March 22, 2007, University of California, Berkeley; Luis Rico, telephone interview by Alexandra M. Nickliss, March 22, 2007, Development Office, University of California, Berkeley. As of February 3, 2016, the market value of the Hearst Scholarship fund is approximately $1,500,000 and generates about $49,500 per year to distribute in scholarships. Thanks to Rita d'Escoto, Donor Relations and Funds Manager, Financial Aid and Scholarships Office, University of California, Berkeley, for the 2016 information on the PAH Scholarships.

22. "National University Rankings," *U.S. News and World Report*, http://colleges.usnews.rankingsandreviews.com/best-colleges/rankings/national-universities, accessed October 29, 2013; Karin Fischer, "American Universities Yawn At Global Rankings," *Chronicle of Higher Education*, October 4, 2013, 24–5; Berkeley Art Museum and Pacific Film Archive, "Roma Pacifica: The Phoebe Apperson Hearst International Architectural Competition and the Berkeley Campus, 1896–1930," December 8, 1999–April 23, 2000, pamphlet; Designing the Campus of Tomorrow: The Legacy of the Hearst Architectural Plan, Present and Future, February 10, 2000, organized by the Center for Studies in Higher Education, University of California, Berkeley; University of California, "The New Century Plan: Vision Statement," n.d., p. 1 (original in author's possession). Rankings of undergraduate and graduate programs of colleges and universities, such as the *U.S. News and World Report* and Jack Gourman's, *The Gourman Report*, are controversial. See Elizabeth F. Farrell and Martin Van Der Werf, "Playing the Rankings Game," *Chronicle of Higher Education*, May 25, 2007, A11–A12, A14, A16, A18–19; Martin Van Der Werf, "Rankings Methodology Hurts Public Institutions," *Chronicle of Higher Education*, May 25, 2007, A13; Jeffrey Salingo, "What the Rankings Do for 'U.S. News,'" *Chronicle of Higher Education*, May 25, 2007, A15; Gourman, *Gourman Report*, 49.

23. Charles Burress, "Outrageous Science": UC Berkeley's Highly Praised Anthropology Department Turns 100," *San Francisco Chronicle*, February 6, 2002, A17, A18; Matt Ziol, "Museum Renaming Sparks Campus Ire," *Daily Californian*, April 16, 1992, 1, 5; Muir Macpherson, "Controversial Name Change," *Daily Californian*, April 21, 1992, 1, 8; Gourman, *Gourman Report*, 7. "Associations representing private colleges and universities, state universities and large research universities" are working on gathering their own statics and information to publish in response to the *U.S. News and World Report* college rankings. See Alan Finder, "Colleges Join Forces on a Web Presence to Let Prospective Students Research and Compare," *New York Times*, July 4, 2007, A15; Eric Hoover, "The 'U.S. News' Rankings Roll On," *Chronicle of Higher Education*, September 7, 2007, A45–A46. I'm grateful to Anne Hyde for providing insight into the politics to rename the University of California Museum.

24. See www.thecenturyclubofcalifornia.org; www.phoebehearstpreschool.org.

25. See www.pta.org; National Cathedral School, "The Arts at NCS; Commencement '07; 2006–2007 Annual Report," *National Cathedral School Magazine* (Fall 2007). See www.ncs.cathedral.org.

26. See www.pta.org, www.VistAsilomar.com; Clemens, *Standing Ground*, vi–vii, chap. 16.

27. DuBois, *Feminism and Suffrage*, 42; Boris, "Class Returns," 74–87.

28. PAH to Orrin Peck, December 22, 1886, PC; "Mrs. Hearst is for Suffrage," no newspaper name, January 2, 1913, newspaper clipping, GPAHP.

29. PAH to Caroline Severance, July 9, 1912, CSC; Flexner, "Anna Howard Shaw," 3:277. Shaw passed away on July 2, 1919.

Bibliography

UNPUBLISHED AND ARCHIVAL SOURCES

Alice Fletcher Papers. Smithsonian Institution, National Anthropological Archives, Washington DC.

Alfred L. Kroeber Correspondence and Papers. Bancroft Library, University of California, Berkeley.

Bancroft, Hubert Howe. "Life of George Hearst." Unpublished page proofs prepared for *Chronicles of the Kings*, 1887–1890. Bancroft Library, University of California, Berkeley.

Bangs, Jean Murray. Maybeck. Miscellaneous Clip File, Environmental Design Archives, University of California, Berkeley.

Belcher, John. "A Journey to California." John Belcher Collection, College of Environmental Design Archives, 1999–98, University of California, Berkeley.

Brooks, Adele S. "Phoebe Apperson Hearst: A Life and Some Letters." Unpublished, incomplete manuscript, ca. 1926. George and Phoebe Apperson Hearst Papers. Bancroft Library, University of California, Berkeley.

California. "An act to make women eligible to educational offices. The Statues of California Passed at the Twentieth Session of the Legislature 1873–74." Sacramento: G. H. Springer, State Printer, 1874. http://192.234.213.35/clerkarchive.

Caroline Severance Collection. Huntington Library, San Marino CA.

Center for Studies in Higher Education, "Designing the Campus of Tomorrow: The Legacy of The Hearst Architectural Plan, Present and Future," February 10, 2000, University of California, Berkeley.

Century Club of California, San Francisco. Century Club of San Francisco Archives. San Francisco CA.

Charlotte Perkins Gilman Papers. Schlesinger Library, Radcliffe Institute, Harvard University, Cambridge MA.

Chester H. Rowell Papers. Bancroft Library, University of California, Berkeley.

Clark, Edward Hardy. "Reminiscences of the Hearst Family." Oral history transcript, Bancroft Library, University of California, Berkeley, 1967.

Columbian Kindergarten Association Files. Antiochiana, Olive Kettering Library, Antioch College, Yellow Springs OH.

Crawford County, Missouri. Marriage Record. 2 vols. Microfilm reel C2044, Missouri State Archives, Jefferson City MO.

Crawford County Courthouse. Marriage Record (or Book) I. June 14, 1862, Crawford County Courthouse. Steelville MO.

Ellen Davis Conway Collection. Rare Books and Manuscripts Library, Columbia University, New York.

Elizabeth W. Allston Pringle Manuscripts, South Carolina Historical Society, Charleston SC.

Frances Douglas Lummis Papers. Special Collections, University of Arizona, Tucson AZ.

Frank, Judith. Administrator of Phoebe Apperson Hearst Scholarships. Oral interview by Alexandra M. Nickliss, March 22, 2007, University of California, Berkeley.

Franklin County Courthouse. Marriage Book. Vol. "A," 1819 to January 1845, microfilm reel C2388, Archives, Jefferson City MO.

Frederic W. Putnam Correspondence, 1901–1910. Pusey Library, Harvard University, Cambridge MA.

General Federation of Women's Clubs. Minutes. 3 vols. Washington DC: General Federation of Women's Clubs, 1892.

George Hearst and Phoebe E. Apperson. Pre-Nuptial Contract, June 14, 1862. Joint Collection, University of Missouri, Western Historical Manuscript Collection, Columbia, and State Historical Society of Missouri Manuscripts.

George Hearst and Phoebe E. Apperson Marriage Record, June 15, 1862. Missouri State Archives, Records Management and Archives Service, Division of the Office of Secretary of State, Jefferson City MO.

George and Phoebe Apperson Hearst Papers. Bancroft Library, University of California, Berkeley.

George Kincaid Papers. Bancroft Library, University of California, Berkeley.

Gibbons, Virginia S. "Phoebe Apperson Hearst." Century Club of California, San Francisco, undated.

Harriet Bradford Talks about Mrs. Phoebe Apperson Hearst, June 26, 1964. Taped interview. Copy in author's possession. The Phoebe Apperson Hearst Historical Society, St. Clair MO.

Hearst Family Archive. Phoebe A. Hearst. Hearst Corporation, San Francisco CA.

Hearst Family Papers, ca. 1885–1957. Bancroft Library, University of California, Berkeley.

Hearst, George. *Autobiography*. Gift of James B. Dunn, Homestake Mining Company, August 21, 1972. Written by Senator Hearst in 1890. Photocopy of typed transcript. Original in possession of the Homestake Mining Company.

Hearst, Phoebe A. *Personalia*. Volume bound by University of California, Bancroft Library, University of California, Berkeley, no date.

Hearst, Phoebe Apperson. "Remarks by Mrs. Hearst at the Cornerstone Laying of the Hearst Mining Building," November 18, 1902, Bancroft Library, University of California, Berkeley.

Hearst, William Randolph. "Memories of San Simeon and the Hearst Family." Oral history interview conducted by Tom Scott, edited by Pendleton Harris, Robert C. Paulik and Nancy E. Loe. San Simeon CA: Hearst San Simeon State Historical Monument, 1988.

Helen Hillyer Brown and Ella Goodall Cooper Collections. National Bahá'í Archives, Wilmette IL.

Howard, John Galen. "Bird's Eye View: The Phoebe Apperson Hearst Plan for the University of California, 1917." College of Environmental Design Archives, University of California, Berkeley.

Ida Husted Harper Papers. Huntington Library, San Marino CA.

James D. Phelan Correspondence and Papers. Bancroft Library, University of California, Berkeley.

Jane Lathrop Stanford Papers. Special Collections, Stanford University, Stanford CA.

Janet M. Peck Family Papers (1860–1956). California Historical Society, San Francisco CA.

Joint Collection. University of Missouri, Western Historical Manuscript Collection, Columbia MO, and State Historical Society of Missouri Manuscripts.

Kantor, J. R. K. *The Best Friend the University Ever Had*. Pamphlet, Bancroft Library, University of California, Berkeley, 1969.

Louise Sorbier Collection. California Historical Society, San Francisco CA.

Lucy Wortham James Collection. Joint Collection of the Western Historical Manuscript Collection, Columbia MO, and State Historical Society of Missouri Manuscripts.

Mann, Dr. Clair V. "The Story of Dunmoor, Former Home of the William James Family (years 1870 to 1879)." Rolla MO: June 30, 1963. Joint Collection of the Western Historical Manuscript Collection, Columbia MO, and State Historical Society of Missouri Manuscripts.

Margaret Graham Papers. Huntington Library, San Marino CA.

McLaughlin, Donald H. "Careers in Mining Geology and Management, University Governance and Teaching: Transcript, 1970–1971." Oral history interview by Harriet Nathan. Berkeley: Regents of the University of California, c. 1975.

Mount Vernon Ladies' Association of the Union Papers. Mount Vernon Ladies' Association Archives, Mount Vernon VA.

National Cathedral School for Girls Archives. Washington DC.

National Congress of Mothers 1896–1897. Copy from the original minutes, National Parents and Teachers Association, Chicago IL, 1896.

National Society of the Daughters of the American Revolution. Daughters of the American Revolution Library, Washington DC.

National Woman's Party Papers. University of California, Berkeley.

National Young Women's Christian Association Board Archives. Smith College, Northampton MA.

Orrin Peck Correspondence and Miscellany, 1887–1921. California Historical Society, San Francisco CA.

Panama-Pacific International Exposition Papers. San Francisco Ephemera, San Francisco History Center, San Francisco Public Library, San Francisco CA.

Panama-Pacific International Exposition Records, 1893–1929. Bancroft Library, University of California, Berkeley.

Panama-Pacific International Exposition Woman's Board. San Francisco Ephemera Collection, San Francisco History Center, San Francisco Public Library, San Francisco CA.

Peck Collection. Huntington Library, San Marino CA.

Phoebe Apperson Hearst Architectural Competition Correspondence. Bancroft Library, University of California, Berkeley.

Phoebe Apperson Hearst Diary, 1866 and 1873. Phoebe Apperson Hearst Museum, University of California, Berkeley.

Phoebe Apperson Hearst, typed copy of will. From the Los Angeles Museum of Natural History, provided by Burton Benedict and the Lowie Museum, 1995.

Pringle, Elizabeth W. Allston. "In Memoriam: Phoebe Apperson Hearst." Minutes of the Council of the Mount Vernon Ladies' Association of the Union. Fairfax County VA, May 1919.

"Proposed Memorial Phoebe Apperson Hearst, 1842–1919." Bancroft Library, University of California, Berkeley, no date.

Ralph Gregory Archives. Marthasville MO.

"Register of the California Homeopathic Institutions Records, 1884–1984." Finding Aid. Special Collections, Kalmanovitz Library, University of California, San Francisco CA.

Richardson, Leon. "Berkeley Culture, University of California Highlights and University Extension, 1892–1962, an oral history transcript." Interview by Amelia R. Fry. 2 vols. Berkeley: Regional Cultural History Project, 1962.

Ritter, Mary Bennett. "After Five Years," November 19, 1939. San Francisco Biography Collection, San Francisco History Center, San Francisco Public Library.

Sada Cornwall Papers, 1862–1921. Bancroft Library, University of California, Berkeley.

San Francisco Young Women's Christian Association Records. Young Women's Christian Association Archives, San Francisco.

Sarah B. (Ingersoll) Cooper Papers, (1842–1910). Department of Manuscripts and University Archives, Cornell University, Ithaca NY.

Simpson, Anna Pratt. *What Women Are Doing for the Panama-Pacific International Exposition.* Pamphlet, Panama-Pacific International Exposition Woman's Board, San Francisco History Center, San Francisco Public Library, ca. 1915.

Thomas Barry Diary, May–August 1879. Bancroft Library, University of California, Berkeley.

Thomas Mooney Papers. Bancroft Library, University of California, Berkeley.

Travelers' Aid Society Records. San Francisco History Center, San Francisco Public Library.

University of California. Academic Personnel Records Maintained by the Office of the President, University of California, ca. 1910–1985, University of California Archives, Bancroft Library, University of California, Berkeley.

University of California. "Announcement of Dedication of Hearst Hall by Association of Women Students," February 9, 1901, Elizabeth Woodworth Plass Scrapbook, University of California Archives, University of California, Berkeley.

University of California. Archives. Bancroft Library, University of California, Berkeley.

University of California. "Biography Forms for Academic Personnel at the University of California Berkeley, ca. 1900–1965," Bancroft Library, University of California, Berkeley.

University of California. "Biography Form for Phoebe Apperson Hearst." Biographies, Inactive, E-H, Secretary of the Chief of Staff of the Regents of the University of California, Office of the President of the University of California, Oakland CA.

University of California. Department and Museum of Anthropology Records. Bancroft Library, University of California, Berkeley.

University of California. Minute Book. University of California Archives. Bancroft Library, University of California, Berkeley.

University of California. Minutes of the Academic Council, Bancroft Library, University of California, Berkeley.

University of California. "University of California Press Notices Related to the Phoebe Hearst Architectural Plan." 2 vols. *California Architect and Buildings News*, January 1896, microfilm. Bancroft Library, University of California, Berkeley.

University of California. Records of the Office of the President. Bancroft Library, University of California, Berkeley.

University of California. Records of the Regents of the University of California, 1868–1933. Bancroft Library, University of California, Berkeley.

University of Pennsylvania Museum of Archaeology and Anthropology Museum Archives. University of Pennsylvania, Philadelphia.

Wallace, Janette Howard. "Reminiscences of Janette Howard Wallace: Daughter of John Galen Howard." Bancroft Library, University of California, Berkeley.

Women's Education and Industrial Union Board Papers. Schlesinger Library, Radcliffe College, Harvard University, Cambridge MA.

William Carey Jones Correspondence and Papers, ca. 1884–1918. Bancroft Library, University of California, Berkeley.

William Randolph Hearst Papers, 1874–1951 (bulk 1927–1947). Bancroft Library, University of California, Berkeley.

William Pepper Manuscripts. Van Pelt Library, University of Pennsylvania, Philadelphia.

William Emerson Ritter Correspondence and Papers, ca. 1879–1944. Bancroft Library, University of California, Berkeley.

Young Women's Christian Association, San Francisco. Pacific Coast Students' Conference of the Young Women's Christian Association. Capitola CA, May 18–28, 1900.

Young Women's Christian Association. "Statistical Material; Figure for the Young Women's Christian Association Work Done at the Panama Pacific International Exposition, San Francisco, California, February 20–December 4, 1915." Year Book Containing Dictionary and Statistical Material of The Young Women's Christian Associations of the United States of America 1915–1916. New York: National Board of the Young Women's Christian Association of the United States of America, 1916.

PUBLISHED SOURCES

Adam, Thomas. *Buying Respectability: Philanthropy and Urban Society in Transnational Perspective, 1840s to 1930s.* Bloomington: Indiana University Press, 2009.

———. *Philanthropy, Patronage, and Civil Society.* Bloomington: Indiana University Press, 2004.

Adams, Katherine H., and Michael L. Keene. *Alice Paul and the American Suffrage Campaign.* Urbana: University of Illinois Press, 2008.

Ahlstrom, Sydney E. *A Religious History of the American People*. New Haven: Yale University Press, 1972.

Alcoff, Linda. "Cultural Feminism versus Post-Structuralism: The Identity Crisis in Feminist Theory." *Signs: Journal of Women in Culture and Society* 13 (Spring 1988): 405-36.

Alexander, Adele Logan. "Adella Hunt Logan, the Tuskegee Woman's Club, and African Americans in the Suffrage Movement." In *Votes for Women! The Woman Suffrage Movement in Tennessee, the South, and the Nation*, edited by Marjorie Spruill Wheeler, 71–104. Knoxville: University of Tennessee Press, 1995.

Allen, Ann Taylor. "Feminism, Social Science, and the Meanings of Modernity: The Debate on the Origin of the Family in Europe and the United States, 1860–1914." *American Historical Review* 104 (October 1999): 1085–1113.

————. "Gender, Professionalization, and the Child in the Progressive Era: Patty Hill Smith, 1868–1946." *Journal of Women's History* 23 (Summer 2011): 112–36.

————. "Spiritual Motherhood: German Feminists and the Kindergarten Movement, 1848–1911." *History of Education Quarterly Special Issue: Educational Policy and Reform in Modern Germany* 22 (Autumn 1982): 319–39.

Allen, H. S. "The Phoebe Hearst Architectural Competition for the University of California." *American Monthly Review of Reviews: An International Magazine* 20 (October 1899): 433–41.

Allgor, Catherine. *Parlor Politics in Which Ladies of Washington Help Build a City and Government*. Charlottesville: University Press of Virginia, 2000.

Alpern, Sara, Joyce Antler, Elisabeth Perry Israels, and Ingrid Winther Scobie, eds. *The Challenge of Feminist Biography: Writing the Lives of Modern American Women*. Urbana: University of Illinois, 1992.

Altschuler, Glenn C. *Race, Ethnicity, and Class in American Social Thought, 1865–1919*. Arlington Heights IL: H. Davidson, 1982.

American Historical Review Roundtable. "Historians and Biography." *American Historical Review* 114 (June 2009): 573–661.

Anderson, Douglas Firth. "Through Fire and Fair by the Golden Gate: Progressive Era Protestantism and Regional Culture." PhD diss., Graduate Theological Union, University of California Berkeley, 1988.

———. "'We Have Here a Different Civilization': Protestant Identity in the San Francisco Bay Area, 1906–1909." *Western Historical Quarterly* 23 (May 1992): 199–221.

Anderson, Karen. "Work, Gender, and Power in the American West." *Pacific Historical Review* 61 (November 1992): 481–99.

Antler, Joyce. "Lucy Sprague Mitchell." In *Notable American Women: The Modern Period*, edited by Barbara Sicherman and Carol Hurd Green, with Ilene Kantrov and Harriette Walker, 484–87. Cambridge MA: Belknap Press with Harvard University Press, 1980.

Appleby, Joyce. *Inheriting the Revolution: The First Generation of Americans.* Cambridge MA: Harvard University Press, 2000.

———. *The Relentless Revolution: A History of Capitalism.* New York: W. W. Norton, 2010.

———. "The Social Consequences of American Revolutionary Ideals in the Early Republic." In *The Middling Sorts: Explorations in the History of the American Middle Class*, edited by Burton J. Bledstein and Robert D. Johnston, 31–49. New York: Routledge, 2001.

Arendt, Hannah. *The Human Condition.* Chicago: University of Chicago Press, 1958.

Armitage, Susan. "'Revisiting 'The Gentle Tamers Revisited': The Problems and Possibilities of Western Women's History—An Introduction." *Pacific Historical Review* 61 (November 1992): 459-62.

———. "Women and Men in Western History: A Stereotypical Vision." *Western Historical Quarterly* 16 (October 1985): 381–95.

Aron, Cindy. *Working at Play: A History of Vacations in the United States.* New York: Oxford University Press, 1999.

Babcock, Barbara Allen. "Clara Shortridge Foltz: Constitution-Maker." *Indiana Law Journal* 66 (Fall 1991): 849–940.

———. "Essay: Clara Shortridge Foltz 'First Woman.'" *Arizona Law Review* 30 (1988): 673–717.

Baker, Jean H. "Getting Right with Women's Suffrage." *Journal of the Gilded Age and the Progressive Era* 5 (January 2006): 7–17.

Baker, Orin C. *Travelers' Aid Society in America: Principles and Methods.* New York: Funk and Wagnalls, 1917.

Baker, Paula. "The Domestication of Politics: Women and American Political Society, 1780–1920." *American Historical Review* 89 (June 1984): 620–47.

Baker, Ray Stannard, ed. *Woodrow Wilson: Life and Letters, Armistice March 1–November 11, 1918*. Garden City NY: Doubleday, Page, 1939.

Baltzell, E. Digby. *Philadelphia Gentlemen: The Making of a National Upper Class*. Illinois: Free Press, 1958.

———. *The Protestant Establishment: Aristocracy and Caste in America*. New York: Random House, 1964.

Bancroft, Hubert Howe. *The Biography of George Hearst Prepared for "The Chronicles of the Kings."* 2 vols. San Francisco: History Company, n.d.

———. *Chronicles of the Builders*. Vol. 2. San Francisco: History Company, ca. 1890.

Banner, Lois W. "AHR Roundtable: Biography as History," *American Historical Review* 114 (June 2009): 579–86.

———. *American Beauty: A Social History Through Two Centuries of the American Ideal and Image of the Beautiful Woman*. New York: Alfred A. Knopf, 1983.

Barry, John M. *The Great Influenza: The Epic Story of the Deadliest Plague in History*. New York: Viking, 2004.

Barry, Kathleen. "The New Historical Synthesis: Women's Biography." *Journal of Women's History* 1 (Winter 1990): 75–105.

Barth, Gunther. *Instant City: Urbanization and the Rise of San Francisco and Denver*. Albuquerque: University of New Mexico Press, 1988.

———. "Metropolitan and Urban Elites in the Far West." In *The Age of Industrialism in America: Essays in Social Structure and Cultural Values*, edited by Frederic Cople Jaher, 158–87. New York: Free Press, 1968.

Batzell, Rudi. "'Labor of Social Reproduction': Work and Gendered Power in the History of Capitalism, 1870–1930." *Journal of the Gilded Age and Progressive Era* 15 (July 2016): 310–30.

Beard, Mary. *Woman as Force in History: A Study in Traditions and Realities*. New York: Collier, 1946.

Bederman, Gayle. *Manliness and Civilization: A Cultural History of Gender and Race in the United States, 1880–1917*. Chicago and London: University of Chicago Press, 1995.

Beers, Dorothy Gondos. "The Centennial City 1865–1876." In *Philadelphia: A 300-Year History*, edited by Russell F. Weigley. New York: W. W. Norton, 1982.

Beeton, Beverly. *Women Vote in the West: The Woman Suffrage Movement 1869–1896.* New York: Garland, 1986.

Bender, Thomas. "Wholes and Parts: The Need for Synthesis in American History." *Journal of American History* 73 (June 1986): 120–36.

Benedict, Burton. *The Anthropology of World's Fairs: San Francisco's Panama Pacific International Exposition.* Berkeley: Lowie Museum of Anthropology; London; Berkeley: Scolar Press, 1983.

Berch, Bettina. *The Woman behind the Lens: The Life and Work of Frances Benjamin Johnston, 1864–1952.* Charlottesville: University Press of Virginia, 2000.

Bergland, Barbara. *Making San Francisco America: Cultural Frontiers in the Urban West 1846–1906.* Lawrence: University Press of Kansas, 2007.

Berkeley, Kathleen C. "'Colored Ladies Also Contributed': Black Women's Activities from Benevolence to Social Welfare, 1866–1896." *The Web of Southern Social Relations: Women, Family, and Education*, edited by Walter Frazer Jr., R. Frank Sounders Jr., and John L. Wakelyn, 181–203. Athens: University of Georgia Press, 1985.

Blackwell, Marilyn S., and Kristen T. Oertel. *Frontier Feminist: Clarina Howard Nichols and the Politics of Motherhood.* Lawrence: University Press of Kansas, 2010.

Blair, Karen. *The Clubwoman as Feminist: True Womanhood Redefined, 1868–1914.* New York: Holmes and Meier, 1980.

———. "General Federation of Women's Clubs." In *The Reader's Companion to U.S. Women's History*, edited by Wilma Mankiller et al. Boston: Houghton Mifflin, 1998.

Bledstein, Burton J. *The Culture of Professionalism: The Middle Class and the Development of Higher Education in America.* New York: W. W. Norton, 1978.

Bledstein, Burton J., and Robert D. Johnston, eds. *The Middling Sorts: Explorations in the History of the Middle Class.* New York: Routledge, 2001.

Block, Sharon. *Rape and Sexual Power in Early America.* Published for the Omohundro Institute of Early American History and Culture, Williamsburg VA. Chapel Hill: University of North Carolina Press, 2006.

Blow, Susan. "Kindergarten Education." *Education in the United States: A Series of Monographs*, edited by Nicholas Murray Butler. Albany NY: J. B. Lyon, 1904.

Boisseau, T. J., and Abigail M. Markwyn, eds. *Gendering the Fair: Histories of Women and Gender at World's Fairs*. Urbana: University of Illinois Press, 2010.

———. "World's Fairs in Feminist Historical Perspective." In *Gendering the Fair: Histories of Women and Gender at World's Fairs*, edited by T. J. Boisseau and Abigail Markwyn. Urbana: University of Illinois Press, 2010.

Bonfils, Winifred Black. *The Life and Personality of Phoebe Apperson Hearst*. San Francisco: John Henry Nash, 1928.

Booth, Marilyn, and Antoinette Burton, eds. "Editor's Note: Critical Feminist Biography II." *Journal of Women's History* 21 (Winter 2009): 8–12.

Bordin, Ruth. *Frances Willard: A Biography*. Chapel Hill: University of North Carolina Press, 1986.

———. *Women and Temperance: The Quest for Power and Liberty, 1873–1900*. Philadelphia: Temple University Press, 1981.

Boris, Eileen. "Class Returns." *Journal of Women's History* 25 (Winter 2013): 74–87.

Botting, Eileen Hunt, ed., and introduction. *A Vindication of the Rights of Woman by Mary Wollstonecraft*. New Haven: Yale University Press, 2014.

Bourdieu, Pierre. *Distinction: A Social Critique of the Judgment of Taste*. Translated by Richard Nice. Cambridge MA: Harvard University Press, 1984.

———. *The Field of Cultural Production: Essay on Art and Literature*, edited and introduced by Randal Johnson. New York: Columbia University Press, 1993.

———. "Structures, Habitus, Power: Basis for a Theory of Symbolic Power." In *Culture/Power/History: A Reader in Contemporary Social Theory*, edited by Nicholas B. Dirks, Geoff Eley, and Sherry B. Ortner, 155–99. Princeton NJ: Princeton University Press, 1994.

Boutelle, Sara Holmes. *Julia Morgan, Architect*. New York: Abbeville Press, 1988.

Boylan, Anne M. "Claiming Visibility: Women in Public/Public Women in the United States, 1865–1910." In *Becoming Visible: Women's Presence in Late Nineteenth-Century America*, edited by Janet Floyd, Alison Easton, R. J. Ellis, and Lindsey Traub, 17–40. Amsterdam: Rodopi, 2010.

———. "Evangelical Womanhood in the Nineteenth Century: The Role of Women in Sunday Schools." *Feminist Studies* 4 (October 1978): 62–80.

———. *The Origins of Women's Activism in New York and Boston, 1797–1840.* Chapel Hill: University of North Carolina Press, 2002.

———. *Sunday School: The Formation of an American Institution, 1790–1880.* New Haven: Yale University Press, 1988.

———. "Timid Girls, Venerable Widows, and Dignified Matrons: Life Cycle Patterns Among Organized Women in New York and Boston, 1797–1840." *American Quarterly* 38 (Winter 1986): 779–97.

———. "Women and Politics in the Era before Seneca Falls." *Journal of the Early Republic* 10 (Fall 1990): 363–82.

———. "Women in Groups: An Analysis of Women's Benevolent Organizations in New York and Boston, 1797–1840." *Journal of American History* 71 (December 1984): 497–523.

Bremner, Robert H. *From the Depths: The Discovery of Poverty in the United States.* New York: New York University Press, 1956.

———. "'Scientific Philanthropy,' 1873–1893." *Social Science Review* 30 (June 1956): 168–73.

Brennan, Margaret Lynch. *The Irish Bridget: Irish Immigrant Women in Domestic Service in America, 1840–1930.* Syracuse NY: Syracuse University Press, 2009.

Bristow, Nancy K. *The American Pandemic: The Lost Worlds of the 1918 Influenza Epidemic.* New York: Oxford University Press, 2012.

Brown, Elizabeth, and Alan Fern. "Introduction." In *Revisiting the White City: American Art at the 1893 World's Fair.* Organizers Carolyn Kinder Carr and George Gurney. Washington DC: National Museum of American Art; National Portrait Gallery, 1993.

Bryce, James. *The American Commonwealth.* 2 vols. London: Macmillan, 1888.

Buchanan, James A., and Gail Stuart, eds. *Comprising the History of the Panama Canal and A Full Account of the World's Greatest Exposition, Embracing the Participation of the State and Nations of the World and Other Events at San Francisco, 1915.* Compiled by the Pan-Pacific Press Association of San Francisco, 1916.

Buechler, Steven M. "Elizabeth Boynton Herbert and the Woman Suffrage Movement, 1870–1896: *Signs: Journal of Women in Culture and Society* 13 (Autumn 1987): 78–97.

————. *The Transformation of the Woman Suffrage Movement: The Case of Illinois, 1850–1920*. New Brunswick NJ: Rutgers University Press, 1986.

Buhle, Mary Jo. *Women and American Socialism, 1870–1920*. Urbana: University of Illinois Press, 1981.

Burkhardt, Frederick et al., eds. *Dictionary of American Biography*. New York: Charles Scribner's Sons, 1964.

Burnham, John Chynoweth. "Milicent Washburn Shinn." In *Notable American Women, 1607–1950: A Biographical Dictionary*, edited by Edward T. James, Janet Wilson James, and Paul S. Boyer, 3: 285–88. Cambridge MA: Belknap Press of Harvard University Press, 1971.

Burrow, James G. *Organized Medicine in the Progressive Era: The Move Toward Monopoly*. Baltimore: Johns Hopkins University Press, 1977.

Burton, Antoinette. *Burdens of History: British Feminists, Indian Women, and Imperial Culture, 1865–1915*. Chapel Hill: University of North Carolina Press, 1994.

Butler, Judith. *Gender Trouble: Feminism and the Subversion of Identity*. New York: Routledge, 1990.

Butsch, Richard S., ed. *For Fun and Profit: The Transformation of Leisure into Consumption*. Philadelphia: Temple University Press, 1990.

Cardwell, Kenneth H. *Bernard Maybeck: Artisan, Architect, Artist*. Santa Barbara CA and Salt Lake City: Peregrine Smith, 1977.

Cardwell, Kenneth H., and William C. Hays. "Fifty Years from Now." *California Monthly* (April 1954): 20–26.

Carnes, Mark C., and Clyde Griffen, eds. *Meanings of Manhood: Constructions of Masculinity in Victorian America*. Chicago and London: University of Chicago Press, 1990.

Carpenter, Frank G. *Carp's Washington*. New York: McGraw-Hill, 1960.

Catt, Carrie Chapman, and Nettie Rogers Shuler. *Woman Suffrage and Politics: The Inner Story of the Suffrage Movement*. Reprint. Introduction by T. A. Larson. Seattle: University of Washington Press, 1969.

Century Club of California, San Francisco. *Twenty-Fourth Annual Report for the Year Ending May 22, 1912*. San Francisco: John R. McNicoll Printing Company.

Chandler, Arthur. *The Biography of San Francisco State University*. San Francisco: Lexikos Press, 1986.

Childs, Margaretta P. "Elizabeth Waties Allston Pringle." In *Notable American Women*, 1607–1950: *A Biographical Dictionary*, 3 vols., edited by Edward T. James, Janet Wilson James, and Paul S. Boyer. Cambridge MA: Harvard University Press, 1971.

Clarke, Edward H. *Sex in Education or, A Fair Chance for Girls*. 1873. Reprint; New York: Arno Press and *New York Times*, 1972.

Clemens, Dorothy Thelen. *Standing Ground and Starting Point: 100 Years with the University YWCA*. Berkeley: University YWCA, 1990.

Cocks, Catherine. *Doing the Town: The Rise of Urban Tourism in the United States, 1850–1915*. Berkeley: University of California Press, 2001.

Cohen, Lizabeth. "Citizens and Consumers in the Century of Mass Consumption." In *Perspectives on Modern America: Making Sense of the Twentieth-Century*, edited by Harvard Sitkoff, 145–61. New York: Oxford University, 2001.

Cohen, Nancy. *The Reconstruction of American Liberalism, 1865–1914*. Chapel Hill: University of North Carolina Press, 2002.

Coker, William Francis. *Organismic Theories of the State; Nineteenth Century Interpretations of the State as Organism or as Person*. New York: Columbia University, 1910.

Cole, Douglas. *Franz Boas: The Early Years, 1858–1906*. Seattle: University of Washington Press, 1999.

College Equal Suffrage League of Northern California. *Winning Equal Suffrage in California: Reports of Committees of the College Equal Suffrage League of Northern California in the Campaign of 1911*. San Francisco CA: National College Equal Suffrage League, 1913.

Collier, Jane F. "Women in Politics." In *Woman, Culture, and Society*, edited by Michelle Zimbalist Rosaldo and Louise Lamphere. Stanford CA: Stanford University Press, 1974.

Columbian Kindergarten Association. *First Statement of the Columbian Kindergarten Association for the Year Ending April 30, 1894*. Washington DC, 1894.

Conn, Steven. *Museums and American Intellectual Life, 1876–1920*. Chicago: University of Chicago Press, 1998.

Cooper, John Milton, Jr. *The Warrior and the Priest: Woodrow Wilson and Theodore Roosevelt*. Cambridge MA: Belknap Press of Harvard University Press, 1983.

Cossitt, Rev. F. R. *The Life and Times of Rev. Finis Ewing One of the Fathers and Founders of the Cumberland Presbyterian Church*. Louisville KY: Rev. Lee Roy Woods, Agent for the Board of Publication of the Cumberland Presbyterian Church, 1853.

Cott, Nancy F. *The Bonds of Womanhood: "Woman's Sphere" in New England, 1780–1835*. New Haven: Yale University Press, 1977.

———. "Giving Character to Our Whole Civil Polity: Marriage and the Public Order in the Late Nineteenth Century." In *U. S. History as Women's History: New Feminist Essays*, edited by Linda K. Kerber, Alice Kessler-Harris, and Kathryn Kish Sklar, 107–21. Chapel Hill: University of North Carolina Press. 1995.

———. *Grounding of Modern Feminism*. New Haven: Yale University Press, 1987.

———. *Public Vows: A History of Marriage and the Nation*. Cambridge MA: Harvard University Press, 2000.

Crawford County History Book Committee. "Steelville Presbyterian." *Crawford County Missouri History*. Paducah KY: Turner, 1987.

Cremin, Lawrence A. *American Education: The Metropolitan Experience 1876–1980*. New York: Harper and Row, 1988.

Crocker, Ruth, *Mrs. Russell Sage: Women's Activism and Philanthropy in Gilded Age and Progressive Era America*. Bloomington: Indiana University Press, 2006.

Croly, Jenny June Cunningham. *The History of the Woman's Club Movement*. New York: Henry G. Allen, 1898.

Cronon, William. *Changes in the Land: Indians, Colonists, and the Ecology of New England*. New York: Hill and Wang, 1983.

Cronon, William, George Miles, and Jay Gitlin, eds. *Under an Open Sky: Rethinking America's Western Past*. New York: W. W. Norton, 1992.

———. "Becoming West: Toward a New Meaning for Western History," In *Under an Open Sky: Rethinking America's Western Past*, edited by William Cronon, George Miles, and Jay Gitlin, 3–27. New York: W. W. Norton, 1992.

Crosby, Alfred W. *America's Forgotten Pandemic: The Influenza of 1918*. 2nd ed. New York: Cambridge University Press, 2003.

Cross, Robert D. "Grace Hoadley Dodge." In *Notable American Women, 1607–1950: A Biographical Dictionary*, edited by Edward T. James, Janet Wilson James, and Paul S. Boyer, 1:489–92. Cambridge MA: Belknap Press of Harvard University Press, 1971.

Dahlgren, Mrs. Madeleine Vinton. *Etiquette of Social Life in Washington.* 5th ed. Philadelphia: J. B. Lippincott, 1881.

Darnell, Regna. "The Emergence of Academic Anthropology at the University of Pennsylvania." *Journal of the History of the Behavioral Sciences*, 6 (January 1970): 91.

Darney, Virginia Grant. "Women and World's Fairs: American International Exposition, 1876–1904." PhD diss., Emory University, 1982.

Davies, Wallace Evan. "Caroline Webster Schermerhorn Astor." In *Notable American Women, 1607–1950: A Biographical Dictionary*, edited by Edward T. James, Janet Wilson James, and Paul S. Boyer, 1:62–64. Cambridge MA: Belknap Press of Harvard University Press, 1971.

Davis, Florence Pearl. "The Education of Southern Girls from the Middle of the Eighteenth Century to the Close of the Antebellum Period." PhD diss., University of Chicago, 1951.

Davis, Kathy. "Critical Sociology and Gender Relations." In *The Gender of Power*, edited by Davis, Kathy, Monique Leijenaar, and Jantine Oldersma. Newbury Park CA: Sage, 1991.

Davis, Kathy, Monique Leijenaar, and Jantine Oldersma. *The Gender of Power.* Newbury Park CA: Sage, 1991.

Davis, Susan G. *Parades and Power: Street Theatre in Nineteenth-Century Philadelphia.* Philadelphia: Temple University Press, 1986.

Decker, Peter. *Fortune and Failures: White Collar Mobility in Nineteenth-Century San Francisco.* Cambridge MA: Harvard University Press, 1978.

de Cos, Patricia L. *History and Development of Kindergarten in California: Prepared for the Joint Legislative Committee to Develop a Master Plan for Education— Kindergarten Through University.* Sacramento: California Research Bureau, April, 2001.

deFord, Miriam Allen. *They Were San Franciscans.* Caldwell ID: Caxton Printers, 1947.

Degler, Carl N. "Charlotte Anna Perkins Stetson Gilman." In *Notable American Women, 1607–1950: A Biographical Dictionary*, edited by Edward T. James, Janet Wilson James, and Paul S. Boyer. 3 vols. Cambridge MA: Belknap Press of Harvard University Press, 1971.

———. *In Search of Human Nature: The Decline of Revival of Darwinism in American Social Thought.* New York: Oxford University Press, 1991.

DeMott, Benjamin. *The Imperial Middle: Why Americans Can't Think Straight About Class*. New York: William Morrow, 1990.

Deutsch, Sarah. *Women and the City: Gender, Space, and Power in Boston 1870–1940*. New York: Oxford University Press, 2000.

Dexter, Ralph W. "Frederic Ward Putnam and the Development of Museums of Natural History and Anthropology in the United States." *Curator* 9 (June 1966): 150–55.

———. "The Putnam-Kroeber Relations in the Development of American Anthropology." *Journal of California and Great Basin Anthropology* 11, no. 1 (1989): 91–96.

———. "The Role of F. W. Putnam in Developing Anthropology at the American Museum of Natural History." *Curator* 19 (December 1976): 303–10.

Dirks, Nicholas, Geoff Eley, and Sherry B. Ortner, eds. *Culture/Power/History: A Reader in Contemporary Social Theory*. Princeton NJ: Princeton University Press, 1994.

Douglass, John Aubrey. *The California Idea and American Higher Education*. Stanford CA: Stanford University Press, 2000.

Draper, Joan. "The École des Beaux-Arts and the Architectural Profession in the United States: The Case of John Galen Howard." In *The Architect: Chapters in the History of the Profession*, edited by Spiro Kristof, 209–37. New York: Oxford University Press, 1977.

DuBois, Ellen Carol. *Feminism and Suffrage: The Emergence of an Independent Women's Movement in America, 1848?–1869*. Ithaca: Cornell University Press, 1978.

———. *Harriot Stanton Blatch and the Winning of Woman Suffrage*. New Haven: Yale University Press, 1997.

———. *Woman Suffrage and Women's Rights*. New York: New York University Press, 1998.

———. "Working Women, Class Relations, and Suffrage Militance: Harriot Stanton Blatch and the New York Woman Suffrage Movement, 1894–1909." *Journal of American History* 74 (June 1987): 34–58.

DuBois, Ellen, Mari Jo Buhle, Temma Kaplan, Gerda Lerner, and Carroll Smith-Rosenberg. "Politics and Culture in Women's History: A Symposium." *Feminist Studies* 6 (Spring 1980): 26–64.

DuBois, Ellen Carol, and Lynn Dumenil. *Through Women's Eyes: An American History with Documents.* 4th ed. New York: Bedford/St. Martin's, 2016.

DuBois, Ellen Carol, and Linda Gordon. "Daughters Writing: Toward a Theory of Women's Biography." *Feminist Studies* 9 (Spring 1983): 80–102.

Duffin, Lorna. "The Conspicuous Consumptive: Woman as an Invalid." In *The Nineteenth-Century Woman: Her Cultural and Physical World*, edited by Sara Delamont and Lorna Duffin, 26–56. New York: Barnes and Noble, 1978.

Dye, Nancy Schrom, and Daniel Blake. "Mother Love and Infant Death, 1750–1920." *Journal of American History* 73 (September 1986): 329–53.

Edelman, Susan Scheiber. "'A Red Hot Suffrage Campaign': The Woman Suffrage Cause in California, 1896." *California Supreme Court Historical Society Yearbook* 2 (1995): 51–131. Reprint of 1993 publication.

The Elite Directory for San Francisco and Oakland. San Francisco: Argonaut Publishing Company, 1879. Hathi Trust Digital Library, University of California, Berkeley.

Epstein, Barbara Leslie. *The Politics of Domesticity: Women, Evangelism, and Temperance in Nineteenth Century America.* Middletown CT: Wesleyan University Press, 1981.

Epstein, Cynthia Fuchs. "Women and Elites: A Cross-National Perspective." In *Access to Power: Cross-National Studies of Women and Elites*, edited by Cynthia Fuchs Epstein and Rose Laub Coser, 3–15. London: George Allen and Unwin, 1981.

Ethington, Philip J. *The Public City: The Political Construction of Urban Life in San Francisco, 1850–1900.* New York: Cambridge University Press, 1994.

Ewald, Donna, and Peter Clute. *San Francisco Invites the World: The Panama-Pacific International Exposition of 1915.* San Francisco: Chronicle Books, 1991.

Fanning, Patricia J. *Influenza and Inequality: One Town's Tragic Response to the Great Epidemic of 1918.* Amherst: University of Massachusetts Press, 2010.

Feinstein, Karen Wolk. "Kindergartens, Feminism, and the Professionalization of Motherhood." *International Journal of Women's Studies* 3 (January–February 1980): 28–38.

Fellman, Anita Clair, and Michael Fellman. *Making Sense of Self: Medical Advice Literature in Late Nineteenth-Century America.* Philadelphia: University of Pennsylvania Press, 1981.

Ferrier, William Warren. *Origin and Development of the University of California.* Berkeley: Sather Gate Book Shop, ca. 1930.

Field, Corrine T. *The Struggle for Equal Adulthood: Gender, Race, Age, and the Fight for Citizenship in Antebellum America.* Chapel Hill: University of North Carolina Press, 2014.

Finkelstein, Barbara. "The Moral Dimensions of Pedagogy: Teaching Behavior in Popular Primary Schools in Nineteenth-Century America." *American Studies* 15 (Fall 1974): 79–89.

————. "Pedagogy as Intrusion: Teaching Values in Popular Primary Schools in Nineteenth-Century America." *History of Childhood Quarterly* 2 (Winter 1975): 349–78.

Finnegan, John Patrick. *Against the Specter of the Dragon: The Campaign for Military Preparedness.* Westport CT: Greenwood Press, 1974.

Finnegan, Margaret. *Selling Suffrage: Consumer Culture and Votes for Women.* New York: Columbia University Press, 1999.

Fischer, Christiane. "Women in California in the Early 1850s." *Southern California Quarterly* 60 (Fall 1978): 231–53.

Fischer, David Hackett, and James C. Kelly. *Bound Away: Virginia and the Westward Movement.* Charlottesville: University Press of Virginia, 2000.

Fischer, Sue, and Kathy Davis. *Negotiating at the Margins: The Gendered Discourses of Power and Resistance*, edited by Sue Fischer and Kathy Davis, 3–20. New Brunswick NJ: Rutgers University Press, 1993.

Fisher, Berenice. "Wandering in the Wilderness: The Search for Women Role Models." *Signs: Journal of Women in Culture and Society* 13 (Winter 1988): 211–33.

Fitzpatrick, Ellen. *Endless Crusade: Women Social Scientists and Progressive Reform.* New York: Oxford University Press, 1990.

Flack, James Kirkpatrick. *Desideratum in Washington: The Intellectual Community in the Capital City, 1870–1900.* Cambridge MA: Schenkam, 1975.

Flanagan, Maureen A. *America Reformed: Progressives and Progressivisms 1890s–1920s.* New York: Oxford University Press, 2007.

————. *Seeing with Their Hearts: Chicago Women and the Vision of the Good City, 1871–1933.* Princeton NJ: Princeton University Press, 2002.

Fletcher, S. S. F., and J. Welton. *Froebel's Chief Writings on Education.* New York: Longman's, Green, 1912.

Flexner, Eleanor. "Anna Howard Shaw." *Notable American Women, 1607–1950: A Biographical Dictionary*, edited by Edward T. James, Janet Wilson James, and Paul S. Boyer, 3:277. Cambridge MA: Belknap Press of Harvard University Press, 1971.

Forte, H. S. "Biographical Sketches, Randolph W. Apperson." *Pen Pictures from the "Garden of the World."* Santa Clara County CA: Lewis, 1888.

———, ed. *Pen Pictures from the "Garden of the World."* Santa Clara County CA: Lewis 1888.

Foucault, Michel. *Power/Knowledge: Selected Interviews and Other Writings, 1972–1977*, edited by Colon Gordon; translated by Colon Gordon, Leo Marshall, John Mephan, and Kate Soper. New York: Pantheon Books, 1972.

Fox, Daniel M. *Engines of Culture: Philanthropy and Art Museums.* Madison: State Historical Society of Wisconsin, 1963.

Fox, Greer Litton. "'Nice Girl': Social Control of Women Through a Value Construct." *Signs: Journal of Women in Culture and Society* 2 (Summer 1977): 805–17.

Fox, Richard Wrightman, and T. J. Jackson Lears, eds. *The Power of Culture: Critical Essays in American History.* Chicago: University of Chicago Press, 1993.

Frankel, Noralee, and Nancy S. Dye, eds. *Gender, Class, Race, and Reform in the Progressive Era.* Lexington: University Press of Kentucky, 1991.

Franzen, Trisha. *Anna Howard Shaw: The Work of Woman Suffrage.* Urbana: University of Illinois Press, 2014.

Free, Laura E. "Money Changes Everything." *Reviews in American History* 41 (Sept. 2013): 467–72.

Freedman, Estelle. "Separatism as Strategy: Female Institution Building and American Feminism, 1870–1930." *Feminist Studies* 5 (Fall 1979): 512–29.

———. "Separatism Revisited: Women's Institutions, Social Reform, and the Career of Miriam Van Waters." In *Feminism, Sexuality, and Politics: Essays by Estelle B. Freedman*, 37–55. Chapel Hill: University of North Carolina Press, 2006.

Freeman, John E. "University Anthropology: Early Departments in the United States." Paper read before the Kroeber Anthropological Society, April 25, 1964, Berkeley, California." *Kroeber Anthropological Society Papers* no. 32 (Spring 1965): 78–90.

Gamber, Wendy. *The Female Economy: The Millinery and Dressmaking Trades, 1860–1930.* Urbana: University of Illinois Press, 1997.

García, Miroslava Chávez. *Negotiating Conquest: Gender and Power in California, 1770s to 1880s.* Tucson: University of Arizona Press, 2004.

Garnett, Porter. *Stately Homes of California.* Boston: Little, Brown, 1915.

———. "Stately Homes of California." *Sunset, the Pacific Monthly* 32 (April 1914): 843–47.

Gebhard, David, and Harriette Von Breton, organizers. *Architecture in California, 1868–1968.* Exhibition to celebrate the Centennial of the University of California. Santa Barbara CA: Standard Printing of Santa Barbara, ca. 1968.

Geertz, Clifford, "Thick Description: Toward an Interpretive Theory of Culture." In *The Interpretation of Cultures: Selected Essays,* 3–30. London: Fontana Press, 1993.

Geidel, Peter. "Alva E. Belmont: A Forgotten Feminist." PhD diss., Columbia University, 1992.

Geiger, Roger L. *The History of Higher Education: Learning and Culture from the Founding to World War II.* Princeton NJ: Princeton University Press, 2014.

Gere, Anne Ruggles. *Intimate Practices: Literacy and Cultural Work in U.S. Women's Clubs, 1880–1920.* Urbana: University of Illinois Press, 1997.

Gettleman, Marvin E. "Charity and Social Classes in the United States, 1874–1900, I." *American Journal of Economics and Sociology* 22 (April 1963): 313–29.

Gilb, Corinne L. "Clara Shortridge Foltz." In *Notable American Women, 1607–1950: A Biographical Dictionary,* edited by Edward T. James, Janet Wilson James, and Paul S. Boyer, 1:641–43. Cambridge MA: Belknap Press of Harvard University Press, 1971.

———. "Laura de Force Gordon." In *Notable American Women, 1607–1950: A Biographical Dictionary,* edited by Edward T. James, Janet Wilson James, and Paul S. Boyer, 2:68–69. Cambridge MA: Belknap Press of Harvard University Press, 1971.

Gilkeson, John S. *Anthropologists and the Rediscovery of America, 1886–1965.* New York: Cambridge University Press, 2010.

Gillmore, Inez Haynes. *The Story of the Woman's Party.* New York: Harcourt, Brace, 1921.

Gilmore, Glenda Elizabeth. *Gender and Jim Crow: Women and the Politics of White Supremacy in North Carolina 1896–1920*. Chapel Hill: University of North Carolina Press, 1996.

Ginzberg, Lori D. "'Moral Suasion Is Moral Balderdash': Women, Politics, and Social Activism in the 1850s." *Journal of American History* 73 (December 1986): 601–22.

———. *Untidy Origins: A Story of Women's Rights in Antebellum New York*. Chapel Hill: University of North Carolina Press, 2005.

———. *Women and the Work of Benevolence: Morality, Politics, and Class in the Nineteenth-Century United States*. New Haven: Yale University Press, 1990.

Gittell, Marilyn, and Teresa Shtob. "Changing Women's Roles in Political Volunteerism and Reform of the City." *Signs: Journal of Women in Culture and Society* 5 (Spring 1980): s67–s78. Supplement.

Glauert, Ralph Edward. "Education and Society in Antebellum Missouri." PhD diss., University of Missouri, 1973.

Glenn, Evelyn Nakano. *Unequal Freedom: How Race and Gender Shaped American Citizenship and Labor*. Cambridge MA: Harvard University Press, 2002.

Golden, Janet. *A Society History of Wet Nursing in America*. New York: Cambridge University Press, 1996.

Golden Gate Kindergarten Association. *Golden Gate Kindergarten Association Annual Reports*. vol. 1. San Francisco: Golden Gate Kindergarten Association, 1879.

———. *Decade Report: Tenth Annual Report of the Golden Gate Kindergarten Association for the Year Ending October 6, 1889*. San Francisco: George Spaulding, 1889.

———. *Eleventh Annual Report of the Golden Gate Kindergarten Association for the Year Ending October 6, 1890*. San Francisco: George Spaulding, 1890.

———. *Fifth Annual Report of the Golden Gate Kindergarten Association for the Year Ending October 6, 1884*. San Francisco: George Spaulding, 1884.

Good, Cassandra A. *Founding Friendships: Friendships between Men and Women in the Early American Republic*. New York: Oxford University Press, 2015.

Goode, James N. *Capital Losses: A Cultural History of Washington's Destroyed Buildings*. Washington DC: Smithsonian Institution Press, 1979.

Goodier, Susan. *No Votes for Women: The New York Anti-Suffrage Movement.* Urbana: University of Illinois Press, 2013.

Gordon, Ann D., ed. *African American Women and the Vote, 1837–1965.* Amherst: University of Massachusetts Press, 1997.

———, ed. *The Selected Papers of Elizabeth Cady Stanton and Susan B. Anthony.* 5 vols. New Brunswick NJ: Rutgers University Press, 1997.

Gordon, Linda. "If the Progressives Were Advising Us Today, Should We Listen?" *Journal of the Golden Age and Progressive Era* 1 (April 2002): 109–21.

Gordon, Lynn D. "Co-Education on Two Campuses: Berkeley and Chicago, 1890–1912." In *Woman's Being, Woman's Place: Female Identity and Vocation in American History*, edited by Mary Kelly, 171–93. Boston: G. K. Hall, 1979.

———. *Gender and Higher Education in the Progressive Era.* New Haven: Yale University Press, 1990.

Gourman, Jack. *The Gourman Report: Rating Undergraduate Programs in American and International Universities.* 11th ed. Los Angeles: National Education Standards, 2006.

Gowans, Alan. *Styles and Types of North American Architecture: Social Function and Cultural Expression.* New York: Harper Collins, 1992.

Graham, Sara Hunter. *Woman Suffrage and the New Democracy.* New Haven: Yale University Press, 1996.

Gramsci, Antonio. *Selections from the Prison Notebooks.* New York: International, 1971.

Green, Constance McLaughlin. *The Secret City: A History of Race Relations in the Nation's Capital.* Princeton NJ: Princeton University Press, 1967.

———. *Washington: A History of the Capital 1800–1950.* 2 vols. Princeton NJ: Princeton University Press, 1962–63.

Green, Natalie Coffin. "The YWCA and the San Francisco Exposition." *Women's International Quarterly* 1 (July 1915): 238–40.

Greene, Charles S. "The Hearst Architectural Competition of the University of California." *Overland.* Second series, 34 (July 1899): 66–73.

Gregory, Ralph. "George Hearst in Missouri." *Bulletin Quarterly of the Missouri Historical Society* (January 1965): 75–86.

Guinn, Lisa. "Anne Wittenmyer and Nineteenth-Century Women's Usefulness." *Annals of Iowa* 74 (Fall 2015): 351–77.

Gullett, Gayle. *Becoming Citizens: The Emergence and Development of the California Women's Movement, 1880–1911.* Urbana: University of Illinois Press, 2000.

―――. "'Our Great Opportunity': Organized Women Advance Women's Work at the World's Columbian Exposition of 1893." *Illinois Historical Journal* 87 (Winter 1994): 259–76.

Gustafson, Melanie. "Partisan Women in the Progressive Era: The Struggle for Inclusion in American Political Parties." *Journal of Women's History* 9 (Summer 1997): 8–30.

―――. "Partisan and Nonpartisan: The Political Career of Judith Ellen Foster, 1881–190." In *We Have Come to Stay: American Women and Political Parties 1880–1960,* edited by Melanie Gustafson, Kristie Miller, and Elisabeth Perry. Albuquerque: University of New Mexico Press, 1999.

―――. *Women and the Republican Party, 1854–1924.* Urbana: University of Illinois Press, 2001.

Gustafson, Melanie, Kristie Miller, and Elisabeth I. Perry, eds. *We Have Come to Stay: American Women and Political Parties 1880–1960.* Albuquerque: University of New Mexico Press, 1999.

Gustafson, Sandra M. *Eloquence Is Power: Oratory and Performance in Early America.* Published for the Omohundro Institute of Early American History and Culture. Williamsburg VA: Chapel Hill: University of North Carolina Press, 2000.

Haber, Samuel. *The Quest for Authority and Honor in the American Professions, 1750–1900.* Chicago: University of Chicago Press, 1991.

Habermas, Jürgen. "Hannah Arendt's Communications Concept of Power." *Social Research: An International Quarterly* 44 (Spring 1977): 3–24.

―――. *The Structural Transformation of the Public Sphere: An Inquiry into a Category of Bourgeois Society.* Translated by Thomas Berger with the assistance of Frederick Lawrence. Cambridge MA: MIT Press, 1989.

Haberstein, Robert W., and William M. Lamers. "The Pattern of Late Nineteenth-Century Funerals." In *Passing: The Vision of Death in America,* edited by Charles O. Jackson, 91–102. Westport CT: Greenwood Press, 1977.

Hall, Peter Dobkin. *The Organization of American Culture, 1700–1900: Private Institutions, Elites, and the Origins of American Nationality.* New York: New York University Press, 1982.

Haller, John S., Jr. *The History of American Homeopathy: The Academic Years, 1820–1935*. New York: Pharmaceutical Products Press, Imprint of the Haworth Press, 2005.

Hallowell, A. Irving. "The Beginnings of Anthropology in America. In *Selected Papers from the American Anthropologist, 1898–1920*, edited by Frederica de Laguna, 83–90. Washington DC: American Anthropological Association, 1960.

Handler, Richard. "Review Essays: Cultural Theory in History Today." *American Historical Review* 107 (December 2002): 1512–1520.

Harper, Ida Husted. *The Life and Work of Susan B. Anthony*. 3 vols. 1898. Reprint, New York: Arno and *New York Times*, 1969.

Harris, Marvin. *The Rise of Anthropological Theory*. New York: Thomas Y. Crowell, 1968.

Hatch, Nathan O. *The Democratization of American Christianity*. New Haven: Yale University Press, 1989.

Hayden, Dolores. *The Grand Domestic Revolution: A History of Feminist Designs for American Homes, Neighborhoods and Cities*. Cambridge MA: MIT Press, 1981.

Hayes, Margaret Calder. "A Weekend in the Country." *California Monthly* 91 (October 1980): 25.

Hays, William Charles. "Some Interesting Buildings at the University of California: The Work of Bernard Maybeck, Architect." *Indoors and Out* 2 (May 1906): 70–75.

Hearst, Austine. *The Horses of San Simeon*. San Simeon CA: San Simeon Press, 1985.

Hearst, William Randolph, Jr., with Jack Casserly. *The Hearsts: Father and Son*. Niwot CO: Roberts Rinehart, 1991.

Heilbrun, Carolyn G. *Writing a Woman's Life*. New York: Ballantine Books, 1988.

Hemphill, Dallett. *Bowing to Necessities: A History of Manners in America, 1620–1860*. New York: Oxford University Press, 1999.

Herndl, Diane Price. *Invalid Women: Figuring Feminine Illness in American Fiction and Culture*. Chapel Hill: University of North Carolina Press, 1993.

Hewitt, Nancy A. *Women's Activism and Social Change: Rochester, New York, 1822–1872*. Ithaca NY: Cornell University Press, 1984.

Hilkey, Judy. *Character Is Capital: Success Manuals and Manhood in Gilded Age America*. Chapel Hill: University of North Carolina Press, 1997.

Higginbotham, Evelyn Brooks. *Righteous Discontent: The Women's Movement in the Black Baptist Church, 1880–1920.* Cambridge MA: Harvard University Press, 1993.

Himmelfarb, Gertrude. *Darwin and the Darwinian Revolution.* 1959. Reprint, Chicago: Elephant Paperback edition, Ivan R. Dee, 1996.

―――. *Poverty and Compassion: The Moral Imagination of the Late Victorians.* New York: Knopf, 1991.

Hine, Darlene Clark. "'We Specialize in the Wholly Impossible': The Philanthropic Work of Black Women." In *Lady Bountiful Revisited: Women, Philanthropy, and Power,* edited by Kathleen D. McCarthy, 70–93. New Brunswick NJ: Rutgers University Press, 1990.

Hine, Darlene Clark, Wilma King, and Linda Reed. *"We Specialize in the Wholly Impossible": A Reader in Black Women's History.* Brooklyn: Carlson, 1995.

Hinsley, Curtis M. "Essay 1. Anthropology as Education and Entertainment: Fredric Ward Putnam at the World's Fair." In *Coming of Age in Chicago: The 1893 World's Fair and the Coalescence of American Anthropology,* edited by Curtis M. Hinsley and David R. Wilcox. Lincoln: University of Nebraska Press, 2016.

Hinsley, Curtis M., and David R. Wilcox, eds. *Coming of Age in Chicago: The 1893 World's Fair and the Coalescence of American Anthropology.* Lincoln: University of Nebraska Press, 2016.

Hoffert, Sylvia D. *Alva Vanderbilt Belmont: Unlikely Champion of Women's Rights.* Bloomington: Indiana University Press, 2012.

Hoffman, Nancy. *Women's "True" Profession: Voices from the History of Teaching.* Old Westbury NY: Feminist Press and New York: McGraw-Hill, 1981.

Hoganson, Kristin. "Cosmopolitan Domesticity: Importing the American Dream, 1865–1920." *American Historical Review* 107 (February 2002): 55–83.

Hogeland, Ronald W. "'The Female Appendage': Feminine Life-Styles in America, 1820–1860." *Civil War History* 17 (June 1971): 101–14.

Homberger, Eric. *Mrs. Astor's New York: Money and Social Power in a Gilded Age.* New Haven: Yale University Press, 2002.

Hopkins, Joseph G. E. *The Concise Dictionary of American Biography.* New York: Scribner's Sons, 1964.

Hopkins, Marion E. "The Lunch Room of the Young Women's Christian Association." *Association Monthly* 4 (March 1910): 52–54.

Horowitz, Daniel. *The Morality of Spending: Attitudes toward the Consumer Society in America, 1875–1940*. Baltimore: Johns Hopkins University Press, 1985.

Horowitz, Helen Lefkowitz. *Campus Life: Undergraduate Cultures from the End of the Eighteenth Century to the Present*. Chicago: University of Chicago Press, 1987.

———. *Culture and the City: Cultural Philanthropy in Chicago From the 1880s to 1917*. Lexington: University Press of Kentucky, 1976.

———. "'Nous Autres': Reading, Passion, and the Creation of M. Carey Thomas." *Journal of American History* 79 (June 1992): 68–95.

Houde, Mary Jean. *Reaching Out: A Story of the General Federation of Women's Clubs*. Chicago: Mobium Press, 1989.

Howard, John Galen. "The Architectural Plans for the Greater University of California." *University Chronicle* 5 (January 1903): 273–91.

Hyde, Anne Farrar. *An American Vision: Far Western Landscape and National Culture, 1820–1920*. New York: New York University Press, 1990.

Hymes, Dell. "Alfred L. Kroeber." *Language* 37 (January–March 1961): 1–28.

Igler, David. "The Industrial Far West: Region and Nation in the Late Nineteenth Century." *Pacific Historical Review* 69 (May 2000): 159–92.

International Kindergarten Union, Committee of Nineteen. *Pioneers of the Kindergarten Movement in America*. New York: Century, 1924.

Irwin, Inez. *The Story of the Woman's Party*. New York: Harcourt, Brace, 1921.

Issel, William, and Robert Cherny. *San Francisco, 1865–1932: Politics, Power, and Urban Development*. Berkeley: University of California Press, 1986.

Jacklin, Kathleen. "Sarah Brown Ingersoll Cooper." In *Notable American Woman, 1607–1950: A Biographical Dictionary*, edited by Edward T. James, Janet Wilson James, and Paul S. Boyer, 1:380–82. Cambridge: Belknap Press of Harvard University Press, 1971.

Jacknis, Ira. "A Museum of Anthropology, 1891–1901," edited by Roberta J. Park and J. R. K. Kantor. *Chronicle of the University of California: The University at the Turn of the Century Then and Now*, no. 4 (Fall 2000): 47–77.

———. "A Museum Prehistory: Phoebe Hearst and the Founding of the Museum of Anthropology, 1891–1901," edited by Roberta J. Park and J. R. K. Kantor. *Chronicle of the University of California: The University at the Turn of the Century Then and Now*, no. 4 (Fall 2000): 47–77.

———. "Patrons, Potters, and Painters." In *Collecting Native America, 1870–1920*, edited by Shepard Krech III and Barbara H. Hall, 137–171. Washington DC: Smithsonian Institution Press, 1999.

Jackson Street Kindergarten. *Second Annual Report of the Jackson Street Free Kindergarten Association for the Year Ending October 6th, 1881.* San Francisco: George Spaulding, ca. 1881.

Jacob, Kathryn Allamong. *Capital Elites: High Society in Washington, D.C. after the Civil War.* Washington DC: Smithsonian Institution Press, 1995.

Jaher, Frederic. *The Urban Establishment: Upper Strata in Boston, New York, Charleston, Chicago, Los Angeles.* Urbana: University of Illinois Press, 1982.

James, Edward T., Janet Wilson James, and Paul S. Boyer, eds. *Notable American Women, 1607–1950: A Biographical Dictionary.* 3 vols. Cambridge MA: Belknap Press of Harvard University Press, 1971.

James, Janet Wilson. "Emma Jacobina Christiana Marwedel." In *Notable American Women, 1607–1950: A Biographical Dictionary*, edited by Edward T. James, Janet Wilson James, and Paul S. Boyer, 2:506–8. Cambridge MA: Belknap Press of Harvard University Press, 1971.

James Foundation. *Lucy Wortham James 1880–1936: Founder of the Lucy Wortham James Memorial in the New York Community Trust.* St. James MO: The James Foundation, ca. 1971.

Jameson, Elizabeth. "Women as Workers, Women as Civilizers." *Frontiers* 7, no. 3 (1984): 1–8.

Janeway, Elizabeth. "On the Power of the Weak." *Signs: Journal of Women in Culture and Society* 1 (Autumn 1975): 103–9.

Jefferis, B. G. (Benjamin Grant), and J. L. (James Lawrence) Nichols. *Search Lights on Health: Light on Dark Corners; A Complete Sexual Science and a Guide to Purity and Physical Manhood; Advice to Maiden, Wife, and Mother; Love, Courtship and Marriage.* Naperville IL: J. L. Nichols, 1895.

Jeffrey, Julie Roy. *Frontier Women: The Trans-Mississippi West, 1840–1880.* New York: Hill and Wang, 1979.

Jensen, Joan M., and Ricci Lothrop. *California Women: A History.* San Francisco: Boyd and Fraser, 1987.

Jensen, Joan M., and Darlis A. Miller. "The Gentle Tamers Revisited: New Approaches to the History of Women in the American West." *Pacific Historical Review* 49 (May 1980): 173–213.

Jensen, Kimberly. *Mobilizing Minerva: American Women in the First World War.* Urbana: University of Illinois Press, 2008.

Johnson, Joan Marie. "Following the Money: Wealthy Women, Feminism, and the American Suffrage Movement." *Journal of Women's History* 27 (Winter 2015): 62–87.

Johnston, Carolyn. *Sexual Power: Feminism and the Family in America.* Tuscaloosa: University of Alabama Press, 1992.

Jones, William Carey. *Illustrated History of the University of California.* Rev. ed. Berkeley: Students' Cooperative Society, 1901.

Jordy, William H. *American Buildings and Their Architects: The Impact of European Modernism in the Mid-Twentieth Century.* Garden City NY: Doubleday, 1972.

Jung, Maureen. "Capitalism Comes to the Diggings: From Gold-Rush Adventure to Corporate Enterprise." In *California History: A Golden State: Mining and Economic Development in Gold Rush California,* edited by James Rawls and Richard J. Orsi. Sesquicentennial Issue 77, no. 4 (Winter 1998/1999): 52–77. Published in association with the California Historical Society. Berkeley: University of California Press.

Kaeppler, Adrienne L. "Paradise Regained: The Role of Pacific Museums in Forging National Identity." In *Museums and the Making of "Ourselves": The Role of Objects in National Identity,* edited by Flora E. S. Kaplan, 19–44. London: Leicester University Press, 1994.

Kammen, Michael. *Mystic Chords of Memory: The Transformation of Tradition in American Culture.* New York: Alfred A. Knopf, 1991.

Kaplan, Flora E. S. *Museums and the Making of "Ourselves": The Role of Objects in National Identity.* London: Leicester University Press, 1994.

Kastner, Victoria. *Hearst Ranch: Family, Land, and Legacy.* Forward by Stephen Hearst. New York: Abrams, 2013.

Katz, Sherry. "Socialist Women and Progressive Reform." In *California Progressivism Revisited,* edited by William Deverell and Tom Sitton. Berkeley: University of California Press, 1994.

Kaufman, Martin. *Homeopathy in America: The Rise and Fall of a Medical Heresy.* Baltimore: Johns Hopkins University Press, 1971.

Kaufman, Polly Welts. *Women Teachers on the Frontier.* New Haven: Yale University Press, 1984.

Keller, Morton. *Affairs of State: Public Life in Nineteenth Century America.* Cambridge MA: Harvard University Press, 1977.

Kelley, Mary. *Learning to Stand and Speak: Women Education, and Public Life in America's Republic.* Chapel Hill: University of North Carolina Press, 2006.

Kelly, Joan. "Doubled Vision of Feminist Theory: A Postscript to the 'Women and Power' Conference." *Feminist Studies* 5 (Spring 1979): 216–27.

Kemble, John Haskell. *The Panama Route 1848–1869.* Berkeley: University of California Press, 1943.

Kennard, June A. "Review Essay: The History of Physical Education." *Signs: Journal of Women in Culture and Society* 2 (Summer 1977): 835–42.

Kennedy, Kathleen. *Disloyal Mothers and Scurrilous Citizens: Women and Subversion During World War I.* Bloomington: Indiana University Press, 1999.

Kerber, Linda K. "A Constitutional Right to Be Treated Like Ladies: Women and the Obligations of Citizenship." In *U. S. History as Women's History: New Feminist Essays,* edited by Linda Kerber, Alice Kessler-Harris, and Kathryn Kish Sklar, 17–35. Chapel Hill: University of North Carolina Press, 1995.

———. *No Constitutional Right to Be Ladies: Women and the Obligations of Citizenship.* New York: Hill and Wang, 1998.

———. "Separate Spheres, Female Worlds, Woman's Place: The Rhetoric of Women's History." *Journal of American History* 75 (June 1988): 9–39.

———. *Women of the Republic: Intellect and Ideology in Revolutionary America.* Chapel Hill: University of North Carolina Press, 1980.

Kessler-Harris, Alice. *Out to Work: A History of Wage-Earning Women in the United States.* New York: Oxford University Press, 1982.

———. "The Wages of Patriarchy: Some Thoughts about Continuing Relevance of Class and Gender." *Labor Studies in Working-Class History* 3 (Fall 2006): 7–21.

———. *A Woman's Wage: Historical Meanings and Social Consequences.* Updated ed. Lexington: University Press of Kentucky, 1990.

———. "Why Biography?" *American Historical Review* 114 (June 2009): 625–30.

Keyssar, Alexander. *The Right to Vote: The Contested History of Democracy in the United States*. New York: Basic Books, 2000.

Kimble, Grace Eleanor. *Social Work with Travelers and Transients: A Study of Travelers' Aid Work in the United States*. Chicago: University of Chicago Press, 1935.

Kipp, Laurie F. Maffly. *Religion and Society in Frontier California*. New Haven: Yale University Press, 1994.

Kloppenberg, James T. *Uncertain Victory: Social Democracy and Progressivism in European and American Thought, 1870–1920*. New York: Oxford University Press, 1986.

Komter, Aafke. "Gender, Power, and Feminist Theory." In *The Gender of Power*, edited by Kathy Davis, Monique Leijenaar, and Jantine Oldersma, 42–62. London: Sage, 1991.

Konolige, Kit, and Frederica Kit. *The Power of Their Glory: America's Ruling Class, the Episcopalians*. New York: Wyden Books, 1978.

Kristof, Spiro, ed. *The Architect: Chapters in the History of the Profession*. New York: Oxford University Press, 1977.

Kroeber, Alfred L. "Frederic Ward Putnam." *American Anthropologist*, n.s., 17 (October–December 1915): 712–18.

———, ed. *Phoebe Apperson Hearst Memorial Volume*. University of California Publications in American Archaeology and Ethnology. Vol. 20. Berkeley: University of California Press, 1923.

Kroeber, Theodora. *Alfred Kroeber: A Personal Configuration*. Berkeley: University of California Press, 1970.

Kunzel, Regina G. *Fallen Women, Problem Girls: Unmarried Mothers and the Professionalization of Social Work 1890–1945*. New Haven: Yale University Press, 1993.

Lansing, Michael J. "'The Women Are Voluntarily Organizing Themselves': Gender and Grassroots Democracy in the Nonpartisan League." Paper presented at the Western History Association Conference, Newport Beach CA, October 15, 2014.

———. *Insurgent Democracy: The Nonpartisan League in North American Politics*. Chicago: University of Chicago Press, 2015.

Lasch, Christopher. "Alva Erskine Smith Vanderbilt Belmont." In *Notable American Women, 1607–1950: A Biographical Dictionary*, edited by Edward T. James, Janet Wilson James, and Paul S. Boyer, 1:126. Cambridge MA: Belknap Press of Harvard University, 1971.

Leach, William. *True Love and Perfect Union*. New York: Basic Books, 1980.

Lears, T. J. Jackson. *No Place for Grace: Antimodernism and the Transformation of American Culture, 1880–1920*. Chicago: University of Chicago Press, 1981.

Lebsock, Suzanne. *The Free Women of Petersburg: Status and Culture in a Southern Town, 1784–1860*. New York: W. W. Norton, 1984.

———. "Women and American Politics, 1880–1920." In *Women, Politics, and Change*, edited by Louise A. Tilly and Patricia Gurin, 35–62. New York: Russell Sage, 1990.

Leepson, Marc. *Flag: An American Biography*. New York: Thomas Dunne Books, St. Martin's Press, 2005.

Leiby, James. *Carroll Wright and Labor Reform: The Origin of Labor Statistics*. Cambridge MA: Harvard University Press, 1960.

Lerner, Gerda. "New Approaches to the Study of Women in American History." In *Liberating Women's History: Theoretical and Critical Essays*, edited by Berenice A. Carroll, 349–56. Urbana: University of Illinois Press, 1976.

———. "Reconceptualizing Differences among Women." *Journal of Women's History* 1 (Winter 1990): 106–22.

Lessoff, Alan. *The Nation and Its City: Politics, "Corruption," and Progress in Washington D.C., 1861–1902*. Baltimore: Johns Hopkins University Press, 1994.

Lessoff, Alan, Daniel T. Rodgers, Catherine McNicol Stock, Charles Postel, and Robert D. Johnston. "Forum: Populists and Progressives, Capitalism and Democracy." *Journal of the Gilded Age and Progressive Era* 13 (July 2014): 377–443.

Levenstein, Harvey. *Seductive Journey: American Tourists in France from Jefferson to the Jazz Age*. Chicago: University of Chicago Press, 1998.

Levine, Lawrence W. *Highbrow/Lowbrow: The Emergence of Cultural Hierarchy in America*. Cambridge MA: Harvard University Press, 1988.

Lewis, Oscar. *Here Lived the Californians*. New York: Rinehart, 1957.

Limbaugh, Ronald. "Making Old Tools Work Better: Pragmatic Adaptation and Innovation in Gold-Rush Technology." In *California History: A Golden State: Mining and Economic Development in Gold Rush California*, edited by

James Rawls and Richard J. Orsi. Sesquicentennial Issue 77, no. 4 (Winter 1998/1999): 24–51. Published for the California Historical Society. Berkeley: University of California Press.

Lipschultz, Sybil. "Hours and Wages: The Gendering of Labor Standards in America." *Journal of Women's History* 8 (Spring 1996): 114–136.

Litwicki, Ellen. "From the 'ornamental and evanescent' to 'good, useful things': Redesigning the Gift in Progressive America." *Journal of the Gilded Age and Progressive Era* 10 (October 2011): 467–505.

Lloyd, Moya. *Beyond Identity Politics: Feminism, Power and Politics*. Thousand Oaks CA: Sage, 2005.

Long, Frederick Alexandre. "The 'Kingdom Must Come Soon': The Role of A. L. Kroeber and the Hearst Survey in Shaping California Anthropology, 1901–1920." Master's thesis, Simon Fraser University, 1998.

Longstreth, Richard. *On the Edge of the World: Four Architects in San Francisco at the Turn of the Century*. Berkeley: University of California Press, 1998.

Lord, Eliot. *Comstock Mining and Miners*. 1883. Reprint, Berkeley: Howell-North, 1959.

Lowenthal, David. "Identity, Heritage, History." In *Commemorations: The Politics of National Identity*, edited by John R. Gillis, 41–60. Princeton NJ: Princeton University Press, 1994.

Lowie, Robert H. "Reminiscences of Anthropological Currents in America a Half Century Ago." *American Anthropologist*, series 2, 58 (December 1956): 995–1016.

Lundardini, Christine. *From Equal Suffrage to Equal Rights: Alice Paul and the National Woman's Party, 1910–1928*. 1986. Reprint, New York: New York University Press, 2000.

Lundardini, Christine, and Thomas J. Knock. "Woodrow Wilson and Woman Suffrage: A New Look." *Political Science Quarterly* 95 (Winter 1980–1981): 655–71.

Lyons, Clare A. *Sex among the Rabble: An Intimate History of Gender and Power in the Age of Revolution, Philadelphia, 1730–1830*. Chapel Hill: Published for the Omohundro Institute of Early American History and Culture, Williamsburg, Virginia, by the University of North Carolina Press, 2006.

MacCannell, Dean. *The Tourist: A New Theory of the Leisure Class*. New York: Schocken Books, 1976.

Mackaman, Douglas Peter. *Leisure Settings: Bourgeois Culture, Medicine, and the Spa in Modern France*. Chicago: University of Chicago Press, 1998.

Macleod, Dianne Sachko. *Enchanted Lives, Enchanted Objects: American Women Collectors and the Making of Culture, 1800–1940*. Berkeley: University of California Press, 2008.

Mankiller, Wilma et al., eds. *The Reader's Companion to U. S. Women's History*. Boston: Houghton Mifflin, 1998.

Mann, George S. *Genealogy of the Descendants of Richard Man of Scituate, Mass. Preceded by English Family Records, and an Account of the Wrentham, Rehoboth, Boston, Lexington, Virginia, and Other Branches of the Manns Who Settled in This Country*. Boston: Press of David Clapp and Son, 1884.

March, David D. *The History of Missouri*. 2 vols. New York: Lewis, 1967.

Marchand, C. Roland. *The American Peace Movement and Social Reform, 1898–1918*. Princeton NJ: Princeton University Press, 1972.

Margadant, Jo Burr, ed. *The New Biography: Performing Femininity in Nineteenth-Century France*. Berkeley: University of California Press, 2000.

Marilley, Suzanne M. *Woman Suffrage and the Origins of Liberal Feminism in the United States, 1820–1920*. Cambridge MA: Harvard University Press, 1996.

Mark, Joan. *A Stranger in Her Native Land: Alice Fletcher and the American Indians*. Lincoln: University of Nebraska Press, 1988.

Markus, Thomas A. *Buildings and Power: Freedom and Control in the Origin of Modern Building Types*. New York: Routledge, 1993.

Markwyn, Abigail M. "Constructing 'an epitome of civilization': Local Politics and Visions of Progressive Era America at San Francisco's Panama-Pacific International Exposition." PhD diss., University of Wisconsin, Madison, 2006.

———. *Empress of San Francisco: The Pacific Rim, the Great West and California at the Panama-Pacific International Exposition*. Lincoln: University of Nebraska Press, 2014.

———. "Encountering 'Woman' on the Fairgrounds of the 1915 Panama-Pacific Exposition." In *Gendering the Fair: Histories of Women and Gender at World's*

Fairs, edited by T. J. Boisseau and Abigail Markwyn, 169–86. Urbana: University of Illinois, 2010.

―――. "Queen of the Joy Zone Meets Hercules: Gendering Imperial California at the Panama-Pacific International Exposition." *Western Historical Quarterly* 47 (Spring 2016): 51–72.

Marsden, George G. *The Soul of the American University: From Protestant Establishment to Established Nonbelief.* New York: Oxford University Press, 1994.

Marshall, Susan E. *Splintered Sisterhood: Gender and Class in the Campaign against Woman Suffrage.* Madison: University of Wisconsin Press, 1997.

Martin, Theodora Penny. *The Sound of Our Own Voices: Women's Study Clubs, 1860–1910.* Boston: Beacon Press, 1987.

Massey, Mary Elizabeth. *Women in the Civil War*, with an introduction to the Bison Book edition by Jean V. Berlin. Lincoln: University of Nebraska Press, 1994.

Materson, Lisa. *For the Freedom of Her Race: Black Women and Electoral Politics in Illinois, 1877–1932.* Chapel Hill: University of North Carolina Press, 2009.

Matthews, Glenna. "Forging a Cosmopolitan Civic Culture: The Regional Identity of San Francisco and Northern California." In *Many Wests: Place, Culture, and Regional Identity*, edited by David M. Wrobel and Michael C. Steiner, 211–34. Lawrence: University Press of Kansas, 1997.

―――. *The Rise of the Public Woman: Woman's Power and Woman's Place in the United States, 1630–1970.* New York: Oxford University Press, 1992.

May, Henry F. *Protestant Churches and Industrial America.* New York: Octagon Books, 1963.

Maybeck, Jacomena. *Maybeck: The Family View.* Berkeley: Berkeley Architectural Heritage Association, 1980.

McCarthy, Kathleen D., ed. *Lady Bountiful Revisited: Women, Philanthropy, and Power.* New Brunswick NJ: Rutgers University Press, 1990.

―――. *Noblesse Oblige and Cultural Philanthropy in Chicago, 1849–1929.* Chicago: University of Chicago Press, 1982.

―――. *Women's Culture: American Philanthropy and Art, 1830–1930.* Chicago: University of Chicago Press, 1991.

McCaughey, Robert A. *Stand, Columbia: A History of Columbia University in the City of New York, 1754–2004.* New York: Columbia University Press, 2003.

McCoy, Esther. *Five California Architects*. New York: Reinhold, 1960.

McDonald, Kenneth. "The Presbyterian Church and the Social Gospel in California 1890–1910." *American Presbyterians* 72 (Winter 1994): 241–25.

McGerr, Michael. "Political Style and Women's Power, 1830–1930," *Journal of American History* 77 (December 1990): 864–85.

McGovern, James R. "The American Woman's Pre-World War I Freedom in Manners and Morals." *Journal of American History* 55 (September 1968): 315–33.

McVicker, Donald. "Essay 6. Patrons, Popularizers, and Professionals: The Institutional Setting of Late Nineteenth-Century Anthropology in Chicago." In *Coming of Age in Chicago: The 1893 World's Fair and the Coalescence of American Anthropology*, edited by Curtis M. Hinsley and David R. Wilcox. Lincoln: University of Nebraska Press, 2016.

Mead, Rebecca. *How the Vote Was Won: Woman Suffrage in the Western United States, 1868–1914*. New York: New York University Press, 2004.

Melendy, Howard Brett. *The Governors of California: Peter H. Burnett to Edmund G. Brown*. Georgetown CA: Talisman Press, 1965.

Miller, Jean Baker. "Women and Power." In *Rethinking Power*, edited by Thomas E. Wartenberg. Albany: State University of New York Press, 1992.

Mitchell, Timothy. "Society, Economy, and the State Effect." In *State/Culture: State-Formation after the Cultural Turn*, edited by George Steinmetz. Ithaca NY: Cornell University Press, 1999.

Mitchell, Wesley C. "The Backward Art of Spending Money." *American Economic Review* 2 (June 1912): 269–81.

Monoson, S. Sara. "The Lady and the Tiger: Women's Electoral Activism in New York City before Suffrage." *Journal of Women's History* 2 (Fall 1990): 100–135.

Moore, Sarah J. "Manliness and the New American Empire at the 1915 Panama-Pacific Exposition." In *Gendering the Fair: Histories of Women and Gender at World's Fairs*, edited by Bouisseau and Markwyn. Urbana: University of Illinois, 2010.

Morantz, Regina Markell. "Making Women Modern: Middle Class Women and Health Reform in 19th Century America." *Journal of Social History* 20 (Summer 1977): 491–507.

Morgan, Francesca. *Women and Patriotism in Jim Crow America*. Chapel Hill: University of North Carolina Press, 2005.

Moss, Andrea G. Radke. *Bright Epoch: Women and Coeducation in the American West*. Lincoln: University of Nebraska Press, 2008.

Mowry, George. *The California Progressives*. 1951. Chicago: Quadrangle Books, 1963.

Muncy, Robyn. *Creating a Female Dominion in American Reform 1890–1930*. New York: Oxford University Press, 1991.

Murolo, Priscilla. *The Common Ground of Womanhood: Class, Gender, and Working Girls' Clubs, 1884–1928*. Urbana: University of Illinois Press, 1997.

Murray, Stephen O. *American Anthropology and Company: Historical Explanations*. Lincoln: University of Nebraska Press, 2013.

Murray, W. W. "Wyntoon." *Siskiyou Pioneer in Fact and Folklore* 3, no. 1 (1958): 12–20.

Myres, Sandra L. *Westering Women and the Frontier Experience 1800–1915*. Albuquerque: University of New Mexico Press, 1982.

Nasaw, David. *Andrew Carnegie*. New York: Penguin Group (USA), 2006.

———. *The Chief: The Life of William Randolph Hearst*. Boston: Houghton Mifflin, 2000.

Nash, Gerald D. *State Government and Economic Development: A History of Administrative Policies in California, 1849–1933*. Berkeley: Institute of Governmental Studies, University of California Press, 1964.

Nerad, Maresi. "The Situation of Women at Berkeley between 1870 and 1915." *Feminist Studies* 7 (Spring 1987): 67–80.

Newman, Louise M. "Reflections on Aileen Kraditor's Legacy: Fifty Years of Woman Suffrage Historiography, 1965–2014." *Journal of the Gilded Age and Progressive Era* 14 (July 2015): 291–316.

———. *White Women's Rights: The Racial Origins of Feminism in the United States*. New York: Oxford University Press, 1999.

Nickliss, Alexandra M. "Phoebe Apperson Hearst: The Most Powerful Woman in California." PhD diss., University of California, Davis, 1994.

———. "Phoebe Apperson Hearst's 'Gospel of Wealth,' 1883–1901." *Pacific Historical Review* 71 (November 2002): 575–605.

Norris, James D. *The Story of the Maramec Iron Works, 1826–1876*. Madison: State Historical Society for Wisconsin, 1972.

Norton, Mary Beth. *Founding Mothers and Fathers: Gendered Power and the Forming of American Society*. New York: Alfred A. Knopf, 1996.

Nunis, Doyce. "Kate Douglas Smith Wiggin." In *Notable American Women, 1607–1950: A Biographical Dictionary*, edited by Edward T. James, Janet Wilson James, and Paul S. Boyer, 3:605–7. Cambridge: Belknap Press of Harvard University Press, 1971.

Odegard, Peter H. *Pressure Politics: The Story of the Anti-Saloon League*. New York: Columbia University Press, 1928.

Older, Fremont. *My Own Story*. New York: Macmillan, 1926.

Older, Fremont, and Cora Older. *The Life of George Hearst, California Pioneer*. San Francisco: Printed for William Randolph Hearst by John Nash, 1933.

Oldersma, Jantine, and Kathy Davis. "Introduction." In *The Gender of Power*, edited by Kathy Davis, Monique Leijenaar, and Jantine Oldersma, 1–18. London: Sage, 1991.

O'Leary, Cecilia Elizabeth. *To Die For: The Paradox of American Patriotism*. Princeton NJ: Princeton University Press, 1999.

Opdycke, Sandra. *The Flu Epidemic of 1918: America's Experience in the Global Health Crisis*. New York: Routledge, 2014.

Orsi, Richard J. *Sunset Limited: The Southern Pacific Railroad and the Development of the American West, 1850–1930*. Berkeley: University of California Press, 2005.

Ortner, Sherry B. "Is Female to Male as Nature Is to Culture?" In *Woman, Culture, and Society*, edited by Michelle Zimbalist Rosaldo and Louise Lamphere, 67–87. Stanford CA: Stanford University Press, 1974.

Otten, C. Michael. *University Authority and the Student: The Berkeley Experience*. Berkeley: University of California Press, 1970.

Owens, Billie Louis, and Robert J. Owens. *Sons of Frontiersmen: History and Genealogy of Rowland, Whitmire and Associated Families*. Canon City CO: Billie Louise and Robert James Owens, 1976.

Owens, Col. Robert J., USAF Ret. *The Whitmires of Whitmire, SC and Kin: History & Genealogy of the Descendants of George Fredrick Whitmire with a Genealogy of Many of the Maternal Lines*. 2 vols. Canon City CO: Robert James Owens, 1989.

Park, Robert J. "A Gym of Their Own: Women, Sports, and Physical Culture at the Berkeley Campus, 1876–1976," edited by Janet Ruyle. *Chronicle of the University of California: A Journal of University History* 1, no. 2 (Fall 1998): 21–47.

Parmenter, Ross. "Zelia Maria Magdalena Nuttall." In *Notable American Women, 1607–1950: A Biographical Dictionary*, edited by Edward T. James, Janet Wilson

James, and Paul S. Boyer, 2:640–42. Cambridge MA: Belknap Press of Harvard University Press, 1971.

Parsons, Talcott. *Max Weber: The Theory of Social and Economic Organization*, edited by Talcott Parsons, translated by A. M. Henderson and Talcott Parsons. New York: Oxford University Press, 1947.

Pascoe, Peggy. *Relations of Rescue: The Search for Female Moral Authority in the American West, 1874–1939*. New York: Oxford University Press, 1990.

Paul, Rodman. *Mining Frontiers of the Far West, 1848–1880*. New York: Holt, Rinehart, and Winston, 1963.

Penn, Rosalyn Terborg. *African American Women in the Struggle for the Vote, 1850–1920*. Bloomington: Indiana University Press, 1998.

Peterson, Jon A. "The Hidden Origins of the McMillan Plan for Washington DC, 1900–1902." In *Historical Perspectives on Urban Design: Washington, D.C., 1890–1910.*Conference proceedings, held October 7, 1983, Gelman Library, George Washington University, edited by Antoinette J. Lee, 3–18. Washington DC: Center for Washington Area Studies, George Washington University, 1983.

Peterson, Richard H. *The Bonanza Kings: The Social Origins and Business Behavior of Western Mining Entrepreneurs, 1870–1900*. Lincoln: University of Nebraska Press, 1971. Reprinted 1977.

———. *Bonanza Rich: Lifestyles of the Western Mining Entrepreneurs*. Moscow: University of Idaho Press, 1991.

———. "Philanthropic Phoebe: The Educational Charity of Phoebe Apperson Hearst." *California History* 64, no. 4 (Fall 1985): 284–315.

———. "The Philanthropist and the Artist." *California History* 66 (December 1987): 278–318.

———. "The Spirit of Giving: The Educational Philanthropy of Western Mining Leaders, 1870–1900." *Pacific Historical Review* (August 1984): 309–36.

Petrik, Paula. *No Step Backward: Women and Family on the Rocky Mountain Mining Frontier, Helena, Montana, 1865–1900*. Helena: Montana Historical Society Press, 1987.

Pfeffer, Mike, *Southern Ladies and Suffragists: Julia Ward How and Women's Rights at the 1884 New Orleans World's Fair*. Jackson: University Press of Mississippi, 2014.

Pitkin, Hanna Fenichel. *The Concept of Representation*. Berkeley: University of California Press, 1967.

Pitts, Yvonne. "Disability, Scientific Authority, and Women's Political Participation at the Turn of the Twentieth-Century United States." *Journal of Women's History* 24 (Summer 2012): 37–61.

Pliley, Jessica R. *Policing Sexuality: The Mann Act and the Making of the FBI*. Cambridge MA: Harvard University Press, 2014.

Prager, Susan Westerberg. "The Persistence of Separate Property Concepts in California's Community Property System, 1849–1975." *UCLA Law Review* 24 (October 1976): 1–82.

Putnam, Jackson K. *Modern California Politics*. 4th ed. San Francisco: Boyd and Fraser, 1996.

Prytanean Alumnae. *The Prytaneans: An Oral History of the Prytanean Society, Its Members and Their University, 1901–1920*. Berkeley: Prytanean Alumnae, 1970.

Quataert, Jean H. *Staging Philanthropy: Patriotic Women and the National Imagination in Dynastic Germany, 1813–1916*. Ann Arbor: University of Michigan Press, 2001.

Quinn, Elisabeth Lasch. *Black Neighbors: Race and the Limits of Reform in the American Settlement House Movement, 1890–1945*. Chapel Hill: University of North Carolina Press, 1993.

Rankin, Charles. "Teaching: Opportunity and Limitation for Wyoming Women." *Western Historical Quarterly* 21 (May 1990): 147–70.

Ratner, Lorman A., Paula T. Kaufman, and Dwight L. Teeter Jr. *Paradoxes of Prosperity*. Urbana: University of Illinois Press, 2009.

Reed, Christopher Robert. *"All the World Is Here!": The Black Presence at White City*. Bloomington: Indiana University Press, 2000.

Reinstein, Jacob Bert. *Address of Regent J. B. Reinstein at a Special Meeting of the Regents of the University of California*. San Francisco: Woodward, 1898.

———. "The University of California Competition." *American Architect and Building News*, November 1896.

Remus, Emily A. "Tippling Ladies and the Making of Consumer Culture: Gender and Public Space in Fin-de-Siècle Chicago." *Journal of American History* 101 (December 2014): 751–77.

Reuben, Julie A. *The Making of the Modern University: Intellectual Transformation and the Marginalization of Morality*. Chicago: University of Chicago Press, 1996.

Rice, Richard B., William B. Bullough, and Richard J. Orsi. *Elusive Eden: A New History of California*. New York: McGraw-Hill, 1996.

Richards, Greg. "Introduction: Culture and Tourism in Europe." In *Cultural Tourism in Europe*, edited by Greg Richards. Oxford, UK: CAB International, 1996.

Ridge, Martin. "The American West: From Frontier to Region." *New Mexico Historical Review* 64 (April 1989): 125–41.

Riley, Glenda. *Female Frontier: A Comparative View of Women on the Prairie and the Plains*. Lawrence: University Press of Kansas, 1988.

———. *Inventing the American Woman: An Inclusive History*. 2 vols. 2nd ed. Wheeling IL: Harlan Davidson, 1995. First printed in 1986 and 1987 (combined volume).

Ritter, Mary Bennett. *More than Gold in California 1849–1933*. Berkeley: Professional Press, 1933.

Robb, George. "Enterprising Women." *Journal of Women's History* 26 (Spring 2016): 166–71.

Robinson, Charles Mulford. *The Improvement of Towns and Cities of the Practical Basis of Civil Aesthetics*. 3rd rev. ed. New York: G. P. Putnam's Sons, 1907.

———. *Modern Civic Art or the City Made Beautiful*. New York: G. P. Putnam's Sons, 1903.

Robinson, Judith. *The Hearsts: An American Dynasty*. Newark: University of Delaware Press, 1991.

Rodgers, Daniel T. *Atlantic Crossings: Social Politics in a Progressive Age*. Cambridge MA: Belknap Press of Harvard University Press, 1998.

———. "Capitalism and Politics in the Progressive Era and in Ours." *Journal of the Gilded Age and Progressive Era* 13 (July 2014): 379–86.

———. "In Search of Progressivism." *Reviews in American History* 10 (December 1982): 113–32.

Rogers, Naomi. "The Proper Place of Homeopathy: Hahnemann Medical College and Hospital in an Age of Scientific Medicine." Medical Philadelphia Issue. *Pennsylvania Magazine of History and Biography* 108 (April 1984): 179–201.

Roland, Carol. "The California Kindergarten Movement: A Study in Class and Social Feminism." PhD diss., University of California, Riverside, 1980.

Rosaldo, Michelle Zimbalist. "Woman, Culture, and Society: A Theoretical Overview." In *Woman, Culture and Society*, edited by Michelle Zimbalist Rosaldo and Louise Lamphere, 17–42. Stanford CA: Stanford University Press, 1974.

Rosaldo, Michelle, and Louise Lamphere, eds. *Woman, Culture, and Society*. Stanford CA: Stanford University, 1974.

Rosenberg, Carroll Smith. "The Female World of Love and Ritual: Relations between Women in Nineteenth-Century America." *Signs: Journal of Women in Culture and Society* 1 (Autumn 1975): 1–29.

Ross, Dorothy. *The Origins of American Social Science*. New York: Cambridge University Press, 1991.

———. "Susan Blow." In *Notable American Women, 1607–1950: A Biographical Dictionary*, edited by Edward T. James, Janet Wilson James, and Paul S. Boyer, 1:181–82. Cambridge MA: Harvard University Press, 1971.

Ross, Elizabeth Dale. *The Kindergarten Crusade: The Establishment of Preschool Education in the United States*. Athens: Ohio University Press, 1976.

Rossiter, Margaret W. *Women Scientists in America: Struggles and Strategies to 1940*. Baltimore: Johns Hopkins University Press, 1982.

Rotundo, Anthony. *American Manhood: Transformations in Masculinity from the Revolution to the Modern Era*. New York: Basic Books, 1993.

Roty, Amelie Oksenberg. "Power and Powers: A Dialogue between Buff and Rebuff." In *Rethinking Power*, edited by Thomas Wartenberg, 1–13. Albany: State University of New York Press, 1992.

Royster, Jacqueline Jones, ed. *Southern Horrors and Other Writings: The Anti-Lynching Campaign of Ida B. Wells, 1892–1900*. Boston: Bedford Books, 1997.

Russett, Cynthia Eagle. *Sexual Science: The Victorian Construction of Womanhood*. Cambridge MA: Harvard University Press, 1989.

Ruyle, Janet. "Dean Lucy Sprague, the Partheneia, and the Arts." *Chronicle of the University of California* 1, no. 1 (Fall 1998): 65–74.

Ryan, Mary P. "American Parade: Representations of the Nineteenth-Century Social Order," in *The New Cultural History*, edited by Lynn Hunt, 131–53. Berkeley: University of California Press, 1989.

———. *Civic Wars: Democracy and Public Life in the American City during the Nineteenth Century*. Berkeley: University of California Press, 1997.

———. "Civil Society as Democratic Practice: North American Cities during the Nineteenth Century." *Journal of Interdisciplinary History* 29 (Spring 1999): 559–84.

———. *The Cradle of the Middle-Class: The Family in Oneida, New York, 1790–1865*. New York: Cambridge University Press, 1981.

———. "Gender and Public Access: Women's Politics in Nineteenth-Century America." In *Habermas and the Public Sphere*, edited by Craig Calhoun, 259–88. Cambridge MA: MIT Press, 1992.

———. "'A Laudable Pride in the While of Us': City Halls and Civic Materialism." *American Historical Review* 105 (October 2000): 1131–70.

———. "The Power of Women's Networks: A Case Study of Female Moral Reform in Antebellum America." *Feminist Studies* 5 (Spring 1979): 66–85.

———. *Women in Public between Banners and Ballots, 1825–1880*. Baltimore: Johns Hopkins University Press, 1990.

Rydell, Robert W. *All the World's a Fair; Visions of Empire at American International Expositions*. Chicago: University of Chicago Press, 1984.

———. "Rediscovering the 1893 Chicago World's Columbian Exposition." In *The White City: American Art at the 1893 World's Fair 1893*. Organized by Carolyn Kinder Carr and George Gurney, 19–61. Washington DC: National Museum of American Art; National Portrait Gallery, 1993.

Sanchez, Regina Markell Morantz. *Sympathy and Science: Women Physicians in American Medicine*. New York: Oxford University Press, 1985.

Sander, Kathleen Waters. *Mary Elizabeth Garrett: Society and Philanthropy in the Gilded Age*. Baltimore: Johns Hopkins University Press, 2008.

San Francisco Blue Book, Season 1910–1911. San Francisco: Charles C. Hoag, 1911.

San Francisco Board of Supervisors. "In Memoriam: Mary W. Kincaid." *San Francisco Municipal Reports for Fiscal Year 1914–1915*. San Francisco: Neal Publishing, 1917.

Sapiro, Virginia. *A Vindication of Political Virtue: The Political Theory of Mary Wollstonecraft*. Chicago: University of Chicago Press, 1992.

Scharff, Virginia. "Else Surely We Shall All Hang Separately: The Politics of Western Women's History," Special Issue: Western Women's History Revisited. *Pacific Historical Review* 61 (November 1992): 535–55.

————. "Lighting Out for the Territory: Women, Mobility, and Western Place." In *Power and Place in the North American West*, edited by Richard White and John M. Findlay, 287–303. Seattle: University of Washington Press, 1999.

Scharlach, Bernice. *Big Alma: San Francisco's Alma Spreckels*. San Francisco: Scottwall Associates, 1995. Reprint, Berkeley CA: Heyday, 2015.

Schuele, Donna. "'None Could Deny the Eloquence of This Lady': Women, Law, and Government in California, 1850–1890,"edited by John F. Burns and Richard Orsi. *California History: Taming the Elephant: Politics, Government, and Law in Pioneer California* 81, no. 3/4 (2003): 169–198.

Scott, Anne Firor. "Almira Lincoln Phelps: The Self-Made Woman in the Nineteenth Century." In *Making the Invisible Woman Visible*, edited by Anne Scott, 89–106. Urbana: University of Illinois Press, 1984.

————. "The Ever Widening Circle: The Diffusion of Feminist Values from the Troy Female Seminary, 1822–1872." *History of Education Quarterly* 19 (Spring 1979): 3–25.

————. *Natural Allies: Women's Associations in American History*. Urbana: University of Illinois Press, 1991).

————. *The Southern Lady: From Pedestal to Politics 1830–1920*. Chicago: University of Chicago Press, 1970.

————. "What, Then, Is the American: This New Woman?" In *Making the Invisible Woman Visible*, edited by Anne Scott, 37–63. Urbana: University of Illinois Press, 1984.

Scott, Joan Wallach. "Deconstructing Equality-versus-Difference: Or, the Uses of Poststructuralist Theory for Feminism." *Feminist Studies* 14 (1988): 33–50.

————. "Gender: A Useful Category of Historical Analysis." *American Historical Review* 91 (December 1986): 1053–75.

————. *Only Paradoxes to Offer: French Feminists and the Rights of Man*. Cambridge MA: Harvard University Press, 1996.

Scott, Mel. *American City Planning Since 1890*. Berkeley: University of California Press, 1971.

Sears, John F. *Sacred Places: American Tourist Attractions in the Nineteenth Century*. New York: Oxford University Press, 1989.

Sewell, Jessica. *The Everyday City; Public Space in San Francisco, 1890–1915*. Minneapolis: University of Minnesota, 2011.

Shammas, Carole. "Re-Assessing the Married Women's Property Acts." *Journal of Women's History* 6 (Spring 1994): 9–30.

Shapiro, Michael Steven. *Child's Garden: The Kindergarten Movement from Froebel to Dewey*. University Park: Pennsylvania State University Press, 1983.

Simpson, Anna Pratt. *Problems Women Solved, Being the Story of the Woman's Board of the Panama-Pacific International Exposition; What vision, enthusiasm, work and co-operation accomplished*. San Francisco: The Woman's Board, 1915.

Sklar, Kathryn Kish. *Florence Kelley and the Nation's Work: The Rise of Women's Political Culture, 1830–1900*. New Haven: Yale University Press, 1995.

———. "The Historical Foundations of Women's Power in the Creation of the American Welfare State, 1830–1930." In *Maternalist Politics and the Origins of Welfare States*, edited by Seth Koven and Sony Michel, 43–93. New York: Routledge, 1993.

———. "Hull House in the 1890s: A Community of Reformers." *Signs: Journal of Women in Culture and Society* 10 (Summer 1985): 658–77.

———. "Organized Womanhood: Archival Sources on Women and Progressive Reform." *Journal of American History* 75 (June 1988): 176–208.

Sklar, Kathryn Kish, and Thomas Dublin, eds., *Women and Power in American History: A Reader*. 3rd ed. 2 vols. Upper Saddle River NJ: Prentice Hall, 2009. First published 1991 and 2002.

Skocpol, Theda. *Diminished Democracy: From Membership to Management in American Civic Life*. Norman: University of Oklahoma Press, 2003.

Smith, Daniel Scott. "Family Limitation, Sexual Control and Domestic Feminism in Victorian America." *Feminist Studies* 1 (Winter–Spring 1973): 40–57.

Smith, Duane A. "Mother Lode for the West: California Mining Men and Methods," edited by James Rawls and Richard J. Orsi, 149–73. Sesquicentennial Issue. *California History: A Golden State: Mining and Economic Development in Gold Rush California* 77, no. 4 (Winter 1998/1999). Published for the California Historical Society. Berkeley: University of California Press.

Smith, Kathy Simpson. *We Have Raised All of You: Motherhood in the South, 1750–1835*. Baton Rouge: Louisiana State University Press, 2013.

Smith, Rev. James. *History of the Christian Church, From Its Origin to the Present Time; Compiled from Various Authors. Including a History of the Cumberland*

Presbyterian Church, Drawn from Authentic Documents. Nashville: Printed and Published at the Cumberland Presbyterian Office, 1835.

Sneider, Allison L. *Suffragists in an Imperial Age: U. S. Expansion and the Woman Question 1870–1929*. New York: Oxford University Press, 2008.

Solomon, Barbara Miller. *In the Company of Educated Women*. New Haven: Yale University Press, 1985.

Southern, David W. *The Progressive Era and Race: Reaction and Reform, 1900–1917*. Wheeling IL: Harland Davidson, 2005.

Spain, Daphne. *Gendered Spaces*. Chapel Hill: University of North Carolina Press, 1992.

Sparks, Edith. *Capital Intentions: Female Proprietors in San Francisco, 1850–1920*. Chapel Hill: University of North Carolina Press, 2006.

Stadtman, Verne A., comp. and ed. *The Centennial Record of the University of California*. Berkeley: Regents of the University of California, 1967.

Stanton, Elizabeth Cady, and Susan B. Anthony, eds. *History of Woman Suffrage*. 2 vols. New York: Fowler and Wells, 1881.

Stanton, Elizabeth Cady, Susan B. Anthony, Matilda Joslyn Gage, and Ida Husted Harper, eds. *History of Woman Suffrage*. 6 vols. Rochester NY: Susan B. Anthony, 1881–1922. Reprint edition produced in electronic form by Louisville KY: Bank of Wisdom, 1999.

Starr, Kevin. *Americans and the California Dream, 1850–1915*. Reprint edition. New York: Oxford University Press, 1986.

State of California. *Journal of the Assembly during the Sixteenth Session of the Legislature of California, 1865n66*. Sacramento: O.M. Clayes, State Printer, 1866.

Steinmetz, George, ed. *State/Culture: State-Formation after the Cultural Turn*. Ithaca NY: Cornell University Press, 1999.

Steward, Julian H. *Alfred Kroeber*. New York: Columbia University Press, 1973.

Stocking, George W., Jr. *A Franz Boas Reader: The Shaping of American Anthropology, 1883–1911*. Chicago: University of Chicago Press, 1974.

Stowe, William W. *Going Abroad: European Travel in Nineteenth Century American Culture*. Princeton NJ: Princeton University Press, 1994.

Strober, Myra H., and Audri Gordon Lanford. "The Feminization of Public School Teaching: Cross-sectional Analysis, 1850–1880." *Signs: Journal of Women in Culture and Society* 11 (Winter 1986): 212–35.

Stromquist, Shelton. *Reinventing "The People": The Progressive Movement, the Class Problem, and the Origins of Modern Liberalism*. Urbana: University of Illinois Press, 2006.

Susman, Warren I. *Culture as History: The Transformation of American Society in the Twentieth Century*. New York: Pantheon, 1984.

Sutcliffe, Anthony. *Towards the Planned City: Germany, Britain, the United States and France 1780–1914*. Oxford, England: Basil Blackwell, 1981.

Swager, Sally. "Educating Women in America." *Signs: Journal of Women in Culture and Society* 12 (Winter 1987): 333–72.

Swanberg, W. A. *Citizen Hearst: A Biography of William Randolph Hearst*. New York:, Macmillan, 1961.

Swift, Fletcher Harper. *Emma Marwedel, 1818–1893: Pioneer of the Kindergarten in California*. Vol. 6, no. 3 of University of California Publications in Education. Berkeley: University of California Press, 1931.

Taber, Loren B., and Vivian A. Prindle. "College of Physicians and Surgeons of San Francisco." *California Historical Society Quarterly* 30 (March 1951): 67–71.

Task, Jeffrey. *Things American: Art Museums and Civic Culture in the Progressive Era*. Philadelphia: University of Pennsylvania Press, 2012.

Terrell, Mary Church. "The Justice of Woman Suffrage." In *Votes for Women! The Woman Suffrage Movement in Tennessee, the South, and the Nation*, edited by Marjorie Spruill Wheeler. Knoxville: University of Tennessee Press, 1995.

Tetrault, Lisa. *The Myth of Seneca Falls: Memory and the Women's Suffrage Movement, 1848–1898*. Chapel Hill: University of North Carolina Press, 2014.

Thoresen, Timothy H. H. "Paying the Piper and Calling the Tune: The Beginnings of Academic Anthropology in California." *Journal of the History of the Behavioral Sciences* 2 (July 1975): 257–75.

Thurner, Manuela. "'Better Citizens without the Ballot': American Anti-Suffrage Women and Their Rationale during the Progressive Era." *Journal of Women's History* 5 (Spring 1993): 33–60.

Tichenor, Daniel J. "The Presidency, Social Movements, and Contentious Change: Lessons from the Woman's Suffrage and Labor Movements." *Presidential Studies Quarterly* 29 (March 1999): 14–25.

Todd, Frank Morton. *The Story of the Exposition; Being the Official History of the International Celebration Held at San Francisco in 1915 to Commemorate the*

Discovery of the Pacific Ocean and the Construction of the Panama Canal. 5 vols. New York: G. P. Putnam's Sons, Knickerbocker Press, 1921.

Trease, Geoffrey. *Grand Tour*. London: Heinemann, 1967.

Turner, Paul V. *Campus: An American Planning Tradition*. An Architectural History Foundation Book. Cambridge MA: MIT Press, 1987.

Tyack, David, and Elisabeth Hansot. *Learning Together: A History of Coeducation in American Schools*. New Haven: Yale University Press, 1990.

United States Congress. *Memorial Addresses on the Life and Character of George Hearst (A Senator from California) Delivered in the Senate and House of Representatives, March 25, 1892 and February 24, 1894*. Washington DC: Government Printing Office, 1894.

University of California. *Annual Report of the Secretary to the Board of Regents of the University of California for the Year ending June 30, 1897*. Berkeley: University of California Press, 1898.

———. *Bancroftiana*. Berkeley: University of California, 1973.

———. *Biennial Report of the President on Behalf of the Regents, to His Excellency the Governor of the State, 1888*. Sacramento: J. D. Young, 1889.

———. *Biennial Report of the President on Behalf of the Regents, to His Excellency the Governor of the State, 1890*. Sacramento: A. J. Johnston, 1891.

———. *Biennial Report of the President on Behalf of the Regents, to His Excellency the Governor of the State, 1896–1898*. Berkeley: University Press, 1898.

———. *Biennial Report of the President on Behalf of the Regents, to His Excellency the Governor of the State, 1898–1900*. Berkeley: University Press, 1900.

———. *Biennial Report of the President on Behalf of the Regents, to His Excellency the Governor of the State, 1900–1902*. Berkeley: University of California Press, 1902.

———. *Biennial Report of the President on Behalf of the Regents, to His Excellency the Governor of the State, 1906–1908*. Berkeley: University of California Press, 1908.

———. *Blue and Gold 1903*. Berkeley: Published by the Junior Class of the University of California, 1902.

———. *The Department of Anthropology of the University of California*. Berkeley: University Press, 1905.

———. "The Organic Act of 1868 to Create the University of California, Alameda County, California," *Prospectus of the University of California at Berkeley*, 5–34. San Francisco: Excelsior Press, Bacon and Company Printers, 1868.

Vander Velde, Lewis G. *The Presbyterian Churches and the Federal Union 1861–1869*. Cambridge MA: Harvard University Press, 1932.

Vandewalker, Nina C. *The Kindergarten in American Education*. New York: Macmillan, 1908.

Vapnek, Laura. *Breadwinners: Working Women and Economic Independence 1865–1920*. Urbana: University of Illinois Press, 2009.

Veblen, Thorstein. *The Theory of the Leisure Class: An Economic Study in the Evolution of Institutions*. New York: Macmillan, 1899. Reprinted with a review by William Dean Howells. New York: Augustus M. Kelley, 1975.

Vesey, Lawrence. *The Emergence of the American University*. Chicago: University of Chicago, 1965.

Vogel, Ken. *Maramec Iron Works, 1825–1876: Chronological Listing, Explanation of Listings, and Supplements, August 1, 1969*. Revised by David Copeland. St. James MO: James Foundation, August 1984.

Vogel, Morris J. *The Invention of the Modern Hospital, Boston 1870–1920*. Chicago: University of Chicago Press, 1980.

Wade, Richard C. *Urban Frontier: The Rise of Western Cities, 1790–1830*. 2nd ed. Cambridge MA: Harvard University, 1967.

Wall, Joseph Frazier. *Andrew Carnegie*. New York: Oxford University Press [1970].

Walsh, James P. "Regent Peter C. Yorke and the University of California, 1900–1912." PhD diss., University of California, Berkeley, 1970.

Walsh, Mary Roth. *"Doctors Wanted: No Women Need Apply": Sexual Barriers in the Medical Profession, 1835–1975*. New Haven: Yale University Press, 1977.

Waldstreicher, David. *In the Midst of Perpetual Fetes: The Making of American Nationalism, 1776–1820*. Chapel Hill: University of North Carolina Press, 1997.

Ward, Vivian L. "Phoebe Apperson Hearst's Influence on the Kindergarten Movement in California." Master's thesis, Chapman College, 1967.

Ware, Susan. "The Book I Couldn't Write: Alice Paul and the Challenge of Feminist Biography." *Journal of Women's History* 24 (Summer 2012): 13–36.

Ware, Susan and Stacy Braukman, eds., *Notable American Women: A Biographical Dictionary Completing the Twentieth Century*. Cambridge MA: Belknap Press of Harvard University Press, 2004.

Wartenberg, Thomas E., ed. *Rethinking Power*. Albany: State University of New York Press, 1992.

Watson, Mary. *San Francisco Society: Its Characters, Its Characteristics*. San Francisco: Francis, Valentine, 1887.

Watson, Paula D. "Carnegie Ladies, Lady Carnegies: Women and the Building of Libraries." *Libraries and Culture: A Journal of Library History* 31 (Winter 1996): 159–196.

Waugh, Joan. *Unsentimental Reformer: The Life of Josephine Shaw Lowell*. Cambridge MA: Harvard University Press, 1997.

Weimann, Jeanne. *The Fair Women: The Story of the Woman's Building; World's Columbian Exposition, Chicago, 1893*. Chicago: Academy Chicago, 1981.

Welter, Barbara. "The Cult of True Womanhood, 1820–1840." *American Quarterly* 18 (Summer 1966): 151–74.

———. *Dimity Convictions: The American Woman in the Nineteenth Century*. Athens: Ohio University Press, 1976.

Westbrook, Robert B. *John Dewey and American Democracy*. Ithaca NY: Cornell University Press, 1991.

Wheeler, Benjamin Ide. *The Abundant Life*, edited by Monroe E. Deutsch. Berkeley: University of California Press, 1926.

Wheeler, Charles Stetson. *In the Matter of the Estate of Phoebe A. Hearst, Deceased Brief in Behalf of William Randolph Hearst, Transferee and Residuary Legatee and of the Executors*. San Francisco: Press of the James H. Barry Company, March 21, 1921.

Wheeler, Marjorie Spruill. *New Women of the New South: The Leaders of the Suffrage Movement*. New York: Oxford University Press, 1993.

———, ed. *One Woman, One Vote: Rediscovering the Woman Suffrage Movement*. Troutdale OR: New Sage Press, 1995.

———, ed. *Votes for Women! The Woman Suffrage Movement in Tennessee, the South, and the Nation*. Knoxville: University of Tennessee Press, 1995.

White, Richard. *"It's Your Misfortune and None of My Own": A History of the American West*. Norman: University of Oklahoma Press, 1991.

White, Richard, and John M. Findlay. *Power and Place in the North American West*. Seattle: University of Washington Press, 1999.

Whitmire Area History. Clinton: Intercollegiate Press, 1980.

Wiebe, Robert. *The Search for Order: 1870–1920*. New York: Hill and Wang, 1967.

———. *The Segmented Society: An Introduction to the Meaning of America*. New York: Oxford University Press, 1975.

Wilcox, David R. "Essay 3. Anthropology in a Changing America: Interpreting the Chicago 'Triumph' of Frank Hamilton Cushing." In *Coming of Age in Chicago: The 1893 World's Fair and the Coalescence of American Anthropology*, edited by Curtis M. Hinsley and David R. Wilcox. Lincoln: University of Nebraska Press, 2013.

Wilkins, Thurman. "Alice Cunningham Fletcher." In *Notable American Women, 1607–1950: A Biographical Dictionary*, edited by Edward James, Janet Wilson James, and Paul S. Boyer, 1:631–33. Cambridge MA: Belknap Press of Harvard University Press, 1971.

Williams, R. Hal. *The Democratic Party and California Politics 1880–1896*. Stanford CA: Stanford University Press, 1973.

Wilson, William H. *The City Beautiful Movement*. Baltimore: Johns Hopkins University Press, 1989.

Wister, Frances Anne, ed. *Biographical Sketch Sara Yorke Stevenson (1847–1921)*. Philadelphia: Civic Club of Philadelphia, 1922.

Woloch, Nancy. *A Class By Herself; Protective Laws for Women Workers, 1890s–1990s*. Princeton NJ: Princeton University Press, 2015.

Women's Educational and Industrial Union. *First Annual Report, 1888–1889*. San Francisco: Murdock, 1889.

———. *Report of the WEIU for Year Ending May 7, 1879*. Boston: 4 Park Street, 1879.

Wood, Mary I. *The History of the General Federation of Women's Clubs: For the First Twenty-Two Years of Its Organization*, with an introduction by Sheila M. Rothman. Farmdale NY: Distributed by Dabor Social Science Publications, c. 1978.

Woodbridge, Sally B. *John Galen Howard and the University of California: The Design of a Great Public University Campus*. Berkeley: University of California Press, 2002.

————. *Maybeck: Visionary Architect*. New York: Abbeville Press, 1992.

Woody, Thomas. *A History of Women's Education in the United States*. 2 vols. New York: Science Press, 1929.

Wright, Doris Marion. "The Making of Cosmopolitan California: An Analysis of Immigration, 1848–1870." *California Historical Society Quarterly* 19 (December 1940): 323–43.

————. "The Making of Cosmopolitan California—Part II: An Analysis of Immigration, 1848–1870." *California Historical Society Quarterly* 20 (March 1941): 65–79.

Wright, Gwendolyn. *Moralism and the Model Home: Domestic Architecture and Cultural Conflict in Chicago, 1873–1913*. Chicago: University of Chicago Press, 1980.

————. "On the Fringe of the Profession: Women in American Architecture." In *The Architect: Chapters in the History of the Profession*, edited by Spiro Kristof, 280–308. New York: Oxford University Press, 1977.

Wrobel, David M. "Beyond the Frontier-Region Dichotomy." *Pacific Historical Review* 65 (August 1996): 401–29.

Wrobel, David M., and Michael C. Steiner, eds. *Many Wests: Place, Culture, and Regional Identity*. Lawrence: University Press of Kansas, 1997.

Wyatt-Brown, Bertram. *Southern Honor, Ethics and Behavior in the Old South*. New York: Oxford University Press, 1982.

Yeo, Eileen Janes. *The Contest for Social Science: Relations and Representations of Gender and Class*. London: Rivers Oram Press, 1996.

Zagarri, Rosemarie. *Revolutionary Backlash: Women and Politics in the Early American Republic*. Philadelphia: University of Pennsylvania Press, 2007.

Zahniser, J. D., and Amelia R. Fry. *Alice Paul: Claiming Power*. New York: Oxford University Press, 2014.

Zunz, Oliver. *Philanthropy in America: A History*. Princeton NJ: Princeton University Press, 2012.

Index

Page numbers in italic indicate illustrations

GH = George Apperson Hearst

PAH = Phoebe Apperson Hearst

WH = William Randolph Hearst

AAA (American Archaeological Association), 258

ACA (Association of Collegiate Alumnae), 212, 236

Addams, Jane, xxviii, 128, 173, 310, 404–5

Adler, Felix, 90

Adriatic (steamer), 69

AES (American Exploration Society), 253–55, 258

African Americans: inequalities faced by, 23, 172–74, 266; kindergarten opportunities for, 171–72; in Maramec, 19; PAH's attitudes toward, 173–74, 266; in the suffrage movement, 379–80, 532n2; in Washington DC, 172

African American women: in educational reform, 174–75; excluded from GFWC, 149, 151; inequalities faced by,

172–73; in the suffrage movement, 532n2; YWCA policies for, 357

Albertson, J. A., 97

alcoholism, 114–16

allopaths, 97

AMA (American Medical Association), 97, 98

American Archaeological Association (AAA), 258

American Economic Review, 106

American Exploration Society (AES), 253–55, 258

American Medical Association (AMA), 97, 98

American Museum of Natural History (New York City), 265

American Purity Alliance, 360

American West: coeducation in, 23; demographics, 15; emigration to, 3, 5–6; hardships in, 14–16; notions of

from, 188; on women's rights, 143–44

California Model Kindergarten, 90

California Suffrage Constitutional Amendment Campaign (CSCACA), 371

Campbell, Mary Grafton, 137, 144

Camp Sesame (CA), *154*, 155

Canney, F. E. J., 97

capitalism, 9, 15, 80, 136, 182

Carey, Joseph, 392

Carnegie, Andrew, xviii, xxv, 97, 127

Catt, Carrie Chapman, 372, 377

Cauterets (spa), 84–85

Century Club, xxi, 141–48, 427, 470n43, 474n75

CESL (College Equal Suffrage League), 380–82, 384–86

Champ Clark Women's League, 387

Champney, Edward F., 353–54

Charter Day (UC), *300*

Chicago American, 424

Chicago Examiner, 398

Chicago Herald, 288, 294

Chicago Tribune, 149

child-raising: for economic independence, xxiv, 16–17, 127, 133–34; experienced by PAH, 8–13; shifting attitudes toward, 49; use of wet nurses, 39

children: coeducation in the West, 23, 89; cultivating citizenship in, 23, 70, 91; PAH's love of, xxi, 82, 89. *See also* education; kindergarten reform

Christmas gift-giving (PAH's), 318–19

citizenship: labor as element of, 93; racial inequalities in, 174, 266; taught to children, 23, 70, 91;

women's duties in, 2, 70, 382, 403; women's rights of, 235–36. *See also* suffrage movement

City Beautiful movement, 176, 232, 425

City of New York (ship), 127

city planning, 162–64, 213, 215, 233

Civil War, 20, 34

CKA (Columbian Kindergarten Association), xxi, 164–69, 171–72

Clark, Champ, 387–88, 516n27

Clark, Edward Hardy, Jr., 160, 178, 234–35, 292, 295, 304, 306, 423, 424, 465n85

Clark, Richard A., 424

Cleveland, Frances Folsom, 135

Cleveland, Grover, 152

Cliff Dwellers collection, 251, 253

coeducation, 23, 89, 94, 98, 183

College Equal Suffrage League (CESL), 380–82, 384–86

Collins, Elizabeth, 24–26

Colorado, 368

Columbian Kindergarten Association (CKA), xxi, 164–69, 171–72

Columbia University, 268, 276–77

Committee of One Hundred, 125, 145

Committee of Vigilance (1856), 36

common schools, 14, 20, 23

Comstock, Anthony, 360

Congress (U.S.): honoring GH, 154; and the kindergarten movement, 164, 167, 168–69; Mann Act of, 360; and the PPIE, 308–10; and the suffrage movement, 392, 394, 415; women excluded from, 180

Italy, 74–75, 162

tectural design, 216–17; attitudes toward PAH, 216–17, 407–9; attitudes toward powerful women, 193, 370, 490n17; body metaphors describing, 112–13; child raising roles, 49; constraints placed on women, xix, 44–45, 72, 87, 169, 255, 297, 299–301, 324–28, 330–31, 364, 371, 409, 413; in educational politics, 94–95; expectations of manhood, 25, 56; expecting submission from women, 66; gender disparities in wages, 449n33; and gender equality, 13, 236; and the GFWC, 150; in kindergarten reform, 168–69; in the medical profession, 98–103; on moral protection, 344; PAH as equal to, 151–52, 199, 203, 421–22; PAH's acceptance by, 187; PAH's power over, xxii, 101–3, 160, 169, 181–82, 295–301; PAH working with, 158–60, 168–69, 178, 181–82, 349–54, 413–14; in partisan politics, 146, 147, 309–10; philanthropic work of, xxiv–xxv; power of, xvii, xviii–xix; in the PPIE, 307–8; protection myth, 68, 137–38, 402, 406, 417; role in museums, 246; at UC, 210–11, 212, 228, 229, 234–36, 243; viewing women as dependent, 404; women's independence as threatening to, 211

Merriam, John C., 273, 278, 282

Merrill, Mary S., 318–19, 338–39, 343, 352, 353, 355, 360–62, 433n1

middle class: changing child raising roles in, 49; expectations of women in, 327–28; impacts of railroads on, 67–68; middling sorts, 5; visiting rituals, 59. *See also* social classes

middling sorts (social class), 5

Miller, John F., 106

Mills College, 415

minimum wage, 136, 355–57, 530n102

mining department (UC), 183, 193, 194–95, 210, 220–21, *222*, 223, 225, 229

mining industry: and California politics, 42; economic decline impacting, 44; GH in, 26–27, 32, 38–41, 44, 56, 57, 105–6; PAH's fascination with, 16

Mission architectural style, 177–78

Missouri: demographics, 15; emigration to, 3, 5–6, 445n5; hardships in, 14–16; marriage laws, 31, 451n44; population statistics, 448n24

Mitchell, Wesley, 106

money: challenges created by, 68; conspicuous consumption, 35, 46, 96, 132, 170, 289, 314; and cultural capital, 224; Cumberland Presbyterian beliefs on, 9; expectations for elite women, xx–xxii, xxvii, 286; GH's control over, 64–67; impact of World War I on, 416; PAH's control over, 87–88, 106–7; PAH's skill managing, 64, 71–72, 75, 106–7, 151–52, 158–61, 167, 192, 423; in PAH's upbringing, 9–10; PAH's views on, 22, 46–47, 126; political gift-giving, 318–19; political reform agenda communicated by, xxvi–xxviii, 55–56, 87, 109, 145, 175, 246; power through, xvii, xviii–xix,

to, xxvii–xxviii, 109–10; PAH's
involvement in, xix, xxi–xxii, 88,
89, 92–95, 124, 289, 307, 311–12,
320–28, 411; PAH's reputation for
results in, 164, 204; and power,
xxiv–xxv, 95; power of the press
in, 373–76; in the PPIE, 307–12; of
the PPIE Woman's Board, 320–28,
344; similarities to partisan politics,
319; of the suffrage movement, 391;
of the Travelers' Aid Society, 344,
348; unethical methods used in,
147; of the WEIU, 136–41; women's
involvement in, 134, 148–49; of the
YWCA, 330, 331, 335–38, 344
politics (partisan): during the 1896
presidential election, 375–76; of the
1916 presidential election, xv–xvi;
California suffrage campaign, 368–
76; Century Club's participation
in, 143, 147–48; gender differences
in, 309–10; GFWC's involvement in,
150–51; GH's career in, 103–4, 105–
6, 113–14; and kindergarten reform,
168–69; and the mining industry,
42; PAH's approach to, xxvii–xxviii,
109–10; PAH's dislike of, 113–14,
124, 168, 315, 388; PAH's impacts
on, 427; PAH's power in, 152; and
power, xxiv–xxv, 95; power of the
press in, 373–76; power through
voting, xv–xvi, 367–68; in the
PPIE, 307–10; pressure-group
tactics, 144; role of high-society
affairs in, 121–23; role of networks
in, 87–88; in San Francisco, 36, 125,

141, 143; similarities to voluntary
association politics, 319; in UC
board of regents appointments,
198; unethical methods used in, 147;
women's involvement in, xix, 141,
143, 387; WRH's involvement in,
305–6. *See also* suffrage movement
Polk, Willis, 217
Populist Party, 375
poverty: in Germany, 78; in Ireland,
77; in Missouri, 15; PAH's interest
in, 77–78; and the protection myth,
138–39; in scientific philanthropy,
xxv, 83, 166–67; social Darwinism
on, 166; viewed as sin, 114–15
Powell, John Wesley, 261
power: architectural design symbolizing, 162–64, 229–30, 271, 415; in
child raising, 49; and death, 420;
and gender, xviii–xx; in the GFWC,
149; lack of recognition for PAH's,
206–7, 217, 407–9, 421–22, 490n17;
limits of, 274–84, 299–301, 322–28;
of men in architecture, 216–17; PAH
exerting, 92, 345–46, 428–29; of
PAH in academic politics, 200, 221,
225, 229–30, 239–40, 244, 263–64,
274–84, 291, 296, 298–301; of PAH
in partisan politics, 208; of PAH in
reform politics, xxviii, 93–95, 165,
180–82; of PAH over men, xxii, 101–
3, 160, 169, 181–82, 295–301; of PAH
over WRH, 207; PAH's acquisition
of, 161; PAH's balanced approach to,
169, 244; PAH's competency exerting, xvii, 152, 225, 232; PAH's over

power (*continued*)

UC architectural plan, 210, 217–19, 221; PAH's strategy to achieve, 161–62, 200–201; PAH's views on women possessing, 372; of PAH through networking, 247; of the PPIE Woman's Board, 322–28, 351; of the press, 218–19, 373–76; public *versus* private, 332, 345–46; through money, xviii–xix, xxiv–xxv, 93, 207, 246, 259–61, 263, 291, 294–95, 299–301; through voting, xv–xvi, 367–68; of UC Board of Regents, 200, 280; women's acquisition of, xvii–xviii, xxii, 139, 150–51, 370, 428–29; and the YWCA's political agenda, xxii, 335–38

PPIE (Panama-Pacific International Exposition): board of directors, 320, 322–28, 344, 347, 350–54, 359–63, 392–93; contract with Woman's Board, 322–28; finances of, 307, 322–23, 362–64, 520n52; formation of, 317; groundbreaking ceremony, *356*; Hacienda political events, 313–16; images of, *355*, *356*; Joy Zone at, 359–63, 530n108; lobbying Congress, 308–10; moral protection at, 344, 346–49; opening day, 357–58; PAH's involvement in, xxi–xxii, 311–16, 364–65; partisan politics in, 307–10; postcard campaign, 308–9; suffragist exhibit at, 389, 392–95; TAS's role at, 336, 343, 345, 346–49, 361–62; and the Woman's Board's formation, 317; women's involvement in, 308–9, 310–11, 328; YWCA Building at, 349–57, *358*, *359*; YWCA's work at, 329, 335–36, 345, 523n75

PPIE Woman's Board: addressing complaints, 358–63; bylaws of, 320; contract with board of directors, 322–28; finances of, 317, 322–23, 351–54, 363–64, 520n52; formation of, 317; limited power of, 323–28, 344, 347; members of, 317, 318–19, 517n35; moral protection responsibilities, 343–49; PAH as honorary president, xxii, 319–22, 384, 389; PAH's support of, 317–19; in the Preparedness Day parade, 403–6; progressive reform work of, 342–43; responsibilities of, 328, 343–45; and the TAS, 346–49; and the YWCA Building, 349–57

Preger, Wilhelm, 128

prenuptial agreement (PAH's), 32–34

Preparedness Day parade (1916), 399–407

preparedness movement, 398–407

Price, Camilla, 43

Pringle, Elizabeth W. Allston, 1, 11, 12, 13, 316, 402, 415

prohibition, 89, 287, 531n108

Prohibition Party, 144

prostitution, 360

PSRA (Public School Reform Association), 144

PTA (Parent and Teacher Association), 427

Sex in Education (Clarke), 234–35

Shah of Persia, 71

Shaw, Anna Howard, 369–70, 377, 379–81, 389, 391, 428–29, 548n29

Shaw, R. Norman, 215

Shepard, A. D., 339

Shinn, Milicent W., 144, 189–90, 198, 369

Shrader-Breymann, Henrietta, 128

Shuey, Sarah I., 198

Silver Street Kindergarten, 90

Simpson, Anna Pratt, 308, 313, 317, 320, 322, 323

slavery, 6, 15, 19, 24

social classes: in the American West, 3, 19; body metaphors describing, 112–13; British high-society model, 59; classification criteria, 433n1, 448n28; in Europe, 76–78; functional hierarchies, 449n32; hierarchies displayed at PPIE, 359; middle classes, 5, 49, 59, 67–68; PAH's family category in, xvii, 5; PAH's views on, 94; PAH's views on lower, 125–26, 133, 138–39, 228, 260; seen in museum building, 259–61; status symbols for, 45; visiting rituals, 59. *See also* elite class

social Darwinism, 166, 258–59, 359, 404

social events: expectations of wealthy women, xxvii–xxviii, 46–47; GH's dislike of, 46, 117; at the Hacienda, 313–16; hosted by the Jameses, 19; increased status through, xxviii, 61–62, 117–18, 121–23; money spent on, 509n72; moral criticism

of, 287–88; PAH's use of, xxvii–xxviii; political nature of, xxviii, 43, 121–23; in Washington DC, 117–18, 120–23, 287–88

social science, 115, 130, 235, 277, 348–49

Solomons, Hannah Marks, 140–41, 145

Sorbier, Louise, 139, 140, 369

Southern Pacific Railroad, 338–39, 379

spas (health resorts), 84–85

Sperry, Mary, 372

Sprague, Lucy, 106, 241

Spreckels, Claude, 311

Spreckels, Ellis, 311

Sproul, Robert Gordon, 240–41

Stallard, Joshua, xxx

Stanford, Jane Lathrop, 91, 94, 118, 121, 135, 372, 376

Stanford, Leland, 154, 209, 338–39

Stanford University, 209

Stanton, Elizabeth Cady, 367, 377

Steelville Academy, 17

Stephens, William D., 421, 422

Stevens, Doris, xvi, 393, 411–12, 434n2

Stevenson, Matilda Coxe, 266

Stevenson, Sara Yorke, 252–53, 256–58, 262, 296

St. Francis Hotel (San Francisco), xv–xvi, 310

St. James Hotel (London), 70–71

Stoneman, George, 104, 105–6

St. Paul's School (Concord, NH), 86

Stump, Irwin C., 159–60, 477n6

suffrage movement (California): and the 1895 Woman's Congress, 368–71; 1896 campaign, 371–76; and the 1896 Woman's Congress, 371–72; 1911 campaign, 377–79, 381–82, 384–85; and the CESL, 380–82, 384–86; Dreamland Rink rally, 384–85; newspapers supporting, 373–76, 534n14; PAH's support of, xvi, 197, 367–69, 371, 372–73, 376–79, 382–86; passage of amendment, 324; voting as political power, 382

suffrage movement (national): and the 1895 Woman's Congress, 368–71; and the 1896 Woman's Congress, 371–72; and the 1912 presidential election, 387–89; during the 1916 presidential election, 410–13; advocates of, 143–44; Alva Belmont's contributions to, 383–84, 413; and the CESL, 380–82, 384–86; and the Congressional Union, 389–98, 410; critics of, 399, 404; and the Equal Franchise Society, 383–84; exhibit at PPIE, 392–95; GFWC's position on, 149, 151; leadership changes, 377, 379–80; and municipal elections, 441n7; newspaper support of, 398; and the NWP, xv–xvi, 391, 394, 396–98, 404–5, 410–14, 538n51; PAH's support of, xv–xvi, 367–69, 370, 371, 372–73, 376–79, 388–89, 396–97, 412–13; passage of amendment, 415, 428–29; President Wilson's opposition to, 388, 410–11; President Wilson's support of,

416; protest parades, 403; racism in, 379–80, 532n2; radical wings, 377, 383, 389–91, 401–3, 409–13, 535n18; recruiting wealthy elite women, 197, 372; St. Francis Hotel luncheon, xv–xvi, 410–11; "votes for women" slogan, 535n16; voting as political power, xvi, 367–68, 382; and war preparedness, 401–7; WEIU's position on, 140

Suffragist (newspaper), 309

Sullivan, Louis, 195, 217

Swanberg, W. A., 465n85, 466n3

Swett, John, 89, 112

Taft, William Howard, 388, 516n27

TAS (Travelers' Aid Society), 336, 343–49, 361–62

Taylor, Edward R., 469n34

Taylor, Elizabeth Kittle, 399–401, 403, 404

Taylor, Harriet, 331, 335, 339

teaching (profession): as alternative to marriage, 14; professionalization of, 93–94, 175; in rural common schools, 14, 20, 23; in San Francisco politics, 112; training schools for, 134, 174–75; wages of, 21–22, 166, 172, 449n33; women in, 14, 17, 91, 93–94. *See also* education; kindergarten reform

Tebtunis Papyri, 253

temperance, 89, 287, 531n108

Terrell, Mary Church, 532n2

Tevis, Lloyd, 65–67, 69, 110

Thaw, Mary Copley, 266

White, Laura Lovell, 308–9, 310, 319, 369

Whitmire, Henry (PAH's grandfather), 2, 3, 4–6

Whitmire, Ruth Hill (PAH's grandmother), 2, 3, 4–6

Whitmire Campground (MO), 1, 5–6, 15–16

Whitney, Charlotte Anita, 319, 380–81, 393, 397

Wiggin, Kate Douglas, 168

Wilbur, Ray Lyman, 419, 422

Willard, Mary, 135

Wilson, Jessie Woodrow, 336–37

Wilson, Woodrow, xv–xvi, 357, 387–89, 398–99, 410–11, 412–13, 416

Wittenmore, Margaret, 412–13

Wollstonecraft, Mary, 16

Woman's Christian Temperance Union (WCTU), 89, 90, 91, 148, 287, 360, 399, 531n108

Woman's Congress (1895), 368–71

Woman's Congress (1896), 371–72

Woman's Congress Association of the Pacific Coast (WCAPC), 368–72

Woman's Pavilion (Philadelphia exposition), 81–82

Woman's Peace Party, 399, 404–5

women: at the 1893 World's Columbian Exposition, 176; in academic politics, 197–98, 264; access to money, 9, 64, 322; acquisition of power by, xvii–xviii, xviii–xix, 336–38, 428–29, 436n3; arguments against education for, 234–35; body metaphors describing, 112–13; changing child raising roles, 49; civilizing role of, 81, 266; constraints placed on, xix, 324–28, 330–31, 364; demographics of in California, 36, 452n53; domestic role of, 14, 115, 150, 369, 382; economic dependency of, 184–85; economic independence for, xxiii–xxiv, 11, 16–17, 89, 91, 93–94, 137, 241–42; educational opportunities for, 13–14, 161, 180–82, 241–42; in educational reform, 134–35, 174–75; employment in medical profession, 96, 98–103, 235–36; employment in sewing, 241–42; employment in teaching, 17, 91, 93–94; excluded from Congress, 180; expectations of, xxiii, 2, 7–10, 28, 35, 38, 59, 66, 83, 229, 327–28; and gender equality, 13, 236; in health reform, 239–40; independence as threatening to men, 211; in kindergarten reform, 89–92, 95, 134–35, 169; labor protection for, 354–57; male protection myth, 68, 137–38, 406, 417; marching in parades, 398–407; in marriage laws, 31, 33; men's attitudes towards power of, 193, 370; moral protection, 360–63; as museum collectors, 262; PAH's legacy for, 226–27, 424–25, 426–27; PAH symbolizing gender equality, 151–52, 203; in partisan politics, 95, 141–48, 309–10, 368; at the Philadelphia exposition, 81–82; protection myth, 138–39, 417; role in World War I, 416; role of networks women (*continued*)

for, 338; social classification of, 433n1; spending money, 64, 106; "true womanhood" trope, 2, 8; as UC faculty, 233–34, 235–36, 240–41; as UC students, 182–86, 188–91, 196–97, 210–13, 224–31, 234–36, 239–40, 243, 244, 424–25; viewed as dependent, 23, 404; viewed as submissive, 66, 171; viewed as weak, 96; visiting rituals of, 59; wage disparities, 449n33; and the WEIU, 136–41; western womanhood ideals, xxiii, 17. *See also* African American women; elite class women; PPIE Woman's Board; suffrage movement

Women's Anthropological Society, 266

Women's Educational and Industrial Union (WEIU), 136–41, 144

Women's Political Union (WPU), 395

working class: impact of 1918–1919 influenza epidemic on, 419; impact on California suffrage amendment, 386; in Ireland, 77–78

working class women: economic barriers to education of, 241–42; labor protection for, 354–57; protection myth, 138–39; WEIU's work with, 136–40

World's Columbian Exposition (1893 Chicago), 151, 161, 170–71, 176–77, 188, 245–46, 252

World War I, 399–401, 416

WPU (Women's Political Union), 395

Wright, Carroll D., 165, 168

Wynn, Emily, xxiii–xxiv

Wynn, Mattie, xxiii–xxiv

Wyntoon Castle, 268–71, 424; image of, *270*

Wyoming Territory, 143, 368

YMCA (Young Men's Christian Association), 47, 329

Young Men's Christian Association (YMCA), 47, 329

Young Women's Christian Association (YWCA). *See* YWCA (Young Women's Christian Association)

YWCA (Young Women's Christian Association): Asilomar conference and training center, xxii, 329, 332, 336, 338–41, 427, 523n75, 525n84; building, 349–56, *358*, *359*; financial challenges, 351–54; Hacienda Conference, 332–33, 334–38, 340, 341, 524n82; and moral protection at PPIE, 345, 346–49; national board, 330, 341–42; PAH's contributions to, xxi–xxii, 294, 329–30, 427–28, 524n82; political agenda of, 330, 331, 333, 342–43; position on suffrage, 393; at the PPIE, 329, 335–36, 342–43, 349–57, 393, 523n75; supporting the Mann Act, 360; and the TAS, 343, 345, 346–49